Teaching Adventure Education Theory

BEST PRACTICES

BOB STREMBA, EdD
Fort Lewis College

CHRISTIAN A. BISSON, EdD
Plymouth State University

EDITORS

Human Kinetics

Library of Congress Cataloging-in-Publication Data

Teaching adventure education theory : best practices / editors, Bob Stremba, Christian A. Bisson.
p. cm.
Includes bibliographical references.
ISBN-13: 978-0-7360-7126-0 (soft cover)
ISBN-10: 0-7360-7126-1 (soft cover)
1. Adventure education--Study and teaching. I. Stremba, Bob, 1947- II. Bisson, Christian A., 1964-
LC1038T43 2009
378.1'784--dc22

2008033928

ISBN-10: 0-7360-7126-1
ISBN-13: 978-0-7360-7126-0

The Web addresses cited in this text were current as of October 2008, unless otherwise noted.

Acquisitions Editor: Gayle Kassing, PhD; **Developmental Editor:** Jacqueline Eaton Blakley; **Special Projects Editor:** Anne Cole; **Assistant Editors:** Derek Campbell and Lauren B. Morenz; **Copyeditor:** Joyce Sexton; **Proofreader:** Joanna Hatzopoulos Portman; **Permission Manager:** Martha Gullo; **Graphic Designer:** Bob Reuther; **Graphic Artist:** Denise Lowry; **Cover Designer:** Keith Blomberg; **Photographer (cover):** Bob Stremba; **Photo Asset Manager:** Laura Fitch; **Visual Production Assistant:** Joyce Brumfield; **Photo Production Manager:** Jason Allen; **Art Manager:** Kelly Hendren; **Associate Art Manager:** Alan L. Wilborn; **Cover Art:** KOLB, DAVID A. *EXPERIENTIAL LEARNING: EXPERIENCE AS A SOURCE OF LEARNING & DEVELOPMENT, 1st, © 1984.* Reproduced by permission of Pearson Education Inc., Upper Saddle River, New Jersey; **Illustrator:** Tim Offenstein; **Printer:** Sheridan Books

Printed in the United States of America 10 9 8 7 6 5 4 3 2 1

Human Kinetics
Web site: www.HumanKinetics.com

United States: Human Kinetics, P.O. Box 5076, Champaign, IL 61825-5076
800-747-4457
e-mail: humank@hkusa.com

Canada: Human Kinetics, 475 Devonshire Road Unit 100, Windsor, ON N8Y 2L5
800-465-7301 (in Canada only)
e-mail: info@hkcanada.com

Europe: Human Kinetics, 107 Bradford Road, Stanningley, Leeds LS28 6AT, United Kingdom
+44 (0) 113 255 5665
e-mail: hk@hkeurope.com

Australia: Human Kinetics, 57A Price Avenue, Lower Mitcham, South Australia 5062
08 8372 0999
e-mail: info@hkaustralia.com

New Zealand: Human Kinetics, Division of Sports Distributors NZ Ltd., P.O. Box 300 226 Albany, North Shore City, Auckland
0064 9 448 1207
e-mail: info@humankinetics.co.nz

Contents

Preface

Willi Unsoeld was an educator who played a leading role in bringing Outward Bound to the United States in the 1960s. Noted for his climbs of Mt. Everest and other high peaks around the world, Willi was asked, "Why don't you stay out there in the wilderness, in the mountains?" His reply, paraphrased, was "Because that's not where people are" (Schoel and Stratton 1990, p. 130).

This book grows out of that paradox. It seems that Willi was reminding us of a perspective important for those growing into the profession of adventure education today—that it's not just about climbing mountains, paddling class IV rivers, and skiing extreme powder. It's about how our relationship with adventure and wilderness can help us relate better with people and our community.

To transfer Willi's paradox a little further, this book is really about teaching indoors, for those who like to teach in the outdoors. It's for teachers of students who would rather be outdoors but who often find themselves inside classrooms. And it's for all those who want to bring the active learning, the critical reflection, and the interdependent community that a challenging outdoor environment facilitates back off the mountain and into the classroom. But before scaring you back into the wilderness, we want to point out that many of the lessons in this book can at least partially be brought back into the outdoors. Good teaching uses methods that work in both environments.

PURPOSE

Adventure education may be compared to a developing individual. Over the past two or three decades the discipline has grown beyond childhood, and maybe even through a period of rebellious adolescence, to a point where its pedagogy is accepted as producing sound educational outcomes. The first edition of *Mountaineering: The Freedom of the Hills* (Manning) appeared in 1960 as a textbook for students and instructors participating in organized climbing courses. Since then we have seen a growing list of books covering the many technical skills of wilderness travel and outdoor pursuits. This has been followed by professional journals and publications from organizations including Project Adventure and the Association for Experiential Education that have provided tools and perspectives about how to use adventure activities to promote character development. More recently, we have seen books by writers, including Karen Warren (1995), that examine in greater depth the philosophical, historical, psychological, and social foundations of experiential education.

But the maturity of adventure education is especially evidenced through the rather recent arrival of textbooks designed to help an increasing number of college undergraduates, attracted to the discipline, become thoroughly prepared outdoor leaders, adventure instructors, and competent facilitators. Such texts include those by Priest and Gass (2005); Prouty, Panicucci, and Collinson (2007); Gilbertson and colleagues (2006); Beard and Wilson (2006); and Martin and colleagues (2006).

The purpose of *Teaching Adventure Education Theory: Best Practices* is to provide a toolbox of lessons for those who prepare adventure educators concerning the *why* behind the *what*—the theories, models, and concepts that inform the practice. This book can serve as a sort of instructor's manual for those using the texts just mentioned, as well as other books, in their teaching.

This book, then, is for college and university professors teaching adventure education, outdoor education, outdoor recreation, and related disciplines. It is for college education, physical education, and exercise science faculty who are integrating experiential education methodologies into their own teaching practice and into the content presented to their students. It will be useful for graduate students learning the pedagogy of experiential education, and for those educators involved with training staff of camps and outdoor programs. This book is also applicable to secondary school teachers who are bringing theory, philosophy, and group development into their teaching.

The ultimate impact of this text is in the hands of those educators using it. In our own teaching of aspiring adventure educators, we've noticed that students rather easily embrace the technical and field-based skills—backpacking, rock climbing, white-water paddling, mountaineering, and so forth. Sometimes they ask, Why should a skilled practitioner know about theory, philosophy, and history anyway? Often the underlying issue is that students want or need their classroom experience to be as involving as the field environment, because this is how they learn best. The lessons in this text can help create such involvement. They are supplied by a collection of talented educators who have experience engaging college students in the academic and cognitive dimensions of a discipline that many students at first perceive to be limited to technical skills and kinesthetic learning. But we have also seen college adventure education students develop to the point where they are excited about writing a research paper on Kurt Hahn or teaching their peers a model of comfort zones, for example. Perhaps this happens because these students themselves had the opportunity to experience the kinds of engaging pedagogy provided by our contributors.

FEATURES

This text provides the adventure education instructor with a collection of educational strategies that use experiential and involving processes that students expect in the outdoors but that are generally applied here to classroom settings. Our assumption is that those who teach this material will already have some knowledge about and experience with the content of what they are teaching. The lessons provided here suggest a way to teach this content; but because good teaching is an organic and evolving process, this collection of best practices is available for instructors to choose from and modify to fit their own teaching style and their students' learning needs. It is not our intent to standardize or homogenize the curriculum for preparing adventure educators, but to offer resources from which to choose.

Thirty-four lessons are provided in a variety of categories related to adventure education. In addition to a lesson plan detailing activities and teaching suggestions, each lesson includes an overview of the lesson's theory to give the instructor background conceptual material. However, we encourage instructors to practice what they often preach to their students: Overprepare and be ready to change your plan on a moment's notice. Therefore, before teaching a lesson, consult the references that are included to take yourself farther down the path that you will be taking your students on.

The CD-ROM accompanying this text provides access to electronic versions of handouts, visual aids, and other pertinent materials for teaching the lessons. Because the lessons cover a wide range of subjects and use a diverse range of teaching strategies, you will notice a range of materials on the CD-ROM. Some lessons include PowerPoint presentations, while others employ guided discussion and use a minimum of props. This range of accompanying materials is analogous to the variety of teaching methodologies employed by our contributors, as well as by adventure education instructors generally. Each lesson includes a background handout as an option to provide to students before or after your teaching of the lesson. Student handouts and activities available on the CD-ROM appear in thumbnail form within the lesson, and an icon denotes accompanying PowerPoint® presentations and other materials.

ORGANIZATION

We have witnessed common themes and content areas taught in many academic adventure education degree programs and appearing in many of the recent texts used in these programs. The lessons in this book attempt to cover many of these topics, but there will undoubtedly be gaps.

The first part of this book frames the remaining nine parts. Chapter 1 describes the adventure education curriculum found in many college preparation programs, also discussing the rationale for students to know theory and the ways in which the broader competencies in adventure education often align with colleges' liberal arts outcomes. Chapter 2 explores the common pedagogical threads that weave through effective adventure education teaching processes, and the challenges and rewards of teaching this material.

The remainder of the text comprises college-level lesson plans for the actual teaching of the theoretical core curriculum. Part 2 provides lessons for teaching instructional theory and curriculum design processes. Part 3 provides a variety of lessons for teaching the history of adventure education. Part 4 has tools to help students learn about the educational and philosophical foundations of the discipline, including lessons on John Dewey's contributions. Part 5 provides strategies for teaching some of the central theories supporting our field practices, including optimal arousal theory, self-efficacy, locus of control, and the concept of flow. Part 6 offers indoor and outdoor strategies for teaching adventure education's leadership models and theories. Part 7 is about helping our students create a better world, presenting strategies for teaching ethical and social justice issues. Because this discipline often uses outdoor pursuits to help individuals build interpersonal and intrapersonal skills, part 8 focuses on teaching the models and theories of group development and social psychology. Part 9 presents the tools for teaching some of the processing and facilitation models so universal to our practice. And part 10 shows some creative ways to teach the human-to-nature connection that is so central to why we do what we do.

We hope this book inspires you to help prepare aspiring adventure educators, outdoor leaders, and group facilitators by providing optimal and engaging opportunities for them to embrace the theory that informs their practice.

REFERENCES

Beard, C., and J.P. Wilson. 2006. *Experiential learning.* 2nd ed. London: Kogan Page.

Gilbertson, K., T. Bates, T. McLaughlin, and A. Ewert. 2006. *Outdoor education: Methods and strategies.* Champaign, IL: Human Kinetics.

Manning, H., ed. 1960. *Mountaineering: The freedom of the hills.* Seattle, WA: The Mountaineers.

Martin, B., C. Cashel, M. Wagstaff, and M. Breunig. 2006. *Outdoor leadership: Theory and practice.* Champaign, IL: Human Kinetics.

Priest, S., and M.A. Gass. 2005. *Effective leadership in adventure programming.* 2nd ed. Champaign, IL: Human Kinetics.

Prouty, D., J. Panicucci, and R. Collinson. 2007. *Adventure education: Theory and applications.* Champaign, IL: Human Kinetics.

Schoel, J., and M. Stratton, eds. 1990. *Gold nuggets: Readings for experiential education.* Beverly, MA: Project Adventure.

Warren, K., M. Sakofs, and J.S. Hunt, eds. 1995. *The theory of experiential education.* Dubuque, IA: Kendall/Hunt.

Acknowledgments

Writing and editing *Teaching Adventure Education Theory: Best Practices* has been a journey a lot like a backcountry climbing expedition. A group of dedicated, tenacious individuals from the adventure education and publishing communities came together to reach a goal that became attainable only through one another's synergism. Along the path we have all benefitted from the unique contributions and patient persistence offered by all. Because the editors and lesson contributors are very involved in teaching endeavors that often take us into the field with students for weeks at a time, we often found that "swinging leads," to use a climbing term, on this book became the strategy that propelled this book to completion.

We extend special gratitude to Human Kinetics editor Gayle Kassing for her initial enthusiasm, wonderful suggestions, and ongoing cheerleading as we've conceived and prepared the manuscript for this book. We give our greatest gratitude to developmental editor Jackie Blakley. Without her hard work, tenacious attitude, and golden patience we would never have completed this manuscript. We especially thank all those who have contributed their creative lessons to this book. We hope the larger community of learners benefits from these gracious colleagues as much as we have. We extend a deeply felt thank you to all the workshop participants who came to our presentations to showcase some of their best teaching practices at the 2005, 2006, and 2007 Association for Experiential Education International Conferences. Your enthusiasm about this project convinced us to not only get it started but also to finish it.

Finally, we would like to thank the adventure education college students whose eagerness for becoming effective outdoor instructors inspired this book. In particular, Chris Mulcahy and Ryan McMahon, adventure education graduates from Plymouth State University, New Hampshire, each took on the challenge of serving as teaching assistants for courses in the degree program that are more demanding for both student and instructor—the courses that teach the theory, models, and concepts of adventure education. With Chris's and Ryan's curiosity, tenacity, and creativity we were able to offer learning experiences that were much more engaging than would have been possible without their dedicated work. Bob also thanks the adventure education students at Fort Lewis College in Durango, Colorado, for serving as willing participants as he tried out many of the lessons contributed in this book.

On a personal note, Bob would like to express his most loving thanks to his parents, Violet and Henry Stremba, for being the true inspirers over the decades for his path of adventure and teaching.

Lastly, Christian would like to thank his wife Julie and his son Luc. Their infinite patience and heartfelt support have made this project possible. "My loved ones, I owe you both many hours of play and family adventures."

PART I

Introduction to Teaching Adventure Education Theory

The 34 lessons in this book stand on a pedagogical foundation of interdisciplinary content and student involvement.

Chapter 1, "The Unique Curriculum of Adventure Education," describes common threads of the adventure education curriculum found in many college preparation programs. The discipline of adventure education accomplishes its purpose through a synthesis of knowledge and practices from several other established disciplines, including philosophy, history, psychology, education, and the natural sciences. A set of core competencies of outdoor leadership also exists. Well-prepared adventure educators engage with a multidisciplinary set of learning outcomes, including knowledge of theory, that often encompass more global outcomes of liberal arts education. One of the notable aspects of the adventure education curriculum is the use of parallel processes—experiential strategies of teaching that help students learn the models and processes of experiential education. A student knowing the *why* behind the *what*—who is armed with a strong theoretical foundation balanced by real experience with technical skills in the field—is more holistically prepared to assume the responsibilities of an adventure educator.

Chapter 2, "Teaching Theory, Facts, and Abstract Concepts Effectively," explores the theoretical curriculum of adventure education, including the challenges and rewards of teaching this material. Many students are attracted by the technical skills of outdoor adventure since those tasks involve direct experiences, cooperation, real problems, and authentic assessment. Consequently, students often expect to learn more abstract subjects such as history, philosophy, education theories, leadership theories, public land politics, risk management theories, and social psychology theories via instructional strategies that are also engaging and experiential. This chapter reviews experiential models for teaching abstract concepts, including a cone of experience that applies to all effective teaching. We see that proper sequencing of activities, reading, and writing to enhance learning outcomes apply to an outdoor challenge course curriculum as well as to a classroom-based theory course. Case studies, dramatizations, skits, role plays, games, open-ended questions, discussions based on direct experience, and mini-lectures all have their place in teaching adventure education theory. In a society that increasingly requires public and private institutions to be accountable for their actions, a new focus on assessment of learning has emerged, and this text presents a summary of formative, summative, formal, and informal assessment strategies.

Understanding the common threads of the adventure education curriculum, including its interdisciplinary, holistic, and liberal arts connections, lends credibility to the instructor's teaching of the theories and models of our discipline. Using engaging teaching strategies and employing learning-centered forms of assessment will help instructors make students' learning experience as engaging and rewarding as any great outdoor expedition or technical outdoor skill class.

CHAPTER 1

The Unique Curriculum of Adventure Education

Picture this: A group of 10 students and two college faculty is backpacking in the mountains for 12 days, as part of a course for the adventure education college degree program. Last semester these students took a paddling course in which they successfully read currents and deftly negotiated class III rapids down a swift river they were kayaking. Next semester they will be on the second pitch of a multipitch rock climb, gaining confidence in leading successive 5.8 to 5.10 pitches, using skills they are learning in their lead rock climbing course.

Now picture this: These same students are in the university library spending hours researching the philosophies of John Dewey and Kurt Hahn for a 15-page paper for their adventure education philosophy and theory course. The professor has told the class that they will learn about experiential education by largely creating this course, and the students must first understand the theoretical foundations that have shaped experiential education. Students are asked to describe what they need to learn in order to be an informed adventure educator, and they will be held accountable for demonstrating what they have learned.

Finally, picture this: Adventure education students are in a mock courtroom, arguing for the defense of their client, an outdoor program that has had two of its participants die of injuries sustained in a mountaineering accident. For their testimony, this "defense team" has had to read hundreds of pages about legal issues, risk management, accreditation standards, and the ethics of risk for their course on organization and administration of adventure education this semester.

Many college students studying adventure education are initially drawn to active learning in the outdoors, where the "classroom" may be the top of a mountain. They are easily drawn to the technical skills of the discipline and eagerly engage in backpacking, climbing, mountaineering, skiing, and paddling. But other times the classroom will be back on campus, within four walls, where students are engaged in reading, writing, critical thinking, and provocative discussions. They may also have a professor who is adept at creating experiences in the classroom that engage students just as much as does navigating a new river. The common thread is that students are very involved in their learning, and the faculty who teach these students need to develop lessons that bring the mountain into the classroom in order to create this student involvement.

Much is expected of adventure education students. They need to be intellectually curious, committed to involvement, and interested in maturing into self-motivated learners. Some of their learning occurs hands-on and in the field, but much of the learning for a thoroughly prepared adventure educator also occurs through a good deal of reading, writing, research, and collaborative class presentations. Adventure education graduates may work with youth or adults in positions that do not know the 8-to-5 schedule. Therefore, the well-prepared adventure educator has a balance of not only skills but also curiosity, gained in the classroom and library as well as in the field in a way that requires beyond-full-time commitment.

PROFESSIONAL PREPARATION OF ADVENTURE EDUCATORS

Over the past few decades the number of people engaging in outdoor adventure pursuits for recreational, educational, developmental, and therapeutic purposes has increased dramatically. With this has come an increase in the number of college degree programs and other organizations that prepare adventure educators to work in the organizations that serve these participants. Many college programs are called adventure education or outdoor education. However, other programs in outdoor recreation, outdoor leadership, leisure studies, management (parks, recreation, and tourism), and related areas frequently share similar curricular features, including theoretical and conceptual bases that have evolved from such disciplines as the social and behavioral sciences, the natural sciences, and the humanities. In addition, seasonal and year-round adventure and recreation programs now often include components in their staff training sessions that focus on the *why* behind the *what*—for example, Mitten's group development model discussed in lesson 26 of this book—to prepare staff to work more effectively with their participants.

Higher education programs in adventure and outdoor education have progressed beyond "camping for credit" (Levi 1989), and our responsibility in preparing outdoor leaders and adventure educators is to ignite their interests in building a strong foundation to support their passions for action. Priest and Gass (2005) describe a skill wall of building blocks representing components of effective outdoor leadership training. They note, "The capabilities to perform technical skills in an environmentally sound manner—the hard skills—are common among outdoor leaders. . .Unfortunately, the abilities to instruct, organize, and facilitate participants in adventure experiences—the soft skills—are less common in preparing outdoor leaders" (p. xiii). Metaskills include effective communication, flexible leadership style, decision making, and experience-based judgment and are often considered the "glue" that holds the blocks of the skill wall together. So, this assortment of hard skills (or what we call *field skills*), soft skills (or *interpersonal skills*), and metaskills rests on a thoughtful theoretical foundation of social psychology, history, and philosophy. We would add that an effective foundation also includes preparation in how to interpret and conduct research, and emphasize that the foundational theories, models, and concepts extend up through the field skills, interpersonal skills, and metaskills levels.

Priest and Gass' skill wall shows a synthesis of earlier studies (Priest 1987) describing 12 key elements, or *critical* core competencies, of effective outdoor leadership:

1. Technical skills
2. Safety skills
3. Environmental skills
4. Organizational skills
5. Instructional skills
6. Facilitation skills
7. Flexible leadership style
8. Experience-based judgment
9. Problem-solving skills
10. Decision-making skills
11. Effective communication
12. Professional ethics

Priest and Gass, 2005, pp. 3-6.

It is interesting to note that beyond the first three elements—the technical, safety, and environmental skills—the remaining nine elements represent competencies that are often supported by useful theoretical or conceptual models; and these models are typically taught in college degree programs that prepare adventure educators. Figure 1 shows some of the typical college courses associated with the 12 elements of effective leadership. This core theoretical curriculum, then, forms not only a

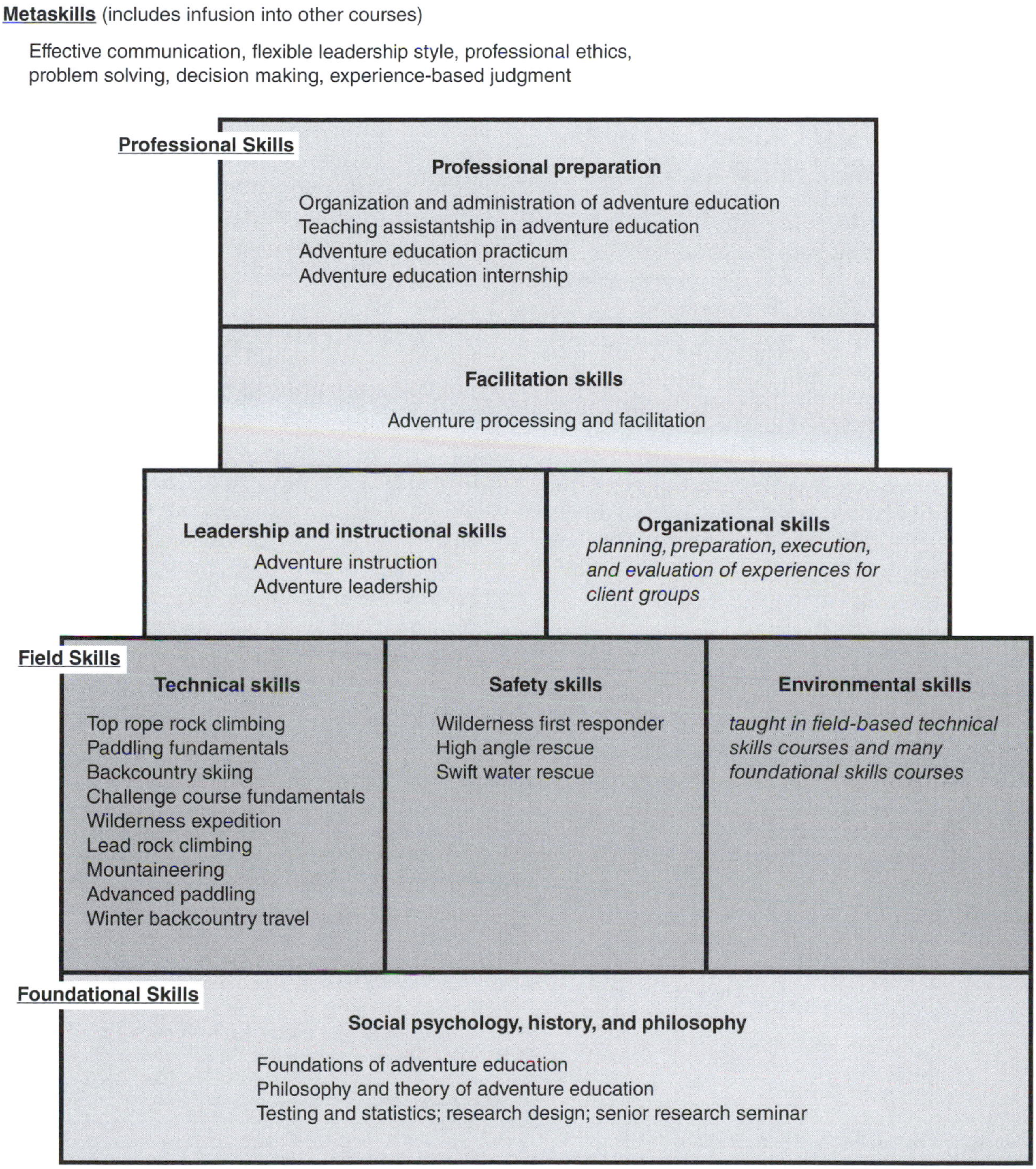

Metaskills (includes infusion into other courses)

Effective communication, flexible leadership style, professional ethics, problem solving, decision making, experience-based judgment

Professional Skills

Professional preparation

Organization and administration of adventure education
Teaching assistantship in adventure education
Adventure education practicum
Adventure education internship

Facilitation skills

Adventure processing and facilitation

Leadership and instructional skills

Adventure instruction
Adventure leadership

Organizational skills

planning, preparation, execution, and evaluation of experiences for client groups

Field Skills

Technical skills

Top rope rock climbing
Paddling fundamentals
Backcountry skiing
Challenge course fundamentals
Wilderness expedition
Lead rock climbing
Mountaineering
Advanced paddling
Winter backcountry travel

Safety skills

Wilderness first responder
High angle rescue
Swift water rescue

Environmental skills

taught in field-based technical skills courses and many foundational skills courses

Foundational Skills

Social psychology, history, and philosophy

Foundations of adventure education
Philosophy and theory of adventure education
Testing and statistics; research design; senior research seminar

FIGURE 1 The effective adventure educator skill wall, showing typical college courses in which the skills are taught.

Adapted, by permission, from S. Priest and M.A. Gass, 2005, *Effective leadership in adventure programming,* 2nd ed. (Champaign, IL: Human Kinetics), xiii.

foundation, but also an integral structure for the entire training that students need in order to become effective adventure educators.

ADVENTURE EDUCATION AND THE LIBERAL ARTS

The process of learning the theoretical and conceptual models infused with many of the 12 core elements, however, also enhances skills and perspectives in analysis, problem solving, communication, and making a positive contribution to the community—broader competencies that effective adventure educators will find useful in their work. These broader areas often align with a liberal arts mission of many colleges and universities, suggesting the value of adventure education philosophy and theory in preparing individuals for a world beyond just technical skill competency. Table 1 shows an example of such an alignment.

The discipline of adventure education accomplishes its purpose through a synthesis of knowledge and practices from a number of other established disciplines, including philosophy, history, psychology, education, and the natural sciences. Therefore, well-prepared adventure educators engage with a multidisciplinary set of learning outcomes, including knowledge of theory, that often encompass more global liberal education outcomes.

WHY KNOW THEORY?

Students aspiring to be adventure educators sometimes resist learning about theory, models, and concepts, perhaps believing that these are abstractions disconnected from the natural environment in which they are most comfortable. We can help these individuals expand their intellectual comfort zones by pointing out that theories and models are not merely abstract

TABLE 1 Example of Alignment Between Liberal Arts Education Outcomes and Adventure Education Theoretical and Conceptual Components

Institution-wide liberal education outcomes	Adventure education alignment
■ **Learning as inquiry:** The ability to use modern methods to access, analyze, interpret, and apply a wide range of information, data, and appropriate sources	■ Conceptual courses covering the foundations of adventure education, philosophy and theory of adventure education, and research on adventure education require students to use library, Internet, professional journal, and other resources.
■ **Critical thinking as problem solving:** The ability to analyze, synthesize, evaluate, and apply information in order to solve complex problems	■ The outcome of students' use of the above-mentioned resources includes research papers, individual and group projects, and class presentations addressing ethical, land-use, client service, risk management, and organizational problems in adventure education. ■ The balance of philosophy, theory, and practical skills in the outdoor environment provides ample opportunities to demonstrate the critical thinking and problem-solving skills necessary for success and survival.
■ **Communication as intellectual contribution:** The ability to contribute to scholarly understanding of a subject by balancing complexity and clarity of argument, clear conceptual organization of evidence, and adaptation to context and audience	■ A senior research seminar, postinternship presentations, and experiential lessons that students develop and teach in the field and classroom require students to synthesize, evaluate, and clearly communicate information to a variety of peer, academic, and professional audiences.
■ **Action as responsible application of academic learning:** The ability to use all of the above to make positive contributions to one's community and the larger society	■ The basis of adventure education rests on applying experience with analysis and reflection to lead to more informed action. ■ Practicums, teaching assistantships, internships, and service learning provide opportunities for community and societal contributions.

Column 1: Adapted, by permission, from Fort Lewis College, "College-Wide Liberal Education Outcomes." [Online]. Available: www.fortlewis.edu/about_flc [July 28, 2008].

concepts dreamed up by an anemic academic cloistered deep inside a research library. Rather, a mountain instructor accumulating lots of field experience, for example, began to see some patterns that explained how varying one's leadership style to match the situation, conditions of the environment, and people on the climb produced better results. Thus, the conditional outdoor leadership theory (Priest and Gass 2005) provides a map for the leader to consult to produce effective results again and again.

As Prouty and colleagues (2007) point out, "Theories can help us understand how and why something happens," and "having a theoretical understanding of the adventure experience can help us design more effective adventure education experiences for our students" (p. 27). Iso-Ahola (1980) notes that "nothing is more practical than a good theory" (p. 55). And what's more practical for the adventure educator than being able to promote success and safety between the client and the sometimes-challenging environment?

Effective adventure education practitioners, perhaps unknowingly, are good empirical and applied researchers. They observe what's going on with their clients in the wilderness and how leadership and group dynamics are occurring, and they strive to facilitate a repetition of what works well. Babbie (1995) discusses how such research can build useful theory: "We want to understand, and we want some ability to predict what will happen in the future. At least we'd like some idea about the likely consequences of the various options available to us. We want to do what will produce the results we want" (p. 468). So, the theories that the lessons in this book teach can help you give students the tools to do what works again and again.

THE PARALLEL PROCESS OF TEACHING AND LEARNING

Karen Warren (1995) describes a model for teaching experiential education theory, first posing this challenge:

> How can we teach a theory of what we practice? How can we come down off the ropes course . . . or put away our New Games props, and sit down in the classroom to learn experiential education philosophy? How can discussions about Dewey's ideas, lesson plans, Summerhill, moral development, ethics of teaching, motivation, and a host of other questions grounded in the foundations of experiential education come alive in a classroom setting? How can we give future teachers a sound theoretical framework to use in teaching experientially? The answer, of course, is experientially. (p. 250)

Here Warren describes a process of teaching, in this case using experiential pedagogy, that parallels the outcomes of students' learning about experiential education. The editors of this book have each taken Warren's student-directed classroom challenge to implement the second scenario presented in the introduction to this chapter. In a college course on the philosophy and theory of adventure education, students are asked to address four questions, inspired by Keith King (2002), starting on the first day of class:

> What do you want to learn?
>
> How do you want to learn it?
>
> How will you know when you've learned it?
>
> What will be the consequences of not learning it?

Within the broad boundaries of the learning objectives on the course syllabus, students must reach some agreement about how the course is going to be conducted. There is initial disequilibrium in being handed a great deal of freedom with little structure. There is anxiety about having to decide things they have minimal experience with. Some students begin to enjoy a process requiring introspection, analysis, and responsibility, while others impatiently just want to get on with it.

All this that is now happening in the classroom is very similar, at least in process, to what students will be encountering as adventure educators in the field, on the ropes course, and even in their own classroom, perhaps, later as teachers. Students coming to an Outward Bound or National Outdoor Leadership School (NOLS) course, for example, are launched into a new environment. They may initially be out of their comfort zones, just as our college students are at the beginning of their course in philosophy and theory of adventure education.

Our participants in the field may be anxious about relying on a rope when they are up 40 feet on a climb, just as the students in the classroom are anxious about what they need to decide. And in both the classroom and the field we have a small community of individuals with different needs, learning styles, and social skills, all coming together for some common experience. What a wonderful way for aspiring adventure educators to learn about self-efficacy, risk, and group development. They learn the theory as they experience the process.

Experiential learning models include a reflection component, and in this spirit we note a couple of things we've learned in teaching about adventure philosophy and theory in a student-directed classroom. First, there is risk, both for the student and for the instructor. Students often feel academic risk because the old rules for getting grades are now ambiguous at first. They may experience social risk, because they must closely interact with their peers on questions that will have consequences. Students often answer the question, "How do you want to learn it?" by saying they want to largely teach the class themselves. So there are risks involving public speaking and preparation. The risks to the instructor include the dilemma that students may not choose to learn some of the topics the instructor deems important. There is the risk in academia of poor course and instructor evaluations from students who think "He didn't teach me anything." But again, experiencing risk—together as students and instructors—provides a vibrant and dynamic process for learning about risk theory.

The second lesson we've learned from the student-directed classroom grows out of the first, regarding instructor risk. How do students know what they should be learning, when they are taking a course to learn "it"? Isn't this like expecting an outdoor leader who is at a level of unconscious incompetence, who doesn't know what he or she doesn't know, to safely conduct a group on challenging technical terrain? Our response has come back to the issue of creating balance: The instructor makes some choices about key content that students should know and also gives students some choices about other content, course learning processes, and even grading models. Such balances will need to be struck differently depending on the instructor's values, student academic and social maturity, and the collective class personality. Again, this is analogous to the balance that adventure educators must always create with their groups in the field. The student-directed classroom, then, is one example of the use of parallel process in education—creating and embracing a process of risk, for example, to teach about risk.

SUMMARY

Many of the lessons in this book present creative parallel processes of teaching and learning. We can show students the power they gain with knowing how to transfer their knowledge from the classroom to the mountain. In the outdoors, the risks come from the natural environment and the decisions leaders must make in response to it. In the classroom, risks come from academic challenges and sometimes the social environment. With well-constructed, experiential lessons we can create opportunities for students to take risks with peers in the classroom that are analogous to the risks they take in the backcountry.

In this text you will find such parallel processes—experiential strategies to take students out of their academic comfort zones, using Christian Bisson's lesson on arousal theory, or Bob Stremba's lesson on edgework, for example, to help aspiring adventure educators understand why people embrace risk and why disequilibrium is a component of character development.

A student knowing the *why* behind the *what*—who is armed with a strong core theoretical foundation balanced by real experience with technical skills in the field—is more holistically prepared to assume the responsibilities of an effective adventure educator.

REFERENCES

Babbie, E. 1998. *The practice of social research.* 8th ed. Belmont, CA: Wadsworth.

Fort Lewis College. 2007. College-wide liberal education outcomes. www.fortlewis.edu/about_flc/ (accessed June 2007).

Iso-Ahola, S.E. 1980. *The social-psychology of leisure and recreation.* Dubuque, IA: Brown.

King, K. 2002. Questions to promote student-directed learning. Personal communication.

Levi, C. 1989. Camping for credit. Personal communication.

Priest, S. 1987. *Preparing effective outdoor pursuit leaders.* Eugene, OR: Institute of Recreation Research and Service.

Priest, S., and M.A. Gass. 2005. *Effective leadership in adventure programming.* 2nd ed. Champaign, IL: Human Kinetics.

Prouty, D., J. Panicucci, and R. Collinson. 2007. *Adventure education: Theory and applications.* Champaign, IL: Human Kinetics.

Warren, K. 1995. The student-directed classroom: A model for teaching experiential education theory. In *The theory of experiential education,* eds. K. Warren, M. Sakofs, and J. Hunt. Dubuque, IA: Kendall/Hunt.

CHAPTER 2

Teaching Theory, Facts, and Abstract Concepts Effectively

Attitudes toward teaching and learning in academia have changed a great deal in the past 50 years (Davis 1993). However, the traditional model of instruction continues to prevail (Johnson 1995; Wurdinger 2005). Even though studies have demonstrated that using more engaging and experiential instructional strategies is yielding greater academic success and higher student satisfaction, we are still delivering theories, facts, models, or concepts via a didactic form of instruction. Our blind commitment to didactic instruction is so ingrained that higher education institutions are still designing and building classrooms to support instruction via lectures. These classrooms are often called "lecture halls" so that no one gets the wrong expectation about what will be happening inside. It is also interesting to note that courses in American universities are still categorized as either "lecture," "lab," or "activity" classes. Strangely, more credits per contact hour (e.g., 3 lecture credits = 37.5 contact hours) are awarded for "lecture"-designated classes than for hands-on "lab" or "activity" classes (e.g., 1 activity credit = 25 contact hours), as if experiential lessons, which take more time, are of lesser value in academia.

Many excellent teachers are pushing for changes in instructional strategies. Likewise, students who have been exposed to effective, engaging, and experiential forms of instruction are also asking, sometimes expecting, to learn from real and meaningful experiences, cooperative work, problem solving, and fun, engaging activities. This yearning for effective teaching strategies is even more present in adventure, outdoor, and experiential education.

The great majority of students studying in our respective fields are seeking vocational training that will prepare them to lead, teach, instruct, facilitate, coordinate, or direct adventure-related programs. Therefore, we include in our curriculum classes focusing on the development of their technical skills—such as outdoor pursuit activities, emergency care skills, or environmental care practices. Many of these classes become the most popular in our programs since they involve direct experiences, cooperation, real problems, and authentic assessment. Consequently, we should not be surprised to discover our students expecting us to teach and instruct more abstract subjects such as history, philosophy, education theories, leadership theories, public land politics, risk management theories, and social psychology theories via instructional strategies that are also engaging and experiential.

The challenge we face as instructors is that theories, facts, models, or concepts are mostly abstract in character. When the topic of instruction is less tangible than paddling a canoe or building a litter, it can sometimes be difficult to find ways to create lessons that are engaging and experiential.

This chapter reviews the principles of effective teaching in academia as well as the various teaching strategies used throughout the lesson plans presented in this text. A special section of the chapter is reserved for a review of essential assessment strategies.

PRINCIPLES OF EFFECTIVE TEACHING

A principle is a fundamental rule explaining the working of a device or process. Therefore, by presenting here the few essential principles influencing the effectiveness of the teaching-learning process, we want to emphasize that being a good teacher requires not only the use of good teaching strategies—which will also be presented later—but also the application of some fundamental pedagogical rules.

Using the Experiential Learning Model to Teach Abstract Concepts

The experiential learning model proposed by Kolb (1984) has been widely reproduced and accepted as a viable model to implement experiential learning strategies (figure 2). Although many other scholars and educators (Pfeiffer and Jones 1980; Joplin 1981; Priest 1990; Wurdinger and Priest 1999) have proposed variations on the model, the basic elements of an "experience" and a "reflection" remain the two constants that essentially define the experiential learning model.

Therefore, applying the experiential learning model to a lesson about an abstract topic or concept challenges us to create and offer some form of experience in our lesson. This is often easier said than done, but the idea is quite simple. If we want to teach the theoretical leadership model, we should simply place each student in a leadership role and then help the student reflect on his or her experience as a leader. This is easy to accomplish if we have many days to dedicate to this experience, as in a wilderness expedition. In a 60- to 120-minute period, creating an experience in leadership becomes a little more difficult, but not impossible. Although it is true that experiential learning is more time-consuming and that college and university weekly class schedules do not always give us the luxury of time, we can—as seen in this book—create lessons that offer short but engaging and meaningful experiences through which the theoretical concepts can be applied or tested.

You will notice that in this text, most of the lessons include some form of concrete experience that helps connect the learners with the

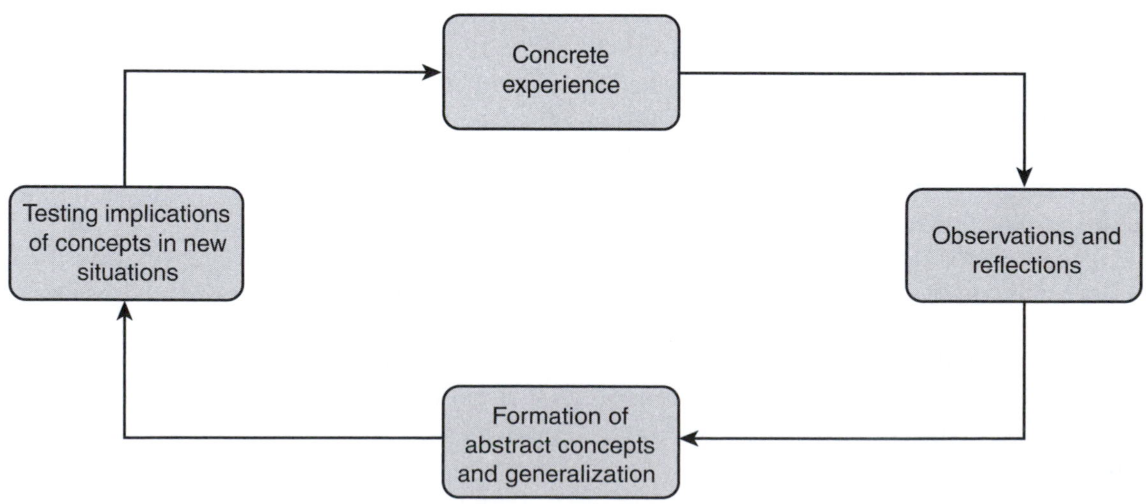

FIGURE 2 Kolb's experiential learning cycle.

KOLB, DAVID A., *EXPERIENTIAL LEARNING: EXPERIENCE AS A SOURCE OF LEARNING & DEVELOPMENT*, 1st, © 1984. Electronically reproduced by permission of Pearson Education, Inc., Upper Saddle River, New Jersey.

subject of the lesson. At times the experience is a game or an activity; in other cases it is a simulation, a role play, or a skit. At times the lesson involves the learners in metaphoric problem solving, a case study, or a real issue.

Regardless of the teaching strategies used, what is essential to increase our students' involvement—even in our theory classes—is to create and provide concrete experiences. Some argue that all teaching strategies—even the most didactic ones—can be construed as experiences. Although this is correct with reference to the broad definition of "experience," we can also agree with John Dewey's contention: "The belief that all genuine education comes about through experience does not mean that all experiences are genuinely or equally educative" (1938, p. 25). This is why it is very important to look carefully at the type of experiences we create for our lessons. Is the experience relevant to the student, is it meaningful, is it engaging? To address the issue of how experiential your "experience" is, we look next at the different levels of experience you can use in your lessons.

Cone of Experience

In the second edition of their text on experiential learning, Beard and Wilson (2006) present a model adapted from Edgar Dale's *cone of experience* (figure 3). Their interpretation of Dale's model offers a gradient of experience in which the learner interacts with the subject being learned through a sample of teaching strategies that offer gradually more or fewer degrees of abstraction.

The model suggests that to share factual information, we often select the use of written

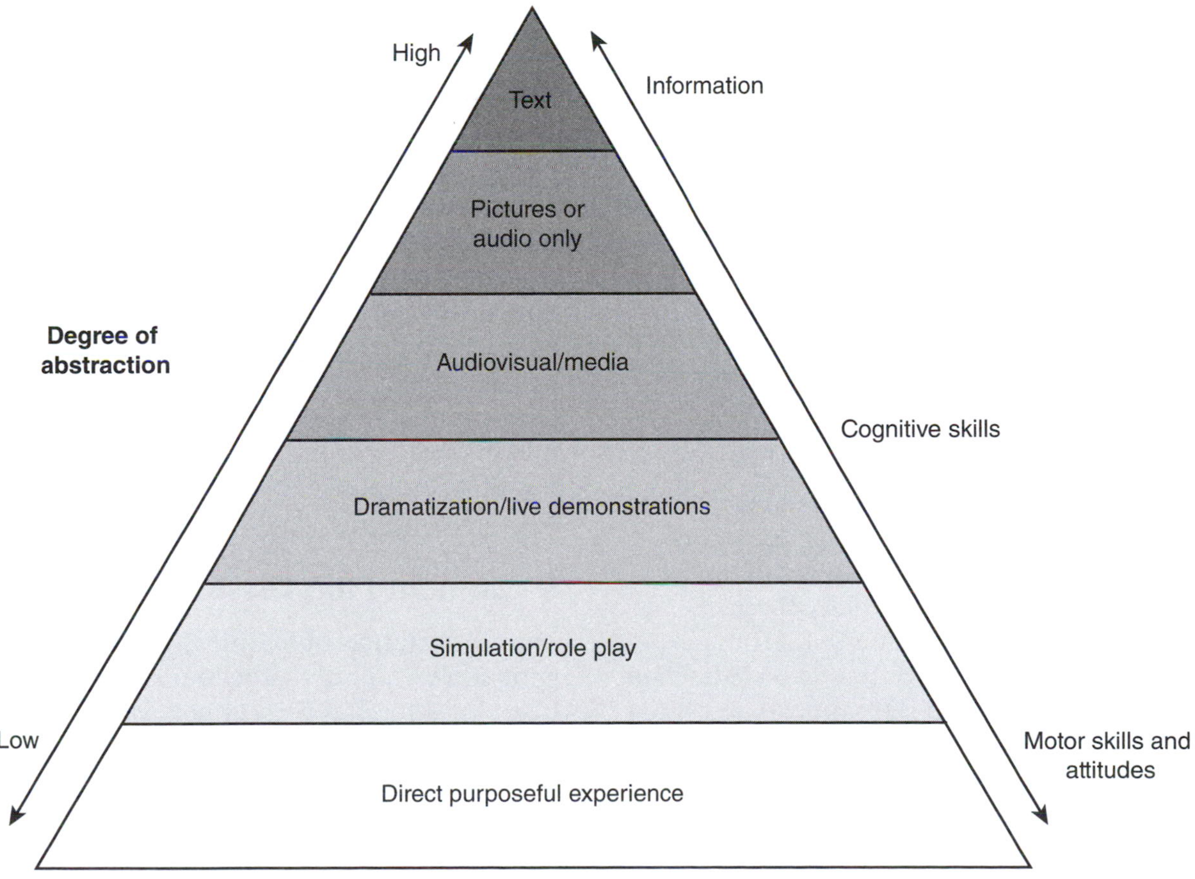

FIGURE 3 Beard and Wilson's adaptation of Dale's cone of experience.

Adapted, by permission, from C. Beard and J.P. Wilson, 2006, *Experiential learning: A best practice handbook for educators and trainers*, 2nd ed. (Philadelphia, PA: Kogan Page), 108. Also from Dale. *Audiovisual methods in teaching*, 1E. © 1969 Wadsworth, a part of Cengage Learning, Inc. Reproduced by permission. www.cengage.com/permissions

material such as that in a text or a lecture that provides only audio inputs. Both levels of experience provide a limited amount of stimuli for the learners, which often leads them to lose focus or limit their mastery of the concepts. For instance, if we require our students to read about outdoor leadership theories or if we simply lecture about the topic while using visual aids, we have created a learning experience that will keep the theoretical concepts quite abstract or irrelevant in the minds of our students.

Lower in the cone, the use of audio-visual material and media such as movies or animation seems to provide more stimuli and decrease the degree of abstraction. Therefore, we can argue that if one shows a movie clip representing outdoor leadership strategies in action, one's students will gain a greater understanding of the concepts since they can associate these concepts with observable behaviors. But their involvement is still very passive. The cone of experience indicates that similar to the use of multimedia, a live demonstration in front of the learner will decrease the abstraction level of the topic but still offer only a passive participation in the experience. Beard and Wilson (2006) suggest that these forms of instruction are more appropriate to the acquisition of content knowledge or the development of cognitive skills.

At the bottom of the cone, we find strategies that increase the level of engagement in the experience and also lower the level of abstraction of the topic being studied. For instance, if we choose to involve students in a skit, a role play, or a simulation about leadership, we allow them to directly experience all the nuances associated with or hidden in the theoretical model. Finally, if we place them in a real leadership situation, as in a wilderness expedition, with real clients, then the abstraction of the leadership model disappears and their understanding of the model becomes highly relevant. Beard and Wilson (2006) recommend that these teaching strategies be used for the development of technical skills or attitudes.

Although we agree with Beard and Wilson (2006), we also feel that not only technical skills and attitudes can be developed via more engaging forms of experiences. Our contention is that all forms of educational outcomes, including content knowledge (e.g., factual information), skills (e.g., cognitive skills, technical skills, social skills), or values (e.g., relating to attitudes, character building, moral development, and ethical issues), can be developed via more engaging and experiential teaching strategies. This becomes more evident when we look closely at the various teaching strategies employed throughout the lesson plans in this text.

Using Isomorphic Activities to Teach Theoretical Models

Priest and Gass (2005) define an isomorph as "an idea, object, or description that is identical in form or structure—but not necessarily composition or function—to another idea, object, or description" (p. 216). In other words, isomorphic activities are designed to reproduce theoretical concepts or models with equivalent structures throughout the activity.

For instance, in the lesson from Stremba about the edgework theory (see lesson 30), by using concentric circles to represent various degrees of comfort zones, the instructor employs an isomorphic activity to illustrate the abstract concepts of emotional or psychological barriers. Using isomorphic games or activities can allow you to engage your students in direct, fun, and meaningful experiences that will help them understand or appreciate theories, concepts, or models that are for the most part inherently abstract. In this text you will find many examples of lessons that include the use of isomorphic games or activities to teach abstract concepts.

Sequencing the Lesson

The importance of sequencing activities to enhance learning and other outcomes in adventure education has been largely accepted as an essential component of any effective instructional strategy (Bisson 1999; Rohnke and Butler 1995). What we should acknowledge here is that sequencing activities in a challenge course curriculum is as important as sequencing learning activities in a theory lesson.

Sequencing activities in your lesson might imply choosing to start the lesson with an activity, posing a problem, or providing some basic information. It also means varying your teaching strategies throughout the lesson—intermixing teaching strategies such as activities, games, discussion, mini-lecture, small group exercise, role play, and guest speakers.

As on a challenge course, there is no magic sequence (Bisson 1999), but one can follow principles of varying activities to enhance learning. These principles are simple. First, to capture students' attention and get them intrigued by a new concept while respecting an experiential learning model, start the lesson with an activity followed by a discussion, a mini-lecture, or both. Second, to prepare students to resolve a complex problem or practice a new set of skills based on sound theoretical principles, start the lesson with a mini-lecture, then move to an activity, a role play, or a small group problem-solving experience. By doing so, you will still offer an effective learning experience known as *information assimilation* (Coleman 1976). Third, it is essential to remember that many scholars from a wide variety of disciplines (Birkel 1973; deWinstanley and Bjork 2002; Johnson 1995; McKeachie 1980; Olmsted III 1999; Penner 1984; Shakarian 1995) have shown that lecturing is effective only if, first and foremost, it lasts a short period of time—between 10 and 15 minutes. This means that if you use lecturing, you should always infuse your presentation with active learning strategies such as discussion, writing, games, questioning, role play, and demonstration.

Reading and Writing to Enhance Learning

Using written material to teach theoretical concepts is a valid and proven practice. Textbooks, articles, stories, Web sites, news clips, and quotes can provide a background perspective regarding a specific topic or theory. In relation to sequencing, readings can be done before, during, or after the lesson.

- **Reading before the lesson.** A teacher can assign a reading to prepare the students to participate in an activity. This can be construed as *front-loading,* whereby the students acquire concepts and new vocabulary before participating in a class experience. For instance, assigning specific readings about a controversial issue will help prepare students for a class debate or discussion.
- **Reading during the lesson.** A teacher can assign short readings to emphasize a point or generate controversy about concepts that have already been accepted by the students. Reading during a lesson could include a sharing of students' writing about a topic or point of view. For example, asking students to share-read each other's educational philosophy will enable them to better discuss and comment on their respective belief systems.
- **Reading after the lesson.** A teacher can assign materials for students to read to further explore information that has been learned during the lesson. Additional reading can allow students to develop new questions or find new applications for theories, concepts, or facts learned in class. For instance, assigning students to visit and read a Web site dedicated to Kurt Hahn can help students further explore his impact on education across nations.

Using Technology in the Classroom

One advantage provided by a classroom environment is the ability to use multimedia technology to enhance the learning experience of students. Chalkboards, whiteboards, and flip charts are all very useful to support group discussion or group work, but having access to a computer and a classroom projector can greatly enhance a mini-lecture, demonstration, or discussion. Furthermore, if the classroom is connected to the World Wide Web, it becomes easy to bring in information, images, or video from around the world. With the right technology, one could even bring in a guest speaker from another continent.

Using multimedia in the classroom has become increasingly popular. However, like any other instructional tool, multimedia can be abused. The key point to remember is that audio-visual aids should support the learning and not distract from it.

STRATEGIES FOR EFFECTIVE TEACHING

Many of us are familiar with the analogy between the carpenter and the effective teacher. Usually, the comparison goes as follows: "A skilled educator is like a skilled carpenter, using a variety of tools to build knowledge, skills, or values." Although the analogy is powerful, it is incomplete unless we take the time to add a qualification: "But there is a distinction between skilled carpenters and master carpenters; so, like master carpenters, master teachers know which tools to use for what purpose and for which learner." What is interesting about these comparisons is that the first one elegantly reminds us that teaching is a science (e.g., involving knowledge of the strategies and how people learn) while the second suggests that teaching is also a craft. As with any master craftsperson, it takes years of experience, a perceptive mind, and diligence to reflect on one's work to approach a level of mastery.

The next section deals with the science of teaching. Developing your craft comes with experience. Be aware that the following strategies represent only a small sample of all possible teaching strategies pertinent to the instruction of abstract concepts. We decided to highlight these strategies because you will find all of them in the various lesson plans in this book.

Lecturing

We discuss the teaching strategy of lecturing not because it is a predominant method used by this book's editors and contributors, but simply because its presence in academia is so prevalent while also strongly criticized. We suggest that lecture is, as Birkel (1973) pointed out, more a victim than a villain.

Lecturing is perhaps the oldest teaching strategy and still the most widely used in colleges and universities throughout the world (McKeachie 1980). The classic image of a savant passing on his or her knowledge to passive and ignorant students may be what comes to mind when we hear the word "lecture." Although this image suggests an oppressive form of instructor–pupil relationship, the reality is that lecture can be something else. It can be engaging, and by this we do not imply that "listening" is a form of engagement. A lecture can be engaging if we create a dialogue instead of a one-way speech. It can be engaging if it includes questions, invites participation, or does not require students to take notes but to simply focus on the dialogue.

You will notice that some lesson plans in this text propose the use of lectures, but you will also notice that these are identified as mini-lectures that should not last more than 10 to 15 minutes each. Research on concentration from Stuart and Rutherford (1978) suggests that student concentration rises sharply to reach a maximum in 10 to 15 minutes and falls steadily thereafter.

Lecture should be used to present new materials, challenge theory, and share possible applications in the real world. It should not be used to literally review what has been read or what is written on the board or the PowerPoint slide.

As mentioned earlier, mini-lectures can be placed between activities or small group discussions. They can be enhanced by a demonstration, by a skit or role play, or by the planting of questions in the audience in advance.

Lectures can be fun. They can use humor, can be delivered in character, or can use visual aids that will generate laughter. As McKeachie (1980) said, "Effective lecturers combine the talents of scholar, writer, producer, comedian, showman, and teacher in ways that contribute to student learning" (p. 25).

Sullivan and McIntosh (1996) summarize the characteristics of an effective mini-lecture in contrast to an ineffective lecture (see table 2). In the effective mini-lecture, with the learners actively engaged, the teacher involves students through a highly interactive and participatory approach using a variety of teaching techniques. By contrast, in an ineffective lecture, with the learners passively engaged, the teacher speaks and student interaction is minimal. Consequently, the learners' minds quickly wander to more interesting topics.

You can find good examples of effective mini-lectures in lesson 9, lesson 23, and lesson 34.

TABLE 2 Comparing Effective and Ineffective Lectures

Characteristics of the effective lecture	Characteristics of the ineffective lecture
Educator-student interaction	100% educator talk, with limited or no interaction
Two-way communication	One-way communication
Educator-student questions	Few if any questions (educator or student)
Shared responsibility for active learning	Dependence of students on educator for all information
Small group, problem-solving activities	No student activities
Variety of supporting media	No supporting media
Limited note taking required (students have copies of lecture notes)	Extensive note taking required
Lasting no more than 10 to 15 minutes	Lasting more than 15 minutes

Adapted with permission of Jhpiego. From: Sullivan R. and McIntosh N. 2006. *Delivering Effective Lectures*. Strategy Paper #5. Baltimore, Maryland.

Dramatization

Dramatization has been a popular alternative in teaching or group therapy for many years (Blatner 2006). Role-playing, also known as "sociodrama," is a derivative of psychodrama, a powerful group therapy method developed in the mid-1930s by psychotherapist Jacob L. Moreno (Blatner 2006).

Today, sociodrama or role play has been effectively adapted to many fields of study in higher education. This teaching method is very popular in medical, business, and law schools. In these environments, role play is ideal for helping students understand through direct experience the complexity of human interaction. In addition, role play allows future practitioners to (1) practice effective communication strategies, (2) implement problem solving, and (3) become more self-aware. According to Blatner (2002), this set of outcomes represents the interdependence of three basic categories of skills essential for the development of thinking.

Because of its high level of direct involvement and its potential for promoting reflection and active learning, role-playing as been adopted by many adventure educators as an ideal teaching strategy to instruct human behavior–related content. In areas from leadership to small group dynamics theories or history and ethics, role-playing has been used to enhance learning. A research study from McCarthy and Anderson (2000) indicates that role play and collaborative exercise are more effective than the traditional teacher-centered lecture.

Variations on role plays are plentiful. Different variations of the strategy can allow you and your students to delve more deeply into the conflicts presented in the role play. The following are a few of these variations.

1. **Role reversal:** In this variation, the players are aware that at any moment during the role play the instructor can request a role reversal, meaning that the roles of two or more people are to be exchanged.
2. **Doubling:** In doubling, the principal actors are always paired with other actors who play the role of their subconscious or the "inner voice." At any time during the role play, the inner voice can be heard to express the feelings that the characters are experiencing. This technique allows a deeper understanding of inner conflict as would be appropriately illustrated during a role play about an ethical dilemma. You can even assign two inner voices to a main character to illustrate the struggle that one faces when making an ethical decision.
3. **The replacement:** This variation is similar to role reversal, but this time the exchange happens between players and spectators. At a given moment, the

instructor can stop the action and invite spectators to take the roles of the actors. This technique allows the introduction of new perspectives on the issue at hand.

4. **The directors:** The instructor can ask the players to stop their action—as in a freeze frame—and then invite the spectators to direct the action. Again, this allows the infusion of new ideas and new behaviors but is less intimidating for spectators since they will only be directing and not be on stage.

Although the terms *role play, skit, sketch,* and *simulation* are often used interchangeably, we would like to propose here a simple classification scheme. Role play, as mentioned before, is a synonym for sociodrama; hence the content most often involves serious issues like dealing with conflict, giving feedback, and reviewing important historical events. In addition, role plays are planned in advance, often requiring the instructor or the students to prepare a short script, a sort of guideline or theme that will help the students (actors) frame their improvisation.

In contrast to role play, skits or sketches are defined as short and most often humorous plays in which the players are improvising the content with little or no direction from the teacher. Skits are best used when the content of the message is less important than the potential a situation has for satirical treatment. It is not the best dramatic strategy to use for teaching specific appropriate or professional behaviors. For instance, asking students to improvise skits to teach Leave No Trace principles might lead them to transmit inaccurate information if they have not carefully studied the recommended practices. On the other hand, asking students to improvise a skit about what poor expedition behavior looks like is a sure way to entertain the class while sending a submessage about what is acceptable and unacceptable behavior during a wilderness expedition.

Finally, simulations differ from role plays and skits in that they are more appropriately used when the entire class is involved in a full-scale process for the purpose of testing new skills. For instance, simulations are often used in first aid training or leadership development; the classic "leader of the day" strategy is essentially a simulation. Simulation can also be used to teach about risk management via the reconstruction of a full-scale mock trial based on a true outdoor-related accident.

You can find good examples of effective role plays in lesson 4, "Visionary and Actionary," and lesson 7, "Adventure Education History Roundtable."

Case Studies

According to Boehrer and Linsky (1990), case studies originated in the teaching of law and medicine. However, today this teaching strategy is extremely popular in business education as well as in ethics classes in philosophy. With this technique, the students are presented with a real or fictional life problem and invited to resolve it in small groups or with the entire class.

To be effective, the case study needs to present a written scenario with relevant information including facts, background, context, sequence of events, and potential consequences for various actions. A case study can be inspired by current, historical, or hypothetical events. Obviously, the more real the case is, the more engaged the students may be, especially if you use a story you have personally experienced as a professional adventure educator. There is much to be said about the motivation created by a question such as "What would you have done in my place?"

Case studies are an excellent teaching strategy for applying concepts, theories, or professional responses to a realistic situation within a safe learning environment. Make sure that your students have learned or are learning the abstract concepts necessary to properly resolve the case. Remember also to remain neutral or play "devil's advocate" when the solutions to the case study are presented by your students. Your role is to facilitate their reflection or the application of the theory they are trying to use.

Games and Activities

Using games and activities to enhance learning is not foreign to outdoor, adventure, or experiential educators. We have a plethora of texts and guide books covering myriad games that focus on group or individual skill development. The idea of using play as a valid form of pedagogy has been substantiated by many scholars (Bisson and Luckner 1996; Levy 1978). Their contention is that play is an innate human behavior and that although it is often associated with young children, "play potential" still exists within adults, especially young college students.

Games or activities can take many forms. They can be metaphoric, as on challenge courses, or they can be literal, as in a mock game show used to review class content. What is essential is that the game or the activity be designed and used to accomplish a few essential goals: (1) capture the attention of the learners, (2) promote participation, (3) promote cooperation, and (4) enhance learning. That is, games must be carefully selected, adapted, or designed to meet the goal of the lesson. As explained earlier, using games with an isomorphic structure can help students experience abstract concepts or the components of a theoretical model firsthand.

Activities often pose a mental problem or a physical challenge that needs to be resolved. The problem or challenge is often a metaphor or a fantasy inspired by the subject being studied. Activities that pose problems are seen by students as a good way to test their abilities and social skills. Activities can be used to help students discover theoretical concepts or facts regarding politics, history, or research in adventure education.

You can find good examples of effective games in lesson 3, "Using Backward Design"; lesson 12, "Creating the Right Amount of Challenge"; and lesson 23, "Be Safe Out There," to name a few. To read about effective activities, look at lesson 5, "A History of Adventure Education in the United States"; lesson 6, "Creating History"; or lesson 13, "I Think I Can" for a small sample.

Discussions

Discussion is perhaps the "poster child" for teaching strategies used to promote active learning in academia (McKeachie 2002). As with lecture, its popularity is surpassed only by its misuse. Discussion seems to be ostensibly easy to use; however, leading or stimulating an effective discussion is easier said than done.

Adventure educators are used to the challenges associated with leading discussion, especially when they try to process adventure activities. It is important to apply basic processing strategies when facilitating a discussion. First and foremost, the art of questioning lies at the center of any successful discussion.

Open-ended questions will elicit more responses than questions calling for "yes" or "no" answers. Moving from the general to the specific will help students tackle more complex issues. Using synthesis, evaluative, or analytical questions, as suggested by Bloom (1956), will help students deepen their understanding of theories and concepts in adventure education—will explain the "why" behind the "what." Questions like "What, if any, outcomes can you predict?" will promote the development of synthesis skills to find abstract relations between concepts and propose new sets of outcomes. Questions like "Explain why you agree or disagree with . . ." will encourage students to evaluate theories by looking for internal evidence in the theoretical construct as well as testing the construct through external criteria. Questions like "How would you classify . . .?" will help students analyze evidence by looking for relationships and organizational structure in the elements of a theory (Bloom 1956).

Discussions are easier to generate if they are based on direct experience. So, using a group discussion either with the entire class or in a subgroup or dyad—after a game, activity, role play, skit, demonstration, film, or guest speaker—is more effective than using an opening question.

Using writing in the class can ease the discussion process and allow more alternative points of view to surface when the students exchange and argue their positions. Give time for them to write and make sure they know that this writing will not be collected or graded. Explain that the writing is only a tool for them to use to collect their thoughts and process the questions.

A popular variation on group discussion is the "fishbowl conversation." In a fishbowl conversation, five or six students sit in a circle at the center of a room (i.e., the fishbowl) while the rest of the class sits on the outside and silently and carefully listens to the inner-circle discussion. Two essential variations to the fishbowl exist. In the open fishbowl, an extra chair is added to the inner circle and left empty until someone from the outer circle decides to join the circle. At that time, someone from the fishbowl must volunteer to join the outer group. This process is repeated until everyone has had the chance to join the fishbowl. The second variation is called the closed fishbowl. In this variation, all the inner-circle chairs are occupied. When the time is appropriate, the instructor can call for a rotation, and all the members of the fishbowl move to the outer circle while volunteers from the outside group take a place in the inner circle.

Promoting participation during discussion can be a challenge. McKeachie (2002) and Davis (1993) remind us that a successful discussion also depends on the level of participation by the students. Both authors indicate that creating a safe and familiar social environment is essential to help students who are timid feel comfortable about speaking in their subgroup or in class. Adventure educators are often well trained in creating a positive classroom culture. Before involving your students in group discussions, make sure that they know each other and that they have found commonalities or have shared fun learning experiences together.

You can find examples of effective use of discussion in lesson 20, lesson 32,and lesson 33.

ASSESSING LEARNING

In 1995, Barr and Tagg proposed a new paradigm for college and university teachers. They argued that the traditional "teaching-centered" curriculum was no longer viable in a society that increasingly requires public and private institutions to be accountable for their actions. They challenged the old model in which the function of the college teacher was to teach—mainly via lectures and assigned reading—while the role of the student was to learn. If the student failed to learn, the responsibility rested on the student's shoulders, not the instructor's (Suskie 2004). Barr and Tagg (1995) proposed a shift from a teaching-centered or instructor-centered to a more learning-centered or learner-centered curriculum. Faculties that embrace the learning-centered paradigm recognize that the role of the teacher is to ensure learning by creating effective learning environments and using effective learning strategies. These faculties are also aware that learning is not the sole responsibility of the student but is a responsibility shared between teachers and learners.

To accomplish this renewed vision of the teacher's role, a new focus on assessment of learning and outcomes has emerged throughout the higher education community. Assessment is no longer confused with grading or evaluation but is now used to provide essential feedback to the learner as well as the educator. The following is a brief review of various forms of assessment and their application to effective teaching strategies.

Formative Assessment

Formative assessment is generally defined as a set of formal or informal assessment strategies that are conducted throughout the learning-teaching process. It is designed to provide immediate or prompt feedback to the learner and the instructor on the development of the learner's knowledge, skills, or values.

The task of formative assessment is not limited to an instructor; it can also be performed by the learners or their peers. It is important to understand that formative assessment is not necessarily used for grading purposes. Its main value is in providing feedback on the learning and indicating whether the learning objectives are being met.

Summative Assessment

In contrast to formative assessment, *summative assessment* is generally conducted at the end of the course or the teaching unit to evaluate the amount of learning accumulated by the students. It is often performed via a formal strategy such as a test, quiz, or paper that will be used to assign a grade. Completion of the summative assessment normally means that the specific learning experience has ended;

therefore the feedback provided is meaningful but perhaps not as useful as with the formative assessment.

Formal and Informal Assessment

As mentioned before, assessment can be either formal or informal. *Formal assessments* usually take the form of a written document, such as a test, quiz, or paper. *Informal assessment,* which usually occurs in a more casual manner, uses observation, inventories, checklists, rating scales, rubrics, performance and portfolio assessments, participation, peer evaluation and self-evaluation, and discussion.

Formative Judgment

Formative judgment is defined by Cangelos (2000) as the direct observation of behavior indicating a change in learning that will affect the instructor's current or future teaching strategy. Similar to formative assessment, formative judgment is performed during the learning-teaching process and influences mostly the teacher's teaching plan. It is not feedback to the student, but feedback to the teacher. Many lesson plans in this text involve the use of formative assessment and formative judgment, while only a few propose the use of summative assessment tools to measure the students' learning on the given topic.

SUMMARY

Effectively teaching abstract concepts and theories related to adventure, outdoor, or experiential education requires more than just fun games and activities. Pedagogical principles essential to creating an effective education experience include using the experiential learning cycle, knowing the gradient of experience we can create, developing isomorphic activities, properly sequencing the learning experience, using writing and reading to enhance cognitive learning, and enhancing the experience via the use of technology in the classroom. Proven teaching strategies that can enhance experiential learning include mini-lectures, dramatization, games and activities, group case studies, and discussion. Basic assessment principles that promote a shift in our assessment from a traditional teaching- or instructor-centered to a more learning- or learner-centered curriculum are desirable in experiential education.

Understanding principles of effective teaching, using engaging teaching strategies, and using learning-centered forms of assessment will help you deliver theoretical or abstract concepts in adventure, outdoor, or experiential education that will make the students' experience as engaging and rewarding as any great outdoor expedition or technical outdoor skill class.

REFERENCES

Barr, R., and J. Tagg. 1995. From teaching to learning: A new paradigm for undergraduate education. *Change* 27,(6):12-25.

Beard, C., and J.P. Wilson. 2006. *Experiential learning: A best practice handbook for educators and trainers.* Philadelphia: Kogan Page.

Birkel, L.F. 1973. The lecture method: Villain or victim? *Peabody Journal of Education* 50,(4):298-301.

Bisson, C. 1999. Sequencing the adventure experience. In *Adventure programming,* eds. J.C. Miles and S. Priest. State College, PA: Venture.

Bisson, C., and J. Luckner. 1996. Fun in learning: The pedagogical role of fun in adventure education. *Journal of Experiential Education* 19,(2):107-112.

Blatner, A. 2002. *Role playing in education.* www.blatner.com/adam/pdntbk/rlplayedu.htm (accessed June 24, 2007).

Blatner, A. 2006. Enacting the new academy: Sociodrama as a powerful tool in higher education. *ReVision* 28,(3):30-35.

Bloom, B.S. 1956. *Taxonomy of educational objectives: The classification of educational goals.* New York: Susan Fauer.

Boehrer, J., and M. Linsky. 1990. Teaching with cases: Learning to question. In *The changing face of college teaching,* ed. M.D. Svinicki. New Directions for Teaching and Learning, No. 42. San Francisco: Jossey-Bass.

Cangelos, J.S. 2000. *Assessment strategies for monitoring student learning.* New York: Longman.

Coleman, J.S. 1976. Difference between experiential and classroom learning. In *Experiential learning: Rationale, characteristics and assessment,* ed. M.T. Keeton. San Francisco: Jossey-Bass.

Davis, B.G. 1993. *Tools for teaching.* San Francisco: Jossey-Bass.

Dewey, J. 1938. *Experience and education.* New York: Free Press.

deWinstanley, P.A., and R.A. Bjork. 2002. Successful lecturing: Presenting information in ways that engage effective processing. In *Applying the science of learning to university teaching and beyond,* eds. D.F. Halpern and M.D. Hakel. New Directions for Teaching and Learning, No. 89, 19-31.

Johnson, G. 1995. *First steps to excellence in college teaching.* Madison, WI: Magna.

Joplin, L. 1981. On defining experiential education. *Journal of Experiential Education* 4,(1):17-20.

Kolb, D.A. 1984. *Experiential learning.* Englewood Cliffs, NJ: Prentice Hall.

Levy, J. 1978. *Play behavior.* New York: Wiley.

McCarthy, J.P., and L. Anderson. 2000. Active learning techniques versus traditional teaching styles: Two experiments from history and political science. *Innovative Higher Education* 24,(4):279-294.

McKeachie, W.J. 1980. Improving lectures by understanding students' information processing. In *Learning, cognition, and college teaching,* ed. W.J. McKeachie. New Directions for Teaching and Learning, No. 2, 25-35.

McKeachie, W.J. 2002. *Teaching tips: Strategies, research, and theory for college and university teachers.* Boston: Houghton Mifflin.

Olmsted III, J.A. 1999. The mid-lecture break: When less is more. *Journal of Chemistry Education* 76,(4):525-527.

Penner, J.G. 1984. *Why many college teachers cannot lecture.* Springfield, IL: Charles C. Thomas.

Pfeiffer, J.W., and J.E. Jones. 1980. *The 1980 annual handbook for group facilitators.* San Diego: University Associates.

Priest, S. 1990. Everything you always wanted to know about judgment, but were afraid to ask. *Journal of Adventure Education and Outdoor Leadership* 7,(3):5-12.

Priest, S., and M. Gass. 2005. *Effective leadership in adventure programming.* Champaign, IL: Human Kinetics.

Rohnke, K., and S. Butler. 1995. *Quicksilver: Adventure games, initiative problems, trust activities, and a guide to effective leadership.* Dubuque, IA: Kendall/Hunt.

Shakarian, D. 1995. Beyond lecture: Active learning strategies that work. *Journal of Physical Education, Recreation and Dance* 66,(5):21-24.

Stuart, J., and R.J.D. Rutherford. 1978. Medical student concentration during lectures. *Lancet* 2:514-516.

Sullivan, R.L., and N. McIntosh. 1996. Delivering effective lectures. JHPIEGO strategy paper No. 5. www.reproline.jhu.edu/English/6read/6training/lecture/delivering_lecture.htm (accessed June 24, 2007).

Suskie, L. 2004. *Assessing student learning. A common sense guide.* Bolton, MA: Anker.

Wurdinger, S. 2005. *Using experiential learning in the classroom: Practical ideas for all educators.* Lanham, MD: Scarecrow Education.

Wurdinger, S., and S. Priest. 1999. Integrating theory and application in experiential learning. In *Adventure programming,* eds. J.C. Miles and S. Priest. State College, PA: Venture.

PART II

Instructional Theory

When students who are preparing to be adventure educators first teach something, they often fall back on teaching methods that are familiar but ineffective for even their own learning. It's curious to observe students who say they are hands-on learners teach a lesson using a lecture style, with their "students" as passive recipients of information. Or, these beginning teachers overuse a set of methods they have found engaging, but fail to similarly involve those they are teaching. Effective methods of teaching prospective adventure educators how to teach begin with the pedagogical theories and models that describe why these methods work to promote learning. In this part of the book, Kate Cassidy, Mary Breunig, and Alison Rheingold provide lessons that help adventure educators move beyond their own, perhaps limited, experiences as recipients of teaching to develop lessons that account for different learning styles and focus on intended learning outcomes. Their lessons show us how to teach adventure educators and teachers to teach, and thereby provide a useful foundation for the subsequent lessons in this book.

In the first lesson, "Addressing Multiple Ways of Knowing in Adventure Education," Kate Cassidy invites adventure educators to include a variety of teaching strategies to create meaningful learning adventures for their students. Howard Gardner (1983) initially proposed seven different intelligences—linguistic, musical, logical-mathematical, visual-spatial, bodily-kinesthetic, interpersonal, intrapersonal—and later added an eighth, naturalist intelligence. He asserted that, barring brain damage, all individuals possess the potential of all the intelligences. Cassidy's lesson has students identify their own strongest as well as underdeveloped intelligences and then engage in a set of learning activities that demonstrate the eight different intelligences. The result is that they have an opportunity to redefine and appreciate differences in intelligence as an asset rather than a deficit, and to use this framework to create better learning experiences for their own students.

Lesson 2, "Multiple Intelligence Theory and Learning Styles" by Mary Breunig, continues from Kate Cassidy's multiple intelligence framework lesson by providing a useful reminder that stretching one's comfort zone can apply not only to outdoor adventure pursuits, but also to more interpersonal and reflective experiences. This lesson includes a set of interactive strategies for adventure educators to use in a variety of contexts, including instruction and curriculum design, risk-taking activities, and wilderness trips. Using Gardner's theory of multiple intelligences (1983, 1993) and Kolb's (1984) experiential learning cycle, students and teachers can understand and design lessons that appeal to the variety of learning styles and intelligences that exist in a classroom as well as on backcountry adventures. Breunig's lesson helps students understand that a person whose learning style favors bodily-kinesthetic activities may feel very comfortable taking part in physical experiences but may quickly become uncomfortable when taking part in a storytelling exercise, for example.

The third lesson, "Using Backward Design: A Methodology to Develop Experiential Lessons" by Alison Rheingold, gives experiential educators a powerful set of tools to design lessons that begin with a focus on what students will learn, rather than what new and fun game or activity the teacher may want to use. By ending rather than beginning their lesson planning with choosing learning activities, educators start with the intended learning outcomes. The outcomes then drive the process; everything flows from what one wants the student to learn. Rheingold's lesson suggests that planning how to assess student learning outcomes is the second step and that finally, after completing these two steps, one should plan the actual experiences that students will engage in. National and state standards—although many people think of them as a hindrance—can actually be of assistance in this process, because by using these standards educators start with a broad road map, without which one can be directionless.

All three lessons in part II help teach or are themselves based on David Kolb's (1984) experiential learning cycle, which has been a pivotal construct in the field of adventure education.

REFERENCES

Gardner, H. 1983. *Frames of mind.* 2nd ed. New York: Basic Books.

Gardner, H. 1993. *Multiple intelligences: The theory in practice.* New York: Basic Books.

Kolb, D.A. 1984. *Experiential learning: Experience as the source of learning and development.* Englewood Cliffs, NJ: Prentice Hall.

LESSON 1

Addressing Multiple Ways of Knowing in Adventure Education

Kate J. Cassidy

Adventure facilitators should recognize the multiple means by which participants can both challenge themselves and engage in reflective activities to maximize the learning potential of an experience. Choosing activities that span the intelligences allows learners to "solve problems in culturally meaningful ways and create products that reflect their cultural perspectives" (Reiff 1997, p. 302). Multiple intelligence theory provides a simple framework to help adventure facilitators think of alternative conceptions of adventure, reflection, risk, and facilitation. This lesson will demonstrate the importance of addressing multiple ways of knowing when one is designing lessons or curriculum.

Background

> Accepting that we have multiple intelligences democratizes intelligence in the interest of inclusivity; it allows us to redefine and appreciate difference in intelligence as an asset rather than a deficit. (Weil 2004, p. 224)

General intelligence theory—or *g-theory*—is based on the idea that a human's capacity to learn is innate, varies in amount between people, and is stable over a person's life span. This perspective was put forward by the psychologist Alfred Binet, who created what is now popularly known as the IQ test. In the early 1900s, Binet was asked to create an assessment that would predict which students might succeed or fail in school in order that resources might be allocated accordingly. At that time, it was believed that verbal and mathematical skills were most valuable in society. Today, people are more aware of the cultural bias, reinforcement of privilege, and marginalization that are inherent in this unitary perspective of capabilities (Kincheloe 2004).

The theory of multiple intelligences was introduced by Howard Gardner (1983) in his book *Frames of Mind*. Gardner challenged traditional g-theory by arguing for a multidimensional and context-aware perspective on intelligence. He defined intelligence as "the ability to solve problems or fashion products that are of consequence in a particular cultural setting or community" (Gardner 1993, p. 15). Gardner initially proposed seven different intelligences—linguistic, musical, logical-mathematical, visual-spatial, bodily-kinesthetic, interpersonal, and intrapersonal—and later added an eighth, naturalist intelligence. He asserted that barring brain damage, all individuals possess the potential of all the intelligences. Gardner's theory states that each person's profile of strengths in the intelligences is unique and that everyone has the potential to develop each intelligence throughout her or his lifetime. Gardner also cautioned that however useful it might be to separate the intelligences analytically, it must be remembered that the intelligences are integrated with one another in practice (Gardner 1983).

Following is a short description of each intelligence (Gardner 1983, 1993; Hoerr 1996; Lazear 1999).

- **Verbal-linguistic:** Characteristic of this intelligence is an appreciation for the different uses of language. This intelligence involves the ability to communicate effectively, as well as a sensitivity to the meanings and sounds of words. It includes an interest in the practical uses of language.
- **Logical-mathematical:** This intelligence involves a sensitivity to logical or numerical patterns. It can be used to examine relationships, understand large abstract concepts, and solve complex problems.
- **Musical-rhythmic:** Characteristic of musical intelligence is the connection to, and skillful use of, melody, rhythm, and tone.
- **Bodily-kinesthetic:** With this intelligence, the body is used to understand and act upon the world. Bodily-kinesthetic intelligence is the ability to use the body in highly differentiated and skilled ways, and for expressive as well as goal-directed purposes. It involves the capacity to work with objects using both fine and gross motor skills.
- **Visual-spatial:** Visual-spatial intelligence involves the realm of images, patterns, colors, designs, textures, and pictures. This way of knowing allows people to manipulate an object through space and to understand how an object would appear from a different angle or if it were reversed.
- **Interpersonal:** Interpersonal intelligence is the understanding of others. It is the ability to relate to other people's perspectives and to develop an understanding of how they feel.
- **Intrapersonal:** Intrapersonal intelligence involves looking inward and investigating the self. It is the ability to access one's own emotions and motivations; to know one's strengths, weaknesses, and desires; and to use this information to plan and direct one's life.
- **Naturalist:** This intelligence relates to recognizing and appreciating the natural world. It involves such capacities as the ability to discriminate among living things and cultural artifacts and to recognize and classify plants, minerals, animals, and other natural elements within one's environment.

Multiple intelligence theory is not without criticism. Some theorists argue that the inferences made from the research Gardner used to support the theory are unsubstantiated; others feel that the theory still represents a compartmentalized and traditional view of human capabilities (see Kincheloe 2004; Klein 1997; Waterhouse 2006; White 1998). Nevertheless, the theory has proved to be a useful framework for educators to think about abilities broadly (Sternberg 1994). Gardner articulates what experiential educators have always known intuitively: that people learn and know in a variety of ways. Although Western schooling has traditionally valued a profile strong in logical-mathematical and verbal-linguistic intelligences, individuals with different intelligence profiles are successful in the real world. Gardner's theory adds credence to the idea that educators should provide holistic experiences that allow students to develop their multiple intelligences (Weil 2004). As Elliot Eisner writes of Gardner and his theory, "He has provided not only significant leads for researchers to pursue, but extremely important implications for developing a more equitable approach to education" (Eisner 1994, p. 560).

Adventure education programs focus on intrapersonal and interpersonal development through the use of adventurous challenges and reflection. It is important for adventure facilitators to consider different ways of knowing in order to create a positive learning and social environment for each unique participant. Traditionally many adventure programs have emphasized physical challenge, but it is valuable to consider "challenge" from a wider perspective. Canoeing and climbing may be challenging for some, while drama, music, journaling, and storytelling may be challenging and meaningful to others. Using the theory of multiple intelligences to create experiences that are meaningful to each individual may help learners feel open to expressing themselves when participating and sharing their perspectives with others.

Perceived risk is also an important component of adventure education programs (Priest and Gass 2005). Each individual's perception of risk is different and may be physical, social, psychological, or spiritual (Martin, Franc, and Zounkova 2004). A person with a profile high in bodily-kinesthetic intelligence may feel very comfortable taking part in physical activities, but may quickly become uncomfortable when taking part in a storytelling exercise. Thinking in terms of multiple intelligences allows adventure educators to consider a variety of ways in which individuals may experience risk.

Adventure facilitators can also benefit by having an awareness of their personal comfort level with different intelligences. This awareness will help facilitators become sensitive to the potential to be biased in selecting activities that reflect their own strongest intelligences.

To maximize the potential of an experience, adventure facilitators should recognize the multiple means by which participants can both challenge themselves and engage in reflective activities (Martin, Franc, and Zounkova 2004). Choosing activities that span the intelligences allows learners to "solve problems in culturally meaningful ways and create products that reflect their cultural perspectives" (Reiff 1997, p. 302). Multiple intelligence theory provides a simple framework to help adventure facilitators think of alternative conceptions of adventure, reflection, risk, and facilitation.

RESOURCES

Eisner, E.W. 1994. Commentary: Putting multiple intelligences in context: Some questions and observations. *Teachers College Board Record,* 95(4):555-560.

Gardner, H. 1983. *Frames of mind.* 2nd ed. New York: Basic Books.

Gardner, H. 1993. *Multiple intelligences: The theory in practice.* New York: Basic Books.

Hoerr, T.R. 1996. *Implementing multiple intelligences: The new city school experience.* Bloomington, IN: Phi Delta Kappa Educational Foundation.

Kincheloe, J. 2004. *Multiple intelligences reconsidered.* New York: Peter Lang.

Klein, P.D. 1997. Multiplying the problems of intelligence by eight: A critique of Gardner's theory. *Canadian Journal of Education,* 22(4):377-394.

Lazear, D. 1999. *Eight ways of teaching.* Arlington Heights, IL: Skylight.

Martin, A., D. Franc, and D. Zounkova. 2004. *Outdoor and experiential learning: An holistic and creative approach to programme design.* Burlington, VT: Gower.

Priest, S., and M.A. Gass. 2005. *Effective leadership in adventure programming.* Champaign, IL: Human Kinetics.

Reiff, J.C. 1997. Multiple intelligences, culture and equitable learning. *Childhood Education,* 73(5):301-304.

Sternberg, R.J. 1994. Reforming school reform: Comments on "Multiple intelligences: The theory in practice." *Teachers College Board Record,* 95(4):561-569.

Waterhouse, L. 2006. Multiple intelligences, the Mozart effect, and emotional intelligence: A critical review. *Educational Psychologist,* 41(4):207-225.

Weil, D. 2004. Howard Gardner's third way: Toward a postformal redefinition of educational psychology. In *Multiple intelligences reconsidered,* ed. J. Kincheloe, 221-235. New York: Peter Lang.

White, J. 1998. *Do Howard Gardner's multiple intelligences add up?* London: Institute of Education, University of London.

Lesson Plan

PURPOSE

This lesson will invite students to consider the importance of addressing multiple ways of knowing in order to create meaningful learning adventures for all participants.

OBJECTIVES

As a result of this lesson, students will be able to . . .

1. *Affective and psychomotor:* participate in multiple activities to experience how they respond to each of the multiple intelligences.
2. *Cognitive:* consider and discuss the value of recognizing different ways of knowing and being engaged.
3. *Cognitive:* explain multiple intelligence theory, how it presents another way of thinking about intelligence, and how one can adopt it as a useful framework when thinking about appropriate challenges and reflection activities in adventure education.
4. *Cognitive:* assess and describe their own profile of intelligences, as well as ways in which their profile might affect their style of facilitating adventure education.
5. *Cognitive:* describe, synthesize, and apply the principles learned by contributing to a class compilation describing the intelligences and proposing an adventure activity that touches on a variety of intelligences.

DURATION

90 minutes

GROUP SIZE

6 to 30

LOCATION

Best conducted indoors

EQUIPMENT

- Flip chart paper, eight sheets
- Markers in a variety of colors
- One shoebox for every 6 to 10 students
- Waxed paper or tissue paper
- Tape
- Six white index cards for every 6 to 10 students
- A stopwatch
- Small slips of paper, one per student
- Background handout (on CD-ROM)
- Paper and pen for each student

RISK MANAGEMENT CONSIDERATIONS

None

STUDENT PREPARATION

- Ask students to reflect on the following questions in their journal. Reflections may include drawings or collages to illustrate thoughts.
  - How have the ways in which you learn, the things that you like, and the tasks you perform well been helpful or not helpful in your schooling?
  - Why does traditional schooling often treat people the same in terms of what is taught and how it is taught? What are the positive and negative sides of this traditional approach?
  - Does an adventure program treat all people the same in what is taught and how it is taught?
  - Can or should alternative activities using art, music, drama, or other atypical ways of meeting challenges be used in an adventure program? What are the positive and negative aspects of doing this?
- After writing their reflections, students should complete the Multiple Intelligence Quiz (or another multiple intelligence self-assessment selected by the instructor) and read the Background handout. Both documents are provided on the CD-ROM.
- Supplementary reading assignments may also be drawn from the following suggested sources:
  - Gardner, H. 1983. *Frames of mind.* 2nd ed. New York: Basic Books.
  - Gardner, H. 1993. *Multiple intelligences: The theory in practice.* New York: Basic Books.
  - Martin, A., D. Franc, and D. Zounkova. 2004. *Outdoor and experiential learning: An holistic and creative approach to programme design.* Burlington, VT: Gower.

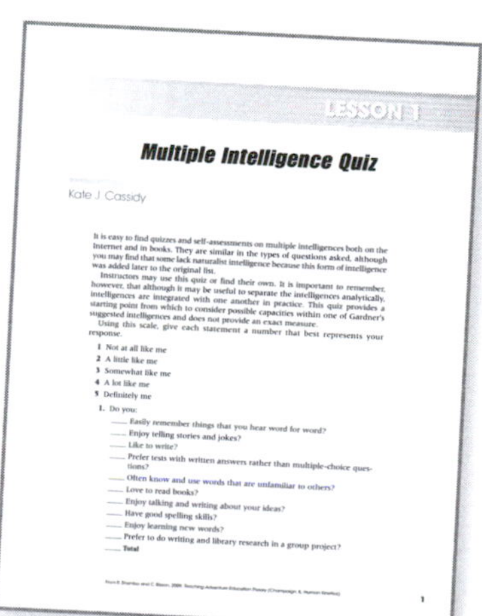

LESSON 1

Multiple Intelligence Quiz

Kate J. Cassidy

It is easy to find quizzes and self-assessments on multiple intelligences both on the Internet and in books. They are similar in the types of questions asked, although you may find that some lack naturalist intelligence because this form of intelligence was added later to the original list.

Instructors may use this quiz or find their own. It is important to remember, however, that although it may be useful to separate the intelligences analytically, intelligences are integrated with one another in practice. This quiz provides a starting point from which to consider possible capacities within one of Gardner's suggested intelligences and does not provide an exact measure.

Using this scale, give each statement a number that best represents your response.

1 Not at all like me
2 A little like me
3 Somewhat like me
4 A lot like me
5 Definitely me

1. Do you:
   - ___ Easily remember things that you hear word for word?
   - ___ Enjoy telling stories and jokes?
   - ___ Like to write?
   - ___ Prefer tests with written answers rather than multiple-choice questions?
   - ___ Often know and use words that are unfamiliar to others?
   - ___ Love to read books?
   - ___ Enjoy talking and writing about your ideas?
   - ___ Have good spelling skills?
   - ___ Enjoy learning new words?
   - ___ Prefer to do writing and library research in a group project?
   - ___ **Total**

1

INSTRUCTOR PREPARATION

- **Posters.** Write the term for each of the intelligences on one of eight sheets of large flip chart paper. Divide each sheet into two sections. On the top write "Strong intelligence," and on the bottom write "Undeveloped intelligence."
- **Pen-hole box.** Poke a hole (with diameter about the size of a pen) through one end of a shoebox. Cut the bottom off the box. Next, tape a piece of waxed paper over the bottom so that light can get in but you cannot clearly see what is inside. Draw pictures using markers of different colors on three index cards (one set of three per box). Each picture should involve nature images and words. Sample pictures are shown in figure 1.1. (These pictures have an advanced degree of difficulty as they have been created to play with assumptions and encourage disagreement and discussion around students' recall.) Reproduce these images, or create your own, using markers of a variety of colors. Tape down the lid of the box so that it stays in place but can be removed when you need to switch index-card pictures.
- **Group-poem slips.** Create enough small slips of paper that you can give one to each student in the class. On each slip, write one of these sentences:
  - This is a poem to celebrate unique individuals.
  - This is a poem about how people solve problems together.
  - This is a poem about a team.

LESSON CONTENT AND TEACHING STRATEGIES

To pique interest, post the questions from the students' journal assignment on the board. Then lead a discussion on students' reflections to start the class.

Activity 1: Identify Your Intelligence

Place the multiple intelligence posters (blank except for the headings) throughout the room. Using their quiz scores as reference, ask students to write their names on the three poster sheets that identify their strongest intelligences and the three poster sheets that list their most undeveloped intelligences. When everyone is finished, gather the sheets and put them together in one place where everyone can see them. Take some time to look at the results as a class. Let students talk about and compare their results.

Ask students:

- Are there any commonalities in our class as to intelligences that are stronger or less developed?
- Did the results of the quiz reflect what you thought your intelligences or capabilities would be?
- Can we find two people who have the same strong intelligences but who like very different things?

Ensure that the following educational concepts are addressed during or after the discussion:

- Everyone is different in his or her profile of intelligences; each person is strong in some intelligences and has other intelligences that are underdeveloped.
- All learners have the potential to develop all of their intelligences throughout their lives.

the fox ran after
after and all the
way home...com
pleting another
day in the life of
a rabbit!!

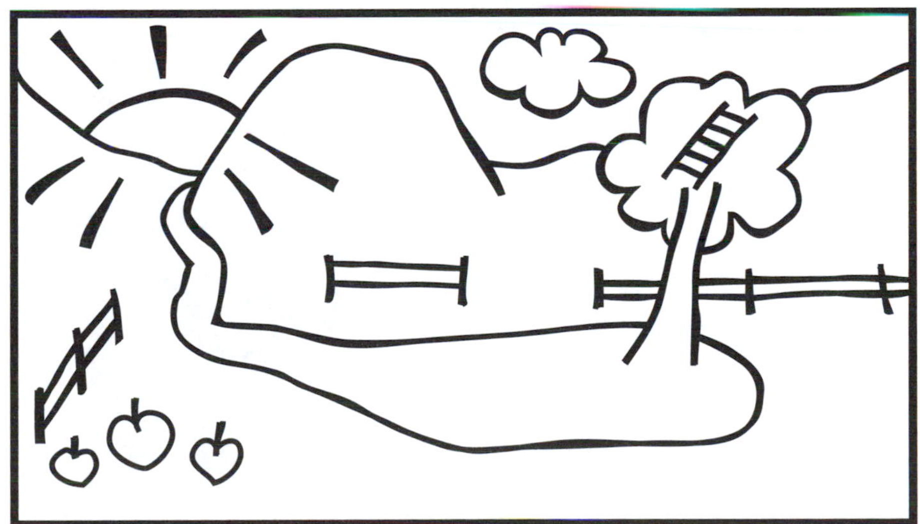

FIGURE 1.1 Pictures for the pen-hole box activity should involve nature images and words.

- What is meaningful in terms of activities, skills, and products varies among people.
- The fact that two people have similar profiles of intelligences doesn't mean that they will come to know in exactly the same way, like the same things, or be good at the same things.
- Quizzes such as the one the students took prior to class are useful for reflecting on a topic but cannot adequately capture a person's capabilities, so the results may differ from what a person considers to be true.

Activity 2: Pen-Hole Box

1. Put one of the three index-card pictures inside the box, taped to the end opposite the hole. Have the class sit in a circle. For this activity to be effective, each circle should be no larger than 6 to 10 people. For larger classes, form numerous circles and give each one a box. In the middle of the circle, place a blank index card and markers of the same color as the drawing inside the box.
2. Provide the following instructions: "I will act as timer in this activity. When I say 'go,' one at a time each member will have 10 seconds to look at the picture as it gets passed around the circle. After my signal that the time is up for each

Students work together to reproduce the picture inside the box as closely as possible.

Photograph by Kendel O'Hara.

individual, he or she will pass it to the next person in the circle. The box will travel around the circle to each member of the group only once. The goal of this activity is for your group as a whole to reproduce the picture inside the box as closely as possible. When your group is satisfied with the picture you have produced, we will compare your group drawing with the one in the box. After you have compared the pictures, your group will have 2 minutes to plan strategy for the next round. There will be three rounds in total using the three pictures. A new picture will be put into the box before each round."

3. Although the group may assume that they should wait until everyone has seen inside the box before they can begin drawing, they can start drawing at any point (you may wish to leave this ambiguous in your instructions so that the group may come to this conclusion during strategy planning sessions).
4. Have the class split into groups of three to six people to discuss the activity. How were ideas generated? How were problems addressed? What was the pace of the activity—were a lot of ideas generated at first and then just fine-tuned over the three pictures, or did ideas build evenly as the activity progressed? Ask the group to discuss these questions and then create a musical rhythm (stomping feet, clapping, etc.) that represents the process of the activity. When they are done, each group will show their rhythm to the class and explain how they came up with it.
5. Ask each group to consider what insights they can take away from the activity that may pertain to future group work. Ask each group to create a tableau (drama) of important learning outcomes that they will be taking away. When each group is ready, have them present to the larger group and explain the insights demonstrated within their tableau.

Activity 3: Group Poem

1. Hand out one group-poem slip per student. Ask students to think about the Pen-Hole Box activity (or just life in general) in relation to the sentence they receive. For 3 minutes they must freewrite continuously on the topic suggested by the sentence. If they get stuck, they can repeat a word or rewrite the sentence, but they must write continuously for the full 3 minutes.
2. Next, divide the class into three groups based upon their sentence. Ask the groups to discuss what they wrote and then create a poem that starts and ends with the sentence they were given. In between the assigned sentences, each member of the group will contribute *one line or portion of a line* from their free write. For example, if a group has four members, the poem will have six lines. The following is an example of a group poem that celebrates uniqueness in individuals.

    This is a poem to celebrate unique individuals.
    Different lives, different meanings
    Taking in everyone's opinions
    More than just skin color, religion, language
    Free to be me, free to be you
    This is a poem to celebrate unique individuals.

3. The class now has three separate poems representing each of the three sentences. You will next merge these three poems into one full-group poem with three stanzas. Ask a volunteer from each of the three groups to read their

stanza aloud. The poem will be read out loud in the order (a) "This is a poem to celebrate unique individuals . . ."; (b) "This is a poem about how people problem solve together . . ."; and (c) "This is a poem about a team. . . ."

CLOSURE

As a class, discuss what intelligences were used during the different parts of the activity and reflection exercises. Students should note that most of the activities incorporated more than one intelligence. Ask students to think about whether they felt more comfortable during certain activities than others. Do their likes and dislikes correspond to the intelligences that they identified as strong or underdeveloped? Did using any of the intelligences make them uncomfortable? How might this translate to a person's teaching style preferences? Talk about the tendency of instructors to teach using the ways of knowing with which they are most comfortable. Can challenges and reflection activities that touch multiple ways of knowing play a role in adventure programs? What would be the advantages and disadvantages? What challenges might using such activities pose?

ASSESSMENT OF LEARNING

- **Assembling a class multiple intelligence book.** It is recommended that the following two assignments be graded. Give students the opportunity to make changes to anything that might be incorrect and improve their grade. The final product will be assembled into a class book for each student to take away.
  1. Have students prepare a one-page poster describing an intelligence in which they feel strong. This one page will include the name of the intelligence, a short description of the intelligence, and ways to incorporate the intelligence in adventure programming. This page may be illustrated in any manner (e.g., using art, decoupage, a concept map) and must include sources.
  2. Have students find an activity, game, or reflection exercise that incorporates an intelligence that they need to develop. They are to describe the activity, citing its source, the intelligences it touches upon, the type of program in which it might be used, ages for which it might be most appropriate, any adaptations needed to make it accessible, risk management considerations, and materials needed. Consider whether there might be an appropriate time during the course to have the students present their activity to the class.
- **Reflection sheet.** Students should return to their prelesson journal entries and write one to two pages about the ways in which their ideas have changed or stayed the same. This reflection can be graded.

LESSON 2

Multiple Intelligence Theory and Learning Styles

Mary C. Breunig

Students learn in a variety of ways. Many respond well to a "traditional" teaching methodology with its emphasis on auditory learning, and others respond less favorably to such methods. Experiential learning provides one methodological framework for educators to address the various learning styles and intelligences of students in the classroom. This lesson introduces Kolb's (1984) experiential learning cycle as one framework to help educators design lessons that address learners' various intelligences and learning styles.

Background

Howard Gardner's (1983) theory of multiple intelligences, a psychological and educational theory, suggests that an array of different kinds of "intelligences" exists in human beings. Each individual manifests varying levels of these different intelligences and thus a unique cognitive profile (Gardner 1983). Multiple intelligence theory was relatively radical when it was introduced. Gardner (1983) pointed out that IQ tests measure primarily verbal, logical-mathematical, and some spatial intelligence. Believing that there are many other kinds of intelligence that are important aspects of human capabilities, he proposed his theory of multiple intelligences. The original theory included seven separate intelligences; in 1999, Gardner added two more. According to Gardner, the nine intelligences include verbal-linguistic intelligence, logical-mathematical intelligence, visual-spatial intelligence, musical-rhythmic intelligence, bodily-kinesthetic intelligence, interpersonal intelligence, intrapersonal intelligence, existential intelligence, and naturalist intelligence.

Gardner believes that education in general (not just IQ tests) was designed to teach to a certain kind of intelligence, which may also be referred to as a *learning style*. Learning styles are simply different approaches to or ways of learning. The three predominant learning styles are *visual, auditory,* and *tactile* or *bodily-kinesthetic*. Visual learners need to see the teacher's body language and facial expression to fully understand the content of a lesson. Auditory learners learn best through verbal presentations or lectures, discussions, talking things through, and listening to what others have to say. Bodily-kinesthetic learners learn best through a hands-on approach, actively exploring the physical world around them.

Gardner (1983) was concerned that these three learning styles were, by definition, too narrow. He was also concerned that most schools adopted a methodological approach to teaching and learning that appealed to those learners who were predominantly auditory and visual and less to those who were bodily-kinesthetic or who had intelligences that were different from the three predominant learning styles. This, in part, led to the theory of multiple intelligences. Because both teachers and students have various intelligences and predominant learning styles, both teachers and students need not only to understand these differences but also to design lessons that appeal to the variety of learning styles and intelligences that exist in a classroom or wilderness trip setting.

For example, when I first started teaching within the postsecondary outdoor and adventure education classroom, I was struck by the number of students who were nontraditional, bodily-kinesthetic learners. I began to consider, mostly through trial and error, how to teach for a bodily-kinesthetic learning style within a traditional (predominantly lecture-based) post-secondary learning context. In doing so, I also came to the realization that not all students were bodily-kinesthetic learners. I learned that what was needed was a mixed-methods approach to teaching and learning about adventure education theory that appealed to a variety of learning styles. Research on multiple intelligence theory and experiential education theory provided me with the necessary background knowledge to explore this in practice.

When teaching outdoor and environmental education and outdoor leadership, I realized that teaching students about how to employ Kolb's (1984) experiential learning cycle provided them with one framework to help them design their own lessons. The result is that I employ this cycle in my own teaching and encourage students to use it when they teach as a means to address learners' various intelligences and learning styles.

RESOURCES

Fogarty, R., and J. Stoehr. 1995. *Integrating curricula with multiple intelligences: Teams, themes, and threads.* Palatine, IL: IRI/Skylight.

Gardner, H. 1983. *Multiple intelligences: The theory in practice.* New York: Basic Books.

Gardner, H. 1999. *Intelligence reframed. Multiple intelligences for the 21st century.* New York: Basic Books.

Kolb, D.A. 1984. *Experiential learning.* Englewood Cliffs, NJ: Prentice Hall.

Lazear, D. 1991. *Seven ways of teaching: The artistry of teaching with multiple intelligences.* Palatine, IL: IRI/Skylight.

Lesson Plan

PURPOSE

For students to be able to use theories of multiple intelligences (Gardner 1983, 1999) and Kolb's (1984) experiential learning cycle to design adventure education lessons that can be applied across a variety of settings, including at camp, on wilderness trips, or in a more traditional classroom setting.

OBJECTIVES

As a result of this lesson students will be able to . . .

1. *Cognitive and psychomotor:* explain multiple intelligence (MI) theory (Gardner 1983, 1999) and the three primary learning styles after engaging in a variety of activities.
2. *Cognitive:* design a lesson that integrates all aspects of Kolb's experiential learning cycle: experience, observation and reflection, formation of abstract concepts and generalizations, and testing implications in new settings.
3. *Cognitive and psychomotor:* design lesson plans that integrate at least one aspect of adventure education, that appeal to three or more intelligences and learning styles, and that include the experiential learning cycle.
4. *Cognitive and psychomotor:* describe and demonstrate classroom strategies incorporating a variety of teaching methodologies.

DURATION

1 hour, 20 minutes

GROUP SIZE

30 to 50

LOCATION

Indoor space with room to move

EQUIPMENT

- Small musical instruments
- Puzzles
- Board games
- Children's books
- Climbing and other outdoor-oriented magazines
- Balls and Frisbees
- CD player and CDs
- Art supplies for drawing
- State or provincial curriculum documents (obtained online)
- Computer and LCD projector

RISK MANAGEMENT CONSIDERATIONS

None

STUDENT PREPARATION

Have students read about multiple intelligence theory (MI) prior to the lesson; use the Background handout (on the CD-ROM), as well as any other resources you choose. Students should have an understanding of the seven (plus two) multiple intelligences before being engaged in the lesson (Fogarty and Stoehr 1995; Gardner 1983, 1999; Lazear 1991).

INSTRUCTOR PREPARATION

Come to class a bit early and set out multiple intelligence "stations." The stations could include the following:

- Musical intelligence—provide musical instruments or a CD player and CDs.
- Linguistic intelligence—set out games (Scrabble or Boggle) or some books.
- Logical-mathematical intelligence—set out Sudoku or other math games, or selected puzzles, or both.
- Spatial intelligence—provide art supplies.
- Intrapersonal intelligence—offer opportunities for some students to be alone, giving them time and materials for drawing or journaling.
- Interpersonal intelligence—provide opportunities for some students to engage in group activities using the games, storytelling, or kids' books.
- Bodily-kinesthetic intelligence—set out balls, Frisbees, and so on.
- Naturalist intelligence—ask students to go outside and find something in nature that resonates with them; then have them write about it.
- Existential intelligence—prepare a list of philosophically oriented questions for students to consider discussing. Two examples are "What is the central purpose of outdoor recreation?" and "Many outdoor educators propose that outdoor recreation is a means to attain a just citizenry. What is meant by a just citizenry?"

Place the stations around the room; that is, locate the music in one spot, the puzzles in another, the board games in another, and so on.

LESSON CONTENT AND TEACHING STRATEGIES

Welcome students to the class and inform them that they are going to start with an activity.

Activity 1: MI Stations

1. Ask students to go to a station that appeals to them and to "play" for 10 minutes. They can move around if they want to; they don't have to stay at one station.
2. After the 10 minutes, ask students to return to their seats. Ask them what drew them to a particular station. What did they do and why? Tell them that, in essence, each of them has different intelligences and that they were drawn to certain stations and activities partly as a result of these intelligences. Tell them that you used this activity as a means to introduce the day's lesson on multiple intelligence theory.

Activity 2: PowerPoint and Mini-Lecture on Identifying Your Intelligences

Launch the PowerPoint presentation (see CD-ROM). Define multiple intelligence theory (slide 2). Inform students that this was a relatively radical theory when it was introduced.

Gardner (1983) pointed out that IQ tests measure primarily verbal, logical-mathematical, and some spatial intelligence. Believing that there are many other kinds of intelligence that are important aspects of human capabilities, he proposed his theory of multiple intelligences, which included seven distinct intelligences. In 1999, he added two more. Show slide 3 for the 7 + 2 intelligences.

Gardner believes that education in general was designed to teach to a certain kind of intelligence, which may also be referred to as a *learning style*. Ask students what the three predominant learning styles are and then provide them with the definition for each (slide 4). Ask students about their own K through 12 and postsecondary experiences. Ask them which learning style seems to fit best with their own educational experiences. In other words, most teachers and professors employ a teaching methodology that would appeal to which predominant learning style(s)? Ask them what their predominant learning style as adventure education students is (most will likely respond that it is bodily-kinesthetic or naturalist).

Tell them that you imagine it must be challenging to be a bodily-kinesthetic learner who is trying to learn through predominantly auditory and occasionally visual means. Tell them that this is, in part, what Gardner had in mind when he came up with the theory of multiple intelligences. Remind students that it is important for them to think about the fact that not every learner learns through visual-auditory lessons. On the other hand, they must also be attentive to the fact that even if many of them are bodily-kinesthetic learners, not all people in their classrooms or on their wilderness trips will be kinesthetic learners. Students therefore need not only to understand these differences but also to design lessons that appeal to a variety of learning styles and intelligences.

Activity 3: MI Survey

1. Ask students to fill out the MI survey located at http://www.ldrc.ca/projects/miinventory/mitest.html. Remind them that this alone will not provide sufficient information to unequivocally determine their intelligences, but will give them some information that they can use to begin to understand their MI "leanings."
2. Have students get into small groups to discuss their intelligences (preferably in mixed intelligence groups). Ask them to begin to consider what some of the implications of having a dominant intelligence might be for them with reference to their own learning and teaching. Ask each group to ensure that there is one student to record (take notes) and one student to report their findings back to the whole class.
3. Have the reporter from each group do a 2-minute report on how his or her group responded to the question about implications of the MI and learning styles theories for teaching and learning.
4. Tell students that teaching or leading trips in a way that appeals to a variety of learning intelligences and learning styles may be important in light of their conclusions. Mention that Kolb's (1984) experiential learning cycle provides one framework students can use to design lessons that appeal to a variety of intelligences (see slide 5). Review the cycle with students. Tell them that preparation was added because without adequate preparation an experience may hold less value. Use this particular lesson as an example: "Because you read about multiple intelligence theory before coming to class today, you were somewhat prepared to engage in the first activity and to discuss it. Without that reading, I might have had to spend more time with you initially introducing the topic. In addition, because you had done the reading, I am already addressing the visual learners, also called spatial learners. I could then engage the bodily-kinesthetic learners in an activity before using the PowerPoint to

emphasize the intent of the lesson for the auditory learners, also called linguistic learners. Do you see how this can work?"

Activity 4: Write a Lesson Plan

Pull out the state or provincial curriculum documents that you retrieved online. Ask students to get into small groups and to design lessons using the experiential learning cycle (Kolb 1984). You may also distribute the Write a Lesson Plan handout on the CD-ROM as a guide. It lists specifications for the lesson plan and includes a rubric that can be used to assess the completed lessons. (The PowerPoint slide with Kolb's cycle should be displayed on the screen for the purposes of this lesson.) Tell students that depending upon the interests of their small group, they could design either an outdoor-oriented lesson (e.g., how to set up a tent or light a stove) or a K through 12 school-based lesson (using the curriculum documents). In either case, students will be employing the experiential learning cycle as a framework. Students should also be reminded of the importance of designing the lesson for the multiple and varied intelligences of the learners in the classroom. Do this by referring back to the PowerPoint or providing students with a handout that lists and gives examples of the multiple intelligences. You can first practice a lesson with the class as a whole if this would be helpful.

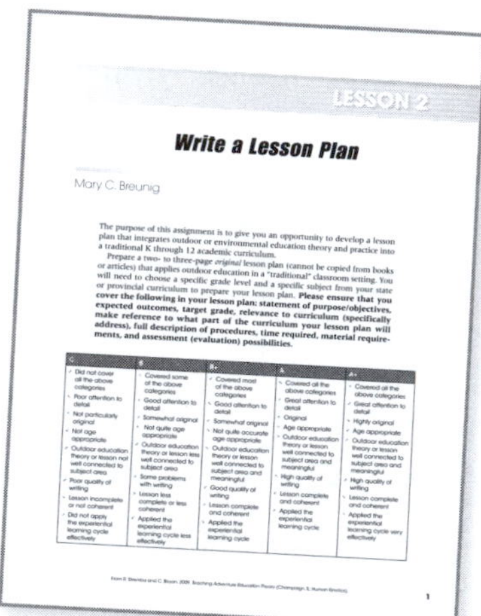

LESSON 2

Write a Lesson Plan

Mary C. Breunig

The purpose of this assignment is to give you an opportunity to develop a lesson plan that integrates outdoor or environmental education theory and practice into a traditional K through 12 academic curriculum.

Prepare a two- to three-page *original* lesson plan (cannot be copied from books or articles) that applies outdoor education in a "traditional" classroom setting. You will need to choose a specific grade level and a specific subject from your state or provincial curriculum to prepare your lesson plan. **Please ensure that you cover the following in your lesson plan: statement of purpose/objectives, expected outcomes, target grade, relevance to curriculum (specifically make reference to what part of the curriculum your lesson plan will address), full description of procedures, time required, material requirements, and assessment (evaluation) possibilities.**

C	B	B+	A	A+
Did not cover all the above categories Poor attention to detail Not particularly original Not age appropriate Outdoor education theory or lesson not well connected to subject area Poor quality of writing Lesson incomplete or not coherent Did not apply the experiential learning cycle effectively	Covered some of the above categories Good attention to detail Somewhat original Not quite age appropriate Outdoor education theory or lesson less well connected to subject area Some problems with writing Lesson less complete or less coherent Applied the experiential learning cycle less effectively	Covered most of the above categories Good attention to detail Somewhat original Not quite accurate age appropriate Outdoor education theory or lesson well connected to subject area and meaningful Good quality of writing Lesson complete and coherent Applied the experiential learning cycle	Covered all the above categories Great attention to detail Original Age appropriate Outdoor education theory or lesson well connected to subject area and meaningful High quality of writing Lesson complete and coherent Applied the experiential learning cycle	Covered all the above categories Great attention to detail Highly original Age appropriate Outdoor education theory or lesson well connected to subject area and meaningful High quality of writing Lesson complete and coherent Applied the experiential learning cycle very effectively

1

CLOSURE

Have students regather as a large group. Ask them questions such as "What is one thing you now know about multiple intelligences that you didn't know before?" or "How can you use Kolb's model in your own teaching?"

ASSESSMENT OF LEARNING

Ask students if they have any questions about what they did today when designing lesson plans. Let them know that you will take all of the assignments and create a lesson plan booklet for each student so that everyone leaves the class with many new lesson plans.

LESSON 3

Using Backward Design

A Methodology to Develop Experiential Lessons

Alison Rheingold

As experiential educators we are often focused on what students will be doing instead of what they will be learning. We learn a new game or activity and immediately want to turn around and use it with our students. We imagine all the laughter, all the meaningful engagement in learning that will take place. While we are skilled at coming up with fun ways to engage learners of all ages, we are not as good at defining what it is we want our students to actually get out of the experience.

This lesson will demonstrate how to design lessons or curriculum that will create meaningful learning experiences for students. Also, because experiential educators in schools and other settings are faced with the challenge of meeting standards set in place at the national, state, district, and organizational levels, this lesson explores how we can embrace this challenge and begin to see these standards as an opportunity instead of a hindrance.

Background

Many experiential educators are in need of a model for designing lessons, curriculum, or programs. Understanding by Design (UBD), as proposed by Grant Wiggins and Jay McTighe (2005), provides a guide for best practices for those who want to do more than just create a series of engaging activities. In combination with an action-reflection method of facilitating experiences (i.e., David Kolb's [1984] experiential learning theory), the concept of UBD offers a structure that allows the educator to plan not only the learning experience but also the assessment and the intended outcomes.

Educators may typically start their planning by thinking of ways to engage students. Instead, with UBD (also called *backward design*), they end with that step. For experiential educators this is often a great challenge; but, by ending their planning with the learning activities, educators create the opportunity to start with the intended learning outcomes. The outcomes then drive the process: Everything flows from what one wants the student to learn. After the intended learner outcomes are defined, one then plans the assessment. This also is a step that may not feel natural to experiential educators. In UBD, assessment means "acceptable evidence," and the educator plans the products that students will create to demonstrate learning. Finally, after going through these two steps, the educator plans the actual experiences in which students will engage.

So, the first step in backward design is to plan the learning outcomes, called *desired results.* Determining the desired results can be a lengthy process depending on the length of the lesson, curriculum, or program. For the purpose of this lesson, the process of creating desired results can be simplified into two categories: *established goals* and *student understandings.* Established goals refer to the big-picture outcomes that drive the whole lesson. They often are the frameworks, guidelines, or standards that one works from—provided at the national, state, or district level in public schools or at the organizational level with specific programs. Student understandings refer to what students or participants will actually learn during a lesson or portion of the curriculum—also thought of as lesson outcomes or lesson objectives.

The second step in the backward design process is to plan the assessment. Assessment in experiential learning can take many forms and should focus on students' demonstrating that they have accomplished, or are working toward, the learning outcomes. This lesson does not focus on explaining teaching methods for designing effective assessments, but general concepts can be covered: Assessment should happen both during the lesson and at the end; assessment should add to learning, not detract from it; students should be engaged in self-assessment; assessment should be meaningful and should contribute to the overall process (Black & William 1998). Ultimately, assessment should provide feedback to the teacher and learner about what has been learned and what the next steps should be.

Finally, one plans the learning experiences. Kolb-like models of the experiential learning cycle provide a model that fits well with the general process of UBD. Experiences or activities should include processing. Intentionally planning the processing as part of the lesson or learning experience means that the act of reflecting, analyzing, and applying is an active process that aids the learning and can be a means for assessment.

Project Adventure's *Adventure Curriculum for Physical Education* provides an example of the backward design process. The desired results are modeled after national standards for physical education (produced by NASPE, the National Association for Sport and Physical Education). Each lesson has lesson outcomes, and the activities were selected because they provide a vehicle for students to reach those outcomes. Assessment is embedded not as an afterthought but as a step in the process. Discussion questions flow through the experiential learning cycle and are meant to be a guide for teachers—some of whom, though they do not consider themselves experiential educators, are teaching an experiential lesson.

National and state standards actually can be of assistance in this process, though many people think of them as a hindrance. By using these standards, educators start with a broad road map; without it, one can be directionless. Wiggins and McTighe (2005) provide information on how to change standards and frameworks into useful tools for developing lessons.

Understanding by Design provides a process for designing effective experiential lessons and curriculum. By starting with outcomes and ending with the development of engaging learning experiences, educators can create meaningful opportunities for their students.

RESOURCES

Black, P. and D. William. 1998. Assessment and classroom learning. *Assessment in Education: Principles, Policy, and Practice, 5 (1)7.*

Dyson, B., & Brown, M. (2005). Adventure education in your physical education program. In J.L. Lund & D. Tannehill (Eds.), *Standards-Based Physical Education Curriculum Development.* Boston: Jones and Bartlett Publishers.

Kolb, D.A. 1984. *Experiential learning: Experience as the source of learning and development.* Englewood Cliffs, NJ: Prentice Hall.

National Association for Sport and Physical Education. 2004. *Moving into the future: National standards for physical education.* Reston, VA: American Alliance for Health, Physical Education, Recreation and Dance.

Panicucci, J., A. Kohut, L. Faulkingham, A. Rheingold, and N. Stratton. 2003. *Adventure curriculum for physical education—Middle School.* Beverly, MA: Project Adventure.

Wiggins, G., and J. McTighe. 2005. *Understanding by design.* Alexandria, VA: Association for Supervision and Curriculum Development.

The following is a good description of the experiential learning cycle:

www.wilderdom.com/experiential/elc/ExperientialLearningCycle.htm

The following are resources for looking at standards:

edstandards.org/Standards.html—Developing Education Standards

www.education-world.com/standards/national/index.shtml—National Education Standards

www.mcrel.org/standards-benchmarks/—Mid-continent Research for Education and Learning

www.nap.edu/readingroom/books/nses/html/—National Science Education Standards

www.aahperd.org/naspe/—National Association for Sport and Physical Education

www.ymca.net

www.outwardbound.org/aboutus.vp.html

Lesson Plan

PURPOSE

For students to explore how the combination of curriculum development methodology presented in *Understanding by Design* (Wiggins and McTighe 2005) and the basic idea of Kolb-like experiential learning cycles can help experiential educators develop effective lessons, design curriculum, or both.

OBJECTIVES

As a result of this lesson students will be able to . . .

1. *Cognitive:* describe the difference between curriculum or lessons that are designed as a series of activities and those that are designed as a series of lesson outcomes.
2. *Cognitive:* define and explain the concept of backward design.
3. *Cognitive:* describe how beginning with organizational, district, state, or national standards can be a strategy for lesson or curriculum design and a justification for using experiential methodologies to teach content.
4. *Cognitive:* design a lesson that uses the concept of backward design.

DURATION

Two 60-minute sessions

GROUP SIZE

6 to 30

LOCATION

Indoors

EQUIPMENT

- Take-a-Stand cards
- 30 tossable items, varying in shape and size
- Boundary rope, 60 feet (18 meters)
- Two buckets
- Handouts of a variety of different standards, frameworks, and organizational goals

RISK MANAGEMENT CONSIDERATIONS

Make sure to use soft, throwable items for the Mass Pass activity.

STUDENT PREPARATION

It would be helpful for students to have a basic understanding of the experiential learning cycle.

INSTRUCTOR PREPARATION

None

LESSON CONTENT AND TEACHING STRATEGIES

Say to students, "As experiential educators we are often focused on what students will be doing instead of what they will be learning. We learn a new game or activity and immediately want to turn around and use it with our students. We imagine all the laughter, all the meaningful engagement in learning that will take place. [Add an example, from your own work, of when you have started planning by thinking of great activities and then figured out why you wanted to use them.] While we are skilled at coming up with fun ways to engage learners of all ages, we are not as good at defining what it is we want our students to actually get out of the experience. This lesson will demonstrate how to design lessons or curriculum that will create meaningful learning experiences for your students. Also, because experiential educators in schools and other settings face the challenge of meeting standards set in place at the national, state, district, and organizational levels, it is worthwhile exploring how we can embrace this challenge and begin to see these standards as an opportunity instead of a hindrance."

Activity 1: Take-a-Stand

1. Begin by placing a large card at each of the four corners of the room, one saying "Strongly agree," one saying "Agree," one saying "Disagree," and one saying "Strongly disagree." Point out their locations to your students. Tell students that

you will read a series of statements. They are to listen to each statement and decide whether they strongly agree, agree, disagree, or strongly disagree with it. Without taking a lot of time, they should then move to the sign that represents their position. For the sake of the discussion there is no standing in the middle; students need to decide which sign best represents their thoughts. Make sure to tell students that there are no wrong places to stand: The point of the activity is to stimulate thinking and conversation, not to discover the "correct" answers. Read one statement, let students go to their spots, and then ask someone from each area to describe why he or she chose that placement. Continue with as many statements as time permits. Choose from the following statements:

- District, state, and national standards restrict the creativity of teachers.
- No real learning happens during an activity, only through the reflection process after an activity or learning experience has ended.
- Sometimes experiential education can be "hands-on without being minds-on."
- Having a challenge course is more important than knowing how to use it.
- It is more important to know the activities that students will engage in than what they will learn.
- True experiential education does not need assessment.
- Letter grades are inherently against the premise of experiential education.
- The phrase "structured self-discovery" is an oxymoron.
- There is a difference between a sequence of activities and a sequence of lesson objectives.

2. Read this quote from *Understanding by Design* (2000): "All activity-based, as opposed to standards-based-teaching, shares a weakness . . . little in the design asks students to derive intellectual fruit from the unit. One might view this activity oriented approach as 'faith in learning by osmosis.'"
3. To close this activity, ask each student to turn to a partner and share thoughts stimulated by the activity while answering the following questions:
    - What did you notice about your feelings toward the different questions? Did you notice any patterns in where you placed yourself?
    - Did anyone's response surprise you?
    - Which question stimulated the most "thinking for yourself"?
    - Can you think of any questions related to this topic that you would like to see others' positions on?

Activity 2: PowerPoint Presentation

Following the partner conversations, ask students to return to their seats and turn their attention to the PowerPoint presentation (see CD-ROM). Begin by reviewing the learning outcomes for this lesson. Then present the slides with the following comments:

Slide 2: Stages of the Backward Design Process

- For many people it is counterintuitive to start with outcomes. By asking yourself the broad question, "What do I actually want people to learn?" you will begin an intentional process of planning and implementing the lesson.

- Although we will not go into depth about the second step, assessment, it is important to be thoughtful about not only how you are going to assess student learning, but also what you will accept as evidence of learning.
- Ending the process with creating meaningful learning experiences means that you have used activities as the vehicle for reaching the outcomes, not chosen the activities and only later identified the outcomes more or less as a by-product. That is, instead of saying "I want to have people climb on the high challenge course; now I've got to figure out why," you have said "I want to challenge my students to learn how to rely on other people for support; I will use belayed climbing as a means to reach that end."

Slide 3: Lesson, Unit, or Curriculum Design Model

- This is a visual representation of the backward design model.
- You have to build the foundation first, starting with broad information and working your way toward specifically what you will do with students.

Slide 4: Identifying Desired Results

- There are two steps in determining what you want students or participants to learn. The first is to create broad statements that encompass the big picture of what you want to teach. These, according to Understanding by Design (UBD), are called the established goals. At the state, national, or organizational level they are often called curriculum standards, frameworks, or guidelines.
- The second stage is to determine what you hope students will learn during the specific lesson or learning experience. This outcome should be measurable and visible. It should be one that can actually occur during the lesson.

Activity 3: Mass Pass

This activity, from *Adventure Curriculum for Physical Education—Middle School* (Panicucci et al., 2003), is used as presented in the book to show how a lesson can be designed on the basis of the UBD principles.

Setup Using rope, create a fairly large square (15-25 feet or about 5-8 meters per side). Make sure that the square has clearly defined corners. In one corner

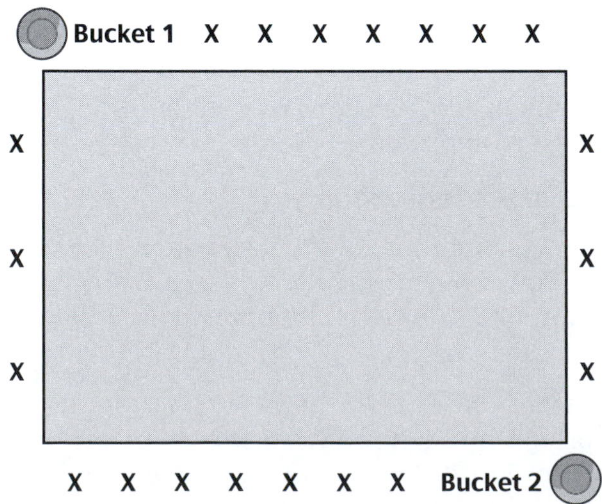

FIGURE 3.1 Mass Pass activity setup.

place one of the buckets (bucket 1), and in the opposite corner place the other bucket (bucket 2). Place all of the tossable items into bucket 1. See figure 3.1. The *X*s represent group members.

Framing "This activity requires your group to transport multiple objects around the perimeter of the square. An ability to plan effectively is needed to succeed, yet there is also opportunity for creative thinking in devising strategy. I'll give you all the rules and then I'll give you some time to plan."

Procedure Because there are multiple steps to the directions, consider writing out the main points on a flip chart or whiteboard.

1. The goal for the team is to increase their score over several (minimum of four) successive rounds and to maximize their score in the last round. Give the rules and then allow for some planning time. Points are scored according to how many objects end up in bucket 2 over a 90-second period.
2. All objects must start inside bucket 1 at the beginning of every round.
3. Time for each round starts when the first object is removed from bucket 1.
4. All sides of the square must be occupied by at least one student.
5. Once a person has chosen a side, she or he may not switch sides within a round.
6. Every participant must touch the object after it leaves bucket 1 and before it lands at the end in bucket 2.
7. Objects may not be passed to anyone to the immediate right or left; in other words the object must "skip" at least one person when it is passed.
8. Points are earned for each object that is placed successfully inside bucket 2.
9. Whenever an object is being passed, it must always cross over the inside of the boundary area (i.e., it cannot be passed around the corner on the outside of the perimeter of the square or behind anyone).
10. Any time an object is dropped outside of the boundary marker it must return to the first bucket to be re-entered into the tossing pattern, if it is to be used in the round.
11. If an object is dropped inside the boundary markers, it may not be retrieved and is lost for the duration of that round.
12. No member of the team may step inside the perimeter boundary during a round. If such a touch occurs, all the objects must be returned to the start.
13. All actions must stop when the time is up. At that time, the objects in bucket 2 are counted and the score is tallied.
14. Scoring: 10 points for every fleece ball, 20 points for every Frisbee (or other designations depending on your objects).
15. Give planning opportunities between each round so that your class can continually improve their time.

Discussion Debrief the lesson by asking questions that are relevant to the lesson objectives as stated on the PowerPoint slide. Consider the following questions:

- What skills did the group demonstrate that helped you be successful in this activity?
- What got in the way of your success?
- What was your individual contribution toward the success of the group? Were

you able to share your ideas? If not, what hindered this process?

- What will you do differently the next time you and this group encounter a problem to solve?

End the lesson by looking at PowerPoint slides 5 through 10, which detail the design explained in *Adventure Curriculum for Physical Education* and how this lesson, Mass Pass, fits into the bigger picture of the book *Understanding by Design*. Make sure to point out the connection between the NASPE (National Association for Sport and Physical Education) standards and the curriculum's desired results (established goals). As shown on slide 5, the curriculum is also divided into themes, which separate the different grade levels into subject areas. The themes for the middle school level are problem solving, respect for differences, self-esteem, and compassion.

Activity 4: Create a Sample Lesson

Present PowerPoint slide 11. Depending on how familiar students are either with state and national standards for various academic subject areas or with organizational guidelines and goals or program objectives, spend time explaining how standards and guidelines are developed and how they are used. Hand out samples of different standards, frameworks, and objectives that represent a wide range of subject areas, age levels, and programs. (See list of sources for looking at standards.) Ask students to select a set of standards in which they are interested. Have them get into groups of three or four and work their way through the process of backward design to create a learning experience that would help students work on the broad standard or guideline. Students should specifically show the following:

- How have they changed the standard into something useful (established goals)?
- What is the specific lesson outcome?
- What is the activity in which students will engage?

Because this is meant to be an exercise, or practice for the real thing, do not give students all that much time. Their plan should not be elaborate, though it should show how the learning experience will flow through the experiential learning cycle. Make sure to review this information if needed.

Ask each group to briefly present what they worked on. Give feedback to each group, specifically around their connection between the established goal, the lesson outcome, and the activity or experience.

Activity 5: Homework

For homework to be presented in the next class session, have students think about actual lessons that they need to create. Are they currently teaching or working with groups? If they are not, have students imagine a scenario in which they would like to be teaching or working.

Have students determine whether there are relevant standards, frameworks, or program objectives that apply to their lesson. Even if they are not working in a school or programmatic setting, it can be helpful to use standards as a starting place. Students should create a set of goals that broadly define what they hope their students or participants will learn. They should do this by altering or using existing standards or developing standards from scratch. The second step will be for students to create the lesson outcomes. The final step will be to design the meaningful learning experience. Learning experiences should clearly reflect how they will address the stages of the experiential learning cycle. Although assessment is not a part of this lesson, students may choose to include how they will determine whether their students have achieved the intended outcomes.

Students present their developed lessons to the class. During this time, have students assess each other's work by looking for the key elements necessary to effectively develop experiential lessons.

CLOSURE

After all presentations are complete, have students pair back up with their partner from the Take-a-Stand activity. With their partner they should discuss the following questions:

- What is one key learning from this lesson that you will take with you?
- How has your thinking about curriculum and lesson planning shifted since the beginning of this lesson?
- What do you think the difference is between planning a series of learning experiences and planning a series of learning outcomes?
- What next steps can you take to apply your learning from this lesson to your own teaching practice?

ASSESSMENT OF LEARNING

- At the end of activity 4, students present their work.
- Activity 5 serves as a culminating assessment of learning in this lesson.
- Assessing each other during the lesson development discussion also serves as a form of assessment.

PART III

History

Like other professionals, adventure educators need to know the historical roots of their profession. They need to know about the origins of the educational movement that led to the creation of outdoor education, environmental education, adventure education, and experiential education. They need to know about the people who have pioneered the educational use of the natural environment, adventure-based activities, and hands-on learning. They need to understand the cultural and political factors that influenced the development of these new forms of education.

In this section, we present four lessons that will help your students acquire and appreciate the historical foundation of adventure education. Contrary to a traditional history lesson, all the lessons presented in this part engage learners in discovering or even experiencing the historical events and people that shaped our profession.

Christian Bisson's lesson 4, "Visionary and Actionary: The Influence of Hahn and Petzoldt on the Development of Adventure Education," focuses on Kurt Hahn and Paul Petzoldt; two dominant figures in the history of adventure education. Hahn is presented as a *visionary,* someone who had a clear vision of the role of education and the learning experiences that can develop spirit, body, and citizenship in the youth of the world. This lesson highlights the challenges and strengths that allowed Hahn to pursue his dreams as an educator. In contrast to Hahn, Petzoldt is presented as an *actionary,* someone who took direct action in the development of a very important school focused on the development of young professional outdoor leaders. Although the two men never worked together, the lesson considers how both are interconnected in the history of adventure education. Through group problem solving, mini-lectures, and role play, students learn to appreciate Hahn and Petzoldt's lasting influences.

In lesson 5, "A History of Outdoor Adventure Education in the United States," Ed Raiola and Marty O'Keefe focus on the rich history of outdoor education and adventure education in the United States. Although they recognize the important role played by Outward Bound and its founder Kurt Hahn, their lesson also reveals that our historical roots are multiple and far-reaching. The lesson explores the development of not only adventure education but also experiential education, the organized camping movement, conservation education, nature study, and outdoor education. Through personal reflection and group problem solving, the lesson allows students to recognize and describe the prominent philosophical and historical roots of outdoor education and adventure education, their effects on the current and future trends in the field, and the various events, people, and organizations that helped develop and shape the field.

In lesson 6, "Creating History: Exploring the Past and Future of Adventure Education," Jacquie Medina brings history to a personal level. Because too often students doubt the relevance of a history lesson, this lesson helps them discover the significance of individuals and events that have influenced modern adventure education. From acquiring a new understanding of the individuals and events that have come before us, students can better understand their current contributions and future directions in the ongoing historical path of adventure education. In this lesson, students develop and analyze an adventure education history time line that weaves together relevant adventure education historical facts and their own professional experiences. Through this process of blending the past and present, student learning is fostered and critical thinking is augmented by the synthesis and formulation of ideas for future directions in adventure education. In brief, your students will begin to see themselves as active participants in the evolution of adventure education.

Finally, history comes to life in Brad Daniel's lesson 7, "Adventure Education History Roundtable." The lesson not only teaches the history of outdoor education, adventure education, environmental education, and experiential education, but it also demonstrates that studying history can be engaging, exciting, and fun. This lesson uses three experiential methods—role play, concept mapping, and time line construction—to engage students and enhance their abilities to remember what they have learned. It focuses on the key figures in adventure education, the roles that these people played in the history of our field, the interconnections between these key people and various outdoor-related organizations, and the similarities and differences between various types of educators who worked or still work with the great outdoors to promote learning.

LESSON 4

Visionary and Actionary

The Influence of Hahn and Petzoldt on the Development of Adventure Education

Christian A. Bisson

Young professionals in adventure education or outdoor recreation may not realize that their profession was not created in parallel with the development of the X Games. They need to know that adventure education has its roots in Europe and America and that particular people played important roles in the development of outdoor professions. Two of the most influential people in our history are Kurt Hahn and Paul Petzoldt. This lesson explores Hahn as a *visionary,* someone who had a clear vision of the role of education and the learning experiences that can develop spirit, body, and citizenship in the youth of the world. In contrast, Petzoldt is presented as an *actionary,* someone who took direct action in the creation of a very important school focused on the development of young professional outdoor leaders. Although the men never worked together, they are interconnected in the history of our profession. Through group problem solving, mini-lectures, and role play, students participating in this lesson will learn to appreciate Hahn's and Petzoldt's lasting influences.

Background

Kurt Hahn and Paul Petzoldt can be perceived, each with his special contributions, as the fathers—if not the grandfathers—of modern adventure-based education. Hahn has been labeled by historians and scholars as a visionary (Miner 1999; Richards 1999; Flavin 1996), while Petzoldt could be more appropriately labeled an actionary, as Petzoldt consistently displayed an action-oriented philosophy as an educator and a reformer of outdoor leadership training. Although the two men never met or worked together, they are indirectly connected when it comes to the history of adventure-based education as a medium for education or the development of the adventure programming profession. Hahn's philosophy on the education of active and compassionate young citizens via outdoor challenges and adventures strongly influenced Petzoldt's desire to educate young people about the art and craft of leading others in the great outdoors. Although Petzoldt did not fully agree with the Outward Bound philosophy, he found it very inspiring. Jane Howard from *Life* magazine reported how Petzoldt described his connection with Hahn's Outward Bound:

> "I owe a great debt to Outward Bound," he says. "I disagree with their emphasis on toughness for its own sake, because I think toughness should only come through doing things that are fun. But I think Outward Bound is great, and it convinced me of the importance of something further—something I'd had in the back of my mind all along: giving people proper technical training to take kids outdoors (which is plenty tough, all right, but plenty of fun, too). All the organizations that tried to do this—the YMCA, the Scouts, the church groups—meant well, but they were stymied because they just didn't have the know-how. Not that you aren't doing a city kid a great favor if you take him to the country and say, 'Look, this is a tree, this is a flower, this is a rabbit.' But I saw a need for something more—something that might require more stamina and energy than Outward Bound, and yet be more fun." (Howard 1969)

Outward Bound was an influence on Petzoldt in 1963 during his short tenure at the Colorado Outward Bound School—the first Outward Bound school in America—when he worked for the newly opened outdoor school as chief instructor for mountaineering.

Aside from this obvious connection, Hahn and Petzoldt share a common life theme: perseverance. Both experienced countless trials and tribulations while seeking to make a difference in society. It was Hahn's grand vision to develop a passionate citizen, while Petzoldt had a hands-on passion for sharing his deep love for the mountains and adventures. It is both Hahn's vision and Petzoldt's action that adventure educators around the world can celebrate when they study the history of our profession. While Hahn gave us the foundations for adventure-based curriculum (i.e., challenge, learning, compassion, service, and self-growth), Petzoldt gave us the foundations for the adventure-based profession (technical skills, leadership skills, judgment, environmental responsibility, and safety).

KURT HAHN

Kurt Hahn was born in 1886 into an upper-class Jewish family living in Berlin, Germany. Hahn was athletic; he played tennis and field hockey and developed a passion for track and field events, especially sprinting and jumping—particularly the standing jump, which was widely practiced at the time (Flavin 1996). He was also intellectual; he developed a passion for the English culture, as well as the work of ancient philosophers such as Plato.

He studied at Oxford University from 1904 to 1906 and soon developed a passion for education. Interested in youth movements and youth development, he studied the work of Sir Robert Baden-Powell (scout movement), Cecil Reddie (education reformist), Thomas Arnold (school headmaster and historian), and many other educators and progressive thinkers (James 2000; Richards 1991).

In 1920, Hahn fulfilled his dream of serving youth by becoming the headmaster of a new German school called Salem, meaning "Peace" in Hebrew. There he was able to develop and put into practice his educational philosophy, which held that the development of youth as young citizens was often more important than their academic training. At Salem, Hahn's teachers and pupils were asked to follow seven "laws":

1. Give children opportunities for self-discovery.
2. Have children meet with triumph and defeat.

3. Give children the opportunity for self-effacement in the common cause.
4. Provide periods of silence.
5. Train the imagination.
6. Make games important but not predominant.
7. Free the sons of the wealthy and powerful from the enervating sense of privilege.

Already in the '20s and early '30s, Salem's laws established the foundation for Hahn's educational philosophy, which would become more clear later on. His tenure at Salem ended abruptly in 1933, when he was arrested and put in jail for his political views against the Nazi party and also because he was a Jewish educator involved in the training of young Germans. This was a situation that Hitler addressed only one month after he came to power by implementing his first anti-Semitic decree, forcing all Jews involved in public services or education to "retire" (Flavin 1996). Hahn's arrest obviously reflected an oppression that was more political than ethnic at this early stage of the Nazi government. It was Hahn's defiance toward the new regime that precipitated his arrest.

In 1932 in response to Hitler's public support for five storm troopers who had been sentenced to capital punishment after murdering a young Communist, Hahn wrote this in a letter to Salem's alumni: "It is a question now in Germany of its Christian civilization, its reputation, its soldierly honor; Salem cannot remain neutral. I call on all members of the Salem association who are active in the SA or SS to terminate their allegiance either to Hitler or Salem" (Flavin 1996, p. 1).

Luckily, Hahn was able with the help of British friends to be deported to England just a few months after his arrest. But he had lost everything—his school, his mission, and his country.

In 1934, after being pressured by his English friends to lead a new school based on the principles of Salem, Hahn opened the Gordonstoun School in Morayshire County (Scotland) with only two students. A third, and important, student would eventually join the school: Prince Philip of Greece, who later would marry Queen Elizabeth II and become His Royal Highness the Duke of Edinburgh (Richards 1991). But Gordonstoun would see its growth hindered when England declared war on Hitler's Germany. In 1940 Hahn was forced to leave Gordonstoun and relocate his school to Plas Dinam (Wales), since the military had commissioned the old Gordonstoun castle.

However, the departure from Gordonstoun allowed Hahn to pursue another element of his educational vision—the dispersion of his philosophy to all the youth of England. In 1937, Hahn created a program called the Moray Badge scheme, which helped Gordonstoun pupils as well as young people in the nearby village benefit from Gordonstoun's unusual curriculum. Initially, the scheme had only three components: (1) fitness—running, jumping, throwing; (2) outdoor adventure—expeditions; and (3) skill development—crafts, hobbies, projects.

Rapid success associated with the Moray Badge scheme led Hahn to expand the scheme to all other counties in England; this would potentially allow him to reach millions of young English men and women. In 1938 the Moray Badge scheme gave birth to the County Badge scheme, which included a fourth component so essential to Hahn—service.

It is important to understand that the schemes were designed to be self-practiced. The youth would get information about the four areas of challenge and then be required to work toward achieving certain benchmarks in each area before receiving the badge. However, at one point, an intensive summer program was created to introduce the County Badge scheme. This program took the form of 28 days of training to promote and develop a foundation in all four areas of the scheme. It was this intensive training that provided the framework for the development of the Outward Bound experience.

In 1941, Laurence Holt, the father of one of Hahn's pupils at Gordonstoun and a co-owner of the Blue Funnel Shipping Company, approached Hahn with the need for a training program for young sailors working in the commercial fleet. Holt felt that the young sailors were having difficulty surviving the stress and adversity created by the war and the potential of shipwreck during the blockade of the British Isles by the German submarines, or U-boats (Richards 1991). It was the combination of Holt's needs and financial backing and Hahn's desire to keep on developing and promoting the County Badge scheme that gave birth to the Outward Bound program, which offered its first course beginning on October 14, 1941 (Richards 1991). Holt himself proposed the name "Outward Bound" because of its nautical connotation, referring to "the moment a ship leaves the pier or the safety of a sea port." Hahn did not like the new name and would have preferred to keep the new program under the County Badge scheme umbrella; but since Holt was the financial backer, the new name was adopted. This drove the division between Outward Bound and the County Badge scheme even though there were commonalities in the function and practices of the two programs. It is important to note here that although Holt had a concrete need to build character in young sailors, the program was catering not only to young commercial sailors but also to many other young professionals such as firemen and police cadets or other youth on leave from their regular schools or about to join the British army (Miner 1999). Holt himself admitted and promoted the idea that training at Outward Bound was less training *for* the sea than *through* the sea (Miner 1999).

In 1946, the newly created Outward Bound trust began the expansion of the program by promoting the development of new Outward Bound schools in England, other parts of Europe, and Africa as well as in other Commonwealth countries.

As the Outward Bound residential experience gained popularity, Hahn never forgot his vision of a national scheme that would allow a greater number of young people to embrace his educational philosophy and become productive and compassionate citizens. In 1956, with the help of Sir John Hunt (the expedition leader who successfully placed two men on the summit of Mt. Everest in 1953) as well as the help of his former Gordonstoun pupil, Prince Philip, Hahn was able to see his vision come to life when the County Badge scheme was endorsed by Prince Philip and became what we know today as the Duke of Edinburgh's Award scheme. This scheme includes all of Hahn's essential curricular components:

1. Service—helping people in the community
2. Skills—covering almost any hobby, skill, or interest
3. Physical recreation—sport, dance, and fitness
4. Expeditions—training for, planning, and completing a journey on foot or horseback or by boat or cycle
5. Residential project—a purposeful enterprise with people not previously known to the participant (this last component is reserved only for the gold-level award of the scheme)

The scheme is offered to youth from 14 to 25 and has inspired a multitude of other countries (41 countries as of 2007) to adopt or adapt it to their own youth. In 1979, the Carter administration created the American equivalent of the Duke of Edinburgh's Award scheme, the Congressional Award, which includes four program areas:

1. Volunteer public service
2. Personal development
3. Physical fitness
4. Expedition/exploration

In 1962, another enterprise of Hahn's led to the creation of the Atlantic College. Hahn's desire to use education as a means to ensure peaceful relationships between youth and future leaders of various nations prompted him to found a college that would include the classic Hahnian curriculum—service, fitness, skills, and adventure—but within an international environment where youth from around the world would learn to build lasting friendships and reverence for all the cultures of the earth. The mission and success of the Atlantic College led to the creation of 10 other colleges with similar educational goals and partnered in a consortium known as the United World Colleges, which was founded in 1967. The United World College–USA was established in Montezuma, New Mexico, in 1982.

In the meantime the Outward Bound movement kept on expanding its reach and influence in other countries. Outward Bound came to America with the help and vision of Josh Miner, a former Gordonstoun teacher who was present when the first Outward Bound school was created in Aberdovey, Wales. Miner, with the help of other private school teachers from the American East Coast, adopted the principles of Hahn's philosophy and created the Colorado Outward Bound School (COBS) in 1962.

Bringing Outward Bound to America was pivotal to the expansion of adventure-based education in the USA. Soon after COBS was created, other Outward Bound schools opened in the Midwest and the South and on the East Coast. As we will see later, the National Outdoor Leadership School itself was created as a response to the arrival of COBS. But the influence of Outward Bound in the USA has been much more diverse. Notably, it was the Outward Bound (OB) curriculum that led to the development of Project Adventure in 1971 under the leadership of Jerry Pieh, a former OB instructor himself and the son of Bob Pieh, the founder of the Minnesota Outward Bound School (now known as Voyageur Outward Bound). The adaptation of the OB curriculum to the public schools via the use of artificial adventure environments such as challenge courses and artificial rock climbing walls was so successful that in 1981, what had been a nationally awarded education curriculum became a company on its own (Project Adventure, Inc.) under the leadership of Dick Prouty and Karl Rohnke. Today, Project Adventure, Inc. is still committed to the propagation of adventure-based curriculum for schools and community groups.

The development of the OB curriculum in America was also behind the development of the Association for Experiential Education. In 1974, the First North American Conference on Outdoor Pursuits in Higher Education was held at Appalachian State University with the help of college professors and OB staff. Subsequently, two more conferences on adventure-based learning, one in Estes Park, Colorado, and one in Toronto (the Association for Experiential Education), were created in 1977.

More recently, the influence of OB in the United States brought about the creation in 1992 of the Expeditionary Learning School Outward Bound (ELSOB). ELSOB is based on the OB philosophy and adapted to the academic requirements of elementary schools.

Kurt Hahn's life was full of disabling challenges. At the age of 19, while rowing bareheaded on a particularly sunny day, he suffered a serious heatstroke injury. This event left him unable to venture into the outdoors for long during the summer months. No longer could he enjoy the lengthy treks or sailing voyages he had once found so rejuvenating and stimulating. But it was from this disability—as well as the other challenges he faced, such as his incarceration under the Nazi government, his exile to England, and the closure of Gordonstoun during World War II—that Hahn developed his philosophy toward life and the multiple challenges that it throws at us: Only the human spirit can be the source of courage and tolerance of adversity. This is why he adopted the concept of his friend Dr. Zimmerman and made it the central theme in his teaching through challenge and adventure. Hahn eloquently said about Dr. Zimmerman:

> He considered it less important to develop the innate strength in a boy than to make him overcome his innate weakness. "Your disability is your opportunity," he used to say to a boy who thought that certain standards were out of his reach. He was radiant when he succeeded in defeating a boy's defeatism, but not more radiant than the boy himself who had learned a great lesson. . . .

Hahn knew that it is through the conscious pushing of self that one can truly achieve one's own full potential. And no one more than Hahn himself believed in and experienced this life-changing philosophy firsthand.

In the end, it is remarkable that Hahn's vision about educating youth as virtuous citizens not only inspired his work until his death in 1974 but also inspired so many other educators and government officials to adopt or adapt his educational philosophy, based on a simple desire to allow young people to develop to their utmost potential. Hahn's affection for the French dictum "Plus est en vous," which means "There is more in you (than you think)," was at the center of his educational philosophy. But more than anything else, Hahn developed his school curricula award schemes to address six social concerns that remain relevant today, which he referred to as the declines in modern society:

1. Decline of fitness due to modern methods of locomotion
2. Decline of initiative and enterprise due to the widespread disease of spectatoritis
3. Decline of memory and imagination due to the confused restlessness of modern life
4. Decline of skill and care due to the weakened tradition of craftsmanship
5. Decline of self-discipline due to the ever-present availability of stimulants and tranquilizers
6. Decline of compassion due to the unseemly haste with which modern life is conducted

It was Hahn's solutions to these declines via the development of physical fitness, technical skills and crafts, a spirit of adventure, and compassion for others through service that enabled Hahn to succeed in his vision and directly influence the development of adventure-based programs.

PAUL PETZOLDT

Paul Petzoldt was born in Iowa, in 1908, into a poor farming family. The last born into a family of nine, Petzoldt had a brief childhood. The family lost their father in 1911, which not only created a void for young Paul but also exacerbated the family's financial situation. Soon the family had to disband, and Paul moved with his mother to Idaho. In his teenage years, Paul was already on his own, moving from job to job to make ends meet. His education had been limited, but his desire to learn about the world was vibrant and unlimited. However, feeding oneself came before schooling in these years, so Paul hit the road early on to pursue his passion for adventure. He had read many mountaineering stories from Europe and wanted to experience the mountains for himself.

At 16 years old, Petzoldt's passion for the great outdoors and an adventurous life led him and a friend (Ralph Herron) to the foot of the Grand Teton in Wyoming. It was there that with courage and a lot of luck, Petzoldt had his first real mountaineering experience (see "The Grand Teton"). It was also on the Grand Teton that Petzoldt learned that climbing mountains and exploring the great outdoors required skills, knowledge, and common sense. The Teton experience also led Petzoldt to develop an interest in safety and proper preparation for outdoor expeditions.

Fortitude led Petzoldt to embrace the world of mountain guiding. Soon after his exploit on the Grand, Petzoldt was asked by professional and amateur climbers from the East Coast to lead them up the Grand Teton. Through his guiding on the Grand he met influential people like the dean of St. George's Chapel at Windsor Castle who allowed him to visit, study, and climb in Europe.

It was also fortitude that allowed Petzoldt to join the first American expedition to K2. when an enlisted member was forced to cancel his participation at the last minute. On K2 Petzoldt further developed his understanding of wilderness expedition and the importance of sharing common goals to develop effective leadership skills and to encourage good expedition behavior. On K2, Paul proved himself as a strong climber, establishing a new high-altitude auxiliary oxygen record and accurately verifying that the mountain was climbable.

From K2, Petzoldt pursued his curiosity about India. Although Petzoldt was not a religious man, he learned more about Indian culture and mysticism by living and working at a medical clinic led by an American physician, Dr. Johnson. The physician and his wife were followers of a spiritual leader, S. Sewan Singh. As a guest of the Johnsons, Petzoldt eventually brought his first wife, Bernice, to the spiritual colony. The couple spent a few months enjoying the Johnsons' hospitality, but soon a conflict between Bernice and Dr. Johnson's wife about spiritual truth and religion led to the events of a tragic evening when Petzoldt accidentally hit the frail Dr. Johnson with full force while running away from a dangerous situation. The old doctor fell hard to the ground and later died of his head injuries. This accident has remained as a smear on Paul Petzoldt's reputation. But the reality, it seems, was that the death was a tragic accident and not a murder as has often been suggested in legends about Petzoldt's life.

Petzoldt would have admitted that he was not a saint, and his life brought him many friends but also a few enemies. His passion for adventures and the mountains and an ongoing quest to make it big financially created stress in his numerous marriages—four in all. Bernice, his first wife, even attempted to kill Petzoldt while he was asleep. Bernice Petzoldt was suffering from mental depression and stress, and perhaps even schizophrenia (which had been present in her family). The rough lifestyle of a mountain guide, as well as the stress caused by homesteading in Wyoming, perhaps pushed Bernice over the edge. Petzoldt recounted that one evening he woke up from his sleep and discovered Bernice standing above him with a large piece of wood in her hands, ready to hit him on the head. He escaped, but afterward he felt that Bernice needed medical attention and that their marriage might be coming to an end. Petzoldt's next two wives left him because of his adventurous and unstable lifestyle.

Throughout his life, Petzoldt tried his luck at many jobs and professions; he was a farmer, a ranch hand, a used car salesman, and a professional poker player. He even tried to become a professional rodeo cowboy, and he worked as a clerk for the Department of Agriculture. During World War II he was the mountaineering and chief ski instructor for the Army 10th Mountain Division, and most of all Petzoldt was a mountain guide and educator. Petzoldt said, "I didn't take the responsibilities that most people desire to have of a steady job and where I had to go and work every day for the rest of my life for Sears and Roebuck. I'd rather die than do that. But I'm living the kind of life I want to live" (Ringholz 1997, p. 8).

It was only in his early 60s that Petzoldt finally saw his luck turning and found a focus in his professional life. In 1961, Petzoldt was living in Lander, Wyoming, where Dottie, his new girlfriend and soon-to-be second wife was working at the local radio station. There, at the foot of the Wind River Range, Petzoldt had opened a small climbing school (the American School of Mountaineering) for the local kids. A year later he read an article in *Reader's Digest* about the new OB school that had recently opened in Marble, Colorado. To his astonishment, Petzoldt discovered that the chief instructor at COBS was his old army buddy, Tap Tapley. Petzoldt contacted Tapley in 1962 at the end of the first instructional season at COBS. He visited COBS soon afterward and was so impressed by the school and its vision that he accepted Tapley's invitation to return to Marble the next season to work as its chief mountaineering instructor. After accepting the offer, Petzoldt spent the summer of 1963 working for COBS.

At the end of the first summer at COBS, Petzoldt knew that OB was in great need of qualified instructors. He had observed that many of the teachers employed at OB had limited skills, knowledge, or experience in the Rockies. He begged the school director, Josh Miner, to give him 10 days before the next season to train the OB instructors in a variety of outdoor living and traveling skills. The next summer his plea bore fruit, and the first American OB staff training was implemented. But Petzoldt found that 10 days was too short and felt that perhaps more intensive and longer training was required. At the same time, he had developed a great concern for the quality of wild places and had even testified before Congress in favor of the 1964 Wilderness Act. But he also felt that the act was missing something and that laws alone would not help protect wilderness areas. Petzoldt knew that the solution was in education and that only through the teaching of proper skills and attitudes could the conservation movement really make a difference in the American wilderness.

So, during and after his second season at OB, Petzoldt thought about the problem and eventually came up with the idea of creating a new OB school in Lander. This school would focus on training young people in outdoor leadership skills so that in return they themselves would be able to lead their friends, families, Boy or Girl Scout groups, or church youth organizations. The school would also provide an alternative to the antisocial behavior young people displayed when they were lacking real adventures, but the experience would not push them physically or emotionally as severely as the regular OB curriculum did to help young people build character and tolerance for adversity. This new school would be the next step in their training as safe and skilled users of wild places so that they could enjoy as well as protect such places.

Soon Petzoldt submitted a proposal to Outward Bound USA. He wrote to Miner in 1964 about his plan: "My personal wishes, of course, would be to have an Outward Bound Leadership School here (Lander), drawing principally on the students who have finished a course in another Outward Bound school and who, then, are ready to profit by the training that we could give them here to make them real outdoor leaders for their communities, or, if you wished, for other Outward Bound schools in the future" (Ringholz 1997, p. 183). Unfortunately, Petzoldt's proposal was turned down by OB, mostly because it was felt that the Wyoming location would be too close to the existing OB school in Marble, Colorado. The OB officials did not want the two schools to compete for the same potential students. In addition, in Petzoldt's vision of the new school, the entire Wind River Range would be the classroom and no base camp with dormitories and shower house would be needed. The OB officials had a different vision; they wanted a base with barracks, offices, garages, and so on. Realizing that the proposal was going nowhere, Petzoldt decided to forget about OB and move along with his plan on his own. In 1965, with the backing of three affluent Lander residents (Jack Nicholas, an attorney; William Ericson, a physician; and Ed Breece, a legislator), who formed the nucleus of the early board of trustees, he established the National Outdoor Leadership School (NOLS) (Bachert 1999).

However, Petzoldt's new school would not have been possible without the help of his old friend Tap Tapley. Tapley was brought in by Petzoldt as codirector of the school, and together they overviewed everything from administrative tasks to field supervision. The first course, which began on June 8, 1965, was attended by 43 young men from 20 states. The course lasted four weeks and included travel in small patrol groups with instructors and frequent visits from Paul or Tap. Each student was required to lead for the day, and at the end of the course the patrol traveled on their own without instructors. Interestingly, right from the beginning, Petzoldt established new environmental practices that had students camping away from water to protect scenic beauty, or washing their dishes away from any water sources to avoid contaminating them. Trash was either burned or carried out; wastewater from cooking was placed in sump holes; and tramped or charred campfire areas were covered. Petzoldt used to say to his students, "The basic thing to remember is to camp and pass through an area and leave no trace of you being there" (Ringholz 1997, p. 188). Needless to say, Petzoldt was ahead of his time with his minimum-impact camping practices.

From 1965 to 1969, NOLS grew steadily; but in 1970 after the TV presentation of a special documentary on Paul Petzoldt and NOLS called *30 Days to Survival*, the enrollment jumped dramatically. In 1965, the school had graduated 83 students; in 1970 the number of graduates reached almost 1,000 (Bachert 1999). Consequently, NOLS began to expand by offering new courses in new areas; the Wind River Range was becoming too small for all these patrols. Branches were opened in Connecticut, Tennessee, Baja Mexico, Alaska, and Washington State. To help with the growing demand for specialized equipment, Petzoldt opened an outdoor equipment factory and retail store called Paul Petzoldt Wilderness Equipment (PPWE). This was a for-profit organization while NOLS remained a not-for-profit entity. Soon the rapid growth of the schools forced Petzoldt to take on many business loans to develop his new business venture. PPWE provided all the equipment to NOLS; it also sold specialized camping equipment to other organizations and in retail stores, but NOLS was by far its principal customer. Petzoldt directed the school as well as the factory, and soon this unusual business situation led his wife to worry about his financial decision making. When Dottie opened her own bank account to protect her savings, Petzoldt saw this as the beginning of a rift between them. In 1973 they were divorced. Petzoldt had difficulty separating the two financial entities, the school and the equipment company; and since one was taxable and the other was not, mixing the incomes and expenses soon became a serious issue for the school board of directors. Consequently, in 1975, under pressure from the Internal Revenue Service, the board was forced to remove Petzoldt as school director, stating that "he no longer serves in any capacity with the NOLS" (Ringholz 1997, p. 202). But not all was bad for Petzoldt in 1975; after a long-distance romance with a friend he had met on a safari in Mozambique, he proposed to and married his third wife, Joan Brodbeck from Milwaukee.

In the late '70s, a group of college professors from the Midwest and the East Coast expressed to Petzoldt their concern regarding the abuse outdoors lovers were inflicting on the newly designated wilderness areas. Petzoldt had always known that legal rulings about land use were not enough and that only through education could outdoor users develop a new land ethic. After a meeting on the subject, three teachers decided to try apply their new solution by bringing groups of college students to Driggs, Wyoming, where Petzoldt had established his new headquarters after losing NOLS. Frank Lupton from Western Illinois University, Charles Gregory of Pennsylvania State University, and Jack Drury from New York's North Country Community College were the first teachers to bring their students to study new ways to recreate in the wilderness. The week's experience was so successful that soon afterward Petzoldt started to offer more specialized courses for college students studying recreation, park management, forestry, conservation, and other related outdoor fields.

In 1977, Petzoldt, with the support of Frank Lupton, Charles Gregory, and Robert Christie, chartered a nonprofit organization, the Wilderness Use Education Association, which in 1980 was renamed the Wilderness Education Association (WEA). The WEA is a certification body that is dispersed throughout sponsoring colleges and universities. It includes an 18-point curriculum focused on developing outdoor leaders in three main areas: technical skills, leadership skills, and instructional skills. Even in his 70s, well past the age of retirement, Petzoldt spent thousands of hours promoting the new certification program. He visited conferences and a multitude of universities and colleges to encourage higher institutions to become affiliates of WEA (Teeters & Lupton 1999).

In his personal life, the '80s brought the "old man of the mountain" a measure of peace and happiness with his last companion. Petzoldt had met his fourth wife, Ginny, in 1970 at the New York premiere of *30 Days to Survival.* Ginny's son Wilton had been killed in Vietnam in 1969, and she and Petzoldt were to become friends for many years. They had met at the premiere because Wilton had attended the second NOLS season in 1966, and when he died his mother had requested that in lieu of flowers, friends and family could give donations to NOLS in his memory since his experience at the school had been so important to him. When Petzoldt's third marriage to Joan reached a rapid impasse for financial reasons and Ginny lost her husband, Petzoldt rekindled his friendship with her, and they married in 1987.

Petzoldt successfully climbed the Grand Teton one last time in 1984, at the respectable age of 76. In 1995, he received an honorary doctoral degree from the University of Idaho. He wrote three successful books and presented lectures about judgment, leadership, and conservation, also telling many tall tales about his numerous adventures. It was his love for the great outdoors, adventures, and education that led him to provide the profession with a set of skills and competencies that distinguish the outdoor recreationist from the outdoor professional. After reading about Petzoldt's life work and learning of his vibrant spirit of enterprise, one can only conclude that his influence on the adventure-based education profession was undeniable and profound.

RESOURCES

Bachert, D. 1999. The National Outdoor Leadership School: 40,000 wilderness experiences and counting. In *Adventure programming,* eds. J.C. Miles and S. Priest. State College, PA: Venture.

Flavin, M. 1996. *Kurt Hahn's school and legacy.* Wilmington, DE: Middle Atlantic Press.

Garvey, D. 1999. A history of the Association for Experiential Education. In *Adventure programming,* ed. J.C. Miles and S. Priest. State College, PA: Venture.

Howard, J. 1969. Last mountain man? Not if he can help it. *Life,* December 19.

James, T. 2000. Kurt Hahn and the aims of education. www.kurthahn.org/writings/james.pdf (accessed January 16, 2007).

Miner, J.L. 1999. The creation of Outward Bound. In *Adventure programming,* eds. J.C. Miles and S. Priest. State College, PA: Venture.

Petzoldt, P.K. 1995. *Teton tales.* Merrillville, IN: ICS Books.

Prouty, D. 1999. Project Adventure: A brief history. In *Adventure programming,* eds. J.C. Miles and S. Priest. State College, PA: Venture.

Richards, A. 1991. The genesis of Outward Bound. www.kurthahn.org/writings/GenesisofOB.pdf (accessed January 16, 2007).

Richards, A. 1999. Kurt Hahn. In *Adventure programming,* eds. J.C. Miles and S. Priest. State College, PA: Venture.

Ringholz, R.C. 1997. *On belay!: The life of legendary mountaineer Paul Petzoldt.* Seattle, WA: The Mountaineers.

Teeters, C.E., and F. Lupton. 1999. The Wilderness Education Association: History and change. In *Adventure programming,* eds. J.C. Miles and S. Priest. State College, PA: Venture.

Lesson Plan

PURPOSE

The purpose of this lesson is to introduce students to the work and accomplishments of Kurt Hahn and Paul Petzoldt and the influence they had on the field of adventure education.

OBJECTIVES

As a result of this lesson students will be able to . . .

1. *Cognitive:* explain the contributions of Kurt Hahn to the field of adventure education.

2. *Cognitive:* explain the contributions of Paul Petzoldt to the field of adventure education.
3. *Cognitive:* explain the relationship between the Outward Bound school movement and the creation of the National Outdoor Leadership School.

DURATION

Two sessions of 100 minutes each

GROUP SIZE

10 to 25 students

LOCATION

Indoors (you will need a multimedia classroom)

EQUIPMENT

- 48 foam board rectangles (12 by 5 inches, or 30 by 12 centimeters)—optional
- Printout of Historical Research Pursuit Activity Labels [CD-ROM]
- One copy of figure 4.1 [CD-ROM]
- Six copies of Seeded Questions [CD-ROM]
- One roll of flagging tape
- A few rolls of poster tape
- Multiple copies of articles or chapters about Kurt Hahn, Paul Petzoldt, OB, NOLS, WEA, Association for Experiential Education, Project Adventure, and the United World Colleges
- Costumes for impersonating Kurt Hahn and Paul Petzoldt
- Multimedia equipment for the PowerPoint presentation
- Classroom with a connection to the Internet—optional

RISK MANAGEMENT CONSIDERATIONS

None applicable for this lesson

STUDENT PREPARATION

No prelesson preparation required

INSTRUCTOR PREPARATION

Before the lesson, you should organize and prepare your materials as follows:

1. Collect and print various articles about Kurt Hahn, Paul Petzoldt, OB, NOLS, WEA, Association for Experiential Education, Project Adventure, and the United World Colleges. (See Resources list for potential sources on Hahn, Petzoldt, and these organizations.) Make two copies of each document you decide to use.
2. Print the activity labels from the CD-ROM. 

3. Cut foam board rectangles (12 by 5 inches) and glue one label on each. This is optional; you could use the labels without the foam board or could laminate the labels to protect them for future use.
4. Collect the rest of the materials suggested for the lesson (flagging tape and poster tape).
5. Collect items for creating Hahn's and Petzoldt's costumes. Hahn's costume may include a jacket with a blazon on the front pocket, a white shirt, a tie, and a book (Plato's *The Republic*. Petzoldt's costume may include a wool plaid jacket, a French beret or a toque, a pair of hiking boots, and an ice axe or walking stick.

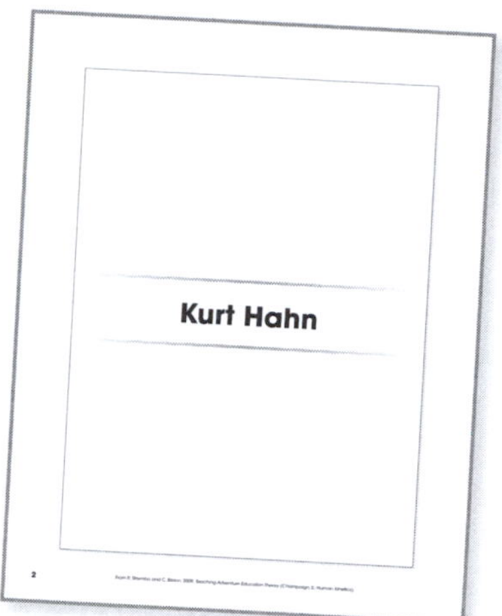
Kurt Hahn

▶ Kurt Hahn costume.

Courtesy of Jamie Hannon.

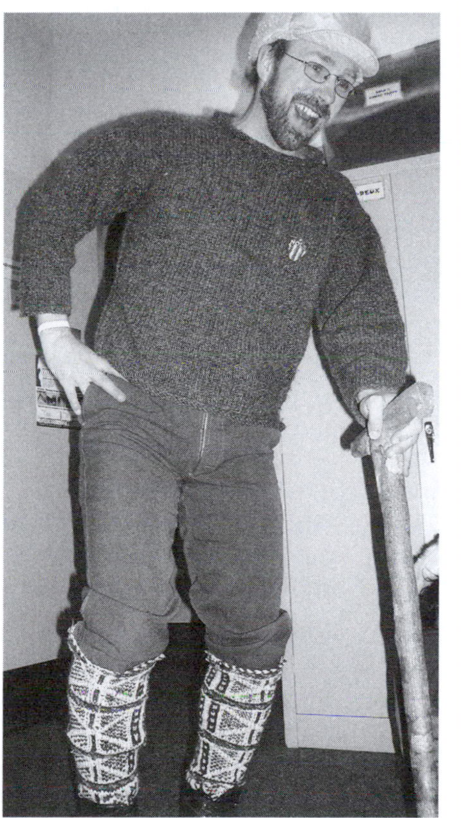

▶ Paul Petzoldt costume.

Courtesy of Jamie Hannon.

LESSON CONTENT AND TEACHING STRATEGIES

Begin the first session of the lesson by posing these questions to your class:

- Can you tell me how old the field of adventure education is?
- Is adventure education an American, English, Canadian, Australian, or New Zealand invention?

- Did adventure education evolve from summer camp?
- Who has influenced or is still influencing our field of study?

Let the students propose various answers to these questions, but don't be surprised if their knowledge of adventure education is limited or erroneous. At one point, thank them for their input and tell them that in light of their answers, you would like them to undertake a group challenge, called "Historical Research Pursuit."

Activity 1: Historical Research Pursuit

Explain to students that as a class, they will research and put together a historical flowchart (see figure 4.1; also included on CD-ROM) representing the relationship and influence of two fathers of adventure education, Kurt Hahn and Paul Petzoldt. Explain that they will also find names of other people or groups of people who helped or have been influenced by Hahn and Petzoldt. Challenge them to create this detailed historical flowchart on the classroom floor and to indicate the historical connections between Petzoldt, Hahn, and all these relevant people or organizations. But before they get started, explain the following rules:

- You may use all the written resources made available to you.
- You may use a computer to search the Internet.
- Everyone must be involved.
- You must match the appropriate date with the appropriate person or organization.
- You must represent the relationship between people and organizations using the flagging tape.
- You must create the flowchart in chronological order from left to right.
- You will have 15 to 20 minutes to complete the task.

After you have answered any questions that the students may have, lay on the floor all the historical labels mounted on the foam boards and give students access to all the information and equipment (e.g., flagging tape and computer with Web access).

During the challenge, help here and there by asking questions or giving positive feedback about people's findings to keep them on task. Once the time is over or the class has completed the task, conclude the experience with a few questions, such as the following:

- Is everyone comfortable with the layout of the historical flowchart?
- Are all the dates and people or organizations correctly matched?
- Are all the important relationships properly represented?

Tell students that they will have the opportunity to make changes to their historical flowchart during the next part of the lesson. Explain that you would like to use two mini-lectures to look at the lives and influence of Kurt Hahn and Paul Petzoldt. Tell them that they will be invited during the mini-lecture to correct any mistakes they find in their historical flowchart.

Activity 2: Mini-Lecture and PowerPoint on Kurt Hahn

Prepare to conduct a mini-lecture on Kurt Hahn with the PowerPoint presentation on the CD-ROM.

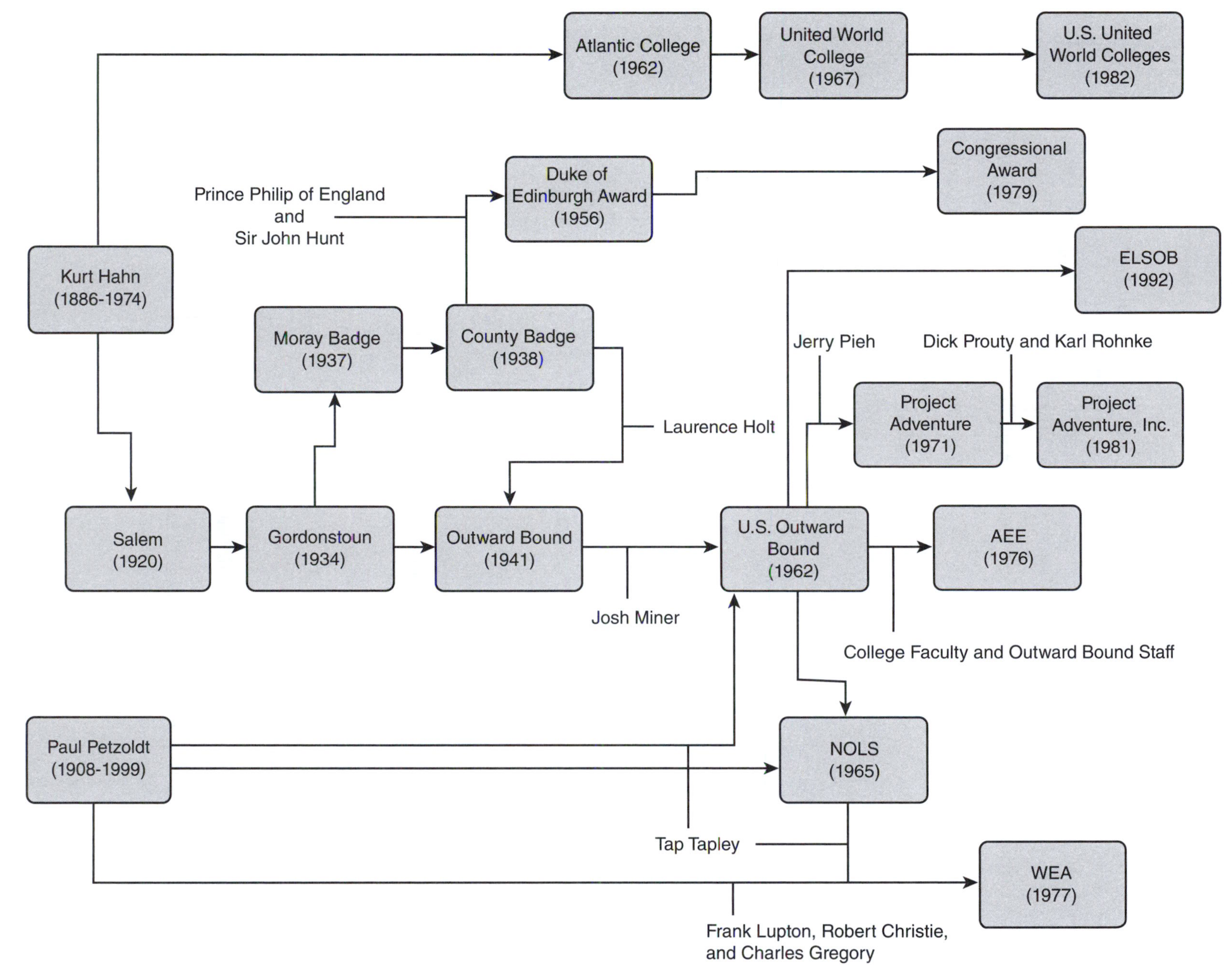

FIGURE 4.1 Historical flowchart.

Kurt Hahn: Visionary Begin the presentation by emphasizing the idea that Hahn was a *visionary*—he helped create schools and curricula, but he was not the outdoor or adventure educator they might expect him to have been. He never led mountain or sailing expeditions; he was fond of physical activities but was not an accomplished outdoorsman (slide 1).

Biographic Facts and Early Years Move quickly over slides 2 and 3, which review Hahn's birth and death as well as his youth through the time he took the position of headmaster at Salem. Pause and remind your students that they can change anything they want on their historical flowchart.

Philosophy Slides 4 and 5 offer a glimpse of Hahn's educational philosophy. Invite students to read the list of the six declines of modern life. Ask them what they think about the declines Hahn was concerned with—are these declines still a threat to our youth today? Are they relevant to today's education system? How do they relate to adventure education? Ask students also to pay close attention to the quote "Your disability is your opportunity"; explain that this theme will follow Hahn throughout his career in education.

The Salem School (1920) When you introduce slide 6, let students read the seven laws of the Salem school and ask them if these laws make sense to them. Do any of the laws seem confusing? Explain laws that students are not sure they understand.

The Salem School (1933) For slide 7, explain why Hahn was put in jail; use a storytelling technique here to relate the story of the young Communist who was killed in front of his mother by two Nazi youths. Explain how Hitler praised the young Nazis for their actions and how Hahn responded. Tell the story (see the Background section, page 54) of the letter Hahn wrote to the Salem alumni explaining that they could be Salem alumni or could belong to the Nazi party but not both.

Gordonstoun School (1934) With slide 8, review Hahn's work at Gordonstoun and point out that again he was forced to abandon his school. Explain why Hahn's meeting with Laurence Holt was so important. Explain that Holt was the partner of a large merchant shipping company and that his concern about the blockade by the German U-boats led him to seek Hahn's help to create a new school. This school would help young sailors gain life experience, character, and tolerance for adversity in the event that their ships were sunk by the German submarines, which would force them to survive on the open sea.

Outward Bound (1941) Slide 9 will allow you to summarize the original and still-prevailing philosophy behind the OB school movement. If your classroom is connected to the Internet, one option in your mini-lecture is to visit the Outward Bound Canada Web site, where you can view a short video presenting the history of Outward Bound. However, before starting the video, ask the students to find answers to the following questions as they watch the video:

1. What does "outward bound" mean to a sailor?
2. Who was an important patron of Outward Bound?
3. According to Hahn, who should have access to the Outward Bound experience?
4. What were and are the goals of Outward Bound?

Once the video is over, ask students to work in groups of three or four to compare notes about their findings. When everyone has found the right answers, present the rest of the slide.

If your classroom is not connected to the Internet, simply present the talking points on slide 9, which explain that OB is a character-building school where "the experience is less a training *for* the sea than *through* the sea, and so benefits all walks of life." Tell students that the school motto was, and still is, "To serve, to strive and not to yield."

Outward Bound in the United States and Around the World With slide 10, show the present international distribution of OB schools. Then, if it is appropriate for you, show slide 11 to review where and how OB started in America. Don't forget to mention that COBS has been renamed Outward Bound Wilderness but that it is still based in Golden, Colorado. Before moving on, remind your students that they can change anything they want about their historical flowchart.

Duke of Edinburgh's Award (1956) Slide 12 will introduce your class to the award scheme that Hahn created with the help of his friend and former pupil, Prince Philip, the Duke of Edinburgh. Here you could explain that it was a profound desire to disseminate his teaching philosophy to all youth, regardless of their socioeconomic background, that inspired Hahn to create award schemes. The first one was the local Moray Badge scheme, which took form in 1936. This youth achievement scheme quickly inspired the creation of the larger County Badge scheme. Later on, the idea became so popular that the Duke of Edinburgh and Lord John Hunt, leader of the first successful ascent of Mt. Everest, joined Hahn's effort to create a truly national youth award, the Duke of Edinburgh's Award.

Youth Award Schemes Around the World and in the United States With slide 13, show the present international distribution of the national youth award schemes. Then, if it is appropriate for you, show slide 14 to review which national youth award was inspired directly by the Duke of Edinburgh's Award. Before moving on, remind your students that they can change anything they want about their historical flowchart.

United World College (1967) One last contribution from Kurt Hahn deserves to be explored, so introduce slide 15. This slide reviews the creation of the College of the Atlantic in 1962, which became the United World Colleges in 1967.

United World Colleges Around the World and in the United States With slide 16, show the present international distribution of the many United World Colleges. Then, if it is appropriate for you, use slide 17 to show which preparatory school in America is part of the United World Colleges group. Before moving on, remind your students that they can change anything they want about their historical flowchart.

Kurt Hahn's Legacy and Resources With slides 18 and 19, summarize Kurt Hahn's legacy. Finally, encourage students to learn more about Kurt Hahn by presenting slide 20, which refers to two excellent books about Kurt Hahn and the development of OB.

Activity 3: Mini-Lecture and PowerPoint on Paul Petzoldt

Prepare to conduct a mini-lecture on Paul Petzoldt with the PowerPoint presentation on the CD-ROM.

LESSON 4

Paul Petzoldt: Actionary Begin the presentation by emphasizing that Petzoldt was an *actionary;* in contrast to Kurt Hahn, Petzoldt was an experienced outdoorsman, a talented and pioneer American mountaineer, and a man who consistently took action to accomplish his goals (slide 1).

Biographical Facts and Early Years Move quickly over slides 2 through 5, which review Petzoldt's birth and death as well as his youth and early guiding years on the Grand Teton. With slide 3, make sure you take the time to tell the story of his first climb of the Grand Teton (see The Grand Teton on the CD-ROM; provide it as a handout to students before the lesson if you desire). Explain also that Petzoldt had an adventurous spirit that led all him over the world, from a canvas tent at the foot of the Grand Teton to Windsor Castle after he befriended Sir Alfred Bailey, private chaplain to the King and Queen of England. On slide 4, review some of his contributions to modern mountaineering, for example a communication system between climbers (On Belay–Climbing–Climb) or his famous high-altitude climbing technique—one step per breath. But most of all, make sure your students understand that Petzoldt was critical of the European mountain guiding techniques that led clients up the mountain without any instruction on safety, judgment, or technical skills. With slide 5, help students understand that Petzoldt was a man who tried his luck at many professions before realizing that it was when he was teaching in the mountains that he was at his best.

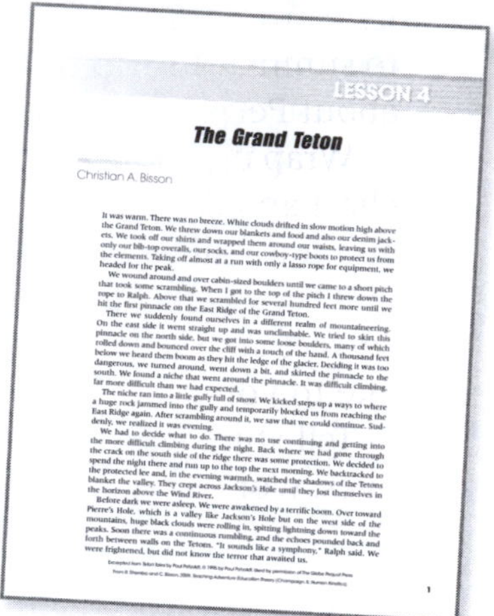

LESSON 4

The Grand Teton

Christian A. Bisson

It was warm. There was no breeze. White clouds drifted in slow motion high above the Grand Teton. We threw down our blankets and food and also our denim jackets. We took off our shirts and wrapped them around our waists, leaving us with only our bib-top overalls, our socks, and our cowboy-type boots to protect us from the elements. Taking off almost at a run with only a lasso rope for equipment, we headed for the peak.

We wound around and over cabin-sized boulders until we came to a short pitch that took some scrambling. When I got to the top of the pitch I threw down the rope to Ralph. Above that we scrambled for several hundred feet more until we hit the first pinnacle on the East Ridge of the Grand Teton.

There we suddenly found ourselves in a different realm of mountaineering. On the east side it went straight up and was unclimbable. We tried to skirt this pinnacle on the north side, but we got into some loose boulders, many of which rolled down and bounced over the cliff with a touch of the hand. A thousand feet below we heard them boom as they hit the ledge of the glacier. Deciding it was too dangerous, we turned around, went down a bit, and skirted the pinnacle to the south. We found a niche that went around the pinnacle. It was difficult climbing, far more difficult than we had expected.

The niche ran into a little gully full of snow. We kicked steps up a ways to where a huge rock jammed into the gully and temporarily blocked us from reaching the East Ridge again. After scrambling around it, we saw that we could continue. Suddenly, we realized it was evening.

We had to decide what to do. There was no use continuing and getting into the more difficult climbing during the night. Back where we had gone through the crack on the south side of the ridge there was some protection. We decided to spend the night there and run up to the top the next morning. We backtracked to the protected lee and, in the evening warmth, watched the shadows of the Tetons blanket the valley. They crept across Jackson's Hole until they lost themselves in the horizon above the Wind River.

Before dark we were asleep. We were awakened by a terrific boom. Over toward Pierre's Hole, which is a valley like Jackson's Hole but on the west side of the mountains, huge black clouds were rolling in, spitting lightning down toward the peaks. Soon there was a continuous rumbling, and the echoes pounded back and forth between walls on the Tetons. "It sounds like a symphony," Ralph said. We were frightened, but did not know the terror that awaited us.

1

The Outward Bound Years Slide 6 will help your students understand or verify the connection they might have found between OB and Paul Petzoldt. So explain briefly how Petzoldt got involved with COBS. Add as many details here as you want, such as the reason he chose to open his wilderness school (NOLS) in Lander, Wyoming—simply because this was where his girlfriend at the time lived and worked.

The NOLS Years (1965-1969) With slide 7, on the NOLS years, review the early development of NOLS from its creation in 1965 up to 1970. Here again, add anecdotes such as the "I Owe You" ticket that Petzoldt gave to students who did not have the money to take his NOLS course. Or explain that Petzoldt had to create his own outdoor equipment company (PPWE) simply because he could not find on the market the equipment he needed for his new school.

The NOLS Years (1970-1974) With slide 8, explain how enrollment in NOLS boomed after the documentary *30 Days to Survival* was presented on TV in 1970 during a program called *The Alcoa Hour.*

The NOLS Years: From 1975 to Today Slide 8 shows how after the documentary, NOLS was able to expand throughout North America. With slide 9, explain why Petzoldt was removed from his position as director at the school. Explain why the Internal Revenue Service felt that it was not appropriate for a not-for profit school like NOLS and a for-profit outdoor equipment company (PPWE) to be led by the same person. Ask students why they think the Internal Revenue Service felt this way. Conclude the NOLS era with slide 10, which depicts the international expansion of NOLS as a school. Pause and remind students that they can change anything they want about their historical flowchart.

Wilderness Education Association Introduce the creation of the WEA by using slide 11. Explain the purpose of the association, and with slides 12 and 13 let your students discover the WEA 18-point curriculum. Ask them where they think they might have strengths and weaknesses as an outdoor leader according to the WEA curriculum. This could lead to an interesting discussion about academic and professional training.

Paul Petzoldt's Legacy With slide 14, review the contributions Paul Petzoldt made to the field of adventure education. Conclude the presentation with slide 15 to summarize who Paul Petzoldt was. With slide 16, suggest further readings by or about Petzoldt that might interest students who want to learn more about him.

Wrap up this session by inviting students to look carefully at their historical flowchart and to modify anything they want about it. When everyone is in agreement about the flowchart, give the students a copy of the historical flowchart on Hahn's and Petzoldt's influence (figure 4.1) to compare with their own flowchart. Let them correct anything on their flowchart as needed and then see if two of them would like to volunteer to place their flowchart on the wall using poster tape.

Tell students that they have explored only the tip of the iceberg regarding the lives, work, and contributions of these two fathers of adventure education. Explain that for the next part of the lesson, you would like everyone to be ready to interview Kurt Hahn and Paul Petzoldt in person. To get prepared to meet and interview these great guest speakers from the past, each student should read one article or book chapter about Hahn and one about Petzoldt. Indicate that students can find many articles about these men by searching on the Web or by reading the articles you have given them to enable them to complete the historical flowchart.

Activity 4: Guest Speakers From the Past

Begin the second part of the lesson on the historical influence of Hahn and Petzoldt by reviewing the historical flowchart that students have created and that is now ideally displayed on the classroom wall.

Explain that you are very excited that they will be able to soon meet these two men who have influenced our profession so much. But before the guest speakers come, ask students to form groups of three or four and discuss what questions they would like to ask the guests. During this time, pull four to six students aside, one at the time, and ask them to participate in the next part of the class by reading a seeded question (see Seeded Questions on the CD-ROM) when appropriate, for instance when no one else is asking questions. While they are finishing their discussions, leave the classroom and dress up as Kurt Hahn.

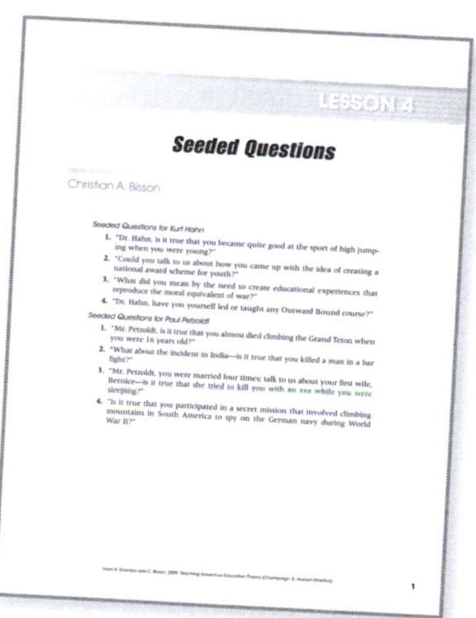
LESSON 4

Seeded Questions

Christian A. Bisson

Seeded Questions for Kurt Hahn

1. "Dr. Hahn, is it true that you became quite good at the sport of high jumping when you were young?"
2. "Could you talk to us about how you came up with the idea of creating a national award scheme for youth?"
3. "What did you mean by the need to create educational experiences that reproduce the moral equivalent of war?"
4. "Dr. Hahn, have you yourself led or taught any Outward Bound course?"

Seeded Questions for Paul Petzoldt

1. "Mr. Petzoldt, is it true that you almost died climbing the Grand Teton when you were 16 years old?"
2. "What about the incident in India—is it true that you killed a man in a bar fight?"
3. "Mr. Petzoldt, you were married four times: talk to us about your first wife, Bernice—is it true that she tried to kill you with an axe while you were sleeping?"
4. "Is it true that you participated in a secret mission that involved climbing mountains in South America to spy on the German navy during World War II?"

1

Kurt Hahn When you are ready, walk into the classroom and greet the class with a gentle "gutentag." To get into the character, try to mix a German and a British accent and walk slowly to your chair to show your age. You can also ask a nearby "fräulein" or "mein herr" to lower the shade in the classroom since the sun fatigues you. Be ready to answer any questions students might have about Kurt Hahn's life; so before the activity, make sure that you have extensively read about him. If the students are shy or unprepared, don't forget that you planted a few questions with four to six students, and call on them if needed. If you do not know the answers to these questions, you can create your own set of seeded questions.

When the interview with Kurt Hahn seems to be slowing down, excuse yourself, explaining that you have another important meeting with former President Jimmy Carter regarding the American Congressional Award he helped create. Bid the class a sweet "auf wiederschauen."

Outside the classroom, quickly put on your Paul Petzoldt costume and get ready for the next interview.

Paul Petzoldt When ready, walk into the classroom and give the class a resounding "hello!" To get into the character, walk slowly, using your ice axe to support yourself, and go around shaking hands and commenting on how honored you are to be here. Be joyful, have a few belly laughs, look distracted, and ask where the students want you to sit or stand. Be ready to answer any questions they might have about Paul Petzoldt's life, so make sure you have read extensively about him. Again, if your students are shy or unprepared, remember that you planted a few questions with four to six students, and call on them if needed. If you do not know the answers to these questions, you can create your own set of seeded questions.

When the interview with Paul Petzoldt seems to be slowing down, excuse yourself, explaining that you have heard of a mountain nearby that has to be climbed. So give them a big "good bye and good luck."

Once you have returned to class, apologize for missing the guest speakers and ask a few questions about the students' first impression of the two gentlemen. Ask them if they better understand why one was labeled a "visionary" and the other an "actionary." Also ask what they think was the greatest contribution each of these two men made to the field of adventure education. Finally, ask if they think that the two men would have gotten along if they had met.

CLOSURE

For closure, invite your students to look at the historical time line they have created, and ask them to imagine where their name could be placed on the time line. What would be their professional involvement with the field of adventure education, and for which branch of the time line do they see themselves contributing to the future of adventure education?

Often this closure can lead to some very interesting exchanges between your students.

ASSESSMENT OF LEARNING

A formative assessment will occur during the creation of the historical flowchart. In addition, the types of questions students ask the guest speakers, Hahn and Petzoldt, will give you an idea of their depth of reading and comprehension about the life and influence these two men had on adventure education.

LESSON 5

A History of Outdoor Adventure Education in the United States

Ed Raiola and Marty O'Keefe

The rich history of outdoor adventure education in the United States is typically traced to Outward Bound and its founder, Kurt Hahn, but its roots are much deeper and farther reaching than that. The pioneers of outdoor adventure education were men and women with a vision of the impact that group-focused outdoor learning and living could have on the lives of participants. This lesson allows you to explore with your students the people, organizations, and events that have shaped what we today call outdoor adventure education.

Background

Although many researchers trace the origin of adventure education to Kurt Hahn, founder of Outward Bound, prior events and people made Hahn's era, the mid-20th century, a ripe time in history for Outward Bound to come to the United States and create the wave of momentum that is still building today. To explore the development of adventure education we must go back to the beginnings of experiential education, the organized camping movement, conservation education, nature study, outdoor education, and environmental education, as well as experiential education. They each influenced and shaped what we now call adventure education.

It's important to understand that adventure education is a form of experiential education. So, the earliest roots of adventure education are traced to the philosophical teachings of experiential educators such as Comenius, Rousseau, and Pestalozzi. During the 19th century the organized camping movement used adventure and the outdoors as educational tools. Key figures include Mr. and Mrs. Gunn and their Gunnery School, as well as Laura Mattoon, an educator who taught at a private girls' school and led expeditions for girls in the New Hampshire wilderness. The development of the national and state parks and the founding of organizations like the Appalachian Mountain Club were important events at the end of the 19th century as well.

The 20th century experienced substantial development in such organizations as the American Camping Association, Boy and Girl Scouts, the progressive education movement, and public school programs using the environment and overnight camping as part of the curriculum to continue the growth of adventure education. From the 1960s to the present there has been a rapid development in school camping; public and private outdoor programs such as Outward Bound, the National Outdoor Leadership School, and Project Adventure; and professional organizations such as the Association for Experiential Education and the National Recreation and Park Association.

RESOURCES

Martin, B., C. Cashel, W. Wagstaff, and M. Breunig. 2006. *Outdoor leadership theory and practice.* Champaign, IL: Human Kinetics.

Prouty, D., J. Panicucci, and R. Collinson. 2007. *Adventure education: Theory and applications.* Champaign, IL: Human Kinetics.

Raiola, E., and M. O'Keefe. 1999. Philosophy in practice: A history of adventure programming. In *Adventure programming,* eds. J.C. Miles and S. Priest, 45-53. State College, PA: Venture.

Lesson Plan

PURPOSE

In this lesson students will learn to recognize and describe the prominent philosophical and historical roots of outdoor adventure education; their effects on current and future trends in the field; and the various events, people, and organizations that helped develop and shape the field of outdoor adventure education.

OBJECTIVES

As a result of this lesson students will be able to . . .

1. *Cognitive:* recognize and describe six to eight prominent North American outdoor adventure education organizations and their contributions within the field.
2. *Cognitive:* recognize and describe the prominent philosophical and historical roots of outdoor adventure education and their effects on current and future trends in the field.
3. *Cognitive:* recognize and describe the various events, people, and organizations that helped develop and shape the field of outdoor adventure education.
4. *Affective:* recognize and describe, through reflection and a written exercise, a personal event, person, or organization that has had a major impact on how they perceive themselves in relation to outdoor adventure education.

DURATION

50 to 90 minutes

GROUP SIZE

6 to 30 students

LOCATION

Indoor space large enough to accommodate the group size

EQUIPMENT

- 3- × 5-inch index cards—five per student
- Tape for attaching cards to wall or board
- Flat surface such as a wall to put a time line on and attach cards to (see activity 1 for details)
- Historical time line from Raiola and O'Keefe—a copy for each group of three students (see "Time Line: A History of Adventure Education in the United States" on CD-ROM)

RISK MANAGEMENT CONSIDERATIONS

None applicable for this lesson

STUDENT PREPARATION

Either before or after the lesson, students should read the Background section on the CD-ROM. Students can also read the chapter by Raiola and O'Keefe (1999) titled "Philosophy in Practice: A History of Adventure Programming."

INSTRUCTOR PREPARATION

Put a date line on the board or wall using the dates from the Time Line: A History of Outdoor Adventure Education in the United States handout on the CD-ROM. Adjust the time periods based on the size of the board or wall space. You may want to limit the date line to five or six time periods if you have a small group. Sample dates are 1600s to 1860; 1860s to early 1900; 1900 to 1930s; 1940 to 1960s; 1970s; 1980 to the present. (See activity 1 explanation for more details.)

LESSON CONTENT AND TEACHING STRATEGIES

Begin the class with a short perspective piece about history and the reasons to explore its value to us. We often use a short story about the need to continue to look back, dive into, and play around with history. For example, most people believe that outdoor adventure education started with Outward Bound or the National Outdoor Leadership School (NOLS). Understanding our historical roots can help each of us bring a broad perspective to what we see and understand and help us glean more knowledge and understanding about what we do and why we do it. We also need to continue to look at history to search for voices and stories that have not yet been heard and told (for example, women's voices and stories).

Activity 1: Historical Time Line

Hand out five 3 × 5 cards to each person. Give students 3 minutes to reflect on the following question and respond by writing on one of the cards: "Think of a person, event, or organization that has had a major impact on how you perceive yourself in relation to outdoor adventure education. Be as descriptive as possible (who, what, where, when, why)."

On the remaining four cards, have students reflect and respond to the following prompt: "List important events, people, and organizations in the history of outdoor adventure education and their dates." Students should use one card for each event, person, or organization. If students have not read the assigned chapter, have them simply list events, people, or organizations that they are aware of.

Have them come up to the board and tape their personal event cards near the appropriate dates on the time line. For example, a student who listed "camping education movement" or "L.B. Sharp" would tape that card near the 1920s or 1930s, respectively.

For a creative way to divide students, first request that the whole group line up alphabetically by the first letter of one of the important events, people, or organizations that they listed on their card. Then divide them into groups of three. Have the small groups look at all their historical cards and have each small group decide what date they think or know is correct for each event, person, or organization. Then ask an individual representative from each group to go up to the board and place all the cards on the dates that their group agreed on.

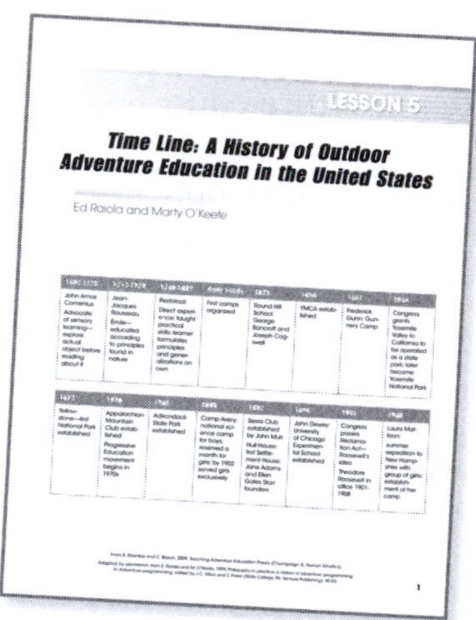
LESSON 5

Time Line: A History of Outdoor Adventure Education in the United States

Ed Raiola and Marty O'Keefe

Optional additional activity: You prepare beforehand individual 3 × 5 cards depicting important dates, events, people, or organizations that you want to focus on during the lesson and hand those out to each group to add to the time line.

Hand out copies of the time line handout from the CD-ROM and ask your students to compare it to the time line and events they have listed. Have the students correct any mistakes on the time line.

Focus on key points as a large group. For example: People were doing adventure education long before Outward Bound and the National Outdoor Leadership School. Consider the first organized camps in the 1800s, women leading programming in the early 1900s, how the development and evolution of adventure emerged from experiential education, the organized camping movement, conservation education, nature study, outdoor education, and environmental education.

Depending on the size of the class, have students share their personal story in either a large or a small group, explaining what they wrote about on their personal history card at the beginning of class. Have the students take their cards and do one or both of the following, depending upon time:

- Place their personal history card on the time line according to chronology, that is, based on when they had the experience.
- Place their card with a card that identifies a movement or organization with a focus or philosophy similar to the focus or philosophy behind the experience that they had.

Have a short discussion with the large group highlighting the overall history of adventure education and the students' connection to it. Use the following focus questions or create your own:

- What events and people helped prepare and create the way for you to have the type of adventure education experience that you described on your personal experience card?

- What historical roots can you see or connect to the event, organization, or person you described on your personal experience card?

CLOSURE

End the lesson by asking students to think about current issues that may help or hinder the growth or evolution of adventure education. Examples may include overpopulation, development of new high-tech tools or toys, loss of natural resources, growth of adventure travel, and aging population.

ASSESSMENT OF LEARNING

In small groups, students will recognize and describe the prominent organizations (American Camping Association, Outward Bound, National Outdoor Leadership School, Project Adventure, Wilderness Education Association, and Association for Experiential Education) and their contributions within the field of outdoor adventure education by participating in the historical time line activity.

In the large group discussion, students will recognize and describe the prominent philosophical and historical roots of outdoor adventure education (experiential education, the organized camping movement, conservation education, nature study, outdoor education, and environmental education) and their effects on current and future trends in the field.

In small and large group discussion and through personal reflection, students will recognize and describe a personal event, person, or organization that has had a major impact on how they perceive themselves in relation to outdoor adventure education.

LESSON 6

Creating History

Exploring the Past and Future of Adventure Education

Jacquie Medina

The significance, wisdom, and efforts of individuals and the events that have influenced adventure education can be overlooked if students do not understand the application of this information to themselves or their work. By understanding individuals and events from the past and how they apply to us, we can better understand our contributions and future directions in the historical path of adventure education. In this lesson students will develop and analyze an adventure education history time line that weaves together relevant adventure education components and the students' personal and professional experiences. Through this process of blending the past and present, students begin to see themselves as active participants in the evolution of adventure education.

Background

Synthesizing and summarizing contributing factors in adventure education history is no small task, as there has yet to emerge any consensus on a clear definition of adventure education (Raiola and O'Keefe 1999). In general, adventure education has been identified as a branch of outdoor education emphasizing the development of interpersonal and intrapersonal skills through experiences that often involve elements of "excitement, uncertainty, real or perceived risk, effort, and interactions with the natural environment" (Raiola and O'Keefe, p. 46). However, adventure education experiences may or may not occur in the out-of-doors. The historical factors contributing to adventure education history are woven within the related areas of outdoor leadership, experiential education, environmental education, and outdoor education and recreation (Drury et al. 2005; Martin et al. 2006; Miles and Priest 1990; Moore and Driver 2005; Raiola and O'Keefe 1999; Priest and Gass 2005; Prouty, Panicucci, and Collinson 2007). Writings in these broader topic areas will provide you with greater depth and breadth of facts that you may wish to include in your history time line.

People, events, organizations, and laws are among the contributing factors to adventure education history. One can argue that the history of adventure education can be traced back to ancient Greece, Egyptian explorers, and tribal communities (Hunt 1999; Neill 2006). Adventure education is rooted in the early philosophies and teachings of individuals such as Plato, Aristotle, Rousseau, William James, and John Dewey (Hunt 1999; Priest and Gass 2005). These ideas of experiential learning and the integration of our senses and the environment in the learning process, along with the role of adventure in fostering lessons of virtue, have influenced people and programs that have significantly contributed to the development of adventure education.

Fredrick William Gunn, recognized for implementing camping as part of an educational program at the Gunnery School for Boys in 1861, subsequently began the organized camping movement. In 1902, the first summer camp for girls in the United States was started by Laura Mattoon. Believing that camping was a means of building character, Mattoon and eight campers hiked and swam in the New Hampshire mountains and lakes, slept in tents, and built their own furniture. In addition, Mattoon was a contributing member in the Camp Directors' Association of America developed in 1910, which in 1935 changed its name to the American Camping Association (Martin et al. 2006; Raiola and O'Keefe 1999).

The beginning of the scouting movement is associated with Lord Robert Baden-Powell, who founded the Boy Scouts in Britain in 1907 and helped to establish the Girl Guides in 1911. The Boy Scouts were introduced in the United States in 1910 by the efforts of William Boyce, and Juliette Gordon Lowe was instrumental in bringing the Girl Guides to the United States in 1912. This organization eventually became known as the Girl Scouts in the United States (Martin et al. 2006).

The conservation and designation of national and state parks and wilderness areas have also been essential in the development of adventure education. The availability and preservation of lands and water for adventure experiences can be attributed to early acts including, but not limited to, the operation of Yosemite National Park as a state park beginning in 1864, the establishment of Yellowstone as the first national park in 1872, the development of the National Park Service in 1916, the implementation of the Wilderness Act in 1964, and that of the National Trails System Act and National Wild and Scenic Rivers Act, both in 1968 (Moore and Driver 2005).

Throughout summaries of adventure education history and related fields, certain people and organizations have consistently emerged as integral to the development of adventure education. One of the most significant figures is Kurt Hahn, who is recognized as the founder of Outward Bound in 1941 in Aberdovey, Wales. Hahn's educational philosophy emphasized helping students build character and become responsible and contributing members of society. The adventurous outdoor experiences involved in Outward Bound were "less training *for* the sea than *through* the sea" (Miner and Boldt 1981, p. 33). In 1962, Colorado Outward Bound School became the first Outward Bound School in the United States.

Paul Petzoldt, another significant individual in adventure education history, was the chief instructor for Colorado Outward Bound School. It was through his experiences with Outward Bound and mountain guiding that he was spurred to develop the National Outdoor Leadership School (NOLS). Petzoldt felt that training was needed to prepare outdoor leaders to lead individuals into the wilderness and developed NOLS in 1965 to train people for this role. In 1977, Petzoldt, along with Frank Lupton, Charles Gregory, and Bob Christie, founded the Wilderness Use Education Association (renamed Wilderness Education Association [WEA] in 1978). The WEA was intended to train outdoor leaders through universities, colleges, and outdoor organizations. The WEA mission involves promoting professionalism within outdoor leadership, thus improving the safety of outdoor trips and enhancing the conservation of wild outdoors (Drury et al. 2005; Teeters and Lupton 1999).

In 1971, Project Adventure evolved from a three-year grant awarded to Hamilton-Wenham Junior-Senior High School for developing a curriculum that would apply Outward Bound principles to the classroom. The grant was the beginning of the continued growth of Project Adventure, which today includes national and international offices. Project Adventure has been instrumental in designing and installing challenge ropes courses, training teachers in adventure curriculum, and publishing numerous adventure education books (Prouty 1999).

Along with the growth of adventure education has been the development of professional organizations including the Association of Experiential Education, the Association for Challenge Course Technology, and most recently the Professional Ropes Course Association. Organizations like these provide professionals with resources such as forums for collaboration and growth, challenge course building standards, and accreditation standards (Association for Challenge Course Technology 2006; Priest and Gass 2005; Professional Ropes Course Association 2006).

RESOURCES

Association for Challenge Course Technology. 2006. www.acctinfo.org.

Drury, J.K., B.F. Bonney, D. Berman, and M.C. Wagstaff. 2005. *The backcountry classroom: Lessons, tools, and activities for teaching outdoor leaders.* 2nd ed. Guilford, CT: Falconguide.

Hunt, J. 1999. Philosophy of adventure education. In *Adventure programming,* eds. J.C. Miles and S. Priest, 115-122. State College, PA: Venture.

Martin, B., C. Cashel, M. Wagstaff, and M. Breunig. 2006. *Outdoor leadership: Theory and practice.* Champaign, IL: Human Kinetics.

Miles, J.C., and S. Priest, eds. 1990. *Adventure education.* State College, PA: Venture.

Miner, J., and J. Boldt. 1981. *Outward Bound, USA: Learning through experience in adventure based education.* New York: Morrow.

Moore, R.L., and B.L. Driver. 2005. *Introduction to outdoor recreation.* State College, PA: Venture.

Neill, J. 2006. History of outdoor education. Wilderdom Web site: www.wilderdom.com.

Priest, S., and M.A. Gass. 2005. *Effective leadership in adventure programming.* 2nd ed. Champaign, IL: Human Kinetics.

Professional Ropes Course Association. 2006. About the PRCA. www.prcainfo.org.

Prouty, D. 1999. Project adventure: A brief history. In *Adventure programming,* eds. J.C. Miles and S. Priest, 93-101. State College, PA: Venture.

Prouty, D., J. Panicucci, and R. Collinson. 2007. *Adventure education: Theory and applications.* Champaign, IL: Human Kinetics.

Raiola, E., and M. O'Keefe. 1999. Philosophy in practice: A history of adventure programming. In *Adventure programming,* eds. J.C. Miles and S. Priest, 45-53. State College, PA: Venture.

Teeters, C., and F. Lupton. 1999. The wilderness education association: History and change. In *Adventure programming,* eds. J.C. Miles and S. Priest, 77-83. State College, PA: Venture.

Lesson Plan

PURPOSE

The purpose of this lesson is to allow students to develop an understanding of adventure education history and its relationship to the students' educational paths, to critically analyze past and present trends, and to synthesize and formulate ideas for future directions of the adventure education field.

OBJECTIVES

As a result of this lesson students will be able to . . .

1. *Cognitive:* demonstrate knowledge and understanding of the significant individuals, organizations, and events within the development of adventure education history.
2. *Cognitive:* integrate personal and professional experiences in adventure education into adventure education history and relate these experiences to significant components of adventure education history.
3. *Cognitive:* analyze and identify patterns, themes, and relationships that emerge or develop throughout adventure education history.
4. *Cognitive:* synthesize the components and trends in adventure education history to formulate and propose new ideas and trends for the future of adventure education.

DURATION

90 to 120 minutes

GROUP SIZE

Approximately 8 to 18 students

LOCATION

Indoors or outdoors. Outdoor materials (e.g., stones, pinecones, sticks, line in the sand, length of rope or webbing) can be used to represent historical components or the time line. A large open space on a wall or on the ground is needed for laying the time line and placing the history time cards on it.

EQUIPMENT

- Indoor or outdoor time line prop (e.g., rope, sticks, newsprint, paddles, dry erase board)
- 4- × 6-inch note cards—one to three note cards per person, plus one per group
- 3- × 5-inch note cards—three per person
- List of adventure education historical readings and significant people, events, organizations, laws, and so on (see Key People and Events in Adventure Education History on the CD-ROM)
- Activity handouts (Analysis of the Time Line and Future Directions of Adventure Education activities on the CD-ROM)
- Tape, paperclips, string (means of attaching history time cards to time line prop)
- Multiple color markers or string (specific to time line prop)

RISK MANAGEMENT CONSIDERATIONS

None applicable to this lesson

STUDENT PREPARATION

- Students should read the Background document included on the CD-ROM. Students can also read from the following sources in preparation for this lesson. If possible, it may be helpful to place these texts on reserve at the library.
  - Drury, J.K., B.F. Bonney, D. Berman, and M.C. Wagstaff. 2005. *The backcountry classroom: Lessons, tools, and activities for teaching outdoor leaders.* 2nd ed. Guilford, CT: Falconguide.
  - Martin, B., C. Cashel, M. Wagstaff, and M. Breunig. 2006. *Outdoor leadership: Theory and practice.* Champaign, IL: Human Kinetics.
  - Miles, J.C., and S. Priest, eds. 1990. *Adventure education.* State College, PA: Venture.
  - Moore, R.L., and B.L. Driver. 2005. *Introduction to outdoor recreation.* State College, PA: Venture.
  - Priest, S., and M.A. Gass. 2005. *Effective leadership in adventure programming.* 2nd ed. Champaign, IL: Human Kinetics.
  - Prouty, D., J. Panicucci, and R. Collinson. 2007. *Adventure education: Theory and applications.* Champaign, IL: Human Kinetics.
  - Raiola, E., and M. O'Keefe. 1999. Philosophy in practice: A history of adventure programming. In *Adventure programming,* eds. J.C. Miles and S. Priest, 45-53. State College, PA: Venture.
  - Teeters, C., and F. Lupton. 1999. The wilderness education association: History and change. In *Adventure programming,* eds. J.C. Miles and S. Priest, 77-83. State College, PA: Venture.
- In addition, students should be given a copy of Key People and Events in Adventure Education History (CD-ROM). If desired, you can use this as a sample to build a list that meets your class needs. For example, regional, state, and local contributions can be added to the list, as well as the history of your school's adventure education program or state and local parks, events, and people that have made a contribution to adventure education history.
- *History time cards:* Whether components are assigned or self-selected, each student will have one to three components from the adventure education history list to explore in depth. Students will prepare a history time card and informational summary to be shared with the class during the history time line development. History time cards are 4- × 6-inch note cards with a picture, design, or symbol representing the historical component on one side and a brief summary of pertinent information on the other side. A sample time card is included on the CD-ROM.
- Students must also create and bring to class three 3- × 5-inch personal history time cards listing the following, respectively: (1) the student's name and the date

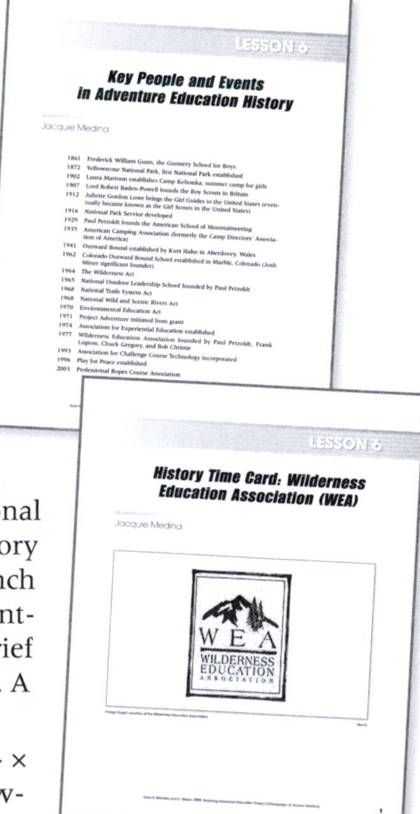
LESSON 6

Key People and Events in Adventure Education History

Jacquie Medina

1861 Frederick William Gunn, the Gunnery School for Boys
1872 Yellowstone National Park, first National Park established
1902 Laura Mattoon establishes Camp Kehonka, summer camp for girls
1907 Lord Robert Baden-Powell founds the Boy Scouts in Britain
1912 Juliette Gordon Lowe brings the Girl Guides to the United States (eventually became known as the Girl Scouts in the United States)
1916 National Park Service developed
1929 Paul Petzoldt founds the American School of Mountaineering
1935 American Camping Association (formerly the Camp Directors' Association of America)
1941 Outward Bound established by Kurt Hahn in Aberdovey, Wales
1962 Colorado Outward Bound School established in Marble, Colorado (Josh Miner significant founder)
1964 The Wilderness Act
1965 National Outdoor Leadership School founded by Paul Petzoldt
1968 National Trails System Act
1968 National Wild and Scenic Rivers Act
1970 Environmental Education Act
1971 Project Adventure initiated from grant
1974 Association for Experiential Education established
1977 Wilderness Education Association founded by Paul Petzoldt, Frank Lupton, Chuck Gregory, and Bob Christie
1993 Association for Challenge Course Technology incorporated
1996 Play for Peace established
2003 Professional Ropes Course Association

LESSON 6

History Time Card: Wilderness Education Association (WEA)

Jacquie Medina

and location of birth, (2) the student's earliest experience in adventure education, and (3) the student's most recent experience in adventure education. Use the same development format that was used to create the 4- × 6-inch history time cards. Color coding the note cards provides a visual emphasis when students are analyzing the time line for trends and patterns.

INSTRUCTOR PREPARATION

Mark the time line with centuries and decades and locate the time line so that it is accessible for all students to attach history time cards to. Indoor time line options may include a length of newsprint, dry erase board, or string (on which time cards can be hung). Outdoor time line options (although these could be used indoors as well) may include space that allows for a length of newsprint paper, rope, or a line drawn in the sand or created using sticks, paddles, and so on. Provide a method for placing history time cards on the time line (tape, clips, rocks, etc.).

LESSON CONTENT AND TEACHING STRATEGIES

The lesson is divided into three activities: (1) time line development, (2) analysis of the time line, and (3) time line synthesis and formulation of future directions in adventure education.

To begin, ask the students to reflect on their own lives and to recall a historical moment that has penetrated their memory. For this example, the historical moment does not need to be related to adventure education. Ask two to three students to share with their classmates the historical moment that comes to mind. After they cite these examples, ask the students "What makes these moments memorable?"

Use the students' examples to transition to the historical components that they explored for this lesson. Pose the following questions:

- Have these components also emerged as memorable or significant within adventure education history?
- Why have these components emerged as significant?
- What relationships exist between these components and others on the time line?
- How do these components apply to you as a student or as an outdoor professional?

This lesson is designed to promote student understanding of adventure education history by helping the students answer the question "How does this apply to me?" Make a conscious effort to state the following goal for this lesson:

"By understanding the individuals and events that have come before us and how they apply to us, perhaps we can better understand our own contributions and future directions."

Activity 1: Development of the Time Line

Now that you have the students' attention, ask the students to place two of their 3- × 5-inch cards on the time line: the one with their name, birth date, and birth location and the one detailing their earliest experience in adventure education. Allow the students time to look at the time cards that have been placed on the time line. Point out any unique aspects you notice such as similar birth dates, years, or locations and similarities or differences among students' earliest experiences. Emphasis should be on facilitating the students' ability to see themselves as participating and contributing beings within the historical path of adventure education.

Next, use one of the students' earliest experiences as a link to a significant adventure education historical component. For example, one of the students may have participated in Girl Scouts or Boy Scouts, attended a summer camp, or visited a national park or wilderness area. Ask the student who has the history time card listing the Girls Scouts or Boy Scouts to place the history time card on the time line and then share with the class the selected history component and the summary information provided on the back of the card.

At this point, your role is to facilitate the students' understanding of adventure education history through sharing the history time cards and placing them on the time line. Encourage students to make connections between the historical information placed on the time line and the history time cards they have not yet shared. Pose questions such as these:

- How does the history component on your time card relate to the time cards already placed on the time line?
- What is one of the earliest dates in adventure education history on the time cards you are still holding?
- In relation to what organization or event was this individual [any person on the time line] instrumental?
- What other historical events occurred during this decade [any decade on the time line]?

As in the beginning of the lesson, continue to use the students' "earliest adventure experience time cards" to introduce new time cards or links among the material. The order in which time cards are actually placed on the time line may be chronological or may reflect the relationships that the students see among the material. However, the order in which you present the material may vary based on the number of students in the class and the historical components selected for discussion. When approximately half of the history time cards have been placed on the time line, have the students add their third 3- × 5-inch note card, the one that represents their most recent adventure education experience. Use these new time cards to make additional links to the remaining history time cards, specifically more recent events in adventure education history. Continue to facilitate student learning by sharing of knowledge through posing questions.

Be prepared to add history time cards to the time line for components on the adventure education history list that were not selected by students; world events that provide context to the developmental path of adventure education; or dates, individuals, and events that represent your institution or program's adventure education history.

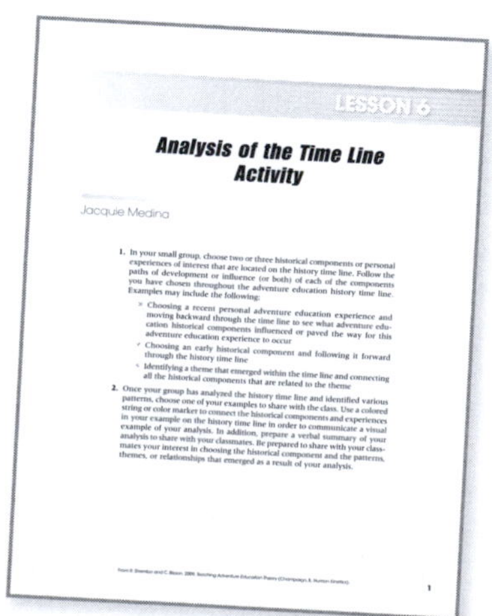

LESSON 6

Analysis of the Time Line Activity

Jacquie Medina

1. In your small group, choose two or three historical components or personal experiences of interest that are located on the history time line. Follow the paths of development or influence (or both) of each of the components you have chosen throughout the adventure education history time line. Examples may include the following:
   - Choosing a recent personal adventure education experience and moving backward through the time line to see what adventure education historical components influenced or paved the way for this adventure education experience to occur
   - Choosing an early historical component and following it forward through the history time line
   - Identifying a theme that emerged within the time line and connecting all the historical components that are related to the theme
2. Once your group has analyzed the history time line and identified various patterns, choose one of your examples to share with the class. Use a colored string or color marker to connect the historical components and experiences in your example on the history time line in order to communicate a visual example of your analysis. In addition, prepare a verbal summary of your analysis to share with your classmates. Be prepared to share with your classmates your interest in choosing the historical component and the patterns, themes, or relationships that emerged as a result of your analysis.

1

Activity 2: Analysis of the Time Line

Once the time line has been developed, divide the class into pairs or groups of three and provide each group with an Analysis of the Time Line activity handout (on CD-ROM). Explain the activity, emphasizing that each group will choose two to three historical components or personal experiences of interest that are located on the time line. The purpose of the activity is to follow the path of development and influence throughout adventure education history of each of the components they have chosen. The following are examples of specific activities:

- Choose a recent personal experience and move backward through the time line to see what adventure education historical components influenced or paved the way for that experience to occur.
- Choose an early historical component and follow it forward through the history time line.
- In place of an event or experience, have the students identify a theme that emerged throughout the time line and connect all historical components that are related to that theme.

Once the small groups have analyzed the time line and identified various patterns, have each group choose one of their examples to share with the class. Provide each group with a different color string or marker to connect the historical components and experiences on the history time line in order to communicate a visual example of their analysis. In addition, provide student groups with the opportunity to verbally summarize and share with their classmates the outcome of their analysis. Facilitate a discussion of the individual and combined paths that students have identified using the string or markers. Questions may include the following:

- What are some of the earliest historical components that have affected or made possible your adventure education experiences today?
- How might your experience be different today with the removal of one of the events listed in your path?
- How have world events or social change affected the development of adventure education?
- What events, people, laws, or organizations have only recently influenced adventure education? What do you think brought these factors into being?
- What, if any, patterns or themes have been cyclical throughout the time line?

As the instructor, you play a vital role in fostering the students' critical analysis of the time line. Be prepared to lead a short discussion on a particular area of student interest (e.g., differentiation of Outward Bound, National Outdoor Leadership School, and Wilderness Education Association). Consider introducing themes that the students may not have addressed in their analysis such as the impact of risk management, leadership development, social and political events, or international and regional influences on adventure education.

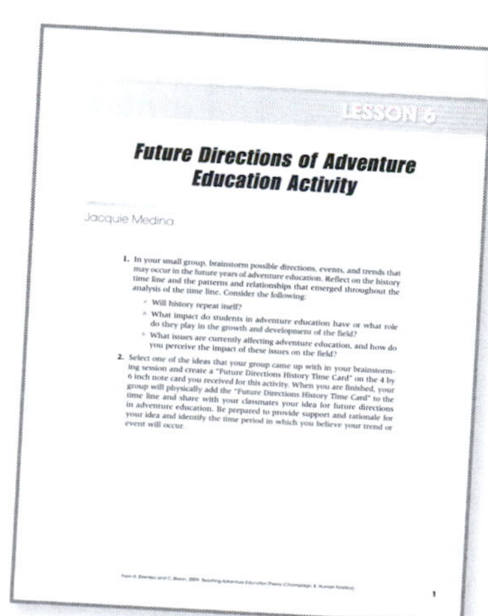

LESSON 6

Future Directions of Adventure Education Activity

Jacquie Medina

1. In your small group, brainstorm possible directions, events, and trends that may occur in the future years of adventure education. Reflect on the history time line and the patterns and relationships that emerged throughout the analysis of the time line. Consider the following:
   - Will history repeat itself?
   - What impact do students in adventure education have or what role do they play in the growth and development of the field?
   - What issues are currently affecting adventure education, and how do you perceive the impact of these issues on the field?
2. Select one of the ideas that your group came up with in your brainstorming session and create a "Future Directions History Time Card" on the 4 by 6 inch note card you received for this activity. When you are finished, your group will physically add the "Future Directions History Time Card" to the time line and share with your classmates your idea for future directions in adventure education. Be prepared to provide support and rationale for your idea and identify the time period in which you believe your trend or event will occur.

1

Activity 3: Future Directions of Adventure Education

Following the analysis of the time line, students return to their small groups to brainstorm possible directions, events, and trends that may occur in the future years of adventure education. Provide students with the Future Directions of Adventure Education activity handout (on CD-ROM) and a 4- × 6-inch note card. Encourage students to consider the following:

- Referring to the string and marker patterns presented by all groups during the analysis, do you think history will repeat itself?

- What impact do students in adventure education like yourselves have on the growth and development of the field, or what role do they play in this growth?
- What issues are currently affecting adventure education, and how do you perceive the impact of these issues on the field?

Following their brainstorming session, student groups select one of their ideas and create a "future directions history time card" to be added to the history time line. Groups take turns physically adding their future directions time card to the time line and sharing with their classmates their ideas for the future directions of adventure education. Groups should provide support and rationale for their ideas and articulate the time period during which they believe these developments will occur.

CLOSURE

To move from the future directions activity, revisit the statement of the goal for the lesson: By understanding the individuals and events that have come before us and how they apply to us, perhaps we can better understand our own contributions and future directions. Ask the students to consider the following:

- What do you now know about the individuals and events in adventure education history that came before you?
- How do these historical components apply to you?
- What can you—or we—contribute to adventure education?
- How will our actions and inactions affect the future of adventure education?

ASSESSMENT OF LEARNING

Assessment of learning and lesson objectives occur throughout the lesson and can be documented by the following:

- The student demonstrates knowledge and understanding of the significant individuals, organizations, and events within the development of adventure education history through the accurate development of history time cards, oral summary of historical components, and placement of the history time cards within the appropriate historical time period.
- The student identifies and articulates relationships between his or her personal and professional experiences in adventure education and significant components of adventure education history during the development and analysis of the history time line.
- The student demonstrates analysis and identification of patterns, themes, and relationships that emerged or developed throughout adventure education history by presenting a visual example and an oral summary of his or her analysis to classmates.
- The student synthesizes the components and trends in adventure education history and proposes and substantiates future directions in adventure education.

LESSON 7

Adventure Education History Roundtable

Brad Daniel

Learning the history of adventure education can be exciting and fun for students. This lesson uses three experiential methods—role play, concept mapping, and time line construction—to engage students and enhance their abilities to remember what they have learned. It focuses on the key figures in adventure education, the roles that these people played in the history of adventure education, the interconnections between these key people and various adventure education organizations, and the similarities and differences among various types of educators who deal with the outdoors.

Background

The following section contains resources useful to this lesson. It begins with an overview of the history of adventure education, primarily in North America. It includes a list of some of the important figures in the history of adventure education including several theorists whose work bears directly on the field. It closes with a list of useful resources on the history of adventure education.

This section is intended to give the reader a brief overview of the history of adventure education. For a fuller description, it will be helpful to read the other Backgrounds at the beginning of each history lesson along with the resources presented in the bibliography. Students participating in the lesson are expected to research their assigned character in detail.

The historical development of adventure education involved many people, organizations, and movements that spanned the globe. At its core, adventure education emphasizes direct experience as a means for learning about self, others, and the world. This core tenet, along with the theoretical foundation that underlies adventure education, can be traced back to philosophers (e.g., Aristotle, Plato) and educators (e.g., John Amos Comenius, Jean-Jacques Rousseau, Johann Heinrich Pestalozzi), yet it is a field defined and informed by a variety of disciplines, including experiential education, outdoor education and leadership, conservation education, environmental education, and outdoor recreation (Martin, Cashel, Wagstaff, and Breunig 2006; Hunt 1999; Raiola and O'Keefe 1999; Priest and Gass 2005; Miles and Priest 1990). More recently, adventure education has assimilated ideas and theories drawn from modern and progressive education (e.g., John Dewey, David Kolb), wilderness expedition programs (e.g., Kurt Hahn, Paul Petzoldt), psychology and sociology (e.g., Abraham Maslow, William James, Albert Bandura, Mihalyi Csikszentmihalyi), and organized camping (e.g., Robert Baden-Powell, Laura Mattoon, Abbie Graham) (Martin, Cashel, Wagstaff, and Breunig 2006; Hunt 1999; Raiola and O'Keefe 1999; Miles and Priest 1990).

Early adventure education was heavily influenced by activities in the United Kingdom. In 1907, Englishman Robert Baden-Powell established the scouting movement in Britain, emphasizing practical outdoor activities. This movement influenced the Boy Scouts' first camp experiment (1909-10), Camp Backett, as well as the establishment of Girl Guides, which was run initially by Agnes Baden-Powell. Juliette Lowe brought the concept to the United States, founding what would become the Girl Scouts of America. Laura Mattoon started the first summer camp for girls in the United States to educate girls using experience-based learning. She was a member of the Camp Directors' Association of America, an organization that would become the American Camping Association in 1935 (Martin, Cashel, Wagstaff, and Bruening 2006; Raiola and O'Keefe 1999).

By the 1930s, resident camping programs and the organized camping movement were growing in the United States. One camp director, Abbie Graham, authored a popular inspirational book *The Girls' Camp: Program-Making for Summer Leisure* (New York: The Woman's Press, 1933). Outdoor immersion experiences were becoming increasingly popular.

In 1941, the first Outward Bound program was conducted by Kurt Hahn in Aberdovey, Wales. Within 10 years, Outward Bound had expanded to other parts of the world and was introduced to North America in the early 1960s by Josh Miner, who formed the Colorado Outward Bound School (COBS). One well-known speaker for Outward Bound was Willi Unsoeld, a U.S. climber and member of the first American expedition to summit Mt. Everest on May 22, 1963. In the United States, COBS was followed by other outdoor adventure education programs, including the Minnesota Outward Bound School (founded in 1962 by Bob Pieh and later named Voyageur) and the National Outdoor Leadership School (NOLS). NOLS was created and managed in 1965 by Paul Petzoldt and Ernest "Tap" Tapley, who had worked previously at Colorado Outward Bound. The purpose of NOLS was to teach outdoor skills and develop outdoor leaders.

As adventure education blossomed, it began to be incorporated into formal educational institutions. Lloyd B. Sharp, an outdoor education pioneer in the United States, noted, "That which ought and can best be taught inside the schoolrooms should there be taught, and that which can best be learned through experience dealing directly with native materials and life situations outside the school should there be learned" (Knapp 1996, p. 77). In agreement with Sharp, Julian Smith founded the National Outdoor Education Project in 1955, which was intended to enrich and extend school curricula through adventures in the outdoors. Other organizations began to spring up as well. For example, Jerry Pieh created Project Adventure (1971) in order to provide adventure-based learning activities in schools. (In subsequent terms, Project Adventure was directed by Bob Lentz, Karl Rohnke, and Dick Prouty.) By 1974, Project Adventure had spread to 400 schools after receiving additional funding. It has been heavily involved in the development of challenge and ropes courses, portable initiatives, group games, and teacher training (Prouty 1999).

Also in 1974, the first North American Conference on Outdoor Pursuits in Higher Education was held at Appalachian State University in Boone, North Carolina. The Association for Experiential Education (AEE) was born just a few years later (Garvey 1990).

In 1977 and 1978, Paul Petzoldt, who earlier had worked as chief instructor for the Colorado Outward Bound School and founded the National Outdoor Leadership School, was instrumental in forming another organization, the Wilderness Education Association (WEA). Founded by Petzoldt, Dr. Frank Lupton, Robert Christie, and Charles Gregory, it was first known as the Wilderness Use Education Association (WUEA). The name was changed to the Wilderness Education Association (WEA) in 1980 (Drury, Bonney, Berman, and Wagstaff 2005).

As adventure education became incorporated into school curricula and matured as a field, a body of literature from several disciplines contributed to the theoretical foundation. For example, John Dewey, considered by many to be the founder of modern experiential education, argued for learning based on experience-based reflection. David Kolb constructed a model based on Dewey's experiential learning process that consists of concrete experiences, observation and reflection on those experiences, concept formation, and generalization. Abraham Maslow's theories pertaining to the *hierarchy of needs, optimal stress,* and *peak experiences* helped adventure education programmers to understand participants' needs and to develop better programs. Simon Priest, an adventure educator and coauthor of the *Adventure Experience Paradigm,* explained an individual's response based on the dynamic interaction between competence and risk. Albert Bandura's work on *social cognitive theory* proved helpful because it was based on the concept of self-efficacy, or "the belief in one's abilities to organize and execute the courses of action required to produce given attainments" (Bandura 1997, p. 3). Many other theorists from an array of academic disciplines continue to influence the development of adventure education. These ideas, models, and theories, including those mentioned above, are reviewed in many introductory adventure education texts such as *Outdoor Leadership: Theory and Practice* by Martin, Cashel, Wagstaff, and Breunig (2006) or *Effective Leadership for Adventure Programming* by Priest and Gass (2005).

Today, the field of adventure education has matured considerably with well-integrated experiential and intellectual components, including peer-reviewed journals and professional organizations. The number of professional organizations, such as the Association for Challenge Course Technology, the Professional Ropes Course Association, and the Association of Outdoor Recreation and Education (AORE), is growing (Priest and Gass 2005). Adventure education has made great strides both in depth and rigor. Clearly, the field of adventure education has come a long way from its humble origins.

Following is a list of some of the more influential figures in adventure education history:

Robert Baden-Powell (England)

Established the scouting movement.

Abbie Graham (USA)

Camp director, author of inspirational writings for girls; wrote *The Girls' Camp: Program-Making for Summer Leisure* (New York: The Woman's Press, 1933).

Kurt Hahn (Germany)

Founded Outward Bound.

Lord John Hunt (Britain)

Leader on an early Mt. Everest expedition, director of the Duke of Edinburgh Award Scheme, founding member of the Mountain Leadership Training Board.

Bob Lentz (USA)

First director of Project Adventure.

Juliette Low (USA)

In 1912 founded the Girl Guides in the United States, which became the Girl Scouts of America in 1913 (incorporated in 1915).

Laura Mattoon (USA)

Helped to create the American Camping Association; started a camp to educate girls using experience-based learning.

Josh Miner (USA)

Brought Outward Bound to the United States.

Paul Petzoldt (USA)

Worked for Outward Bound, founded the National Outdoor Leadership School and later the Wilderness Education Association.

Bob Pieh (USA)

Founded the Minnesota Outward Bound School.

Jerry Pieh (USA)

Established Project Adventure.

Dick Prouty (USA)

Author, educator, and third director of Project Adventure.

Karl Rohnke (USA)

Second director of Project Adventure. Author of many popular books that incorporated adventure education concepts into mainstream education.

Lloyd B. Sharp (USA)

Outdoor education pioneer who argued "that which ought and can best be taught inside the schoolrooms should there be taught, and that which can best be learned through experience dealing directly with native materials and life situations outside the school should there be learned."

Julian Smith (USA)

Founder of the National Outdoor Education Project.

Willi Unsoeld (USA)

American climber, member of the first American expedition to summit Mt. Everest on May 22, 1963; speaker for Outward Bound.

Following is a list of some theorists who have influenced the development of adventure education.

Albert Bandura

Known for *social cognitive theory* based on the concept of self-efficacy—the belief in one's abilities to organize and execute the courses of action required to produce given attainments.

Mihalyi Csikszentmihalyi

Known for his *flow theory,* referring to an experience that is engrossing, intrinsically rewarding, and outside the parameters of worry and boredom.

John Dewey

Considered by many to be the founder of modern experiential education.

David Kolb

Constructed a model based on Dewey's experiential learning process by which a concrete experience would be followed by observation and reflection, thereby leading to the formation of an abstract concept and generalization.

Abraham Maslow

Known for theories pertaining to the *hierarchy of needs* and *peak experiences.*

Simon Priest

An adventure educator and coauthor of the *adventure experience paradigm,* which explains the individual's behaviors based on the dynamic interaction between competence and risk.

RESOURCES

Bandura, A. 1997. *Self-efficacy: the exercise of control.* New York: W.H. Freeman and Company.

Drury, J.K., B.F. Bonney, D. Berman, and M.C. Wagstaff. 2005. *The backcountry classroom: Lessons, tools, and activities for teaching outdoor leaders.* 2nd ed. Guilford, CT: Falconguide.

Garvey, D. 1990. A history of the AEE. In *Adventure Education,* eds. J.C. Miles and S. Priest, 75-82. State College, PA: Venture.

Graham, A. 1933. *The girls' camp: Program-making for summer leisure.* New York: The Woman's Press.

Hunt, J. 1999. Philosophy of adventure education. In *Adventure programming,* eds. J.C. Miles and S. Priest, 119-128. State College, PA: Venture.

Knapp, C. 1996. *Just beyond the classroom: Community adventures for interdisciplinary learning.* Charleston, WV: ERIC Clearinghouse on Rural Education and Small Schools.

Martin, B., C. Cashel, M. Wagstaff, and M. Breunig. 2006. *Outdoor leadership: Theory and practice.* Champaign, IL: Human Kinetics.

Miles, J.C., and S. Priest. 1990. *Adventure education.* State College, PA: Venture.

Priest, S., and M.A. Gass. 2005. *Effective leadership for adventure programming.* 2nd ed. Champaign, IL: Human Kinetics.

Prouty, D. 1999. Project adventure: A brief history. In *Adventure programming,* eds. J.C. Miles and S. Priest, 93-101. State College, PA: Venture.

Raiola, E., and M. O'Keefe. 1999. Philosophy in practice: A history of adventure programming. In *Adventure programming,* eds. J.C. Miles and S. Priest, 45-53. State College, PA: Venture.

Lesson Plan

PURPOSE

The purpose of this lesson is to illustrate the interconnections among some of the key people, events, and organizations in the history of adventure education.

OBJECTIVES

As a result of this lesson, students will be able to . . .

1. *Cognitive:* identify key figures in the history of adventure education in North America and describe their contributions to the field.
2. *Cognitive:* explain the interconnections between key people and organizations in the history of adventure education in North America.
3. *Affective/psychomotor:* participate in a roundtable discussion–role play that allows each student to role-play a key person in the history of adventure education.
4. *Cognitive:* describe similarities and differences among adventure educators, outdoor educators, experiential educators, environmental educators, and adventurers.

DURATION

50 to 150 minutes with additional preclass assignments and postclass follow-up. This lesson can be done as a stand-alone or as part of a longer unit consisting of several days or classes. The lesson can be offered over the course of a week through a sequence of three 50-minute lessons or two 1.5-hour lessons.

GROUP SIZE

6 to 25 students

LOCATION

Indoors, outdoors, or both. The area needs to be large enough to allow the group to sit in a circle. Presenting the lesson outdoors usually enhances the experience.

EQUIPMENT

- Two pieces of blank 11- × 17-inch paper for each student
- Color pencils or pens
- Props and costumes as determined by each student based on his or her assigned character
- A large ball of yarn and 50-foot (15-meter) rope (optional)
- Three packs of colored index cards (optional)

RISK MANAGEMENT CONSIDERATIONS

Low physical risk. There could be some social risk for students who have trouble speaking in front of others. They may feel a little uncomfortable.

STUDENT PREPARATION

Each student is asked to research an important figure (see suggested list in the Background section on the CD-ROM) in the history of adventure education using authoritative resources. Then students compose a one-page list of bulleted points about the figure. The list of educators should include adventure educators (e.g., Paul Petzoldt, Kurt Hahn, Joshua Miner, Karl Rohnke) as well as others whose ideas and theories have influenced the field (e.g., David Kolb, Abraham Maslow, John Dewey). When assigning people, you may want to include one or two people who may not be considered adventure educators in order to encourage follow-up discussion about the definition of adventure educators and adventure education. This can provide fodder for rich discussion. For example, you could assign someone to research and play John Muir or Aldo Leopold to stimulate discussion about the areas of overlap and interconnection between the fields of adventure education and environmental education. The students have two weeks to complete this preclass research assignment before the actual class session takes place. They are instructed to research the following topics regarding their assigned person:

- Why is the person considered important in the history of adventure education?
- Who or what influenced the person to pursue his or her career (mentor, author, formative life event, personal life experiences)?
- What are the person's direct or indirect key contributions to the field of outdoor education (e.g., publications, theories)?
- If applicable, what key organizations did the person found or work for?

INSTRUCTOR PREPARATION

Before teaching the lesson, the instructor should read the overview of the history of adventure education contained in the Background section. Instructors will find it helpful to read the resources presented in the Background as well.

All materials should be procured prior to the first class. You might want to consider videotaping the roundtable discussion or taking pictures of the students while they are in character. Make index cards and markers available to allow students to make name tags to wear or to place in front of them.

LESSON CONTENT AND TEACHING STRATEGIES

In the class preceding the roundtable discussion, instruct the students to come to the next class in character as their assigned figure in order to participate in a roundtable discussion. They should be prepared to introduce themselves as their assigned characters; to play their characters in role; and to show and describe their characters' key contributions to the adventure education field, including books, theories, activities, and any organizations with which they were affiliated. This will be done informally rather than through individual, formal presentations. During this role-play exercise, the students, in character, should explain why they are considered important in the history of adventure education. This discussion should include who or what influenced them (e.g., a mentor, an author, an organized wilderness expedition, an experience).

In addition, students will find it helpful if you demonstrate the difference between simply presenting facts, figures, and tidbits of information about the person and actually "play the person in role" by using stories and narrative to share what the person did. For example, using Aldo Leopold as an example, you might say this:

> "Hi, I'm Aldo Leopold. It is a pleasure to be here with all of you. I'm not sure if I fit the classic definition of an adventure educator although I certainly have had my share of adventures, and I love to share them with others. For instance, I will never forget the time I was out hunting with friends when we shot an old wolf. When we got close to her, we saw the "fierce green fire" go out in her eyes as she died. It was an important experience for me that influenced my thinking about the relationship between humans and the environment. I published these ideas, including one referred to as the land ethic, in my book *A Sand County Almanac. . . .*"

Activity 1: Roundtable Discussion

Preface the lesson by describing and demonstrating the process of *concept mapping.* Draw an example on the board consisting of several interconnected bubbles. Instruct the students to have an 11 × 17 piece of paper out and to use pens or color pencils to create a rough concept map–time line illustrating the interconnections among key people (e.g., John Dewey, Kurt Hahn, Paul Petzoldt), publications (e.g., *Journal of Experiential Education, Experience and Education* by John Dewey), theories (e.g., optimal arousal, adventure experience paradigm, cognitive dissonance theory), and organizations (e.g., Outward Bound, NOLS, Project Adventure, WEA, and AEE). Have the students use bubbles or boxes to represent these categories and draw lines between them to indicate their connections. For example, a bubble with the name of Paul Petzoldt might be connected to several other bubbles respectively named Outward Bound, NOLS, and WEA. Students can label the connecting lines to indicate how the bubbles are linked. A possible variation to the concept map is to use it as a historical time line. If you choose to have your students do this, tell students that the bubbles should be arranged chronologically from one side of the page to the other along a spectrum, with key years indicated on the horizontal axis.

Begin the roundtable discussion by inviting each student to introduce his or her character by name only. Encourage the students to decide on their own when to share with the group depending on whom or what their figure was connected to. For example, if one student represents Kurt Hahn, the next student, representing Josh Miner, might choose to go next because of the connection to Outward Bound. A student playing Paul Petzoldt may then choose to go next to connect Outward Bound to NOLS.

Once everyone has had the opportunity to introduce his or her character, jump-start the roundtable discussion by asking a few questions or sharing some observation about who is here today. Ask questions like "Mr. Hahn, is it true that the creation of the first Outward Bound program was related to the merchant-shipping industry, and can you tell us more about yourself and about the first Outward Bound?" or "Miss Mattoon, is it true that you were personally involved with the creation of the American Camping Association, and can you tell more about yourself and how ACA began?" These questions will help get the ball rolling, and soon people should feel comfortable jumping in.

Throughout the activity, keep energizing the discussion and make sure that everyone has the opportunity to discuss his or her historical contribution. Your role as moderator is to ask connecting or guiding questions to prompt discussion should the conversation begin to drag. For example, you might say, "Thank you, Mr. Miner, for telling us about yourself. Is anyone else here connected to the organization (Outward Bound) that he has just told us about?"

Remind students to keep developing their concept maps throughout the roundtable discussion. Explain to students that the concept map constructed in class will serve as a rough draft. Each of them will have the opportunity to redo or revise his or her own concept map before turning it in for a grade in the next class. Encourage students to be creative. For example, some may choose to color code their maps (e.g., blue representing people, green representing publications, red representing organizations, and brown representing theories or paradigms).

Bring closure to the roundtable when appropriate, and make sure that you thank everyone for participating.

Consider the following two variations of the activity:

- **Variation 1:** Have the students construct a time line of adventure education on the classroom wall using colored index cards, tape, and yarn. Color code the time line by having the students write the names of people on cards of one color, organizations on cards of another color, and so on. Tape or tack the cards to the wall in chronological order, and then tape or tack the ends of short pieces of yarn to the cards in order to show the connections between key people, publications, and organizations. Students can use this group-constructed time line to revise or reorganize their concept maps. As teacher, you can use the time line as a visual aid throughout the course.

- **Variation 2:** After the roundtable discussion, have group members physically arrange themselves along a piece of rope that represents a time line. Students will stand or sit at a place on the line that represents an important event in the life of their assigned person. The teacher gives either a large ball of yarn or a long piece of yarn to one student to start. Then the yarn is used to illustrate connections between the people. Each character will hold the yarn somewhere along its length and then pass the ball of yarn to another figure who indicates that he or she would like to receive it. To refer back to the earlier example, the student portraying Kurt Hahn may pass the ball of yarn to the student portraying Josh Miner, while the latter student describes how they are connected. The web of interconnections in adventure education slowly begins to emerge. Depending on how large the ball of yarn is (or how many individual pieces you have if you choose to cut them instead), it can be passed to characters more than once.

CLOSURE

Ask the students how they would define adventure education, how their definition has changed as a result of the lesson (if it has), and whether all of the people represented in the exercise fit their definition of adventure educators. This can provide for a very interesting discussion. More specifically, you could ask what the difference is, if any, between the following:

- An outdoor educator and an adventure educator
- An adventure educator and an environmental educator
- An adventure educator and an experiential educator
- An adventure educator and an adventurer

Finally, ask students what questions this lesson has raised in their minds regarding the history of adventure education.

ASSESSMENT OF LEARNING

Assessment of learning can occur at the end of the section on adventure education history in several ways:

- You can quiz students orally at the end of the class, or at the beginning of the next class, about the key people, places, and events by asking questions such as "How would you describe Paul Petzoldt's connections to Outward Bound, NOLS, and WEA?" or "Why are Dewey's ideas considered important in the history of adventure education?"
- You can grade students' individual versions of their concept map–time line illustrating the history of adventure education and the interconnections among the key people, publications, and organizations.
- You can give a written test to assess whether the students can match key historical figures with publications, organizations, or theories.

PART IV

Educational and Philosophical Foundations

The lessons in this part of the book, about the educational and philosophical foundations of adventure education, help the student apply the models and structures developed by John Dewey, David Kolb, and others from the previous part's lessons on teaching the historical highlights of the discipline.

Students on the path to becoming adventure educators can benefit by looking first at the broad road map of possible professional destinations. Bob Stremba's lesson 8, "The Four Uses of Outdoor Adventure Programming," includes activities that demonstrate Miles and Priest's (1999) four categories of adventure programming: recreational, educational, developmental, and therapeutic. Because one size no longer fits all, programs must tailor adventure activities to meet the needs and goals of particular individuals and groups. Such specialization requires staff with the experience and skill sets to match these different needs; and practitioners who have not only the technical skills, but also the educational and psychological skills, are better prepared to provide the higher levels of programming that promote greater client change.

Christian Bisson's lesson 9, "Philosophical Influences in Outdoor, Adventure, and Experiential Education," will help aspiring adventure educators develop a strong educational foundation that informs their practice. This lesson includes a creative "musing forest" to help students understand how some of the big ideas of our discipline's influencers can be the first steps toward developing their own educational philosophy. The thinking of Socrates, Rousseau, Descartes, and others helped form philosophies of rationalism, empiricism, and pragmatism. These early philosophers, along with John Dewey more recently, are a small sample of philosophers, thinkers, and educators who have inspired or influenced the epistemology of adventure education, outdoor education, and experiential education. Therefore, effective adventure educators stand on the shoulders of these giants when reflecting on and writing their own educational philosophy, which becomes a cornerstone of their own educational practice.

The remaining two lessons in this part immerse the student in the progressive education philosophy of John Dewey (1938) and the experiential learning cycle provided by David Kolb (1984). Mary Breunig's lesson 10, "Teaching Dewey's *Experience and Education* Experientially," uses common objects found in adventure experiences, such as a climbing rope, along with Kolb's model to teach Dewey's philosophy—an example of the parallel process of teaching and learning introduced in chapter 1. One of the goals of this lesson is for the student to understand the difference between an educative and a miseducative experience and apply this understanding to wilderness and classroom learning. In lesson 11, "How Do We Learn? An Exploration of John Dewey's Pattern of Inquiry," Leslie Rapparlie uses the activity known as "minefield" in a reflective journey in order for students to employ a specific component of experience to explore their own quest for knowledge. Her lesson points out that knowing how to use and create educative experiences is essential for all adventure educators since experience is the basis of all their work. The tools presented in this lesson for comprehending how people learn can enrich the learning experience of both the learner and the educator.

The lessons in this part give the adventure educator a solid starting point for applying models and concepts of progressive education and experiential learning to a variety of programs and client groups with whom they may work.

REFERENCES

Dewey, J. 1938. *Experience and education.* New York: Simon & Schuster.

Kolb, D.A. 1984. *Experiential learning.* Englewood Cliffs, NJ: Prentice Hall.

Miles, J.C. and S. Priest, eds. 1999. *Adventure programming.* State College, P.A.: Venture.

LESSON 8

The Four Uses of Outdoor Adventure Programming

Bob Stremba

Students who are preparing to be adventure educators should understand how outdoor activities are used so that they can make informed choices about the match between their interests and professional opportunities. Along a continuum of four programming use models—from *outdoor recreation,* through *adventure* or *outdoor education,* to *developmental adventure,* and finally to *therapeutic adventure*—the level of change in participants or clients becomes higher and more intentional. The skill set required of staff to best match these programs becomes deeper and more complex as well, progressing from technical and risk management skills in outdoor recreation to technical, risk management, facilitation, client assessment, and treatment planning skills at the therapeutic adventure level.

Background

With the proliferation of outdoor and indoor adventure programs in recent years has come a focus on specific populations and client groups. No longer operating as one-size-fits-all, programs can tailor adventure activities to meet the needs and goals that are particular to different kinds of individuals and groups. Such specialization requires staff with the experience and skill sets to match these different needs.

Miles and Priest (1999) identify four categories of adventure programming "based on whether they change the way people feel, think, or behave: recreational, educational, developmental, and therapeutic" (p. xiii).

Webb (1999) explains that recreational adventure programs provide enjoyment, entertainment, renewal, and skill development. Outdoor recreation consists of leisure activities engaged in for their own sake or in order to maintain a healthy, physically active lifestyle; and these activities generally occur in natural settings (Martin et al. 2006).

Like outdoor recreation, outdoor education occurs in the natural environment, but "it is a method of teaching and learning that emphasizes direct, multisensory experiences . . . and uses an integrated approach to learning by involving the natural, community, and individual environments" (Gilbertson et al. 2006, p. 5). Although somewhat simplistically, the difference between outdoor recreation and outdoor education can be illustrated through the role of a staff person operating in these programs. A climbing guide, for example, is charged with the responsibility of getting her clients to the top of the mountain and back down again safely. The emphasis is on recreational adventure and enjoyment of the experience itself. The focus of a climbing instructor is to teach his students to reach the top of the mountain and safely get back down so that they achieve the skills to climb mountains again on their own, without a guide or instructor. Both the guide, working for a recreationally focused program, and the instructor, working for a school or other educational program, must have skills in technical mountaineering, risk management, and leadership; but the instructor must also know how to create learning progressions and assess student learning so that the students can do the activity again.

Outdoor education and adventure education share the characteristics of teaching skills and perspectives that individuals can use beyond their initial outdoor or adventure experience. But there are also some differences between the two. Outdoor education typically occurs in or through the outdoors. Adventure education often occurs outdoors, but some professionals say it can also occur indoors, in schools or conference rooms, as long as the five central characteristics of adventure are present. Horwood (1999) describes these adventure characteristics as "uncertain outcome, risk, inescapable consequences, energetic action, and willing participation" (p. 9). In addition, adventure education has a focus on the use of adventure activities to help individuals and groups develop intrapersonal and interpersonal skills, including the confidence to embrace challenge or the ability to work more effectively in groups. In the mountain climbing example, an adventure educator would use skills in group facilitation and debriefing to help individuals apply climbing a mountain to handling other challenges at school, or to help a group understand the connections between the interdependence required of a climbing team and a work team to achieve success.

The boundaries among the levels of adventure programming are dynamic, and a program can certainly use adventure at more than one level. Such is the case as we move from adventure education to developmental adventure, which is often, but not always, applied to remedy personal or group dysfunction (Hirsch 1999). "Developmental activities employ a range of adventure programming options such as wilderness expeditions, initiative tasks, challenge courses, residential camping, base camping, and outdoor pursuits. They adhere to the tenets and procedures of experiential education to engage participants in thought-provoking reflection that is assumed will result in the growth or development of individuals and/or groups" (pp. 14-15). In addition to needing the technical and risk management skills to conduct adventure activities at an outdoor recreational level, as well as the facilitation and debriefing skills to conduct activities at an educational level, the person working in developmental adventure also has advanced processing skills for creating metaphors, knowledge about organizational or corporate culture, and client assessment skills to properly develop and implement a program having lasting value.

The fourth level of adventure programming, therapeutic adventure, uses all the kinds of adventure activities that the previous three levels do; but adventure therapy programs intentionally focus on "creating circumstances likely to engender change in participants" (Gillis and Ringer 1999, p. 31). These programs work with client populations such as at-risk youth needing to reduce dysfunctional behaviors like substance abuse, ineffective coping skills, and aggression. In addition to having skills at the recreational, educational, and developmental levels, people working in therapeutic adventure must know about client assessment, treatment planning, intervention, and follow-up. Because of the breadth and depth of skill sets required in therapeutic adventure, staff teams are often formed. The team as a whole possesses the skills that any single individual may have difficulty achieving in one lifetime (Gillis and Ringer 1999).

The continuum describing the four levels of adventure programming is presented in table 8.1. Notice that as one progresses along the continuum from outdoor recreation, through adventure or outdoor education, to developmental adventure, and finally to therapeutic adventure, the level of change in participants or clients becomes higher and more intentional. The skill set required of staff working in these programs becomes deeper and more complex as well, progressing from technical and risk management skills in outdoor recreation to technical, risk management, facilitation, client assessment, and treatment planning skills at the therapeutic adventure level.

TABLE 8.1 The Continuum of Four Levels of Adventure Programming in Relation to Client Change

	Outdoor recreation	Adventure or outdoor education	Developmental adventure	Therapeutic adventure
Description	Organized free-time activities engaged in for their own sake and involving an interaction between the participant and nature Aimed at having fun, learning new activities or skills, becoming energized Changes the way people feel by entertaining, reenergizing, or revitalizing them (play)	Activities aimed at understanding concepts through adventure, that is, learning the importance of working together as a team and of support (interpersonal relationships) or the value of healthy risk taking (intrapersonal relationships) Changes the way people think—new attitudes that can transfer to daily life	Experiences that improve behaviors and attitudes (i.e., communication, teamwork, trust) through adventure; emphasis on transfer to home, work, or school Changes the way people behave	Activities that reduce dysfunctional behaviors such as substance abuse, ineffective coping skills, and aggression; client population sometimes court referred; emphasis on transfer to home, work, or school Changes malbehavior
Staff skills	Technical, group leadership, business management, program development, risk management, natural resources skills	Outdoor recreation staff skills *plus* instructional/ teaching skills, technical and process leadership, group facilitation skills	Adventure education staff skills *plus* high-level facilitation (framing, metaphors) skills; knowledge of organizational cultures	Developmental adventure staff skills *plus* therapeutic, treatment planning, and behavior management skills; skills with special populations
Examples of jobs	Recreation leader, trip guide, parks manager, resort staff	Adventure educator, outdoor instructor, environmental educator	Experience-based facilitator or trainer for a corporation or organizational development program	Adventure therapist for a youth-at-risk or residential program

Low → Intentional level of change in participant or client → **High**

Adapted from S. Priest and M.A. Gass, 2005, *Effective leadership in adventure programming*, 2nd ed. (Champaign, IL: Human Kinetics), 23.

Finally, the umbrella that encompasses almost all levels of adventure programming is experiential education. The Association for Experiential Education (AEE) includes in the definition of experiential education that there must be reflection, critical analysis, and synthesis; that experiences are structured to require the learner to take initiative, make decisions, and be accountable for results; and that the outcomes of experience cannot be totally predicted (AEE 2003). One or more of these characteristics are generally present in the last three levels of adventure programming, but a recreational adventure program must include elements of reflection, analysis, and synthesis, in addition to fun and play, to be considered experiential. Bungee jumping, for example, would be considered recreation or adventure amusement but would not be considered adventure education.

RESOURCES

Association for Experiential Education (AEE). 2003. Definition of experiential education. www.aee.org/ndef.html (accessed August 2007).

Gilbertson, K., T. Bates, T. McLaughlin, and A. Ewert. 2006. *Outdoor education: Methods and strategies.* Champaign, IL: Human Kinetics.

Gillis, H.L. Jr., and T.M. Ringer. 1999. Adventure as therapy. In *Adventure programming,* eds. J.C. Miles and S. Priest, 29-37. State College, PA: Venture.

Hirsch, J. 1999. Developmental adventure programs. In *Adventure programming,* eds. J.C. Miles and S. Priest, 13-27. State College, PA: Venture.

Horwood, B. 1999. Educational adventure and schooling. In *Adventure programming,* eds. J.C. Miles and S. Priest, 9-12. State College, PA: Venture.

King, K. 1988. The role of adventure in the experiential learning process. *Journal of Experiential Education,* 11(2):4-8.

Martin, B., C. Cashel, M. Wagstaff, and M. Breunig. 2006. *Outdoor leadership: Theory and practice.* Champaign, IL: Human Kinetics.

Miles, J.C., and S. Priest, eds. 1999. *Adventure programming.* State College, PA: Venture.

Priest, S., and M.A. Gass. 2005. *Effective leadership in adventure programming.* 2nd ed. Champaign, IL: Human Kinetics.

Webb, D.J. 1999. Recreational outdoor adventure programs. In *Adventure programming,* eds. J.C. Miles and S. Priest, 3-8. State College, PA: Venture.

Lesson Plan

PURPOSE

For students to understand the differences among the four ways in which outdoor adventure activities are used in order to make more informed choices pertaining to the match between their interests and professional opportunities.

OBJECTIVES

As a result of this lesson students will be able to . . .

1. *Psychomotor and affective:* experience activities that demonstrate the four levels of outdoor adventure programming—recreational, educational, developmental, and therapeutic.
2. *Cognitive:* describe the characteristics of the four levels of outdoor adventure programming—recreational, educational, developmental, and therapeutic.

3. *Cognitive:* describe how to use rock climbing or another adventure activity with a client group at each of four levels—recreational, educational, developmental, and therapeutic.
4. *Affective:* experience emotions at the intrapersonal dimension and support at the interpersonal dimension connected with a perceived risk at the adventure education level of adventure programming.
5. *Cognitive:* describe the difference between adventure education and adventure amusement.

DURATION

90 to 120 minutes; longer if an actual climbing site or indoor climbing wall is used as part of each of the four activities

GROUP SIZE

15 for activities included in lesson; larger groups can be divided into smaller activity groups.

LOCATION

Indoors or outdoors

EQUIPMENT

- A soft throwable object such as a rubber chicken or a sponge
- Tent pole(s) 10 to 12 feet (3-3.7 meters) long; one pole for every 10 to 12 students in the group
- 20 to 25 feet (6-7.6 meters) of climbing webbing or retired climbing rope
- Computer connected to an LCD projector for the PowerPoint presentation

RISK MANAGEMENT CONSIDERATIONS

For activities 3 and 4, the instructor should be familiar with and teach students proper spotting and safety procedures.

STUDENT PREPARATION

- Students can read the Background included with this lesson (on CD-ROM). 
- Students can read one or more of the following:
  - Gilbertson et al. 2006. Chapter 1: “Defining Outdoor Education.”
  - Martin et al. 2006. Chapter 1: “The Journey Begins.”
  - Miles and Priest 1999. Chapter 1: “Recreational Outdoor Adventure Programs”; chapter 2: “Educational Adventure and Schooling”; chapter 3: “Developmental Adventure Programs”; chapter 4: Adventure as Therapy.”
  - Priest and Gass 2005. Preface.

INSTRUCTOR PREPARATION

Assemble the materials listed. Determine areas that are sufficient in size to accommodate your group for the lesson activities. Find two trees or objects about 15 feet (4.5 meters) apart to set up activity 3.

LESSON CONTENT AND TEACHING STRATEGIES

This lesson uses four activities to have students experience the four levels of use of outdoor adventure—recreational, educational, developmental, and therapeutic. Most of these activities can be done indoors or outdoors; however, Alaskan baseball will require more indoor space such as a gymnasium. To help students generalize and transfer the concepts beyond the activities, discussions about how students can apply the concepts to a more field-based activity such as rock climbing are included. However, given sufficient time and resources, the instructor could include short climbing experiences at an actual climbing site or an indoor climbing wall.

To introduce the lesson, show slides 1 and 2, while asking students to think about an adventure activity, such as backpacking, rock climbing, whitewater paddling, mountaineering, ropes courses, and so on. Briefly describe the four levels of the adventure pursuits continuum as presented in the theory synthesis. Tell students, "We will be experiencing four ways in which adventure programming can be used."

Activity 1: Alaskan Baseball (Recreational Adventure)

Divide the class into two equal teams. Then provide the following instructions: "We are about to play a game of baseball, although the rules of this baseball game are a bit different. This rubber chicken [or other throwable object] in my hand will serve as the ball and one person from our group will be the bat."

"Here is how we play: Team A will throw this rubber chicken as far away as possible. Once they do that, Team B will need to run and retrieve the chicken. While Team B is running, Team A will quickly form a tight cluster, and one member of Team A will run in circles around this tight cluster. For every full rotation around the team cluster, Team A will earn a point."

"Meanwhile Team B has retrieved the rubber chicken and has now formed a single-file line. The first person in Team B's line passes the chicken under the legs to the next teammate, who then passes the chicken over the head to the next teammate, who then passes it under the legs, and so on until it reaches the end of the line. Once the chicken has reached the end of Team B's line, they all shout STOP! Then Team B throws the rubber chicken as far away as possible. Team A now retrieves the chicken and passes it over, under, over, under while Team B forms a cluster and earns points for each full rotation."

Explain that this process continues until the groups are thoroughly exhausted, until the throwing gets out of control, or until you call it off.

After the activity, gather the students for a discussion. Ask them to consider how to apply the activity they just did to teaching beginning rock climbing to a public group. You could ask, "What safety preparations will you implement?" Responses may include that the instructor recons the climbing site, fits participants with harnesses and helmets, and has a first aid kit ready. You might also ask, "How will you teach participants climbing skills?" Responses may include having a "ground school" where the instructor demonstrates knots and tie-in procedures, belaying procedures, and communication between climber and belayer and then has participants practice these procedures on the ground. Finally, participants may watch the instructor actually demonstrate basic climbing moves on the rock; they may then put into practice what they have just seen by climbing a route with the instructor supervising from the ground.

Close the discussion by saying that the manner in which the group played Alaskan baseball is an example of how an activity can be used *recreationally,* with the purpose of having fun and becoming energized. Similarly, other activities such as rock climbing can be used recreationally, with the staff member presenting instructions about how to do the activity, describing any safety practices, then simply monitoring to make sure that the group remains on track. For example, in outdoor or indoor recreation, the staff person functions as a leader, trip guide, or climbing guide.

Activity 2: Helium Stick (Educational Adventure)

Have a multisection tent pole, approximately 10 to 12 feet (3-3.7 meters) long, available for every 10 to 12 students. Starting with the pole at shoulder height and parallel to the ground, all persons in the group must have the pole resting on their index finger, which is pointing straight in front of them. With every person's finger maintaining contact with the pole, the group must lower the pole to the ground. If any finger loses contact with the pole, the group must return the pole to shoulder height and start over. If the group gets stuck, you can stop the task and ask the group to discuss their strategy, then continue with the activity.

Following the helium stick activity, engage students in a discussion using questions such as these:

- What worked for you in this activity? What was not effective?
- What solutions were suggested and how were they received?
- What would an outside observer have seen as your strengths and weaknesses?

Ask students to consider how to apply the activity they just did to teaching beginning rock climbing to a school group: "In addition to the preparations and strategies for climbing as a recreational activity, as discussed after we played Alaskan baseball, what can you think of here to include a focus on education?" Responses may include offering climbers encouragement and group support when they are frozen with anxiety, and at the end discussing feelings and application of successes and newfound confidence to situations at home, work, and school.

Close the discussion by saying that what the group has just done—engaging in the helium stick activity, followed by application to rock climbing—provides an example of how adventure activities can be used *educationally.* In outdoor or indoor education, the staff person functions as an instructor or educator.

Activity 3: The High Road (Developmental Adventure)

Attach a 20-foot (6-meter) length of nylon webbing or a section of retired climbing rope between two trees, approximately 5 feet (1.5 meters) off the ground.

Developmental adventures are often framed metaphorically, so describe the following scenario (Priest and Gass 2005, pp. xi-xii) to the student group:

> You are on the staff of a health care company that is having troublesome issues regarding working together. Your company has contracted the services of a corporate adventure training program that will use adventure experiences to help you resolve some of your company's issues. In your business, your work group is known as one that starts projects well, but it also seems that things quickly go awry. Sometimes the best-laid plans just don't work out. Your needs as a staff include building trust, working more efficiently together (things take too much time now), and better project planning. Hopefully, improvements in these internal areas will improve external areas like customer service.

Tell students: "So, your project here is to take the high road and get your group from this side of the line (webbing) to the other. This hurdle must be successfully overcome. A successful outcome includes taking the high road—going over, not under, the hurdle. It also includes safety, so you will need to use proper spotting and lifting procedures, making sure that people are supported once off the ground. It also includes quality—you can't touch the line. How will you take the high road and maintain safety and quality? Recall what you need to work on. You have a time limit of 20 minutes, with a bonus if you complete the project in under 15 minutes and a consequence for every minute it takes over 20 to finish."

Be sure to mention the metaphors that a corporate trainer might use to help a group draw comparisons between the High Road activity and the client group's concerns and the problems to solve (see table 8.2).

TABLE 8.2 Examples of Metaphors for Developmental Adventure Programming

Client issue	High Road activity	Rock climbing
Partnership, teamwork	Developing a collaborative plan to get over the webbing line	Tandem climbing—two climbers (i.e., workplace mentor and mentee) climb a route "held together" by plastic tape tied to each climber's harness
Taking directions from someone who sees the bigger picture (ground coach) and project implementer	Roles—some people take roles as givers of directions (GODs), others as implementers of directions	Blindfolded climber with sighted belayer
Difficult project or assignment	Processing questions about perceived risk in the activity and at work	Processing questions about what the "crux" is for you in the activity and at work
Trust, asking for help	Questions about asking for help in the activity, for example asking for support from spotters on both sides of the line, and at work	Questions about how the belayer elicits trust from the climber and how trust is developed or lost at work

Ask students to consider how to substitute rock climbing, or another outdoor or indoor adventure activity, for the activity they just did to help develop better behavior in a corporate group. "In addition to the preparations and strategies for climbing as recreation and education, what can you think of to include a developmental focus?"

Close the discussion by saying that what the group has just done—engaging in the High Road activity, followed by application to rock climbing—provides an example of how adventure activities can be used *developmentally.* In this form of outdoor or indoor education, the staff person functions as a facilitator or trainer.

Activity 4: Trust Lean (Therapeutic Adventure)

Describe the following scenario (Priest and Gass 2005, p. xii) to the student group:

> As an adventure professional, you work in a substance abuse program for youth, focusing on enhancing communication between adolescents with drug addictions and their parents. Your program uses adventure experiences as adjunctive therapy to established treatment plans. Your focus for this therapy session is to redirect interaction between a

14-year-old son and his mother or father; the two have become emotionally separated in this single-parent family. Current symptoms of the son's behavior include substance abuse, low self-esteem, and a strong fear that his parent will abandon him.

Demonstrate the trust lean: Ask for two student volunteers. One will role-play the 14-year-old son while the other role-plays the parent. Demonstrate and explain that the "parent" stands behind the "son" in a position with hands up for support, one foot behind the other so that the parent remains balanced and is available to help the son balance his life. The son stands in front of the parent with hands across his chest. The instructor describes falling procedures for the student role-playing the son—keep feet together, body rigid, and then, upon direction, fall into the arms of the parent. Mention the therapeutic metaphor: "Staying straight will help you be successful here and improve your relationship with your parent." Then, instruct the son to fall backward into the arms of his parent.

Conduct a discussion, with the two student volunteers remaining in their roles as parent and son, using questions that focus on these aspects:

- Connections between staying straight in the trust lean and in life
- Trust between son and parent
- The parent's being there for the son
- Clear communication

Ask students to apply the processes of the trust lean to using beginning rock climbing to help clients change dysfunctional behavior. Ask focus questions such as these:

- Besides the preparations and strategies for climbing as recreation and education, what can you include so that the activity has a therapeutic focus?
- Consider and then discuss how rock climbing can serve as a therapeutic metaphor for healthy risk taking, persistence, trust, and clear communication.

Close the discussion by saying that what has just occurred—the trust lean, followed by application to rock climbing—provides an example of how adventure activities can be used *therapeutically.* In this form of outdoor or indoor education, the staff person functions as a therapist.

Activity 5: Mini-Lecture and PowerPoint on the Adventure Programming Continuum

Show slides 3 through 6 to review the experiences in which students just participated. Continue with the PowerPoint, and as images (on CD-ROM) are shown, add comments such as the following to illustrate the differences among the four levels of outdoor pursuits:

- *What is outdoor recreation?* (show slide 7)—leisure activities that can include backpacking, rock climbing, and canoeing, as well as gardening, dog walking, and sitting in a park
- *What is outdoor education?* (show slide 3)—activities that take place primarily through involvement with the natural environment and that comprise environmental education and adventure education
- *What is adventure education?* (show slide 8)—the branch of outdoor education using human-powered outdoor pursuits such as backpacking and rock climbing to focus on interpersonal and intrapersonal relationships

Here, pause the PowerPoint slide show to illustrate the difference between adventure education and adventure amusement. Ask students to close their eyes and recall the most embarrassing moment they have had during the past year. Tell them that in a minute you will ask them to open their eyes and will call on one student to come to the front of the class and describe this embarrassing moment. Ask them to focus on their feelings while imagining that they will be the one describing their most embarrassing moment. After a few moments' pause, ask students to open their eyes. Now tell students that you are *not* going to ask anyone to come to the front of the class to describe his or her most embarrassing moment.

Then ask, "What were your feelings when you imagined yourself as the one describing your most embarrassing moment to the class?" Point out that feelings of anxiety are typical in this situation just as they are when one is about to engage in a new adventure activity. The commonality is that both scenarios involve some perceived risk—social risk in the case of disclosing an embarrassing moment, and perceived physical risk in the case of rappelling down a rock face. There may even be more real risk in the social, classroom situation. In addition, adventure education's focus on intrapersonal relationships means that there is an intentional, often facilitated reflection that allows participants to use the adventure experience to explore feelings and internal reactions to situations. The focus on interpersonal relationships often includes support provided by the group and the instructors for individuals to take perceived risks and as a result feel more able to embrace other challenges they may encounter in life.

As an option, ask if any students actually do want to describe their most embarrassing moment to the class group. Ask such volunteers what they need in order to feel safe with such self-disclosure. This may include agreements from the class to listen nonjudgmentally and to maintain confidentiality within the group. These agreements can then be related to the support component of interpersonal relationships, a distinguishing feature of adventure education.

Returning to the PowerPoint, explain the following difference between adventure education and adventure amusement: In adventure education, participants or students have some control or choice over their degree of involvement; and their actions, judgments, and decisions during the adventure process have some effect on the outcomes of the experience. Adventure amusement, however, includes activities in which clients have little or no involvement in decisions that could affect the outcomes. Examples of adventure amusement include bungee jumping, a guided raft trip, and some guided climbing trips.

- *What is developmental adventure?* (show slide 9)—The use of adventure activities to help groups of people improve behaviors and attitudes such as communication, teamwork, and trust. The adventure educator uses a variety of processing experiences to then help people transfer their new learning back to home, work, or school.
- *What is therapeutic adventure?* (show slide 10)—The use of adventure activities to help individuals replace dysfunctional behaviors such as use of substances, inadequate coping skills, and acting-out behavior with healthier intrapersonal and interpersonal behaviors

Explain that as we go from outdoor recreation to outdoor/adventure education, then to developmental adventure and therapeutic adventure, emphasis is on increasing levels of client change. Therefore, the staff skills through this continuum of outdoor pursuits must include higher levels of training in facilitation, counseling, client assessment, and, ultimately, psychotherapy. The person having skills in therapeutic adventure can provide recreational programming, but the person skilled in using outdoor pursuits only for recreational purposes is less prepared to facilitate adventure experiences that can result in more transformative, behavior-changing outcomes.

Ask students, "Have you been involved as a participant or staff person in a program that operates at any of these four levels? For example, scouts, ski lessons, summer camp?" Also ask, "What occurred in your program at one or more of these four levels?"

On the PowerPoint, show Keith King's (1988) quote (slide 11) about experiential learning, and ask students to describe how the program involved *stress, striving, self-direction, sacrifice, goal setting, perfecting skills,* and *working cooperatively.* Explain that these are the characteristics of experiential education, the umbrella that covers the discipline of adventure education.

Optional Activities

In the weeks following this lesson, include one or more of these learning activities:

- Invite speakers into class from programs representing each of the four levels of outdoor pursuits. For example, a manager of a community parks and recreation program or a climbing guide represents the recreational level of outdoor programming. An instructor from a program such as Outward Bound or NOLS represents the adventure/outdoor education type of program. A facilitator of corporate or organizational development programs represents the developmental level of programs. A person working in a therapeutic adventure or wilderness therapy program may discuss his or her experience at the therapeutic level of outdoor pursuits programming. As part of each presentation, reinforce how the program matches one or more levels of outdoor pursuits programming. As a variation, take the class on a field trip to each of the four types of programs.
- Have students individually or in small groups research a program of interest, including conducting an interview with a professional working in the program. Encourage the class group to choose programs that encompass all four levels of outdoor pursuits. Have students present their findings to the class, along with a brief review of how the program they researched matches the characteristics of recreational, educational, developmental, or therapeutic programming.

CLOSURE

End the lesson by showing slide 12. Remind students that they have engaged in four levels of adventure programming—recreational, educational, developmental, and therapeutic. It's useful for aspiring adventure educators to understand the differences among these levels so that they can be prepared with the skills and experiences that best match the needs of client groups with whom they wish to work.

ASSESSMENT OF LEARNING

- For each of four levels of adventure programming—recreational, educational, developmental, and therapeutic—students will describe how to use rock climbing or another adventure activity with a client group.
- In a concluding discussion, students will be able to relate their involvement in an outdoor program to characteristics of one or more of the four levels of adventure programming.

LESSON 9

Philosophical Influences in Outdoor, Adventure, and Experiential Education

Christian A. Bisson

Like any emerging field of study, adventure education has looked to the past to find allies. Scholars have reviewed the writings of philosophers and educators to build an argument for the use of adventure activities, the natural environment, or direct experience to promote learning and growth. Young adventure educators often have the same desire to confirm their instinctive feeling or thinking about the importance of learning through outdoor adventure experiences. As future professionals, they need to develop a sound educational philosophy regarding their profession—a philosophy that can be substantiated by the work of influential writers and thinker, past or present. This lesson is designed to help your students take their first steps in discovering their own educational philosophy. Via hands-on activities, the lesson introduces the writing of philosophers and educators who have influenced adventure education epistemology.

Background

When practiced in an outdoor environment, adventure education is concerned with three basic epistemological questions. First, can we rationalize the use of risk and adventure activities to promote learning? Second, can we rationalize the use of an outdoor setting to promote learning? Third, can we rationalize the use of direct experiences to promote learning? Finding answers to these questions can provide us with the historical and philosophical foundation that has influenced, and perhaps still influences, generations of adventure educators.

Scholars in our field such as Crosby (1981), Hammerman and colleagues (2001), Donaldson and Vinson (1979), Wurdinger (1995), Warren and colleagues (1999), and Itin (1999), to name only a few, have presented us with convincing historical and philosophical arguments for learning through adventure, nature, and direct experiences. These authors, like many others, have built a rationale for adventure education, outdoor education, or experiential education by looking into the history of Western philosophy. They reviewed the work of Greek philosophers such as Socrates, Plato, and Aristotle to justify the use of risk and direct experience to develop moral citizens (Wurdinger 1995). They also looked at the writing of educators and philosophers from the 17th century such as Rousseau, Comenius, and Pestalozzi to justify education through our senses and the natural world (Hammerman, Hammerman, and Hammerman 2001). In addition, they considered various philosophical schools of thought from the 17th and 18th centuries that cumulated at the end of the Enlightenment era with the work of the German philosopher Immanuel Kant. Reflection on knowledge and how it is acquired helped bridge the gap between the continental rationalism of Descartes and the empiricism of Hume. This bridge still helps us to establish the philosophical rationale for promoting learning through experience and reflection (Crosby 1981). Finally, scholars in adventure or experiential education have extensively referred to the work of 20th-century American philosopher John Dewey to justify experiential education as an essential and powerful approach to learning and social change (Itin 1999). Although it is evident that by its nature, adventure education has always been associated with experiential learning and outdoor education, it is also useful to separate the various components of this pedagogical approach to build a more thorough philosophical argument for its application. Let's now look at each epistemological question separately.

RATIONALIZING RISK AND ADVENTURE ACTIVITIES TO PROMOTE LEARNING

Wurdinger (1995) indicates that philosophical influences on adventure education can be traced back to antiquity in the writing of Socrates, Plato, and Aristotle. In the thought of Socrates (469-399 BC), adventure educators can find support for their belief in "hands-on" learning, since Socrates said that "human nature cannot know the mystery of an art without experience . . ."; Wurdinger sees this as an assertion that experience is essential to acquiring knowledge (1995).

In Socrates and his student, Plato (427-347 BC), we can find the ideological roots for the belief not only that learners should acquire new skills by practicing these new skills, as an apprentice practices potting to learn the art of pottery, but also that morality and virtues can be learned through experience (Hunt 1990; Wurdinger 1995). For instance, Socrates, and later Plato, believed that to learn social virtues, children should experience these virtues themselves. They argued that to become courageous, wise, just, and temperate, one must participate in experiences that require one to be courageous, wise, just, and temperate (Priest and Gass 2005). In addition, Wurdinger (1995) suggests that Plato's commitment to learning through experience went as far as proposing that if risk is necessary for learning, then risk should be taken. For instance, in his treatise on society and education, *The Republic,* Plato uses the words of his master to support his position on risk taking. In the dialogue between Socrates and Glaucon on how young people should be educated, Socrates asks, "If risks must be run, should one not run them where success will improve people?" (Wurdinger 1995, p. 17). From this, Wurdinger (1995) believes that we can find the philosophical influence of Plato on Kurt Hahn, who revolutionized the teaching of morality and virtues in pre- and post-World War II youth by using adventurous and potentially risky outdoor experiences to develop in them virtues such as compassion, courage, and resiliency.

According to Wurdinger (1995), the writings of Aristotle (384-322 BC), a student of Plato, can also be used to justify risk and adventure in education. Wurdinger (1995) states that like Plato, Aristotle believed that youth can acquire certain virtues such as courage only by being exposed to risk-taking situations. To support his argument, Wurdinger quotes Aristotle: ". . . it is by action that some become just and others unjust, and it is by acting in the face of danger and by developing the habit of feeling fear or confidence that some become brave men and others cowards." Here, Aristotle not only allows us to justify the use of risk and fear to develop virtues, but also provides us with the rationale that practicing these virtues is essential to the development of a just and moral citizen.

In the end, we can conclude that the predominant philosophers from Greek antiquity gave us the following philosophical rationale for adventure education: (1) Knowledge is based on experience; (2) we should use experiences to develop virtues in youth so we can develop a better society; (3) taking risks is important for learning certain virtues.

RATIONALIZING THE USE OF AN OUTDOOR SETTING TO PROMOTE LEARNING

Outdoor education scholars such as Hammerman et al. (1980, 2001), Gilbertson et al. (2006), and Neill (2007) state that the elements of a philosophical basis for teaching in nature can be found in the writings and philosophy of Comenius, Rousseau, and Pestalozzi.

John Amos Comenius (1592-1670) is known as the father of modern education. He strongly promoted universal access to education, arguing that all children, from the rich to the poor—the intelligent and the ignorant, the boys and the girls—should be sent to school. For his views and his courage, Comenius is often referred to in his homeland, the Czech Republic, as the "teacher of nations." However, his ideas on education not only influenced social reforms in Europe but also inspired the development of a more "natural" way to teach children. Outdoor educators have attributed to Comenius the belief "that children learn best through the use of their senses" (Gilbertson et al. 2006). In a paper on the philosophy of outdoor education, James Neill (2007) noted that Comenius "was a strong advocate of sensory learning who believed that the child should experience the actual object of study before reading about it. He thought the use of the sense—seeing, hearing, tasting, and touching—were the avenues through which children were to come in contact with the natural world. In preparation for the later study of natural sciences, children should first gain acquaintance with objects such as water, earth, fire, rain, plants, and rocks."

The ideas promoted by Comenius also influenced the Franco-Swiss philosopher and educator Jean-Jacques Rousseau (1712-1778). In one of his most recognized works about education, *Émile ou de l'éducation,* Rousseau expressed his fundamental belief that man is naturally good and that if a child is removed from the negative influences of an urban life, he can grow into a moral and productive adult. Although *Émile* is not as much a practical treatise on education as a fictional work depicting Rousseau's philosophy about education, many scholars in outdoor education have referred to Rousseau's use of sensory experiences in nature as validation for the need to offer outdoor education experiences to children at a young age (Hammerman 1980; Gilbertson et al. 2006). Perhaps the most often-used quote from Rousseau to rationalize the use of the senses in the education of children is ". . . our first teachers are our feet, our hands, and our eyes. To substitute books for all these . . . is but to teach us to use the reasons of others" (Neill 2007). Beyond Rousseau's promotion of sensory and natural exploration of the world by children, we can also find an ally in Rousseau when he proclaims that a good education should include rigorous physical activities and a close connection with the natural world (Neil 2007).

Another influential thinker who is often referred to, when we are rationalizing the use of outdoor places as a suitable environment for learning, is the Swiss educator Johann Heinrich Pestalozzi (1746-1827). A contemporary of Rousseau, Pestalozzi took up the impracticable ideas found in *Émile ou de l'éducation* and explored how they might be developed and implemented. He opposed memorization and strict discipline and pioneered the use of tactile objects in the teaching of natural science. He also supported the idea that the teacher should ask questions and that children should be free to explore the world to find answers (Hammerman 1980). Pestalozzi urged teachers to take their pupils out of the classroom, saying, "Lead your child out into nature, teach him on the hilltops and in the valleys. There he will listen better, and the sense of freedom will give him more strength to overcome difficulties. But in these hours of freedom let him be taught by nature rather than by you. Let him fully realize that she is the real teacher and that you, with your art, do nothing more than walk quietly at her side" (Neill 2007).

We can conclude that the predominant educator-philosophers from Europe's 17th and 18th centuries gave us the following philosophical rationale for adventure education: (1) Children should be encouraged to use all their all senses when learning; (2) learning close to nature can help create a moral person; and (3) the natural world provides a good place to learn.

RATIONALIZING THE USE OF DIRECT EXPERIENCES TO PROMOTE LEARNING

Although an argument for experiential learning has already been presented through the work of Socrates, Plato, Aristotle, Comenius, Rousseau, and Pestalozzi, many scholars in adventure education have researched the history of Western philosophy to find inspiration and justification for the field of adventure education. One of these scholars is April Crosby. Crosby (1981) studied experiential education as a philosophy of education within the historical evolution of Western epistemology.

Crosby (1981) explained that early in the history of Western philosophy, an epistemological dilemma emerged between the knowing mind (subjective) and the knowable mind (objective). For instance, Plato felt that no one could really know the Forms, or the essence of what is reality, since the Forms can be reached *only* through the dialectic process (reflection or *theoria*). He indicated that our senses place too much emphasis on the world around us and that this perception cannot be trusted to lead us to the truth about the reality of the world. Similarly, Aristotle believed that our understanding of the reality of the world was separated between *theoria* and praxis, or subjective theoretical wisdom and practical wisdom. Crosby (1981) summarized these ideas by proposing that the teaching implication of these dichotomies was "How do we get the knowing mind in touch with its object of knowledge, the world?" (p. 11).

It was this epistemological dilemma about knowledge and reality that eventually led to the creation of two distinctive schools of thought during the Enlightenment era. One camp, led by the French philosopher Descartes (1596-1650), was known as continental rationalism. The word "continental" was added to the word "rationalism" simply because the philosophical movement was preponderant on the European continent. The genesis of the movement was the idea that only the thinking process or reason can allow us to truly know something. This implied that sciences such as mathematics and logic are knowable since they can emerge from reason alone.

The opposite camp, empiricism, led by the Scottish philosopher David Hume (1711-1776), proposed that true knowledge could be acquired only through direct and objective observation of the world.

The solution to this impasse between rationalism and empiricism was proposed by Immanuel Kant, the German philosopher. Kant saw the problem with Descartes' rationalism and Hume's empiricism and proposed that "we cannot use what we perceive unless it is ordered according to certain categories (e.g., space, time, causation). Kant hypothesized that because of the structure of the human mind, we would never receive experience except as already organized by our active, structuring mind" (Crosby 1981, p. 14). The bridge between reason and experience proposed by Kant allows us to combine the two in a new pedagogy in which experience and reflection on the experience are no more in a battle between subjective and objective.

More than a century later, the American educator and philosopher John Dewey (1859-1952) picked up the debate and found himself agreeing with many of Kant's arguments about the order in which our mind organizes our experiences. However, Dewey felt that the dichotomy between reason and reflection was driven by the quest for the truth about reality, and that a better epistemology of education would focus on knowing values instead of theoretical abstractions (Crosby 1981). Dewey, along with William James, is often recognized as one of the founders of the philosophical school of pragmatism. For Dewey and other pragmatists, education should aim not at the teaching of mere dead fact; rather, the skills and knowledge that students learn should be integrated fully into their lives as persons, citizens, and human beings (Priest and Gass 2005). Dewey says it best: "The very problem of mind and body suggests division; I do not know of anything so disastrously affected by the habit of division as this particular theme. . . . The evils which we suffer in education, in religion, in the materialism of business and the aloofness of 'intellectuals' from life, in the whole separation of knowledge and practice—all testify to the necessity of seeing mind-body as an integral whole" (Dewey 1984, p. 25).

In the end, we can surmise that philosophers and educators throughout Western civilization have given us the following philosophical rationale for experiential education: (1) Reflection is essential to learning; (2) direct experience and observations of the subject learned are valuable to the learner; (3) both experience and reflection are essential for learning; and (4) the knowledge, skills, or values learned in education must be relevant and practical for the learner.

RESOURCES

Crosby, A. 1981. A critical look: Philosophical foundations of experiential education. *Journal of Experiential Education,* 4(1):9-16.

Dewey, J. 1984. *The collected works of John Dewey: Later works. Volume 3: 1927-1928 Essays, reviews, miscellany,* ed. J.A. Boydston. Carbondale, IL: Southern Illinois University Press.

Donaldson, G.W., and R. Vinson. 1979. William James: Philosophical father of experiential education. *Journal of Experiential Education,* 2(2):6-8.

Gilbertson, K., T. Bates, T. McLaughlin, and A. Ewert. 2006. *Outdoor education: Methods and strategies.* Champaign, IL: Human Kinetics.

Hammerman, W.M., ed. 1980. *Fifty years of resident outdoor education (1930-1980): Its impact on American education.* Martinsville, IN: American Camping Association.

Hammerman, D.R., W.M. Hammerman, and E.L. Hammerman. 2001. *Teaching in the outdoors.* Danville, IL: Interstate.

Hunt, J.S. 1990. Philosophy of adventure education. In *Adventure education,* eds. J.C. Miles and S. Priest, 119-128. State College, PA: Venture.

Itin, M.C. 1999. Reasserting the philosophy of experiential education as a vehicle for change in the 21st century. *Journal of Experiential Education,* 22(2):91-98.

Neill, J. 2007. Philosophy of outdoor education. www.wilderdom.com/Philosophy.html (accessed December 12, 2007).

Priest, S., and M. Gass. 2005. *Adventure programming.* Champaign, IL: Human Kinetics.

Warren, K., M. Sakofs, and J.S. Hunt. 1999. *The theory of experiential education.* Dubuque, IA: Association for Experiential Education.

Wurdinger, S. 1995. *Philosophical issues in adventure education.* Dubuque, IA: Kendall/Hunt.

Lesson Plan

PURPOSE

The purpose of this lesson is to allow students to explore the thinking of various philosophers and educators so that they can better appreciate the philosophical roots of outdoor, adventure, and experiential education. In addition, this lesson is a stepping-stone toward developing their own educational philosophy.

OBJECTIVES

As a result of this lesson students will be able to . . .

1. *Affective and psychomotor:* participate in an experience that provides an opportunity to directly explore the thoughts of philosophers and educators of the past.
2. *Cognitive:* explain the difference between empiricism and continental rationalism.
3. *Cognitive:* explain the respective limitations associated with empiricism and continental rationalism.
4. *Affective and psychomotor:* participate in an experience that provides an opportunity to directly explore and contrast the application of empiricism and continental rationalism.
5. *Cognitive:* explain the philosophy of John Dewey and its influence on the development of experiential education.
6. *Affective:* demonstrate a personal appreciation for the thinking and influence of some philosophers and educators.

DURATION

90 to 120 minutes

GROUP SIZE

Appropriate for 12 to 25 students

LOCATION

Indoors and outdoors (you will need a multimedia classroom and access to a nearby forest to complete the Musing Forest activity).

EQUIPMENT

- Philosopher quotes (see handouts on the CD-ROM)
- Musing Forest sign (see Musing Forest sign on the CD-ROM)
- 20 plastic paper covers (8.5 by 11 inches)
- 20 pipe cleaners
- A small bell
- Four cactus pears
- One steak knife
- Four plates
- Four copies of the Description of the Cactus Pear handout (on the CD-ROM)
- Multimedia equipment for the PowerPoint presentation

RISK MANAGEMENT CONSIDERATIONS

The Cactus Pear Dilemma activity might challenge some students, so make sure that any volunteers for this activity have the opportunity to choose their level of challenge.

STUDENT PREPARATION

No specific preparation is needed before the lesson.

INSTRUCTOR PREPARATION

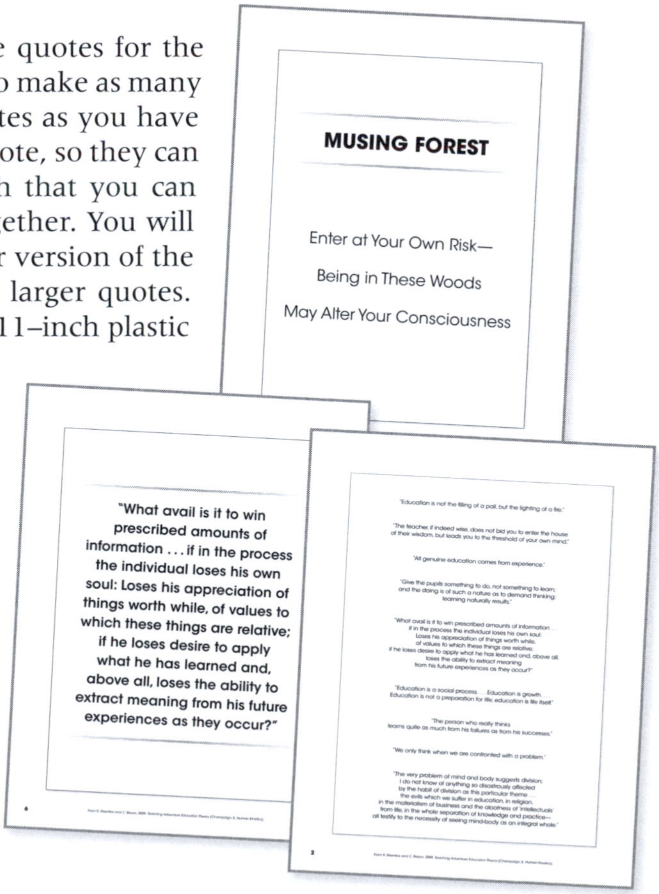

Before class, print and prepare all the quotes for the Musing Forest activity. You will need to make as many copies of the small version of the quotes as you have students in your class. Cut out each quote, so they can used individually, and sort them such that you can clip all the copies of a given quote together. You will need to print only one set of the larger version of the quotes. Now, assemble the small and larger quotes. Each large quote goes into an 8.5- by 11–inch plastic paper cover (see photo on page 117). Place the corresponding small quotes in the same plastic cover. Also print one copy of the Musing Forest sign and place it in its own plastic cover.

Once you have prepared all your material, use a nearby wooded area and randomly install all the quotes to create the "Musing Forest." Use the pipe cleaners to attach the quotes to the branches.

Finally, don't forget to purchase the cactus pears at your local grocery store; they can normally be found in the exotic fruit section. If your grocery store does not carry cactus

Place the quotes in plastic covers and hang them on branches with pipe cleaners.
Christian Bisson

pears, buy any other unusual fruits or vegetables, such as star fruits, pomegranates, or guavas. Make sure you get the right information from the Web if you choose to use a fruit other than the cactus pear.

LESSON CONTENT AND TEACHING STRATEGIES

Begin your lesson by explaining that you would like the class to explore the thinking of philosophers and educators who have influenced and are still influencing the fields of outdoor, adventure, and experiential education. Follow up by stating that to this end the class will go outside to a nearby wooded area to explore a "musing forest." The students may ask, "What is a musing forest?" Explain that a quiet stroll in the woods has often been a source of inspiration to philosophers and thinkers and that you would like to invite them to have the same experience. When everyone is ready, move the class outside.

Activity 1: The Musing Forest

Bring your class to the edge of the forest where you have previously placed this sign:

MUSING FOREST

ENTER AT YOUR OWN RISK—BEING IN THESE WOODS

MAY ALTER YOUR CONSCIOUSNESS

At the site, give this brief disclaimer regarding the possibility that the quiet stroll they are about to take in the forest might affect their thinking or consciousness regarding learning and teaching.

After presenting the disclaimer, do the following:

1. Invite everyone to take a silent stroll in the Musing Forest.
2. Specify the geographical limits of the Musing Forest so that students do not wander too far and get lost.
3. Explain that in the forest, they may encounter wisdom trees and that these trees have special leaves with thought-provoking quotes on them. Explain that they are welcome to pick the leaves (the quotes) from any of the wisdom trees and that they can collect as many quotes as they wish.
4. Finally, indicate that when they hear the sound of a bell, they should return to where they are presently standing.

If there are no questions, send the class on their quiet stroll and wait a good 10 to 15 minutes so that everyone has the opportunity to visit many, if not all, of the wisdom trees.

When all the students are back, ask if they were all able to find at least one wisdom leaf or quote that rang true to them. You should get positive answers, but if some people found no interesting quotes, ask them why. Then ask the students to try to complete the next challenge, which is to find someone else who has the same collection of quotes that they do. Let them mingle and search for few minutes; then inquire how many people were able to find someone else with an identical collection of quotes. Obviously, the answer should be no one.

The processing that follows this activity will normally lead your students to explain that no two people could have collected the same quotes because each of them has a different perspective or philosophy on teaching and learning. At this point you can only agree with them and explain that by completing this little stroll in the Musing Forest they have taken their first steps toward the development of their own educational philosophy.

To wrap up the activity, explain to the students that the next part of the lesson will allow them to discover which philosophers and educators their favorite quotes came from. Ask them to keep their quotes so that they can look for the authors in the next part of the lesson.

Activity 2: Mini-Lecture and PowerPoint: Influential Philosophers, Part 1

Introduce the PowerPoint (on CD-ROM) by explaining that you will review in chronological order, from ancient Greece to the 20th century, the philosophers and educators who generated the quotes they found in the Musing Forest. Remind them to look for the authors of their favorite quotes.

Use slides 2 through 4 to review the teaching of Socrates, Plato, and Aristotle. Introduce these philosophers' quotations and their respective educational philosophies. Slide 5 presents a "So What?" summary of what we can borrow from the thinkers of antiquity to make an argument for learning through experiences, and even risk-based activities when necessary. But also indicate that these arguments do not necessarily support the use of a natural environment for learning.

Slides 6 through 8 review the teaching of Comenius, Rousseau, and Pestalozzi. Introduce these authors' quotations and their respective educational philosophies. Slide 9 presents a "So What?" summary of what we can borrow from the thinkers of the 17th and 18th centuries to make an argument for direct experiences through all the senses and for teaching in the great outdoors. But also point out that these arguments do not provide clear support for the use of experience with reflection or a pragmatic approach to learning.

Slides 10 and 11 review the thinking of the French philosopher Descartes, as well as the premise underlying the school of thought known as continental rationalism. Present the information on the slides and then transition to an activity (slide 12) that will challenge Descartes' philosophy.

Activity 3: The Cactus Pear Dilemma

For this activity, ask for eight volunteers who are adventurous and who like to try new experiences. Once you have this group of eight, ask them to separate themselves into two groups of four.

Now explain that the rest of the class will also participate in this activity; they will be the judge of both groups' arguments regarding a simple question. Present slide 12 to introduce the question: Can continental rationalism resolve the cactus pear dilemma? In other words, members of both groups will have to answer the question: Do I like cactus pears or not? The rest of the class will judge which of the two groups they will trust the most with respect to their answers to that question.

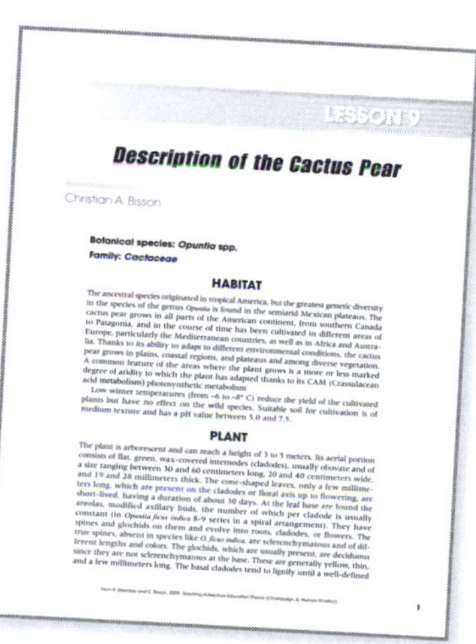
LESSON 9

Description of the Cactus Pear

Christian A. Bisson

Botanical species: ***Opuntia*** **spp.**
Family: ***Cactaceae***

HABITAT

The ancestral species originated in tropical America, but the greatest genetic diversity in the species of the genus *Opuntia* is found in the semiarid Mexican plateaus. The cactus pear grows in all parts of the American continent, from southern Canada to Patagonia, and in the course of time has been cultivated in different areas of Europe, particularly the Mediterranean countries, as well as in Africa and Australia. Thanks to its ability to adapt to different environmental conditions, the cactus pear grows in plains, coastal regions, and plateaus and among diverse vegetation. A common feature of the areas where the plant grows is a more or less marked degree of aridity to which the plant has adapted thanks to its CAM (Crassulacean acid metabolism) photosynthetic metabolism.

Low winter temperatures (from −6 to −8° C) reduce the yield of the cultivated plants but have no effect on the wild species. Suitable soil for cultivation is of medium texture and has a pH value between 5.0 and 7.5.

PLANT

The plant is arborescent and can reach a height of 3 to 5 meters. Its aerial portion consists of flat, green, wax-covered internodes (cladodes), usually obovate and of a size ranging between 30 and 60 centimeters long, 20 and 40 centimeters wide, and 19 and 28 millimeters thick. The cone-shaped leaves, only a few millimeters long, which are present on the cladodes or floral axis up to flowering, are short-lived, having a duration of about 30 days. At the leaf base are found the areolas, modified axillary buds, the number of which per cladode is usually constant (in *Opuntia ficus indica* 8-9 series in a spiral arrangement). They have spines and glochids on them and evolve into roots, cladodes, or flowers. The true spines, absent in species like *O. ficus indica*, are sclerenchymatous and of different lengths and colors. The glochids, which are usually present, are deciduous since they are not sclerenchymatous at the base. These are generally yellow, thin, and a few millimeters long. The basal cladodes tend to lignify until a well-defined

1

Give four cactus pears to one of the groups of four, along with a knife and plates, and invite them to taste the cactus pears. The members of the other group of four will each receive a copy of a summary fact sheet about the cactus pear (on CD-ROM) and read about this Southwestern fruit.

Once the groups have tasted the cactus pears and read the fact sheets, ask each volunteer to tell the judges, based on his or her personal experience, if he or she likes or dislikes cactus pears. After all the volunteers have presented their opinion, invite the judges to deliberate and decide which group they would trust the most if they wanted to decide whether or not to try a cactus pear.

Use slide 13 to conclude the exercise. Restate the original question: Can continental rationalism alone resolve the cactus pear dilemma? The answer is that knowledge and understanding cannot come from our rational mind alone. Our senses must be involved; direct experience with the subject being studied must be made available.

Activity 4: Mini-Lecture and PowerPoint: Influential Philosophers, Part 2

Return to the PowerPoint presentation and introduce the philosophy of Hume, who was a proponent of empiricism. As with Descartes, present the information on the slides (slides 14 and 15) and then transition to a mini-activity (slide 16) that will challenge Hume's philosophy.

Slide 16 introduces a challenge by posing a simple question: Can empiricism alone resolve the Adelson checker-shadow dilemma? Professor Edward Adelson of MIT creates optical illusions that defy our senses. The illustration on the slide presents two squares on a checkerboard; square A is near the upper edge of the board, and square B is near the middle under the shadow cast by a cylinder. The question this poses is simple: Are square A and square B the same shade of gray?

Let the students answer the question based on what they see. Their answer will be that square A and square B are not the same shade of gray. Leave them with this answer and move on to the next slides.

Use slide 17 to conclude the exercise. First revisit the question about the squares: Are square A and square B the same shade of gray? The answer is yes. The students will not believe you at first, so click a second time to show the proof. With the proof, they will have to admit that as with all the other optical illusions, they cannot trust only their visual cortex. Follow up with an open-ended "why?" Their answer should lead them to realize that their senses have limitations and that their cognitive abilities can reveal the reality of what they are seeing.

Restate the original question: Can empiricism alone explain the shade-of-gray dilemma? The answer is that knowledge and understanding cannot come only from our senses. Our reason must be involved; direct experience without rationalization can lead to false assumptions.

Slide 18 will allow you to present a solution to the conflict between continental rationalism and empiricism. Introduce the thinking of Kant (see the Background section in this lesson for more details) and state that the concept of "experience with reflection" offers a philosophy of learning and teaching that is much more correct than the dichotomy offered by Descartes and Hume.

Activity 5: Mini-Lecture and PowerPoint: Influential Philosophers, Part 3

Introduce slide 20 to bring the presentation to the last era of study, the 20th century. Summarize John Dewey's role in the development of experiential education and quickly summarize the tenets of pragmatism. You can explain that pragmatism is mainly concerned with consequences, utility, and practicality of reflection on either thoughts or actions—meaning experiences.

Slides 21 through 24 will help you present quotes from Dewey that your students might have found in the Musing Forest. You will discover that many of Dewey's quotes are the most popular among students, especially this one: "All genuine education comes from experience." It is interesting to ask students to comment on Dewey's quotes and to explain why they like some of them so much. This often leads the class into a meaningful discussion. Slide 25 summarizes the thinking of Dewey and his commitment to meaningful and experiential forms of education.

The last slide (slide 26) will help your students ponder who among this small sample of philosophers and educators most influences them. This is the perfect time to reinforce the challenge they will soon face in reflecting and in writing their own educational philosophy.

CLOSURE

As you conclude the lesson, remind the class that you have reviewed only a small sample of philosophers, thinkers, and educators who have inspired or influenced the epistemology of adventure education, outdoor education, and experiential education. Invite them to search for and read more about the philosophical roots of our professions and to keep collecting wisdom leaves (quotes) as they stroll along the path of past and present thinkers.

ASSESSMENT OF LEARNING

A formative type of assessment occurs during both classroom activities, the cactus pear dilemma and the Adelson checker-shadow dilemma. During these activities, it is easy to receive feedback from your class on the level of understanding they have about the nature and limitations of empiricism and continental rationalism.

It is easy to perform a summative assessment when your students complete, submit, and then present their personal educational philosophy to their peers. This assessment normally comes a few weeks later, so they will have time to read more about influential philosophers and educators.

LESSON 10

Teaching Dewey's Experience and Education *Experientially*

Mary C. Breunig

This lesson plan introduces learners to some of the experiential education theory found in John Dewey's seminal book *Experience and Education.* Key concepts from the book are taught experientially, with Kolb's (1984) experiential learning cycle used as the framework for this mixed-methods approach (lecture, experience, and guided discussion) to teaching about experiential education theory.

Background

According to the Association for Experiential Education (AEE 2004), experiential education is both a philosophy and a methodology in which educators purposefully engage with learners in direct experience and focused reflection to increase knowledge, develop skills, and clarify values. Central to this definition is the distinction between experiential education as methodology and as philosophy. This distinction suggests that there is a difference between experiential learning and experiential education.

Clifford Knapp, a prominent experiential educator, helps to highlight the difference between experiential learning and experiential education. Knapp (1992) explains that experiential learning consists of four distinct segments: "(a) active student involvement in a meaningful and challenging experience, (b) reflection upon the experience individually and in a group, (c) the development of new knowledge about the world, and (d) application of this knowledge to a new situation" (pp. 36-37). Figure 10.1 helps to illustrate the experiential learning cycle.

This cycle helps to illustrate how experience, reflection, new knowledge, and application can be employed as a way of teaching experientially. Many experiential educational initiatives are based on this learning cycle. Experiential education employs both methodology (experiential way of teaching) and philosophy as part of the educative process. Experiential education as philosophy implies that there is an intended aim toward which the experiential learning process is directed.

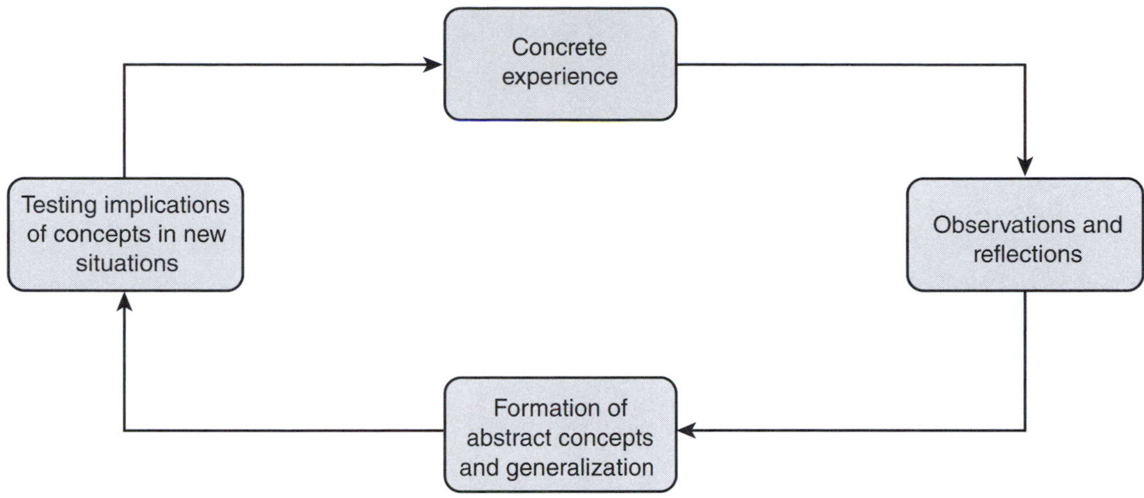

FIGURE 10.1 Kolb's (1984) experiential learning cycle.

Many of my own early experiences in learning about experiential education theory both as a student and as a professor, were rooted in learning about the theory presented within the book, including the experiential continuum, student-centered teaching and learning, freedom of experience, and educative and miseducative experiences, among others. Dewey is often cited as one of the founding fathers of experiential education, and much of the early work of the progressivists laid the groundwork for our present-day understanding of experiential education theory (Breunig 2005).

That said, many experiential educators learn and teach about experiential and alternative pedagogies but have done so fairly traditionally through lecture and some discussion. My own knowledge about some of the key theoretical concepts in *Experience and Education* (Dewey 1938), one of the seminal books related to experiential education theory, and other experiential education theory was acquired through a fairly traditional teaching methodology that was predominantly didactic. When I started to teach Dewey's book myself, I initially replicated my own experiences with this method of learning, employing lecture as a means to transmit aspects of the key knowledge found within the book. But students did not always "get it," because many outdoor recreation students are predominantly bodily-kinesthetic learners rather than visual or auditory learners. There is a different, more involving approach to teaching experiential education theory—one that employs a mixed methodological approach to teaching and learning experiential education theory.

Dewey's *Experience and Education* can be learned through an experiential approach that is more "in sync" with the theory being taught and that appeals to the primarily bodily-kinesthetic learning style of students. This can occur while one heeds Dewey's (1938) advice not to reject the old in reaching for the new. In other words, we can combine mini-lecture, experiential activities, and guided discussion as a means to teach about experiential education theory. In this sense, we bring the theories of experiential education into congruence with experiential teaching practices as they relate to *Experience and Education*.

RESOURCES

Association for Experiential Education. 2004. What is experiential education? www.aee.org (accessed February 23, 2004).

Breunig, M. 2005. Experiential education and its potential as a vehicle for social change. *Academic Exchange Extra,* 4:1-15.

Dewey, J. 1938. *Experience and education.* New York: Simon & Schuster.

Knapp, C. 1992. *Lasting lessons: A teacher's guide to reflecting on experience.* Charleston, WV: ERIC Clearinghouse on Rural Education and Small Schools.

Kolb, D.A. 1984. *Experiential learning.* Englewood Cliffs, NJ: Prentice Hall.

Lesson Plan

PURPOSE

To introduce students to some of the experiential education theory in Dewey's seminal book, *Experience and Education.* The goal is to acquaint students with this theory using an experiential methodology that appeals to the bodily-kinesthetic learning style of many outdoor recreation students.

OBJECTIVES

As a result of this lesson students will be able to . . .

1. *Cognitive and psychomotor:* develop and teach a lesson, using experiential processes, about Dewey's theory as explained in *Experience and Education.*
2. *Cognitive and psychomotor:* discuss and correctly describe at least three key elements of Dewey's theory.
3. *Cognitive:* develop their own classroom strategies to teach experiential education theory as a result of their own participation in an experiential process of learning theory.

DURATION

80 minutes

GROUP SIZE

15 to 25

LOCATION

Indoor space with room to move

EQUIPMENT

- One retired dynamic climbing rope
- Shoelaces or cordelette (one per person)
- Flip chart paper and markers
- PowerPoint projector

RISK MANAGEMENT CONSIDERATIONS

None

STUDENT PREPARATION

- Students should have already learned about Kolb's (1984) experiential learning cycle and be able to identify and define the four components of the cycle (experience, observation and reflection, formation of abstract concepts and generalizations, and testing implications in new settings) in addition to a fifth (added) component (preparation). See slide 2 of the PowerPoint presentation.
- Students should also have an understanding of the three learning styles: auditory, visual, and bodily-kinesthetic.
- Students should read Dewey's *Experience and Education* prior to the lesson and prepare a written reading response for the day of the lesson, highlighting some of the key concepts in the book and defining some of the specialized vocabulary in this lesson.

INSTRUCTOR PREPARATION

None

LESSON CONTENT AND TEACHING STRATEGIES

Review Kolb's (1984) experiential learning cycle (see slide 2 of PowerPoint presentation on the CD-ROM). Ask students if they have impressions, comments, or questions about *Experience and Education.* Answer initial questions if there are any. Inform students that the day's lesson will take an experiential approach to learning elements of the theory contained within the book.

Activity 1: Graffiti Walk

Have students write on the flip chart paper, or the chalkboard, some of the key theoretical concepts presented in Dewey's *Experience and Education.* Explain that this is a graffiti walk and that they should try to cover the paper or board with as many concepts as possible.

Circle those concepts that are most relevant, in your view, to experiential education and those that the lesson will focus on. Mention that it is not possible to cover all of the topics. This lesson focuses on the following key theoretical concepts: overt action, rules and social control, impulse and desire, freedom, movement or activity as a means but not an end, and educative versus mis-educative experiences.

Define miseducative and educative experiences (slide 3) and emphasize that this is a central theme throughout Dewey's book.

Activity 2: Overt Action

Have students divide up into pairs. Ask one of the students in each pair to take a shoelace or piece of cordelette. Ask the other student to write down on a piece of paper how he or she would instruct someone verbally about how to tie an overhand knot. Then, without using any demonstration, this second student reads the directions to the first student, asking that person to follow the directions exactly as given. Ask students to show their results.

Now have students reverse roles and ask the student who just wrote the directions to take the shoelace or cordelette. Ask the student who just tied the overhand knot to use any form of communication he or she chooses (demonstration, verbal communication, drawing, etc.) to inform the other student about how to tie an overhand knot. Ask students to show their results.

In most cases, the demonstration method, overt action, will produce better results than verbal instructions alone. Explain what the term *overt action* means (Dewey 1938) and provide a definition (slide 4 from the PowerPoint presentation).

Explain how Kolb's (1984) experiential learning cycle provides one rationale for the use of overt action. This cycle is an important tool to use when one is designing lesson plans and when one is teaching. Explain that when students were able to tie the overhand knot by using some experience alongside some observation and demonstration, overt action, the results of the knot-tying activity were more positive than with the method of knowledge transmission, simple verbal instructions, used in the first round of knot tying. Invite further questions and comments.

Point out that desks, books, and pens and paper are all examples of what Dewey refers to as *objective conditions*, and refer back to this term on the graffiti walk board. Explain that in many ways these objective conditions help provide some of the minimum necessary structure (Dewey 1938) that is so central to learning. Also emphasize that the objective conditions may inhibit learning because while they may to some extent enable the passive, quiet behavior so often valued in schools, they may also inhibit students' freedom (Dewey 1938). Explain that overt action and freedom are valued aspects of experiential and adventure education but may be less valued by traditional pedagogies that favor the transmission of knowledge and visual and auditory learning styles over the bodily-kinesthetic learning style.

Activity 3: Educative Experience

Move to an open space and provide students with a dynamic climbing rope. Tell them to do something with it, with the reminder that they cannot do something that will be harmful either emotionally or physically to any member of the group. Tell them that they have 5 minutes. It is likely that there will be a period of chaos, and within the 5-minute time frame the students may organize themselves and actually do something or may not.

Ask whether overt action, giving them a climbing rope and encouraging them to do something with it, was educative for them. It is likely that most will say no, but some may say yes. Ask what they learned. Ask if the activity could have been more educative.

Lead into a discussion about impulse and desire. Mention that sometimes overt action is how students' natural impulses and desires find expression. According to Dewey, not all overt action, not all impulses and desires, are educative. Some may be miseducative. Dewey (p. 64) suggests that the ideal aim of education is creation of the power of self-control over students' natural impulses and desires. Students develop self-control when an instructor uses her greater maturity of experience to provide minimum necessary structure (often in the form of objective conditions) to facilitate an experience for students that combines some structure and some freedom (often in the form of overt action) to design educative experiences.

Mention that designing experiences with the "right" amount of minimum necessary structure is no easy task, and draw parallels between Dewey's conclusions about this and instructing wilderness trips. More freedom, overt action, may actually inhibit learning or educative experiences, resulting in a higher level of risk both in learning and in instructing trips. If students and trip participants are always afraid or the environment is always chaotic or unpredictable, experiences may actually be less educative or even mis-educative.

Dewey (1938) emphasized that educative experiences cannot be either/or. They must combine objective conditions and overt action. He suggests that the experiential continuum (see slide 5) is one way to achieve this combination. More recently, Kolb's (1984) experiential learning cycle has helped to frame this idea. Together these resources provide educators with a means to consider how to plan lessons or how to instruct trips. Slide 5 lists the components of the experiential learning cycle alongside the experiential continuum in parentheses.

CLOSURE

- If time allows, have students form small groups and try to design a lesson plan or plan a trip using the experiential continuum or the experiential learning cycle. Using slide 5, provide students with a sample lesson to illustrate. For example, Brock University, where I teach, is located on the Niagara Escarpment, and we have the Bruce Trail running through campus. To teach students about the geology of the area, I tell them that the Niagara Escarpment is a World Biosphere Reserve (the preparation stage of the cycle). At the escarpment we examine the layers of rock and make observations about the nature of the escarpment (the experience stage of the cycle). We then reflect (the next stage of the cycle) on the unique qualities of this area, and next discuss the implications for ways of preserving the area (formation of abstract concepts and generalizations). Students are then encouraged to consider how their individual actions can affect the nature of this particular area and any area in which they may live or travel. Students are asked to identify what they can do to help protect fragile areas (testing implications in new settings).
- If time is too short to do the first suggested closure activity, ask students to discuss some of the implications of the experiential continuum or the experiential learning cycle for their own learning and future teaching experiences. How could they use these ideas in practice? What resonates with them? How do the experiential continuum and the experiential learning cycle address various learning styles? How does the experiential learning cycle address some of Dewey's concerns as explained in *Experience and Education*? Depending on the group of students, the instructor may have to ask additional questions or use various prompts to help students make these connections. Remind students of some of the concepts that were presented during the lesson and some of the other concepts within Dewey's book that also relate to experiential and adventure education (slide 6).
- Another possible closure activity is to have students do the graffiti walk again, seeing if they have additional comments or insights about the concepts as compared to what they learned from the first walk. The relevant PowerPoint slides can be used to reinforce Dewey and Kolb.

ASSESSMENT OF LEARNING

- Ask each small group from the final discussion, just described, to record their responses and to report them back to the class. Or, ask them to actively apply one of the concepts that they have learned to an upcoming experience and then report back to the class, either orally or in writing.
- A quiz can be given on some of the key theoretical concepts.
- Ask students to design lesson plans, as a graded assignment, using the experiential continuum and experiential learning cycle framework.

LESSON 11

How Do We Learn?

An Exploration of John Dewey's Pattern of Inquiry

Leslie E. Rapparlie

In some ways, "experiential education" has become a catch phrase among educators across the world. While experiential means of teaching may not fit into every curriculum, one can easily notice the immediate results when hands-on experience engages the mind. But experiential education does not have to be used simply to teach material; it can be used to allow students to literally explore the process that occurs when they learn.

This lesson presents a concrete activity that can be used with students to investigate John Dewey's "pattern of inquiry." Once students gain an understanding of the process that takes place each time they question and learn a topic, they may be able to better contextualize other lessons and materials across disciplines. Moreover, understanding the pattern of inquiry can create a passion for lifelong learning—the ultimate goal for all students!

Background

John Dewey, considered one of the forefathers of experiential education, developed a progressive view of education and the ways in which it needed to be transformed (Kraft 1999). Dewey believed that education must include participation and cooperation and that people "need contact with groups of individuals so that [they] can broaden [their] own personal ideas" (Wurdinger 1997, p. 9). In this way, societal and personal growth are encouraged. Participatory group learning has become an essential element of modern-day adventure education. Individualized ropes course elements, for example, have their place, but broader and more intensive learning almost always occurs in a group setting.

Not only did Dewey believe in creating a stronger sense of community through cooperative learning; he also believed in the introduction of experience into the traditional educational system. It is the responsibility of the educator to create and develop experiences that will lead to learning (Dewey 1938); if the intention of an experience is to control the learner, or if the experience is above the maturity level of the learner, then the educative qualities of the experience are lost. Additionally, Dewey emphasized that the "individual is in control of his or her own learning, and determines what is of most interest and value. When individuals are forced to participate they sometimes resist, or may feel captive and obligated to learn what the instructor wants them to learn" (Wurdinger 1997, p. 12). Thus, the "primary responsibility of educators is that they not only be aware of the general principle of the shaping of actual experience by environing conditions, but that they also recognize in the concrete what surroundings are conducive to having experiences that lead to growth" (Dewey 1938, p. 40). It is these concepts of experience that are at the heart of adventure education.

While providing experiences sits at the core of Dewey's philosophy, a specific component of experience, which Dewey termed the *pattern of inquiry (POI),* reflects the philosopher's ideas on how people use an experience to gain knowledge about a topic or concept. The POI is a cyclical process, detailing the journey of learning instead of the ultimate destination. Dewey believed that true learning comes from a passionate quest for knowledge that develops a thirst for lifelong learning.

The first step in this process is to have an opportunity to test the knowledge students already have (Wurdinger and Priest 1999). This opportunity comes in the form of an experiential inquiry. The learner must be interested in an idea, want to know more about it, and become engaged in an experience to gain additional knowledge. This inquiry, an *indeterminate situation,* is an experience without a known outcome. From this indeterminate situation, learners begin to question and challenge the problem at hand. Out of the questioning arises the formation of cognitive ideas, concepts, and potential resolutions to the situation—or a *determinate situation.* To conclude the POI, a learner uses these ideas and concepts in other situations, testing their validity and either adopting them to knowledge or abandoning them for ideas with stronger resonance. Dewey's POI can be represented by figure 11.1.

It is the cyclical nature of Dewey's POI that points to the importance of lifelong inquiry. The POI can take place in isolated form, or several POIs can occur at the same time. For example, a novice backpacker may have the large POI of the expedition that is taking place. Within the trip, other, less complex POIs may also occur,

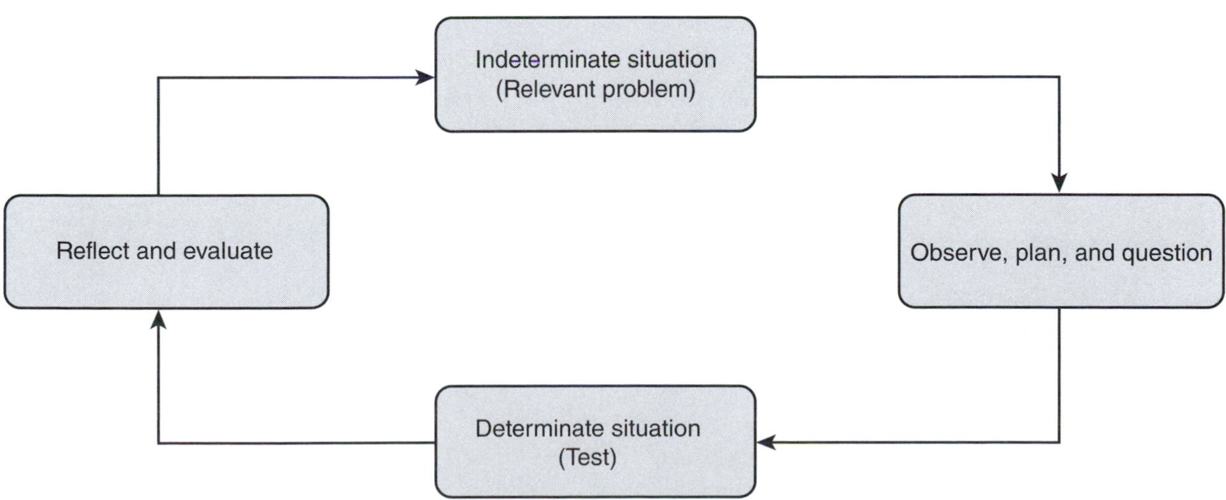

FIGURE 11.1 Visual representation of Dewey's pattern of inquiry.

like the most efficient way to light the stove, how to stay warm at night, how to hang a bear bag, or how to use a map and compass. All of this information is being confronted at the same time. Each time the stove is lit, for example, information from the last experience of lighting the stove is being used. On the whole, all the information gained from the expedition will be taken into the next expedition and so forth. This, Dewey claimed, is the learning process of life in both academic and nonacademic settings (Kraft 1999).

Knowing how to use and create educative experiences is essential for all adventure educators since experience is the basis of all their work. Dewey developed strong ideas about how experience is processed by the human brain and how it leads to learning. The POI can be a tool for comprehending how people learn and can enrich the learning experience of both the learner and the educator.

RESOURCES

Dewey, J. 1938. *Experience and education.* New York: Collier Books.

Kraft, R.J. 1999. Experiential learning. In *Adventure programming,* eds. J.C. Miles and S. Priest, 181-186. State College, PA: Venture.

Wurdinger, S.D. 1997. *Philosophical issues in adventure education.* Dubuque, IA: Kendall/Hunt.

Wurdinger, S.D., and S. Priest. 1999. Integrating theory and application in experiential learning. In *Adventure programming,* eds. J.C. Miles and S. Priest, 187-192. State College, PA: Venture.

Lesson Plan

PURPOSE

To expose students to Dewey's POI and how it might apply to their lives. As a foundation of experiential education, exposure to the POI is essential for all adventure educators.

OBJECTIVES

As a result of this lesson students will be able to . . .

1. *Cognitive:* explain Dewey's educational philosophy on the pattern of inquiry and how it applies to adventure education.
2. *Cognitive:* describe how the pattern of inquiry applies to lifelong learning.
3. *Psychomotor and affective:* participate in an experience that explores their personal style of learning.

DURATION

60 to 75 minutes

GROUP SIZE

6 to 30

LOCATION

Indoors or outdoors (a space big enough for students to move around in)

EQUIPMENT

- Paper and pens or pencils
- Large rope or piece of webbing
- Various objects of different shapes and sizes (i.e., fleece balls, stuffed animals, blocks of wood, etc.)
- Blindfolds

RISK MANAGEMENT CONSIDERATIONS

You will be asking the students to blindfold each other and lead each other around the room or open space outside, so be aware of anything that might cause slips, trips, or falls. Also, be careful to tend to the emotional safety of the students, ensuring that they can opt out of being blindfolded if need be.

STUDENT PREPARATION

In preparation for this lesson, students should read chapters 3, 6, and 7 of *Experience and Education* by John Dewey and pages 8 through 12 of *Philosophical Issues in Experiential Education* by Scott Wurdinger.

INSTRUCTOR PREPARATION

Before class begins, the activity you will use throughout the lesson should be set up in an area where the students cannot see it. Use a piece of long rope or webbing to create a border. To start, you will form a circle or other basic geometric shape. The size of the bordered area depends on the group size; but as a rule of thumb, the smaller the shape, the more difficult the activity will be. Within the border, toss the various objects (stuffed animals, fleece balls, wood planks, etc.) so that they are scattered throughout. The more objects inside the border, the more complicated the task will be.

LESSON CONTENT AND TEACHING STRATEGIES

Once the students arrive, ask them to define, on sheets of paper cut into fourths, the words *experience, observe, test,* and *reflect.* Have the students set the papers aside for now.

Activity 1: The Assisted Walk and Easy Minefield

Students should find a partner. One person in each partner team is then blindfolded. Once these students are blindfolded, they should sit down and wait. Bring the nonblindfolded partners to the location where the activity is set up and explain the problem that they are about to solve. Once you have finished the explanation, the participants will retrieve their blindfolded partner and guide them to the activity without touching them.

Traditionally this activity is known as "minefield," but you may want to use a metaphor that is more appropriate for your class and the theme of the course. You can call the activity whatever you wish and use the metaphor that best fits your class. For example, you might have the students imagine the setup before them as an expedition they are about to embark on. One end of the border represents the trailhead; the other end is the terminus of a successful trip. The goal is to get the blindfolded partner safely from the trailhead to the terminus. All the objects the blindfolded partner will encounter within the "expedition," however, are obstacles to inhibit the safe completion of the trip. These obstacles may be events like bad weather, injuries, food poisoning, snakebites, and so on. Emphasize that if while navigating the trip the blindfolded partner touches any of the objects or other travelers (other students), that person's expedition has been compromised and he or she will need to return to the trailhead and try again as many times as necessary to complete the trip safely.

If some pairs finish before others, they should simply wait until all pairs have completed the activity. Students can, however, remove their blindfolds once they are finished. The most important part of the activity is the stipulation that the nonblindfolded partners can never touch their blindfolded partners or enter the expedition (cross over the border) at any point.

▶ Students navigate the minefield.
Leslie Rapparlie

You should allow the students up to 15 minutes to complete the activity. If your minefield was set up in a basic geometric shape, you'll find that most students complete the task relatively quickly. Once the students have concluded this part of the activity, they will have completed the first and second phases of Dewey's POI. First, they were given a task to complete—an indeterminate situation. When they understood the parameters of the task, they could ask questions (observe and question) before they began. Upon completion, they have created a determinate situation and entered the third phase of the POI.

Once everyone has completed the first round of the activity, these are some questions you might want to use for discussion:

- What was it like for the blindfolded people to go through the experience without knowing what they were getting into?

- What was it like to guide someone through this activity?
- For both people, what were the challenges? What was easy?
- What led to your success? What caused you to have to start over?
- If you could do the activity again, would you know how to do it better?

The purpose of these questions is to allow students to understand and reflect on the conclusions they have developed (the fourth part of the POI). Here, they form concepts and ideas about the experience they just had. In order to see if the concepts they have developed from this POI are valid and hold true, have the students repeat the experience—with a slight variation—so that they can experience the POI a second time and see if their conclusions stand up.

Activity 2: Variation on the Assisted Walk and Challenging Minefield

Bring the class back to the area where they cannot see the activity setup and have the partners switch so that each individual gets the experience of being blindfolded and each gets the experience of being the communicator. While they are switching, change the border of the minefield (or you could set up two different minefields before class begins). The second minefield should not be a common geometric shape. A skinny, winding bordered area provides a surprise and a challenge to the students who will expect, as a result of the first run-through of the activity, to master the task immediately.

Again, have the blindfolded partners sit down and wait for their partners to return to them. Take the nonblindfolded students over to the minefield and again explain the rules of the activity. This group of people did not hear the rules the first time, since they were the first blindfolded group. Allow the students up to 20 minutes to finish the activity. Once all pairs have successfully completed the activity, have a brief discussion that includes questions like the following:

- What was easier or more difficult about the second try at this activity?
- Did you carry knowledge from the last attempt with you into the second try? Was it helpful to do that or did this knowledge hinder you in any way?

The purpose of these questions is to explore whether students recognize the "test" phase of Dewey's POI. Questions here should prompt students to think about how knowledge from the first try of this activity played into the second attempt.

Activity 3: Discussion and Mini-Lecture

Ask the students to explore how they solved the problems posed

Students confront a more challenging minefield.

Leslie Rapparlie

by the activity. In small groups or in one large group, depending on the size of the class, have them revisit the words *experience, observe, test,* and *reflect* that they defined at the beginning of class. Mention that these four words represent phases of their experience of the activity they just did. Give them 10 minutes to share their definitions with each other and then agree on how to order the four words according to the way they experienced the phases during the activity. At the end of 10 minutes, have each group report on their discussion.

Introduce the POI. Present figure 11.1. Emphasize these points:

- Dewey stressed that the POI is the way we learn everything, academic and nonacademic.
- The POI can create a love or passion for lifelong learning, or inquiry.
- Several POIs can occur at the same time. For example, you may have a big experience, like an expedition, and within it you also have smaller experiences, like lighting a stove or packing a pack.

CLOSURE

Ask the students to think of a personal experience that supports or refutes Dewey's POI theory and write a few paragraphs about it.

ASSESSMENT OF LEARNING

- Ask students to think about the activity they just experienced. Then ask whether they found that their learning during the experience occurred as Dewey suggests in the POI model. Their ability to discuss the topic should indicate the extent to which they understand the material.
- Review students' writings from the closure.

PART V

Theoretical Foundations

Although many adventure education students have experienced firsthand the effects of adventure programming theory, they know little about the work and influence of social psychologists and researchers such as Duffy, Bandura, and Csikszentmihalyi. As future professionals in adventure education, they must understand how people are motivated or afraid to participate in adventurous activities. They must also understand how their instruction can help their participants find the courage to attempt new challenges. They need to be able to recognize healthy and unhealthy behaviors their participants display as the participants reflect on their successes and failures while attempting adventure activities. Finally, they need to understand the role of risk in the adventure curriculum, its power and its limitations. The four lessons in this section present all of these important concepts, but most important, they immerse students in the practical nature of the theories.

For instance, in lesson 12, "Creating the Right Amount of Challenge: Optimal Arousal Theory and the Adventure Experience Paradigm," Christian Bisson's experiential approach to teaching arousal theory helps the learners to quickly understand the importance of creating flexibility in the level of challenge we offer to our participants. Although we mostly work with small groups, we need to remember that each individual in the group may react differently to our activities. Understanding optimal arousal theory and the principles underlying individual motivation help ensure that we deliver exciting and effective adventure programs to all.

In lesson 13, "I Think I Can: Self-Efficacy Theory in Adventure Programming," Bisson further explores the theoretical concepts of individual motivation by once again using an experiential approach to learning about Bandura's self-efficacy theory. The way we present risky activities can influence the self-efficacy of our students either positively or negatively. Therefore, understanding the principles behind individual aptitudes for attempting new tasks will help aspiring professionals design activities and programs that engage new learners at the most appropriate level. This lesson allows your students to experience firsthand how adventure education instructional strategies can influence participants' self-efficacy.

Bisson's lesson 14, "Attribution Theory in Adventure Programming," considers the work of Heider and Weiner in attribution theory. The lesson stresses the importance that our young professional adventure educators understand how their students perceive the world and themselves when it comes to failure and success. Rock climbing is used as a laboratory to observe and identify healthy and unhealthy attribution behavior. This lesson is designed to let students experience firsthand how participants react to success and failure. The lesson also helps them learn how to recognize behavioral cues to assess whether their own students have a predominantly internal or external locus of control.

Finally, in lesson 15, "Flow Theory: Risk Taking and Adventure Experiences," Ed Raiola and Marty O'Keefe present another lesson on the role of risk in adventure education as well as our duty to carefully use risk to foster growth in our participants. The lesson focuses on understanding the potential positive and negative impact of risk on participants, the different types of risk (i.e., physical, intellectual, and emotional), the role of risk in personal growth and development, and why some risks are more appealing than others. Raiola and O'Keefe use an experiential approach to teach the concept of flow as explained by Csikszentmihalyi. In the end, the lesson encourages students to carefully match risk and challenge in their adventure programming so that their participants will be more likely to understand how to include positive risk taking in their lives.

LESSON 12

Creating the Right Amount of Challenge

Optimal Arousal Theory and the Adventure Experience Paradigm

Christian A. Bisson

Using activities that present risk and challenges is at the heart of adventure education. However, it is essential for adventure professionals to keep in mind that all adventure activities may not fit all our participants. Although we mostly work with small groups, we need to remember that each individual in the group may react differently to our activities. Understanding the principles underlying individual motivation and the optimal arousal theory will help ensure that we deliver exciting and effective adventure programs to all. This lesson is designed to help your students experience firsthand how adventure activities influence motivation and learning through arousal.

Background

Two important theoretical texts related to adventure education, *Outdoor Adventure Pursuits* by Alan Ewert (1989) and *Effective Leadership in Adventure Programming* by Simon Priest and Michael Gass (2005), include discussions of optimal arousal theory. Presented in both texts as an essential theoretical model to explain the motivation or behavior of individuals participating in adventure-based activity, the optimal arousal theory is a fundamental theoretical model that needs to be introduced to future professionals in adventure education or recreation.

The model was introduced in the 1950s through the work of Elizabeth Duffy (1957) on the physiological responses to "emotional activation," as it was named at the beginning of Duffy's studies. The model simply states that each organism, or individual, naturally seeks external stimuli of an appropriate level in order to perform at optimal potential or to feel optimal satisfaction. The initial research on optimal arousal focused on identifying the relationship between arousal or activation and the level of the motivating or emotional value of the situation to the individual (Duffy 1957). Duffy hypothesized that differences in level of arousal in a given individual "are accompanied by differences in the quality of performance;

the relationship may be graphically represented by an inverted U-shaped curve" (p. 273). Adapted from Ellis (1973), figure 12.1 represents this quadratic relationship, with one side indicating a level of arousal that could be associated with stimulation characterized by eustress and the other side indicating a level of arousal that could be associated with stimulation characterized by distress.

Priest and Gass (2005) explained the model by saying that people may be overaroused or underaroused. When someone is underaroused by an environment or an activity, his or her performance or level of motivation may decrease. Motivation may also decrease when one is overaroused. Consequently, somewhere between being over- and underaroused is an emotional condition labeled "optimal arousal," a point where the level of stimulation or challenge leads to the highest level of performance or motivation for the individual.

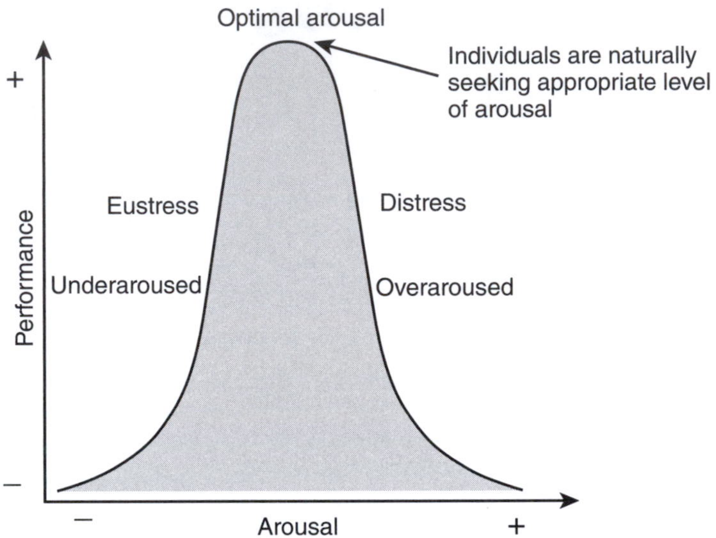

FIGURE 12.1 The optimal arousal theory.

Adapted from M.J. Ellis, 1973, *Why people play* (Englewood Cliffs, NJ: Prentice Hall). Used by permission of the author.

Ewert (1989) indicated that the best way to achieve the right level of arousal for each individual is to appropriately increase the level of uncertainty and dissonance by (1) increasing the number of choices that can be made, (2) increasing the complexity of a challenge, and (3) creating a stimulus overload. Thus Ewert (1989) suggested that the instructor can control the level of arousal.

Controlling the factors influencing the level of arousal empowers the instructor to select the appropriate activities, the level of challenge, and the pace at which the adventure experience is presented. The goal, obviously, is to create a level of arousal appropriate for each participant.

Extrapolating from the optimal arousal theory, we can entertain the idea that a similar model could apply to the level of perceived risk and the amount of arousal experienced by participants. By replacing level of performance with level of risk in the inverted U-shaped model, we can hypothesize that when the real or perceived risk is too low, some participants in an adventure experience may be underaroused or even bored. When the risk is too high or perceived as too high, some participants may be overaroused, and this may keep them from participating or even lead them to quit altogether. Figure 12.2 illustrates this adaptation.

Therefore, as suggested by Ewert (1989) and earlier Martin and Priest (1986), as well as Priest and Baillie (1987), controlling the level of real and perceived risk in adventure activities can lead to the appropriate level of stimulation or arousal.

Inspired by other models pertaining to risk, motivation, flow, and arousal, Martin and Priest (1986) proposed the "adventure paradigm;" a model that explains how varying the level of risk according to the participant's level of competence can lead to participants in adventure programs to five possible conditions of challenge: (1)

exploration and experimentation, (2) adventure, (3) peak adventure, (4) misadventure, and (5) devastation and disaster. Figure 12.3 illustrates the proposed relationship between risk and competence.

The model defines risk as "the potential to lose something of value" and competence as "the capability of individuals to deal with the demands placed on them by their environment" (Priest and Gass 2005, p. 49).

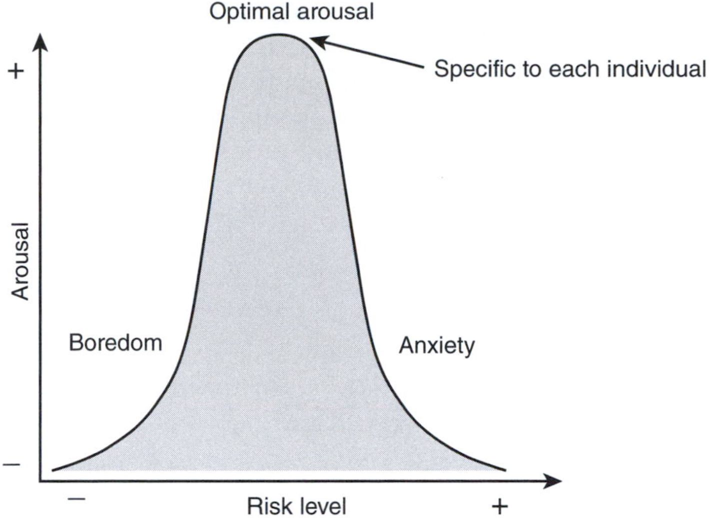

▶ **FIGURE 12.2** Level of risk versus level of arousal.

Adapted from M.J. Ellis, 1973, *Why people play* (Englewood Cliffs, NJ: Prentice Hall). Used by permission of the author.

Obviously, what this model tells us is that there are conditions or experiences we want to promote and others that we should stay away from. We should progress from the condition of exploration and experimentation through the condition of adventure and eventually expose our participants to a peak adventure condition. Consequently, as we have seen with the optimal arousal theory, it is essential to attempt to match the level of perceived risk with the level of competence for each participant.

These essential theoretical concepts can and should be applied in all adventure programs, as strongly argued by Hopkins and Putnam (1993) in their discussion of the "problem of the match" (pp. 101-102). In explaining the need to match the level of challenge appropriately to each participant, Hopkins and Putnam suggest that sequencing activities with an increasing level of challenge or perceived risk

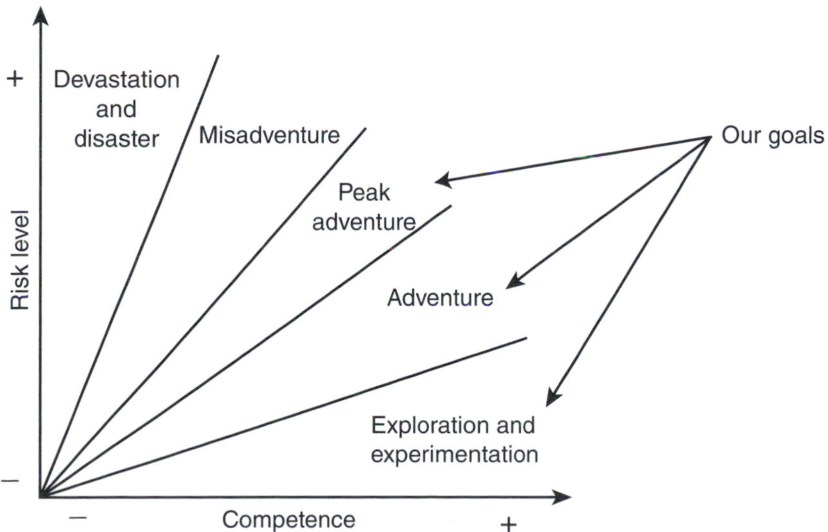

▶ **FIGURE 12.3** Adventure paradigm.

Adapted from P. Martin and S. Priest, 1986, "Understanding the adventure experience," *Journal of Adventure Education* 3 (1): 18-21. Adapted by permission of Peter Martin.

will allow participants to remain motivated (i.e., aroused) by a condition of challenge associated with eustress but not elicit fear (i.e., overarousal) because the level of challenge appears too difficult or too dangerous. Therefore, one could say that the need to have flexible adventure programs, which allow practitioners to carefully match risk and arousal or risk and competence, leads to the conclusion that the notion of various levels of challenges is essential in planning as well as in implementing adventure programs.

RESOURCES

Duffy, E. 1957. The psychological significance of the concept of "arousal" or "activation." *Psychological Review,* 64(5):265-275.

Ellis, M.J. 1973. *Why people play.* Englewood Cliffs, NJ: Prentice Hall.

Ewert, A.W. 1989. *Outdoor adventure pursuits: Foundations, model, and theories.* Columbus, OH: Publishing Horizons.

Hopkins, D., and R. Putnam. 1993. *Personal growth through adventure.* London: David Fulton.

Martin, P., and S. Priest. 1986. Understanding the adventure experience. *Journal of Experiential Education,* 3(1):18-21.

Priest, S., and R. Baillie. 1987. Justifying the risk to others: The real razor's edge. *Journal of Experiential Education,* 10(1):16-22.

Priest, S., and M. Gass. 2005. *Effective leadership in adventure programming.* Champaign, IL: Human Kinetics.

Lesson Plan

PURPOSE

The purpose of this lesson is to allow students to experience the optimal arousal theory for themselves so that they can better appreciate the need to plan challenges with multiple levels of arousal.

OBJECTIVES

As a result of this lesson students will be able to . . .

1. *Affective and psychomotor:* participate in an experience that provides various levels of arousal and be able to explain their behavior and their respective levels of arousal during the various stages of the activity.
2. *Cognitive:* explain how the optimal arousal theory relates to the level of risk used in adventure education.
3. *Cognitive:* explain the five conditions of challenge according to the adventure experience paradigm.
4. *Cognitive:* explain the theoretical foundation supporting the need to offer various levels of challenge to participants in adventure programming.
5. *Cognitive:* demonstrate the ability to apply the principles underlying optimal arousal theory and the adventure experience paradigm by planning a flexible adventure curriculum for a specific adventure activity.

DURATION

50 to 60 minutes

GROUP SIZE

Appropriate for 6 to 25 students

LOCATION

Indoors and outdoors (you will need a flat outdoor space large enough to accommodate the size of the group you are working with)

EQUIPMENT

- 12 to 20 fleece balls
- 6 to 10 bean-stuffed animals
- 6 to 10 tennis balls
- One ice axe
- 6 to 10 water balloons
- One small bottle of perfume

RISK MANAGEMENT CONSIDERATIONS

Be aware that some people may be allergic to perfume. Although no one will come into physical contact with the perfume, some people may feel uncomfortable knowing that a perfume is being used in the activity. This will actually work perfectly with the optimal arousal theory.

STUDENT PREPARATION

No specific preparation is needed before the lesson.

INSTRUCTOR PREPARATION

Prepare the water balloons ahead of time. Take one of the water balloons and apply some perfume to it to simulate a balloon filled with perfume. Place the fake perfume balloon in an airtight plastic food container. You will be placing all the props into an activity bag to keep them hidden. Be careful not to prepare the fake perfume balloon too early, as over time the alcohol in the perfume will dissolve the membrane. Collect the rest of the props (throwing objects) and place them in the activity bag. In doing so, organize them by weight, placing them into the bag from heaviest (in the bottom of the bag) to lightest (on top)— ice axe, water balloons, tennis balls, bean-stuffed animals, fleece balls.

LESSON CONTENT AND TEACHING STRATEGIES

Begin by telling the students that you will explore with them the theoretical concepts and practical application of the optimal arousal theory, as well as the relationship between risk levels and arousal, and finally help them better understand the importance of the adventure experience paradigm.

Make a compelling argument for the purpose of the lesson by sharing a situation you have personally experienced that relates to the optimal arousal theory and the adventure experience paradigm. For instance, you could recount an experience such as the following to illustrate the importance of understanding these theories and models:

"Early on in my career as a wilderness instructor, I received many good evaluations, but once in a while in a course evaluation a student would write, 'I was expecting the course to be more challenging' or 'I found the course harder than I had expected.'"

Then you could ask such questions as these:

- Why may some students not be pleased with the level of challenge offered by a course?
- How can we optimize the experience of each participant?
- Can we manipulate a program to ensure the optimal level of satisfaction in our participants?

Once the students' curiosity has been aroused, explain that to help them answer these questions you would like to lead them in a short adventure activity and then see what can be learned about risk, individual level of arousal, and individual level of competence. Before going outside to do the activity, explain that at the end of the lesson you will allow them to work in small groups to find practical application to these theoretical concepts.

Activity 1: What Goes Up Must Come Down

Move the group outside into an open area that is level and safe. Make sure that the space is large enough to allow people to run away from the center of the activity. The area can have a soft surface like grass or a hard surface like pavement, though a hard surface may provide a better effect.

Now share a few rules specific to this activity:

- Participants can move away from the center of the group if they choose to.
- If participants move, they should attempt to move away safely.
- If they decide to stay immobile, they cannot look up.
- If they decide to stay immobile, they must remain standing and keep their eyes open.

Gather the group together and then have people randomly disperse themselves around you. Explain that after you have counted to three, they will throw objects above their heads. Show them the first set of objects; start with the softest objects (fleece balls). Ask if the group would be willing to throw this type of object up in the air. They will definitely say yes, so count to three and throw all the fleece balls in the air. Repeat this process for each heavier type of object (bean-stuffed animals, tennis balls, and water balloons). Conclude with a final round, which will include more water balloons and the fake perfume balloon. You should feel their excitement increase as you introduce increasingly heavier objects.

When the water balloons are introduced, there are always some people in a group who will get very excited. When you introduce the fake perfume balloon, saying that you filled it with your grandmother's perfume, you will discover that half, if not more, of the students will want to throw it up but will run away before it comes back down. Finally, between each throw, remind people that they can always choose to stay in place but not look up. Or they can choose to walk away from the drop zone. Again, you should see behavior changes as the activity progresses.

There are many ways to process this activity, but the following questions are in keeping with the basic goals of your processing session.

- Did any of you notice a difference in behaviors as the experiment progressed?

Group participating in the activity "What Goes Up Must Come Down."
Courtesy of Jeremy Meyer.

- How many of you were excited when we used the soft objects?
- How many of you were excited when we used the heavier objects?
- What happened to the group when I suggested using the water balloons?
- How many of you walked away when we used the water balloon?
- Why did you walk away?
- How many of you walked away when I used the perfume balloon?
- Why did you walk away?
- Would you say that as we progressed in this game, the level of risk increased?
- How would you define risk? [the potential of losing something of value, or potential loss]
- Give me some examples of "potential loss" in this game.
- What are some examples of "potential loss" in adventure education?
- What is the "ultimate loss" in adventure education? [death]
- What is "perceived risk"?
- Was there any perceived risk in the game we just played? [the fake perfume balloon] This could be a good time to indicate that the perfume balloon was not filled with perfume (or later on when reviewing the theory in the classroom).
- Would you say that as we progressed in this game, the level of excitement or arousal increased?

- How would you define arousal? [level of external stimuli received in a period of time]

Once you feel that you have covered enough of these questions, explain that you have prepared a visual aid that should help the students conceptualize the theoretical models supporting their findings.

Activity 2: Mini-Lecture and PowerPoint on Arousal Theory and the Adventure Paradigm

Once everyone is back the classroom, introduce the PowerPoint presentation (on CD-ROM) as an aid to visualize and explain what happened during the What Goes Up Must Come Down activity.

As you go through the slides, emphasize the following concepts by encouraging the students to make connections between what is on the slide and what happened outdoors.

Optimal Arousal Theory

With slide 2, introduce Ellis' (1973) model representing his optimal arousal theory. As you present the model, emphasize the following concepts associated with human arousal behavior.

- Like infants, adolescents and adults need external stimuli.
- Lack of stimuli is unhealthy; psychological experimentation on external-stimulus deprivation showed that a healthy person cannot be placed in isolation for more than three days without causing harm to their mental health.
- Levels of stimuli that are too low create apathy (boredom).
- Levels of stimuli that are too high create too much stress (anxiety).
- People will naturally seek the appropriate level of stimuli in their life.

At the end, help the students notice that as the level of arousal increases in a participant, it creates greater performance through good stress—*eustress*. However, if the level of arousal keeps increasing past an optimal level, the participant's performance decreases because too much arousal creates bad stress—*distress*. Make sure you emphasize the idea that the relationship between performance and level of arousal is specific to each one of us.

Risk Level Versus Arousal Slide 3 presents an adaptation of Ellis' model. Lead students to notice that we could substitute "risk levels" for "competence" to create a new model that combines risk and arousal. Indicate that like Ellis' optimal arousal theory, this model supports the construct that each individual will have a specific level of optimal arousal when exposed to risk.

Moderate Risk Taker With the next slide (slide 4) ask your students to indicate, through a show of hands, if any of them experienced the following progression in their level of arousal during the activity:

- Soft objects (i.e., fleece balls)—low level of arousal
- Heavier objects (i.e., bean-stuffed animals and tennis balls)—moderate level of arousal
- Water balloons—high or optimal level of arousal
- Water balloons and perfume balloon—too much arousal

- Ice axes—extreme arousal (When you present this option, pull the ice axe out of the bag and ask how many of them, in all honesty, would have run away from the drop zone if the group had thrown six ice axes like this one in the air. The healthy response is that all of them would have run away.)

If many students identify their behavior through this slide, tell them that they might be identified as "moderate risk takers," which is a norm for most participants when it comes to physical risk taking.

High Risk Taker Slide 5 reviews the possible arousal level for hypothetical "high risk takers." This group is usually smaller in a normal population; but since your students are mostly outdoor adventure lovers, you might see a large group of people identify with this scenario when you ask if any of them recognize their behavior in this slide:

- Soft objects (i.e., fleece balls)—low level of arousal
- Heavier objects (i.e., bean-stuffed animals and tennis balls)—low level of arousal
- Water balloons—moderate level of arousal
- Water balloons and perfume balloon—high or optimal level of arousal
- Ice axes—extreme arousal

Low Risk Taker Slide 6 reviews the possible arousal level for hypothetical "low risk takers." Don't be surprised if no students, or only a few, identify themselves as shown on this slide, since most would probably find the activity too tame for their taste. In any case, ask if any of them recognize their behavior in this slide:

- Soft objects (i.e., fleece balls)—moderate level of arousal
- Heavier objects (i.e., bean-stuffed animals and tennis balls)—high or optimal level of arousal
- Water balloons—too much arousal
- Water balloons and perfume balloon—extreme arousal
- Ice axes—extreme arousal

Adventure Experience Paradigm Slide 7 introduces another model inspired by Ellis' work on arousal theory. The model is known as the adventure experience paradigm, conceived by Martin and Priest (1986). As you present this slide, define the following terms as proposed by Martin and Priest (1986):

- *Risk* is defined as the potential of losing something of value.
- *Competence* is defined as the combination of skill, attitude, knowledge, behavior, confidence, and experience that one uses to deal effectively with the demands placed on one by the surrounding environment.

Once you have defined the terms representing the two axes, explain the various levels of adventure included in the paradigm:

- Exploration and experimentation
- Adventure
- Peak experience

- Misadventure
- Devastation and disaster

Emphasize that our goal as adventure educators is to provide an effective experience for each of our participants.

So What? At this point in the presentation (slide 8), help your students understand the practical application of these theoretical models. Help them realize through a series of questions that ultimately our goal is to match individual level of competence to the level of risk in our adventure activities. Consequently, your students should conclude that to achieve this goal, our programs need to be flexible and to offer more than one level of risk and challenge.

We Have Choices To prove your point, present slide 9 to show the choices we can make to create more flexible levels of challenge (e.g., risk or perceived risk) in our programs. Once the students get the idea, ask them to come up with a list of factors or conditions we can use to create adventure or perceived risk. Their list might include but not be limited to the following:

- Height
- Speed
- Darkness
- Isolation
- Terrain difficulty
- Water depth

Once you have a good list of factors or conditions, lead the group into the final activity, which will challenge them to create more flexible levels of challenge for specific outdoor activities.

Activity 3: Small Group Professional Challenge

Separate the class into groups of three to five. Assign an adventure education program (See the Small Group Professional Challenge handout on CD-ROM) scenario to each small group. Some groups may have the same scenario if your class is larger than 20. Ask the students to discuss their scenario and to come up with a solution that applies the theoretical principles they have just explored.

Note that the backpacking program scenario will require a topographic map on which yo have placed a departure point (A) and a point of arrival (B). select an area on the map that provides multiple traveling options via trails with various level of challenge (i.e., length, elevation gain, river crossing), as well as an obvious off-trail traveling option.

You might need to go around and help some of the groups understand what artificial environments for paddling (i.e., man-made obstacle on a white-water river section or an artificial paddling training course) and caving (i.e., man-made underground labyrinth) are.

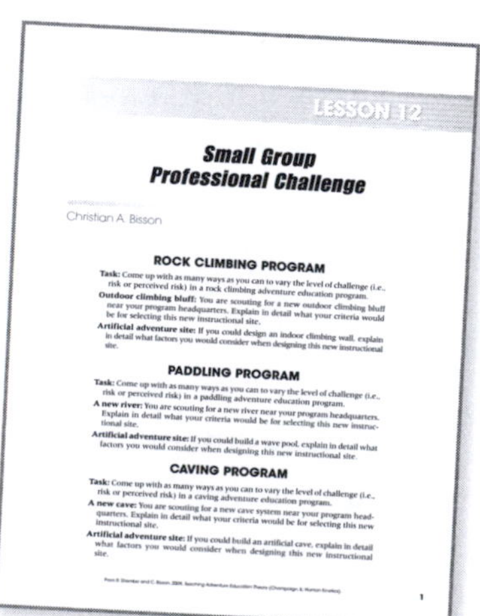

LESSON 12

Small Group Professional Challenge

Christian A. Bisson

ROCK CLIMBING PROGRAM

Task: Come up with as many ways as you can to vary the level of challenge (i.e., risk or perceived risk) in a rock climbing adventure education program.

Outdoor climbing bluff: You are scouting for a new outdoor climbing bluff near your program headquarters. Explain in detail what your criteria would be for selecting this new instructional site.

Artificial adventure site: If you could design an indoor climbing wall, explain in detail what factors you would consider when designing this new instructional site.

PADDLING PROGRAM

Task: Come up with as many ways as you can to vary the level of challenge (i.e., risk or perceived risk) in a paddling adventure education program.

A new river: You are scouting for a new river near your program headquarters. Explain in detail what your criteria would be for selecting this new instructional site.

Artificial adventure site: If you could build a wave pool, explain in detail what factors you would consider when designing this new instructional site.

CAVING PROGRAM

Task: Come up with as many ways as you can to vary the level of challenge (i.e., risk or perceived risk) in a caving adventure education program.

A new cave: You are scouting for a new cave system near your program headquarters. Explain in detail what your criteria would be for selecting this new instructional site.

Artificial adventure site: If you could build an artificial cave, explain in detail what factors you would consider when designing this new instructional site.

1

CLOSURE

Ask your students if, after completing the last activity, they think it is always easy to provide different levels of challenge. Discuss the various factors that can keep us from offering various levels of challenge, such as the following:

- Time
- Money
- Human resources
- Environmental limitations

Finally, review what has been learned by asking questions such as these:

- How would you describe risk?
- How would you explain the difference between risk and perceived risk?
- How does risk affect your own level of arousal?
- What level of adventure from the adventure experience paradigm do you prefer experiencing when you participate in an outdoor pursuit activity?
- If you were in charge of developing a new adventure education curriculum, what would you do to ensure that the adventure activities you provide are effective for everyone?

ASSESSMENT OF LEARNING

Have each small group share with the rest of the class their solution for their adventure education curriculum scenario. Assess their solutions and provide reinforcement when a solution indicates various levels of challenge and risk to support the optimal arousal theory and the adventure experience paradigm.

The following are examples of appropriate solutions:

- Rock Climbing Scenario: different heights for the climbing route, different levels of difficulty (i.e., 5.4, 5.5, 5.6, 5.7, and 5.8), different levels of exposure
- Paddling Scenario: different levels of difficulty of rapids, different levels of paddling difficulty from one side of the river to the other, possibility of portages
- Caving Scenario: different passage sizes and difficulties
- Backpacking Scenario: different routes offering different levels of challenges (i.e., on trail, off trail, longer or shorter distances)

LESSON 13

I Think I Can

Self-Efficacy Theory in Adventure Programming

Christian A. Bisson

The way we as adventure educators present risky activities can influence the self-efficacy of our students either positively or negatively. Understanding the principles behind individual aptitudes for attempting new tasks will help ensure that we deliver exciting and effective adventure programs to all. Self-efficacy is strongly influenced by adventure programming; therefore it is essential that professionals in this field understand the theoretical construct, the benefits of self-efficacy, and the factors influencing it. This lesson is designed to allow your students to experience firsthand how adventure education instructional strategies can influence participants' self-efficacy.

Background

Bandura defines *self-efficacy* as a person's beliefs about his or her capabilities to learn or perform actions at designated levels (Bandura 1997). Self-efficacy is the central variable within what Bandura and his colleagues call *social cognitive theory* (Schunk and Zimmerman 2006). This theoretical model views human behavior in terms of three influential factors that mutually interact; Bandura (1997) calls this interaction *triadic reciprocity*. In this interaction, factors such as (1) environment variables, (2) behaviors, and (3) intrapersonal factors (i.e., cognitive, affective, and biological) influence one another as presented in figure 13.1.

Bandura (1997) proposed that our actions can affect the environment and how we think about ourselves. Environmental variables can influence our behavior or what we think about who we are. Finally, our thoughts can influence our actions and how we perceive our environment (Schunk and Zimmerman 2006). Thus self-efficacy, or our belief in our own competence, reflects the reciprocal causation suggested by triadic reciprocity. What I think about myself will affect my performance in my activities or how I allow the environment to influence me. This is what every novice student in adventure education experiences when he or she

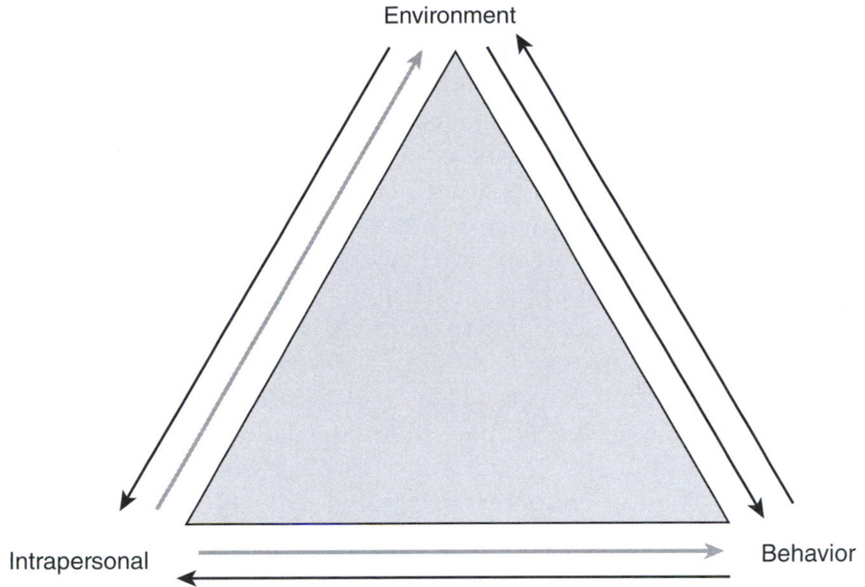

FIGURE 13.1 Relationships among factors influencing individuals according to the social cognitive theory.

faces a new activity, situation, or challenge. Bandura (1997) also indicates that the reciprocal relationships among environment, behavior, and intrapersonal factors such as cognition are not equal in strength. Since it is easier to control our own thinking (i.e., cognition) than it is to control the environment, and since our action (i.e., behavior) can be strongly influenced by our thinking, Bandura (1997) suggests that our thinking can be a strong agent of persuasion (i.e., motivation) and potential outcomes (i.e., performance). The larger arrows in figure 13.1 represent this skewed influence.

According to Bandura, individual self-efficacy may fluctuate in at least three ways: (1) magnitude, (2) strength, and (3) generality.

Magnitude refers to the "degree of certainty" that people experience or display regarding their potential level of success at completing a task. This degree of certainty will be influenced by factors such as perceived risk or perceived task difficulty. For instance, a student who is afraid of heights may be 100% certain that he or she can go near the edge of a cliff but only 50% certain that he or she can perform the rappel exercise proposed by the instructor. Fortunately, magnitude can be modified, as we will see later (Priest and Gass 2005).

Strength or *resiliency* refers to the length of time people hold on to their "expectations of success" despite any negative influence from the environment. For instance, a person can display "low strength" in self-efficacy by rapidly losing his belief that he can succeed at rolling a kayak after failing in his first attempt. On the other hand, a person with "high-strength" self-efficacy will likely continue to attempt to roll her kayak even after one or multiple failures at her Eskimo roll (Priest and Gass 2005).

Generality refers to the degree of transferability between self-efficacy for a specific task to self-efficacy for another task or to general self-efficacy. For example, success at climbing a 5.5 route may help some people build their certainty that they will also be successful at climbing a 5.7 route (i.e., specific self-efficacy) or at speaking in front of a group of strangers (i.e., general self-efficacy). According to Priest and Gass (2005), in terms of its level and type, transfer is easier if the person sees a similarity between tasks. The ability to see connections between tasks can obviously be enhanced via processing techniques.

Bandura's research on self-efficacy revealed that this intrapersonal attribute can be modified by four influencing sources. Some of these sources are internal (i.e., intrapersonal factors) and some are external (i.e., environmental variables). These sources of influences are (1) prior mastery experiences (internal), (2) vicarious experiences (external), (3) emotional arousal (internal), and (4) verbal persuasion (external).

Prior mastery experience, according to research, is the most influential and stable (i.e., strongest) of these sources (Paxton and McAvoy 1998). Research suggests that prior success in identical or similar tasks increases self-efficacy, while failure early on tends to have a greater impact than later failure when one is performing a new task. In addition, success at a task that is associated with effort builds greater self-efficacy than does success attributed to luck, hence the importance of proper sequencing in the level of challenge that we present to our students in adventure education. Another implication is that helping our students recall prior success in a similar task will help increase their belief in their ability to succeed at accomplishing a new task.

Vicarious experience, or observing or hearing about other people who have been successful at a new and challenging task, can also help people gain self-efficacy. Although this source of influence is not as powerful as direct experience, vicarious learning can increase motivation to attempt a new challenge. The implications for adventure education are obvious: Demonstrating a new skill, role modeling, or carefully selecting the sequence in which participants will perform a task can be vital in helping to increase the self-efficacy of some students.

Emotional arousal refers to the level of anxiety or boredom that learners can experience when presented with a new challenge. The right amount of stress, in the realm of eustress, facilitates motivation and has a positive influence on participants' self-efficacy. And avoiding boredom or distress associated with failure or setbacks is essential especially if these two conditions become debilitating. All this suggests that it is essential to create an exciting environment and, again, to select the right level of an adventure challenge.

Verbal persuasion is the least influential of the sources. Nevertheless, motivating and supporting participants through verbal persuasion can help certain students perceive themselves as more likely to succeed. At the same time, verbal encouragement must be appropriate in quantity and in kind for each individual. As leaders, if we misjudge the potential for our students to succeed at a task, we risk inflating the expectations we convey to them via verbal persuasion. In the case of failure, this can have a negative effect on learners and lower their self-efficacy toward future attempts. Along the same lines, overpraising mediocre performance can cause learners to doubt our integrity as well as reduce their self-efficacy (Martin 1999). Finally, verbal coercion, needless to say, is unacceptable; not only can it backfire, it can also breech ethical protocols.

As Ewert (1989) said, "Self-efficacy is the cornerstone of many outdoor pursuits programs" (p. 93). Not only is this theoretical concept based on solid evidence; but also issues of self-efficacy are always present for people exposed to outdoor adventure activities for the first time. Most importantly, Bandura's work has provided us with concrete strategies to help our students improve their specific and general self-efficacy levels.

RESOURCES

Bandura, A. 1997. *Self-efficacy: The exercise of control.* New York: Freeman.

Ewert, A.W. 1989. *Outdoor adventure pursuits: Foundation, models, and theories.* Columbus, OH: Publishing Horizons.

Martin, P. 1999. Practical stories in a theoretical framework. In *Adventure programming,* eds. J.C. Miles and S. Priest. State College, PA: Venture.

Paxton, T., and L. McAvoy. 1998. Self-efficacy and everyday life. In *Proceedings from the Coalition for Education in the Outdoors 4th research symposium,* 32-39. Bradford Woods, IN: Coalition for Education in the Outdoors.

Priest, S., and M.A. Gass. 2005. *Effective leadership in adventure programming.* Champaign, IL: Human Kinetics.

Schunk, D.H., and B.J. Zimmerman. 2006. Competence and control beliefs: Distinguishing the means and ends. In *Handbook of educational psychology,* eds. P.A. Alexander and P.H. Winne. Mahwah, NJ: Erlbaum.

Lesson Plan

PURPOSE

The purpose of this lesson is to allow students to experience the principles of self-efficacy theory through action so that they can better appreciate how the intervention of a trained adventure educator can help improve a participant's self-efficacy.

OBJECTIVES

As a result of this lesson students will be able to . . .

1. *Affective and psychomotor:* participate in an experience that provides an opportunity to directly observe and study self-efficacy–related behaviors.
2. *Cognitive:* explain the theoretical and practical definition of self-efficacy.
3. *Cognitive:* explain the four factors (i.e., prior mastery experiences, vicarious experiences, emotional arousal, verbal persuasion) that influence the development of a client's self-efficacy during participation in an adventure activity.
4. *Cognitive:* explain the theoretical foundation supporting the need to identify and cultivate a high level of self-efficacy in adventure program participants.
5. *Cognitive:* demonstrate the ability to identify and create strategies to cultivate self-efficacy in adventure program participants.

DURATION

90 to 120 minutes

GROUP SIZE

Appropriate for 12 to 25 students

LOCATION

Indoors (you will need a multimedia classroom and a staging area for the Leap of Faith activity)

EQUIPMENT

- A stable platform about 36 to 40 inches (90 to 100 centimeters) high (a table, an office desk, or a low trust-fall platform can work perfectly for this lesson)
- A small landing platform about 16 inches (40 centimeters) wide by 16 inches long and about 12 inches (30 centimeters) high (a solid milk crate with a reinforced top works great; see photo below)
- Four copies of the "Leap of Faith: Instructor's Cheat Sheet" (on CD-ROM)
- Multimedia equipment for the PowerPoint presentation

RISK MANAGEMENT CONSIDERATIONS

The Leap of Faith activity is inherently dangerous. Make sure that the students volunteering for this activity have had no ankle or knee injuries. Spotting during the activity should be mandatory, especially if you use a milk crate for the landing platform.

STUDENT PREPARATION

No specific preparation is needed before the lesson.

INSTRUCTOR PREPARATION

Build the reinforced landing platform if needed. Test the stability of the high platform from which the participants will jump during the Leap of Faith activity.

LESSON CONTENT AND TEACHING STRATEGIES

Begin your lesson by explaining that you would like to explore with your students the Little Engine That Could Theory. Most of them should know about the classic children's book by this title and especially the mantra of the little engine, so ask them to tell you what the little engine said to itself to successfully climb the hill: The answer is the simple but rhythmic and rousing "I think I can, I think I can, I think I can. . . ."

Landing platform used for the "Leap of Faith" activity.
Christian Bisson

Of course, most students will suspect that there is no such thing as the Little Engine That Could Theory, so tell them that it is better known as the *self-efficacy theory* of Albert Bandura.

Then explain that one of the best ways for them to understand Bandura's theory and its application to adventure education will be to begin the lesson with a little experimentation followed by a mini-lecture.

Activity 1: Leap of Faith

Begin the activity by asking for a few students to volunteer as subjects in the experiment on self-efficacy. You can use four volunteers if you have a short period of time to devote to the experiment, or eight or even twelve if you have more time. Carefully explain that the activity will involve some physical risk and that people with a history of injury to their ankles or knees should refrain from volunteering as subjects.

Once you have the number of volunteers you want, ask them to leave the room and wait outside the classroom. While they are outside, prepare the rest of the class for their task.

Explain that the subjects will come in one at a time and participate in a classic adventure activity called Leap of Faith. The activity involves a simple jump from a high platform (36 to 40 inches, or 90 to 100 centimeters) to a lower and smaller landing platform (12 inches, or 30 centimeters). The platforms are placed about 3 to 4 feet (0.9 to 1.2 meters) apart. Each subject will have one attempt at performing the jump. The jump will be considered successful if the subject can safely land and remain on the landing platform.

To perform the experiment, you will need four additional volunteers to play the role of instructors. Each instructor will be in charge of explaining the activity to a particular subject (if you have only four subjects) or to a group of subjects (if you have more than four subjects) and supervising their attempts. You can help the instructors quickly learn their roles by giving them an instructional cheat sheet (see "Leap of Faith: Instructor's Cheat Sheet" on the CD-ROM).

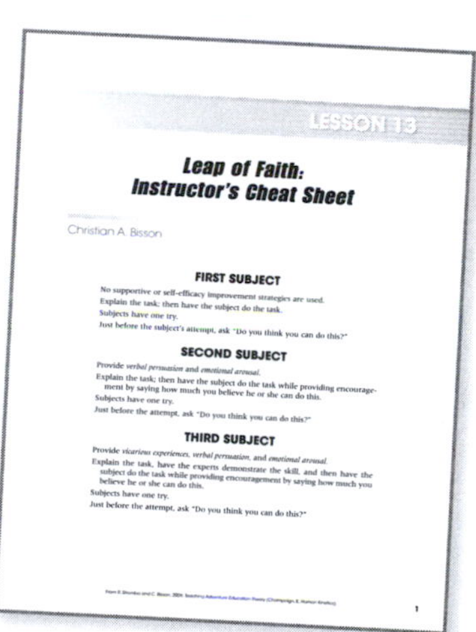

LESSON 13

Leap of Faith: Instructor's Cheat Sheet

Christian A. Bisson

FIRST SUBJECT

No supportive or self-efficacy improvement strategies are used.
Explain the task; then have the subject do the task.
Subjects have one try.
Just before the subject's attempt, ask "Do you think you can do this?"

SECOND SUBJECT

Provide *verbal persuasion* and *emotional arousal.*
Explain the task; then have the subject do the task while providing encouragement by saying how much you believe he or she can do this.
Subjects have one try.
Just before the attempt, ask "Do you think you can do this?"

THIRD SUBJECT

Provide *vicarious experiences, verbal persuasion,* and *emotional arousal.*
Explain the task, have the experts demonstrate the skill, and then have the subject do the task while providing encouragement by saying how much you believe he or she can do this.
Subjects have one try.
Just before the attempt, ask "Do you think you can do this?"

1

Finally, explain that you will need two more volunteers to demonstrate the Leap of Faith activity. These two expert students, preferably a male and a female, will take the time to practice and become comfortable and efficient at performing the jump. They will practice while you are out of the classroom briefing the subjects. Also explain that active spotting is essential in this activity.

Next, back in the classroom, explain that each subject or group of subjects will receive a different treatment designed to affect their self-efficacy. (The following description assumes four groups of subjects but would also apply to each subject individually if there were only four subjects in all—subject 1, subject 2, etc.). Group 1 subjects will receive no supportive or self-efficacy improvement strategies. They will receive only the instruction regarding the activity. Indicate that the instructor will ask subjects one simple question just before their attempt: "Do you think you can do this?" Emphasize that after this question has been asked, instructors and spotters need to be very attentive to the subjects' verbal and nonverbal responses.

Subjects in group 2 will receive verbal persuasion and emotional arousing in the form of positive encouragement and cheers. Again, just before their attempt, they will be asked the question "Do you think you can do this?"

Subjects in group 3 will receive verbal persuasion, emotional arousing, and vicarious experience. This time the task will not only be explained but will also be demonstrated by the expert students. Like the group 2 subjects, these subjects will hear encouragement and cheering before performing the jump.

Subjects in group 4 will receive verbal persuasion, emotional arousing, vicarious experience, and a chance to develop prior mastery experience. They will develop prior mastery by practicing from a lower starting point such as a chair. Subjects in this group will also hear encouragement and cheers before performing the jump and will see a demonstration by the expert students as well.

As the instructors learn their role and the expert students practice the jump while being spotted, meet with the subjects and explain that they will be asked to come in one at a time and to carefully follow the instructions they receive.

When everyone is ready, begin the experiment. Guide the instruction when needed and supervise for safety. Keep reminding the instructors and the spotters to pay attention to the responses of the subjects when subjects are asked if they think they can complete the task successfully.

When all the subjects have completed the task, take time to thank all the volunteers, especially the subjects. Have the class take a short break or move directly to the mini-lecture.

Activity 2: Mini-Lecture and PowerPoint on Self-Efficacy Theory

When everyone is ready, introduce the self-efficacy PowerPoint presentation (on the CD-ROM) as a visual aid to explain Bandura's theory as well as to explain what happened during the Leap of Faith experiment.

The title slide (slide 1) brings back the humor in the opening statement about the Little Engine That Could theory. It might elicit chuckles from the students, which is a good way to start a mini-lecture.

Move quickly over slide 2 to give your students a sense of who Albert Bandura is and what he has done in social psychology.

With slide 3, take the time to carefully explain Bandura's definition of self-efficacy. Make sure the students understand that self-efficacy refers to people's *belief* in their ability to be successful in a task and that this belief will determine how they feel, think, motivate themselves, and behave when facing new or similar tasks. In addition, discuss the difference between general and specific self-efficacy. Make sure you stress that specific self-efficacy may not always transfer to other specific tasks. For instance, it may be that a person develops a high level of self-efficacy for rock climbing but not for public speaking.

With slides 4 through 6, review with your students the advantages of developing in oneself a healthy level of self-efficacy. Similarly, review slides 7 through 9 to consider the disadvantages of having a low level of self-efficacy.

After you have defined self-efficacy and presented an argument for its development in all our participants, it is time to look at the four factors that can influence the development of self-efficacy: (1) prior mastery experiences, (2) vicarious experiences, (3) emotional arousal, and (4) verbal persuasion. Slides 10 through 14 introduce the four sources and explain each one. Note that slides 11 through 14 will allow you not only to define each source of self-efficacy but also to outline the ramifications of these principles in the field of adventure programming. Therefore, make sure to solicit input from your students on the slides that say "So What?" This is a great opportunity to get your class involved and to assess if they understand the meaning of each source.

Follow up these explanations by presenting slide 15. The figure (figure 13.2) on this slide should help you summarize the effectiveness level for each of the factors that influence the development of self-efficacy. Emphasize that as professional adventure educators, they have many strategies to use in order to influence their clients' self-efficacy, and that they should know which ones to use in particular situations to achieve the best result.

Once students understand the theoretical framework for the self-efficacy theory, it is time to connect the theory with practice. So, introduce slide 16 to begin the

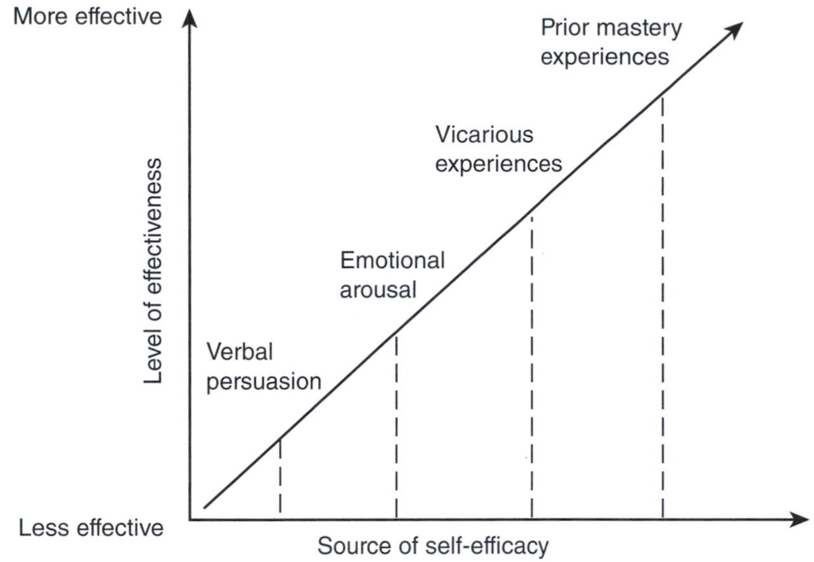

FIGURE 13.2 Sources of self-efficacy and their effectiveness levels.

analysis of the Leap of Faith activity. Explain that for the next 20 minutes or so you would like to have a group discussion about the experiment. More specifically, you would like the students to help one another answer the following questions:

- What strategies were used to influence the level of self-efficacy in each subject?
- What were the responses of the subjects to the question "Do you think you can do this?"
- What was the end-result performance of each subject?
- Did the behavior of the subjects match Bandura's theory?

Slides 17 through 20 will help you and the class analyze each subject or group of subjects. Make sure that you solicit input from the subjects and their own analysis of their experience. At the end of slide 20, bring the class back to the ultimate question: Did the behavior of the subjects match Bandura's theory?

End this mini-lecture with a final reference to the "Little Engine" joke by presenting slide 21, which is animated.

CLOSURE

As you conclude your lesson, remind the class that understanding self-efficacy theory and the strategies we can use to help our clients modify their perception is an essential skill for any professional adventure educator. Remind them that in the spirit of John Dewey, we can say that in adventure education, theory without practice is worthless, but practice without theory could be dangerous.

ASSESSMENT OF LEARNING

Formative assessment occurs throughout the lesson, especially at the end of the PowerPoint presentation when the class discusses the events and outcomes of the Leap of Faith activity.

You can also use a more summative form of assessment during the following week by giving the class a short quiz on the subject.

LESSON 14

Attribution Theory in Adventure Programming

Christian A. Bisson

Adventure educators need to understand how their students can perceive the world and themselves when it comes to failure and success. Using adventure activities is an ideal way to observe attribution behavior and to influence it if it is unhealthy. Adventure curricula are authentic and therefore provide immediate feedback to people about their ability. However, the perception our students have of their performance could be incorrect if their locus of control is skewed by an unhealthy image of self, perhaps that of a timid or an arrogant personality. This lesson is designed to let your students experience firsthand how participants react to success and failure. The lesson will also help them learn how to recognize behavioral cues to assess whether their own students have a predominantly internal or external locus of control.

Background

Attribution theory was initially proposed by Heider (1958) and later developed as a more rigorous theory in the work of Weiner (1985, 1986). In his work, Heider suggested that people perceive the result of an action (i.e., performance) by looking at factors within themselves (internal) or within their environment (external). Basically, Heider suggested the obvious, that people consider internal or external causes when explaining their performances (Heider 1958). Although Heider was right about the role of these two causal factors in people's performance or action attribution, the reality regarding how we explain what we do or what happens to us is rather more complex.

The idea had to wait until 1985 before being improved by the work of Weiner. Weiner (1985, 1986) picked up Heider's idea of internal and external attribution and added two more dimensions, or sets of factors, to explain how people attribute causation in their lives. Weiner (1985, 1986) suggested that causation could be not only internal or external but could also be stable or unstable and controllable or uncontrollable.

STABILITY

Stable factors are factors that are fairly permanent or enduring within the self or within the environment. One's physical abilities, cognitive skills, and emotional aptitudes are good examples of internal stable factors, while external stable factors could be represented by the reality of the task in its level of difficulty or the standards established by others to determine success or failure.

Unstable factors are more temporary or transitory. Like the stable factors, they can be found within the person or within the environment. Internal unstable factors can be represented by the level of effort one gives toward accomplishing a task or the level of self-motivation one develops to perform an action. External unstable factors are defined as chance, fortitude, serendipity, accident, and coincidence.

LOCUS OF CONTROL

Locus of control can be defined as the perception people have regarding their ability to control the events that happen to them. People will either believe that they are in control of certain actions or events (internal) or that they are not in control of these actions or events (external). Controllable internal factors can be associated with one's level of planning, preparation, work, or training before a performance, or with a lack of focus or laziness. Uncontrollable external factors are often associated with the actions of others, such as the level of support they show when one is attempting to complete a task, or actions they take to hinder performance or provide a challenge. Uncontrollable external factors can also be attributed to the environment, for example weather, temperature, and altitude.

LOCUS OF CAUSALITY

Locus of causality is defined by Weiner (1986) as the internal or external attribution of causality as originally proposed by Heider. Again, someone expressing an internal attribution relates the causality of events or actions to him- or herself, while someone expressing an external attribution relates the causality to others within the situation.

BIASES IN ATTRIBUTION

Researchers in social psychology have discovered that we have a natural tendency to attribute the behavior of others to internal factors, whereas we tend to attribute events that we experience to external factors; this is particularly true when the end result of an action or behavior is failure. For instance, as instructors we might readily attribute misbehavior on the part of a student to internal factors, such as a lack of focus or commitment to learning, while attributing a poor class experience to external factors such as distractions caused by student misbehavior. This tendency to overestimate the influence of internal factors in others and underestimate the importance of internal factors in oneself, especially within the context of failure, is the reason teachers sometimes fail to recognize that student misbehavior may be the result of a boring and unengaging lesson (external) due to their own lack of preparation and effort (internal) (Martin 1999).

THE ROLE OF ATTRIBUTION IN ACHIEVEMENT MOTIVATION

It is proposed that when the context is appropriate, meaning that one's success has truly been caused by controllable and stable factors, attributing performance to oneself (internal) will lead to feelings of pride and will provide motivation to repeat a performance or engage in new experiences. On the other hand, attributing failure to an internal locus because of controllable and stable factors will lead to a sense of shame and can hinder future performance or participation in the same or a similar task (Weinberg and Gould 2003). Table 14.1 illustrates the effects of attribution on achievement motivation.

TABLE 14.1 Effect of Attributions on Achievement Motivation

Attributions	Psychological results
Stability factors	**Expectancy of future success**
Stable	Increase expectancy of success
Unstable	Decrease expectancy of success
Causality factors	**Emotional influence**
Internal cause	Increase pride or shame
External cause	Decrease pride or shame
Control factors	**Emotional influence**
Within one's control	Increase motivation
Out of one's control	Decrease motivation

Adapted, by permission, from R. Weinberg and D. Gould, 2007, *Foundations of sport & exercise psychology*, 4th ed. (Champaign, IL: Human Kinetics), 64.

As a professional adventure educator, Martin (1999) asks two very good questions about encouraging attribution in participants and offers the corresponding answers:

1. Should I encourage an *internal* attribution for this person in this situation?

   An internal attribution will be laying causal explanation with the participant. This may be appropriate if the person has control over his or her capacity to improve but needs encouragement to reapply himself or herself or work harder, if he or she has succeeded deservedly, or if the person needs to be encouraged to understand his or her limitation. (p. 173)

2. Should I encourage an *external* attribution for this person in this situation?

   An external attribution lays causal explanation with the situation. This may be appropriate if the person has reached the limit of his or her capabilities, if he or she has succeeded without effort or application, or if the situation was not as it initially seemed and was, or became, beyond his or her control. (p. 173)

As you can see, the answers to these questions are very specific to the individual, his or her behavior or performance, and the situation (task difficulty). This is why it is important that adventure educators carefully observe the behavior of participants when exposing them to activities with high perceived risk. The participants' responses, their performance, and the context in which that performance is completed all play a role in determining what attribution you will promote or reinforce. Table 14.2 gives examples of attributions an instructor should promote in a student participating in a climbing program.

TABLE 14.2 Healthy and Unhealthy Attribution and the Proper Response by the Instructor

Reality: Success or failure during a climbing experience	Perception: Participant says ...	Attribution	Action instructor should promote ...
Success because of ... physical strength, effort, and good climbing technique.	I was lucky, this was an easy route, and my belayer helped me.	Unhealthy	**Stable** **Internal** **Controllable**
Failure because of ... bad luck, hard route, and spinning climbing hold.	I am not strong enough, I am not focused, and I used poor technique.	Unhealthy	**Unstable** **External** **Uncontrollable**
Failure because of ... lack of physical strength, effort, and poor climbing technique.	I was unlucky, this route was too hard, and my belayer pulled me off.	Unhealthy	**Stable** **Internal** **Controllable**
Success because of ... good luck, easy route, and help from the belayer.	I am in good physical shape, I stayed focused, and I used good footwork.	Unhealthy	**Unstable** **External** **Uncontrollable**
Failure because of ... lack of physical strength, effort, and poor climbing technique.	I am out of shape, I am not focused, and I chose my sequence of moves poorly.	Healthy	**Stable** **Internal** **Controllable**
Success because of ... good luck, easy route, and help from the belayer.	I was lucky, this was an easy route, and my belayer helped me.	Healthy	**Unstable** **External** **Uncontrollable**
Success because of ... physical strength, effort, and good climbing technique.	I am in good physical shape, I stayed focused, and I used good footwork.	Healthy	**Stable** **Internal** **Controllable**
Failure because of ... bad luck, hard route, and spinning climbing hold.	I was unlucky, this route was too hard, and the last hold spun.	Healthy	**Unstable** **External** **Uncontrollable**

In the end, it is important to remember that although promoting an internal attribution is generally believed to be better and healthier, promoting an external attribution is more appropriate in certain situations. If a young male participant displays "machismo" and bravado after failing at an easy task when he obviously did not put effort or focus into succeeding, it is appropriate for the instructor to help him realize that he cannot blame anyone but himself for his failure. Conversely, if a young female participant fails at a very difficult task not because of a lack of inner strength or physical abilities but still displays signs of a misplaced "humility," it is appropriate for the instructor to help her realize that she cannot blame herself for the failure, but instead that the situation was simply impossible to overcome at the moment.

It is essential to remember that this role played by an adventure education instructor—that of an honest mirror—is crucial to the development of healthy attribution in many, if not most, participants in adventure education or adventure therapy programs.

RESOURCES

Hattie, J.A., H.W. Marsh, J.T. Neill, and G.E. Richards. 1997. Adventure education and Outward Bound: Out-of-class experiences that have a lasting effect. *Review of Educational Research*, 67:43-87.

Heider, F. 1958. *The psychology of interpersonal relations.* New York: Wiley.

Martin, P. 1999. Practical stories in a theoretical framework. In *Adventure programming*, eds. J.C. Miles and S. Priest. State College, PA: Venture.

Weinberg, R., and D. Gould. 2003. *Foundations of sport and exercise psychology.* Champaign, IL: Human Kinetics.

Weiner, B. 1985. An attribution theory of achievement motivation and emotion. *Psychology Review* 92:548-573.

Weiner, B. 1986. *An attribution theory of achievement motivation and emotion.* New York: Springer-Verlag.

Lesson Plan

PURPOSE

The purpose of this lesson is to allow students to experience the attribution theory for themselves so that they can better appreciate its impact on participants' motivation and internal sense of control.

OBJECTIVES

As a result of this lesson students will be able to . . .

1. *Affective and psychomotor:* participate in an experience that provides an opportunity to directly observe and study attribution theory–related behaviors.
2. *Cognitive:* Explain how attribution theory relates to personal motivation in adventure activities and in life.
3. *Cognitive:* Explain the various factors (i.e.., stability, locus of control, and locus of causality) influencing the attribution of performance outcomes.
4. *Cognitive:* Explain the theoretical foundation supporting the need to identify and cultivate healthy attribution of outcomes in adventure program participants.
5. *Cognitive:* Demonstrate the ability to identify and create strategies to cultivate healthy attribution in adventure program participants.

DURATION

90 to 120 minutes

GROUP SIZE

Appropriate for 6 to 25 students

LOCATION

Indoors, outdoors, or both (you will need a multimedia classroom and access to an indoor or outdoor climbing wall if you choose climbing as your medium for studying attribution theory)

EQUIPMENT

- All necessary equipment needed to rock climb at an indoor or outdoor climbing wall
- Attribution Behavior Survey (on CD-ROM; four surveys for each researcher)
- Rotter's Locus of Control Scale (on CD-ROM; one per student)
- Multimedia equipment for PowerPoint presentation

RISK MANAGEMENT CONSIDERATIONS

If you choose to use a rock climbing experience to introduce attribution theory, you will need to make sure that most students are able to properly belay and use rock climbing equipment.

STUDENT PREPARATION

No specific preparation needs to be completed before the lesson.

INSTRUCTOR PREPARATION

If needed, reserve indoor or outdoor climbing wall. Prepare four climbing routes of various degrees of difficulty, such as one easy (5.4-5.5), two moderate (5.7-5.8), and one hard (5.10-5.11). In addition, in one of the moderate routes, make sure that two or three large key climbing holds are loosened so that they can spin in a way that will challenge the climbers unexpectedly.

LESSON CONTENT AND TEACHING STRATEGIES

Begin your class by explaining that you would like to explore with your students the theoretical concepts of attribution of outcomes to one's performance and the influence of attributions on future personal motivation in adventure programming or in life.

Following your initial explanation of today's topic, most of your students will have little to no clue as to what you are talking about, so follow up with clarification and a motivational statement, for example, "Well, I think the best way for me to introduce you to the concepts behind attribution theory is to take you rock climbing." You should then get a more enthusiastic reaction from the class.

Activity 1: The Climbing Experience

First, a note about why I use rock climbing for this exercise. There are many reasons:

- All my students are already familiar with rock climbing before taking this class.
- This activity will ensure that participants experience success and failure.
- The activity allows me to throw in variables that will enhance the basic attribution categories (i.e., stability, locus of causality, locus of control).
- In rock climbing we can clearly identify success or failure.
- All my students can get involved in the experience.

However, if you do not have easy access to an indoor or outdoor climbing wall, you could substitute another individual adventure activity. For example, students could perform a low-element challenge course activity (e.g., balance beam, fidget ladder, tire swing, flea leap), solo paddle a course through a set of buoys, or ride an obstacle course on a mountain bike. Whatever experience you select, make sure that you can clearly identify success and failure in the students' performance and that the activity has various challenge levels that will ensure both success and failure.

If you use a rock climbing wall for this exercise, bring the class to the climbing wall. Explain that this is not a climbing class and that only a few of them will be climbing today, but that everyone will be involved in this little human behavior experiment. Follow up this disclaimer by asking for volunteers to be the subjects (climbers). If you know your students well, select carefully from the volunteers. If possible, select two males and two females to balance gender in your sample. Then, within the four selected students, try to select a male and a female student each of whom you suspect is self-confident, athletic, and able to climb well. Try also to select a male and a female student each of whom you suspect is more timid and has less climbing experience.

Once you have completed your selection, ask these people to get ready for climbing by putting on a harness and, if necessary, a helmet. No rock climbing shoes are allowed. Now ask for four or eight other volunteers who are proficient at belaying. Pick eight volunteers if you want to use backup belayers. Finally, the rest of the class should be divided into four research groups of equal size. For instance, if you have a class of 24 students, you might have four teams with three researchers each. In any case, make sure that everyone is involved.

While the subject-climbers and the belayers are getting ready, pull the research teams aside and prepare them for their task. Explain that their task is to select a subject-climber and briefly interview him or her after each climb. Tell the researchers that after each climb, they will pull their subject aside and ask him or her this simple question: "To what causes would you attribute your success [or failure]?" Obviously they will ask about causes leading to failure when the climb was unsuccessful and causes leading to success when the climb was successful. Ask them to use the Attribution Behavior Survey (on CD-ROM) to record their subject's responses. Indicate that each researcher needs to complete a form for each climb, so there will be multiple observations of each subject. Ask the researchers to record the exact wording of the subjects and to note any significant nonverbal expression or other cues such as intonation, pauses, or emphasis that support or contradict their responses. Give a few examples of responses that the researchers might receive and how they will record them.

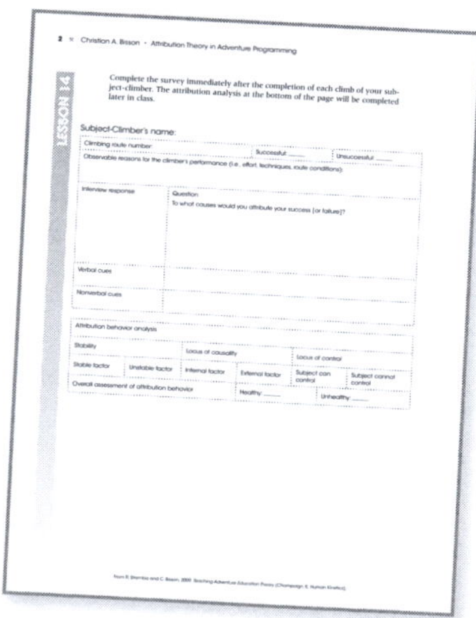
2 ■ Christian A. Bisson • Attribution Theory in Adventure Programming

LESSON 14

Complete the survey immediately after the completion of each climb of your subject-climber. The attribution analysis at the bottom of the page will be completed later in class.

Subject-Climber's name:

Climbing route number: | Successful: ____ | Unsuccessful: ____

Observable reasons for the climber's performance (i.e., effort, techniques, route conditions):

Interview response	Question To what causes would you attribute your success [or failure]?
Verbal cues	
Nonverbal cues	

Attribution behavior analysis

Stability		Locus of causality		Locus of control	
Stable factor	Unstable factor	Internal factor	External factor	Subject can control	Subject cannot control
Overall assessment of attribution behavior			Healthy: ____	Unhealthy: ____	

Return to the climbers and inspect their setup. Now introduce the four climbs, simply listing them by numbers from 1 to 4. Follow up by explaining the respective roles of the subject-climbers, the belayers, and the researchers.

Role of Subject-Climbers

- Each subject will climb all four climbing routes in any order.
- Each subject will have a single attempt at climbing each climbing route.
- A subject's attempt to climb a route will end as soon as the subject reaches the top of the climb and touches the last hold, or when the subject falls or rests on the rope.

Two student researchers interviewing their subject (i.e., climber).
Courtesy of Jeremy Meyer.

- A climb will be considered successful if the subject reaches the top of the climbing route and touches the highest hold on the route.
- A climb will be considered unsuccessful if the subject does not reach the top of the climbing route and touch the highest hold, or if he or she falls or rests on the rope at any time during the climb.

Role of Belayers

- Belayers are responsible for the safety of the subjects and their own safety.
- Belayers are assigned to manage one climbing route only.
- Belayers are allowed to encourage and coach climbers.
- Belayers are responsible for monitoring the progress of the subjects and bringing them down if they are unsuccessful or if they finish the climb.

Role of Researchers

- Researchers are responsible for pulling aside and interviewing their subject.

Female subject completing a climb during a hands-on exercise to study attribution theory.
Christian Bisson

- Researchers are responsible for observing and noting the success or failure of their subject.
- Researchers are responsible for observing and noting the context in which the success or failure of their subject occurred.

When these directions and role clarifications have been presented, start the experience. Obviously, keep monitoring the safety and the interview process during the experience. In addition, when possible, observe the performances of the subjects; this could help you later on when you review the theoretical framework in class.

Once all four climbers have completed the four climbs, take the time to thank everyone for their participation, especially the subjects. Put away the climbing gear and return to the classroom for the next activity.

Interview after the climb.

Christian Bisson

Activity 2: Mini-Lecture and PowerPoint on Attribution Theory, Part 1

Once everyone is back the classroom, introduce the attribution theory PowerPoint presentation (on the CD-ROM) as an aid to visualizing the concepts behind attribution theory. However, before the presentation, explain that you would like all the students to complete a small questionnaire that will help quantify one dimension of their personal attribution behavior, namely their "locus of control." It will not be necessary to explain what locus of control is; simply distribute Rotter's Locus of Control Scale (on CD-ROM) and allow students a good 10 to 15 minutes to complete the questionnaire (slide 2).

Once everyone has completed the questionnaire, explain that the results of the questionnaire will be compiled and analyzed later on, but that for right now they simply need to put their questionnaire away.

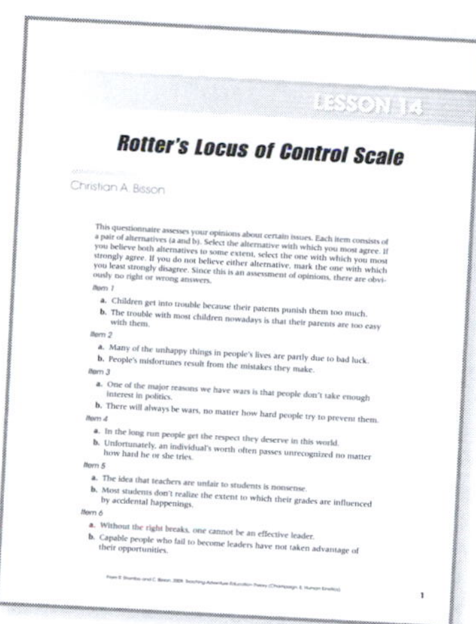
LESSON 14

Rotter's Locus of Control Scale

Christian A. Bisson

This questionnaire assesses your opinions about certain issues. Each item consists of a pair of alternatives (a and b). Select the alternative with which you most agree. If you believe both alternatives to some extent, select the one with which you most strongly agree. If you do not believe either alternative, mark the one with which you least strongly disagree. Since this is an assessment of opinions, there are obviously no right or wrong answers.

Item 1

a. Children get into trouble because their patents punish them too much.
b. The trouble with most children nowadays is that their parents are too easy with them.

Item 2

a. Many of the unhappy things in people's lives are partly due to bad luck.
b. People's misfortunes result from the mistakes they make.

Item 3

a. One of the major reasons we have wars is that people don't take enough interest in politics.
b. There will always be wars, no matter how hard people try to prevent them.

Item 4

a. In the long run people get the respect they deserve in this world.
b. Unfortunately, an individual's worth often passes unrecognized no matter how hard he or she tries.

Item 5

a. The idea that teachers are unfair to students is nonsense.
b. Most students don't realize the extent to which their grades are influenced by accidental happenings.

Item 6

a. Without the right breaks, one cannot be an effective leader.
b. Capable people who fail to become leaders have not taken advantage of their opportunities.

1

Start the PowerPoint presentation by briefly explaining slides 3 and 4, which review the definition of the term "attribution theory" and its historical roots.

Spend some time on slide 5, since it is crucial that the students understand the three basic attribution categories, *stability, causality,* and *locus of control.* This is an appropriate time to connect the third category, locus of control, to the questionnaire they have just completed.

Follow up with slides 6, 7, and 8 to carefully define and give examples of the three categories. At this point you can invite students to recall the climbing experience they have just completed. Make reference to the climber-subjects and their answers to the survey. Explain that soon the research teams, along with their respective subjects and members of the belay teams, will be able to complete the analysis section in their Attribution Behavior Survey.

If there is no question regarding the categories of attribution, introduce the effect of these forms of attribution behavior on one's expectancy of future success (i.e., self-efficacy), self-image, and motivation level (see slide 9).

Before moving on to slide 10, ask the class if they can guess what categories of attribution an instructor should attempt to promote. They will certainly answer "stable, internal, within our control," which is correct in most but not all situations. Explain this by reviewing slide 10.

Activity 3: Instructor Intervention Quiz

To demonstrate the notions explained on the previous slide, invite your class to take the Instructor Intervention Quiz (slides 11-12). Ask the researchers to regroup into their respective research groups. The students who were selected as subjects can also join their respective research teams. Similarly, the belayers and backup belayers can regroup themselves into their two groups.

Explain to the groups that on the basis of each scenario in the quiz, they will have to consider the "true reasons" for success or failure of the climbers and their "perceptions" before submitting their analysis of the health (i.e., healthy or unhealthy) of a climber's perception for that scenario. Finally, explain that they will also need to consider the "true reasons" in each scenario before submitting an action plan according to which the instructor would promote either a stable, internal, and controllable or an unstable, external, and uncontrollable attribution behavior.

For the quiz, you can simply take a census to find out (1) how many groups would analyze the climber's perception as healthy and how many would analyze it as unhealthy, and (2) which groups would propose that the instructor should promote a stable, internal, and controllable attribution behavior and which would propose promoting an unstable, external, and uncontrollable attribution behavior. Or you can "jazz up" the quiz by having only one group submit their answer as in a TV game show. You might then need to provide each group with a noisemaker of some kind to capture the right to respond to the scenario as soon as you have revealed the perception of the climber on the slide.

Conclude the quiz by presenting slide 13 and explaining that in brief, what we need to do as instructors is decide if we need to promote an internal or an external attribution behavior based on the student's performance and his or her perception of that performance.

Activity 4: Climbing Exercise Analysis and Interpretation

Announce that now it is time to put all of this information to good use. Introduce slide 13 and explain the following task:

- In your research team, review the Attribution Behavior Survey for the climbing experience.
- Complete the Attribution Behavior Analysis at the bottom of the page.
- Share your findings with your subject and his or her last belayer and backup belayer.

Give ample time for each research team to complete the analysis and share their findings with the subjects.

Activity 5: What Is Your LOC?

Once the analysis and sharing of findings are complete, introduce slide 14 and invite everyone to self-score his or her own locus of control (LOC) according to the Rotter scale. Ask them to tally their total score and to write it down on a small piece of paper that you will be collecting. Make sure to preserve anonymity by asking students not to place their name on the paper.

While the class is completing this task, draw a continuum line on the board, and label the left end 0, the middle 15, and the right end 29 (figure 14.1).

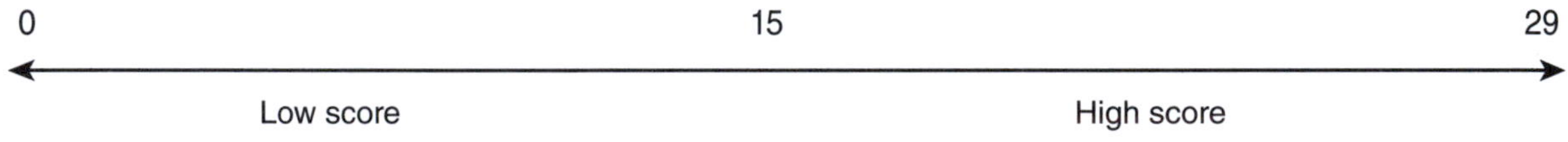

FIGURE 14.1 Rotter's locus of control scale.

When all the students have completed their tally, collect the score sheets and start placing ticks along the continuum line that correspond to the scores on the sheets. Once you have done this, explain that a high score (i.e., above 15) means a tendency toward a more external locus of control and a low score (i.e., below 15) means a tendency toward a more internal locus of control.

At this point it can be interesting to ask the students who volunteered to be the subject-climbers to comment on the analysis they received and their score on the Rotter scale. Are their peers' analysis and their LOC score congruent or mismatched? A great discussion can emerge from this comparison, so be ready to answer questions regarding the accuracy of questionnaires such as Rotter's scale, the specificity of the climbing experience in relation to the attribution behavior, or the skill required to appropriately perceive the emotional state of someone involved in an adventure activity such as rock climbing.

Activity 6: Mini-Lecture and PowerPoint on Attribution Theory, Part 2

Now that the lesson has provided practice and theory regarding attribution behavior, it is time to focus on the "So What?" part of the lesson. Introduce slide 16 and explain that research in adventure education has shown evidence that adventure programs can promote healthy attribution behavior in participants—especially if (1) the program focuses on the development of healthy attribution as an outcome, (2) the levels of challenge are appropriately selected, and (3) the program lasts more than one day.

Finally, the last slide of the PowerPoint presentation will help your class explore the "Now What?" part of the lesson. Introduce slide 17 and ask them to collectively answer this question: How do we promote healthy attribution behavior? Use some guided discovery to solicit and direct their answers.

CLOSURE

As you conclude your lesson, remind your class that understanding attribution theory and the strategies we can use to help our clients modify their behavior is an essential skill for any true professional adventure educator. Remind them that in the spirit of John Dewey, we can say that in adventure education, theory without practice is worthless, but practice without theory could be dangerous.

ASSESSMENT OF LEARNING

A formative assessment is performed throughout the lesson, especially during the Instructor Intervention Quiz (activity 3) as well as during the research teams' analysis and sharing of their findings (activity 4). For instance, by visiting each research team during activity 4, you will be able to assess if they are able to connect the theory and the experience they have recently completed. In addition, the last slide can help you assess if they are able to extrapolate, from their understanding of the theory and hypotheses, appropriate strategies to promote healthy attribution behaviors.

You can also use a more summative form of assessment the following week by giving the class a short quiz on the subject.

LESSON 15

Flow Theory

Risk Taking and Adventure Experiences

Ed Raiola and Marty O'Keefe

Adventure education practitioners must understand that we are all risk takers. But what is risky for one person may not be risky for another, and some risks are more easily taken than others (for example, physical vs. intellectual vs. emotional). Practitioners must also understand the potential that risk has for positive and negative impact on participants, the different types of risk, the role of risk in personal growth and development, and why some risks are more appealing than others. This lesson plan provides aspiring practitioners with a framework that will help them understand how to match risks and challenges for each individual to produce experiences characteristic of the flow state. Through this careful matching of risk and challenge in our programming, participants are more likely to understand how to include positive risk taking in their lives.

Background

Keyes (1985) defines *risk* as "an act involving fear of possible loss" (p. 24). Risks can be physical, emotional, or intellectual. A key component of adventure education is risk taking and the potential for loss. With reference to outdoor adventure education, people typically think of the "high-risk activities" in the physical realm as the most hazardous. Yet when one asks participants what is most risky, they may cite paddling class 5 rapids but are just as likely to cite speaking up during a conflict, sharing ideas within the group, or stepping back and letting someone else take the lead. This highlights the idea that risk is not limited to the physical realm of outdoor adventure education programming.

Why do we need risk? As Quinn (1999) states,

> So the answers to the questions, why risk, why engage the possibility of penalty and discomfort, and why approach one's personal limit, become obvious. Without actively seeking, without attempting to, and going beyond what one already knows one can accomplish, there is no growth. Strenuousness of mind, heart, and body engenders

growth. Where there is no growth, where stagnation is the rule, a human being offers nothing, either to one's self or to society. (p. 151)

Csikszentmihalyi and Csikszentmihalyi's (1999) theory of flow provides a framework for how risk taking can be done in a way that promotes healthy growth. Flow refers to "a state of experience that is engrossing, intrinsically rewarding, and outside the parameters of worry and boredom" (Csikszentmihalyi and Csikszentmihalyi 1999, p. 153). The theory outlines common conditions for the occurrence of flow and characteristics that constitute a feeling of enjoyment, well-being, and competence. The conditions conducive to the flow experience include clarity of goals, immediacy of feedback, and a balance of challenge and skills. The characteristics of the flow experience itself include a feeling of total concentration and absorption in the activity, a sense of control, a loss of self-consciousness, a merging of action and awareness, and a transformation of time. The outcomes of flow include positive affect and self-affirmation for the participant (Csikszentmihalyi and Csikszentmihalyi 1999; Csikszentmihalyi 2000; Voelkl, Ellis, and Walker 2003).

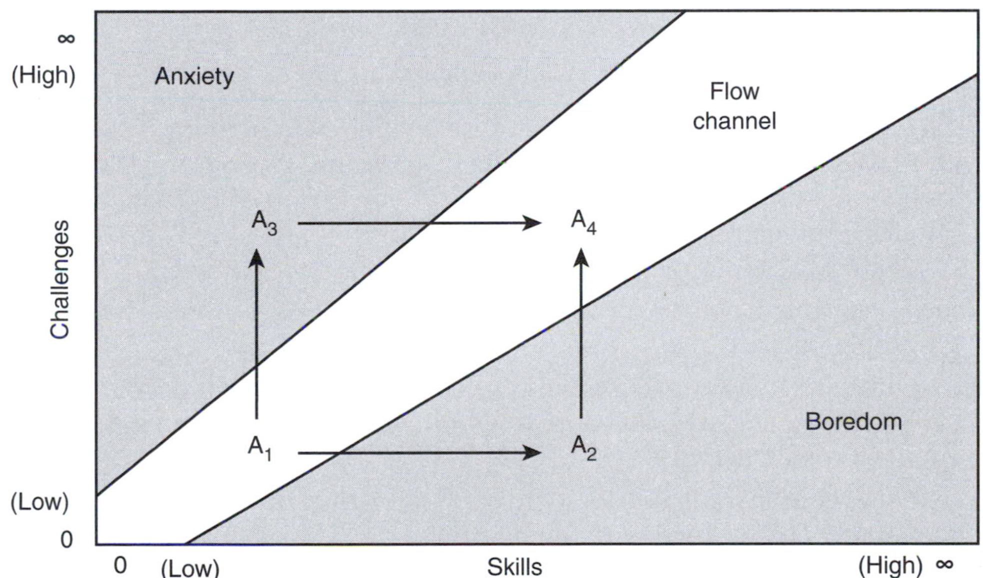

FIGURE 15.1 The flow model.

Figure (adapted), page 74 from FLOW: THE PSYCHOLOGY OF OPTIMAL EXPERIENCE by MIHALY CSIKSZENTMIHALYI. Copyright © 1990 by Mihaly Csikszentmihalyi. Reprinted by permission of HarperCollins Publishers. Also by permission of Random House Group Ltd. and Rider (U.K. and Commonwealth).

This model gives outdoor adventure practitioners a framework for matching risks and challenges for each individual to produce experiences characteristic of the flow state. Through this careful matching of risk and challenge in our programming, participants are more likely to understand how to include positive risk taking in their lives.

RESOURCES

Csikszentmihalyi, M. 1990. *Flow: The psychology of optimal experience.* New York: Harper & Row.

Csikszentmihalyi, M. 2000. The contribution of flow to positive psychology: Science essays in honor of Martin E. P. Seligman. In *The science of optimum and hope,* ed. J.E. Gilham, 387-395. Philadelphia: Templeton Foundation Press.

Csikszentmihalyi, M., and I. Csikszentmihalyi. 1999. Adventure and the flow experience. In *Adventure programming*, eds. J.C. Miles and S. Priest, 153-158. State College, PA: Venture.

Keyes, R. 1985. *Chancing it: Why we take risks.* Boston, Toronto: Little, Brown.

Quinn, W. 1999. The essence of adventure. In *Adventure programming*, eds. J.C. Miles and S. Priest, 149-151. State College, PA: Venture.

Voelkl, J., G. Ellis, and J. Walker. 2003. Go with the flow. *Park and Recreation*, 38(8):20-29.

Lesson Plan

PURPOSE

This lesson explores the role of risk in our lives, dealing with Csikszentmihalyi and Csikszentmihalyi's (1999) theory of flow and how it relates to adventure education. Topics include the various types of risk (psychological, physical, and emotional, as well as real vs. perceived) and the importance of the flow experience in adventure programming.

OBJECTIVES

As a result of this lesson students will be able to . . .

1. *Affective and psychomotor:* participate in several class activities that provide various levels of risk and then discuss in small and large group settings how each student's experience relates to the various types of risk (psychological, physical, and emotional; real vs. perceived).
2. *Cognitive:* recognize and describe the various types of risk (physical, emotional, social, spiritual; real vs. perceived) through readings, discussions, and the lesson plan activity.
3. *Cognitive:* recognize and describe the elements of the flow model and its relationship to adventure education programming through readings, discussions, and lesson plan activity.
4. *Cognitive:* demonstrate the ability to apply the principles of the flow model for use in adventure education programming.

DURATION

90 minutes

GROUP SIZE

6 to 30 students

LOCATION

Indoors

EQUIPMENT

- Whiteboard
- Dry erase markers
- Some type of timing device—a stopwatch will do
- Quotation Reaction Exercise handout (on CD-ROM)
- Multimedia classroom for the PowerPoint presentation

RISK MANAGEMENT CONSIDERATIONS

During the Constant Eye Contact activity, allow for challenge by choice. Challenge by choice allows participants to choose a level of challenge that is appropriate for them during each activity.

STUDENT PREPARATION

Students should read the Background included on the CD-ROM. Students can also read from the following sources before or after this lesson. If possible, these texts could be placed on reserve at the library.

- Csikszentmihalyi, M., and I. Csikszentmihalyi. 1999. Adventure and the flow experience. In *Adventure programming,* ed. J.C. Miles and S. Priest, 153-158. State College, PA: Venture.
- Quinn, W. 1999. The essence of adventure. In *Adventure programming,* ed. J.C. Miles and S. Priest, 149-151. State College, PA: Venture.
- Voelkl, J., G. Ellis, and J. Walker. 2003. Go with the flow. *Park and Recreation* 38(8):20-29.

INSTRUCTOR PREPARATION

Gather teaching aid materials and print the Quotation Reaction Exercise handout (on CD-ROM).

LESSON CONTENT AND TEACHING STRATEGIES

Before students arrive for class, write the following questions on the board. Students will answer the questions individually in a freewrite exercise as the lesson begins.

1. Define risk.
2. Describe a risk you are currently taking in your life and want to continue to take. What are you risking? (Typical responses include coming to college, leaving home, entering into a new relationship, moving to a new town, taking out a loan to pay for college, smoking, driving over the speed limit, participating in some type of adventure activity.)
3. Describe a risk that you are not taking and that you feel satisfied with not taking. What are you not willing to risk? (Typical responses include smoking, unprotected sex, solo free climbing, driving while intoxicated, entering into a relationship, sharing inner feelings with strangers.)
4. Think of someone you perceive as a risk taker. What about this person makes her or him a risk taker in your mind? What traits does this person possess, and what values and key fears?
5. When was the last time you took a risk, and what made the behavior or action risky?

Once students arrive, give them 5 minutes to write down responses to the questions. Once they are finished, ask them to put their responses aside and tell them that you will get back to the responses in a few minutes.

Activity 1: Constant Eye Contact

Have class members line up according to the first letter of a risk that they are currently taking as described in their freewrite. Then get them into pairs by having the line fold in half so that each person is standing across from a partner.

Once the students are in pairs, have them stand close together, toe to toe. Offer challenge by choice. (The idea behind challenge by choice is to give people options, especially when they get to a point of challenge where they may feel stressed or face self-doubt or pressure. When people can choose their own level of challenge and risk, they are more apt to get into "flow" [Csikszentmihalyi and Csikszentmihalyi 1999] and want to continue to risk and grow. If challenge is too high, they may be anxious and not want to continue; if challenge is too low, they may be bored, be unmotivated, and not do well. A possible example of a challenge by choice for this activity might be to choose to step a bit farther apart from their partners than originally requested by the facilitator.) Instruct the partners to make constant eye contact for 3 minutes without looking away, without making any physical contact, and without talking or making any noise. Keep time.

After the 3 minutes, tell the students to take a deep breath and congratulate each other; then ask them to respond as a large group to the following questions:

- Was this activity risky? How? Why?
- Why might the activity not have been risky for some of you?
- Does this experience fit the definition of risk that you came up with in the freewrite at the beginning of class?

Activity 2: Discussion

Bring the class together and ask the students for their personal definitions of risk. Write some of the definitions on the board and compare them. Then write Keyes' definition (Keyes 1985, p. 24) on the board:

> A risk is an act involving fear of possible loss.

Ask a number of students to go up to the board and write down one risk that he or she is taking now. Then ask students to categorize the risks (real vs. perceived; physical, emotional, intellectual, and so on.) Also ask the students to share one of the risks that they identified during the freewrite as a risk they are not willing to take and to explain why this is the case.

Continue the discussion by asking, "What are some risks we take every day or sometimes without thinking?" (Examples include such things as jaywalking, driving a car when the gas gauge registers empty, leaving home on a dark cloudy day without a raincoat or umbrella, operating a power lawn mower while barefoot or in sandals, smoking cigarettes, using a fork or knife to get a piece of bread out of a toaster without first unplugging it, turning electrical appliances on or off while in a bath or shower.) This question is aimed at the notion that we are all risk takers and that what is risky for me may not be risky for someone else, or the notion that some risks are more easily taken than others.

Note that when people think of adventure education they typically view the "high-risk activities" as the most challenging; yet when you ask students in this field what is most risky for them, they do not necessarily cite padding class V rapids. They associate high risk with events or actions like moving away from home, coming to college, entering into or out of a relationship, and having a family. This highlights the idea that risk is not limited to the physical realm.

Activity 3: PowerPoint on the Flow Model

As you refer to the flow model (Csikszentmihalyi 1990), use examples from either the students' experiences elicited during the previous discussions or from your own experience to illustrate the specific conditions, characteristics, and outcomes of flow. For example, if an instructor is teaching a beginning kayaking course, would she want to place the participants on a class III rapid the first time the paddlers are in the boats? No, that would not be appropriately "balancing the challenge and skills" as described under the conditions of flow. Explain what the model depicts in terms of balancing the inherent challenges of an activity with the skill level of the participant in order to avoid anxiety and boredom, with the goal that the participant enter into the state of flow. Next, use the PowerPoint slides to present the conditions, characteristics, and outcomes of flow experiences and the parallels to adventure education (on CD-ROM).

- Now ask the students to look again at the risks they are currently taking (listed on the board) and to explain how those risks fit into the definition of flow and the characteristics of flow.
- Discuss how we can plan for "flow" to happen more for us in our everyday activities or our programs.

Activity 4: Quotation Reaction Exercise

Draw a horizontal line (to represent a spectrum) on the board. Label one end, "Makes sense to me. I can buy into that statement. I can live out that statement." Label the other end, "Does not make sense to me. I cannot buy into that statement. I cannot live out that statement." Tell the students to place themselves somewhere along the spectrum (they do not have to end up at the polar ends but may choose to) after you read each quote. Read to the group individual quotes from the Quotation Reaction Exercise handout on the CD-ROM. Ask the students to indicate their reactions to the quotes by placing themselves somewhere along the spectrum. Then have individual students explain their reasons for where they are on the spectrum.

During discussion of these quotes, the following questions may prove useful as well. "What do you think of this idea of flow?"; "Is it possible to maintain flow for long periods of time?"; "Csikszentmihalyi and Csikszentmihalyi (1999) suggest that school and work should be restructured to provide flow experiences, since they take up so many years of a person's life. What would this look like?"

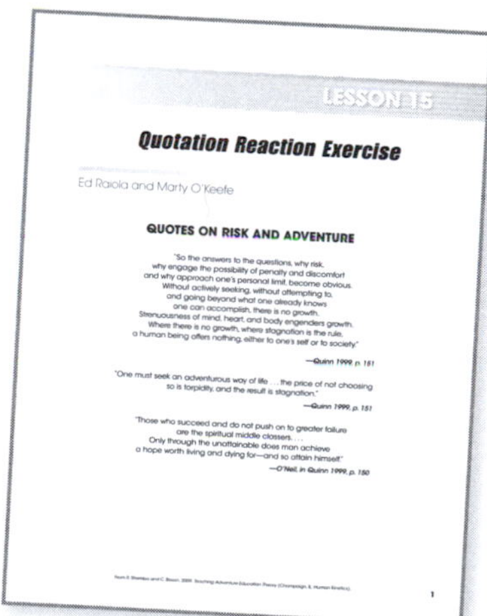
LESSON 15

Quotation Reaction Exercise

Ed Raiola and Marty O'Keefe

QUOTES ON RISK AND ADVENTURE

"So the answers to the questions, why risk, why engage the possibility of penalty and discomfort and why approach one's personal limit, become obvious. Without actively seeking, without attempting to, and going beyond what one already knows one can accomplish, there is no growth. Strenuousness of mind, heart, and body engenders growth. Where there is no growth, where stagnation is the rule, a human being offers nothing, either to one's self or to society."

—Quinn 1999, p. 151

"One must seek an adventurous way of life . . . the price of not choosing so is torpidity, and the result is stagnation."

—Quinn 1999, p. 151

"Those who succeed and do not push on to greater failure are the spiritual middle classers. . . . Only through the unattainable does man achieve a hope worth living and dying for—and so attain himself."

—O'Neil, in Quinn 1999, p. 150

1

Another option for using the quotes is to ask the students to divide themselves into groups of three and hand out copies of the quotes to each small group. Give students 10 to 15 minutes to discuss and explain why they agree or disagree with each quote. Follow up by bringing the class into a large group discussion and ask each small group to explain what they came up with. Ask the groups to first describe the author's point of view, then their own.

CLOSURE

In the final activity, students evaluate and synthesize the main points from this lesson. This serves as a powerful way to close the lesson.

ASSESSMENT OF LEARNING

In small group activities, students will recognize and describe various levels of risk and then discuss how their experience relates to the various types of risk (physical, emotional, social, spiritual; real vs. perceived).

In small and large group activities, students will recognize and describe the elements of the flow model and its relationship to adventure education programming through readings, discussions, and lesson plan activities.

In large group discussions students demonstrate the ability to apply the principles of the flow model for use in adventure education programming.

PART VI

Leadership Theories

Leadership development is a central goal for the participants in many adventure education programs and is therefore also a core piece of most academic and staff training programs that prepare adventure educators. The four lessons in this part show students how to apply models and theories to dynamic field situations so that they can implement a leadership style that best matches the situation and the group. Because adventure leaders must frequently make decisions that affect safety as well as group morale, two of the lessons also include models that help the leader raise the decision-making process to a conscious and intentional level.

In lesson 16, "Conditional Outdoor Leadership Meets Kolb's Learning Cycle," Bob Stremba shows how classroom skits and scenarios are used to examine changing conditions of favorability as described by Priest and Gass' conditional outdoor leadership theory, or COLT (2005). But the COLT model can be adapted beyond outdoor leadership and combined with Kolb's (1984) experiential learning cycle to help adventure educators prepare and teach lessons that account for how favorable the learning environment is.

Further support for a flexible leadership style comes from Denise Mitten's lesson 17, "Three Functions of Leadership Essential to the Welfare of a Group." Through a leadership conundrum experience and skits derived from reflective journal assignments, students learn that a process of shared leadership and decision making usually results in a safer trip and also that the participants have more control over the outcome because they are able to collectively own their successes and failures.

The remaining two lessons in this part employ field-based experiences and classroom role plays to focus on the decision-making elements of adventure leadership. In lesson 18, "Using Situational Leadership Theory in Decision Making," Maurice Phipps shows how the situational leadership theory developed by Hersey, Blanchard, and Johnson (2007) offers a valuable framework for diagnosing a group's needs in a given situation, choosing the right leadership style for that situation, and communicating the style effectively and positively to the group. Lesson 19, "Decision-Making Traps" by Bob Stremba, teaches Ian McKammon's (2004) material about the role of unconscious factors and heuristic assumptions in leader decisions. This lesson also underscores the connection between leadership and teaching by presenting an outcomes-based model for making decisions about when, where, and how to instruct the variety of outdoor skills included in many adventure education programs.

The overall message of these four lessons is that effective adventure educators use an examined and intentional rather than a seat-of-the-pants approach to leadership, decision making, and experiential teaching. One size does not fit all, and leaders need to flex into a style that matches the environment, the group, and the possible hazards to be encountered.

REFERENCES

Hersey, P., K. Blanchard, and D.E. Johnson. 2007. *Management of organizational behavior: Utilizing human resources.* 7th ed. Englewood Cliffs, NJ: Prentice Hall.

Kolb, D.A. 1984. *Experiential learning: Experience as the source of learning and development.* Englewood Cliffs, NJ: Prentice Hall.

McCammon, I. 2004. Decision-making strategies. Decision-making traps. In *The NOLS leadership educator handbook,* eds. J. Gookin and S. Leach, 42-48. Lander, WY: National Outdoor Leadership School.

Priest, S., and M. Gass. 2005. *Effective leadership in adventure programming.* 2nd ed. Champaign, IL: Human Kinetics.

LESSON 16

Conditional Outdoor Leadership Meets Kolb's Learning Cycle

Bob Stremba

Students learning outdoor leadership often assume that their own, often unexamined, style of leadership is natural, or that one style will fit all situations. In reality, of course, the leadership style must change as conditions of the environment and the group, for example, change. Similarly, regarding instruction and learning, the effective teacher flexes her teaching style to best respond to varying conditions of favorability in the classroom and student environment. This lesson helps students draw parallels between the conditional outdoor leadership theory (COLT) and Kolb's experiential learning cycle.

Background

An interesting scenario unfolds among a group of college students in an introductory adventure education course. As part of a lesson about the various purposes for which adventure activities are used, these students are tasked with the classic spider's web exercise, in which they need to get the group from one side of the web to the other, using each hole only once and not touching the web. Although the accomplishment of this activity mostly involves problem solving and communication, the discussion afterward slides into issues about leadership styles and the experiential learning cycle.

During the debriefing after this exercise in one case, a student described how frustrated he had been during the activity because no one took charge, and how he had wanted to jump in and tell people what to do. But he saw that most other students appeared to be content with a lot of talking, laughing, and—in his opinion—pointless conversation. This student stated that such a loose process was not how things were done on the search and rescue team of which he was a member.

CONDITIONAL OUTDOOR LEADERSHIP THEORY

The scene just described illustrates a mistake that leaders sometimes make, particularly those new to a discipline involving leadership development. In their belief, a leadership style that works effectively in one situation is the style to use in all situations. The one-size-fits-all leadership style is often the style the instructor is most comfortable with or the style the instructor has the most personal experience with. But in outdoor adventure pursuits, conditions change rapidly, groups have different levels of experience, and individuals are often developing their technical and interpersonal skills. Very little remains static. Therefore, what is called for is a flexible leadership style that responds to all these changing variables.

Priest and Gass (2005) have taken the research of Hersey and Blanchard (1982) and others to describe a continuum of leadership styles that responds to the changing circumstances or favorability of conditions occurring for the leader and her group:

> We can group these styles into three sets of pairs to define three outdoor leadership styles that form a continuum of decision making power: autocratic (telling or selling), democratic (testing or consulting), and abdicratic (joining or delegating). The autocratic style is characterized by an authoritarian approach in which you hold complete power over decision making and dictate the needed response. The democratic style involves shared decision making, with you and the group working together to solve problems. The abdicratic style is an outgrowth of the laissez-faire, or "leaving to do," approach, in which you abdicate all decision making power to the group and agree to abide by their resolutions. True dictatorial, or all-leader power, and laissez-faire, or all-group power, have limited application in outdoor leadership settings, since negotiated involvement by both parties is often a necessary part of adventure experiences, and effective leadership involves influences from both parties as well. (p. 245)

This continuum of outdoor leadership styles is illustrated in figure 16.1.

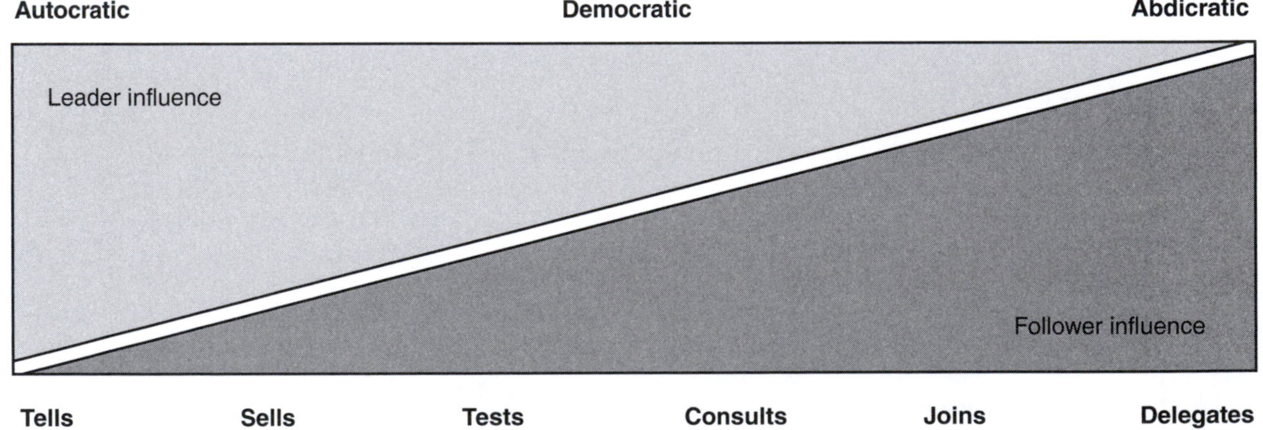

FIGURE 16.1 Continuum of outdoor leadership styles.

Adapted, by permission, from S. Priest and M.A. Gass, 2005, *Effective leadership in adventure programming*, 2nd ed. (Champaign, IL: Human Kinetics), 245.

The leadership style expressed depends on the leader's concern regarding the task to be accomplished and regarding the group and their relationships. These two dimensions, task and relationship, interact and shift in combination with five conditions of favorability, shown in figure 16.2 (Priest and Gass 2005, p. 246). This information about leadership styles (autocratic, democratic, and abdicratic),

Low Favorability	High Favorability
Environmental Dangers	
Bad weather	Good weather
Many perils and hazards	Few perils and hazards
Mostly subjective risks (not easily controlled)	Mostly objective risks (under human control)
Group	
Disintegrated and divided	Cohesive and unified
Distrustful and competitive	Trusting and cooperative
Immature and irresponsible	Mature and responsible
Individuals	
Novice members	Expert members
Incompetent, unskilled, unable	Competent, skilled, able
Unsure, inexperienced, unknowledgeable	Confident, experienced, knowledgeable
Leader	
Deficient and incapable	Proficient and capable
Lacks power base for credibility	Holds strong power base for credibility
Poor judgment, stressed out, fatigued	Sound judgment, in control, fit
Consequences of the Decision	
Problem cloudy and uncertain	Problem clear and defined
Insufficient time and resources available	Sufficient time and resources available
Challenge high with unacceptable outcomes	Challenge low with acceptable outcomes

FIGURE 16.2 A spectrum of conditional favorability.

Adapted, by permission, from S. Priest and M.A. Gass, 2005, *Effective leadership in adventure programming,* 2nd ed. (Champaign, IL: Human Kinetics), 246.

leadership orientations (task and relationship), and conditions of favorability (environmental dangers, competence of individuals, group unity, leader proficiency, and consequences of the decisions the leader is making) all combine to create the conditional outdoor leadership theory, or COLT (Priest and Gass 2005, p. 248), shown in figure 16.3.

Consider an example of a group of novice students on the third day of a 22-day mountain backpacking course, learning about outdoor skills, who arrive at a river crossing. It's early summer, midafternoon, when the runoff is increasing from the mountain snowpack upstream as the daytime temperatures rise. Water depth is above the knees of the shortest person. The river bottom has rocks of various sizes and bad runout, with fast-moving water and a fallen tree forming a strainer just downstream of the spot where the group is considering crossing. The group does

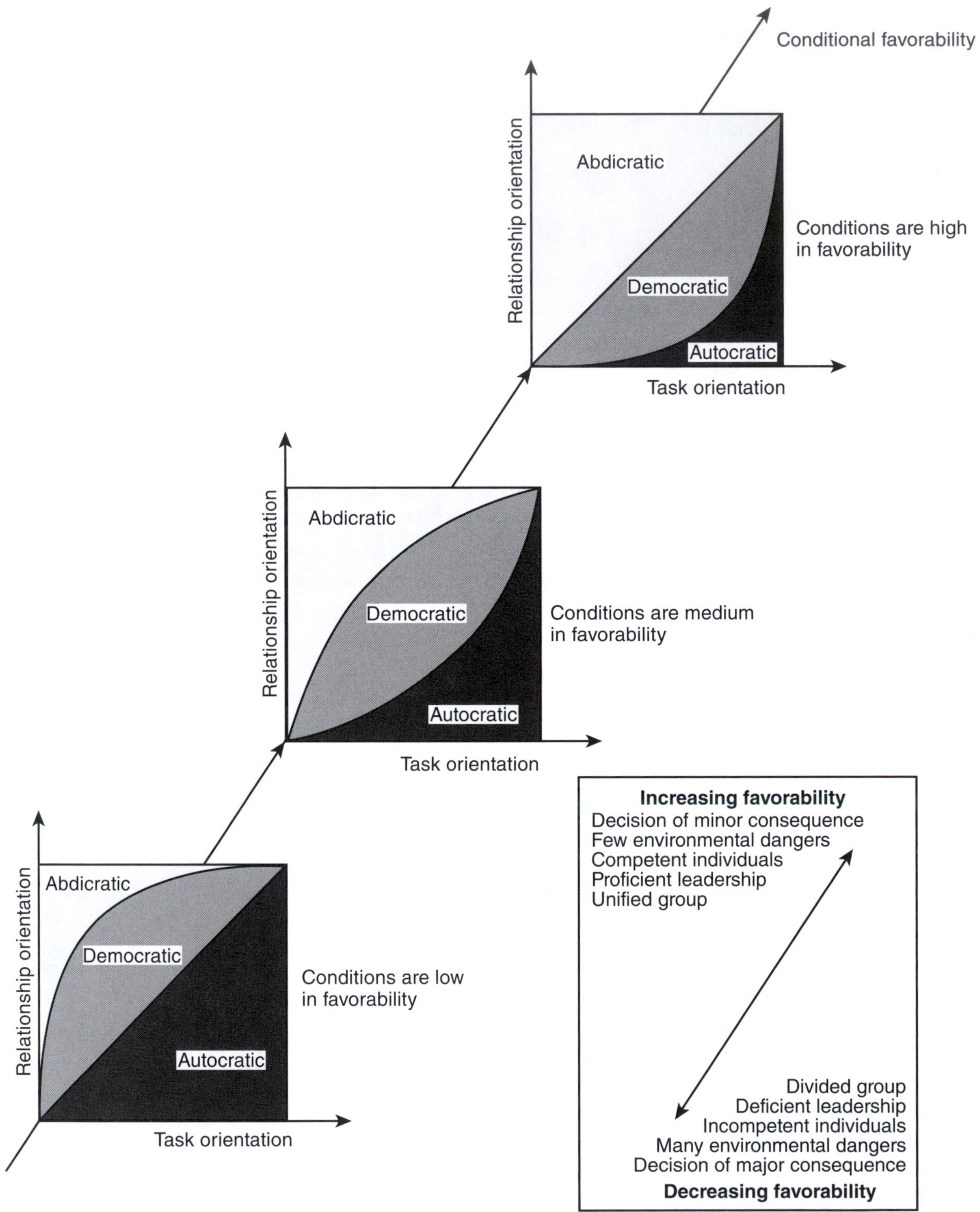

FIGURE 16.3 The conditional outdoor leadership theory (COLT).

Adapted, by permission, from S. Priest and M.A. Gass, 2005, *Effective leadership in adventure programming,* 2nd ed. (Champaign, IL: Human Kinetics), 248.

not have previous experience with judging the river conditions or with the accepted methods to safely cross a river, but they are cohesive and have been getting along well as a group. One student is serving in the role of leader of the day, and after pointing out some of the hazards, says to the group, "I think you can figure out how to cross this river." The leader then steps aside to take a seat on the river bank and watch the group try to conduct the river crossing.

This individual is using a leadership style that does not match the needs of the situation. Among the favorability of conditions, the environmental conditions are low (cold, fast-moving water), and the competence of the individuals was low (novice, unskilled and inexperienced at river crossings). However, conditions of favorability for the group—cohesive and getting along well—are high. This may give the leader a false sense of the group's competence at this new skill. The leader is using an abdicratic style that matches one high condition of favorability, but has failed to account for the bigger picture, which presents several other, lower conditions of favorability to consider. The leader may be more concerned with collaborative relationships within the group when she should be more concerned with the task of getting the novice group safely across the river. A more autocratic, or telling, leadership style is called for here, partly because the consequences of a bad decision are high—hypothermia and possibly serious injury.

Later in the day when the group has camped and is cooking dinner, a more democratic leadership style may be appropriate. By their third day out, individuals have achieved some competence with stove use and meal preparation; and with a little coaching from the leader, they are fairly well able to achieve the goal of a tasty meal while interacting amicably with one another and the leader. The principle the scenario points to is that outdoor leaders cannot anticipate every situation they might encounter, nor can they approach all situations with the same leadership behaviors. They can, however, use conditional outdoor leadership theory to evaluate most situations, utilizing their experience, judgment, and decision-making skills.

KOLB'S EXPERIENTIAL LEARNING CYCLE

David Kolb (1984) is credited with developing the learning model that forms the foundation of adventure education. The first part of this lesson, about the conditional outdoor leadership theory, is taught using Kolb's experiential learning cycle, and then serves as an example to help students understand Kolb's deductive model. Thus, the lesson uses the parallel process described in chapter 1 of this book. The instructor uses experiential methodologies, at first in the background, to teach students about the experiential learning cycle.

In Kolb's model (see figure 16.4), concrete experience precedes theory and is followed by reflection on the experience, with the group pausing to discuss or write about the experience. In adventure education, the experience can be an actual wilderness-based situation, a river crossing, for example, or it can be a structured activity or simulation that the instructor creates in the classroom. Prouty, Panicucci, and Collinson (2007) point out that the discussion or reflection then moves from replaying the experience to making generalizations from the experience. This stage is also known as *abstract conceptualization,* whereby students look back and discover patterns or principles that the current learning experience shares with other past experiences, concepts, or principles they have encountered. Finally, the critical transference or application stage invites students to apply the skills learned in the experience to other activities and situations in their lives at home, school, or work.

The element of risk, which is defined as the potential of losing something of value, is what connects Kolb's experiential learning cycle with adventure education. In this broad context, risk can involve taking a challenging college course in a

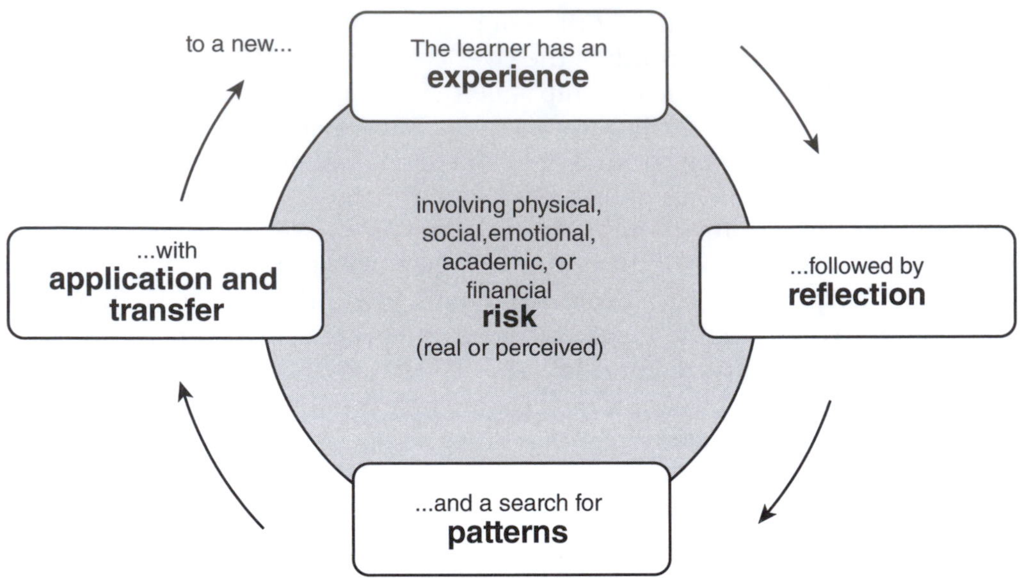

FIGURE 16.4 The experiential learning cycle.

KOLB, DAVID A., *EXPERIENTIAL LEARNING: EXPERIENCE AS A SOURCE OF LEARNING & DEVELOPMENT,* 1st, © 1984. Electronically reproduced by permission of Pearson Education, Inc., Upper Saddle River, New Jersey.

new subject, just as it can involve navigating a challenging set of rapids on a river that the person runs for the first time. Adventure educators understand that if we engage in an experience without having gone through the other components of the experiential learning cycle—reflection, a search for patterns, and application and transfer to a new experience—we have not really engaged in the experiential learning cycle. Adventure educators strive to take their students and clients through the complete experiential learning cycle.

COMBINING COLT WITH KOLB

Adventure educators serve as both leaders in the backcountry and instructors responsible for teaching skills to students. The COLT, therefore, can be adapted beyond leadership to developing and teaching lessons in the outdoors, and to some extent indoors. In learning situations, the conditions of favorability are described somewhat differently than in a leadership context, focusing on how good the learning environment is, as shown in figure 16.2 (p. 179). We still consider the revised conditions of favorability from COLT, as well as a teaching style that shifts between task orientation (how to tie a climbing rope into a harness, for example) and relationship orientation (for example, working with students in small groups).

But we are shifting away from the continuum of autocratic, democratic, and abdicratic styles of leadership and instead focusing on the instructional processes of experience, reflection, generalization, and transfer described in Kolb's experiential learning cycle. In fact, a hands-on experience, from Kolb's model, may be just the solution for the low favorability condition of students who are unmotivated or who have learning disabilities that interfere with attention behavior. However, we should not use Kolb's model to necessarily *start* with experience when conditions of favorability are low in the *leadership* context—when the situation calls for an autocratic leadership style and a lecture mode of instruction, with an experienced instructor telling inexperienced students what to do to be safe and successful. In fact, Prouty, Panicucci, and Collinson note that Kolb's cycle "can begin at any phase;

at times a particular phase can be skipped, emphasized, or minimized due to the circumstances at hand" (p. 37).

So, regarding instruction and learning, it is the teacher's expertise in using Kolb's experiential learning cycle that responds to varying conditions of favorability. In outdoor leadership situations, however, it is the leader's ability to flex among leadership styles that responds to varying conditions of favorability.

RESOURCES

Hersey, P., and K. Blanchard. 1982. *Management of organizational behavior: Utilizing human resources.* 4th ed. Englewood Cliffs, NJ: Prentice Hall.

Kolb, D.A. 1984. *Experiential learning: Experience as the source of learning and development.* Englewood Cliffs, NJ: Prentice Hall.

Priest, S., and M. Gass. 2005. *Effective leadership in adventure programming.* 2nd ed. Champaign, IL: Human Kinetics.

Prouty, D., J. Panicucci, and R. Collinson. 2007. *Adventure education: Theory and applications.* Champaign, IL: Human Kinetics.

Lesson Plan

PURPOSE

For students to be able to apply the conditional outdoor leadership theory and Kolb's experiential learning cycle to their own practice of adventure leadership and instruction.

OBJECTIVES

As a result of this lesson students will be able to . . .

1. *Cognitive:* correctly describe the conditions of favorability occurring in personal leadership situations.
2. *Psychomotor and cognitive:* enact and identify the leadership style that best matches conditions of favorability for in-class scenarios.
3. *Cognitive:* identify the components of Kolb's experiential learning cycle that match the correct parts of the lesson on conditional outdoor leadership theory.
4. *Cognitive and psychomotor:* create and teach a short lesson that uses Kolb's experiential learning cycle while taking into consideration the conditions of favorability.

DURATION

60 to 90 minutes

GROUP SIZE

15 to 30

LOCATION

Indoors

EQUIPMENT

- Two pieces of 20-foot (6-meter) webbing or ropes
- A few medium-size rocks
- One or two kitchen strainers

RISK MANAGEMENT CONSIDERATIONS

None

STUDENT PREPARATION

In preparation for this lesson, students should read the Background included with the lesson (on CD-ROM) or read chapter 18, "Flexible Leadership Style," by Priest and Gass (2005) plus pages 36 to 38 in Prouty, Panicucci, and Collinson 2007.

INSTRUCTOR PREPARATION

Set up a "river" in the classroom using two pieces of 20-foot (6-meter) webbing or ropes parallel to each other and placed 4 to 5 feet (1.2-1.5 meters) apart. Bend the webbing or rope boundaries to resemble a river bend, and place some rocks and a couple of mesh kitchen strainers to symbolize river rocks and strainers.

LESSON CONTENT AND TEACHING STRATEGIES

This lesson begins with an activity about outdoor leadership to illustrate the conditional outdoor leadership theory. This introductory activity parallels the content of the second part of the lesson, on Kolb's experiential learning cycle, by beginning an instructional process with an experience and following up with the theory illustrated by the experience.

Activity 1: Ineffective Leadership Skit

Set up a classroom "river" as just described. Select three to five students, or ask for volunteers ahead of time. Brief these students by telling them that they are part of a mountain backpacking group about to cross a river. They should gather on one "bank" of the classroom "river" and wait for further instructions about crossing the river. Instruct these students that as they attempt to cross the river, they should act as if they are struggling and ultimately get swept off their feet and float downriver. Describe the following scenario to the class:

> A group of novice students is on their third day of a 22-day mountain backpacking course, learning about outdoor skills, when they arrive at a river crossing (point out the classroom "river"). It's early summer, midafternoon, when the runoff is increasing from the mountain snowpack upstream as the daytime temperatures rise. Water depth is above the knees of the shortest person. The river bottom has rocks of various sizes and bad runout, with fast-moving water and a fallen tree forming a strainer just downstream of the spot where the group is considering crossing. The group does not have previous experience with judging the river conditions or with the accepted methods to safely cross a river, but they are cohesive and have been getting along well as a group. One person is serving in the role of leader of the day—I will play that role in the skit.

Playing leader of the day, give the group of volunteer students river-crossing directions using an abdicratic leadership style, in which decision-making power is given to the group. Point out the hazards to the group; then say something like, "I think you can figure out how to cross this river"; then step aside on the "river bank." As the group crosses the river, they should act as if they are struggling and ultimately get swept off their feet and float downriver.

Activity 2: Mini-Lecture and PowerPoint on Conditional Outdoor Leadership Theory

Explain conditional outdoor leadership theory (COLT), as described in the Background and the accompanying PowerPoint presentation (on CD-ROM). Show slides 1 and 2. Point out the axes for task orientation and relationship orientation and the continuum of outdoor leadership styles ranging from autocratic through democratic to abdicratic.

Show slides 3 through 9, and provide examples of the factors to consider in conditions of favorability—environmental dangers, condition of the group, condition of individuals, condition of the leader, and consequences of the decision. Relate these conditions to the river-crossing skit, or ask students to comment about the connections. For example, in the skit the environmental conditions were low (cold, fast-moving water) and the competence of the individuals was low (novice, unskilled and inexperienced at river crossings). However, conditions of favorability for the group (cohesive and getting along well) were high. This may give the leader a false sense of the group's competence at this new skill, with the leader using a style that matches one high condition of favorability, in the skit example, but failing to account for the bigger picture that presents additional lower conditions of favorability to consider. The leader may have been more concerned with collaborative relationships within the group when what was needed was more concern with the task of getting the novice group safely across the river.

Ask for comments in response to the following questions:

- In the skit, what was this group's level of experience?
- What were the leader's behaviors, and what style, from the continuum, was the leader using?
- Did the leadership style match the group's level of experience?

Show slides 10 through 12, and explain that the abdicratic leadership behaviors, with the leader delegating the river-crossing task to the group, did not match the conditions of favorability. This situation called for the leader to use a more autocratic, or telling, style of leadership that focuses on task completion. So there was a mismatch between the experience level of the group and the leadership style of the leader. But experience level is one of five conditions that can change, and therefore the leadership style should change with these changing conditions. In the outdoors these conditions can change rapidly, and a static, one-size-fits-all, leadership style cannot be used in dynamic, changing conditions.

Activity 3: Small Group Discussion

Have students form small groups and briefly share situations in which they have been in a leadership position. Have each small group then choose one of the shared situations and address these questions:

- What were conditions of low and high favorability?
- To what extent did the leadership style and behaviors used by the leader match the conditions of favorability?
- Which of these conditions did the leader have some control over?

- What could the leader have done to help maintain or create conditions of higher favorability in this situation?

Ask each group to report in a manner that avoids repetition, and to comment on the connections they see between their own experience and the COLT model. As the instructor you can provide examples from your own experience in which leadership changed with changing conditions of favorability.

Activity 4: Effective Leadership Skit

Using the same river-crossing scenario as before, change some of the conditions of favorability. For example, conditions of individuals can be changed from novice to moderately experienced at river crossings. The condition of the group can be changed from cohesive and unified to divided and irresponsible. Invite one student to serve as leader of the day and, based on the information he or she now has about the conditional outdoor leadership theory, use a leadership style that matches the new conditions of favorability to instruct the group in the river crossing. You can occasionally "freeze" the action and ask the class for additional ideas of leadership behaviors, or invite other students to join in as leaders of the river-crossing scenario when they want to demonstrate additional leadership strategies that best match the conditions of favorability.

Ask for comments and observations from the class regarding what the leader did differently in this scenario compared to the first one, as well as how these new leader behaviors matched the conditions of favorability better than in the first skit.

Summary statement for COLT: Outdoor leaders cannot anticipate every situation they might encounter. They can, however, use conditional outdoor leadership theory to evaluate most situations, employing their experience, judgment and decision-making skills. Then leaders should flex into the leadership style—autocratic, democratic, or abdicratic—that best matches the conditions of favorability occurring at the time.

Activity 5: Mini-Lecture and PowerPoint on Connecting COLT With Kolb

On the PowerPoint presentation (on CD-ROM), advance to slide 13 about the experiential learning cycle.

Ask students to reflect on the conditional outdoor leadership theory lesson they have just experienced. Explain that they will be deconstructing this lesson in order to learn another model fundamental to experiential education, David Kolb's experiential learning cycle.

Describe the components of the experiential learning cycle as slides 14 through 18 are shown, asking students which parts of the conditional outdoor leadership theory lesson match each component of the experiential learning cycle. (See the Background for more information.) Students should be able to point out the correlations shown in table 16.1.

Point out that risk, which is defined as the potential of losing something of value, is what connects Kolb's experiential learning cycle with adventure education. In this broad context, risk can involve taking a challenging college course in a new subject, just as it can involve navigating a challenging set of rapids on a river that the person runs for the first time.

Ask students to share examples of an experience they have had that involved risk—physical, social, emotional, academic, or financial risk.

Point out that adventure educators must understand that if we engage in an experience without going through the other components of the experiential learn-

TABLE 16.1 Relationship of Kolb's Experiential Learning Cycle to the Conditional Outdoor Leadership Theory Lesson

Kolb's experiential learning cycle components	Conditional outdoor leadership theory lesson
The learner has an *experience*	First skit illustrating ineffective leadership on a river crossing that does not properly match the conditions of favorability
. . . followed by *reflection*	Student responses to questions including "Does the leadership style match the group's level of experience?"
. . . and a search for *patterns*	Small group discussions in which students share situations relating to their own leadership experiences that illustrate conditions of favorability
. . . with *application and transfer* to a new experience.	Second skit in which students illustrate effective leadership on a river crossing that properly matches the conditions of favorability

ing cycle—reflection, a search for patterns, and application and transfer to a new experience—we have not engaged in the experiential learning cycle. Our students' jobs as prospective adventure educators is to take their own students and clients through the complete experiential learning cycle.

Explain that the conditional outdoor leadership theory can also be applied to developing and teaching lessons in the outdoors and to some extent indoors. The conditions of favorability are described a little differently to focus on how good the learning environment is.

Explain the following: For teaching and learning situations we still consider the revised conditions of favorability from COLT, and a teaching style can be used that shifts between task orientation (how to tie climbing webbing into a harness, for example) and relationship orientation (working with students in small groups, for example). But we are shifting away from the continuum of autocratic, democratic and abdicratic styles of leadership and instead focusing on the instructional processes of experience, reflection, generalization, and transfer described by Kolb's experiential learning cycle. In fact, a hands-on experience, from Kolb's model, may be just the solution for the low favorability condition of students who are unmotivated or who have learning disabilities that interfere with attention behavior. So, regarding instruction and learning, it is the teacher's expertise in using the experiential learning cycle that responds to varying conditions of favorability. In outdoor leadership situations, however, it is the leader's ability to flex among leadership styles that responds to varying conditions of favorability. Adventure educators who serve as both instructors and leaders, then, need to be familiar with both the experiential learning process and with flexible leadership styles. See the Background for more information.

CLOSURE

Ask students to form groups of three or four, or use the same small groups as in the earlier discussion exercise. Have each group choose a field instruction topic that can be taught to another small group—for example, stove lighting or tying a climbing rope into a seat harness. The group should then decide what the conditions of favorability for instruction and learning are, using the information in figure 16.2 as a guideline. Conditions of favorability for instruction and learning include, for example, the competency that students already have with the topic, the environmental conditions that are occurring, and previous experience the instructors have teaching the topic.

Each small group plans a lesson using Kolb's experiential learning cycle of experience, reflection, generalization, and transfer for a group with the conditions of favorability for instruction and learning they have chosen. Have small groups pair up, and ask each of the two groups in the pair to teach their lesson to the other group. The teaching group should first inform the learning group what the conditions of favorability are for this scenario.

After the small groups teach their lessons to each other, have students identify the connections between lesson components and Kolb's experiential learning cycle.

ASSESSMENT OF LEARNING

Assessment of learning is built into this lesson as follows:

- **Objective 1.** After experiencing the ineffective leadership style in the river-crossing scenario, students in small groups describe the conditions of favorability occurring in their own personal leadership situations.
- **Objective 2.** Through a second scenario, students enact and identify, via discussion, the leadership style that best matches conditions of favorability.
- **Objective 3.** In a reflective discussion, students identify the components of Kolb's experiential learning cycle that match the correct parts of the lesson on conditional outdoor leadership theory.
- **Objective 4.** Through planning and teaching their own lessons, students create and teach a short lesson that uses Kolb's experiential learning cycle while taking into consideration the conditions of favorability.

LESSON 17

Three Functions of Leadership Essential to the Welfare of a Group

Denise Mitten

Understanding how and when to share leadership roles is an important leadership skill. A trip is safer and the successes and failures of the experience are more readily accessible to the participants if they feel control over the outcome. Appropriate sharing of leadership jobs in the effective and psychological domains is a way to include participants more in the internal process of the trip—and, by extension, in the group accomplishments, both tangible and intangible. Through this lesson students can learn about the responsible, effective, and psychological functions of a leader and learn more about doing all three jobs as a leader as well as sharing the jobs appropriately.

Background

Three functions of leadership are essential to the welfare of a group: *responsible* leadership, *effective* leadership, and *psychological* leadership (Berne 1963; Clarke 1983).

The responsible leader is the person with a title and the person who, if anything goes wrong, is called to account by a higher authority. The responsible leader has the last word on safety issues and must constantly be mindful of safety considerations. This person has the ultimate responsibility for maintaining the goal of the trip or program. As part of the responsible leadership job, the leader is constantly monitoring the group members and thinking about the group's process.

An effective leader makes sure things get done and also may be the one who does those things. This includes taking leadership, for example, in problem solving, getting the canoes loaded, starting dinner, and teaching participants how to kayak. The effective leader gives direction, and the direction is most likely followed.

A *psychological leader* motivates group members and self, encourages and supports group members, and tends to the emotional needs of group members and self and other relationship considerations. For example, when a participant begins to climb at a climbing wall, a leader might ask, "How do you like to be supported while you climb? Would you like us to be verbal with our encouragement and tell you about holds we notice? Would you like us to be quietly attentive and add our ideas when asked? Or what?"

Outdoor leaders need to perform all three of the leadership functions during a trip. While the responsible leadership job is not shared, by the end of a program or trip the participants may be doing a large portion of the day-to-day effective and psychological leadership jobs. If so, this frees the leaders to do deeper work. For example, leaders can work one-on-one to teach more skills. The responsible leader has the job of setting the tone and direction in order for this shared leadership to occur.

Sharing effective and psychological leadership can come about organically or can be delegated (Mitten and Clement 2007). For example, after the facilitator explains an activity, a participant might jump in and suggest a plan for moving forward. Or, on a wilderness trip, a participant might say, "How about if I work on tent setup—anyone want to help?" These are examples of participants sharing the effective leadership job organically (that is, without being told). As an example of a participant's sharing the psychological leadership job, someone might say to a group member starting to climb, "Juan, how do you want support from us? We're here for you and want to honor what you think works best for you."

When participants organically share the effective and psychological leadership jobs, be sure to acknowledge and encourage this behavior. This reinforcement validates both the process and the individual group member's behavior in the eyes of other group members. For example, a leader might say, "Sally, I'm delighted that you are thinking about the jobs we need to do to set up camp tonight, and while a few other people help Sally with the tents, could Isabella and Jason help me with dinner?" Later on in the program or trip when it has become a group norm for participants to share the effective and psychological leadership jobs, the leaders will need less and less to reinforce directives given by participants.

The more the effective and psychological leadership jobs are shared, the more the program or trip and the competencies and accomplishments can be shared by all the group members. One can compare this to drafting in a bicycle club or breaking snowshoe or ski trails. Each person takes a turn at the lead so that the work of leadership is shared and everyone is involved in the trip's success.

Figure 17.1 illustrates the functions and the relationship between leaders and group members. Leaders' functions are responsible, effective, and psychological leadership, while the functions of the group members are effective and psychological leadership.

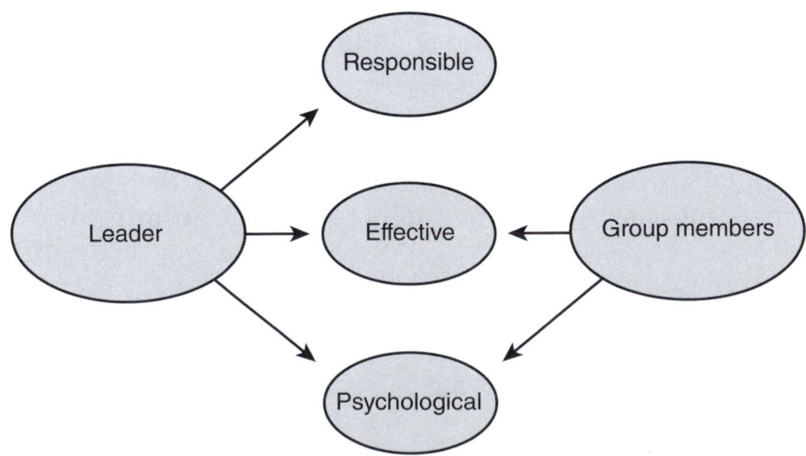

FIGURE 17.1 The three functions of leadership.

Reprinted, by permission, from Project Adventure, 2007, *Adventure education: Theory and applications* (Champaign, IL: Human Kinetics), 81.

RESOURCES

Berne, E. 1963. *The structure and dynamics of groups.* New York: Grove Press.

Clarke, J.E. 1983. *Who, me lead a group?* Winston Press.

Mitten, D., and K. Clement. 2007. Skills and responsibilities for adventure education leaders. In *Adventure based programming and education,* eds. R. Prouty, J. Panicucci, and R. Collinson. Champaign, IL: Human Kinetics.

Lesson Plan

PURPOSE

To draw on the students' past experiences and memories to aid in their understanding of the functions of leadership. This lesson also helps students experience the benefits of shared leadership.

OBJECTIVES

As a result of this lesson students will be able to . . .

1. *Affective:* listen to others and value their experiences.
2. *Affective:* feel the impact of giving voice to their thoughts.
3. *Cognitive:* recognize the need for the three types of leadership.
4. *Cognitive:* describe the three functions or jobs of a leader and be able to systematically practice them to enhance individual group and community experiences.
5. *Cognitive:* be able to select and justify appropriate leadership behavior to increase collaborative leadership among group members.
6. *Cognitive:* develop more skills in meta-cognition, specifically in being able to watch themselves as they perform leadership functions.
7. *Cognitive and affective:* use the three functions of leadership to contribute to the development of a "caring group environment."
8. *Cognitive and affective:* understand that the more the effective and psychological leadership jobs are shared, the more easily the program or trip and the competencies and accomplishments can be shared by all the group members.
9. *Cognitive and psychomotor:* understand the process of journaling through application.

DURATION

Two 50-minute sessions. Students journal between the class sessions.

GROUP SIZE

8 to 40

LOCATION

Indoors or outdoors

EQUIPMENT

- 40 fleece, tennis, or other balls less than 4 inches (10 centimeters) in diameter
- Assembled outdoor gear (the gear you might have in a base camp, including one or more tents, stove, cooking gear, and the like)

RISK MANAGEMENT CONSIDERATIONS

None

STUDENT PREPARATION

Before the class, students read the Background about the three functions of a leader.

INSTRUCTOR PREPARATION

No prelesson preparation needed

LESSON CONTENT AND TEACHING STRATEGIES

Set the stage for the first class session by describing breaking trail in the snow and how taking turns keeps one person from having to do the hard work of all the trailbreaking. If students can go out in the snow and take turns breaking a ski, snowshoe, or walking trail for each other, that would be ideal. During the other three seasons, if you have access to woods that have spider webs across the trails in the mornings, you can take turns breaking trail (getting stuck with spider webs) in that environment. If the outdoor component is not possible, tell a story about taking turns breaking trail or drafting on bicycles. Geese flying in a V-formation is another phenomenon that fits the concept. Students should get the idea that if we all take turns in the leadership position, there is less chance for any one person to become exhausted. At the same time, if all the participants are too tired to break trail and for some reason you all have to keep moving, the designated or responsible leader has to be able to break the trail.

Define and explain the three jobs or functions of a leader. After a short explanation, have students pair-share an experience they have had as a responsible leader or in a group in which there was a responsible leader. Then have students share a few examples in the large group to be sure that everyone is grasping the concept. Do the same for effective and psychological leaders. Have the students share both positive and negative experiences or examples of these three leadership concepts.

Sometimes it is hard for students to grasp the concept of only one responsible leader. For example, on an outdoor trip the head leader is always the responsible leader, even if the program uses the leader of the day (LOD) concept to give students leadership practice. Most people can understand that the head leader must remain the responsible leader because of liability issues, but the reasons are broader than liability. Participants can feel free to try new ways of being in a group, as well as new ways to be effective and psychological leaders, knowing that the responsible leader is their safety valve. Having a designated responsible leader helps keep the trip safe because the roles are clear. As an example, safety expectations and contracts cannot be changed just because the group members are in smaller groups and the responsible leader cannot be in all groups. Certain questions about safety will be referred to the responsible leader, even if the responsible leader asks for student input and opinions, again providing a safety net for the participants.

Describe organic psychological and effective leadership and how these can be recognized and reinforced by the responsible leader, as well as how the responsible leader can delegate psychological and effective leadership tasks. Organic leadership behavior occurs when a participant does an effective or psychological leadership task because she or he sees that it needs to be done rather than because she or he is told to do it. Leadership grows organically from the group members.

Activity 1: Leadership Conundrum

End this first of two class sessions with the following activity. Have the students queue up one behind another in a single-file line. Stand about 15 feet (4.6 meters) in front of the first person and face that person. Have about 40 balls 4 inches (10 centimeters) or less in diameter.

Tell the group members to walk toward you; the front person or leader must catch and hold the balls as you roll or toss them. The goal is for all the students to reach you without dropping any balls. Roll and toss balls moderately quickly so that the front-line leader has too many balls to hold.

Start over, telling the students that now they should figure how to share the leadership job of catching the balls and reaching their goal but that only one person can be out of line at a time. Usually the students will take a turn at catching a couple of balls and then quickly move to the end of the line. Then the next person will catch a couple of balls and move to the line's end. This way the students as a group will be able to catch all of the balls and reach you. Having the students stay in a line symbolizes the orderly or boundaried process of sharing leadership.

Processing Questions

- What did you see happening during this activity?
- What feelings came up for you during this activity?
- What did you think about when the line leader was getting bombarded with balls?
- How did you feel watching the line leader try to catch all the balls?
- What did it feel like to all have a part in catching the balls?
- How did having a part in catching the balls affect your task completion?

Relate this activity back to the trailbreaking example; discuss how sharing effective and psychological leadership functions can help trips run more smoothly, help all participants truly experience the success of the trip, and possibly keep the leader from becoming exhausted.

Activity 2: Journal Assignment

Have the students keep a journal between this class and the next, recording their behavior in the three leadership functions as well as behavior that they observe in others. Students should record positive as well as negative examples. Students turn in the journals before the next class so that you can determine if they are grasping the concepts. On trail, students can also keep a journal.

Activity 3: Fifteen (Plus) Ways to Be a Leader

At the beginning of the second class session, ask students to share some observations from their journal assignments.

Have students divide into groups of three to five people. Using the assembled outdoor gear, have each group prepare an in-depth skit. During the skit, each group shows at least five examples, some positive and some negative, of responsible, effective, and psychological leadership behavior (for the effective and psychological leadership, show both organic and delegated). Because they use a great deal of gear, the skits tend to be authentic and detailed and to provide clear examples. For instance, students may set up camp showing how leadership functions might be displayed. Before they perform the skit, students write out what behaviors they plan to demonstrate. Students watching the skit keep track of the leadership behaviors they see. After the skit, compare the two records.

Activity 4: Leadership Letter to a Colleague

Students write a letter to a colleague about a trip, real or imaginary, telling the colleague about at least three examples of each of the functions of leadership as they occurred on the trip. At least two of the examples should be ones that the letter writer participated in. The student can have been either a leader or a participant on the trip.

CLOSURE

The take-home message from this lesson is that if the leadership is shared in appropriate ways, students learn more about leadership, including judgment and decision making. Also a trip is usually safer, and the successes and failures are more completely shared by the participants.

ASSESSMENT OF LEARNING

- After their pair share, as students participate in discussion, assess whether they are grasping the concepts.
- Students either in small groups or as a whole can compare what the skit performers intended to share and what the watchers observed.
- Use the rubric provided in table 17.1 to assess the leadership letter to a colleague.

TABLE 17.1 Assignment Assessment Rubric

Category	4 points	3 points	2 points	Must revise
Information quality	Information is presented clearly and completely relates to the topic.	Information is presented clearly and mostly relates to the topic.	Information is presented clearly and somewhat relates to the topic.	Paper demonstrates little understanding of the material.
Examples	All examples are specific and relevant. The supporting details or examples enhance the understanding of the main concept.	Most examples are specific and relevant. The supporting details or examples enhance the understanding of the main concept.	Some examples are specific and relevant. The supporting details or examples enhance the understanding of the main concept.	Fewer than three examples are presented for each leadership job, or the examples are not relevant or are not explained well.
Clarity and expression	Ideas are expressed clearly, and the paper and its parts make sense.	One or two ideas or parts of the paper are confusing.	Some ideas or parts of the paper are confusing.	Many ideas or parts of the paper are confusing.
Organization	Information is highly organized with well-constructed paragraphs.	Information is organized with mostly well-constructed paragraphs.	Information is somewhat organized.	The information appears disorganized.
Mechanics	Paper contains no grammatical, spelling, or punctuation errors.	Paper contains almost no grammatical, spelling, or punctuation errors.	Paper has a few grammatical, spelling, or punctuation errors.	Paper has more than five grammatical, spelling, or punctuation errors.

LESSON 18

Using Situational Leadership Theory in Decision Making

Maurice Phipps

Leadership, judgment, and decision making are inseparable components of outdoor leadership. The way leaders delegate decision making to a group, as well as the way they present this transaction, relates to leadership style. Most people have a favored style—the one with which they are comfortable. But because different leadership styles are called for in different situations, leaders must learn about and practice alternative leader styles. The situational leadership theory developed by Hersey, Blanchard, and Johnson (1996) offers a valuable framework for diagnosing a group's needs in a given situation, choosing the right leadership style for that situation, and communicating the style effectively and positively.

Background

According to Hersey, Blanchard, and Johnson (2007), effective use of *situational leadership theory* is dependent on doing three things successfully: *identifying* the specific job, task, or activity; *assessing* the current performance readiness; and *matching* the leader response. *Assessing* readiness refers to a leader's making a judgment about how well the followers can do whatever the task may be; that is, the leader must answer the question, *What is this group's readiness level for this task?* Once this is determined, the leader selects an appropriate leadership style (or one could say that the leader *matches* his or her style) to communicate the decision making.

Communicating the leadership style effectively may be the most difficult of the three tasks. In this context, communication has two vital components: accuracy and positivity. The leader must take great care to portray the chosen style accurately because all leadership styles can be perceived as either positive or negative. For example, the *delegating* style can be perceived by followers as dumping. Accurate communication requires ensuring that followers perceive what the leader intends to be perceived. *Leadership style is the style that is perceived by the follower.* So if the leader perceives that she is *telling* but her followers perceive that she is *selling,* then the style in use is selling.

For communication to be positive, it should be practiced face to face, and on outdoor courses this is often accomplished when students serve as leader of the day. An open communication climate and requests for feedback will help correct inappropriately communicated styles. The leader should always speak with group members in a positive, not a denigrating, way.

Knowledge of leadership styles alone is not sufficient to enable optimum group function. A comprehensive knowledge of how groups develop and the intricacies of group dynamics will help the leader decide the readiness level of the group at a particular time. It will also help the leader decide whether some relationship decisions should have a high priority. Pushing on with the task is a natural thing and often occurs at the expense of relationship building, an important aspect of leadership. If the relationships in the group deteriorate, then deterioration in the task will quickly follow.

The decision-making process described in connection with the journal technique outlined in this lesson can be used in conjunction with the *group dynamics teaching model* (Phipps 1991) to help students understand how relationships and tasks affect readiness levels. Putting these two models together is the *experiential leadership education* systematic approach, which was originally tested through comparison of Wilderness Education Association course groups by Phipps (1986) and further tested with a case study from a NASA-Ames Research Center researcher (Irwin and Phipps, 1994). It is also documented in Phipps and Swiderski (1991) and Ford and Blanchard (1999). Both studies supported the use of a systematic approach and this journal technique.

The decision-making journal described in this lesson is a very effective technique for practicing situational leadership theory. Reviewing the journals provides a way for instructors to check the thinking processes of their students. These results can be "eyeballed" by the instructor and students or plugged into a computer program for analysis in graph form with associated statistical information if more academic depth is required. For information on in-depth analysis, consult *A Systematic Approach to Learning Leadership* (Phipps 1996). Modified Excel programs to produce the graphs and charts are available at http://paws.wcu.edu/phipps/LeadpA.html. An example of the computer analysis can be found in the article by Grube, Phipps, and Grube (2002). Situational leadership materials can be obtained from the Center for Leadership Studies, Escondido, California.

RESOURCES

Cockrell, D., ed. 1991. *The wilderness educator: The Wilderness Education Association curriculum guide.* Merrillville, IN: ICS Books.

Ford, P., and J. Blanchard. 1999. *Leadership and administration of outdoor pursuits. 2nd ed.* State College, PA: Venture Publishing, Inc.

Grube, D., M.L. Phipps, and A.J. Grube. 2002. Practicing leader decision-making through a systematic journal technique: A single case analysis. *Journal of Experiential Education,* 24(1):220-230.

Hersey, P., K. Blanchard, and D.E. Johnson. 2007. *Management of organizational behavior: Utilizing human resources.* 7th ed. New Jersey: Prentice Hall.

Irwin, C., and M.L. Phipps. 1994. The great outdoors and beyond: Common threads in leadership training on land, in the air, and in space. In *Coalition for Education in the Outdoors Research Symposium Research Proceedings.* Bradford Woods, IN: The Coalition for Education in the Outdoors.

Phipps, M.L. 1986. An assessment of a systematic approach to teaching outdoor leadership in expedition settings. Unpublished doctoral dissertation, University of Minnesota.

Phipps, M.L. 1991. The group dynamics teaching model. In *The wilderness educator: The Wilderness Education Association curriculum guide,* ed. D. Cockrell. Merrillville, IN: ICS Books.

Phipps, M.L. 1996. A systematic approach to learning leadership. Unpublished course package. Western Carolina University, Cullowhee, NC.

Phipps, M.L. 1999. Practicing leader decision-making through a systematic journal technique. In *Proceedings of the National Conference for Outdoor Leaders at Brevard,* ed. E. Raiola. Nashville, TN: Wilderness Education Association.

Phipps, M.L., J.L. Mann, and M. Ballard. 1995. The ELSA manual. Unpublished manuscript. Western Carolina University, Cullowhee, NC.

Phipps, M.L., and C.A. Phipps. 1992. Expedition leader style analysis (ELSA) in experiential leadership education. In *Conference Proceedings of the 1991 National Conference for Outdoor Leaders: Public, Commercial, and Non-Profit Partnerships in Outdoor Recreation,* eds. R. Cash and M. Phipps. Gunnison, CO: Western State College.

Phipps, M.L., and C.A. Phipps. 2003. Using the expedition leader style analysis. In *The Proceedings of the 2002 National Conference for Outdoor Leaders,* ed. Paul Brawdy. Bloomington, IN: Wilderness Education Association.

Phipps, M.L., and M.J. Swiderski. 1991. The "soft" skills of outdoor leadership. In *Adventure education,* eds. J.C. Miles and S. Priest. State College, PA: Venture.

Lesson Plan

PURPOSE

To enable students to understand the complexities of leadership and to practice leader decision making.

OBJECTIVES

As a result of this lesson students will be able to . . .

1. *Cognitive:* choose the correct style of leadership based on situational leadership theory.
2. *Cognitive:* distinguish between different individual and group readiness levels.
3. *Cognitive:* prioritize both task and relationship decisions.
4. *Cognitive:* make more informed leadership decisions using judgment and situational leadership.

DURATION

50 minutes, followed by a field trip of three days or more

GROUP SIZE

Field trip—about 10 students

LOCATION

Indoors and an outdoor field trip

EQUIPMENT

- Expedition Leader Style Analysis (ELSA) Inventory and ELSA Score Sheet (on CD-ROM)
- Colored pens—green, blue, orange, and magenta (situational leadership colors)

RISK MANAGEMENT CONSIDERATIONS

Low risk

STUDENT PREPARATION

No prelesson preparation required.

INSTRUCTOR PREPARATION

Gather the materials needed for the lesson.

LESSON CONTENT AND TEACHING STRATEGIES

To begin the lesson, students complete the Expedition Leader Style Analysis (ELSA) inventory before any theory is discussed so that a true representation of the students' favored styles emerges.

Activity 1: ELSA Inventory

Have students complete the ELSA inventory (provided on the CD-ROM) to discover their favored leadership style. The ELSA inventory (Phipps and Phipps 1992; Phipps, Mann, and Ballard 1995) involves selecting forced-choice leader decisions on 12 scenarios on a paper and pencil test that illustrates the styles with which one is comfortable and uncomfortable.

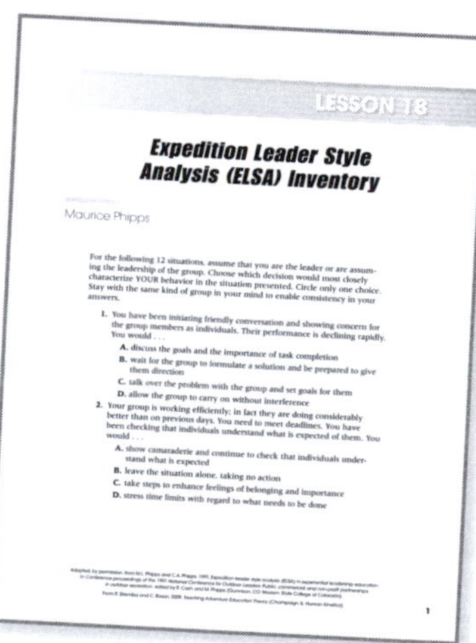
LESSON 18

Expedition Leader Style Analysis (ELSA) Inventory

Maurice Phipps

For the following 12 situations, assume that you are the leader or are assuming the leadership of the group. Choose which decision would most closely characterize YOUR behavior in the situation presented. Circle only one choice. Stay with the same kind of group in your mind to enable consistency in your answers.

1. You have been initiating friendly conversation and showing concern for the group members as individuals. Their performance is declining rapidly. You would . . .
   - **A.** discuss the goals and the importance of task completion
   - **B.** wait for the group to formulate a solution and be prepared to give them direction
   - **C.** talk over the problem with the group and set goals for them
   - **D.** allow the group to carry on without interference
2. Your group is working efficiently; in fact they are doing considerably better than on previous days. You need to meet deadlines. You have been checking that individuals understand what is expected of them. You would . . .
   - **A.** show camaraderie and continue to check that individuals understand what is expected
   - **B.** leave the situation alone, taking no action
   - **C.** take steps to enhance feelings of belonging and importance
   - **D.** stress time limits with regard to what needs to be done

1

Show the situational leadership diagram (see figure 18.1) and explain readiness levels; then explain how, once the readiness level is determined, a corresponding leadership style emerges. Emphasize that the leader must assess the readiness level of participants, select the appropriate leadership style, and communicate the style accurately and in a positive manner.

The key to leader style selection in situational leadership theory is accurate assessment of the maturity or readiness of the follower(s). Then a corresponding leadership style is chosen: *telling, selling, participating,* or *delegating.* To rate the readiness level of the individual or group, it is necessary to judge where they are in the specific task. An R1 is the least ready and a beginner to the task at hand. R1s need and want to be told how to approach the task, as in orientation to a new activity, so the *telling* style is used. The definition of readiness in Hersey, Blanchard, and Johnson's (2007) terms includes being both willing and able.

R2s are eager but sometimes not ready in that they are not yet skilled enough. They often think they are, however, so the situational leader adjusts his or her style to *selling* the decision by adding the "whys" of the decision.

R3s know what they are doing and have the skills but do not feel confident yet, so the situational leader *participates* with them.

Leaders often try to get the group to work interdependently and move to the R4 level. In this case the leader style is *delegating*—participants have the decision making delegated to them.

Give specific examples for each of the readiness levels. For example, if people are erecting a tent for the first time, it would be appropriate for the leader to use a telling style. Rock climbing with groups of different readiness levels is another example. An example using four rock climbing groups with different readiness

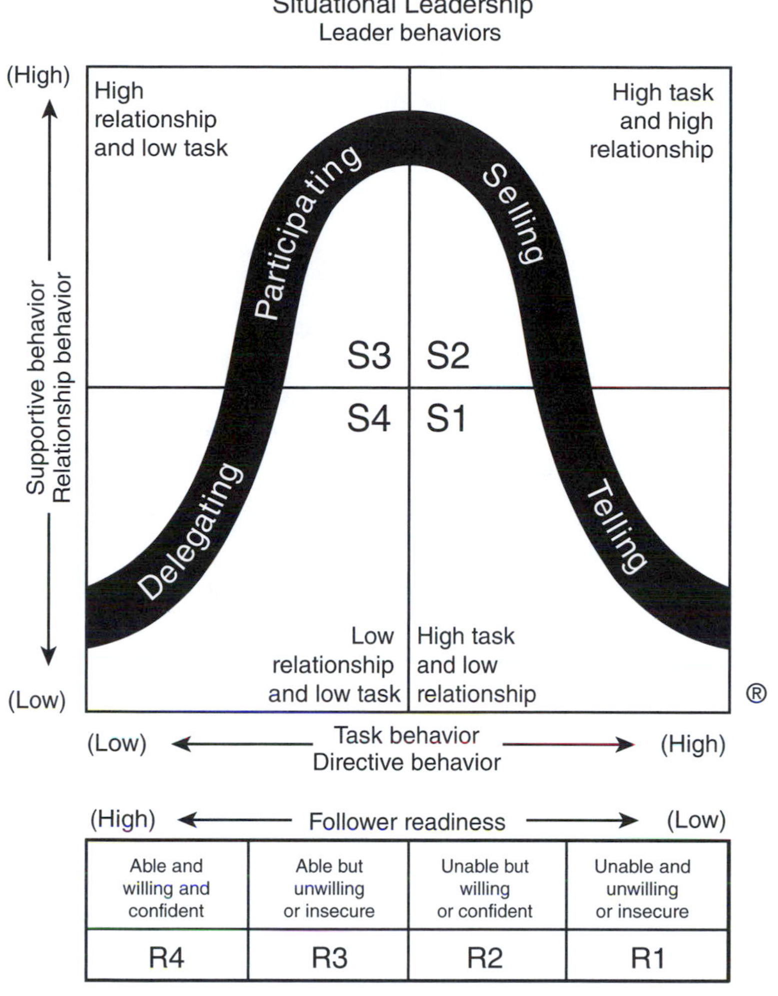

FIGURE 18.1 Situational leadership model.

levels, presented in the same format as the ELSA, will illustrate how to diagnose readiness levels in the task. These are documented in figure 18.2 with the correct situational leader style shown as the answer provided on the CD-ROM.

Activity 2: Small Group Brainstorm

Have small groups brainstorm examples of each readiness level, R1 through R4.

Caution students to beware of confusion about the term "delegating." In the model it refers to the delegating of decision making, not the delegating of a task.

Remind students that the key to the leader style choice is diagnosing the readiness level; after the diagnosis, the corresponding leadership style is used. The other critical factor is communicating that style accurately and positively; for example, telling is used not in a demeaning way but rather in an informing way. If not communicated accurately and positively, delegating can be viewed as dumping instead of entrusting.

B You are about to start a rock climbing class. The group has been out on the trip for four days and is working well as a cohesive group. This is the first day climbing for everyone. You would . . .

A. allow the group to choose anchors and belay each other
B. set up the climbs and be directive in your instruction, and closely monitor everyone
C. give explanations and a rationale for how the climbs are being set up but still be directive
D. assist the group as necessary in setting up the climbs and belaying

C You are about to start a rock climbing class. The group has been out on the trip for four days and is working well as a cohesive group. Participants have done some indoor climbing prior to the trip. You would . . .

A. allow the group to choose anchors and belay each other
B. set up the climbs and be directive in your instruction, and closely monitor everyone
C. give explanations and a rationale for how the climbs are being set up but still be directive
D. assist the group as necessary in setting up the climbs and belaying

D You are about to start a rock climbing class. The group has been out on the trip for four days and is working well as a cohesive group. Participants have had two rock climbing sessions already, including setting anchors and belay practice. You would . . .

A. allow the group to choose anchors and belay each other
B. set up the climbs and be directive in your instruction, and closely monitor everyone
C. give explanations and a rationale for how the climbs are being set up but still be directive
D. assist the group as necessary in setting up the climbs and belaying

A You are about to start a rock climbing class. The group has been out on the trip for four days and is working well as a cohesive group. The group consists of American Mountain Guide certified climbing instructors. You would . . .

A. allow the group to choose anchors and belay each other
B. set up the climbs and be directive in your instruction, and closely monitor everyone
C. give explanations and a rationale for how the climbs are being set up but still be directive
D. assist the group as necessary in setting up the climbs and belaying

FIGURE 18.2 Correct application of styles for four different rock climbing groups.

Gather the students back together and have the small groups share their brainstorming results.

Activity 3: Scoring the Inventory

Have students use the score sheet on the accompanying CD-ROM. Explain that the inventory illustrates students' favored styles and the effectiveness of the chosen styles, so an imbalance would mean that the leader needs to practice some of the other styles. Knowing one's personal preferences regarding leadership style makes one aware of and able to consciously practice the styles one tends not to favor, as well as the dominant and supporting styles. Coloring the quadrants and pie chart to match the situational leadership colors aids in the recognition of the styles. On an outdoor course, students can benefit by practicing all the styles at various times to correspond to the readiness level of the group.

Activity 4: Mini-Lecture on the Decision-Making Journal

Emphasize that instead of settling on a leadership style from a "gut level" perspective, students can practice the situational leadership model using a field journal technique (Phipps 1999). The journal layout is shown in figure 18.3 (also provided on the CD-ROM). The four most important decisions of the day, on a course of about eight days, or of sections such as morning, afternoon, and evening for shorter courses (using 12 decisions a day), should be documented. Students will need time to complete journal entries. However, they need to write down only enough information to enable the instructor to understand the decisions being recorded.

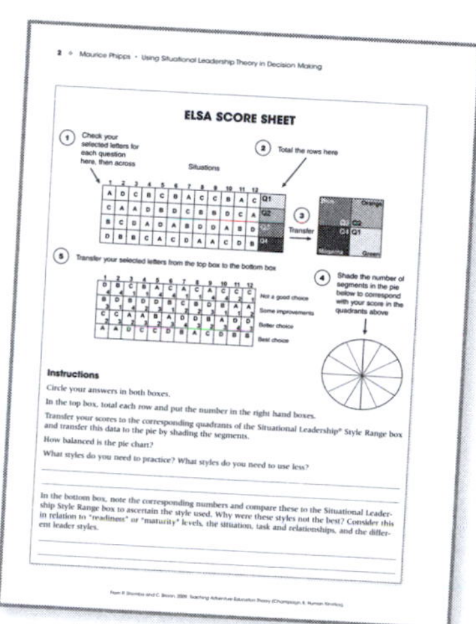

2 • Maurice Phipps • Using Situational Leadership Theory in Decision Making

ELSA SCORE SHEET

① Check your selected letters for each question here, then across

② Total the rows here

Situations

1	2	3	4	5	6	7	8	9	10	11	12	
A	D	C	B	C	B	A	C	C	B	A	C	Q1
C	A	A	D	B	D	C	B	B	D	C	A	Q2
B	C	D	A	D	A	B	D	D	A	B	D	Q3
D	B	B	C	A	C	D	A	A	C	D	B	Q4

③ Transfer →

Q2 Q3 Q4 Q1

⑤ Transfer your selected letters from the top box to the bottom box

1	2	3	4	5	6	7	8	9	10	11	12	
D	B	C	B	A	C	A	C	A	C	C	C	Not a good choice
B	D	B	D	D	B	C	B	D	B	A	A	Some improvements
C	C	A	A	B	A	D	D	B	A	D	D	Better choice
A	A	D	C	C	D	B	A	C	D	B	B	Best choice

④ Shade the number of segments in the pie below to correspond with your score in the quadrants above

Instructions

Circle your answers in both boxes.

In the top box, total each row and put the number in the right hand boxes.

Transfer your scores to the corresponding quadrants of the Situational Leadership® Style Range box and transfer this data to the pie by shading the segments.

How balanced is the pie chart?

What styles do you need to practice? What styles do you need to use less?

In the bottom box, note the corresponding numbers and compare these to the Situational Leadership Style Range box to ascertain the style used. Why were these styles not the best? Consider this in relation to "readiness" or "maturity" levels, the situation, task and relationships, and the different leader styles.

Date ____________________

Choose the four most important decisions that you as a leader made each day or during each course section.

DECISION 1

Describe the situation.

What did you do as the leader? (Or, what would you have done as the leader?)

Why did you do this? (Or, why would you have done this?)

How did you implement this decision? (Or, how would you have implemented this decision?)

continued ▶

▶ **FIGURE 18.3** Decision-making journal page format.

Reprinted, by permission, from M.L. Phipps, 1999, Practicing leader decision-making through a systematic journal technique. In *Proceedings of the National Conference for Outdoor Leaders at Brevard,* edited by E. Raiola (Nashville, TN: Wilderness Education Association).

continued ▶

Circle the participant readiness level at the time of the decision.

R4 **R3** **R2** **R1**

Circle the corresponding leadership style used.

S4 Delegating **S3 Participating** **S2 Selling** **S1 Telling**

Was this decision related to task or relationship or both? Circle your choice.

T **R** **Both**

DECISION 2

Describe the situation.

What did you do as the leader? (Or, what would you have done as the leader?)

Why did you do this? (Or, why would you have done this?)

How did you implement this decision? (Or, how would you have implemented this decision?)

Circle the participant readiness level at the time of the decision.

R4 **R3** **R2** **R1**

Circle the corresponding leadership style used.

S4 Delegating **S3 Participating** **S2 Selling** **S1 Telling**

Was this decision related to task or relationship or both? Circle your choice.

T **R** **Both**

DECISION 3

Describe the situation.

What did you do as the leader? (Or, what would you have done as the leader?)

▶ **FIGURE 18.3** *(continued)*

Why did you do this? (Or, why would you have done this?)

How did you implement this decision? (Or, how would you have implemented this decision?)

Circle the participant readiness level at the time of the decision.

R4 **R3** **R2** **R1**

Circle the corresponding leadership style used.

S4 Delegating **S3 Participating** **S2 Selling** **S1 Telling**

Was this decision related to task or relationship or both? Circle your choice.

T **R** **Both**

DECISION 4

Describe the situation.

What did you do as the leader? (Or, what would you have done as the leader?)

Why did you do this? (Or, why would you have done this?)

How did you implement this decision? (Or, how would you have implemented this decision?)

Circle the participant readiness level at the time of the decision.

R4 **R3** **R2** **R1**

Circle the corresponding leadership style used.

S4 Delegating **S3 Participating** **S2 Selling** **S1 Telling**

Was this decision related to task or relationship or both? Circle your choice.

T **R** **Both**

FIGURE 18.3 *(continued)*

The journal technique forces students to think as a leader on a continual basis, not just when they are leader of the day. Have students complete four or 12 journal entries each day by prioritizing the situations and choosing the most important decisions of the day. These decisions have to be leader decisions, affecting someone else or the group, not personal decisions like deciding to brush one's teeth.

A journal entry should be a description of the student's own leader decision making, not a critique of someone else's decision making. Instructors should discuss the decisions regularly both with the individuals and with the group. Instructors can ask such questions as "What was the readiness level of the group in that situation?"; "Does the leadership style used match that readiness level?"; "Why prioritize that situation?"; and (at times when students forget to do any relationship decisions) "What about doing some relationship decisions; were they not important?"

The journal needs to include sufficient detail that the instructor can understand the information. Too much journal writing on an outdoor course can be demotivating, especially on hard days and late nights. This suggested format is highly practicable, yet gets to the essence of what we as instructors want, to see what students are actually thinking and look at their decision making for the entire course.

Practice is critical for gaining comfort in using less favored leadership styles. Getting sufficient leadership practice during a course can be a problem if the student is leader of the day only one or two times. During an outdoor course, group members who are not leader of the day or an instructor may tend not to pay attention to the decision-making and leadership processes that are occurring. But effective leaders-in-training must always be monitoring the group and situation, diagnosing the readiness levels, adapting leadership styles, and so forth. As the instructor, you need to get everyone on the course to be constantly "switched on," practicing the selecting of appropriate leadership styles all the time.

CLOSURE

The key to success in getting the situational leadership theory across and practicing it effectively in real situations, as well as in students' heads through the journal technique, is the selection of the readiness level, the diagnosis of where everyone is with regard to the task and the situation. Refer to figure 18.1 to check these readiness levels and styles in relation to the model as a whole. To help with the diagnosis of the readiness levels, Hersey, Blanchard, and Johnson detail some specific behaviors in *Management of Organizational Behavior: Utilizing Human Resources*. Remind students that this diagnosis is the key to selecting the most effective style to motivate their followers. During pouncing, common questions concerning readiness are "What R level was the group at during that particular task, R1, R2, R3, or R4?" and "What behaviors were they exhibiting that enabled you to make that judgment?"

ASSESSMENT OF LEARNING

- Students' journals demonstrate their learning.
- The procedure of selecting individual students and checking their thinking is called *pouncing*. This assessment technique motivates students to continually think as a leader instead of taking the day off when they are not leader of the day. If the students know they will be pounced at any time and will be given feedback on their leader decision making, then they will keep

the journal regularly. Effective pouncing helps students analyze readiness levels, appropriate styles, the importance of certain styles, the importance of relationship decisions as well as task decisions, and the importance of some decisions in relation to others. All this helps students analyze more and think more critically.

LESSON 19

Decision-Making Traps

Bob Stremba

Outdoor leaders are constantly taking in information and making decisions based on that information. This lesson explores how the processes of decision making by outdoor leaders can be unconsciously influenced by a variety of decision-making traps. These traps are associated with common decision-making strategies based on heuristics, analysis, expertise, and random choice. The lesson presents an outcomes-based model as a process for making decisions about broader curricular questions, such as when, where, and how to instruct the variety of outdoor skills that are typically part of outdoor leadership courses.

Background

Put yourself into the following scene. It's day 5 of a seven-day backcountry expedition that you are coinstructing as part of an adventure education program or course. This is the second of three backcountry expeditions for the course. You have established a leader of the day (LOD) routine, and today two students are leading your group of 11 (including two instructors) on a route covering 8 or 9 miles in mountainous terrain. It's a warm fall day, but you and your coinstructor have noticed signs of a weather change. The students have previously had instruction in map reading and compass navigation, including declination, and some instruction in mountain weather patterns. The group gets to a trail junction, where they have a choice of two trails—Bog Brook Trail and Rainbow Trail. The trails are about 20 degrees apart, and the magnetic declination in this part of the country is 18 degrees west.

At the trail junction, the LODs ponder the maps and take a compass reading, and other group members add their opinions, sometimes strongly, about which trail to take. The following conversation unfolds among the LODs and other students (designated S 1, S 2, etc.). The coinstructors take notes on the conversation but are not involved in it; they will use these notes as material for a subsequent debriefing about decision making.

S 1: [Looks at LODs and asks] "Which trail do we take?"

LOD 1: "The blazes are this way." [pointing to Bog Brook Trail]

S 2: [Looking at a map] "We want to head north."

S 1: "Both trails connect with the Appalachian Trail."

S 3: "That sign over there says 'Rainbow Trail,' but the arrow on the sign sort of looks like it's pointing between the two trails."

S 2: "Signs can be ambiguous."

LOD 2: "I'm going to check this out." [Scouts a few yards up Rainbow Trail, then returns to the group]

LOD 1: [To LOD 2, who has returned from scouting Rainbow Trail] "Any blazes?"

LOD 2: "No."

S 3: "The blazes go this way. And this trail has more use, and it's wider." [Pointing down Bog Brook Trail] "I think we should go this way."

S 1: "I agree."

Pause here for a moment. What assumptions are the students making, and what experience might they be basing these assumptions on? The conversation at the trail junction continues.

LOD 2: "Let's look at a compass." [Takes out a compass] "This trail's going north, and we need to go north." [Pointing down Bog Brook Trail]

The students decide to take Bog Brook Trail. Within a half mile they meet a large group of other hikers coming from the other direction. The students ask this other group where they are coming from and where they are going. The other group says they are going to Rainbow Trail—the other option back at the junction from which the student group has just come.

S 1: "Hmm. If they're going to Rainbow Trail, isn't that where we should be going?"

LOD 2: [Looks at the compass and takes a hasty and imprecise bearing to try to determine which direction the trail they have been following is heading] "This trail is still heading in the right direction." [Pointing down Bog Brook Trail]

S 2: "We need to get this right, guys! We should go the other way!"

After some further discussion, the group turns around, goes back to the trail junction, and heads up Rainbow Trail, which is the correct choice. A half mile up the trail, they take a break in a clearing off-trail, sit down in a circle, and use their notes on the conversation to debrief the decision-making process.

What are some decision-making traps occurring here? How might students use this field situation to learn more about decision making?

INTRAPERSONAL AND INTERPERSONAL PROCESSES IN DECISION MAKING

Ian McCammon (2004) explains that decision-making strategies describe how people take in information and turn it into a decision. Decision-making styles, on the other hand, describe how a group interacts in coming to a decision. So, in the decision-making process, an interaction between intrapersonal process (strategies) and interpersonal process (styles) is going on.

McCammon further points out that we like to think of ourselves as basically unbiased. We believe that the way we perceive the world is pretty much the way it really is, the way everybody else also perceives it. But our perceptions are at least partially formed by subjective factors like our own experiences and expectations, our perceptions of our own skill level, our confidence, our unconscious insecurities, and the way we want to be perceived by others. In short, a lack of awareness of interpersonal and intrapersonal issues can create a huge blind spot in decision making for the outdoor leader.

The sometimes unconscious intrapersonal processes of decision making, then, can lead the outdoor leader into a variety of traps. The group at the trail junction, for example, used a heuristic decision-making strategy that led them into a familiarity trap. They decided to take the wider trail that had blazes, because a wide trail with blazes was familiar to them. Perhaps they were thinking unconsciously, "Most trails we have been on have had blazes. This new trail also has blazes; that other trail has no blazes. Therefore, our trail must have blazes."

Table 19.1 outlines some common decision-making strategies along with the decision-making traps associated with each. For a more detailed description and examples of the decision-making traps, the reader is directed to the McCammon article, available in the referenced NOLS publication.

The decision-making process involves a number of unconscious processes. The traps are often unconscious because it is uncomfortable to look at intrapersonal issues such as a need to be liked (expert halo) or to acknowledge that we made a wrong decision earlier (consistency trap). So, elevating unconscious thought processes to consciousness is a useful tool for training outdoor leaders about decision making.

TABLE 19.1 Decision-Making Strategies With Associated Decision-Making Traps

Decision-making strategies	Decision-making traps
Heuristic Simple rules of thumb, convenient for novices	a. Familiarity trap b. Acceptance trap c. Consistency trap d. Expert halo trap e. Scarcity trap f. Social proof trap g. Rules trap
Analytic Goals clear and defined; complete information available; leader's experience sufficient for separating relevant from irrelevant factors	a. Quantification trap b. Right answer trap
Expertise Based on real experience and knowledge; common themes recognized	a. Unconscious-incompetent trap b. Challenge/boredom trap c. Popularity trap d. Certainty trap e. Harmony trap
Random choice Short time, minimal consequences, similar outcomes	a. Positive outcome trap b. Gambler trap c. Illusory causation trap d. Control paradox trap

ADDING THE ACCIDENT EQUATION TO DECISION-MAKING TRAPS

Alan Hale (1983) proposed an *accident equation,* in which the potential for an accident is the result of the interaction between human hazards and environmental hazards. Human, or subjective, hazards include attitudes, behaviors, and skills (or lack of skills). Environmental, or objective, hazards, include the places in which the program operates, the activities undertaken, and the equipment used.

Combining Hale's accident equation with an understanding of McCammon's decision-making traps yields an assessment tool that can be applied in the field. Before making a decision that will affect a group of students or clients, the outdoor leader can ask herself some questions. Better yet, she can have a discussion with her coleader about these questions:

1. What human and environmental hazards are present? How dangerous is this situation for this group?
2. Which decision-making traps might be present? What are the unconscious factors that can obscure our ability to see the hazards? (Of course, lack of conscious awareness may in itself obscure the leader's ability to identify these unconscious factors.)
3. How do the hazards and the decision-making traps combine to suggest the best decision in this situation with this group at this time?

Applying this question sequence back to the scene at the trail junction, an experienced leader would see two potential hazards. The fact that students are still learning their map and compass navigation skills suggests a human hazard, and the changing weather presents a possible environmental or objective hazard that could affect the group. We've already noted the presence of the familiarity trap. Perhaps the acceptance trap is operating as well; that is, students will sometimes not question a popular peer, LOD, or instructor even in the face of ample evidence that the person is wrong.

So, we have a human hazard, an impending environmental hazard, and one or two decision-making traps. McCammon (2004) suggests counting the number of hazard clues present, then adding this sum to the number of decision-making traps that could exist, in order to provide new insights about risk taking. Decision making is seldom a linear, logical process; and the third question regarding how the hazards and decision-making traps combine may allow exploration of some of the more qualitative dimensions of decision making. Perhaps in some situations the number of hazards and the number of decision-making traps should be multiplied rather than added together.

Let's apply these three questions to another, more technical outdoor situation with higher consequences. A group of individuals new to winter mountain travel relies for guidance on one of their members who does a lot of recreational rock climbing but lacks an avalanche assessment background. There are at least two human hazards here. The group traverses a fresh snow slope under a new cornice while traveling on cross-country rather than metal-edged backcountry skis; this presents, perhaps, three environmental hazards. To complicate matters, a half hour earlier the group saw three other skiers successfully travel this very route.

Hopefully, this combination of an unskilled leader with novice individuals in a risky environment would not exist in an educational program. But, the example does illustrate the interaction of decision-making traps and the accident equation. This group is falling into the social proof trap because they have just seen others engaged in the activity and thus perceive the risk to be low ("Nothing happened to them, so it must be safe for us"). The individuals and their "leader" are also in the unconscious incompetent trap because they don't know what they don't know. And the positive outcome trap may have grown out of the social proof trap because they assume that positive outcomes are more likely than negative ones ("I'll never get buried in an avalanche"). What's more, the leader himself has fallen into the expert halo trap, or the students perceive the leader in such a way as to place the expert halo on him. This trap is the tendency to ascribe skills and knowledge to someone in one domain when the person shows expertise in another ("This person is a 5.12 climber, so he must know how to navigate in avalanche terrain").

An experienced leader analyzing this situation would identify the human and environmental hazards. In addition, she would see four decision-making traps, for a total of eight or nine factors, adding up to a poor decision-making process. Throwing in the fact that this group really is not conscious of many of the issues that are operating, perhaps we should multiply rather than add the hazards and traps together; this results in a higher number, showing the added flaws in a decision-making process for such a group.

TEACHING STUDENTS DECISION MAKING IN THE FIELD

Instructors of the group in the trail junction scenario told the students at the beginning of the course that as they gained experience the instructors would be less involved in helping them make decisions. Students would get to experience the consequences—success, inconvenience, annoyance—of their decisions. Instructors told them in advance that they might not intervene when the students made a low-stakes "wrong" decision, but that they would clearly say something when the student group was about to make a decision that had high-stakes consequences. In the trail junction dilemma, the instructors stood aside and took notes on the conversations, aware that the worst thing that could happen was that the group would be hiking 8 or 9 miles in the wrong direction, maybe in darkness and rain. The group was well equipped to endure this challenge if they had to. After the LODs corrected their initial errors and returned to the junction to choose the correct trail, the group took a break to debrief the decision-making process. An hour or two was lost, but the students learned through direct experience about assumptions; decision-making traps; and the value of becoming very precise in map reading, applying magnetic declination, and compass skills. To paraphrase Paul Petzoldt, we learn good decision making by first making some wrong decisions.

A proactive variation of the three-question process is described by McCammon. In a "premortem" decision-making test, the group tests a decision that is about to be implemented by imagining the decision or plan failing. In this imagined aftermath of the failure, people point out the hazard clues they missed, along with the decision-making traps that would more likely be evident afterward. Then the group leader asks the question, "What experiences are we basing this decision on?" The group should be identifying domain-specific experiences, rather than gut feelings based on no similar experience.

The three questions listed earlier can be part of the decision-making debriefing process, and, along with the premortem test, can then be used by students before they make subsequent decisions. Thus, the experiential learning cycle has progressed from the initial experience (a "wrong" decision) through the stages of reflection and generalization (the debriefing) to application of the three questions to a new decision-making experience. Educating students to recognize and avoid heuristic and other decision-making traps provides a common language for debriefing and teaching outdoor leaders.

OUTCOMES-BASED MODEL FOR DECISION MAKING

We have been exploring some of the interpersonal and intrapersonal dimensions of decision making and how to bring these ideas into adventure leadership education. But how can this help one learn about decision making within the broader context of the mission and goals of the program for which one is instructing? This raises curricular questions, such as when, where, and how instructors can teach the variety of technical, educational, leadership, human, and professional skills expected. Many programs, such as Outward Bound, use outdoor technical and expedition activities as a means for promoting broader goals of character development.

Consider the following scenario. When planning a nine-day backpacking-based wilderness course, some students notice how close the contour lines are on the map of the desert and canyon region they will be traveling through. The rock climbers in the group salivate at this topographic relief, shifting their focus now to climbing opportunities. But the course objectives focus on expedition travel, human skills (i.e., expedition behavior), professional skills, and to some extent leadership skills. Does recreational climbing fit into these outcomes?

We can begin by specifying the desired outcomes, with the goal of providing experiences that take students to higher levels of mastery within each outcome set. Outcome sets include the following:

- Technical skills
- Educational (instructional) skills
- Leadership skills
- Human skills (i.e., expedition behavior)
- Professional skills
- Foundational (conceptual) skills

Then the course instructors and students can make decisions about the activity, site selection, and timing that best support the delivery of those outcomes. Outward Bound West (2004) includes some of these questions in a course management model provided to instructors. A question that adventure educators and outdoor leaders can ask themselves frequently is, "Will this decision (about activity, site, timing, etc.) best help meet the desired outcomes (educational objectives) of our course, program, or organization?"

SUMMARY

Those learning outdoor leadership benefit from opportunities to make real field-based decisions; experience the positive and negative, but not fatal, consequences of those decisions; and then look back at both the domain-specific and unconscious intrapersonal factors related to their decisions. Decision-making strategies are often based on heuristics, analysis, expertise, and random choice; and each of these strategies is useful when thoughtfully engaged in. But each strategy also brings with it some traps that the leader can fall into unknowingly. Raising awareness of these traps to a conscious level, through openness and debriefing, can provide the student adventure leader with an ongoing process to make more informed subsequent decisions.

RESOURCES

Hale, A. 1983. Safety management for outdoor program leadership. Unpublished manuscript.

McCammon, I. 2004. Decision-making strategies. Decision-making traps. In *The NOLS Leadership Educator Handbook*, eds. J. Gookin and S. Leach, 42-48. Lander, WY: National Outdoor Leadership School.

Outward Bound West. 2004. *Field staff manual.* Outward Bound: Golden, CO.

Priest, S., and M.A. Gass. 2005. *Effective leadership in adventure programming.* 2nd ed. Champaign, IL: Human Kinetics.

Lesson Plan

PURPOSE

For students to understand a model of field-based decision making so that as outdoor leaders they can make decisions that avoid common heuristic traps.

OBJECTIVES

As a result of this lesson students will be able to . . .

1. *Cognitive:* describe orally or in writing the heuristic decision-making traps in a provided scenario.
2. *Cognitive:* describe how a field-based decision will best help meet the educational, human, and technical skill outcomes of an adventure program.
3. *Psychomotor and cognitive:* in a field-based leadership situation, assess hazard cues and decision options, describe unconscious factors that can obscure one's ability to see the hazard cues, and implement a decision that minimizes hazards and heuristic traps.

DURATION

Approximately 1 hour in class. This lesson can be extended into the field through, for example, a multiday backpacking trip in which students rotate through leadership responsibilities.

GROUP SIZE

Up to 30 students

LOCATION

Indoor class with the option of field-based implementation and discussion

EQUIPMENT

- Handout: Decision-Making Traps in Outdoor Leadership (on CD-ROM)
- Any topographic map
- Compass

RISK MANAGEMENT CONSIDERATIONS

If the lesson includes an optional field-based experience that will allow students to assess and implement their decisions, the instructor should inform them in advance that she may not intervene when the students make a low-stakes "wrong" decision, but that she will clearly say something when they are about to make a decision that has high-stakes consequences.

STUDENT PREPARATION

1. Students should read the Background included with this lesson (on CD-ROM) or pages 42 to 48 in J. Gookin and S. Leach, 2004, *The NOLS Leadership Educator Handbook* (Lander, WY: National Outdoor Leadership School.)
2. On the basis of this reading, students should write a two- to three-page reaction paper that critically examines two decisions they have observed leaders make during a backcountry or field-based expedition, including how the decision-making processes relate to at least three of the models, strategies, and so on discussed in all the readings.

INSTRUCTOR PREPARATION

Provide the decision-making handout (on CD-ROM) to students, either electronically or as hard copies.

LESSON CONTENT AND TEACHING METHODS

To focus on the purpose of the lesson, pose the following key questions:

- What are some of the unconscious factors behind field-based decision-making processes?
- How can outdoor leaders use a sound decision-making process?

Activity 1: Leadership Role Play

Invite five students to assist with the scenario provided in the Background for this lesson. The roles these students will enact are two leaders of the day (LODs) and three students on a backpacking trip. ("S 1" is student number one, "S 2" is another student, and so forth. "LOD" denotes each of the two students role-playing the leaders of the day.) The rest of the students should fishbowl the scenario, focusing particularly on the LODs. Ask the fishbowl observers to focus on what they think the decision-making traps in the scenario are. You may want to draw a diagram of the trail junction on a blackboard or whiteboard.

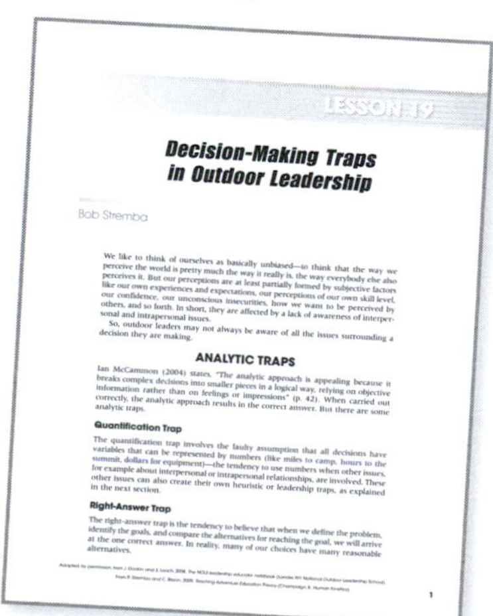

LESSON 19

Decision-Making Traps in Outdoor Leadership

Bob Stremba

We like to think of ourselves as basically unbiased—to think that the way we perceive the world is pretty much the way it really is, the way everybody else also perceives it. But our perceptions are at least partially formed by subjective factors like our own experiences and expectations, our perceptions of our own skill level, our confidence, our unconscious insecurities, how we want to be perceived by others, and so forth. In short, they are affected by a lack of awareness of interpersonal and intrapersonal issues.

So, outdoor leaders may not always be aware of all the issues surrounding a decision they are making.

ANALYTIC TRAPS

Ian McCammon (2004) states, "The analytic approach is appealing because it breaks complex decisions into smaller pieces in a logical way, relying on objective information rather than on feelings or impressions" (p. 42). When carried out correctly, the analytic approach results in the correct answer. But there are some analytic traps.

Quantification Trap

The quantification trap involves the faulty assumption that all decisions have variables that can be represented by numbers (like miles to camp, hours to the summit, dollars for equipment)—the tendency to use numbers when other issues, for example about interpersonal or intrapersonal relationships, are involved. These other issues can also create their own heuristic or leadership traps, as explained in the next section.

Right-Answer Trap

The right-answer trap is the tendency to believe that when we define the problem, identify the goals, and compare the alternatives for reaching the goal, we will arrive at the one correct answer. In reality, many of our choices have many reasonable alternatives.

1

Activity 2: Debrief and Mini-Lecture

Provide the handout, "Decision-Making Traps in Outdoor Leadership" (on CD-ROM). Ask students to consider the trail junction scenario described in the Background section of this lesson and comment on some of the decision-making traps they saw occurring so that they can then explore a process for avoiding the traps.

Form small groups for discussions about the decision-making traps, asking students to identify what factors in the scenario point toward particular traps. The small group discussions can be structured by categories of decision-making traps—heuristic traps, analytic traps, expertise traps, and so on. Ask each group to appoint a note taker to be able to later report discussion highlights to the larger class.

Ask group note takers to report highlights of their discussion, focusing on the decision-making traps that occurred in the scenario and the factors that led toward those traps. As groups take turns reporting to the class, avoid redundancy by asking each reporter to present only those observations that previous reporters have not yet mentioned.

Following the group discussions and reports, conduct a short session that places the students' observations regarding the scenario into a contextual framework of decision making.

Mention that heuristic traps are central to many of the mistakes that occur in decision making. So, the discussion will start with heuristics. Heuristics are generalizations based on one or two pieces of information. They are simple rules of thumb, shortcuts, that we use to guide our decisions. People will rely on these shortcuts even in the face of ample evidence that they are wrong. Ask students in their small groups to refer to the handout and describe one or two heuristic traps operating in the scenario. Two that are commonly identified are the familiarity trap and the acceptance trap.

Explain that decision making is a largely unconscious process. We usually don't know that a heuristic trap is present. So, elevating unconscious thought processes to consciousness can be a useful tool for outdoor leaders to use in order to recognize heuristics. "This is what we're going to do now."

Activity 3: Premortem Decision-Making Trap Test

In order to test a decision about to be implemented by the LODs or the group, we can engage in a premortem decision-making trap test (McCammon 2004). Ask students in their small groups to engage in the following exercise:

From individuals' personal or professional outdoor experience, the group should choose one outdoor leadership decision-making process to analyze. Mention that students may have been a decision maker or an observer or instructor of the decision-making process. They should then imagine that the decision or plan fails.

Consider what are, or were, the hazard clues that were present? Hazard clues include human hazards and environmental hazards. Human, or subjective, hazards include attitudes, behaviors, and skills (or lack of skills). Environmental, or objective, hazards, include the places where the program operates, the activities undertaken, and the equipment used. More information about hazard and accident models can be found in Priest and Gass (2005, pp. 93-94). Ask students to count the hazard clues in the situation they are analyzing.

What decision-making traps were occurring—analytic, heuristic, expertise, random choice, leadership traps? Add up the hazard clues plus the number of decision-making traps. The number of traps, or the trap score, indicates how hard it was to actually be objective about the hazard clues. The more decision-making traps, the harder it is to be objective about your decision. This premortem decision-making trap test is a way to assess how vulnerable the leader is to misreading the situation. A "dangerous decision" score might be the sum or the product of traps and hazard clues. Students and instructors can try this calculation in the field.

Explain that group leaders and members can ask this simple question, "What experiences are we basing this decision on?" They should be coming up with domain-specific experiences, rather than gut feelings based on no similar experience. Gut feelings or intuition may be one of the heuristic traps or simply a random choice.

Indicate that those first four sets of decision-making traps—analytic, heuristic, expertise, and random choice—point to what can go wrong when we're unaware of some of the interpersonal and intrapersonal issues involved in a situation. Explain that next we will look at what can go right. We will turn these four sets of decision-making traps into effective decision-making strategies, which reflect how people actually take in information and turn it into a good decision (McCammon 2004). This is an intrapersonal process; it usually occurs within the leader or decision maker before she presents the decision to the group, using various *decision-making styles* of implementation—for example, directive, consultative, voting, consensus, or delegation.

Have students form four groups or remain in their previous groups from the premortem decision-making exercise; one group is needed for each of the sets of decision-making traps described next. Ask groups to use the outdoor leadership decision they previously discussed but now to discuss in their group examples of this decision-making strategy going right—examples in which few or none of the restricting elements of the decision-making traps are present.

- *Analytic:* Goals are clear and defined. You have complete and accurate information. You have the experience to separate relevant information from irrelevant information. You have enough time and resources to make the decision.
- *Heuristic:* Simple rules of thumb can be correctly applied to this situation. An example is to not have a gap in the group hiking on a trail. Heuristics are quick, and they don't require much analysis; although they are not always correct, the use of heuristics to arrive at the best decision was appropriate.
- *Expertise:* The novice has gained enough experience to recognize and interpret complex patterns. Direct experience plus knowledge promotes recognition of common themes in a variety of experiences.
- *Random choice:* An example is the decision of what to cook for dinner. Little time is required to make the decision, and consequences of the decision are minimal. Here you are choosing between alternatives that produce outcomes so similar that there is no practical way to distinguish between them.

Summarize the group discussion by asking groups to comment on when each decision-making strategy is appropriate. Discuss the pros and cons of each strategy.

The decision-making strategies listed can be useful when implemented under the right conditions, or they can be traps when relied on blindly. We can tell the difference if we are able to engage in an analytical process of determining what could go right if we were to implement the strategy and what could go wrong using the premortem decision-making trap test.

Activity 4: Mini-Lecture on Outcomes-Based Model for Decision Making

Start by stating that so far we have been exploring some of the interpersonal and intrapersonal dimensions of decision making and how to bring these ideas into adventure leadership education. But how can this help someone learn about decision making within a broader context of the mission and goals of the program for which he or she is instructing? This raises curricular questions, such as when, where, and how instructors can teach the variety of technical, educational, leadership, human, and professional skills expected. Many programs, such as Outward

Bound, use outdoor technical and expedition activities as a means of promoting broader goals of character development.

Describe the following scenario. You are part of an instructor team planning a nine-day backpacking-based wilderness expedition for your program. You notice how close the contour lines are on the map of the desert and canyon region you will be traveling through. You enjoy rock climbing, and you expect that some of the students coming on this program would also salivate at this topographic relief, focusing on the climbing opportunities. But the program's objectives focus on expedition travel, human skills (i.e., expedition behavior), and to some extent leadership skills. Does recreational climbing fit into these outcomes?

Explain that we can begin by specifying the desired program outcomes, with the goal of providing experiences that take individuals to higher levels of mastery within each outcome set. Outcome sets include the following:

- Technical skills
- Educational (instructional) skills
- Leadership skills
- Human skills (i.e., expedition behavior)
- Professional skills
- Foundational (conceptual) skills

Then the course instructors and students can make decisions about the activity, site selection, and timing that best support the delivery of those outcomes. Outward Bound West (2004) includes some of these questions in a course management model provided to instructors. A question that adventure educators and outdoor leaders can frequently ask themselves is, "Will this decision (about activity, site, timing, etc.) best help meet the desired outcomes (educational objectives) of our course, program, or organization?"

CLOSURE

Those learning outdoor leadership benefit from opportunities to make real field-based decisions; to experience the positive and negative, but not fatal, consequences of those decisions; and then to look back at the factors related to their decisions. Decision-making strategies are often based on heuristics, analysis, expertise, and random choice; and each of these strategies is useful when thoughtfully implemented. But each strategy also brings some traps that the leader can fall into unknowingly. Raising awareness of these traps to a conscious level can provide the aspiring adventure leader with an ongoing process to make more informed decisions.

ASSESSMENT OF LEARNING

During the discussion of the decision-making scenario, students will describe orally or in writing the heuristic decision-making traps from the scenario.

In addition, one or two students will describe an adventure program or course from their experience or an example provided by the instructor. They will identify the educational, human, and technical skill outcomes of that program, then describe how a field-based decision will best help meet those outcomes. For example, a decision to hike an additional 8 miles over technical, mountainous terrain would be appropriate if the technical skill outcomes included mastery of travel on tallus fields and third-class terrain, but not if the technical skill outcomes were limited to travel in more benign environments.

Finally, if this lesson is extended into the field through, for example, a multiday backpacking trip in which students rotate through leadership responsibilities, students will use the "Quick Assessment of Decision-Making Trap Potential" described in handout 2.

PART VII

Professional Ethics and Social Justice Issues

Part VII includes lessons that address professional ethics and issues of equity among participants when working with diverse populations in a risk-based curriculum. Adventure educators work with participants of diverse gender, ethnicity, sexual orientation, age, ability, belief, wealth, and experience. Therefore, it is essential that young adventure educators learn how to provide and promote equality among their participants. They need to be aware of and committed to equality not only because it is appropriate but also because it is professional and ethical. The lessons selected for this section adopt hands-on experiences and reflection to demonstrate why and how adventure professionals may foster equality of experience among their participants.

Karen Warren's lesson 20, "Introduction to Social Justice in Outdoor Adventure Education," introduces students to the ways in which social privilege affects their outdoor leadership and the experiences of their program participants. It draws students' attention to their perceptions, biases, and identities in a multicultural society and uses lively interactive exercises that spark dialogue and reflection on social justice topics in adventure education.

In lesson 21, "Outdoor Leadership With Gender in Mind," Warren considers how gender-role conditioning and conflicts mediate participants' experience in outdoor adventure. Both male and female leaders and participants are disadvantaged when gender topics go unresolved in the outdoors. This lesson is an attempt to compassionately examine how gender affects the outdoor adventure experience by opening dialogue and reviewing strategies for gender-sensitive outdoor leadership.

In lesson 22, "The First-Generation Condition in Adventure Education," Jackson Wilson, Aya Hayashi, and Alan Ewert discuss the unique issues faced by participants without outdoor adventure experience. In order to successfully educate diverse groups of students, adventure educators need to understand how groups of students differ not only in socioeconomic measures but also in prior experience with the great outdoors. This lesson places all students in the role of a first-generation learner, creating a revealing and powerful experience that will better equip aspiring adventure educators to facilitate inexperienced participants.

Finally, in lesson 23, "Be Safe Out There: Critically Thinking Risk in Adventure Education," Denise Mitten and Martyn Whittingham address the ethical use of risk in adventure education. The lesson emphasizes the use of critical thinking skills to evaluate our work as adventure educators, particularly in relation to our facilitation goals. As a result of this lesson, students will better understand the relationship of problem solving and risk and will learn to evaluate what risks to take, with whom to take a risk, and when to do so. This lesson includes several teaching strategies, including an interactive PowerPoint, a reading, and hands-on activities.

LESSON 20

Introduction to Social Justice in Outdoor Adventure Education

Karen Warren

As the field of adventure education becomes more diverse, outdoor leaders will need skills in working with people who may be different from them in identities of race, class, gender, ability, age, religion, or sexual orientation. Part of helping students learn about how to be socially just outdoor adventure leaders is to facilitate an awareness of their own perceptions, biases, and identities in a multicultural society. This lesson introduces students to the ways in which social privilege affects their outdoor leadership and the experiences of their program participants. It teaches about privilege and oppression by using lively interactive exercises that spark dialogue and reflection on social justice topics in adventure education.

Background

While some would question the applicability of social justice issues in the adventure education curriculum, the use of experiential education to create a socially just society has a long history (Warren 2005). Progressive education theorist John Dewey, one of the major advocates of experiential education, believed that the link between democracy and education was a crucial element in the creation of a just society. Direct experience in a social milieu "is the fundamental method of social progress and reform" (Dewey 1959, p. 30).

Kurt Hahn, the founder of Outward Bound, was also a proponent of social justice in outdoor adventure. Hahn's beliefs were influenced by the writings of Plato, who taught that human beings were responsible for the creation of a just society (James 1995). Hahn developed his schools around principles that would address the social decline of the era, mainly the atrocities of the Hitler regime (Richards 1990). He emphasized the development of compassion in students by impelling them into service to help them become "emancipated from the prison of privilege" (Wilson 1981, p. 11).

Activities in this lesson offer white outdoor educators a way to role-model their spending privilege by making it a part of the curriculum. Many social justice education authors have suggested that students need models of white activists dismantling racism in order to understand their own journey to justice (see Adams, Bell, and Griffin 1997; McIntosh 1990; Warren 1998b; Wise 2005).

Learning about privilege and oppression in an experiential way that engages the affective realms of learning often brings up a range of feelings in students (and teachers) and poses deep questions about the conditioning that each person experiences as a result of living in the North American culture. Commonly, when pulled outside their comfort zone around social justice issues, students rely on distancing avoidance behaviors that may be unconscious or unintentional. While these distancing behaviors arise from a basic need for security and positive self-image, making students aware of these behaviors helps them enter the stages of questioning and unsettledness that are necessary to begin a constructive effort to address social injustice (Edler and Irons 1998). As a facilitator, I alert students to the distancing behaviors early in the lesson and ask them to be aware of how these behaviors can impede the dialogue. Drawing from the work of Edler and Irons (1998), I present the following script addressing distancing behaviors that white people often use in dealing with racism.

DISTANCING BEHAVIORS SCRIPT

In this script, "voices" are objections commonly presented about doing antiracism work. Each objection is followed by the facilitator's explanation of the distancing behavior at the root of the objection. The script is very powerful when used as a large group reading by students and the facilitator.

First voice: Before we can really address white privilege and racism we need to agree on a definition.

Facilitator: This is the Dictionary game. What I've seen happen are protracted debates on terms. At the end of the long drawn-out defining session, no one is any closer to having a common definition, and a lot of time has been spent that could have been used to address the issues.

Second voice: I work at a summer camp and we don't have any kids of color at the camp. It's kind of pointless to talk about racism unless we have people of another race there. So I think we need to recruit some staff of color or kids of color to our program first.

Facilitator: That's the Where Are the Blacks/People of Color (POC) game. It assumes that we need POC at the table in order to address privilege and racism—that there's not a problem until POC are present, that we need help to deal with it, and that help can come only from POC. This game is about asking oppressed groups to educate us, as opposed to our taking responsibility.

Third voice: But I *am* interested in talking about social justice and privilege with my students and trip participants. Do you know of any good group initiatives to do that?

Facilitator: I can be sure that someone will ask this question every time I speak on social justice. This is the Instant Solution game. We'll do a few initiatives, and that means we've covered social justice. But social justice must be woven into every part of the program. We need to take risks to initiate those conversations.

Fourth voice: I have so much privilege as a young white heterosexual male who is in most of the dominant groups. I feel like I'm labeled the bad guy, and it's a huge responsibility to have. I feel guilty and ashamed and like I really can't do anything.

Facilitator: You are experiencing the Little Old Me game. Guilt and shame are stoppers in working on antiracism in this field. Assume that to really deal with privilege and racism in this country you will experience discomfort and bewilderment about personal responsibility. Learning and practicing ways to spend privilege are important.

Fifth voice: My program is willing to do some social justice stuff in our staff trainings, but because we have so much to cover in a week of staff training we can't spend too much time on social justice. It's already a challenge to get in all we have to do.

Facilitator: That's a classic example of the There Are Other Problems Besides Racism game. Yes, there are many issues to deal with, but social justice issues can be addressed in the context of the other challenges. This game is a way of avoiding the issue of racism.

Sixth voice: A group of us in our program have been working to get social justice talked about in outdoor programming. But there is one woman who is very resistant—she makes very subtly racist remarks or finds an exception to everything we bring up, using her experiences with people of color. We've been working to change her, but it's very frustrating.

Facilitator: Sounds like the Find the Racist game. This is a very destructive behavior because it creates a climate of blaming and finger pointing that prevents further discussion and work on addressing racism in white organizations. It's often easier to focus on one group member than to confront our own privilege or internalized racism.

Seventh voice: But this stuff is really complex, and I have my own biases. I feel as if I really need to learn a lot more about antiracist work before I can act and be effective.

Facilitator: You are caught in the After I Become an Expert game. Remember that antiracism work is a journey with no clear destination except equality for all. If you wait until you "arrive" as the perfectly polished antibias expert, you will miss vital opportunities to do valuable work along the way.

In outdoor adventure, many leaders and participants come from dominant groups; therefore, before we can invite people from oppressed communities to participate in programs, we must make the programs themselves welcoming. Examining the paradigms that are foundations of thinking in the outdoor adventure field is critical.

METHODS TRAPS

A prominent goal in teaching about social justice issues in adventure education is to critically analyze contemporary approaches in the field. Drawing from the work of Warren (1998a), this section presents a critical examination of problematic methods used in the outdoor field.

The One-Size-Fits-All Method

The delusive belief that there are generic methods that will work for everyone in a group persists when educators view their learning communities as homogenous groups of students with similar needs. Certainly, a one-size-fits-all method of experiential education is simpler to use and seemingly more efficient, but it fails to acknowledge the social differences that exist in every group.

Rote Methods

Programs that run many groups of students through a standard curriculum often fall into the rote methods trap. Stagnation is the foe of inclusive programming. The use of ropes courses where instructors use routine teaching progressions and "tried and true" methods is an example of this trap. A repetitious use of the tools of experiential education can cause facilitators to be unthinking or mechanistic in the application of their bag of tricks. Formulaic methods familiar to the facilitator but unexamined as to their cultural appropriateness are problematic.

Separating Technique From Theory

The trap of separating technique from theory is particularly pertinent in cultural diversity work as facilitators attempt to "do the right thing" without an understanding of their own biases or the current antibias work theories. Facilitators need training not only in techniques but, more importantly, with respect to the social and cultural backgrounds of their participants and the way in which their own locations in privilege or marginality affect how they teach and facilitate.

For instance, in order to understand the dynamics of a mixed-race outdoor program, facilitators need to understand current theories on racial identity development (Tatum 1997). I have witnessed white facilitators, in the name of inclusivity, break up small groups of students of color who are interacting positively with each other on a course. These facilitators fail to understand that the racial identity development stage of the students of color encourages them to seek out others who are like them for support.

Choosing Experiences Before Goals

Experiential educators are often exposed to compelling and provocative methods, then drawn to use a particular method because of its novelty or because their own experience with it was at one time a formative, life-altering event for them. The result is that the facilitator tries to work that experiential event into the curriculum without regard to the goals of the class or group. With reference to socially just facilitation, the way educators experience the world may be different from the way it is experienced by students from oppressed social groups. To use experiences that are important to facilitators but alienating to students who have different norms and behavioral expectations supports this methods trap.

CONCLUSION

To effectively teach about social justice issues in outdoor adventure, educators will benefit from scrutiny of their own biases and a continuing quest for more information about the complex dynamics of privilege and oppression. The following resources may be useful in that pursuit.

RESOURCES

Adams, M., L. Bell, and P. Griffin, eds. 1997. *Teaching for diversity and social justice: A sourcebook.* New York: Routledge.

Delpit, L. 1995. *Other people's children: Cultural conflict in the classroom.* New York: New Press.

Dewey, J. 1959. *Dewey on education.* New York: Distancing Behaviors College.

Edler, J., and B. Irons. 1998. Distancing behaviors often used by white people. In *Beyond heroes and holidays: A practical guide to K-12 anti-racist, multicultural education and staff development,* eds. E. Lee, D. Menkart, and M. Okazawa-Rey, 114. Washington, DC: Network of Educators on the Americas.

Hooks, B. 1994. *Teaching to transgress: Education as the practice of freedom.* New York: Routledge.

James, T. 1995. Sketch of a moving spirit: Kurt Hahn. In *The theory of experiential education,* eds. K. Warren, M. Sakofs, and J.S. Hunt, 85-95. Dubuque, IA: Kendall/Hunt.

McIntosh, P. 1990. White privilege: Unpacking the invisible knapsack. *Independent School.* http://seamonkey.ed.asu.edu/~mcisaac/emc598ge/Unpacking.html

Richards, A. 1990. Kurt Hahn. In *Adventure education,* eds. J.C. Miles and S. Priest, 67-74. State College, PA: Venture.

Tatum, B.D. 1997. *"Why are all the black kids sitting together in the cafeteria?" and other conversations about race.* New York: Basic Books.

Van Nostrand, C.H. 1993. *Gender-responsible leadership.* Newbury Park, CA: Sage.

Warren, K., ed. 1996. *Women's voices in experiential education.* Dubuque, IA: Kendall/Hunt.

Warren, K. 1997. Where have we been, where are we going? Gender issues in experiential education. *Journal of Experiential Education,* 20(3):117-118.

Warren, K. 1998a. A call for race, gender, and class sensitive facilitation in outdoor experiential education. *Journal of Experiential Education,* 21(1):21-25.

Warren, K. 1998b. Educating students for social justice in service learning. *Journal of Experiential Education,* 21(3):134-139.

Warren, K. 1998c. Old paradigms, new visions: Social justice in outdoor adventure. *Ziplines,* 37:54-55.

Warren, K. 1999. Social justice turning initiative. *Ziplines,* 39:42-43.

Warren, K. 1999. Unpacking the knapsack of outdoor experiential education: Race, gender, and class sensitive outdoor leadership. Unpublished doctoral dissertation, Union Institute, Cincinnati, OH.

Warren, K. 2002. Preparing the next generation: Social justice in outdoor leadership education and training. *Journal of Experiential Education,* 25(1):231-238.

Warren, K. 2005. A path worth taking: The development of social justice in outdoor experiential education. *Equity and Excellence in Education,* 38(1):88-89.

Warren, K., and T. Flippo. 2001. Social justice speak out. *Ziplines,* 42:36-38.

Warren, K., and T.A. Loeffler. 2000. Setting a place at the table: Social justice research in outdoor experiential education. *Journal of Experiential Education,* 23(2):85-90.

Warren, K., and A. Russek. 1997. Social justice in outdoor leadership. ERIC Document Reproduction Service No. ED414 148.

Wilson, R. 1981. *Inside Outward Bound.* Charlotte, NC: East Woods Press.

Wise, T. 2005. *White like me: Reflections on race from a privileged son.* New York: Soft Skull.

Lesson Plan

PURPOSE

To create a safe learning community for students to address social justice topics in adventure education.

OBJECTIVES

As a result of this lesson students will be able to . . .

1. *Affective and cognitive:* explain how social privilege exists and can be mediated in outdoor adventures.
2. *Affective and psychomotor:* participate in several interactive experiences that clarify and reinforce their understanding of social justice concepts in outdoor adventures.
3. *Affective and spiritual:* gain greater self-understanding of the personal effects of privilege and oppression in their own adventure experiences.
4. *Cognitive:* apply socially just outdoor leadership to real-life scenarios.

DURATION

120 minutes

GROUP SIZE

8 to 20 students

LOCATION

Indoors or outdoors

EQUIPMENT

- Daypack (the "knapsack of privilege"), containing a popular outdoor magazine, small first aid kit, outdoor program brochure or catalogue, checkbook, old dirty outdoor clothing, trail map, climbing gear, energy bar, outdoor leadership text
- Privilege bucks (on CD-ROM)
- Soft objects (e.g., small stuffed animals, toilet paper rolls or tissue packets, foam balls, small rubber toys), masking tape, rubber bands, markers, slips of paper, 8-foot-long (2.4 meter-long) rope
- Large sheets of newsprint, masking tape, markers

RISK MANAGEMENT CONSIDERATIONS

As students will be taking emotional risks in this lesson, it is essential to set a climate of safety before the lesson begins. It is critical to time the lesson to take place after the students have gained some sense of comfort and trust with each other. Ground rules or verbal agreements are established or reiterated. Some very useful ground rules include maintaining confidentiality, sharing "airtime," and the idea that it is all right to make a mistake or say something the "wrong way." Emphasize that feelings of guilt, confusion, anger, affirmation, and a range of others may come up and that they are part of the process. Encourage students to sit with those feelings and notice any learning that comes from them.

STUDENT PREPARATION

Students should read the Background document (on the CD-ROM). Students can also read from the following sources in preparation for this lesson. If possible, these articles could be placed on reserve at the library.

- Newbury, L., ed. 2003. Social difference, justice, and outdoor education. *Pathways,* 15(1):2-3.
- Warren, K. 1998a. A call for race, gender, and class sensitive facilitation in outdoor experiential education. *Journal of Experiential Education,* 21(1):21-25.
- Warren, K. 1998c. Old paradigms, new visions: Social justice in outdoor adventure. *Ziplines,* 37:54-55.
- Warren, K. 2002. Preparing the next generation: Social justice in outdoor leadership education and training. *Journal of Experiential Education,* 25(1):231-238.

INSTRUCTOR PREPARATION

Gather all the props you will need for the activities and print and cut the privilege bucks (on CD-ROM).

LESSON CONTENT AND TEACHING STRATEGIES

The lesson starts when you walk quietly into the classroom. Write the following quote on the board and then proceed with the Unpacking the Knapsack of White Privilege activity.

There are some things you learn best in calm and some best in storm.—Willa Cather

Activity 1: Unpacking the Knapsack of White Privilege

This creative drama sets the stage for thinking about and discussing the concept of privilege in outdoor adventure education. It applies the work of Peggy McIntosh (1990) to the outdoor adventure field.

Enter the classroom wearing a daypack that you keep on while you go about your normal class routines. Wear the daypack throughout the session without mentioning why you have it on. This demonstrates the invisibility of privilege in our everyday life.

When you are ready to move into the activity, look around the room and ask your students if they have seen your daypack. They will be puzzled and say it is on your back. Turn around and pretend you don't see it because it's on your back. This drama should go on until the students "convince" you that you have a daypack on your back. Then announce proudly that this is your "knapsack of privilege" and unpack it piece by piece, explaining the white privilege that exists in outdoor adventure.

Use the following script to explain the contents of your knapsack of privilege.

- **Recent outdoor magazine:** "I can pick up my most recent issue of [popular outdoor magazine] and expect to see people of my race represented on the cover and photos inside."
- **Small first aid kit:** "I can get an adhesive bandage out of my first aid kit and know that it will match my skin color because it's 'flesh colored.'"
- **Outdoor program catalogue:** "I can consider going on an outdoor trip with this organization and be assured that people of my race will be on the course with me."
- **Checkbook:** "When I decide to go on the outdoor program and want to pay for it with a check, I can be pretty sure that if people question the validity of my check, it won't be because of my race."
- **Worn, ripped, well-used piece of outdoor clothing:** "I can show up with my favorite dirty old fleece on the course and not worry that people will attribute these choices to my race."
- **Trail map:** "I can hike up the mountain on this map and be reasonably sure that if I meet people on the trail they will be of my own race."
- **Piece of climbing gear:** "I can do really well as a climber and not be a credit to my race."
- **Energy bar:** "I can see my race represented on these bars and be assured that the trip food I am given to eat will include the staple foods that fit with my cultural traditions."
- **Outdoor leadership text:** "When I read this book I can be sure that members of my race will be represented, and that the history of outdoor adventure will show me that people of my color made it what it is."

After you have unpacked the knapsack of privilege, revisit or create ground rules that will allow people to be able to share freely about social justice topics in the class. Relate this to the quote that started the lesson—social justice education can cause a "storm" in people as it asks hard questions and prompts strong feelings. Remind students that social injustice and oppression are not their fault but are their responsibility.

Provide some definitions before moving into the next activity, which is designed to help students understand privilege from a personal perspective.

- *Oppression* is prejudice plus power.
- *Privilege* is a system of advantage granted to or enjoyed by a social group. It is often unconscious or unwanted.
- *Agent* or *dominant* groups are those privileged in the hierarchy of oppression. Their experience in society is viewed as normal and universal.
- *Target* or *subordinate* groups are those disadvantaged or victimized in the hierarchy of oppression. Sometimes group members accept and incorporate the negative images of themselves created by the dominant society. This is called *internalized oppression.*

Activity 2: Privilege Bucks

Distribute three to five copies of the privilege bucks to students (on CD-ROM). Have them think about a social privilege that they have without needing to be conscious of it at all times. Examples of privilege might include being white, Christian, able-bodied, heterosexual, young, male, or middle or upper class. Then invite your students to write on each privilege buck a way they would spend this privilege. Give some examples: "I will spend my white privilege by encouraging the students at the multicultural center to go on my next outdoor trip" or "I will spend my male privilege by including strong female role models in the examples I use as I talk about the history of the outdoors."

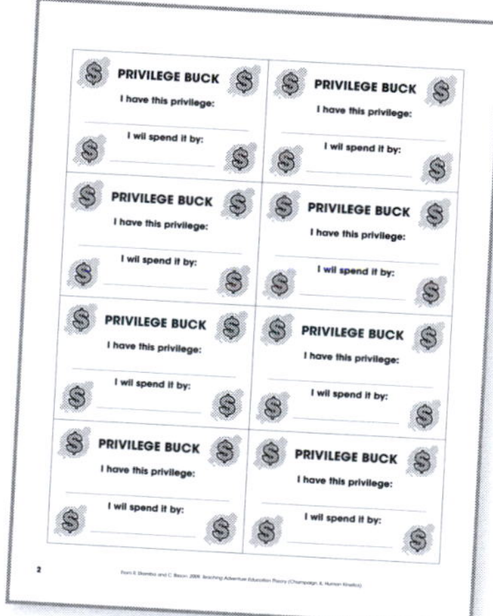

PRIVILEGE BUCK
I have this privilege:
I will spend it by:

PRIVILEGE BUCK
I have this privilege:
I will spend it by:

PRIVILEGE BUCK
I have this privilege:
I will spend it by:

PRIVILEGE BUCK
I have this privilege:
I will spend it by:

PRIVILEGE BUCK
I have this privilege:
I will spend it by:

PRIVILEGE BUCK
I have this privilege:
I will spend it by:

PRIVILEGE BUCK
I have this privilege:
I will spend it by:

PRIVILEGE BUCK
I have this privilege:
I will spend it by:

After students have written on the privilege bucks, have everyone go on a "spending spree" in a whole-group exchange, sharing with group members how they will spend their privilege. Processing questions include the following:

- What were some of your feelings in writing down and sharing your privileges?
- What are some unconscious privileges in the outdoor adventure field?
- How do you think these privileges could be "spent"?

After processing the activities involving the concept of privilege, tell the students that they will move on to applying the social justice definitions to outdoor adventure. They will look specifically at oppression within outdoor programs.

Activity 3: Junkyard Volleyball

This fast-paced game relies on the metaphor of a junkyard to illuminate ideas about the barriers to interrupting oppression in our work and personal life. Distribute two slips of paper to each student. Then have students write down two barriers that they have personally experienced based on these questions:

- What is a challenge you've had in interrupting oppression in your program or organization?
- How have you personally been hurt by oppression?

The participants fasten the slips of paper listing the barriers to the soft toys using rubber bands or masking tape. Divide the class in half, asking the two groups to move to the two sides of the room. Unfold a rope "net" between the groups. When signaled, each group throws its junk into the other group's area. The objective is for the groups to have no junk on their side of the rope when time is called.

After 1 to 2 minutes, stop the action and have people read the slips on two objects near where they are standing. Ask students the following processing questions:

- How did you get the junk out of your space?
- What are the implications of throwing the junk into other people's spaces?
- If we think about the junk as barriers to oppression, what experiences and feelings come up?
- What are the common forms of oppression in the United States (the "isms")? What group is the oppressor? What group is the oppressed? (Note: Have students name the oppressed group without reference to the dominant group. For example, when referring to racism they should name African Americans, Latino or Latina, Asian Americans, and so on instead of "nonwhites.")
- What barriers in interrupting oppression are most challenging to you and why?
- What are some strategies for addressing barriers to antioppression work?
- How do you get support or culture allies in addressing social justice issues in your programs? In yourself?

After students have an understanding of the concepts of privilege and oppression, tell them it is time to move on to applications to outdoor adventure. Talk about how the concept of the "normal" and the "other" plays out in our thinking about outdoor leadership. This next activity will illustrate the concept.

Activity 4: Outdoor Identity

The purpose of this activity is to explore how messages and conceptions of outdoor identity affect our thinking about who can and cannot be outdoor leaders.

Have participants pair up, and give each pair a 6-foot (2-meter) piece of newsprint. Their goal is to draw a life-sized "typical outdoor leader" based on the messages and stereotypes they have experienced about who can lead in the outdoors. Factors that should be represented in their drawings include gender, age, ethnic background, height and weight, sexual orientation, physical abilities, religion, marital or partner status, dress and equipment, class background, political affiliation or activity, and leadership style.

After each group discusses and draws their outdoor leader, have them tape the drawing on the wall and present it to the group.

The paradigm of outdoor identity is revealed through this exercise. Students' life-sized drawings and their descriptions of the drawings are often remarkably similar in their representation of dominant social identity as normative. White men who are heterosexual, in their mid-20s, and tall, thin, and athletic predominate. They have no physical disability but may have a learning disability. They are represented as unmarried or as transiently partnered with no children. Religious leaning is often depicted as nature-based spirituality without formal religious affiliation. Political leaning is often either apolitical or earth activist based. Class background is usually dual; the leader does not have much money now but comes from a middle- or upper-class background. He usually has lots of high-tech gear, but it is depicted as very worn and shabby. The leadership style is charismatic, or laid back, or both.

Some drawings will certainly incorporate exceptions to the dominant view, and it is important to discuss these cracks in the paradigm of outdoor identity, how they come into being, and what perpetuates them.

Sample drawing of "typical outdoor leaders."
Karen Warren

Discuss the following questions:

- What characteristics of outdoor leadership identity support the dominant view of who can be an outdoor leader in the field?
- How do your own background and social identity "measure up" to those of the typical outdoor leader represented in your drawing? How does this make you feel?
- How might a dominant culture perspective of who an outdoor leader is affect that person's leadership?

Activity 5: Outdoor Situations Relating to Social Justice

The final activity in applying social justice topics to outdoor adventure is to work through the scenarios described in the Outdoor Situations Relating to Social Justice handout (on CD-ROM). As a whole group, have the students decide which oppression they want to focus on and address that scenario. Students are invited to give their responses about the underlying issues and their ideas about how they would proceed in the situation if they were the leader. You can add comments based on social justice theory and practice and give some examples of how to address the scenario. The scenarios not addressed in class can be the basis of students' online writing assignment.

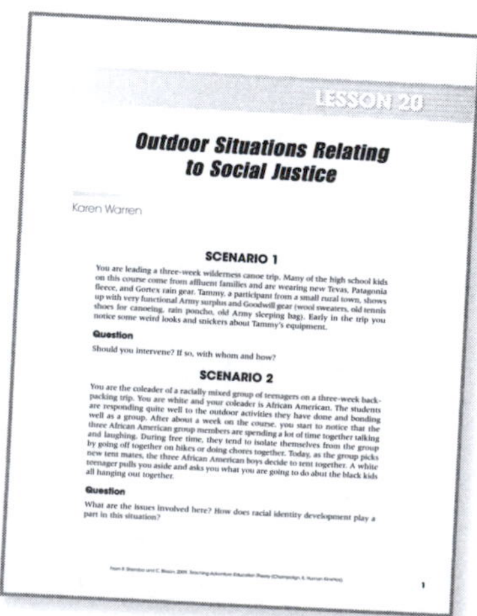

LESSON 20

Outdoor Situations Relating to Social Justice

Karen Warren

SCENARIO 1

You are leading a three-week wilderness canoe trip. Many of the high school kids on this course come from affluent families and are wearing new Tevas, Patagonia fleece, and Gortex rain gear. Tammy, a participant from a small rural town, shows up with very functional Army surplus and Goodwill gear (wool sweaters, old tennis shoes for canoeing, rain poncho, old Army sleeping bag). Early in the trip you notice some weird looks and snickers about Tammy's equipment.

Question

Should you intervene? If so, with whom and how?

SCENARIO 2

You are the coleader of a racially mixed group of teenagers on a three-week backpacking trip. You are white and your coleader is African American. The students are responding quite well to the outdoor activities they have done and bonding well as a group. After about a week on the course, you start to notice that the three African American group members are spending a lot of time together talking and laughing. During free time, they tend to isolate themselves from the group by going off together on hikes or doing chores together. Today, as the group picks new tent mates, the three African American boys decide to tent together. A white teenager pulls you aside and asks you what you are going to do abut the black kids all hanging out together.

Question

What are the issues involved here? How does racial identity development play a part in this situation?

1

CLOSURE

End the class by thanking the students for the risks they took and the respect they have shown for others, themselves, and the subject. Use the metaphor of a journey and encourage them to get support for undertaking the challenges in the journey, look for new routes when the going gets rough, and celebrate accomplishments along the way.

Facilitate a closing circle using the idea of "next steps." All the students have an opportunity to give voice to their next steps in working with social justice in adventure education based on what they have learned in this session.

As this is an introductory lesson in a semester-long course, students will revisit these concepts in a variety of ways in future class periods.

ASSESSMENT OF LEARNING

The final activity, Outdoor Situations Relating to Social Justice, provides a fair assessment of where the students are in their understanding of social justice issues in the outdoor profession.

After class, students do a written reflection piece on the course Web site discussion board about what they learned, what was difficult for them in class, and how they see the subject relating to their own work in the outdoors. The teacher and other students offer comments about the reflection writings on the discussion board as a way to enhance the learning assessment.

LESSON 21

Outdoor Leadership With Gender in Mind

Karen Warren

Outdoor leaders often find that participants' experience in outdoor adventure is mediated by gender-role conditioning and conflicts. Both male and female leaders and participants are disadvantaged when gender topics go unresolved in the outdoors. This lesson is an attempt to compassionately examine how gender affects the outdoor adventure experience by opening dialogue and reviewing strategies for gender-sensitive outdoor leadership.

Background

This lesson draws from the body of literature on gender in outdoor experiential education, in particular from *Women's Voices in Experiential Education* (1996b), edited by Karen Warren.

Warren (1996a) identified five myths of women's outdoor adventure experience that can cause adventure programs to be unresponsive to women's experience (through ignorance rather than intention) and serve as constraints for women at various stages in their pursuit of meaningful outdoor challenges.

THE MYTH OF ACCESSIBILITY

The myth of accessibility is based on the misconception that outdoor experiences are widely available to women. Women's reality doesn't support this notion, as social and economic factors serve to limit women's participation. Women's economic inequity, well documented in their statistically lower earning power, is the first deterrent to involvement in adventure programs. A second deterrent is gender-role conditioning. For a woman deciding between the needs of her loved ones and her own desire for adventure, an outdoor trip may seem frivolous in relation to family needs.

In addition, social conditioning inundates a woman with the insistent caution that the outdoors is no place for her. Not only must she reconcile her own doubts on a personal level (i.e., guilt at leaving the family alone, economic stress, etc.), but a woman also faces substantial societal risks in pursuing adventure experiences. Historically a masculine domain, the wilderness trip is painted by the message bearers of the media and tradition as a scary, uncomfortable, and intimidating event. The moment she steps into the outdoors, her identity is in question. For example, in a content analysis of unisex and women's backpacking guides, Glotfelty (1996) found that the guides written for women tended to focus on psychological messages relating to what it means to be a woman in the outdoors. Perhaps the most significant difference between the two sets of books is that all the women's guides contain a lengthy discussion of femininity. While unisex guides focus on *"how to"* skills, women's guides teach readers *"who to"* be (Glotfelty 1996, p. 442).

THE MYTH OF EGALITARIANISM

The myth of egalitarianism is predicated on the notion that the wilderness is an ideal place to revise prevailing social conditioning. The fallacy of this assumption lies in the fact that the wilderness is not a natural place to break gender stereotypes. When it's pouring rain, the group has been hiking all day, and it's growing dark, the most expedient way to set up camp is for people to do tasks that are comfortable and familiar. In spite of noble intentions of egalitarianism, when efficiency is important in a trying situation, women often do end up cooking.

The mixed-gender wilderness trip also serves as a constant, insidious reminder to women that their intrinsic worth on the course is in doubt. As Appling (1989) observed on National Outdoor Leadership School courses, one often notices

> . . . women avoiding leadership, being fearful of physical challenge, avoiding assertiveness, manifesting feelings of intimidation or inadequate self-esteem. . . . Or tent group dynamics: she does almost all the cooking, he usually sets up the fly, she barely knows the knots to do so herself, he can't cook an edible meal, she gives up weight to him every morning, he makes a point of passing her with it on the trail every day. . . . (p. 11)

The myth of egalitarianism offers a cogent rationale for women-only programs. Women have the opportunity to try out outdoor activities in a supportive atmosphere without immediate comparison to men's adventure experience (McClintock 1996). In co-ed outdoor programs, altering course components involving unconscious discrimination against women is suggested.

THE MYTH OF SQUARE ONE

The myth of square one is apparent at the start of most beginning-level wilderness education courses. Outdoor instructors often assume that beginners arrive with the same lack of skills and similar disadvantages, in other words, that all participants start at square one. Yet due to gender-role socialization, women often lack the precursory experiences in mechanical manipulation and technical training afforded men. In addition, women lack strong outdoor role models in the adventure field. A look at the white man history of adventure education is a case in point (Miles and Priest 1999). The final precursor deficient in a woman's outdoor experience is an internalized assumption of success. A woman who constantly encounters surprise that "she got as far as she did in the wilderness" will soon internalize the message that she is expected to fail.

THE MYTH OF THE SUPERWOMAN

In order to achieve an advanced rank in the outdoor field, female leaders often acquire exemplary competence in outdoor skills, becoming a superwoman unlike the norm. Students no longer have to view her competence for what it is—the ongoing struggle to gain parity in a male-dominated profession.

World-class mountaineer Heidi Howkins (2001) detailed the effects of needing to be a superwoman:

> As the only woman, I knew I had to outperform the others, at least on the way up. This is immature but completely irrefutable. Show me a woman in the mountains who does not feel that she has to try to carry twice as much or do twice as much work as her male partners, and I'll show you someone who is sharing her tent. To stabilize gender dynamics, you have to be unavailable—either engaged with a member of the group or universally respected, out of reach. (p. 183)

The presence of the superwoman on wilderness courses is detrimental. Participants, both men and women, struggle with the dissonance created by the conflict between their indoctrination implying that a woman doesn't belong in the wilderness and the reality of the woman outdoor leader guiding them. The existence of the superwoman gives them a way out of this nagging conflict. Due to her exemplary outdoor achievements, the superwoman is the exception to other women. When she is perceived as unrepresentative of ordinary women, participants are no longer forced to deal with their sexist conditioning; they can keep the same cultural baggage they had when they arrived. Ironically, the exemplary woman outdoor leader loses her status as a role model and ends up being intimidating to female beginners in the field due to an attempt to reconcile gender stereotypes.

THE MYTH OF THE HEROIC QUEST

A metaphor used by adventure programs, the heroic quest model, has been prevalent in literature throughout time. The participant undergoes a real-life experience in the wilderness that parallels the mythical quest of the hero: hearing a call to adventure, leaving home, encountering dragons along the way and slaying them, reflecting on the conquest, and returning home as a hero with a clearer understanding of self.

Yet each stage of a woman's journey in the wilderness is a direct contradiction of the heroic quest model. As Little (2002) found in her study of the meanings of adventure for women, "the label of 'adventure' was perceived by the respondents to build images of danger and extreme challenge, and for these women it could be a struggle to subsequently acknowledge their own achievements" (p. 64). A woman rarely hears a call to adventure; she is often dissuaded from leaving home to engage in adventurous pursuits. A woman's experience often is not compatible with viewing challenges in the wilderness in a militaristic framework; she is more likely to ally herself with the metaphoric dragons than to conquer them. Returning home is also problematic for women. While a man's mythical journey in the wilderness parallels his everyday situation, a woman's does not. Encouraged to be bold and assertive in the outdoors, a man readily transfers this style upon return. The woman who has learned to be strong, assertive, and independent on a wilderness course encounters intense cognitive dissonance back home because these traits are not presently valued for her in society. Finally, women rarely see themselves as heroes in the outdoors (Little 2002).

TERRITORIAL AND LINGUISTIC SEXISM

In addition to the myths of women's adventure experience, it is useful to mention two other factors that influence gender relations in the field: territorial and linguistic sexism.

Territorial sexism refers to the control of a common space as a way to claim and maintain power (Van Nostrand 1993). An example of territorial sexism occurs on the indoor climbing wall or the rock climb site where the instructor teaches to a group arranged in a semicircle around him or her. When the inner circle gathered around the instructor is mostly composed of men and the outer circle of women, territorial sexism exists. While this situation may not be intentional or overt, the result puts women in a more observational role while men maintain a position closer to the action. Since learning technical skills often requires repetitive manipulation of equipment (e.g., knots), the position in the learning environment has an effect on who receives the most experience and instructional assistance.

Linguistic sexism is the use of language to marginalize or invalidate women's experience (Van Nostrand 1993). In the outdoor adventure field, the persistent use of the terms "hard skills" to refer to technical skills and "soft skills" to refer to communication or leadership skills is an example of linguistic sexism. As Jordan (1996) maintains,

> A distinct relationship between the meanings of male, masculine, and hard exists; hard may be characterized as being masculine and, therefore, attributed to men or boys. Since the male sex is more highly valued and attributed more status than the female sex, it is easy to see why, in the past, hard skills have been more highly valued—they are masculine and according to social norms, masculine is the way to be. (p. 209)

Educators interested in removing the language bias evident in the terms "hard" and "soft skills" will teach the importance of using terms such as "interpersonal" or "communication" skills and "technical" skills.

In teaching environments, the inequitable distribution of speaking time is another aspect of linguistic sexism. Research in mixed-gender groups shows that women who speak more than 30 percent of the time are seen as dominating while men, in reality, talk for a longer time than women (Van Nostrand 1993).

Strategies to confront these gender issues in the outdoor adventure field are shown in table 21.1.

TABLE 21.1 Outdoor Leadership Strategies With Gender in Mind

Strategy	Leader actions	Examples
Address territorial sexism	Identify and attempt to change positions in the learning environment that disadvantage women.	Use women to demonstrate a technical skill. Invite women closer to the action.
Address linguistic sexism	Model that language is important: use gender-neutral pronouns, parallel language, and nonsexist outdoor terms, and interrupt sexist joking or teasing.	Use *interpersonal* or *communication skills* instead of *soft skills,* and *technical skills* instead of *hard skills.*
Encourage single-gender learning environments	Promote single-gender learning situations within mixed-gender courses. Advocate for single-gender courses.	Set up all-women's cook or tent groups on a co-ed course.

continued ▶

LESSON 21

TABLE 21.1 *(continued)*

Strategy	Leader actions	Examples
Use positive images	Enact gender-positive role modeling and provide literature and popular culture images showing women in powerful outdoor positions.	Use outdoor teaching material with photos of strong women.
Increase self-awareness	Work to acknowledge and manage your own gender bias by seeking new information and training. Women leaders should avoid the Superwoman role.	Notice how your own conditioning causes you to treat men and women in the outdoors. Attend gender workshops or read about gender in the outdoors.
Teach with sensitivity to gender	Provide instruction that accounts for women's lack of childhood technical conditioning, including repetitive practice of technical skills. Use cooperative and noncompetitive learning environments. Reduce performance pressure.	Review knots often on a climbing course.
Switch roles	Take on leadership roles in contradiction to gender role conditioning.	Male leader teaches cooking while female leader teaches stove repair.

RESOURCES

Appling, L. 1989. Women and leadership. *National Outdoor Leadership School Staff Conference Proceedings,* 9-12. Lander, WY: Appling.

Glotfelty, C. 1996. Femininity in the wilderness: Reading gender in women's guides to backpacking. *Women's Studies,* 25:439-456.

Howkins, H. 2001. *K2: One woman's quest for the summit.* Washington, DC: National Geographic Adventure Press.

Jordan, D.J. 1996. Snips and snails and puppy dog tails . . . The use of gender-free language in experiential education. In *Women's voices in experiential education,* ed. K. Warren, 205-211. Dubuque, IA: Kendall/Hunt.

Little, D. 2002. How do women construct adventure recreation in their lives? Why we need to re-engage with the essence of adventure experience. *Journal of Adventure Education and Outdoor Learning,* 2(1):55-69.

McClintock, M. 1996. Why women's outdoor trips? In *Women's voices in experiential education,* ed. K. Warren, 18-23. Dubuque, IA: Kendall/Hunt.

Miles, J.C., and S. Priest. Eds. 1999. *Adventure programming.* State College, PA: Venture.

Van Nostrand, C.H. 1993. *Gender-responsible leadership.* Newbury Park, CA: Sage.

Warren, K. 1996a. Women's outdoor adventures: Myth and reality. In *Women's voices in experiential education,* ed. K. Warren, 10-17. Dubuque, IA: Kendall/Hunt.

Warren, K., ed. 1996b. *Women's voices in experiential education.* Dubuque, IA: Kendall/Hunt.

Warren, K., and T.A. Loeffler. 2006. Factors that influence women's technical skill development in outdoor adventure. *Journal of Adventure Education and Outdoor Learning,* 6(2):121-134.

Lesson Plan

PURPOSE

To create a safe learning community for students to address gender topics in adventure education.

OBJECTIVES

As a result of this lesson students will be able to . . .

1. *Affective and cognitive*: explain how gender-role conditioning affects the adventure experience.
2. *Cognitive:* apply gender-responsible outdoor leadership to real-life scenarios.
3. *Affective and psychomotor:* participate in several interactive experiences that clarify and reinforce their understanding of gender topics in outdoor adventures.
4. *Affective and spiritual:* gain greater self-understanding of the personal effects of gender in their own adventure experiences.

DURATION

120 minutes

GROUP SIZE

6 to 15 students

LOCATION

Indoors

EQUIPMENT

- Laptop and LCD projector
- Small paper bags, cards, and markers
- Popular outdoor adventure magazines, one for each student

RISK MANAGEMENT CONSIDERATIONS

As students will be taking emotional risks in this lesson, it is essential to set a climate of safety before the lesson begins. Timing the lesson to take place after the students have gained some sense of comfort and trust with each other is critical. Ground rules or verbal agreements are established or reiterated. Some very useful ground rules include maintaining confidentiality, sharing "airtime," and recognizing that it is okay to make a mistake or say something the "wrong way."

STUDENT PREPARATION

Students should read the lesson 21 Background document (on CD-ROM). Students can also read from the following sources in preparation for this lesson. If possible, these texts could be placed on reserve at the library.

- D.J. Jordan, 1996, Snips and snails and puppy dog tails . . . The use of gender-free language in experiential education, in *Women's voices in experiential education,* ed. K. Warren Dubuque, IA: Kendall/Hunt, 205-211.
- K. Warren, 1996, Women's outdoor adventures: Myth and reality, in *Women's voices in experiential education,* ed. K. Warren. Dubuque, IA: Kendall/Hunt, 10-17.

INSTRUCTOR PREPARATION

Before class, gather all the props you will need for the activities.

LESSON CONTENT AND TEACHING STRATEGIES

Start the lesson by giving an overview of the goals of the class and reviewing or establishing ground rules. Emphasize that the aim of learning about gender is not to promote a male–female split but to heal unequal gender relationships of power. Explain that sexism oppresses women and girls and limits their choices in life and at the same time hurts men and boys by punishing them when they go outside of prescribed gender norms.

Have the students write down what they need in order to be able to address gender issues in a safe and supportive climate. Collect these and read them aloud, preserving anonymity, while strategizing how to create that safety. Emphasize that people are in different places on their journey of understanding and that it is important to respect where each person is with regard to the issue.

Introduce the idea of gender-role conditioning in the outdoors by showing the PowerPoint (on CD-ROM) reviewing the messages we get in the outdoor media about men and women in the outdoor setting. Have students view the PowerPoint and share what messages about gender they see in the images. Share some content analysis strategies with them in preparation for the next activity (strategies list in activity 1).

Activity 1: Gender Content Analysis

Messages about race, gender, and class in outdoor adventure come from a number of sources and are reinforced by institutions such as education, the media, and government. This exercise looks at messages about gender promoted by the popular outdoor adventure literature.

For props, use recent copies of popular outdoor adventure magazines depicting the range of outdoor activities (e.g., *Rock and Ice, Climbing, Paddler, Canoe and Kayak, Sea Kayaker, Outside*) and various outdoor leadership skills and foundation texts. Have students survey these magazines and texts, looking for representations of gender in the ads, the photos in the articles, and the text.

Students should use the following content analysis strategies:

- Notice the number of women versus men represented in photos, quotations, and citations. Count these occurrences and determine an overall percentage.
- Notice the position of women in photos and how it applies to competency in the outdoors (e.g., are women primarily in the bow of the canoe while men are in the stern?).
- Notice the activity level of women and men in photos. Are women in passive roles (e.g., are women holding a paddle but not paddling; watching a rock climb)?
- Notice examples of sexualizing or infantizing women (e.g., are women scantily clad? Are they shown as needing protection?).
- Notice the relationship of women and men to risky situations in photos and text (e.g., are women cast as caretakers and men as risk takers?).
- Notice the use or lack of inclusive language.

Depending on the group size, students share their discoveries with the large group or in small groups. Groups brainstorm a synthesis of the gender-based messages about outdoor adventure promoted by this literature.

The content analysis is an effective focus for moving to the next part of the class that relates to personal experiences of gender-role conditioning. Inform students that the next activity is about the gender-role messages they have personally received.

Activity 2: Outside the Bag

Give each student two brown paper lunch bags, markers, and small cards. On the outside of bag 1, students will write their responses to the following question: "What are the outside perceptions, pressures, and messages that exist about male or female outdoor leaders?" The students should answer the question for their own gender.

On the cards in bag 1, students will write words to answer this question: "What do you feel about yourself as a male or female outdoor leader given these pressures or messages?" The students should answer the question for their own gender.

On the outside of bag 2, students will write their answers to this question: "If you could change those outside perceptions, pressures, and messages that exist about male or female outdoor leaders, what would be valued for male or female outdoor leaders?" The students should answer the question for their own gender.

On the cards in bag 2, students write words to answer this question: "How would you feel about yourself as a male or female outdoor leader if you were valued in a different way?" Again, the students should answer the question for their own gender.

Depending on the size of the class, have students share their responses in small groups, dyads, or with the whole group. This activity often gets students thinking about new visions of outdoor leadership they would like to see. As a whole group, ask them to share ideas about how these visions could be achieved in their class, at work, or in personal adventures.

Activity 3: Single-Gender Fishbowls

Tell the students that the single-gender fishbowls will be a way to personalize issues brought up in the readings. Talk about how single-gender environments might seem uncomfortable but have served a purpose in outdoor adventure—they have been a means of advocating for oppressed groups to gather in sanctuary to share common concerns and experiences.

To create the fishbowl, have students of one gender sit in a circle on the floor. They will be the group to discuss while the other-gender students are silent listeners. To relieve the hesitation some people may have about being in the fishbowl, give the usual opportunities to pass during speaking. It is also helpful to have the people on the outside turn their backs so they are facing away from the circle of speakers. Ask participants to use examples from their own experience. The questions are starters, but the dialogue can evolve in the way it needs to. You can usually start with the fishbowl of your own gender and sit in and participate to give the students some role modeling about the levels of disclosure in the dialogue, but be very careful not to direct or dominate the discussion. Have participants swap roles so that the silent listeners get to discuss while the first group becomes the silent listeners.

Women's Fishbowl Questions

- Do women lead differently in the outdoors than men?
- At what times have you felt disadvantaged or advantaged because of your gender in the outdoors?
- What experience do you have of the "superwoman"? (Warren 1996a)
- What are things you would like men in the outdoors to know about your experience in the outdoors?

Men's Fishbowl Questions

- How has sexism hurt you in the outdoors?
- What areas of dealing with gender issues in the outdoors do you find difficult?

- How can female participants (women and girls) be encouraged in the outdoors?
- What are things you would like women in the outdoors to know about your experience in the outdoors?

Activity 4: Strategies for Addressing Gender Issues in the Outdoors

The aim of the final discussion and information sharing is to give students tools for dealing with gender issues that might come up. As students work to resolve gender issues, you should encourage them to speak from personal experience and make their interventions nonjudgmental and respectful by using naming rather than blaming observations. Use the Outdoor Leadership Strategies With Gender in Mind handout (on CD-ROM this is also table 21.1) and discuss strategies that resonate with the students.

Cover the following points in the discussion:

LESSON 21

Outdoor Leadership Strategies With Gender in Mind (Table 21.1)

Karen Warren

- Linguistic sexism. Discuss parallel language as it relates to the Jordan reading (e.g., "ladies" and "men" are not parallel language). Discuss "hard skills" versus "soft skills." Have students brainstorm examples of noninclusive language in the outdoors and alternatives to these examples (e.g., "two-man tents" vs. "two-person tents," "virgin forest" vs. "old-growth forest," "man the tables" vs. "staff the tables").
- Feminist leadership. What would a feminist leadership model look like? How is it different from or similar to outdoor leadership models they know?
- Territorial sexism. How does position in the outdoor learning environment affect acquisition of skills? Ask students to give personal examples.
- Ending sexism. How can male and female leaders work together to rid outdoor programs of sexism?

CLOSURE

Since this lesson is an introduction to gender issues in the outdoors, it is used as a springboard to give attention to gender topics throughout the class. Therefore when a class experience arises that pertains to gender, we take time to discuss it and further our understanding. For example, while we are on the ropes course we look at elements that may be gender biased. Or when we practice teaching technical outdoor skills we might look at how gender-role conditioning affects the teaching and learning. It is important that gender issue education be woven into the entire curriculum, not isolated to one class.

ASSESSMENT OF LEARNING

Learning is assessed in the discussions through students' participation. Students also do a follow-up written reflection on the course Web site discussion board. Students who are interested in gender and the outdoors will often do teaching sessions or write their final paper on the topic as it pertains to their experience.

LESSON 22

The First-Generation Condition in Adventure Education

Jackson Wilson, Aya Hayashi, and Alan Ewert

Many outdoor educators and institutions see the desirability of working with diverse groups of students. For example, in the recent national merger of Outward Bound USA, diversity was included as one of the core values that guides the organization. In order to successfully educate diverse groups of students, educators and institutions need to understand how groups of students systematically differ. This lesson illustrates how first-generation students often differ from other students.

Background

Students differ in many ways, but one major way they differ derives from their family's level of experience with the types of educational programming that the student is currently engaging in. Adventure education students whose parent did not engage in adventure education are considered first-generation adventure education students (McKeachie and Svinicki 2006).

Although within the adventure education literature there appears to be no reference to the first-generation condition, this condition has been thoroughly investigated in the higher education setting (Brown and Burkhardt 1999; Choy 2001; Duggan 2001; Gibbons and Shoffner 2004; Hellman 1996; McConnell 2000; Naumann, Bandalos, and Gutkin 2003; Pascarella et al. 2004; Penrose 2002; Pike and Kuh 2005; Rodriguez 2003; Ryken 2006; Williams and Hellman 1998; Windham, Search, and Jefferson 1996) and in immigration contexts (Chau 2006; Cortes 2006; Ishitani 2005; Stodolska and Alexandris 2004; Urdan and Giancarlo 2001).

The research shows that all first-generation students face some common issues. Families of first-generation students are less likely to be aware of the pressures and benefits of the type of education that the student is experiencing (McKeachie and Svinicki 2006). This unfamiliarity may hamper their ability to motivate their child ("Don't worry, you're almost through the hard part!"), adequately prepare their child ("You should pack this kind of clothing because . . ."), or empathize ("I know what you're talking about—I had a hard time too"). Moreover, the family may be concerned that the educational experience may acculturate their son or daughter and lead to the development of negative views of his or her family of origin (McKeachie and Svinicki 2006). These difficulties have led students to drop out of higher education at a higher rate than their non-first-generation peers (Choy 2001; Ishitani 2005; Ryken 2006).

This lesson mainly addresses the question of how to effectively facilitate adventure education experiences for students; however, your students may ask if it is really important for first-generation students to engage in adventure education experiences. Adventure education experiences are beneficial for many types of students, but they may be especially meaningful for first-generation students. Pascarella and colleagues (2004) found that "in extracurricular activities and noncourse-related interactions with peers, first-generation students tended to derive significantly stronger positive benefits from these involvements than did other students" (p. 272). Stodolska and Alexandris (2004) found that recreational sports were among the primary ways in which immigrants connected with existing communities when they came to the United States. Similarly, the recreational aspect of adventure education can help first-generation students connect with the other students involved. The intimacy of the small group format and the absence of distracting responsibilities often faced by first-generation students may help them overcome the lack of connection that keeps many of these students from fully engaging in formal education and results in lower success rates than for their peers (Pascarella et al. 2004; Pike and Kuh 2005). Moreover, we have found in our roles as practitioners that the diversity of views represented by first-generation students may increase the potential impact of the course for others. Therefore, the participation of first-generation students in adventure education experiences is good for all the students.

Many first-generation students may not engage in adventure education because they are not aware of what adventure experiences are available, what the benefits of participation are, and what the financial options are (Choy 2001). Thus first-generation students may require extra access to mentors prior to participation (Choy 2001; Ishitani 2005; Rodriguez 2003). The adventure education institution could provide this mentoring or could find a partnering community organization like the Pinnacle Scholarship Program. What is important is that a mentor can help students increase their self-efficacy by answering questions and explaining how they can be successful (Gibbons and Shoffner 2004). A mentor can also answer questions that families may have so that they can more effectively facilitate their son's or daughter's success (Rodriguez 2003). In addition, it may be important for students to experience some degree of success in elements of a course before participating in it with their peers (Gibbons and Shoffner 2004).

First-generation students tend to drop out prematurely from educational offerings. If they drop an adventure education course, it is important to frame the experience they had in a way that can help them maximize the benefits they did derive. Students may learn from the experience and choose to engage further in adventure education at a later time (Ishitani 2005; Ryken 2006). After students take a course (or only part of a course), it may be important for them to have opportunities to meet with others who had similar adventure education experiences in order to share and further process what happened (Gibbons and Shoffner 2004).

All students face challenges in adventure education, but it is the role of institutions and instructors to help students turn such challenges into a positive learning experiences. Research shows that first-generation students are more likely than others to encounter challenges that may hinder the learning that they can walk away with. Adventure education instructors and institutions need to be aware of these issues and their possible solutions in order to more effectively facilitate the experiences of students in this group.

RESOURCES

Brown, H.E., and R.L. Burkhardt. 1999. Predicting student success: The relative impact of ethnicity, income, and parental education. Paper presented at the annual forum of the Association for Institutional Research, Seattle.

Chau, W.W.-Y. 2006. The relationship between acculturative stress and spirituality among Chinese immigrant college students in the United States. ERIC Document Reproduction Service No. 491 387.

Choy, S. 2001. *Students whose parents did not go to college: Postsecondary access, persistence, and attainment.* Washington, DC: National Center for Education Statistics.

Cortes, K.E. 2006. The effects of age at arrival and enclave schools on the academic performance of immigrant children. *Economics of Education Review,* 25(2):121.

Duggan, M. 2001. Factors influencing the first-year persistence of first generation college students. Paper presented at the NEAIR Conference, Cambridge, MA.

Gibbons, M.M., and M.F. Shoffner. 2004. Prospective first-generation college students: Meeting their needs through social cognitive career theory. *Professional School Counseling,* 8:91-97.

Hellman, C.M. 1996. Academic self efficacy: Highlighting the first generation student. *Journal of Applied Research in the Community College,* 4(1):69.

Ishitani, T.T. 2005. Studying educational attainment among first-generation students in the United States. Paper presented at the 45th Annual Forum of the Association for Institutional Research, May 30-June 1, San Diego.

Layton, E. 2007. Manager of the Pinnacle Scholars Program. In J. Wilson, ed. Golden, CO. More complete source information to come from author.

McConnell, P.J. 2000. ERIC review: What community colleges should do to assist first-generation students. *Community College Review,* 28(3):75.

McKeachie, W.J., and M. Svinicki. 2006. *McKeachie's teaching tips: Strategies, research, and theory for college and university teachers.* Boston: Houghton Mifflin.

Naumann, W.C., D. Bandalos, and T.B. Gutkin. 2003. Identifying variables that predict college success for first-generation college students. *Journal of College Admission,* 181:4-10.

Outward Bound Wilderness. Pinnacle Scholarship Program. 2007. Retrieved January 31, 2007, from www.outwardboundwilderness.org/scholarships/pinnacle.html.

Pascarella, E.T., C.T. Pierson, G.C. Wolniak, and P.T. Terenzini. 2004. First-generation college students: Additional evidence on college experiences and outcomes. *Journal of Higher Education,* 75(3):420-429.

Penrose, A.M. 2002. Academic literacy perceptions and performance: Comparing first-generation and continuing-generation college students. *Research in the Teaching of English,* 36(4):437.

Pike, G.R., and G.D. Kuh. 2005. First- and second-generation college students: A comparison of their engagement and intellectual development. *Journal of Higher Education,* 76:276-300.

Rodriguez, S. 2003. What helps some first-generation students succeed? *About Campus,* 8(4):17.

Ryken, A.E. 2006. Multiple choices, multiple chances: Fostering re-entry pathways for first generation college students. *Community College Journal of Research and Practice,* 30(8):593.

Stodolska, M., and K. Alexandris. 2004. The role of recreational sport in the adaptation of first generation immigrants in the United States. *Journal of Leisure Research,* 36(3):379-413.

Urdan, T., and C. Giancarlo. 2001. Differences between students in the consequences of goals and goal structures: The role of culture and family obligation. Paper presented at the meeting of the American Educational Research Association, Seattle.

Williams, J.E., and C.M. Hellman. 1998. Investigating self-regulated learning among first-generation community college students. *Journal of Applied Research in the Community College*, 5(2):83.

Windham, P., S. Search, and S. Jefferson. 1996. Demographics: Diversity in more forms. Student demographics, now and the future. ERIC Document Reproduction Service No. 398 951.

Lesson Plan

PURPOSE

Increase current and future outdoor leaders' awareness of issues related to first-generation adventure education students (students whose parents or grandparents have not taken part in similar educational programming).

OBJECTIVES

As a result of this lesson, students will be able to . . .

1. *Affective:* be more empathetic regarding the challenges that first-generation adventure education participants experience and the ways in which they differ from other student groups.
2. *Cognitive:* understand how the first-generation condition may present unique challenges to participants in the adventure education setting.
3. *Cognitive:* develop strategies for helping first-generation adventure education participants and adventure education institutions overcome common first-generation difficulties.

DURATION

45 minutes

GROUP SIZE

10 to 50 students

LOCATION

Indoors

EQUIPMENT

- Three pieces of paper per student—blank sheets of origami-style paper are best
- Multimedia classroom for the PowerPoint presentation
- A copy of the case study for each student (on CD-ROM)

RISK MANAGEMENT CONSIDERATIONS

Some students may become frustrated during the activity. This is intentional, but is something you should be prepared for.

STUDENT PREPARATION

No prelesson preparation required.

INSTRUCTOR PREPARATION

Have copies of the case study ready. In addition, you will need to have made three Japanese paper-folding (origami) sculptures. Many good resources on the

Internet have instructions for creating these simple structures. WannaLearn.com lists Web sites that give easy, step-by-step instructions (www.wannalearn.com/Crafts_and_Hobbies/Origami/). We recommend the crane, ball, and star sculptures because of their simplicity.

LESSON CONTENT AND TEACHING STRATEGIES

This activity is designed to allow all the students to experience some of the emotions that are familiar to first-generation students. Although you could introduce the first-generation concept before you do the activity, we have found that the exercise becomes more meaningful if students gain firsthand experience before they talk about it. The activity simulates the experience of many first-generation students of being expected to achieve at the same level as others even though they have less information and support. The intention is for participants to feel social and internalized pressure to succeed similar to that felt by first-generation students.

Our understanding of the differences characterizing first-generation students is based on the assumption of intergenerational transference of information and social support. Another assumption is that the primary route for this transmission is the family unit. That is, the participant is in the first generation within the family to experience X (adventure education in our case), and the parents have limited firsthand knowledge from which to provide information and social support.

Although the lesson plan presented here is based on origami (Japanese paper folding), you could substitute many other types of activities, such as a dance routine or a navigation exercise using a map and compass. The key is for the activity to be novel for all the students in the group. It also needs to be difficult enough that students will not be able to do it easily without a certain amount of instruction. On the other hand, with some instruction, they should be able to perform the activity in a relatively short period of time (5-10 minutes). Whatever the students' product or performance, you and the students need to be able to easily evaluate how closely it matches the demonstration model you have created.

Activity 1: Experiencing Different Paths

The activity consists of two rounds. Although it may be possible to conduct the exercise with only one instructor, having two instructors is helpful. If you do not have an assistant, you may consider enlisting a student to help. Start by separating the students into four small groups; we'll call them A1, A2, B1, and B2.

In the first round, A1 and A2 form a larger group (group A); B1 and B2 form a second larger group (group B) (figure 22.1 depicts the groups and their respective interactions). You will use step-by-step instruction to teach group A to create a simple origami sculpture, such as a crane, while the second instructor teaches group B to create a different one, such as a ball. It will take 5 to 10 minutes for most students to successfully construct their first sculpture. Students are often surprised and pleased with the results of their efforts. After they complete their sculptures, students may want to have a quick presentation so that everyone can see the work of all the others.

In the second round, the groups are mixed. A1 and B1 are in one group (group 1), while A2 and B2 are in the other group (group 2). The twist in the second round is that groups A1 and A2 are charged with teaching groups B1 and B2, respectively, how to construct a new origami sculpture. Group A1 will teach group B1 the crane sculpture that A1 learned in the first round, while A2 will be charged with trying to teach B2 how to create a sculpture that neither group has previous experience with,

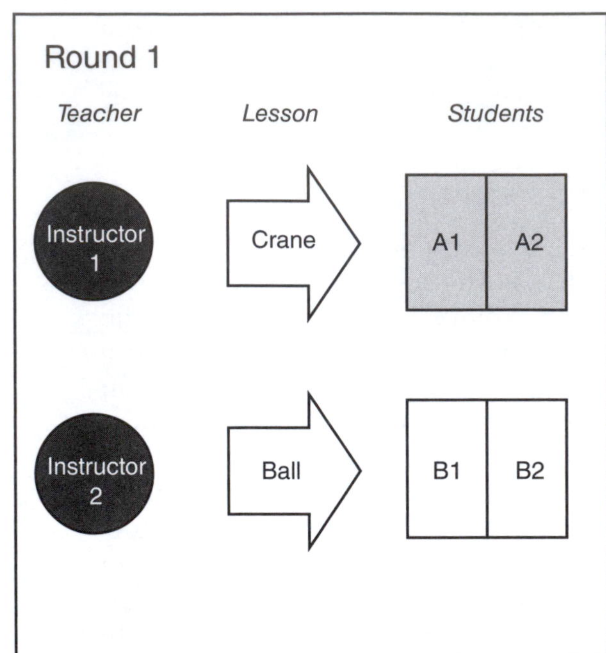

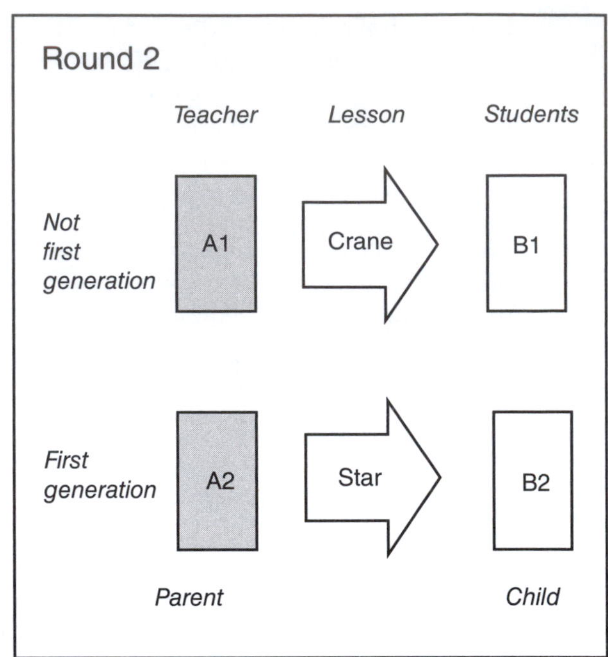

FIGURE 22.1 Logistics for origami activity.

for example a throwing star. Whereas students in group A1 will have the benefit of their recent experience to draw on in teaching B1, those in group A2 will need to base their instruction entirely on the demonstration model of a throwing star.

There are several ways in which you can intensify the students' experience and facilitate the transference of their experience in the activity to a deeper understanding of the first-generation condition. First, you can ask A1 and A2 to refrain from touching any of the paper in the second round. Thus they will not be able to "just do it" for B1 and B2; instead they will have rely on verbal instructions. Second, you can limit the duration of the second round to a period of time that is barely adequate for group 1, but highly unrealistic for group 2. Third, you may offer some type of prize to the group that can finish their sculptures first.

As the paper is incorrectly folded, unfolded, crushed into a ball, and finally made into a sculpture (or left as a crushed ball), you may see both groups straining to achieve victory. However, A2 and B2 may be frustrated because they are expected to perform on the basis of a model while A1 and B1 have the benefit of experience.

This unequal experience between A1 and A2 is intended to represent the lack of information that first-generation parents have to help guide their children compared to the information that other parents have. Parents who have had an adventure education experience (analogous to group A1) can help their son or daughter prepare physically and mentally for a similar experience. In contrast, the parents of first-generation students (analogous to group A2) are in the position of trying to help their children prepare for adventure education even though they have no personal experience of it and may be able to acquire only limited information about it. Adventure education is intended to be challenging for everyone; however, the inequity in information makes preparing for and learning from their adventure education experience even more challenging for first-generation students.

After the activity, conduct a simple processing session. The following are some questions that we have found useful.

About the Experience:

- Was this experience *fair*?
  - What does "fair" mean?
  - Does every experience have to be fair?
- What was it like to be a student in the first round?
  - How was the second round different?
  - Have you had experiences similar to this before?
  - Was the desire to achieve common to both groups in the second round, or was it limited to one?
- How was being an experienced instructor (A1) different from being an inexperienced instructor (A2) in the second round?
  - Have you had experiences similar to this before?

Relationship to Adventure Education:

- How is what happens before and after an education experience important to adventure experience?
- How do the experiences of groups 1 and 2 in the second round compare to those of adventure education students before and after participating in adventure education?
- In what ways would sending your child to an adventure education experience differ if you had had a similar experience yourself and if you had not?
  - What about after the experience?
  - What about from a student's perspective?

Activity 2: Mini-Lecture and PowerPoint on the First-Generation Condition

The intent of this mini-lecture is to give students information about the first-generation condition. Use the PowerPoint presentation on the CD-ROM to support your mini-lecture.

Definition: The first-generation condition is defined as the condition in which an individual engages in an experience, in our case adventure education, that his or her parents (or guardians or caregivers) have not had (McKeachie and Svinicki 2006; slide 2).

Slide 3 illustrates different gradations of the first-generation condition in adventure education (figure 22.2). Some parents may not have participated in any formal adventure education but may have participated in similar activities in an outdoor recreation context. Other parents may never have had an opportunity to experience a nonurban environment. In addition, why parents have had no outdoor recreation or education experiences is just as important as whether or not they have had such experiences.

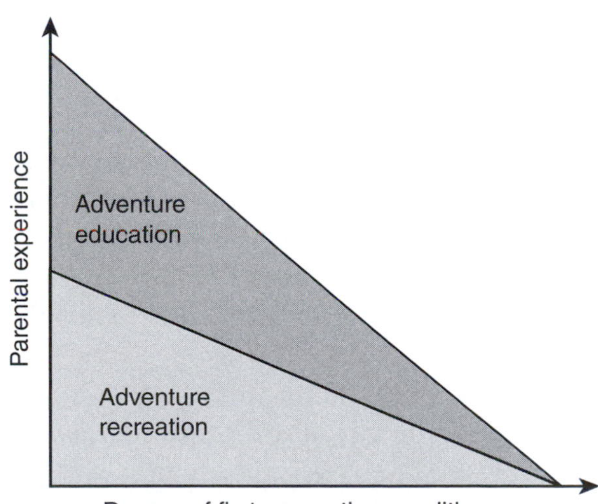

FIGURE 22.2 The first-generation condition is influenced by the degree of parental experience with adventure education.

Explain that practitioners have found that if a student's parents did not participate in adventure education due to cultural mores, racial discrimination, gender roles, or financial barriers, the first-generation condition may have a greater effect on the student (and the family) than on a first-generation student whose parents simply did not choose to engage in adventure education. The degree to which parents have been involved in any aspect of adventure education and the reasons for differing degrees of involvement may affect the extent to which they will be able to be an informational and emotional resource for their son or daughter.

Common first-generation student experiences may include the following (slide 4):

- Not knowing what types of equipment will work
- Not having anyone to advise them about preparing for their experience
- Not having anyone to ask when they have questions such as "What is it like to sleep on the ground?"
- Having parents who are overly concerned about hazards (bears, bad food) that most likely will not be an issue
- Having parents who lack a point of reference ("You're almost through the difficult part!") for when and how to offer encouragement
- Having parents who cannot empathize with their experience

Explain with slide 5 that according to recent research, these conditions could have the following results for students:

- Lack of proper preparation for the experience
- Less engagement in the experience
- Dropping out prematurely
- Inadequately connecting with their family regarding what their experience has meant to them and what they want to do with that experience

Activity 3: Institutional and Instructional Strategies

The next activity is an investigative activity that can be assigned after the lesson. The goal is to have students discover and understand the strategies that adventure education institutions currently use to facilitate first-generation students' success. Have students report their findings during the next class session. Alternatively, they could analyze the case study on page 249.

Choose an adventure education institution that you have worked for, or would like to work for, that enrolls first-generation students. Contact the institution and find out what strategies it uses to maximize the educational experience of first-generation students. Reflect on these strategies, asking the following questions:

- What do the institution and the instructional staff do before, during, and after the adventure education experience?
- What assumptions are implicit in these strategies?
- Which staff positions are involved in this effort?
- Based on your experience in the origami activity and what you know about the first-generation condition, how effective you do believe these strategies are?

- What would you recommend that this organization do differently?
- What constraints might the institution face in trying to implement your recommendations?

The following case study can help your students reflect on the strategies that professional organizations employ to help first-generation students. Ask the class to form groups of three to five, and distribute copies of the case study (on CD-ROM). Then ask them to read the case study and discuss in their small group the strategies that this professional organization employs. When the groups have had time for discussion, move on to the lesson closure activity.

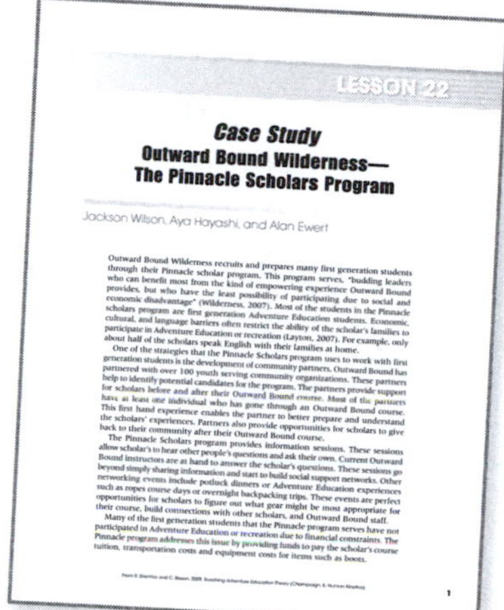
LESSON 22

Case Study
Outward Bound Wilderness—
The Pinnacle Scholars Program

Jackson Wilson, Aya Hayashi, and Alan Ewert

Outward Bound Wilderness recruits and prepares many first generation students through their Pinnacle scholar program. This program serves, "budding leaders who can benefit most from the kind of empowering experience Outward Bound provides, but who have the least possibility of participating due to social and economic disadvantage" (Wilderness, 2007). Most of the students in the Pinnacle scholars program are first generation Adventure Education students. Economic, cultural, and language barriers often restrict the ability of the scholar's families to participate in Adventure Education or recreation (Layton, 2007). For example, only about half of the scholars speak English with their families at home.

One of the strategies that the Pinnacle Scholars program uses to work with first generation students is the development of community partners. Outward Bound has partnered with over 100 youth serving community organizations. These partners help to identify potential candidates for the program. The partners provide support for scholars before and after their Outward Bound course. Most of the partners have at least one individual who has gone through an Outward Bound course. This first hand experience enables the partner to better prepare and understand the scholars' experiences. Partners also provide opportunities for scholars to give back to their community after their Outward Bound course.

The Pinnacle Scholars program provides information sessions. These sessions allow scholar's to hear other people's questions and ask their own. Current Outward Bound instructors are at hand to answer the scholar's questions. These sessions go beyond simply sharing information and start to build social support networks. Other networking events include potluck dinners or Adventure Education experiences such as ropes course days or overnight backpacking trips. These events are perfect opportunities for scholars to figure out what gear might be most appropriate for their course, build connections with other scholars, and Outward Bound staff.

Many of the first generation students that the Pinnacle program serves have not participated in Adventure Education or recreation due to financial constraints. The Pinnacle program addresses this issue by providing funds to pay the scholar's course tuition, transportation costs and equipment costs for items such as boots.

1

Outward Bound Wilderness recruits and prepares many first-generation students through the Pinnacle Scholarship Program. The program serves "budding leaders who can benefit most from the kind of empowering experience Outward Bound provides, but who have the least possibility of participating due to social and economic disadvantage" (Outward Bound Wilderness 2007). Most students in the Pinnacle Scholarship Program are first-generation adventure education students. Economic, cultural, and language barriers often restrict the ability of the scholar's families to participate in adventure education or recreation (Layton 2007). For example, only about half of the scholars speak English with their families at home.

One of the strategies the program uses with first-generation students is the development of community partners. Outward Bound has partnered with more than 100 youth-serving community organizations. The partners help to identify potential candidates for the program. They provide support for scholars before and after their Outward Bound course. Most of the partners have worked with at least one individual who has gone through an Outward Bound course. This first-hand experience enables partners to better prepare scholars and understand their experiences. Partners also provide opportunities for scholars to give back to their community after their Outward Bound course.

The Pinnacle Scholarship Program provides information sessions that allow scholars to hear other people's questions and ask their own. Current Outward Bound instructors are at hand to answer the questions. These sessions go beyond simply sharing information and begin to build social support networks. Other networking events include potluck dinners and adventure education events such as ropes course days or overnight backpacking trips. These events provide perfect opportunities for scholars to figure out what gear might be most appropriate for their course and to build connections with other scholars and Outward Bound staff.

Many of the first-generation students that the program serves have not participated in adventure education or recreation due to financial constraints. The program addresses this issue by providing funds to pay for a scholar's course tuition, transportation, and equipment such as boots.

The program also provides career opportunities. Beyond their initial two- to three-week course, students can apply for scholarships for semester-long courses. Scholars are encouraged to become Outward Bound interns and further develop their skills. Through this path they can become instructors. Other scholars go on to work for other youth-serving programs and become Pinnacle partners.

CLOSURE

Close this lesson by helping your students create a set of best practices for working with first-generation students. This list of practices could be simply a brainstormed list, or students could create an instructional booklet.

It is important to help students understand that the first-generation condition is just one of many ways in which students differ. Although much of the discussion here centers on ways of overcoming challenges common to adventure education students, it is also important to discuss the benefits that diverse students bring to adventure education courses.

ASSESSMENT OF LEARNING

At the end of this lesson students will understand and be able to verbalize what the first-generation condition is and will be able to describe the challenges common to the first generation. They will be able to list various strategies that can be used to specifically address these issues and assess the practicality of these strategies.

LESSON 23

Be Safe Out There

Critically Thinking Risk in Adventure Education

Denise Mitten and Martyn Whittingham

Knowing how to use critical thinking skills to evaluate our work as facilitators helps us truly deliver the programs we promise. This lesson helps students explore critical thinking in relation to our facilitation goals. Students will better understand the relationship between problem solving and risk. In relation to experiential education, when confronted with a risk, students will learn to not just assume that taking the risk is a good thing but to evaluate what risks to take, with whom to take a risk, and when to do so. This lesson includes several teaching strategies, from an interactive PowerPoint to a reading from a storybook to actual activity facilitation.

Background

Education in the critical faculty is the only education of which it can be truly said that it makes good citizens.

—William Graham Sumner, *Folkways*, 1906

The key concepts in this lesson are critical thinking, the use of ethical facilitation to help people work with their fear in adventure education, and understanding and facilitating transfer. The foundations for the subject and content come from psychology, ethics, human development theories, and social theories. Our premise is that in facilitating adventure education programs and in working with fear and risk, we are attempting to help participants understand their own fears and understand how to use those fears to their best advantage. We are helping participants learn how to assess risk, including which risks to choose to take and when to take these risks, as well as how and with whom to take the risks. Actually completing the element in a high ropes course is often subsidiary to this process; and if the focus is primarily on the accomplishment, sometimes more harm than benefit to the participant may result. We are trying to highlight and practice facilitation that enhances the well-being of others and to understand and change and refine facilitation that does harm or diminishes the well-being of others.

CRITICAL THINKING

To extend the thought of Sumner's quote, education in the critical faculty helps make competent facilitators and professionals. "Critical thinking is commonly confused with active involvement in learning (forgetting that active involvement alone is quite compatible with active 'mislearning')" (Paul, Elder, and Bartell 1997). While it is possible to teach critical thinking effectively at the high school or the college and university level, Paul, Elder, and Bartell (1997) found that as a rule this was not occurring. We need to not miss the opportunity to teach students critical thinking skills, because to help them learn and practice these skills is to help them become better practitioners.

Critical thinking involves the ability to assess thinking for quality using the following standards: clarity, accuracy, depth, significance, fairness, precision, relevance, breadth, and logic. The ultimate goal in critical thinking is to foster the development of fair-mindedness, intellectual humility, courage, autonomy, empathy, perseverance, and integrity and confidence in reasoning (see figure 23.1).

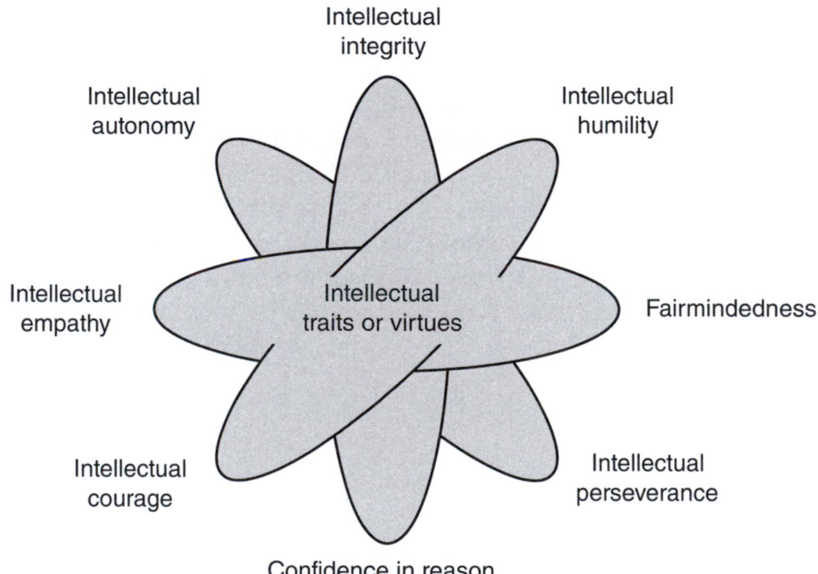

▶ **FIGURE 23.1** Intellectual traits or virtues.

Reprinted, by permission, from R. Paul and L. Elder, 2006, *Critical thinking compentency standards* (Dillon Beach, CA: Foundation for Critical Thinking), 58, www.criticalthinking.org.

We can analyze thinking by identifying its eight elements (see figure 23.2). These elements are examined using the intellectual standards (see figure 23.3). Using ethical reasoning (using critical thinking to highlight whether an act increases or diminishes well-being) and the critical thinking standards, we are more likely to attain standards in our practices that enhance the well-being of participants while minimizing the risk of doing harm to them in any of their personal domains (physical, spiritual, behavioral, emotional, and social). A number of critical thinking handbooks are available, and a conference on critical thinking is held annually; the Web site www.criticalthinking.org is a good source of information.

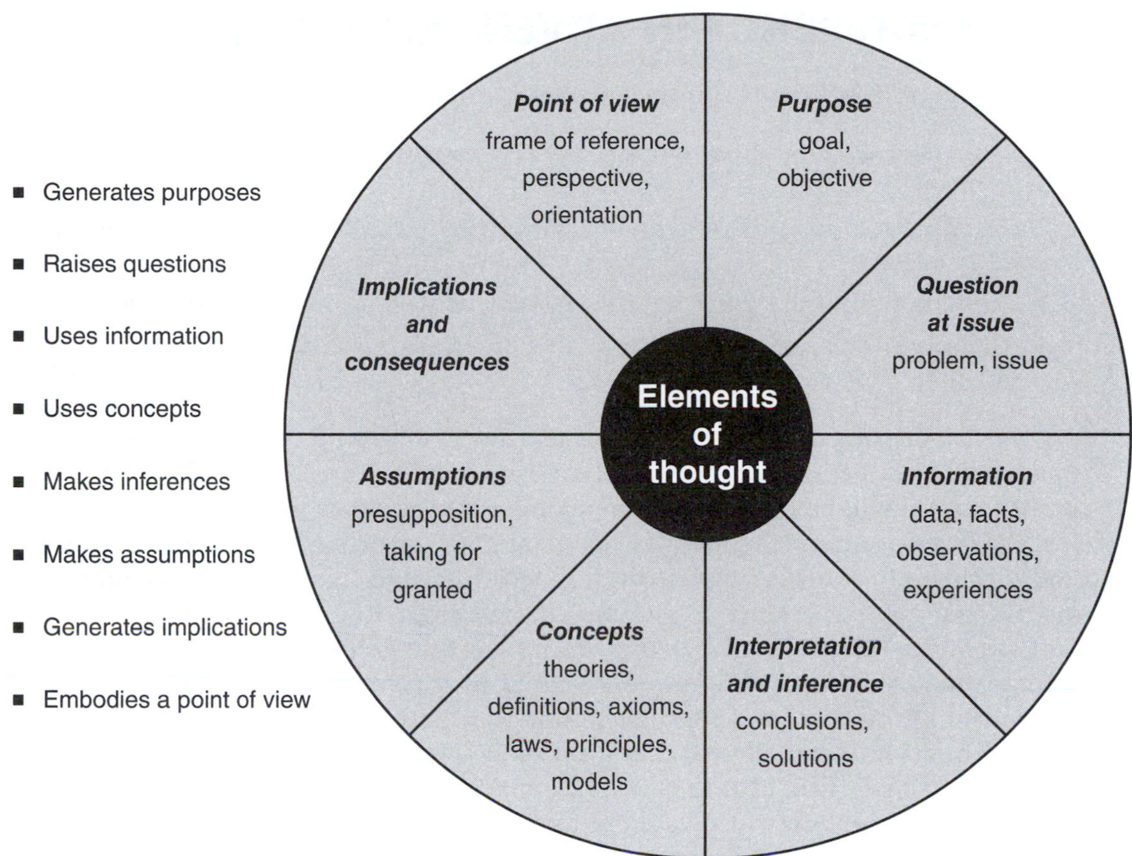

FIGURE 23.2 The elements of ethical reasoning.

Reprinted, by permission, from R. Paul and L. Elder, 2006, *Ethical reasoning* (Dillon Beach, CA: Foundation for Critical Thinking), 16, www.criticalthinking.org.

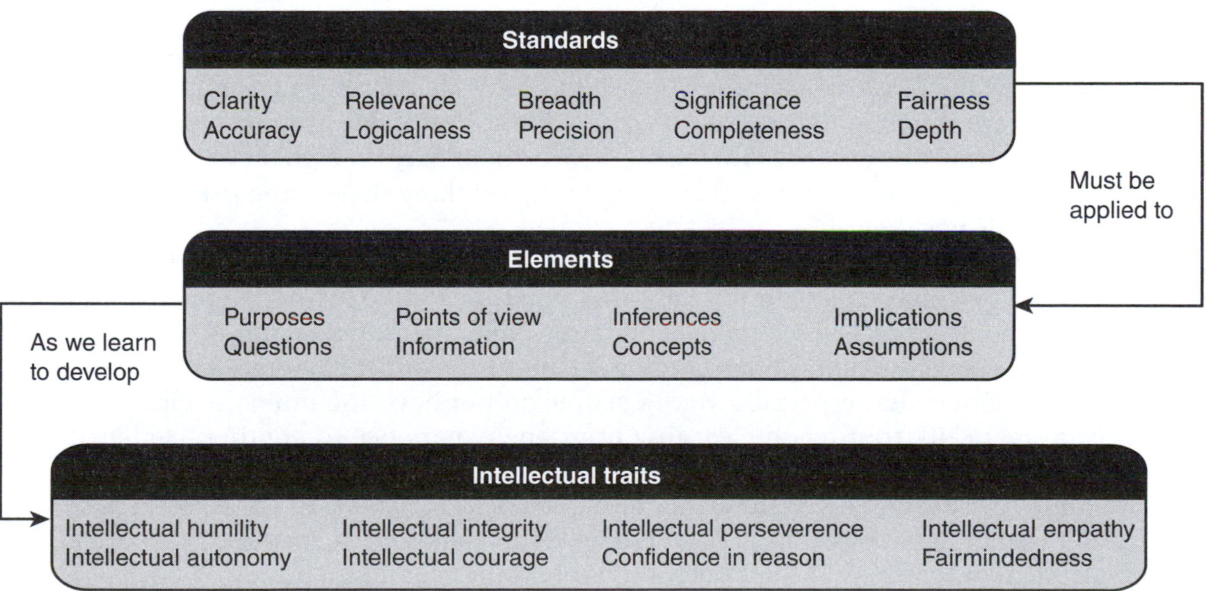

FIGURE 23.3 Critical thinkers routinely apply the intellectual standards to the elements of reasoning in order to develop intellectual traits.

Reprinted, by permission, from R. Paul and L. Elder, 2006, *Critical thinking compentency standards* (Dillon Beach, CA: Foundation for Critical Thinking), 59, www.criticalthinking.org.

TRANSFERENCE IN ADVENTURE EDUCATION

In their role plays, students should consider four areas within transference.

1. Understanding the information, perceptions, and misconceptions participants bring with them to the experience.
2. Building a solid body of knowledge during the activity to have available for transference.
3. Understanding the potential for negative as well as positive transference.
4. Helping the participants to know that the transfer of skills and processes is possible.

First, participants transfer their previous learning to the ropes course experience. In adventure education we talk about and work with transference, hoping that lessons learned will be carried over and generalized to other parts of participants' lives. We don't as often teach facilitators that in fact participants are coming to our programs already transferring lessons learned from their past; this is the transfer process from one experience to another that we hope to initiate during this current experience. A feature of effective teaching is that it elicits from students their preconceptions or preexisting understanding of the material being taught. We explore the knowledge and preconceptions that participants come with. In our work we build on or challenge the initial understandings that participants may have or are transferring into the current experience. In this lesson, students can experience that they may also have initial understandings that may benefit from critical thinking. Showing through example how we can examine our preconceptions helps students understand the importance of this process.

Second, in order to have adequate transfer there must be adequate and accurate learning in the first place. We have to be teaching what we think we are teaching. Concepts that may be clear to us as facilitators may not be clear in the same way to the participants.

Third, we understand that there are possibilities for negative transfer as well as possibilities for positive transfer. As facilitators we need congruence and clarity between our intent and our actual teaching. For example, we may give paticipants positive reinforcement for taking risks. A participant may then go on to other situations and take the same risks that are not safe, thinking that taking risks for their own sake is positive.

Finally, we need to be sure that the participants do not see this learning as contextual, which means in this case that what they have learned applies in the current situation only. Especially at certain developmental ages and for concrete thinkers, processing and understanding metaphors is difficult. Additionally, some research shows that especially young people do not have the brain development to automatically transfer the learning from one experience to another. Odd as it seems, some participants may leave your program thinking "Unless there are 10 other people around me I am not taking any risks." To facilitators, the transfer possibilities may seem obvious; however, if we do not show participants how to use a process in other areas of their lives it often becomes contextualized.

With proper framing and facilitating, people can learn a number of transferable coping skills by working through fear in risky situations. They can learn to assess risk and know if they are facing a cognitive, behavioral, social, physical, or spiritual risk. They can learn to become aware of their anxious cognitions when they are under stress and can learn to change these cognitions. If they experience these anxious cognitions in other stressful situations, they can perhaps change them in those situations too. Other positive gains may include increasing the ability to use helpful self-talk; changing self-perceptions; modifying meaning attributions to create the possibility of hope and change; building skills in making good decisions; using tools to assess risk in its six dimensions; understanding fear and how to manage it and keep thinking and acting; building skills in social support; learning more about understanding, empathizing with, and helping others as they succeed or struggle; and learning to balance needs of the self with needs of others. However, each of these kinds of learning usually requires specific facilitation for that learning as well as the transferences. Otherwise the learning is too often only about the accomplishment of completing an element.

RISK IN ADVENTURE EDUCATION

Risk is the exposure to the possibility of some loss or harm (Gregg 2007). Risk is a cornerstone of most adventure programs. Perceived risk is often used as a central variable in attempts to promote participant growth (Davis-Berman and Berman 2002). Often the actual activity is fairly safe; the facilitators keep the perceived risk high in order to have participants learn to take risks. It is assumed that this risk-taking ability will be generalized into the rest of the participants' lives and create a higher quality of life. On ropes courses we ask participants to make conscious decisions to expose themselves to the chance of loss or harm in order to achieve a desired result. The desired result may be a physical accomplishment, a higher social status in the group, or something else. We tend to think of risk mostly in the physical dimension (e.g., fear of falling), and most ropes courses require physical involvement. We acknowledge that people need to feel emotionally safe in order to take risks and that emotional risks exist; however, teaching about risk often can be more sophisticated. For example, participants can learn the difference in taking an emotional risk, a social risk, a spiritual risk, or a physical risk. Facilitators can help participants understand why it might be beneficial to take a risk and why to specifically choose to or not to take a risk.

Risk is personal or individual. What one person finds risky, another may not see as risky at all. Additionally, risk taking affects all of our domains: physical, social, emotional, spiritual, behavioral, and cognitive. Our facilitation influences each of these domains, sometimes in unanticipated ways. Students and facilitators often benefit from deconstructing some of their current notions of risk. For example, commending a person who takes risks easily and encouraging others to take risks may or may not be beneficial, depending on the context.

As facilitators, most of us agree that it is necessary to know our participants and understand the varied ways in which people approach and use risk. For example, for some participants, risk taking for the sake of risk taking may not be a positive exercise. On the other hand, those same participants might benefit from risk taking if it means standing up for their values in a particular context. It is exactly that sort of personal risk taking—standing up for one's values—that has influenced positive social change. Rosa Parks is an iconic example.

Many people have mis-learned that risk taking builds character. In his book *How to Know God,* Deepak Chopra (2000) articulates what one might say is a primary objection to the use of risk taking alone to build character. In this, Chopra says, there is lack of spiritual intention. He understands that many people use risk to feel powerful and successful. He believes that the concept of "I want to prove myself by taking risks" doesn't add to one's spiritual growth. It can lead to a seemingly stronger ego. The ego, however, will not be satisfied, and so the original problem will not be solved. Instead, the desire to have more power often arises, leading to taking more risks, and so on (Chopra 2000).

Taking risks can help one feel powerful. It also can help one feel superior. This is why the accountant who steals a little money and gets away with it often is intrigued by the idea of trying to steal a bit more and a bit more. In the United States we are in the postmodern period, which is ego focused. We have to consciously not feed into these current cultural values. Even if we don't believe that accomplishments lead to inappropriate feelings of power over others, our participants might take this learning away from an adventure experience because of their past experiences.

In the case of adventure education, risk taking without intention and adequate framing for participants can occur at the expense of the environment and others. That is why our intention as facilitators is so crucial: Have we thoroughly looked at how participants can interpret their experiences, and have we set an intention regarding what we are trying to convey or help participants learn or experience in all of the human domains? For example, a person may see running white-water rapids as taking a risk. When that person successfully runs the rapids, what if she feels as if she has "beaten" the rapids and is better than others who chose not to run the rapids or participate on the trip? Some people climb a mountain and talk about having conquered the mountain. This does not necessarily have to be the outcome, but in our experience, the language and behaviors of leaders can reinforce this sometimes subtle but very real outcome. Chopra refers to this feeling of power as the cheapest way to feed the ego.

Learning that risk taking is a good thing without specific parameters relating to when to take risks, with whom, and what risks to take can promote negative risk-taking behaviors. For people who have had others use power over them in negative ways, as is the case with many at-risk youth, often an obvious interpretation of completing a challenge or risk is to feel powerful. In this sense, risk can be addictive, and there can be negative transferring from a ropes course experience. Some research indicates that risk taking and mastery promote impulsive and egocentric behavior (Whittingham 2005), supporting Chopra's work. Increasingly impulsiveness and lack of impulse control are implicated as risk factors in many psychological disorders, ranging from substance abuse and eating disorders to at-risk behavior such as sexual or violent risk taking (Whittingham 2005). Could we be augmenting the problems we intend to help solve?

On ropes courses, many of us encourage participants to choose their level of participation and therefore their risk. Are we too quick to assume that because the participant has a choice in the amount of risk she or he takes, any drawbacks will be outweighed by the benefits—or have we not thought about the drawbacks of promoting risk taking? Have we thought about what it means to be truly free to choose participation or if that is even possible for participants with certain backgrounds? Have we thought about how this process transfers in terms of spiritual, social, behavioral, cognitive, or emotional development? Have we thought about how intuition plays into risk-taking behavior?

Some people complete ropes course elements and talk about having conquered their fears. However, in *The Gift of Fear,* Gavin de Becker (1997), an expert on the prediction and management of violence, explains why this is not a desired outcome. As he teaches about threat assessment, he explains how to use our fears, rely on intuition, separate real danger from what he calls imagined danger, predict dangerous behavior from others, and move beyond denial so that our intuition will add to our safety. He shows that we have innate survival skills that warn us about risk from strangers, among other risks. Feeling fear is a crucial part of staying safe.

Most of us are in the business of helping people gain competency in the emotional, physical, behavioral, social, spiritual, and cognitive domains. People are not divisible into parts and thus need to be worked with in a holistic manner. By paying more attention to the attributes around the risk taking rather than the risky action in and of itself, we can teach how to assess which risks to take; why, when, and with whom to take them; and how to take them.

Risk is a part of our everyday lives, including the adventures we experience. To be part of a thriving democracy, people need to know how to take risks and how to evaluate context. This includes how to formulate values and now to stand up for one's own values. As adventure facilitators and experiential educators, we can have an important role in teaching people to assess risk and to know the value of taking appropriate risks. We can examine our practices using ethical reasoning to be sure that we are accomplishing our intended goals in facilitation.

RESOURCES

Chopra, D. 2000. *How to know God.* New York: Three Rivers Press.

Davis-Berman, J., and D. Berman. 2002. Risk and anxiety in adventure programming. *Journal of Experiential Education,* 25(2):305-310.

de Becker, G. 1997. *The gift of fear and other survival signals that protect us from violence.* New York: Dell.

Elder, L., and R. Paul. 2003. The thinker's guide to analytic thinking. Dillon Beach, CA: Foundation for Critical Thinking. www.criticalthinking.org.

Gregg, R. 2007. Risk and safety in adventure programming. In *Adventure education: Theory and applications,* eds. D. Prouty, J. Panicucci, and R. Collinson. Champaign, IL: Human Kinetics.

Lionni, L. 1970. *Fish is fish.* New York: Scholastic Press.

Mitten, D. 2005. Spiritual and emotional risks in outdoor activities. *AEE Horizon.*

Paul, R., and L. Elder. 2005. Ethical reasoning. Dillon Beach, CA: Foundation for Critical Thinking. www.criticalthinking.org.

Paul, R.W., L. Elder, and T. Bartell. 1997. California teacher preparation for instruction in critical thinking: Research findings and policy recommendations. California Commission on Teacher Credentialing, Sacramento, California. Dillon Beach, CA: Foundation for Critical Thinking. www.criticalthinking.org.

Ulrich, R.S., R.F. Simons, B.D. Losito, E. Fiorito, M.A. Miles, and M. Zelson. 1991. Stress recovery during exposure to natural and urban environments. *Journal of Environmental Psychology,* 11:201-230.

Vosniadou, S., and W.F. Brewer. 1989. The concept of the earth's shape: A study of conceptual change in childhood. Unpublished paper. Center for the Study of Reading, University of Illinois, Champaign.

Whittingham, M. 2005. Rethinking risk. ACCT Conference, Indianapolis.

ADDITIONAL SUGGESTED READING

Five reasons to stop saying "good job!" by Alfie Kohn. Note: This article was published in *Young Children,* September 2001; and, in abridged form (with the title "Hooked on Praise"), in *Parents Magazine,* May 2000.

Lesson Plan

PURPOSE

To use critical thinking analysis to examine the standards and practices of using risk as a teaching tool and learn about the relationships between judgment, risk, and participant outcomes. Specifically, students learn that through properly facilitated ropes course experiences, participants can develop deliberation and judgment skills, and that this is what we want participants to transfer to other parts of their lives rather than behavioral risk taking.

OBJECTIVES

As a result of this lesson students will be able to . . .

1. *Affective:* understand the relationship between fear and emotions.
2. *Affective:* experience using a critical thinking analysis to examine their beliefs and learn that this sort of analysis can help make their practice more ethical as well as more effective.
3. *Cognitive:* understand the usefulness of risk in adventure activities and how to work with risk to help participants grow in the cognitive, affective, social, physical, behavioral, and spiritual domains.
4. *Cognitive:* learn what some of their misinterpretations of the value of risk may be, as well as the evidence-based understanding of transfer of risk-taking behavior.
5. *Cognitive:* understand that they respond faster emotionally than they do cognitively.
6. *Cognitive:* understand that people develop their beliefs about physical, biological, and psychological phenomena through their experiences and that these beliefs do not necessarily fit the reality or scientific accounts of these phenomena.
7. *Cognitive:* understand more about risk evaluation and the process of transfer of judgment and decision-making skills related to risk taking.
8. *Cognitive:* be able to apply critical thinking processes in their work.

DURATION

180 minutes

GROUP SIZE

6 to 15 students

LOCATION

Outdoors and indoors

EQUIPMENT

- Two large pieces of paper (about 8 feet [2.4 meters] long) and tape to attach them to a wall
- A glass door or glass wall
- Three or four dodge balls
- *Fish Is Fish,* 1970, by L. Lionni (New York: Scholastic Press)

- Optional: video clips (see activity 7 for details)
- Optional: video camera

RISK MANAGEMENT CONSIDERATIONS

You will need a glass door or window that can safely have dodge balls thrown hard at it.

STUDENT PREPARATION

No prelesson preparation required

INSTRUCTOR PREPARATION

Tape the two large sheets of paper to different parts of a wall in your classroom.

LESSON CONTENT AND TEACHING STRATEGIES

Start the lesson by using slide 2 on the PowerPoint presentation (on CD-ROM) to define critical thinking. Explain and discuss with the students the ethical importance of professionals' examining standards and practices in their professions as well as their personal beliefs about the standards and practices. Tell the students that this is what they will do today.

Activity 1: Apple in the Road

Ask the students to consider this scenario: You find an apple in the middle of the road. "Tell me how you think it might have gotten there." In a small class have all the students share their thoughts. Try to come up with as many ways as possible that the apple could have gotten in the middle of the road. Keep the energy high and the ideas flowing. In a class in which you can have two or more groups with three to four people each, divide the class into groups and have the groups do this activity. Set the goal of providing as many explanations as possible. The groups may compete to come up with the most ideas; this helps the process of critical thinking, which is to get beyond our self-imposed limits of what are possible explanations. In the large group share some of the ideas. The primary point is that we sometimes limit our conclusions because of our assumptions. Sometimes we have incomplete understandings, false beliefs, or naïve renditions of concepts about a particular subject.

Many students learning to facilitate ropes courses think that the ropes course builds self-esteem or increases comfort with challenges, and that the reasons to participate in a ropes course experience are quite obvious. However, they often learn that the outcomes people obtain from a ropes course experience are very much dependent on the facilitation of the experience. New students often tend to generalize that the experience builds self esteem and that completing the challenge is "good for you." Have students think of all the reasons they can for people to participate on ropes courses, focusing on beneficial outcomes. Don't hint or coach, but encourage them to think broadly as in the example of the apple. Drawing out and working with existing learning are important for students.

Activity 2: Graffiti Wall

Create a graffiti wall where the students can randomly write down, draw, or in any way illustrate the benefits or reasons they came up with on one of the large sheets of paper that you have taped on the wall. Avoid giving any hints while encouraging students to be as specific as possible. At this point in the lesson it is useful to see what the students believe and especially what misconceptions they may have. Sometimes they have misconceptions and sometimes their understanding is quite limited. Since we all relate new learning to our past experiences or knowledge, it is hard to teach students without knowing what their current knowledge and misconceptions are. Students can fit new learning into their misconceptions without changing their beliefs, which leads to inaccurate learning. A later activity explores this concept more.

Show the students slides 3 and 4, introducing the concept of ethical reasoning (Paul and Elder 2005). Set the stage to use the process of ethical reasoning to examine practices involved in working with participants. Slide 5 provides one definition of "learning" and its impact on future experiences.

Activity 3: Fear and Risk Pop Quiz

Next introduce the pop quiz (see slide 6) about fear and risk on the PowerPoint. Whittingham (2005) introduced this pop quiz as a way to illuminate possible misconceptions about fear and risk and the possible influence of misconceptions on facilitation behavior, as well as students' understanding of how ropes courses can be of educational value. Through use of this quiz more misconceptions may be brought out into the open and discussed (see pop quiz instructor notes that follow).

For each question, ask the students to answer by saying "true," "false" or "depends." When the students have registered their responses, give the correct response, which mostly is "depends." After a few statements, students catch on that "depends" is usually the correct response. However, they will likely continue to think about their beliefs, and it takes more than this quiz to delve into certain misconceptions and see how their new knowledge might affect application or facilitation.

Slide 7: Conquering Fear of Heights Is a Good Thing. Answer: Depends

The purpose of fear is to keep us alive, and we should feel fear at the height of a high ropes course; it is a survival instinct. If the fear is at a maladaptive level, then relieving some of the fear will probably increase the quality of the person's life. Conquering fear of heights so that a person then takes dangerous chances jumping from high places or getting too close to the edge of a rock cliff is not a good thing. There is a correlation between more expertise and less perceived risk, which has been shown to lead to more instructor accidents than participant accidents in rock climbing and high ropes courses.

Slide 8: People Who Are Afraid of Heights Are Likely to Be Fearful People. Answer: Depends

It depends on the person. Some people who are afraid of heights also may be fearful in other areas of life; however, there doesn't seem to be evidence of a correlation such that if people are fearful or timid in one area they are timid in other or all areas. Some instructors teach that people are either high risk takers or low risk takers; some teach that we each lie somewhere on that continuum. Some instructors talk about timid or arrogant personality types with regard to risk taking. Actually, fears and phobias to a large extent usually are quite specific. A person may be very fearful about STDs and choose not to have sex but not be fearful at all about driving fast. Risk-taking comfort may also depend on the domain in life that the risk belongs to. For example, some people are more comfortable taking emotional risks than physical risks and others are more comfortable taking physical risks than spiritual risks. Risk is multidimensional in that we have different tolerances for it in different domains of our lives. Additionally, researchers on participants in certain extreme sports have concluded that these people are not usually high risk takers. They in fact do not see themselves as taking high risks.

Slide 9: People Who Take More Risks Are Happier. Answer: Depends

The correct response is pretty obvious. People who gamble are not always happier. People who take risks and succeed in their career may be happier, so it depends.

Slide 10: An Ability to Take Risks on a High Element or in the Mountains Results in an Ability to Take Risks Elsewhere in One's Life. Answer: Depends

There is no evidence-based research to support this statement, though many outdoor practitioners believe that it is true. What can happen is that a person can begin to feel more comfortable with her body and therefore begin taking more physical risks (cycling to work or recreational rock climbing) in other situations. Remember, people are not typically all risk taking or all timid. Remind students that Indiana Jones was very courageous and deathly afraid of snakes. The correct answer is "depends" because some people will transfer some newfound ability in order to take risks at home, but hopefully the ability to judge which risks to take and when and with whom to take these risks will also be transferred.

Slide 11: People Who Take More Risks Are More Successful in Life. Answer: Depends

Again, it depends on the risks people take as well as their success. For example, a person who takes risks in starting new businesses but does not judge the business climate well enough to choose needed goods or services will not likely be successful in business. Some people take risks by falling in love easily and often, but they may not be successful in relationships. The necessary skill, once again, is judging which risks to take as well as when and with whom.

Slide 12: Increasing One's Ability to Take Risks Is Always a Good Thing. Answer: Not always

It is not *always* a good thing. Bring into the discussion the idea that some people have fear at a maladaptive level and that it is reasonable to want to reduce their fear level, but only to a level that keeps them from undue risk. For example if a person is afraid to drive faster than 30 kilometers per hour, reducing fear so that she can drive 50 kilometers per hour is reasonable; taking away all sense of fear of driving fast is not reasonable.

Slide 13: Summary of Some of the Realities About Risk Taking At this point students should be questioning the belief that risk taking is necessary for personal growth. They should realize that risk is complex and that, just as there are many possible assumptions about the apple in the road, there are many reasons why people take risks as well as potential benefits and losses from risk taking. Additionally, in some cases addictive behavior compels people to take risks. Students should realize that depending on their facilitation they might accidentally promote negative risk-taking behaviors or, if they use deception to create a high perception of perceived risk, may not teach wise risk-taking behaviors. Students should be able to understand that risk aversion in many areas is healthy and that what feels risky is quite individual. A useful question at this time might be: What does promote personal growth?

Activity 4: What Do Our Students Learn?

Use slide 14 to introduce this activity. Have the students reorganize into small groups and ask them to use critical thinking similar to that in the Apple in the Road activity to think of all the learning people might take away from their ropes course programs. For instance, ask them to ponder this question: What intrapersonal skills might people learn from taking part in your program? Additional questions to ask might include the following:

- Can or should all fear be controlled?
- What signals should we get from feelings of fear and how should we use these signals?
- What is the place of intuition in the cost–benefit analysis of risk?
- When might it be courageous to stand up for yourself, and when might it be better to do something you do not want to do because of peer pressure?

You can relate a story about the learning or healing that can occur when a participant says no or does not take the risk to climb. If your students like storytelling, as many do, share this true story about Ann (not her real name).

A half hour into a day rock climbing clinic, which was part of an adventure program for the general public, Ann told a leader that she was going home. The leader, of course, had a pang of concern and disappointment. She asked Ann if there was anything that could be done or changed to help her stay, and Ann told her that nothing could change her mind about needing to leave. The leader said "I'll walk you to your car." En route they chatted about the morning, and Ann told the leader that she was in therapy for sexual abuse and felt too exposed during the clinic. The leader said she understood. As she bid Ann good-bye she asked if she could call later that week to check in.

That week the leader called and invited Ann to join a group on a clinic the next weekend that would have fewer participants. Ann accepted, participated, and seemed to enjoy the clinic. The following week she attended an intermediate climbing clinic. Again, after a half hour she needed to leave. She returned a few weeks later to complete an intermediate clinic. This pattern continued through the Level III Rocks Clinic. Though there were different leaders for the various clinic levels, their handling of the situation was similar. During the clinics the leaders set a tone of warmth and caring and focused on teaching rock climbing. There was no individual or group processing about Ann's pattern other than information sharing from Ann with the leaders; and of course when Ann left, each leader would acknowledge to the other group members that she had left. With a neutral but caring tone they said something to the effect that Ann had decided to leave as she had gone as far as she could that day with her learning about rock climbing.

Months later Ann sent the organization a letter. She shared that being able to say she felt exposed and needed to leave, then leaving without criticism and being welcomed upon her return, supported her healing process and her ability to learn rock climbing skills. Female survivors are often afraid to say they need to leave or to say no. They are afraid that their "no" will be interpreted in a hostile way and that they will be abandoned. In the past, when they were small children, this would have threatened their survival. In this case the value for Ann of saying no, leaving, and returning was substantial. The leaders gave Ann a gift of knowing that she could set her own limits without being abandoned. The leaders were mindful of the goal and continued to provide opportunities for Ann to learn rock climbing. They were mindful of the process and were available and caring while maintaining professional boundaries.

The outcome was possibly different than the leaders would have predicted. We don't usually have participants who leave partway through a clinic and then finish a clinic series in this pattern. However, the outcome in retrospect fit for Ann; and as long as safety and leadership for the other participants are maintained, this sort of consideration is appropriate. This adventure education program was marketed to the general public. The leaders created a safe-feeling atmosphere, thus making it possible for Ann to speak her needs. The organization ran a series of rock climbing clinics designed to teach recreational climbing. The course was not an adventure therapy course; however, adventure education is often therapeutic.

Return to the PowerPoint and use slides 15 and 16 to help students understand what we are trying to do and what we can influence. For slide 15, bring in Dewey's valuation or cost–benefit concept. Participants weigh such questions as "What do I stand to lose or gain?" As well as seeing the possible benefits, participants will consider (or should be taught to consider) possible harmful outcomes including humiliation, shame, social embarrassment, the reinforcement of lack of perceived competence, and the potential of stigmatization. After looking at the relative effects, students can respond to the questions "What is my best decision about what to risk and how to do so?"; "Is there an action that is more appropriate than other actions for this situation?"; and finally, whatever the intended action, "Can I live with the consequences of either success or failure (gain or loss)?"

Slide 16 gives students a process they can use to help participants manage cognitions under stress. First participants decide what action to take (stay on the course, go down, or whatever); then they begin to act (e.g., walk the balance beam log). Facilitators then work with participants to keep thinking while they are acting and not let emotional fear (amygdule) take over. If a participant freezes or becomes very afraid, they work with the person to get back to being able to think through the fear. After the participant completes the element, they help him or her understand and make sense of what has happened so he or she can better use this process in the future. For example, during the debriefing, the facilitator can ask if the participant has ever frozen during any other activity or situation. If the answer is yes, the facilitator can suggest using the same process of stop, evaluate, decide on your action, then keep thinking and acting. In this case a participant may have learned to manage cognitions better, which may help improve behavior in anger management and other areas. Understanding this, students can perhaps see their jobs as facilitators in a different and more complex light. Encourage students to understand the psychological processes at work, how these can be positively affected, and how growth can occur that increases quality of life—or how these psychological processes can be harmed during a ropes course experience. For example, if a facilitator has told group members that being supportive is cheering people on to get as high or as far as they possibly can, then some participants may respond to the cheering, accomplishing the task, yet have silenced their own voices about what they thought was best for themselves. A participant might take away from this experience that he should do what the group wants him to do; this groupthink is very dangerous.

Begin a discussion about how common misconceptions are. Relate this to Dewey and his key conception that the learner constructs meaning from an experience. We have constructed a certain meaning for ourselves, and it may not be the meaning that participants have constructed for themselves. Share some of the following teaching examples or aids with your students:

Many young children experience the earth as flat. When they get to school, they are taught that the earth is round. Many children then visualize the earth as a pancake, which is round (Vosniadou and Brewer 1989). When told that the earth is shaped like a sphere and shown what a sphere looks like, many children visualize the sphere with a pancake on top of it and people standing on the pancake.

Sometimes the knowledge that people bring to a new situation impedes subsequent learning because it guides thinking in wrong directions. For example, people often think that a rock falls faster than a leaf—an everyday assumption based on their physical experiences. Facilitators need to help people change their original conceptions rather than simply use the misconceptions as a basis for further understanding or leaving new material connected to current understanding.

Activity 5: *Fish Is Fish*

Read the book, *Fish Is Fish,* in class. It illustrates how we develop beliefs, in this case about physical and biological phenomena, that fit into our experiences. A fish befriends a tadpole. The fish tells the tadpole that it wants to learn about what's on the land. When the tadpole becomes a frog it reports back to the fish on what it is seeing and learning about on land. The book's illustrations show how the fish interprets what the frog describes. All of the animals look like fish, with some adaptations that incorporate the frog's descriptions, such as fish with wings or with udders. The fish is constructing new knowledge based on its current knowledge, but not in a way that reflects reality.

Activity 6: The Amygdala Is Faster Than Reason!

This activity is placed here to give the students some time to process their thoughts simultaneously with doing an activity that can be fun and rowdy. This activity helps students comprehend that some fears are innate to us and that these fears have had a place in keeping us and our ancestors alive, including fear of falling; fear of heights; and fear of snakes, spiders, and insects. Darwin had a hunch that some fears were hardwired into the brain. Now we know that we have automatic emotional responses to many things, including some fears. For example, specific emotional reactions to certain stimuli (angry faces, happy faces, snakes, spiders) are readily detectable in 400 milliseconds or less following the presentation of the stimuli (Ulrich et al. 1991). People do not think that quickly; therefore the response is from the *amygdala,* or emotional center of the brain, rather than a cognitive response.

To test his theory, Darwin once did an experiment in which he went up to the edge of a snake cage, knowing cognitively that the snake could not strike him. He tried to remain still when the snake attempted to strike at him. He found that no matter how hard he tried, he was unable to overcome his hardwired fear. Experientially, it is useful for the students to have a parallel experience. Tell the students about Darwin's experiment. Then take them to an area where you can have them put their face very close to a large glass door or glass wall. Have a student stand close to the glass and tell him or her that other students will throw dodge balls at his face and not to move or blink. Ask other students to stand on the other side of the glass and to throw the dodge balls hard at their peer's face. Almost all students will involuntarily at least blink, if not draw back, when the first ball comes at them even though they cognitively know that they are safe. It is key for them to have their face very close to the glass and to be looking at the ball. The noise of the ball hitting the glass aids in fear arousal. You can talk about how the amygdala is our personal radar. Its job is to let us know what to fear, what to take an interest in, and what to ignore. In this case it causes our reflex action to kick in. For some people on a ropes course or other perceived risky situation, their amygdala signals fear and they are unable to use reason until they can calm themselves and regroup.

Activity 7: Parallel Process in Action

In this part of the lesson you want to make the point that through using parallel process students may experience stronger positive transference from this lesson. Use video clips to show typical shots of ropes course or climbing wall participants completing elements or climbs. Most likely the students will see people being offered challenges and then encouraged to excel as best they can. They may see the other participants cheering and encouraging. They may or may not see the facilitator actually help participants learn to assess risk in each domain, as the focus is typically on the physical domain or completing the task, or the social domain of both encouraging one another and not letting peers down. Next show a clip in which an instructor or facilitator walks a participant through a series of questions to help him or her decide whether or not to complete an element or climb.

If using a video is not possible, you can demonstrate in the classroom how this might look. The benefit of demonstrating this work is that the students see you teaching in context. Having students watch you do what you will ask them to do is a powerful teaching tool. English teachers use this tool when they demonstrate for students how they themselves write, for example, when they write a poem in front of the class. The students get to see how the teacher's thought process works.

As an example of teaching or facilitating in context, you might set up a role play in your classroom (or on the course if you teach at a course) in which you are the facilitator and one of your students is the participant. Ask the student to role-play someone who is scared. In a classroom you can put a rope on the floor and pretend it is a tightrope. Go through the process of explaining the objective to the student, helping the student use valuation or a cost–benefit analysis to decide whether or not to take the risk, and then helping the student work through fears. Ask questions like "What do you stand to lose or gain?" Use critical thinking skills to probe with follow-up questions such as "How would completing this element affect you socially?" or "If you are feeling scared, how can you check that out with yourself to see if it is a fear you think is useful right now or a fear that you would like to work through right now?" or "In this situation, how would you define success?" You can probe more as the role play progresses. The student sees, hears, and feels you facilitating and likely will be able to repeat this process (parallel process) when facilitating.

Activity 8: Graffiti Wrap-Up and Skits

Use the second piece of wall graffiti paper to have students write some of the possible misconceptions they might have had regarding risk. Give them plenty of time to write. Have a discussion about the misconceptions that were identified and move on to have students in groups of three or four put together a skit in which they help a person through a maladaptive fear, a cost–benefit analysis of a risky situation, or a "freeze" (illustrating the ability to help others manage cognitions under stress) on a ropes course. Have students use the sequence of helping their participants decide whether or not to act; if they decide to act, then act and keep thinking as they act; and finally understand and make sense of what happened as they completed the element. The skills that need to be developed are appropriate risk taking at appropriate times, in appropriate places, with appropriate people, and for appropriate reasons. This judgment skill is built with practice (on the ropes course) and during the debriefing that includes specific examples of transfer possibilities. At this point the critical thinking process is very important. When facilitating, apply the key critical thinking intellectual standards to your facilitation: Be clear, accurate, relevant, logical, and fair.

Because the course I teach is a 300 level, I assume students have had at least a little facilitating experience. Therefore I tape the skits. Knowing that they will see themselves on video "ups the ante" for students, and they tend to produce higher-quality skits. If you want, you can have specific scenarios written up for the students beforehand that focus on what you think they need to practice. As an example, a scenario might involve a young woman, 16 years old, who is three quarters of the way up the ladder to start the grapevine. She has been uncomfortable from the start and now says that she does not want to go any farther. You suspect that she is reacting to a bit of snickering by a couple of the boys in the group and is feeling uncomfortable about showing her backside as she goes up the ladder. There are a number of ways this scenario can go depending on the people doing the role play. In another possible scenario, a football team member is sweating as he begins the cargo net entrance to the course. Then, partway up the net, he freezes. A couple of teammates start encouraging him by saying that he's helping the team as he completes the course.

Debrief the skits, referring back frequently to the information on slides 3 and 4. Watch the video as part of the debrief or, if time is short, watch the video during the next class and do a second debrief after some time has passed. The passage of time and the video can lead to a second and powerful debrief. During the processing, pay attention to your students' responses. Do you see the characteristics of the fair-minded critical person? Can you see how the logic of ethical reasoning has been incorporated? After a brief whole-group discussion, have students in small groups discuss and write reflections about their learning and specifically the final role-play activity. Students tend to have more opportunity for involvement when discussing in small groups. Actually writing their reflections helps them be even clearer about their ideas and thoughts.

CLOSURE

Close by having the students look at the two graffiti sheets and talk about what they see. Some students may be confused after encountering this material; acknowledge that. It is useful to incorporate this material further as you actually do some high elements. If you can do high elements in future sessions, tell the students that you will put into practice some of the ideas discussed today in future classes. In future classes, have students move from their scenarios to facilitate real participants using front-loading and debriefing that take into consideration the material from this lesson. During our class we bring in an elementary group, a high school group, and an adult group over the course of the semester for the students to work with.

Finally, challenge the students to use their meta-cognition skills this week and have them keep track of their risk taking. What risks do they decide to take, why, with whom, and when? When they have chosen to take a risk, do they think about their ability to decide to act, act, and keep thinking as they act while they complete something that is challenging to them (perhaps even in the situation of not procrastinating homework)? Use slides 17 and 18 during this summary and close on slide 19.

ASSESSMENT OF LEARNING

The first graffiti sheet gives an idea of what the students are thinking in terms of the uses and benefits of ropes courses. You can compare the second graffiti sheet with the first to see what changes in thinking might be starting to take place as students add new learning or recognize misconceptions they might have had.

Ongoing formative assessment takes place as you hear students in the discussions and as they share their group work.

The final skits give you an idea of whether or not the students understand the role of fear, risk, risk evaluation, and the use of the ethical reasoning process to guide behavior.

When the students return to class and you collect or discuss their keeping track of their risk taking. You may have a better idea of their grasp of the concepts in this lesson.

PART VIII

Group Development

A collection of supportive individuals with a common purpose is at the heart of many adventure education experiences, and the lessons in this part show students the theories and models behind the process of small group development.

In lesson 24, "Small Group Development in Outdoor Adventure," Karen Warren offers an exercise in which students reflect on their values around group membership, followed by scenarios illustrating the stages of group development, concluding with a game show format to enhance learning. This lesson presents one of the foundational models of group development, that of Tuckman (1965), to help beginning outdoor leaders look more thoroughly at dilemmas that arise on trips.

Kate Cassidy expands on Tuckman's model in lesson 25, "An Alternative to Tuckman: Three Factors in Group Development." She employs variations of the group juggle and helium hoop activities to point out three common concerns that must be addressed during a group's time together: sense of self, sense of group, and sense of purpose. By recognizing and addressing these needs, adventure educators can help groups and the people within them grow and develop. Cassidy's lesson is a useful reminder that the purpose of adventure education is to develop interpersonal and intrapersonal skills and abilities through group problem solving and personal challenges (Priest and Gass 2005).

In lesson 26, "Setting the Stage: How to Get the Group Norms You Want," Denise Mitten introduces a multidimensional model combining concepts from both sequential-stage or successive stage theory and recurring-phase or cyclical theory. Employing discussions and experiences relating to students' favorite trips and healthy versus reactionary bonding, this lesson points out that the group development stages do not always have discrete beginnings or endings, and that groups often cycle through stages again and again as they encounter new and maybe more challenging tasks.

Maurice Phipps' lesson 27, "Setting Group Norms and Expedition Behavior," presents strategies that field-based and classroom groups can use for setting group norms, illustrates concepts in group process and group learning, and outlines skills that will enable a group to stay on track with the agreed-upon behaviors. Petzoldt's (1984) expedition behavior concept, Johnson and colleagues' (1998) cooperative learning theory, and Warters' (1960) group roles all assist in developing high-functioning groups.

The theme of all these lessons is that when adventure leaders know the models of group development, they can better understand that what sometimes look like behavior or motivation problems are really just expected stages that most groups go through, although not always in a linear fashion. This understanding can help the leader avoid drama and respond in ways that can more effectively help a group progress toward success.

RESOURCES

Johnson, D.W., R. Johnson, and A. Smith. 1998. *Active learning: Cooperation in the college classroom.* Edina, MN: Interaction Book.

Petzoldt, P. 1984. *The new wilderness handbook.* New York: Norton.

Priest, S., and M.A. Gass. 2005. *Effective leadership in adventure programming.* Champaign, IL: Human Kinetics.

Tuckman, B.W. 1965. Developmental sequence in small groups. *Psychological Bulletin,* 63(6):384-399.

Warters, J. 1960. *Group guidance: Principles and practice.* New York: McGraw-Hill.

LESSON 24

Small Group Development in Outdoor Adventure

Karen Warren

There are many stage theories of group development. This lesson uses one small group development model and shows how it can be applied in outdoor leadership. Since beginning outdoor leaders often look at dilemmas that arise on their trips as individual problems, it is useful to help them look through the lens of a group development model and implement their leadership strategies and interventions considering group theory. This lesson offers an experiential introduction to small group development in outdoor adventure.

Background

For effectively facilitating group dynamics in adventure education, an understanding of small group development is useful. This lesson draws from the group life cycle stage theory with an application to outdoor leadership and facilitation.

Tuckman (1965) is credited with the initial work on small group development that has been adapted to outdoor adventure education (see Kosseff 2003; Priest and Gass 2005; Martin et al. 2006). In Tuckman's model, groups are viewed as living organisms with a cycle of group life that includes both task functions and social-emotional-integrative or maintenance functions. In outdoor adventure groups, task functions might include setting up camp or hiking up a mountain. Maintenance functions are directed toward enhancing interpersonal relationships and strengthening the group, for example making sure that everyone is included or dealing with conflicts.

In 1977, Tuckman and Jensen reviewed the "new" literature on small group development and amended the previous model to include a termination stage called *adjourning*—a stage that others call *transforming* (Weber 1982). While students should be informed that there are other stage theories of small group development in adventure education (see Garvey and Vorsteg 1995; Fine 1999; Kerr and Gass

1995), this lesson focuses on Tuckman's revised model as one way to look at the group life cycle.

The stages in Tuckman's model include *forming, norming, storming, performing,* and *transforming* or *adjourning.* It should be noted that the stages are not linear but tend to be cycled through and returned to as necessary for the group to mature. Each stage has specific goals that outdoor leaders can facilitate by giving attention to activities and adventures that meld with those goals.

Forming is the orientation stage of the group (Jensen 1979). The group is initiating itself; therefore attention is directed toward forming initial bonds that will develop over time, with emphasis by leaders on the group rather than specific individual differences. The goal of the forming stage is to make everyone feel safe and included. Group members tend to be hesitant and more reserved in this stage as they feel out their place in the group. Activities that focus on commonalities and a sense of belonging within the group rather than individual differences are useful. In this phase the Asian concept of "saving face" is critical and is fulfilled through the selection of activities that don't allow individuals to stand out or be embarrassed or feel awkward in front of their peers and leaders (Becker 1998). In addition, a focus on providing the bottom tier of Maslow's hierarchy of needs is helpful for making group members feel welcome (Fine 1999; Gookin 2006). Tired, hungry, cold, wet students will have difficulty forming a group because they are distracted when their basic needs go unmet.

Norming is the stage of setting the structures of the group that maintain its integrity. Agreements about how to treat other group members and the environment are key in this stage. Leaders help facilitate the development of these agreements, which have been called group rules, working assumptions, or full-value contracts (Schoel and Maizell 2002). It is also a time to introduce safety and risk management guidelines as well as environmental standards such as "Leave No Trace" (Hampton, Cole, and Casey 2003). Group members may also solidify their roles within the group and build healthy relationships (Mitten 1995).

The storming stage can occur at any time in the group process. It is characterized by intragroup conflict in which group members become hostile toward one another and toward the leader(s) (Tuckman 1965). Group members are often testing limits and re-sorting their roles in the group. Conflict resolution allows "a clearer definition of both the task and the various expectations for different group members" (Jensen 1979, p. 41). The role of the leader is to encourage productive storming whereby the resolution of conflict will lead to a more mature group—one that is more capable of achieving its goals.

Since beginning outdoor leaders seem to fear the storming stage more than others, it is beneficial to provide some tools for approaching it. One way to look at limit testing and limit setting is the concentric circle model (see figure 24.1). Since limit setting creates both a sense of safety and a sense of limit testing, leaders should be aware of two layers of limits. In this model, inner-circle limits are nonnegotiable limits. For example, on a trip with youth offenders, those limits might be prohibiting weapons or prohibiting harming themselves or someone else. These are limits a leader does not want to struggle with or have to address. Yet without outer-circle limits, when participants test limits, the inner-circle limits will be the ones that arise. Outer-circle limits in the same example might have to do with such things as taking a smoking break on the trail or wearing shoes in camp. These outer limits can be tested and either upheld or renegotiated depending on the situation. The goal of this model is to keep the limit testing in the outer circle

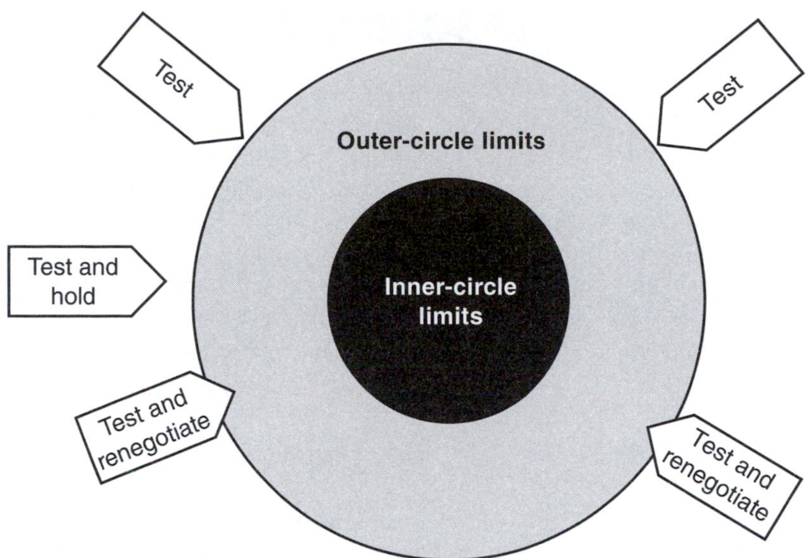

FIGURE 24.1 Limit setting and testing in the storming stage.

to "protect" the inner-circle limits. Without outer-circle limits, participants' testing will occur around intolerable situations that a leader should avoid. A final key point is that when outer-circle limits are tested they cannot be ignored or allowed to drop away. A leader must reassert the limit or modify it through negotiation based on explicit solid reasoning. To abdicate on a previously set limit creates an unsafe climate in the group.

When the group is functioning well, the performing stage has been reached. A leader's role in this stage is to step back and let the group accomplish its work independently of the leader's direct supervision. Leaders should be a source of potential energy, ready to step back in if there is a difficulty but not overshadowing the work of the group. At this stage leaders tend to be consultants rather than authorities (Kosseff 2003). Differences between group members emerge and should be supported in this stage.

The final stage, transforming or adjourning, requires that leaders provide specific support to the group in a way they did not in the performing stage. In North American society, separation, loss, and termination bring up many feelings that people are not taught to deal with effectively. Therefore the "death" of the group can cause a range of feelings in participants, from sadness to relief at the ending (Weber 1982). The transfer of lessons learned to "real life" is complex and not clearly understood (Gass 1995), but this stage is important for solidifying gains made during the experience. As Martin and colleagues (2006) point out, "The group is in disarray again and the leader can assist by recognizing dependency issues, assuring the group that what happened during their experience is important, and fostering transference of the experience" (p. 140).

The leader's role in this stage is to assist in the transition, recognizing that activities and processes that occurred efficiently in the performing stage will take more time. It is also a time when the "home-free" syndrome occurs and both participants and leaders are more susceptible to accidents and misjudgments. Attention to closing activities and evaluative feedback are ways in which groups can celebrate successes and acknowledge failures.

RESOURCES

Becker, R. 1998. Taking the misery out of experiential training. *Training,* 35(2):78-88.

Fine, L.J. 1999. Stage development theory in adventure programming. In *Adventure programming,* eds. J.C. Miles and S. Priest, 193-199. State College, PA: Venture.

Garvey, D., and A.C. Vorsteg. 1995. From theory to practice for college student interns: A stage theory approach. In *The theory of experiential education,* eds. K. Warren, M. Sakofs, and J. Hunt, 297-303. Dubuque, IA: Kendall/Hunt.

Gass, M.A. 1995. Programming the transfer of learning in adventure education. In *The theory of experiential education,* eds. K. Warren, M. Sakofs, and J. Hunt, 131-142. Dubuque, IA: Kendall/Hunt.

Gookin, J., ed. 2006. *NOLS wilderness educator notebook.* Lander, WY: NOLS.

Hampton, B., D. Cole, and D. Casey. 2003. *Soft paths: How to enjoy the wilderness without harming it.* Lander, WY: NOLS.

Jensen, M. 1979. Application of small group theory to adventure programs. *Journal of Experiential Education,* 2(2):39-42.

Kerr, P.J., and M.A. Gass. 1995. A group development model for adventure education. In *The theory of experiential education,* eds. K. Warren, M. Sakofs, and J. Hunt, 285-296. Dubuque, IA: Kendall/Hunt.

Kosseff, A. 2003. *AMC guide to outdoor leadership.* Boston: AMC Books.

Martin, B., C. Cashel, M. Wagstaff, and M. Breunig. 2006. *Outdoor leadership: Theory and practice.* Champaign, IL: Human Kinetics.

Mitten, D. 1995. Building the group: Using personal affirming to create healthy group process. *Journal of Experiential Education,* 18(2):82-90.

Priest, S., and M.A. Gass. 2005. *Effective leadership in adventure programming.* Champaign, IL: Human Kinetics.

Schoel, J. and R.S. Maizell. 2002. *Exploring islands of healing.* Beverly, MA: Project Adventure.

Tuckman, B.W. 1965. Developmental sequence in small groups. *Psychological Bulletin,* 63(6):384-399.

Tuckman, B.W. 2004. Developmental sequence in small groups. *Psychological Bulletin,* 63:384-399.

Tuckman, B.W., and M.C. Jensen. 1977. Stages of small-group development revisited. *Group and Organization Studies,* 2(4):419-427.

Weber, R.C. 1982. The group: A cycle from birth to death. In *NTL reading book for human relations training.* Arlington, VA: NTL Institute.

Lesson Plan

PURPOSE

To introduce students to one of the many theories of small group development and apply it to outdoor adventure education and leadership situations.

OBJECTIVES

As a result of this lesson students will be able to . . .

1. *Affective:* understand more about their own responses in group membership and group leadership situations through a values clarification activity.
2. *Cognitive:* explain the goals of the stages of group development and the leaders' role in each stage.
3. *Cognitive:* apply small group theory to real-life scenarios.
4. *Cognitive:* understand how limit setting and trip planning relate to small group development stages.

5. *Affective and psychomotor:* participate in an interactive experience that assesses and reinforces their knowledge and understanding of small group development theory and practice.

DURATION

120 minutes

GROUP SIZE

6 to 15 students

LOCATION

Indoors

EQUIPMENT

- Laptop and LCD projector
- Three buzzers or sound makers with different sounds
- Pretend microphone—a toy mic, a large carrot, or a flashlight
- Readings available prior to class in course reading packet or on course Web site

RISK MANAGEMENT CONSIDERATIONS

Students will be asked to share some of their personal experiences, so the facilitator should attend to emotional safety by using group ground rules and ensuring other norms of respectful communication.

STUDENT PREPARATION

Students will read the Background handout (on CD-ROM) or read the following:

- Jensen, M. 1979. Application of small group theory to adventure programs. *Journal of Experiential Education,* 2(2):39-42.
- Martin, B., C. Cashel, M. Wagstaff, and M. Breunig. 2006. Facilitating group development. In *Outdoor leadership: Theory and practice,* 133-147. Champaign, IL: Human Kinetics.
- Weber, R.C. 1982. The group: A cycle from birth to death. In *NTL reading book for human relations training.* Arlington, VA: NTL Institute.

INSTRUCTOR PREPARATION

No prelesson preparation required.

LESSON CONTENT AND TEACHING STRATEGIES

To start the lesson, explain that students will learn about small group development by applying a model to outdoor leadership situations. Mention that there are many models and many critiques of group development, and it is important that they keep this in mind as they delve into the topic. Ask if any of the students have a story about a time when they couldn't understand what was happening with their group in the outdoors, or a time when group development affected a trip experience. Students usually have interesting stories that can be referred to later during discussion of the group development model. Remind students that they will be using dialogic learning—that is, all information sharing flows cooperatively and they should interject with their own experiences, comments, and quandaries throughout the lesson.

Activity 1: Forced Choice

This is a focusing activity to help students clarify their values about group membership and claim a position on some of the key points in the reading. An open space with room to move is needed for this activity.

Mention that students will be asked to make a choice on each of several statements and to go to the side of the room designated for that answer. Since this is a forced-choice activity, students need to go to one side or the other—they can't stand in the middle, although they will want to. Remind them that the choice they make does not have to reflect the truth completely; it just has to reflect it more completely than the other choice. After students have made a choice, processing can take several forms: asking individuals why they made the choice they did, or having groups on each side of the room discuss their choices, or having students on opposite sides of the room pair up to discuss their choices. These are the forced-choice statements:

1. When I experience conflict in a group I tend to . . .
   - run and hide in the woods
   - get excited about jumping in and solving it
2. In an outdoor group situation I tend to be . . .
   - more task oriented
   - more maintenance and relationship oriented
3. I like to encourage participation in group activities . . .
   - from behind by nudging
   - from the front by drawing people along
4. I am more comfortable with groups I lead if the participants . . .
   - learn the outdoor skills really well
   - get along really well
5. On an outdoor trip I am more likely to enjoy . . .
   - a night with the group around the campfire
   - an afternoon in the woods by myself away from the group

Explain that the group is a living organism—a unit made up by its members that is constantly influencing and being influenced by its members. Introduce each stage of Tuckman's model by

1. defining the stage,
2. identifying the goals of the stage,
3. describing the leader's role in the stage, and
4. brainstorming appropriate activities for the stage.

See the Background for this information.

Activity 2: Applying Small Group Development Theory to Practice

Once students understand the stages of group development, present the following small group development outdoor leadership scenarios to apply the theory to practice. The scenarios can be provided to small groups of students or worked through by the entire class. After presenting each scenario, pose the questions listed.

1. It is day 3 on a weeklong flat water canoe trip. People have developed into fairly competent paddlers and are having a good time in the hot, sunny weather. Since the policy of your organization is that everyone wear life jackets at all times on the water, you as a leader are dismayed that people keep "forgetting" to put their life jackets on after stops. The final straw is when you are paddling the sweep boat and notice that the paddlers in the three canoes ahead of you have all *taken off* their life jackets and are happily paddling along.
   - What stage of group development is this?
   - According to the goals of that stage, what should you as a leader do?
2. It is the first night of a wilderness backpacking trip. During the initial talk around the campfire, one group member adamantly confronts one of the leaders about her authoritarian attitude. You as the coleader are taken aback because that's not been your experience of your coleader's behavior and no other group members have voiced similar concerns. The rest of the group seems shocked by the outburst of the angry member.
   - What stage of group development is this?
   - According to the goals of that stage, what should you as a leader do?
3. It is three quarters of the way through a canoe trip. Members are getting along well, are enjoying the trip, and are using the canoe camping skills they have been taught. The group arrives at an island where they are planning to camp. It isn't immediately evident where on the island the campsite is. The group members hang out in their canoes waiting for the leader to tell them where to camp.
   - What stage of group development is this?
   - According to the goals of that stage, what should you as a leader do?
4. It is the last night of a weeklong trip. The group is tired, and after dinner people begin to head for their tents to go to bed. At 1:00 a.m. you are awakened by loud laughter and talking as several members return to their tents. At 2:00 a.m. you are awakened again by laughing.
   - What stage of group development is this?
   - What is happening, why, and what can you guess about the quality of the trip?
   - According to the goals of that stage, what should you as a leader do?

It takes practice to see the group through a group lens. We tend to see individual needs. It's important to pay attention to both, as a group member expresses and acts on both individual and group needs. In trip planning, it is critical to take group development stages into consideration. More time is needed in the forming and norming stages as well as in the transforming or adjourning stage, so trip planning should have decreased activities in those stages.

Activity 3: Group Development Game Show

This activity, featuring a PowerPoint presentation (on CD-ROM), is a fun way to assess and solidify learning that students have gained about the theory and practice of facilitating the development of groups in the outdoors. The information comes from the class readings, discussion, and information sharing.

Divide the class into three teams. Place three buzzers or bells with distinctive sounds on a table in front of the screen for the PowerPoint presentation. Each team lines up behind their buzzer and answers the game questions until they rotate out. Depending on the group size, rotation can occur on a wrong answer or on every question.

The MC is introduced and explains the game. A pretend microphone and TV game show host attitude add to the effect. The MC reminds contestants that their answer must be in the form of a question. Categories are explained:

- *Famous Names* are names of people who have made contributions to group development theory and practice.
- In *Name That Stage,* contestants identify the stage of group development that corresponds to the answer.
- In *Spelling,* contestants need to say the word and spell it correctly.
- *What I'd Do* requires contestants to explain what they would do as an outdoor leader in the situation. Sometimes these answers promote great discussions, which can be facilitated during the game or saved until the end to be reviewed. As there are a number of possible answers (some are given in the answer key, but there are also others), the MC (teacher) needs to decide if the answer is correct based on the goals of the particular stage of group development.
- *"C" Words* are words relating to group development that start with the letter *C.*

Using the PowerPoint: A contestant requests a category and dollar amount. Click on the dollar amount for the question. To return to the main game board, click on the highlighted color word(s). Keep score on a whiteboard. Refer to table 24.1 to

TABLE 24.1 Group Game Show Answers (Phrased in the Form of a Question)

	Famous Names	Name That Stage	Spelling	What I'd Do	C Words
100	Who is Tuckman?	What is *forming*?	What is COMMUNICATION?	Set ground rules and safety rules. Review expectations.	What is Conflict?
200	Who is Maslow?	What is *storming*?	What is ADJOURNING?	Pay attention to closing the group. Do a closing activity the night before. Or change the trip so that there is less activity at the end.	What is Cycle or Circle?
300	Who is Jensen?	What is *transforming* or *adjourning*?	What is PERFORMING?	Use "saving face" types of games that include everyone, for example Strong Wind Blows, Fear in a Hat, Group Juggling.	What is Consensus?
400	Who is Weber?	What is *norming*?	What is MAINTENANCE?	Review safety rules and the reason for them. Hold to or renegotiate outer-circle limits.	What is Comfort?
500	Who are Johnson and Johnson?	What is *performing*?	What is RECONNAISSANCE?	Have group set up camp first and if time permits go canoeing later. Attend to Maslow's bottom-tier needs.	What is Cooperative?

determine whether the question has been answered correctly. Some interpretation may be needed, as answers will vary especially in the "What I'd Do" category.

CLOSURE

The class concludes with the faciliator asking if there are any outstanding topics or questions raised by the lesson. These are discussed by the group in class or on the online course Web site.

ASSESSMENT OF LEARNING

- The game show activity serves as a fun way to assess the students' understanding of small group development. Answers that students struggled with in the game show are further clarified after the activity to ensure student comprehension.
- When this lesson is part of a semester-long outdoor leadership class, invite students to go through a continuing examination of the development of the class as a group in relation to what they have learned in this lesson. Using in-class, trip, and online journal discussions, you will be revisiting a stage that the class was in and the goals of that stage that needed to be achieved. For example, you might ask the students to give examples of storming or performing that occurred during a particular class session or a trip and what they did positively to address the group goals during that time.
- Also invite critique of the model and its application as the class group develops. It can be helpful for the facilitator or instructor to be transparent in sharing what he or she is attempting to achieve in relation to the goals of each stage of group development.
- Another assessment tool is to have students write a paper on one stage of group development and explain how they would apply it to an outdoor trip they have been involved with. I have also had students design and describe a new stage or stage theory model of group development. Students have presented these models visually using collages, PowerPoint, or diagrammatic posters.

LESSON 25

An Alternative to Tuckman

Three Factors in Group Development

Kate J. Cassidy

Group development is an essential component of adventure education. This lesson reviews Tuckman's (1965) model of group development and then presents an alternative model (Cassidy 2007, in press) suggesting that group development is influenced by three ever-present factors: individual concerns (sense of self), interpersonal concerns (sense of group), and goal-clarity concerns (sense of meaning). As a result of this lesson, students should understand how to recognize and address these three important concerns in adventure programs to help groups, and the people within them, develop and grow.

Background

The purpose of adventure education is to develop interpersonal and intrapersonal skills through group problem solving and personal challenges (Priest and Gass 2005). Kerr and Gass (1995) describe group development as "one of the cornerstones of adventure education programs" (p. 285). Adventure facilitators should understand the elements involved in a developing group so as to be best able to select appropriate activities and assist groups throughout their development.

TUCKMAN'S MODEL OF GROUP DEVELOPMENT

One of the most common models of group development is Bruce W. Tuckman's model, published in 1965 (Cissna 1984; Gersick 1988; Smith 2005). Tuckman's model is often cited in adventure education practice-based literature (see Cain 2003; Priest and Gass 2005). To create his model, Tuckman conducted a meta-analysis of 50 research-based studies of group development. From this process he created the model popularly known by the rhyming stages: forming, storming, norming, and performing. Adjourning was added in 1977.

A brief review of Tuckman's model (Tuckman 1965; Tuckman and Jensen 1977) is as follows. The first developmental stage, *forming,* refers to issues of orientation, inclusion, and dependency. It is the time when group members become acquainted or familiar with each other and orient themselves to the group. This initial period is sometimes considered stressful for members as they seek to understand the type of group with which they are involved, the behaviors that are acceptable, and their position within the group. During this stage, members are dependent on the leader. The *storming* stage is a period of conflict in the group. Power and authority issues may lead to unrest. Leadership may be questioned. In the next stage, *norming,* groups begin to display cohesion and form a group identity. During this phase, members discuss group process issues such as roles, norms, leadership, and division of labor. In the *performing* stage, full energy is channeled into completing the assigned task. In the last stage, *adjourning,* groups that have a specific termination date turn their attention toward leaving. There may be anxiety about disbanding relationships and the group may reflect on the task to date.

Tuckman synthesized studies about therapy, natural, and laboratory groups as well as t-groups (in which participants seek to increase their sensitivity and emotional expressiveness) in order to create his model. However, it should be noted that 37 of the 50 studies came from psychoanalytic literature on therapy and t-groups. Tuckman (1965) acknowledged that "Generalization must, perforce, be limited to the fact that what has been presented is mainly research dealing with sequential development in therapy groups" (p. 395). Despite this limitation, Tuckman's model has been applied quite broadly in group leadership.

A NEW MODEL OF GROUP DEVELOPMENT FOR PRACTITIONERS

Using an approach similar to Tuckman's, Cassidy (2007) reviewed 44 practitioner-based models. In this research, models were selected evenly from business, education, and therapy literature written by practitioners for practitioners. The results showed that common among practitioner models of group development were three fundamental concerns related to group development: individual concerns (sense of self), interpersonal concerns (sense of group), and goal-clarity concerns (sense of meaning). The group development models Cassidy reviewed suggested that being aware of and addressing these three basic concerns help groups achieve and maintain social and task engagement.

- *Sense of self* refers to the concerns of the individual. Recognizing and valuing each individual member is a critical aspect of group development. Most humans want to feel that they are comfortable, safe, accepted, competent, and respected and are an important member of the groups around them (Maslow 1970). Groups must provide the space in which to honor each individual's needs, background, prior knowledge, and skills throughout the life of the group. This acknowledgement of the unique individual provides a basis for a genuine dialogue that bridges differences in ages, cultures, backgrounds, and opinions. It should be recognized that individuals can sometimes benefit by developing new skills and new levels of introspection to address the needs of sense of self.
- *Sense of group* refers to the group's forming as a community. The basis for meaningful community is set through group norms that respect diversity and healthy

relationships (Mitten 1989). Effective group norms allow the community to work positively together at the same time that individuals are able to share what they consider important aspects of themselves. Open communication, a foundation of care, reciprocity, and a respect for difference are bases for a positive community environment (Noddings 2002; Shields 2000). Group functioning can sometimes improve significantly when members acquire new interpersonal skills.

- *Sense of meaning* exists at the individual as well as the group level. A positive and effective community is based on a shared group vision that respects the goals of each individual (Collins 2001; Stangor 2004). In order for a group to reach productive ends, a shared understanding of the group's vision toward the task at hand must exist. At the same time, participants must see how the experience has personal meaning and is compatible with their own goals in order for their membership to feel relevant. Groups can sometimes benefit by acquiring new goal setting and task-oriented skills to help meet and maintain their purpose.

Cassidy's (2007) model features three factors that separate it from Tuckman's and from some other models of group development. First, this practitioner-based model rests on fundamental concerns rather than predicting and generalizing behaviors. Second, because it is based in concerns it provides flexibility for monitoring, facilitating, and adapting a program to meet each unique group's needs across time. Third, this model shifts the focus of conflict (or storming) from a stage to a possibility that may occur at any point in a group's life due to an unmet concern about sense of self, sense of group, or sense of meaning. These three factors are discussed in greater detail later.

A Focus on Concerns Rather Than Behaviors

In Cassidy's (2007) model emphasis is not placed on predicting and generalizing causes for a group's advancing or becoming arrested in development. This model also shifts away from naming behaviors (such as forming and storming). Instead it focuses on the basic concerns inherent in groups—concerns that should be recognized and addressed throughout the life of the group.

Compatibility With Sequential, Cyclical, and Nonsequential Models

Group development models may be divided into three different types: sequential, cyclical, and nonsequential. Tuckman's model is an example of a sequential stage model suggesting that groups progress in a stepwise, linear manner toward maturity and higher productivity. Another type of group development model can be described as cyclical. In these models, it is suggested that the group may swing back and forth between stages; a shift in stages is thought to occur when new information about the group or the task is encountered. There is also a type of model referred to as nonsequential. This type of model suggests that group development may occur as a result of environmental factors such as time or the context in which the group is located.

Although sense of self, sense of group, and sense of meaning can be considered in a sequential manner to build a new group, research suggests that these concerns are constantly interacting throughout the life of a group and can come to influence the group for any number of internal or external reasons (such as time or context) at any time. Some examples may help clarify this point. A person may affect the group when he or she feels a great sense of pressure or fear and expresses a concern for sense of self. When members face a new task that requires additional interpersonal skills, sense-of-group concerns may come to the surface. A change in plans due to weather, new information, or an impending deadline might make addressing sense of purpose especially important. These examples demonstrate how Cassidy's (2007) model is flexible enough to align with sequential, cyclical, and nonsequential models.

Conflict and Storming as Ongoing Issues

Research (Cassidy 2007) suggests that conflict or storming can occur for multiple reasons: sense of self (for example, people don't feel safe, heard, or accepted), sense of group (perhaps people lack a clear group structure, have communication challenges, or are fighting for leadership), or sense of meaning (people may have multiple opinions on the purpose of the group or feel that the group's purpose does not align with their own personal goals). These conflicts can develop at any time during a group's life. In this way, Cassidy's (2007) model differs from Tuckman's model, in which storming is a discrete stage that the group moves through.

CONCLUSION

An understanding of group development is important for the adventure educator. Tuckman's model of group development may present a limited perspective on group development outside therapy contexts and may not be flexible enough to describe different groups dealing with a variety of internal and external factors over time. McCollom (1990) suggests that even "if we cannot say how groups develop . . . we should at least be able to identify general categories of factors that will shape development" (p. 151). A new group development model is proposed here based on three fundamental concerns that shape groups over time. The model proposes that by helping all the individuals, and the group as a whole, to have their needs met in relation to individual concerns (sense of self), interpersonal concerns (sense of group), and goal-clarity concerns (sense of meaning), the group will be able to reach and maintain full engagement. This model of group development helps facilitators to recognize concerns as they arise and to guide each unique group and the people within the group as they develop and thrive.

RESOURCES

Cain, J. 2003. Exploring the five stages of group formation using adventure-based activities. *Horizons,* 21:23-28.

Cassidy, K. 2007. Tuckman revisited . . . proposing a new model of group development for practitioners. *Journal of Experiential Education,* 29(3):413-417.

Cassidy, K. In press. A contemporary model of experiential education. In *The theory of experiential education* (4th ed.), eds. K. Warren, T.A. Loeffler, and D. Mitten. Dubuque, IA: Kendall/Hunt.

Cissna, K. 1984. Phases in group development. *Small Group Behavior,* 15:3-32.

Collins, J. 2001. *From good to great.* New York: HarperCollins.

Gersick, C.J.G. 1988. Time and transition in work teams: Toward a new model of group development. *Academy of Management Journal,* 31:9-41.

Kerr, J.P., and M.A. Gass. 1995. A group development model for adventure education. In *The theory of experiential education*, eds. K. Warren, M. Sakofs, and J.S. Hunt, Jr., 285-296. Dubuque, IA: Kendall/Hunt.

Maslow, A. 1970. *Motivation and personality.* 2nd ed. New York: Harper & Row.

McCollom, M. 1990. Reevaluating group development: A critique of the familiar models. In *Groups in context*, eds. J. Gillette and M. McCollom, 134-154. New York: Addison-Wesley.

Mitten, D. 1989. Healthy expressions of diversity lead to positive group experiences. *Journal of Experiential Education*, 12(3):17-22.

Noddings, N. 2002. *Starting at home. Caring and social policy.* Berkeley, CA: University of California Press.

Priest, S., and M.A. Gass. 2005. *Effective leadership in adventure programming.* Champaign, IL: Human Kinetics.

Shields, C.M. 2000. Learning from difference: Considerations for schools as communities. *Curriculum Inquiry*, 30(3):275-294.

Smith, M.K. 2005. Bruce W. Tuckman—forming, storming, norming and performing in groups. *The encyclopedia of informed education.* www.infed.org/thinkers/tuckman.htm (accessed January 5, 2007).

Stangor, C. 2004. *Social groups in action and interaction.* New York: Psychology Press.

Tuckman, B.W. 1965. Developmental sequence in small groups. *Psychological Bulletin*, 63:384-399.

Tuckman, B.W., and M.C. Jensen. 1977. Stages of small-group development revisited. *Group and Organizational Studies*, 2:419-427.

Lesson Plan

PURPOSE

This lesson reviews Tuckman's model of group development and then invites students to compare and consider an alternative conception of group development based on three fundamental concerns that are constantly interacting within groups. Students will learn to be aware of and address these three basic concerns to design and lead adventure programs.

OBJECTIVES

As a result of this lesson students will be able to . . .

1. *Affective and psychomotor:* participate in problem-solving challenges to experience how they and others respond to individual concerns (sense of self), interpersonal concerns (sense of group), and goal-clarity concerns (sense of meaning) in different ways.
2. *Cognitive:* create a scenario illustrating how concerns related to sense of self, sense of group, and sense of meaning can manifest.
3. *Cognitive:* discuss how conflict, or storming, is the result of an unmet concern.
4. *Cognitive:* create a scenario illustrating ways in which the group leader may address concerns related to sense of self, sense of group, and sense of meaning.

DURATION

90 minutes

GROUP SIZE

8 to 32

LOCATION

Indoors

EQUIPMENT

- A set of three information sheets for each student (see handouts on CD-ROM)
- Flip chart paper (8-10 sheets)
- Markers (one for every one or two students)
- Blank sheets of paper (one half sheet for each student)
- Hula hoops (one for every eight students)
- Tennis balls (at least two per student)
- Pretzels
- Paper and pen for each student

RISK MANAGEMENT CONSIDERATIONS

Be aware of allergies and health concerns that may relate to giving out pretzels.

STUDENT PREPARATION

Before this lesson, ask students to reflect on the following questions in their journal. Reflections may include drawings or collages to illustrate thoughts.

- Why form groups? What is the best thing about groups? What is the hardest thing about groups?
- Think about the worst, and then the best, group you were ever in. What was the group like? How did people act toward each other? What did you think and feel when you were in that group? How was the group led?
- Do you think groups change over time? If yes, how? If no, why? Do all groups change over time? Do you think group behavior ever declines? Why do you think that does or doesn't happen?

Supplementary reading assignments may be provided from the following books and articles.

- Cain, J. 2003. Exploring the five stages of group formation using adventure-based activities. *Horizons,* 21:23-28.
- Priest, S., and M.A. Gass. 2005. Group development and dynamics. In *Effective leadership in adventure programming,* 65-74. Champaign, IL: Human Kinetics.
- Stangor, C. 2004. *Social groups in action and interaction.* New York: Psychology Press.
- Tuckman, B.W. 1965. Developmental sequence in small groups. *Psychological Bulletin,* 63:384-399.

INSTRUCTOR PREPARATION

Prepare sense-of-self question sheets: Write one question at the top of each flip chart sheet that will help people come to know each other better and at a deeper level than they do currently. The following are sample questions:

- Why are you interested in adventure education?
- Who was your most memorable teacher, and what do you remember most about him or her?

- What is the best group you were ever in, and why?
- Name a memorable outdoor experience you have had in your life.
- What kind of adventure educator do you want to be?
- Name a talent you have.
- Whom do you most admire and why?
- In a group, what role do you like to play?

Post all the question sheets throughout the classroom, along with markers, before students arrive for class.

Prepare group-juggle goal slips. Cut paper in half, so that each student has a half sheet. Write one of the following goals for the group juggle on each slip of paper. More than one student may be given the same goal if you have more than eight students.

- Your goal is to ensure that all ideas are heard.
- Your goal is to ensure that everyone feels involved.
- Your goal is to ensure that every opportunity to be creative is taken.
- Your goal is to complete the activity with the best time.
- Your goal is to ensure that all accomplishments are recognized and celebrated.
- Your goal is to ensure that dropping balls or making a mistake is okay.
- Your goal is to get as many tennis balls as possible into the system.
- Your goal is to memorize every color, texture, and detail in the room.

LESSON CONTENT AND TEACHING STRATEGIES

This lesson is made up of three activities that will allow students to experience the concerns of sense of self, sense of group, and sense of meaning. Debriefing questions are provided for reflecting upon experience.

Activity 1: Exploring Sense of Self

In this activity, demonstrate sense of self by helping the class get to know each other on a deeper and more meaningful level than they do now. Bring a treat (the pretzels) to illustrate care and address physiological needs. Help students consider how sense-of-self concerns may manifest in different people and in different group situations, causing groups and people to act and develop differently.

Flip chart sheets with sense-of-self questions have been prepared and are posted throughout the room along with markers. While waiting for everyone to arrive, have the students travel about and write their thoughts on as many sheets as they wish. They don't have to use complete sentences or put their name beside what they write.

After everyone has written on at least a few sheets, have students get into partners. The goal of this activity is for all the students to learn three unique things that are important to their partner and that the class wouldn't already know about that person. These three pieces of information will be ones people are willing to share with the class at the end of the activity. Students may use the questions on the flip chart paper as a starting point but should not limit themselves to these questions in their quest to find out three unique things. This activity, as all others, should be framed in accordance with challenge-by-choice principles that aim to create a group culture, one that respects the right of individuals to choose their degree and method of participation. As each pair is talking, walk around the class and offer pretzels.

When everyone is ready, have all the students share with the class the three things they discovered about their partner, keeping challenge by choice in mind.

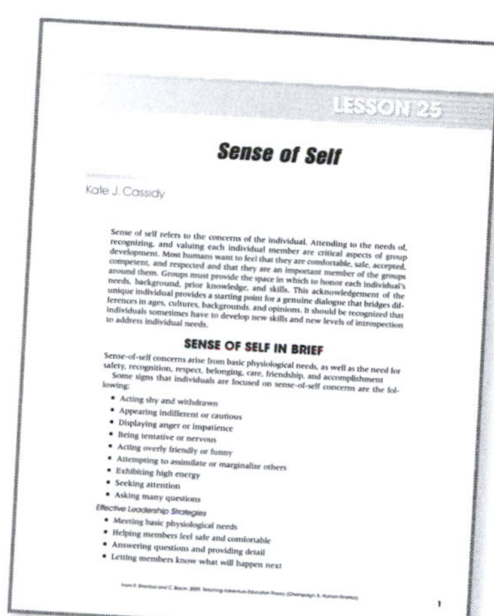

LESSON 25

Sense of Self

Kate J. Cassidy

Sense of self refers to the concerns of the individual. Attending to the needs of, recognizing, and valuing each individual member are critical aspects of group development. Most humans want to feel that they are comfortable, safe, accepted, competent, and respected and that they are an important member of the groups around them. Groups must provide the space in which to honor each individual's needs, background, prior knowledge, and skills. This acknowledgement of the unique individual provides a starting point for a genuine dialogue that bridges differences in ages, cultures, backgrounds, and opinions. It should be recognized that individuals sometimes have to develop new skills and new levels of introspection to address individual needs.

SENSE OF SELF IN BRIEF

Sense-of-self concerns arise from basic physiological needs, as well as the need for safety, recognition, respect, belonging, care, friendship, and accomplishment.

Some signs that individuals are focused on sense-of-self concerns are the following:

- Acting shy and withdrawn
- Appearing indifferent or cautious
- Displaying anger or impatience
- Being tentative or nervous
- Acting overly friendly or funny
- Attempting to assimilate or marginalize others
- Exhibiting high energy
- Seeking attention
- Asking many questions

Effective Leadership Strategies

- Meeting basic physiological needs
- Helping members feel safe and comfortable
- Answering questions and providing detail
- Letting members know what will happen next

1

Finally, ask the class how it feels to have shared this time with classmates. Do people feel more, less, or the same level of comfort with the class after doing this activity?

Hand out the sense-of-self information sheet found on the CD-ROM. Discuss the concerns relating to sense of self and consider the scenario together. Lead a discussion using the questions listed at the end of the scenario.

Activity 2: Exploring Sense of Group

In this activity, demonstrate sense of group by considering what is needed to be an effective community while also helping students to realize that group processes, characteristics, and challenges will vary among groups, causing them to act and develop differently.

Have people get into groups of approximately eight. Give each group a hula hoop. Everyone in the group should be touching the hoop with only his or her two index fingers, which must remain parallel to the ground. Group members cannot pinch, trap, or hold the hoop, only support it. The goal is for all group members to maintain contact with the hoop at all times while lowering it close enough to the ground for all pinkie fingers to touch the floor.

Exploring sense of group with a hula hoop activity.

Courtesy of Susan McGlynn.

Once they are finished, have participants split their group of eight into two groups of four. Give each group a piece of flip chart paper and a marker. Ask them to write clearly. Students are to think of the activity they just did, or other activities they have done with the class or other groups in the past, and list the positive or effective processes and characteristics of the group, guided by the some of the following questions (listed on the board):

- What can an effective group do if they disagree or have conflict?
- What is needed for effective communication within a group?
- How can people show that they truly care for and respect each member of the group?
- How can an effective group handle difference and diversity (of any type)?
- What positive rituals can an effective group have?
- How can people show that they are trustworthy in an effective group?
- What other processes or characteristics can be important in an effective group?

Have students merge their groups of four back into eight. You may lead the class in the discussion or have students debrief as groups of eight. If they are debriefing in small groups, have the following questions on the board as a guide:

- How are the two lists (created by each group of four) the same or different?
- If groups have two different answers to a question, is one wrong?
- Looking at the lists, what characteristic or process is the easiest for a typical group? What is the hardest?
- Do all groups start at the same level of effectiveness?
- Why might it be hard to be an effective group—what challenges do groups face?
- If a group gets along well and is very effective, can you assume that the group will always get along in an effective manner?

Using the previously developed lists (or other ideas of your choosing) and the activity, have each group decide on three to five critical group norms. Ask them to put each norm on a separate sheet of paper and to write as clearly as possible. An example of a norm might be "Don't think about what you are going to say when a person is talking to you—always focus on that person."

Have each group of eight bring their sheets of paper (each sheet with one of the three to five critical norms on it) to the middle of the classroom and lay them on the floor. Without talking, the full class is to cluster similar norms and place them in relation to each other on the floor like a concept map. When they are done, debrief the activity:

- What happened?
- How did people feel about the process and the placement of the norms?
- Why were the norms clustered as they are?

Allow rearranging as the students discuss the process. Then, using the norms on the floor as a guide, facilitate the full group as you create class norms or a class "contract." Discuss possible obstacles to fulfilling the contract.

Hand out the sense-of-group information sheet from the CD-ROM. Discuss the need for sense of group and go over the scenario together. Lead a discussion using the questions listed at the end of the scenario.

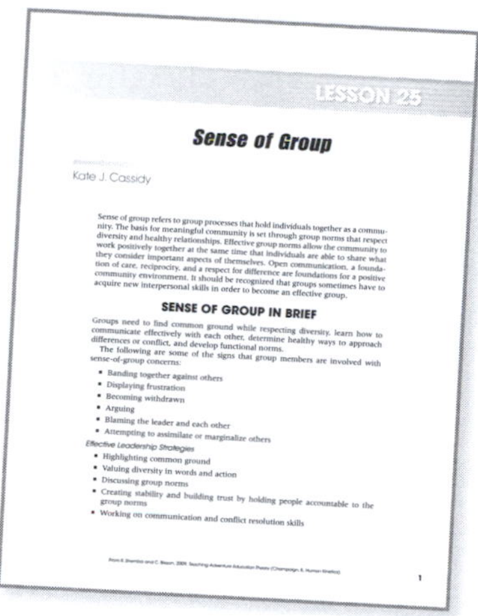

LESSON 25

Sense of Group

Kate J. Cassidy

Sense of group refers to group processes that hold individuals together as a community. The basis for meaningful community is set through group norms that respect diversity and healthy relationships. Effective group norms allow the community to work positively together at the same time that individuals are able to share what they consider important aspects of themselves. Open communication, a foundation of care, reciprocity, and a respect for difference are foundations for a positive community environment. It should be recognized that groups sometimes have to acquire new interpersonal skills in order to become an effective group.

SENSE OF GROUP IN BRIEF

Groups need to find common ground while respecting diversity, learn how to communicate effectively with each other, determine healthy ways to approach differences or conflict, and develop functional norms.

The following are some of the signs that group members are involved with sense-of-group concerns:

- Banding together against others
- Displaying frustration
- Becoming withdrawn
- Arguing
- Blaming the leader and each other
- Attempting to assimilate or marginalize others

Effective Leadership Strategies

- Highlighting common ground
- Valuing diversity in words and action
- Discussing group norms
- Creating stability and building trust by holding people accountable to the group norms
- Working on communication and conflict resolution skills

1

Activity 3: Exploring Sense of Meaning

In this activity, demonstrate sense of meaning by showing that individuals within a group may have different goals. Help the class consider how best to incorporate multiple goals into an overall group goal or vision.

Divide the class into equal circles of 8 to 12 people. Each group is given a tennis ball and told to establish a pattern with the following rules. The ball must start and end with the designated leader. The ball should be thrown to everyone in the group once (the designated leader will receive it twice) but never directly to a person's left or right.

When the groups have established their pattern, hand out the "goal" slips of paper to each participant. Make sure they know not to share their slips with anyone else.

Explain the instructions for the group juggle as follows. With the pattern established a few minutes ago, the group will pass the ball around the pattern as effectively as possible without letting it touch the ground. If it does touch the ground, they must start over. They can add as many balls as they like to the process but must maintain their pattern. Each group is given 4 minutes to complete the task.

After 4 minutes, have the groups stop and share their slips of paper with each other. Ask the groups to come up with an overall group goal that recognizes each individual member's goal in a fulfilling way, and then try the activity again.

To debrief the activity, ask the following questions:

Exploring sense of meaning with the group-juggle activity.

Courtesy of Kendel O'Hara.

- What happened?
- How did people feel about the process?
- What was the group goal?
- How did each group incorporate all of the individual goals?
- How did the person feel whose goal was to notice the detail in the room?

- How did the group address that goal? How did that feel?
- How did the person feel whose goal it was to add as many balls as possible to the process?
- Compare and contrast participants' feelings based on how closely their goal seemed to align with the overall group goal.

Ask the class to consider what they would do if someone's personal goal did not seem to be aligned with the group goal:

- How does an effective group make sure that the group goals are aligned with everyone's personal goals and values?
- Are there ever circumstances in which an individual goal simply does not align with the group? What should a leader do in that circumstance?

Hand out the sense-of-meaning information sheet from the CD-ROM. Discuss the need for sense of meaning and go over the scenario together. Lead a discussion using the questions listed at the end of the scenario.

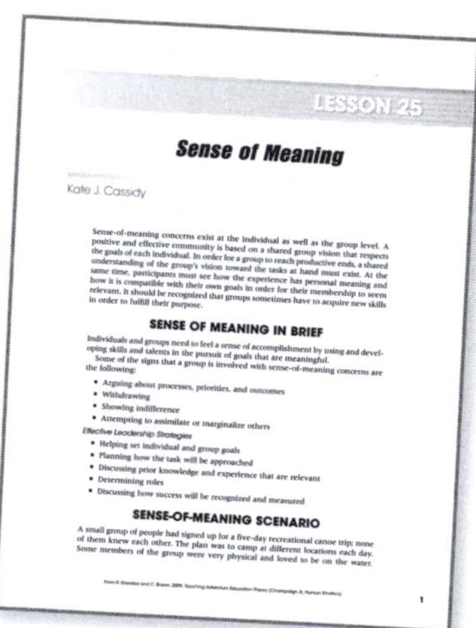
LESSON 25

Sense of Meaning

Kate J. Cassidy

Sense-of-meaning concerns exist at the individual as well as the group level. A positive and effective community is based on a shared group vision that respects the goals of each individual. In order for a group to reach productive ends, a shared understanding of the group's vision toward the tasks at hand must exist. At the same time, participants must see how the experience has personal meaning and how it is compatible with their own goals in order for their membership to seem relevant. It should be recognized that groups sometimes have to acquire new skills in order to fulfill their purpose.

SENSE OF MEANING IN BRIEF

Individuals and groups need to feel a sense of accomplishment by using and developing skills and talents in the pursuit of goals that are meaningful.

Some of the signs that a group is involved with sense-of-meaning concerns are the following:

- Arguing about processes, priorities, and outcomes
- Withdrawing
- Showing indifference
- Attempting to assimilate or marginalize others

Effective Leadership Strategies

- Helping set individual and group goals
- Planning how the task will be approached
- Discussing prior knowledge and experience that are relevant
- Determining roles
- Discussing how success will be recognized and measured

SENSE-OF-MEANING SCENARIO

A small group of people had signed up for a five-day recreational canoe trip; none of them knew each other. The plan was to camp at different locations each day. Some members of the group were very physical and loved to be on the water.

1

CLOSURE

Mention the following points:

- Although every group and every person is different, there are three fundamental concerns that must be addressed during a group's time together: sense of self, sense of group, and sense of meaning. These concerns may show up in a variety of ways and at multiple times over the course of the group's life. By recognizing and addressing these needs, adventure educators can help groups and the people within them grow and develop.
- Although sense of self, sense of group, and sense of meaning can be considered in a sequential manner for program design, it should be recognized that these concerns can dominate the group for any variety of internal or external reasons at any time during the life of a group. This practitioner-based model emphasizes three basic concerns rather than predicting and generalizing behaviors. The model allows for the fact that conflict or storming can occur due to an unmet concern about sense of self, sense of group, or sense of meaning.

ASSESSMENT OF LEARNING

- **Theory:** Students write their own scenario that shows a concern about sense of self, sense of group, or sense of meaning influencing a group, making sure to include visible behaviors and how they should be addressed by the leader.
- **Reflection:** Students return to their prelesson journal entries to reflect upon how their ideas have changed or stayed the same.
- **Reflection:** Students think about the groups they wrote about in their reflection. They identify and describe which of the three basic concerns were most significant in the worst group and give suggestions on how these concerns could have been addressed. Thinking of the best group in which they ever participated, students write about how the basic concerns were being addressed and how.

LESSON 26

Setting the Stage

How to Get the Group Norms You Want

Denise Mitten

One of the most rewarding aspects of an outdoor trip is having a great group experience. Some groups seem to be easy to work with and everything flows well; other groups never seem to get off the ground and the trip is a disappointment. In a well-functioning group, individuals contribute to group decisions, complete group tasks, and feel good about themselves and the group. A well-functioning group is a joy for a leader to work with, and participants, too, have a more positive experience. Sometimes, though, group process and what influences it can be a mystery. This lesson plan is designed to take some of the mystery out of the group formation process and give leaders more skills for intentionally creating the group norms they want to see on trips.

Background

A goal of many adventure education programs is to help participants learn more about being part of a group, which often includes (1) establishing relationships between the leader and members as well as among the members and (2) working together as a team to accomplish tasks (McAvoy et al. 1992). Over 100 theories have been advanced by group dynamists seeking to describe the kinds of developmental changes seen in groups (Forsyth 1990). The common agreement among group dynamists is that groups change over time and that changes occur at both the group level and the individual level. McAvoy and colleagues (1992) present a thorough overview of group dynamic models that have been used in outdoor education.

Most group development models use one of two basic approaches (Hill and Gruner 1973; Shambaugh 1978). In recurring-phase models or cyclical models, theorists assert that certain issues tend to dominate group interaction during various phases of group development, but that these issues can also come up later in the life of the group. This is also referred to as a thematic approach to group development (Napier and Gershenfield 1989).

In a second, sequential-stage or successive-stage approach, theorists seek to identify the typical order of the phases of group development. The amount of time in each stage is determined by the leader's direction or nondirection and the skills and emotional strengths of the members. Some groups never progress beyond early stages.

One can also use a multidimensional model combining concepts from both sequential- or successive-stage theory and recurring-phase or cyclical theory. This type of model emphasizes that the stages do not have discrete beginnings or endings, and that some stages are more thematic; it also recognizes that in adventure education, while the entire trip or program may follow a semblance of sequential phases, groups often cycle through stages again and again as they complete different parts of the program or attend to new and maybe more challenging tasks. Leaders help group members form a cohesive group. With deliberate guidance from the trip leader, group members successfully achieve each of the stages and individuals feel included in, but not ruled by, the group process.

The concept to help students understand is that their adoption and use of one model over another influences the group development and group dynamics. The stages that a group goes through are highly dependent on the beliefs of the leader about the stages as well as the skill of the leader in helping the members develop into a healthy, cohesive group. Encourage leaders to look at a number of models and use a model of group development that fits their values and beliefs.

Many adventure education leaders, without critical examination, use a group model introduced by Tuckman (1965). In Tuckman's model the stages are forming, storming, norming, performing, and adjourning. In the storming phase there is an expectation that participants will experience conflict with one another and that power positions within the group will be worked out, among other things. Both the word "storming" and the anticipation that there will be conflict during this stage set leader expectations that are transferred to participants. Other leaders, however, use a model in which the second stage is called "sorting." With this model it is expected that instead of working out power issues, the group members will sort out operating procedures and responsibilities (for example, "How will we make decisions as a group?"; "What time will we get up in the mornings?"; "What are the tasks that need to be done and who will do what?"). Of course there may be and probably will be conflict in every stage. The leader sets the tone for working with the origins of conflict—unclear communication, role ambiguity, or values differences—and resolving the conflicts accordingly (Mitten and Clement 2007, p. 88).

PARALLEL PROCESS

The concept of parallel process is to do unto others as you want them, in turn, to do unto others. Central to the success of this model is that leaders are conscious role models. Leaders understand that especially in a new setting, participants are watching them for direction and guidance. If leaders treat their participants with care and respect, then participants more likely will treat other participants with care and respect. If you are teaching your participants to be leaders, they will likely replicate in their leadership behavior what you have modeled to them through your actions.

HEALTHY AND REACTIONARY BONDING

Leaders in adventure education are teaching relationship- and community-building skills through their program design and most importantly through the ways in which they form relationships with the participants. To understand how to help group members learn positive community-building skills, it is useful to examine one's own beliefs about communities and relationships. Leaders' understanding of and ability to engage in healthy relationships are integral to positive group cohesion, hence the importance of the concept of creating and maintaining healthy relationships.

For many people, group membership is an unconscious means of regaining the security of the family (whether we would judge the family relationships as healthy or not), and people's relationship skills usually originate from their family experiences (Freud 1922). Studies of groups such as families, therapeutic groups, and combat units support Freud's hypotheses that people join groups simply because they have been in groups since infancy and for reasons that are less than rational (Billig 1976; Janis 1963). Healthy relationships—connections based on mutual respect, trust, and experience with one another—can add to group cohesiveness, enable people to feel good about themselves, and give them opportunities to grow. Relationships that grow out of healthy connections do not happen at the expense of someone or something else. Healthy connections come from individuals' acting on their own desires rather than reacting to an outside stimulus. When people form healthy connections, they enter relationships in which they maintain a separate identity and individual responsibility yet can still function well in a group and feel a sense of authentic belonging. Such relationships often start with common interests, shared experiences, learning together, or accomplishing tasks in an atmosphere of mutual respect and trust. People in healthy relationships feel secure and speak up if they are cold, tired, or hungry or if they have other concerns; and this speaking up helps make trips safer.

In contrast, dependency relationships are reactions against an outside stimulus—stress, hardships, a disliked object or person, or various evils that need to be fought. This form of relationship or bonding is exemplified more by what one is "against" than by what one is "for." In reactionary or dependency bonding, connections usually are maintained only as long as the fight goes on and the crisis continues—that is, as long as the seemingly negative factor exists. Reactionary relationships discourage people from feeling good about themselves and from valuing their own and others' differences.

The misuse of power among people often results in unhealthy or dependency relationships. Family members who connect around secrets, crises, or abuse of another family member learn the misuse of power. They may see others as liking them when they can focus negative energy on something or someone. They usually feel little or no liking based on self-worth or on respect from others, and their dependency relationships reinforce low esteem. A milder example of reactionary or unhealthy bonding might be a relationship formed on the basis of gossiping about another person or shared complaining about spouses. According to Block and Greenberg (1985), relationships formed in reaction typically dissolve, and true intimacy or friendship usually is not achieved.

On outdoor trips, participants' perceptions of the importance of strong connections and the pressure to make quick connections can lead to reactionary bonding. Participants who are connecting in order to survive in the wilderness are making connections in reaction to an outside stimulus. Connecting in order to survive supports the idea that they have to conquer or beat nature and that wilderness is evil and frightening. Unhealthy connections can divide group members, create unsafe conditions, or cause people to compete for food, shelter, and protection. Unhealthy relationships discourage people from pursuing individual goals simultaneously with the group goals and can trap individuals in unhealthy subgroups.

During trips, leaders can purposefully or accidentally create situations that help group members learn or reinforce reactionary or dependency bonding by bonding against nature. Common phrases are "we have to stick together to beat this situation" or "together we can conquer the mountain." However, when participants return to their families and work situations these reactionary or dependency bonds may not be functional.

For some people, bonding or feeling closer under stress feels familiar and even comfortable. This is especially true for people from families in which bonding took place during or after a conflict or abuse. The classic abuse cycle is a buildup to a conflict, then remorse, and finally a honeymoon phase with close bonding. Then the cycle repeats. War is an example in which people bond under stress and when fighting others. However, this type of reactionary or dependency bonding does not lead to community building; nor does it, in the long run, increase self-esteem. In fact, it may teach individuals to create a stressful environment when they want to feel close.

Researchers disagree about the various reasons individuals join groups but agree that people join groups when they are scared. According to Schachter (1959), individuals will affiliate when their opinions, attitudes, or beliefs are shaken. They search for information that will define their own social reality, and affiliation will satisfy this need for information. In a series of studies, Schachter placed subjects in an anxiety-producing situation and then assessed their desire to affiliate with other people. They wanted to affiliate, but only with people experiencing the same misery. Schachter concluded that individuals under stress form groups both to gain information and to reduce anxiety levels. Therefore, putting people in unfamiliar, stressful, and scary situations will produce high group cohesion (Wills 1981; Gerard 1961). However, this does not necessarily help people learn to be part of a group in the absence of a compelling external situation. This notion that group bonding may be due to individuals' fear level is supported by other research findings, including the following:

- Human groups tend to become more cohesive when they face a threatening, rather than a nonthreatening, situation (Kleiner 1960; Pepitone and Kleiner 1957).
- Many animals, including humans, prefer to join with others when they are fearful (Latané and Glass 1968; Schachter 1959).
- Individuals awaiting a negative event, such as receiving a series of painful electric shocks, prefer to wait with others rather than by themselves (Schachter 1959).
- Joining a group is an effective way for people to reduce fear (Kissel 1965).

EXAMINING LEADERS' ASSUMPTIONS

Leaders' goals and assumptions influence their interpretation of participants' behaviors and their own subsequent actions. When working with groups, it is useful for leaders to check to see if they are making assumptions about participants' behavior or character and if their assumptions are based on biases. Our assumptions directly affect the experiences of participants. A leader who sees a person being quiet during the planning phase of a group activity may assume that the participant is (a) not interested, (b) interested but looking for information, (c) too shy to speak, or (d) holding back to give others an opportunity to speak. Mitten's (2003) research on the ethical frameworks that leaders use in decision making indicates that if a leader "blames" the participant for her or his condition, the leader is less likely to help that participant. For example, if a leader sees it as the participant's fault that she or he does not have the skills for an activity, then the leader may be less likely to help that individual acquire the skills. Leaders need to practice the skill of examining their assumptions.

RESOURCES

Billig, M. 1976. *Social psychology and group relations.* New York: Academic Press.

Block, J., and D. Greenberg. 1985. *Women and friendships.* New York: Watts.

Clarke, J.I. 1984. *Who, me lead a group?* San Francisco: Harper & Row.

Forsyth, D. 1990. *Group dynamics.* 2nd ed. New York: Harper & Row.

Freud, S. 1922. *Group psychology and the analysis of the ego.* London: Hogarth.

Gerard, H.B. 1961. Emotional uncertainty and social comparison. *Journal of Abnormal and Social Psychology,* 62:586-592.

Hill, W.F., and L. Gruner. 1973. A study of development in open and closed groups. *Small Group Behavior* ,4(3):355-381.

Janis, I.L. 1963. Group identification under conditions of external danger. *British Journal of Medical Psychology,* 36:227-238.

Kissel, S. 1965. Stress reducing properties of social stimuli. *Journal of Personality and Social Psychology,* 2(3):378-384.

Kleiner, R.J. 1960. The effects of threat reduction upon interpersonal attractiveness. *Journal of Personality,* 28:145-155.

Latané, B., and D.C. Glass. 1968. Social and nonsocial attraction in rats. *Journal of Personality and Social Psychology,* 9:142-146.

McAvoy, L., D. Mitten, J. Steckart, and L. Stringer. 1992. Research in outdoor education: Group development and group dynamics. In *Coalition for Education in the Outdoors research symposium proceedings,* ed. K. Henderson. Bradford Woods, IN: Coalition for Education in the Outdoors.

Meier, J., and A.V. Mitchel. 1993. *Camp counseling.* 7th ed. Madison, WI: Brown & Benchmark.

Mitten, D. 2003. An analysis of outdoor leaders' ethics guiding decision making. UMI No. 3087775.

Mitten, D., and K. Clement. 2007. Skills and responsibilities for adventure education leaders. In *Adventure based programming and education,* eds. D. Prouty, J. Panicucci, and R. Collinson. Champaign, IL: Human Kinetics.

Napier, R., and M. Gershenfield. 1989. *Groups: Theory and experience.* 4th ed. Boston: Houghton Mifflin.

Pepitone, A., and R. Kleiner. 1957. The effects of threat and frustration on group cohesiveness. *Journal of Abnormal and Social Psychology,* 54:192-199.

Schachter, S. 1959. *The psychology of affiliation.* Palo Alto, CA: Stanford University Press.

Shambaugh, P. 1978. The development of the small group. *Human Relations,* 31(3):283-295.

Tuckman, B. 1965. Developmental sequence in small groups. *Psychological Bulletin,* 63:384-399.

Wills, T.A. 1981. Downward comparison principles in social psychology. *Psychological Bulletin,* 90(2):245-271.

Lesson Plan

PURPOSE

To help students see how instrumental a leader can be in influencing group formation and group dynamics and how a leader's perception of group development, as well as the meanings that the leader attaches to participants' behaviors, influences participant growth and group dynamics.

OBJECTIVES

As a result of this lesson students will be able to . . .

1. *Cognitive:* compare, contrast, and question different group development models.
2. *Cognitive:* explain the importance of the initial contact with participants and a positive beginning to the program or trip.
3. *Psychomotor:* demonstrate how to create a welcoming environment for participants that sets the stage for healthy bonding and discourages reactionary bonding.
4. *Cognitive:* select appropriate structural and attitudinal norms to promote during the forming stage of a program or outdoor trip.
5. *Cognitive:* explain and predict the impact of the leader's behavior on group development.
6. *Affective:* communicate effectively and sensitively to learn more about what is motivating participants' behaviors.
7. *Affective:* integrate caring affirmations into one's work with participants.

DURATION

90 minutes

GROUP SIZE

Up to 30 people (15 people is ideal)

LOCATION

This lesson works indoors or outdoors.

EQUIPMENT

- Whiteboard or large paper and markers
- An overhead projector for the worksheets (LCD or other kind; helpful if available)
- Worksheets and handouts (on CD-ROM)
    - Favorite Outdoor Trips worksheet
    - A Group Formation Model Strengthened by Using Affirmations Handout
    - Taking the Group's Temperature worksheet
    - Admit Slips

RISK MANAGEMENT CONSIDERATIONS

None

STUDENT PREPARATION

This lesson is used in the context of teaching about group dynamics. Before the lesson, students should

1. know what structural and attitudinal norms are,

2. complete the Favorite Outdoor Trips worksheet, and
3. read the handout article, "A Group Formation Model Strengthened by Using Affirmations" (on CD-ROM).

INSTRUCTOR PREPARATION

No special prelesson preparation required

LESSON CONTENT AND TEACHING STRATEGIES

This lesson consists of the following segments:

- Discussion of students' favorite outdoor trips (30 minutes)
- Healthy and reactionary bonding (10 minutes)
- The power of saying yes (10 minutes)
- Setting the stage: How do the preceding activities relate to group dynamics? (10 minutes)
- Taking the group's temperature: It's a good sign if . . .; It's a cause for concern if . . . (15 minutes)
- Putting it all together (10 minutes)

Activity 1: Favorite Outdoor Trips

Have students individually complete the Favorite Outdoor Trips worksheet (on CD-ROM). They can do this ahead of time.

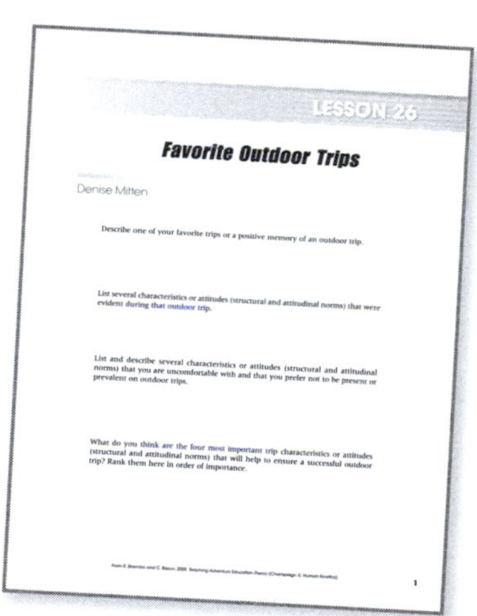

LESSON 26

Favorite Outdoor Trips

Denise Mitten

Describe one of your favorite trips or a positive memory of an outdoor trip.

List several characteristics or attitudes (structural and attitudinal norms) that were evident during that outdoor trip.

List and describe several characteristics or attitudes (structural and attitudinal norms) that you are uncomfortable with and that you prefer not to be present or prevalent on outdoor trips.

What do you think are the four most important trip characteristics or attitudes (structural and attitudinal norms) that will help to ensure a successful outdoor trip? Rank them here in order of importance.

1

Have the students get into dyads and share about one of their favorite or memorable outdoor trips. This helps set the stage for talking about trip characteristics. Back in the whole group, share a few examples.

Move on to the third question on the handout, about negative attitudes. Go around the room and ask each person to name a characteristic or attitude that she or he prefers not to be prevalent on trips. Record these on a whiteboard or a large piece of paper. You can make a gridlike chart or a list. Keep going around the room until you get a general idea of the characteristics the students identify. After making the chart, put a large red "X" through it.

Move on to the fourth question on the handout. Go around the room and ask each person to name the characteristic or attitude that she or he thinks is most important on a trip, and record these on a whiteboard or large piece of paper. For this part of the exercise it is important to record each person's ideas as a set, so go around the room again in the same order and ask each student to name the characteristic or attitude that she or he thinks is second most important. Repeat for the third and fourth most important characteristics or attitudes. The reason to go around one characteristic at a time is to keep the exercise moving and keep everyone involved. Also, students can watch the chart being built starting from the most important characteristics or attitudes. You will end up making a gridlike chart. If you have more than 15 people, you may want to pick 15 people to record their four characteristics. See table 26.1.

TABLE 26.1 Examples of Characteristics and Attitudes That People Want on Outdoor Trips

Lauren	Supportive	Fun	Rugged	Accomplish something
Chandra	Calm	Friendly	Fun	Active
Kramer	Considerate	Peaceful	Helpful	Fun
Mary	Humor	Compassionate	Lively	Thoughtful
Alex	Fun	Relaxing time	New area	Openness

Next, circle several of the lists, making sure to include different types of characteristics. Have students form groups of three or four and ask each group to work with one of the circled lists. For example, say "Three other people go with Lauren, and three people with Mary." The people whose list of characteristics it is become the leaders of that group. It is important that Mary is in the group that uses her list, for example.

After the students get into groups, tell them that now they are to make up a 2 to 4-minute news broadcast advertising their trip. The broadcasts can be radio or television. Encourage the students to be as enthusiastic as possible in their broadcasts, since this will draw participants. They need to describe the trip using at least the four characteristics on the list they are working with. Give them 5 to 10 minutes to create their broadcast. Then share the broadcasts. Debrief by checking the congruency between the listed characteristics and the broadcast. This exercise can be related to how we talk about our trips and how we make our language congruent with our intent. As a side benefit you can relate this to truth in advertising as we promote our programs.

Activity 2: Healthy and Reactionary Bonding

Take a couple of minutes to have the students shake out their arms and legs. For example, they can do the brain gym exercise for 30 seconds: touching the right elbow to the left knee as they lift the knee toward the elbow, and then the same with the left elbow and the right knee.

Begin this segment by telling the students that you would like them to sit comfortably and close their eyes. Give them time to settle in. Tell them to say words that come to mind when you say "We are coming together for peace." As they respond, write their words on the board. Repeat each word as it is offered. Every 10 seconds or so, repeat the statement, "We are coming together for peace." Usually words will flow for 2 or 3 minutes. Then ask people to stand up and shake out their arms and return to their seats.

Ask students to relax and think of words that come to mind when they hear "We are coming together to fight war; we are antiwar." Again, every 10 seconds or when there is a pause, repeat "We are coming together to fight war; we are antiwar. Tell me the words that come to your mind."

Table 26.2 presents an actual list that a group developed for this activity.

Next, observe out loud that the two lists contain a number of the same words (they usually do), and ask the group members whether the lists feel qualitatively different. Typically, the lists will indeed feel qualitatively different. Talk about this difference. Even though both of these situations may be seen as worthwhile, coming together for peace tends to have a more positive feel, often a "nicer" feel. Coming together against war can feel more violent and adversarial. Relate this

TABLE 26.2 Sample of Words That Students Suggested During Activity 2

Coming together for peace		Coming together to fight war; antiwar	
Open-minded	Hope	Teaching	Self-righteous
Relaxation	Curiousness	Energy	Justice
Communicate	Inviting	Compassion	Aggression
Connected	Love	Bold	Hope
Support	Empathy	Hate	Fight
Unity	Listening	Passion	Strategy
Nonjudgmental	Joy	Tactic	Commitment
Tranquility	Sharing	Organize	Information
Justice	Compromising	Goal	Blood
Flexible	Learning	Rage	Buttons
Laughter	Consensus	Courage	

to the idea that healthy bonding is coming together for a mutual goal but not in reaction to something or someone else. Reactionary bonding, which we want to avoid in groups, is coming together to fight someone or some perceived evil. While both types of coming together can involve a positive intent, the reactionary bonding tends to beget more reactionary bonding and instability. Long-term, healthy bonding leads to stability.

Usually the group members describe quite nicely experiences they have had in each kind of bonding situation. Typically they can relate to playground situations in which there may have been an "in" group and an "out" group or other rival factions. Use the visualization as a metaphor about how, as leaders, we'd like our groups to form. We'd like our groups to bond in a healthy rather than a reactionary way. After this discussion, move on to the third activity.

Activity 3: The Power of Saying Yes

How important is giving guidance by saying "yes" or "no"? One leadership characteristic that can help set the tone for a supportive trip atmosphere is that of being positive and supportive. The leader can set an example by saying "yes" or being proactive about what to do rather than about what not to do. Another way to say this is that a leader sets the example to face challenges or problems with resourcefulness and good cheer.

Have two people leave the meeting area so as to be out of hearing range. Explain to the remaining students that as a group they are to think of a task that the two people will have to complete when they return to the room. Examples of task instructions that are appropriate for this activity are "Go up to Fred and touch his right shoulder with your left hand" or "Go to the middle of the room, take off your right shoe, and give it to Cassandra."

Have one of the two people come back in. (The second person does not get to see or hear what happens with the first person.) As the first person tries to complete the task, group members will be helpful by saying "no" if he or she gets off course and remaining silent when he or she is on task. Designate one student as a timer. When the person is done, conduct a short debrief, asking the person who completed the task to speak first and then have the rest of the students share what it felt like to be saying "no." Then move on. The person who just completed the task should remain in the room.

Have the second person come back in. This time the others will be helpful by saying "yes" when the person gets closer to completing the task. No word is spoken except "no" for the first person and "yes" for the second person. Often it helps to have participants practice saying "yes" and otherwise being silent, as groups tend to be better at saying "no." Time the person as she or he completes the task. Again, conduct a short debrief, asking the person who completed the task to speak first, then having the rest of the students share what it felt like to be saying "yes." Be sure to do the "no" exercise first.

Students pick up on the qualitative difference between the two exercises. Sometimes the "yes" activity takes much less time and sometimes not. "No" can produce faster results, and that is why teachers, parents, and facilitators sometimes say "no." Finally, assure the students that there are very appropriate times and places to use the word "no"; we are talking about a general atmosphere, not making a hard-and-fast rule. Another concept operating here is parallel process. How we as leaders treat the participants influences how the participants treat one another. If we are supportive to them, it is more likely that they will be supportive to one another.

Activity 4: Discussion and Mini-Lecture

Discuss the importance of the leader's or instructor's initial contact with participants. Today's focus is on how to use the healthy bonding concept, as well as saying "yes," to set a positive and supportive atmosphere. This supportive atmosphere will aid in establishing the norms that you want with the group members. This initial supportive atmosphere that you model is created in the forming or preaffiliation stage, depending on the group development approach used. We want to establish a warm, welcoming tone and set the stage for healthy bonding by treating the participants how we want them to treat one another.

Ask students to consider the metaphor of house cleaning. "If your parents are visiting or you are going to have company, you make sure that the entranceway and the first room they will see is very clean and tidy. If you make a really good first impression, the visit goes better." Since group members make an almost immediate evaluation of whether they like the leader or the trip, making a positive first impression is important. Another metaphor you can use is that of burnt beans. Ask students if they have ever burned beans. Ask them how easy is it to "doctor" burnt beans so that they are edible. Most will agree that this is next to impossible. Therefore we want to avoid burning the beans. You can print out a poster showing a circle with "Burnt Beans" written inside and a large red "X" through the circle (see the sample in figure 26.1; also included on the CD-ROM).

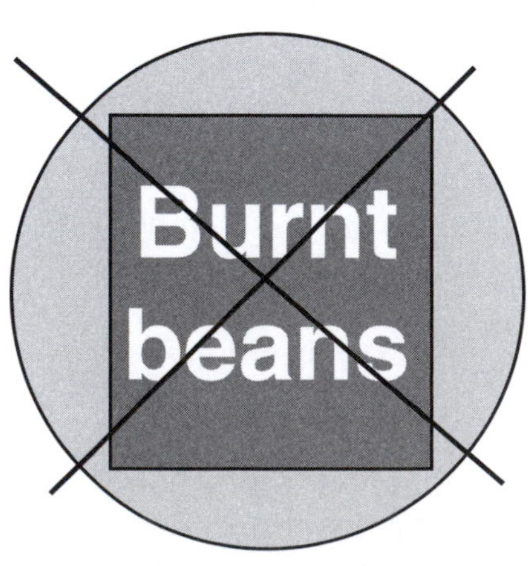

FIGURE 26.1 Burnt Beans poster.

In terms of groups, once participants have formed an opinion about the leader or program (and this happens within the first 3 minutes of contact) and norms have been set, it is very hard to change opinions and norms.

Remind students that there are over 100 models describing group development. These models incorporate and reflect theory; no one model is "correct." Additionally, the leader's influence to a certain extent directs group development. The reading for this lesson uses a model, adapted from Tuckman (1965) and from Garland, Jones, and Kolodny (1965, in Meier and Mitchel 1993), that differs significantly from the Tuckman model in several ways. This adapted model uses sorting rather than storming as the second stage; adds a differentiating stage (also found in Garland, Jones, and Kolodny 1965); and, while presented like a stage model, is more of a matrix (various stages overlap, or a given stage starts within another stage). For example, although norming is the third stage, norms are initiated sometimes even before the group members convene and certainly in the forming stage.

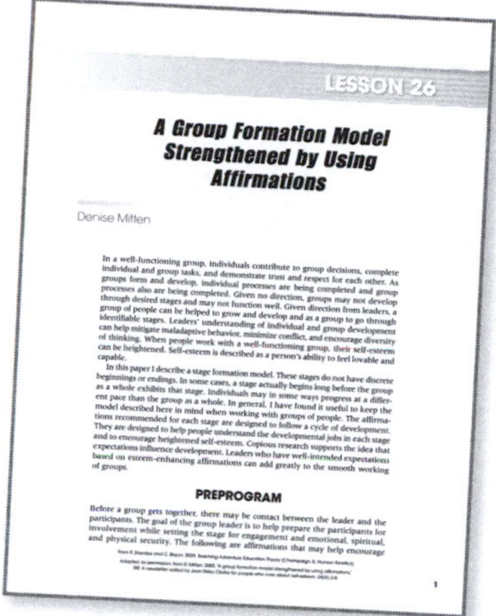

LESSON 26

A Group Formation Model Strengthened by Using Affirmations

Denise Mitten

PREPROGRAM

To derive an example of how leaders subtly influence group development, have the students say what descriptors come to mind when they hear the word "sorting" and which come to mind when they hear the word "storming." This often gives a good idea of how our behavior can follow language. The Garland, Jones, and Kolodny model, found in the text *Camp Counseling* (7th edition) by Meier and Mitchel, uses different stages and different names for the stages than Tuckman's model. Most students have seen or used Tuckman's model. Bring in the information from the article "A Group Formation Model Strengthened by Using Affirmations" about using affirmations during the group's development as an additional way to help initiate desired norms.

Activity 5: Taking the Group's Temperature

Present the Taking the Group's Temperature worksheet (on CD-ROM).

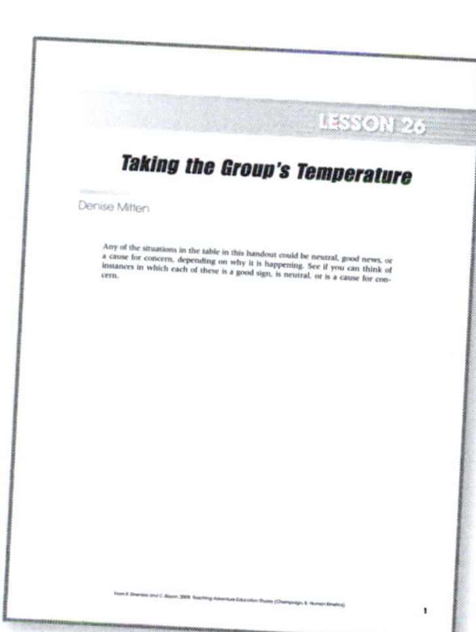

LESSON 26

Taking the Group's Temperature

Denise Mitten

Open with the Mark Twain quote, *It's not what you know that gets you in trouble, it is what you know that just ain't so.* Explain that as leaders we often have preconceived notions about what a certain behavior means. We see others' behavior through our own filters. This exercise helps students learn about some of their own filters.

After completing the worksheet exercise, engage students in a discussion about how, as a leader, one would find out if a behavior was a cause for concern or not. The benefit of processing this exercise is that it helps students develop a plan for checking out behavior before acting on their assumptions.

Activity 6: Putting It All Together

To conclude this lesson, have the students get into small groups and discuss some of the learning. Ask them to come up with four or five specific ways in which they can incorporate new practices into their leadership or apply what they learned today. Also ask them to give specific examples of how they could incorporate affirmations into their leadership behavior. Share the ideas in the large group; you could also have one student compile the list and distribute it to all class members.

CLOSURE

For a group of up to 15 students, go around the room and have all the students report one specific change they could make to their leadership or group work after thinking about the concepts presented in this lesson.

LESSON 26

Leave students with the thought that the leader's energy and attitude have the most influence at the beginning of a trip or program, before norms are established, and that leaders should use this time wisely to initiate the structural and attitudinal norms they would most like to see on a trip.

ASSESSMENT OF LEARNING

- Formative assessment happens throughout as you hear what the students are saying and observe how the discussions are going.
- When reading the students' list in activity 6 on how they can apply this lesson, you can assess their ability to apply the material.
- Either before the lesson ends or the next time you meet with the students, use an Admit Slip (on CD-ROM) to see where any continued confusion might exist.

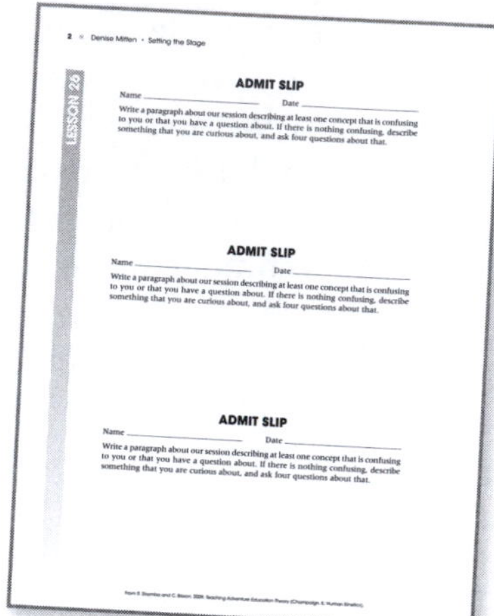

2 ■ Denise Mitten • Setting the Stage

LESSON 26

ADMIT SLIP

Name ______________ Date ______________

Write a paragraph about our session describing at least one concept that is confusing to you or that you have a question about. If there is nothing confusing, describe something that you are curious about, and ask four questions about that.

ADMIT SLIP

Name ______________ Date ______________

Write a paragraph about our session describing at least one concept that is confusing to you or that you have a question about. If there is nothing confusing, describe something that you are curious about, and ask four questions about that.

ADMIT SLIP

Name ______________ Date ______________

Write a paragraph about our session describing at least one concept that is confusing to you or that you have a question about. If there is nothing confusing, describe something that you are curious about, and ask four questions about that.

LESSON 27

Setting Group Norms and Expedition Behavior

Maurice Phipps

Most groups that come together for a specific task develop group norms as they get on with the task. Because there are often cultural differences and different personal standards of behavior, many conflicts can arise as people "bump" into each other over these issues. Such problems can be magnified on expeditions, as recognized by Paul Petzoldt, who referred to group norms as "expedition behavior." One can just let norms develop on their own, but such norms could of course be negative. The alternative is to purposely set group norms or expedition behavior. If the norms are cooperatively set, this can start the group dynamics off positively and provide some standards that the group is willing to conform to.

Background

The small group forms the heart of adventure education field expeditions and is often used as a learning modality in the classroom as well. Johnson, Johnson, and Smith (1998) describe educational groups as follows:

- *Pseudo learning group:* Students are assigned to work together but have no interest in doing so.
- *Traditional learning group:* Students agree to work together without seeing the benefits of doing so—this is basically individual work with talking.
- *Cooperative learning group:* Students are placed together to accomplish shared goals, and they perceive that they can reach their goals only if other group members reach their goals.
- *High-performing cooperative learning group:* The group is cooperative and outperforms expectations given its membership.

Lesson adapted, by permissioon, from M.L. Phipps and C.A. Phipps, 2003, "Group norm setting: A critical skill for effective classroom groups," *MountainRise* 1(1). [Online]. Available: http://facctr.wcu.edu/mountainrise/MR_1_1_PDF/MR_1_1_Phipps.pdf [October 21, 2008].

We all want our student groups to be highly functioning; how can we get them to this point and beyond? The use of cooperative learning, suggested by Johnson, Johnson, and Smith (1998), includes five elements:

1. **Positive interdependence.** The perception must be that one cannot succeed unless everyone else succeeds. Each person's efforts benefit all.
2. **Individual accountability and personal responsibility.** Each member must be accountable for contributing a fair share of the work.
3. **Face-to-face promotive interaction.** Through interpersonal interactions, cognitive learning is increased. Such interaction includes discussions, testing each other, cooperative note taking, shared worksheets, jigsaw-type procedures, and so on.
4. **Interpersonal and small group skills.** Members have the ability to practice effective group skills, including leadership, decision making, trust building, communication, and conflict management.
5. **Group processing.** Members discuss how the group is working. How effective are relationships? Are goals being met, and is the task being accomplished? How well? How can the group improve?

In a high-functioning cooperative learning group, all five elements need to be continually occurring. If the instructor includes all these elements and provides the motivation for group processing, then a higher-functioning team will develop, resulting in greater student learning.

A very important part of cooperative learning is the ability of individuals to function well as a group, that is, to use effective group skills. Group skills include, for example, setting common goals and norms, understanding leadership roles in educational groups, discussing progress in these areas, and working through conflicts. Students also benefit from some basic knowledge of group dynamics and leadership. To set this positive group tone, one must devote some time to the teaching of group skills and group maintenance so that the groups have the skills to be functional rather than dysfunctional. Giving the class a substantial group project (formal cooperative learning) without the group skills to successfully work together can be, in Dewey's (1963) term, "mis-educational."

Providing the time and support for students to learn group skills and group maintenance will not only help prevent mis-education but also allow practice in professional skills often expected in the workplace. This may mean that some course content either must be cut or must be covered by students as homework instead of "in class." What kinds of things can be done to develop a high-functioning group learning community?

To enable the students to begin to function effectively, the setting of group norms and an understanding of how to monitor these norms create a solid foundation. The setting of group norms can not only help students to function well in small groups but also help develop good behavior for other class situations. Imagine a 3-hour evening class with a few students at the back continually chatting through a lecture. Enabling the students to "police" this poor behavior is more effective than the instructor's becoming an austere disciplinarian. Or imagine trying to control behaviors on an expedition in which members are cooped up together 24 hours a day. Positive behavior can be best achieved through effective group norm setting.

Norms in a group will evolve even if nothing purposeful is done; but because these norms might be negative, it is better to set them intentionally than to allow them to just evolve, especially since changing norms is almost always more difficult later on. There are different ways to set norms, but it is essential to emphasize two points: (1) Norms are extremely important, and (2) norms are not to be confused with rules. Rules are often "handed down," and, as they are not cooperatively set, will most likely not be effectively monitored by students. To emphasize the importance of norm setting, one can elicit the students' own group experiences to provide a ray of hope for those who've had negative experiences and to reinforce that students' full participation will ensure that this experience will be more positive.

Setting appropriate behaviors through purposeful group norm setting puts students and instructor on the same page so that guesswork about functional learning and living behaviors is removed. The fact that the behaviors are cooperatively set means that they are more likely to be upheld by class members. The instructor, however, must support students in this endeavor by teaching group skills and giving time for group processing to find out what needs to be fixed so that the class and its project groups can become high functioning. The complexities of group skills, concepts, and processing for college students are addressed in *The Group Book: Effective Skills for Cooperative Groups* (Phipps and Phipps 2000). For expeditions, using information about expedition behavior (Petzoldt 1984 or Drury et al. 2005), along with the processes just outlined for setting norms, can be an invaluable exercise in enabling a cooperative group.

RESOURCES

Dewey, J. 1963. *Experience and education.* New York: Collier Books.

Drury, J.K., B.F. Bonney, D. Berman, and M. Wagstaff. 2005. *The backcountry classroom.* 2nd ed. Helena, MT: Globe Pequot Press.

Hanson, C. 2004. Teaching expedition behavior during the honeymoon. In *Leadership educator notebook: A toolbox for leadership educators,* eds. J. Gookin and S. Leach, 22. Lander, WY: National Outdoor Leadership School.

Johnson, D.W., R. Johnson, and A. Smith. 1998. *Active learning: Cooperation in the college classroom.* Edina, MN: Interaction Book Company.

Petzoldt, P. 1984. *The new wilderness handbook.* New York: Norton.

Phipps, M.L., and C.A. Phipps. 2000. *The group book: Effective skills for cooperative groups.* Sylva, NC: System 4 Services.

Phipps, M.L., and C.A. Phipps. 2003. Group norm setting: A critical skill for effective classroom groups. *MountainRise Electronic Journal,* 1(1):1-8. http://facctr.wcu.edu/mountainrise/archive/vol1no1/issue.html.

Warters, J. 1960. *Group guidance: Principles and practice.* New York: McGraw-Hill.

Lesson Plan

PURPOSE

To establish group norms or expected behaviors in a class or group; to establish expedition behavior for outdoor expedition style-courses.

OBJECTIVES

As a result of this lesson students will be able to . . .

1. *Cognitive:* portray in a skit examples of poor expedition behavior.
2. *Cognitive:* correctly identify which of three categories various examples of expedition behavior relate to.

3. *Cognitive:* practice the group norm–setting process in outdoor leadership situations.
4. *Cognitive:* use norms developed collaboratively by a group to reinforce positive expedition behavior.

DURATION

60 minutes

GROUP SIZE

Any size class divided into groups of three or four students

LOCATION

Indoors

EQUIPMENT

Flip chart and tape for hanging chart paper on a wall, or a large blackboard and chalk, or computer with LCD projector

RISK MANAGEMENT CONSIDERATIONS

This is a low-risk indoor class.

STUDENT PREPARATION

If the class is a regular class, then no preparation is necessary. If the course is an expedition-style course or outdoor leadership course, the students should have read about expedition behavior in chapter 7 of Paul Petzoldt's *The New Wilderness Handbook* (1984) or chapter 12 in *The Backcountry Classroom* (Drury et al. 2005).

INSTRUCTOR PREPARATION

- Familiarity with materials about expedition behavior in Petzoldt 1984 or Drury and colleagues 2005
- Flip chart page or document projected from a computer consisting of three columns, headed "Individual-to-individual behavior," "Individual-to-group behavior," and "Group-to-individual behavior"

LESSON CONTENT AND TEACHING STRATEGIES

Instructors who include group work in their classes often find that a few groups have prepared well and some have barely completed the work. In addition, some students become angry with the instructor because the group project was for a shared grade and they feel that they put more work into it than their partners. What happened here? Isn't group work supposed to be an effective way to teach? Why were some of the groups dysfunctional? When students groan as a significant group project is announced, they have probably been in a dysfunctional group in the past. Most have experienced the situation in which each individual's norms seem to be different. So, if we can get everyone on the same page regarding expected behaviors or norms, we can help avoid unnecessary conflict.

Hanson (2004) describes an engaging strategy to introduce students to expedition behavior—role-playing scenarios illustrating bad expedition behavior, followed by discussion of the problems and the solutions. This lesson employs that strategy.

Activity 1: Role Play

Form student groups of two to four, and give each group one of the following scenarios to role-play and a few minutes to create their skit. The instructor can create other scenarios from her or his experience. Examples of scenarios (Hanson 2004, p. 22) include the following:

- One of you keeps making rude comments about sex, gender, and/or race. When someone else brings this up, you downplay it by saying that you're joking.
- Two of you are up early, making breakfast and breaking camp. A third person is still in his sleeping bag. When the third person gets up to join the others, breakfast is over and you are all now late.
- You're hiking as a group but are having trouble staying together. The person in the lead is blazing down the trail. When the rest of the group catches up, the lead person is well rested and continues down the trail.

Discuss the problems or poor expedition behavior that the skits illustrated. There may be a tendency to also jump to solutions, but save that until the next part of the lesson.

Activity 2: Establishing Group Norms

Allow about 40 minutes for students to cooperatively set group norms during the first class or group meeting.

Explain that the scenarios depicted in the opening activity can be avoided if the group is collaboratively involved in setting norms they agree to live by. To provide the big picture, or boundaries within which group norms are developed, introduce the outline of the course—classroom or field based—including goals, course elements, academic content, and so on.

Explain that Paul Petzoldt (1984), a mountaineer with vast experience of groups in stressful outdoor conditions, referred to norm setting as the setting of expedition behavior.

On the board or flip chart, draw three columns with the headings "Individual-to-individual behavior," "Individual-to-group behavior," and "Group-to-individual behavior." These are the first three of Paul Petzoldt's (1984) behavior headings. Alternatively, have a computer document prepared with these headings and projected onto a screen (table 27.1; also provided on the CD-ROM as a handout for students, if you desire). During the norm brainstorming process, a volunteer student recorder can type suggestions into the document, which can be edited and later distributed electronically or as hard copy to all group members.

TABLE 27.1 Group Norm Categories

Individual-to-individual behavior	Individual-to-group behavior	Group-to-individual behavior
Examples: No put-downs Give praise	Examples: Be on time to meetings Be prepared	Examples: No scapegoats Include everyone in the group

Adapted, by permission, from M.L. Phipps and C.A. Phipps, 2003, "Group norm setting: A critical skill for effective classroom groups," *MountainRise* 1(1). [Online]. Available: http://facctr.wcu.edu/mountainrise/MR_1_1_PDF/MR_1_1_Phipps.pdf. [October 21, 2008].

Ask students to reflect on the skits in the opening activity. Ask which of the three columns relates to each of the issues depicted. For the three scenarios provided by Hanson, described earlier, the connections are as follows:

- The first scenario, about rude comments, illustrates individual-to-individual behavior.
- The second scenario, about a late sleeper, illustrates individual-to-group behavior.
- The third scenario, about a hiking group that doesn't stay together, illustrates group-to-individual behavior.

In small groups the class can brainstorm for each column what behaviors they would like to see in the class as a whole and in small groups working in and out of class. This is also an opportunity to discuss solutions to the problems that the opening activity scenarios presented. For groups about to embark on a field expedition, either some or all headings can be used. The complete set of headings includes "Individual to individual," "Individual to group," "Group to individual," "Group to other groups," "Individual and group to multiple use of the region," "Individual and group to administrative agencies," and "Individual and group to local populace."

Invite students to include both positive and negative suggestions such as "Be supportive" and "Don't be late to meetings." All the suggestions should be added to the lists in the three (or more) columns. Some suggested behaviors may fit all headings but need to be written down only once. As the instructor you can request clarification and amplification of examples so that each norm is well understood by everyone. You can also add suggestions, for example, "No chatting while someone is addressing the whole class." There should be only enough instructor involvement to ensure that it is class norms and not the instructor's rules that are being instituted. Table 27.2 shows an example of a set of norms developed by a class.

TABLE 27.2 Example of Group Norm Setting

Individual to individual	Individual to group	Group to individual
Be considerate. Stay in touch during project. Respect each other's space. Share assignment loads equally. Keep commitments. Be considerate of feelings. Communicate no matter what! Help classmates who miss class. Be supportive. Have patience. No put-downs. Be flexible and agreeable to change. Offer notes if someone misses class. Be open to others' ideas. Take all ideas seriously and be open to them. Don't interrupt. Be enthusiastic. Be responsible for duties and meetings.	Do your fair share. Support each other. Don't talk if someone is speaking to the class. Don't be defensive. Don't use put-downs. Be on time. Don't smoke. Be prepared (bring materials). Notify other members if you can't attend a meeting. Use eye contact. Don't be absent. Control negative comments. Be open and courteous to the entire class. Participate in class discussions. Don't chit-chat in cliques.	Respect an individual's "off" days. Give others a chance to explain themselves. Don't gang up on anyone. Show respect. Listen attentively as a group when an individual is talking. Share helpful ideas. Don't leave while someone is talking. Don't scapegoat. Be on time. Don't make unnecessary noise. Allow everyone to participate. Don't chew gum. Call and remind members of study groups.

Adapted, by permission, from M.L. Phipps and C.A. Phipps, 2003, "Group norm setting: A critical skill for effective classroom groups," *MountainRise* 1(1). [Online]. Available: http://facctr.wcu.edu/mountainrise/MR_1_1_PDF/MR_1_1_Phipps.pdf. [October 21, 2008].

Activity 3: Achieving Consensus and Recording Norms

Once the norms are recorded, the group must reach a consensus to accept the norms, so ask a question such as "Does anyone disagree with any of the norms?" A consensus is reached when the whole class agrees or no one disagrees. If someone takes issue with a suggested norm, this needs to be resolved; the suggestion must be removed or must be modified to get everyone's approval. Having the norm document projected from a computer simplifies this consensus and revision process. Or, have a student write a neat copy that can be subsequently typed and distributed to everyone.

If this process is occurring in the field, use a group journal or ask everyone to write down each norm as presented. Later, if someone wishes to change anything, it is important that the whole group be involved in the change. The consensus-making process is important for building in a sense of ownership and leads to empowerment for the next step, monitoring group norms.

Activity 4: Monitoring Group Norms

After consensus is reached, ask "Who is expected to make sure that everyone keeps to the norms?" or "Who is responsible for addressing situations in which norms are broken?" The answer is *everyone,* which leads into the concept of distributed leadership. Explain that this concept, according to Johnson, Johnson, and Smith (1998), means that anyone who moves the group forward with respect to either task or relationship is taking a leadership role and that in educational groups especially, distributed leadership should be strongly encouraged. Jane Warters (1960) describes this as positive group roles (see figure 27.1).

Explain that all of these roles help move the group forward both in accomplishing tasks and in maintaining positive relationships, but the key role in relation to group norms is that of the standard setter (and keeper). The function of this group role is to set and monitor standards in the group. Emphasize that everyone in the class can perform any of the group roles, and it is especially important for everyone to perform the role of the standard setter/keeper of the group norms. Skills that a good standard keeper requires are the ability to give feedback appropriately and to manage conflict. Both these skills are "group" skills that need to be understood and practiced.

Stress that students have set *their* norms and that *they* are responsible for upholding them. This involves providing peer feedback and nonjudgmentally confronting norm infractions. Remind students that the norms will be revisited on a regular basis.

Activity 5: Revisiting Group Norms

Later in the course or expedition it may be necessary to bring students back to their original agreements regarding group norms. Explain that one of the common pitfalls for an instructor of groups, even if he or she has done a good job of facilitating the setting of group norms, is addressing a norm violation as if it were a personal affront rather than asking the class how they wish to address it. As group norms will be broken, and as students may not address violations, the instructor should check on how well the norms are being kept.

Ask students to write on a piece of scrap paper one thing that they are doing well regarding the norms they have established and one thing that they feel they need to improve on. The students pass their comments to the instructor or a student facilitator, who reads them to the group. This exercise can serve simply as a reminder to do better.

TASK ROLES

Initiating activity: presenting solutions, new ideas, and so on

Seeking opinions: looking for an expression of feeling

Seeking information: asking for clarification of values, suggestions, ideas

Giving information: offering facts, generalizations, relating one's own experience to the group problem

Giving opinions: voicing concerns and values, rather than facts

Elaborating: clarifying examples and proposals

Coordinating: showing relationships among various ideas or suggestions

Summarizing: pulling together related ideas and suggestions

Testing feasibility: making applications of suggestions to situations, examining practicality of ideas

GROUP-BUILDING ROLES

Encouraging: being friendly, warm, and responsive to others; praising others and their ideas

Gatekeeping: trying to make it possible for another member to make a contribution to the group

Standard setting*: expressing standards for the group to use in choosing its content or procedures or in evaluating its decisions; reminding the group to avoid decisions that conflict with group standards (and norms)

Following: going along with decisions of the group, thoughtfully accepting ideas of others

Expressing group feeling: summarizing what the group feeling is sensed to be, describing reactions of the group to ideas

BOTH GROUP-BUILDING AND MAINTENANCE ROLES

Evaluating: submitting group decisions or accomplishments to compare with group standards, measuring accomplishments against goals

Diagnosing: determining sources of difficulties and appropriate steps to take next, analyzing the main blocks to progress

Testing for consensus: tentatively asking for group opinions in order to find out if the group is reaching consensus

Mediating: harmonizing, conciliating differences in points of view, making compromise solutions

Relieving tensions: draining off negative feelings by joking or pouring oil on troubled waters, putting tense situations into a wider context

FIGURE 27.1 Warters' positive group roles.

*Standard setting and keeping is the key group or distributed leadership role for monitoring group roles.

Adapted from J. Warters, 1960, *Group guidance: Principles and practice* (New York: McGraw-Hill).

If conflict over a norm exists, the group should brainstorm reasonable consequences. An example of a consequence suggested by one class for tardiness was that the tardy student would have to answer two questions about homework before sitting down. Again, care must be taken not to reduce the norms to rules, so consequences must be agreed on by the whole class. Of course, both norms and consequences also have to be in sync with the policies of course and the institution or organization, and the instructor should state this explicitly.

Students must and generally do realize that instructors are not handing over their professional responsibilities but rather allowing students to monitor their own behavior. Most students welcome this opportunity and are pleased to be learning the skills needed in order for their groups and the class to work effectively. Occasionally, however, group norm setting and monitoring may not work with a particular individual. Explain that an individual meeting in which the nonconforming student is confronted may be necessary in the case of behavior that affects the whole class.

CLOSURE

The lesson presents a technique for setting group norms, illustrates concepts in group process and group learning, and outlines skills that will enable the group to stay on track with the agreed-upon behaviors. Petzoldt's expedition behavior concept, Johnson and colleagues' cooperative learning theory, and Warters' group roles all assist in developing high-functioning groups.

ASSESSMENT OF LEARNING

- Observe whether students are able to correctly connect examples of poor expedition behavior with Petzoldt's (1984) categories—individual-to-individual behavior, individual-to-group-behavior, and group-to-individual behavior.
- During a classroom- or field-based course, observe and provide students with feedback about how they practice, monitor, and maintain the norms they have established at the beginning.

PART IX

Processing and Facilitation Models

The three lessons in this part complement the lessons in part VIII, "Group Development," by describing creative ways to teach the processing and facilitation models that promote healthy group development.

Lesson 28, "Six Generations of Facilitation" by Bob Stremba, shows how to use the Spider's Web activity described by Gass (1995) to introduce the first six of eight levels (or generations) of facilitation commonly used by adventure educators who work with educational and developmental programs. This lesson points out that the well-prepared adventure educator is able to assess the needs of the group and then conduct activities using strategies that often go beyond a traditional debriefing circle.

One example of a more creative facilitation process is presented by Jacquie Medina in lesson 29, "Visual Reflections: Using Photographs to Facilitate Adventure Experiences." Schon's (1983) theory of reflection-in-action is taught by having students first relate to photos that suggest a story, then act as photojournalists to stimulate and guide a group's processing discussion about the Toxic Waste activity.

Lesson 30, "Growth at the Edge: Expanding Our Comfort Zones" by Bob Stremba, teaches Luckner and Nadler's (1997) edgework model to show that adventure activities, when used to promote change and growth, help individuals expand their comfort zones beyond the adventure itself. In this lesson, blindfolds and mousetraps are used to give adventure education students an experience of disequilibrium so that they can subsequently understand these feelings as experienced by their own clients or students engaged in new adventures.

The models and theories presented in these lessons encourage adventure educators to expand their collection of tools that help individuals make important connections between the adventure experience and their lives back at home, work, or school.

RESOURCES

Gass, M.A. 1995. *Book of metaphors,* vol. 2. Dubuque, IA: Kendall/Hunt.

Luckner, J.L., and R.S. Nadler. 1997. *Processing the experience: Strategies to enhance and generalize learning.* 2nd ed. Dubuque, IA: Kendall/Hunt.

Schon, D.A. 1983. *The reflective practitioner.* New York: Basic Books.

LESSON 28

Six Generations of Facilitation

Bob Stremba

Because adventure activities are increasingly used to help individuals, groups, and organizations learn about challenge, communication, teamwork, and problem solving, facilitators must know how to promote individual and organizational change. With this shift to embrace goals of interpersonal and intrapersonal skill development and behavior change have come increasingly sophisticated levels of processing and facilitation. The well-prepared adventure educator, therefore, is able to assess the needs of the group and then conduct activities using strategies that often go beyond a debriefing circle to include metaphors and front-loading. This lesson introduces the first six of eight levels (or *generations*) of facilitation commonly used by adventure educators working with educational and developmental programs. The lesson serves, therefore, as an overview for students gaining proficiency with the content and processes at least through level 3, and possibly through level 5, of facilitation.

Background

Adventure activities are increasingly being used in educational and developmental contexts to help individuals, groups, and organizations learn about challenge, communication, teamwork, and problem solving. Therapeutic adventure programs help people make changes in behaviors and thought processes that can lead to more functional personal and social skills. With this shift to embrace goals of interpersonal and intrapersonal skill development and behavior change have come increasingly sophisticated levels of processing and facilitation. The well-prepared adventure educator can no longer let the mountain speak for itself except when conducting adventure programming at the recreation level, where client goals are to have fun, be entertained, and perhaps to learn a new technical skill.

Gass (1995) identified six generations of facilitation. Within a decade, two additional levels were developed to better match the needs of therapeutic populations and more mature organizational groups; so Gass and Stevens (2007) now describe eight generations of facilitation, with increasing levels of sophistication and therefore increased training required of the facilitator. These generations, or levels, are (p. 103) as follows:

1. Letting the experience speak for itself—learning by doing
2. Speaking on behalf of the experience—learning by telling
3. Debriefing the experience—learning through reflection
4. Directly front-loading the experience—direction with reflection
5. Isomorphically framing the experience—reinforcement with reflection
6. Indirectly front-loading the experience—indirect reinforcement in reflection
7. Flagging the experience—unconscious reinforcement in reflection
8. Empowering clients to self-facilitate—coaching and reflection

It is useful for individuals learning about the profession of adventure education and facilitation to understand that each generation of facilitation has particular characteristics that match particular kinds of client goals. Facilitators must be able to assess their clients' needs and their own expertise in facilitating an experience to meet those needs in order to remain an ethical professional. For recreational adventure experiences, this client needs assessment typically focuses on the physical readiness of individuals to successfully participate in the activity. For educational programs, the facilitator should be determining the extent to which the planned adventure activities will promote desired learning outcomes. But for developmental and therapeutic groups, the facilitator must also talk with organizational representatives and clients themselves about desired interpersonal and intrapersonal outcomes, and may need to consult client clinical assessment information as well.

The first two generations of facilitation—letting the experience speak for itself and speaking for the experience—are satisfactory approaches for programs having a recreational focus, for example guiding a raft group down a river for fun and excitement. But in many of the educational and developmental programs that beginning and more seasoned adventure educators work with, levels 3 (debriefing), 4 (direct front-loading), and 5 (isomorphic framing) are most commonly employed. Although level 5 is considered an advanced facilitation skill, more programs are expecting staff to be able to help clients create metaphors relating the adventure experience to other aspects of their lives in order to promote transfer of learning.

Table 28.1 summarizes the relationship between facilitation levels, client assessment strategies, and type of adventure program.

For detailed information and examples of facilitation strategies used with each generation or level, consult Priest and Gass (2005, chapters 14 through 17), and Gass and Stevens (2007). The following list summarizes facilitation styles used with levels 1 through 6.

- **Level 1: Letting the experience speak for itself.** After providing a briefing about how to conduct the adventure activity, including safety parameters, have students engage in the activity. At the completion of the activity, say nothing, perhaps refer to how much fun the group seemed to have, or encourage the group to move on to new levels of the activity.
- **Level 2: Speaking on behalf of the experience.** Conduct the adventure activity as would be done at level 1. After the activity, provide feedback and observations on what the group did well, their communication, what you think they need to work on, and how they can apply what they learned.

TABLE 28.1 Levels of Facilitation Suggested for Types of Adventure Programs

<table>
<tr><th></th><th>Outdoor recreation</th><th>Outdoor/adventure education</th><th>Developmental adventure</th><th>Therapeutic adventure</th></tr>
<tr><td>Purpose of program type</td><td>Having fun, learning skills, being entertained.</td><td>Learning new concepts, generating new awareness.</td><td>Improving functional behaviors, developing new behaviors.</td><td>Changing behaviors, thoughts, and unconscious processes.</td></tr>
<tr><td>Planning for facilitation</td><td>Assess client physical abilities.</td><td>Know client's educational objectives and desired outcomes.</td><td colspan="2">Talk to organizational representative and clients themselves about desired goals and outcomes.
Consult client clinical assessments.</td></tr>
<tr><td rowspan="2">Facilitation levels to use</td><td rowspan="2">Level 1: Letting the experience speak for itself (learning by doing). Clients gain new skills but little intrapersonal and interpersonal insight. Client centered.
Level 2: Speaking for the experience (learning by telling). Assess client needs first. Tell clients what they did well, what they learned, and how they can apply this knowledge. But telling can invalidate and alienate participants. Facilitator centered.</td><td colspan="2">Level 3: Debriefing (learning through reflection). Guided group discussion using open-ended questions. Facilitator and client centered.
Level 8: Self-facilitation (coaching and reflection). Facilitator teaches clients reflection and debriefing techniques; clients focus on what is most relevant to them. Client centered after facilitator taught.
Level 4: Directly front-loading (direction with reflection). Highlighting learning objectives before the activity. Facilitator or student centered.</td><td>Level 6: Indirect front-loading (redirection before reflection). Facilitator centered.
Level 7: Flagging the experience (unconscious reinforcement in reflection). Absorbs the client in a natural trance state. Facilitator centered.
Facilitation at these levels requires advanced training.</td></tr>
<tr><td></td><td colspan="2">Level 5: Isomorphic framing; metaphors (reinforcement with reflection). Creating parallel structures between the activity and clients' lives. Requires assessment of clients' needs. Facilitator and student centered.</td></tr>
</table>

Lower → → Change in participant or client → → **Higher**

Adapted, by permission, from M.A. Gass and C.A. Stevens, 2007 Facilitating the adventure process. In *Adventure education: Theory and applications,* by Project Adventure and edited by D. Prouty, J. Panicucci, and R. Collinson (Champaign, IL: Human Kinetics), 101-123, and from S. Priest and M.A. Gass, 2005, *Effective leadership in adventure programming,* 2nd ed. (Champaign, IL: Human Kinetics).

- **Level 3: Debriefing the experience.** Conduct the adventure activity as would be done at level 1 or 2. After the activity conduct a debrief using open-ended questions such as "What happened?"; "What did you notice about leadership during the activity?"; and "What did you learn that you can use elsewhere in your life?"
- **Level 4: Directly front-loading the experience.** This time, begin by introducing the adventure activity, but add a series of questions to focus learning prior to the activity. The following are examples of front-loading questions:
  - What would you like to use this activity to work on?
  - What did you learn from your previous involvement in this activity that you can apply to this attempt?
  - Why might experiencing this activity be important and how does it relate to everyday life? (Gass and Stevens 2007, p. 104)
  - What behaviors might bring about success, and how can the group optimize these behaviors? (Gass and Stevens 2007, p. 105)

  After the activity, debrief with a focus on applying the information from the earlier front-loading discussion.

- **Level 5: Isomorphically framing the experience.** Introduce the adventure activity by having students consider parallels between the activity and other aspects of their lives. Ask students, before beginning the activity, questions such as the following:
  - How can this activity represent something in your life?
  - What will a successful resolution be in this activity and in what the activity represents for you?

  After the activity, the debrief focuses on applying the metaphor, or isomorphic framework; group members "discuss the close similarities between the frame and their experience and see the obvious connections for themselves. For example, clients think, 'If a strategy works here, I can see how it will work in my life as well'" (Gass and Stevens 2007, p. 105).
- **Level 6: Indirectly front-loading the experience.** This style is used primarily with therapeutic programs and by facilitators having more advanced training. The activity is presented using "paradoxical forms, such as double binding (e.g., win–win frames), symptom prescription, symptom displacement, illusion of alternatives, and proactive reframing" (Waltzlawick 1978). For example, for a group of college athletes using the Spider's Web activity to explore their repeated use of sexist language and gender-exclusive behavior, the facilitator begins by describing what often happens in a typical group. "At the beginning, everyone offers lots of suggestions at the same time, but many of the suggestions aren't heard or are ignored. After a while, a couple of dominant males take charge. They get a few men to the other side of the spider's web and then throw some women through like sacks of potatoes, often making embarrassing remarks. Then the same group of dominant males decides how to do the hardest part of the task, which is getting the last person through. In the discussion afterward, everyone agrees that the leadership was sexist and not inclusive." The facilitator then points out to the college athletes that there are other ways to do the spider's web. "Let's see what this group does" (Gass 1995, pp. 6-7).

  If the group indeed performs the activity using the male-dominated approach mentioned in the briefing, the facilitator points out that they succeeded in highlighting some issues they may now want to work on. If the group performs in a more equitable and nonsexist manner, the facilitator comments on their success in using new behaviors. Either approach provides a win–win situation that is integral to indirect front-loading.

Some common threads connect the first three facilitation generations with one another and the second three generations with one another. "The first three generations are used after an activity to bring about change, while the next . . . generations are used by the facilitator before, during, and after the adventure program to bring about change" (Gass and Stevens 2007, p. 103).

In addition, each level of facilitation employs a different level of facilitator-centered versus client-centered approach. A basic distinction concerns the extent to which the discussion of learning from the activity comes from the facilitator versus the extent to which it comes from the client or student group involved in the activity, with the facilitator doing more listening than talking. In adventure education, more lasting learning usually occurs when facilitation of activities occurs in a more student-centered way.

Generations 3, 4, and 5 are most commonly used by adventure educators working with educational and developmental programs. Understanding these levels forms the foundation for facilitators to go on and learn about specific techniques such as the use of open-ended questions, artwork, journaling, photography, and metaphors to promote learning and change with a variety of client groups.

RESOURCES

Gass, M.A. 1995. *Book of metaphors*, vol. 2. Dubuque, IA: Kendall/Hunt.

Gass, M.A., and Stevens, C.A. 2007. Facilitating the adventure process. In *Adventure education: Theory and applications*, eds. D. Prouty, J. Panicucci, and R. Collinson, 101-123. Champaign, IL: Human Kinetics.

Priest, S., and M.A. Gass. 2005. *Effective leadership in adventure programming*. 2nd ed. Champaign, IL: Human Kinetics.

Waltzlawick, P. 1978. *The language of change*. New York: Norton.

Lesson Plan

PURPOSE

For students to be able to choose a level and style of adventure facilitation that accounts for the goals of the program, an assessment of the client, and the facilitator's experience.

OBJECTIVES

As a result of this lesson students will be able to . . .

1. *Kinesthetic:* participate in the spider's web activity conducted in different ways, using up to six different generations or levels of facilitation.
2. *Cognitive and affective:* describe their observations of facilitator language, style, and actions for six generations of facilitation.
3. *Cognitive:* describe common threads among facilitation levels 1 through 3 and among levels 4 through 6.

DURATION

Approximately 60 minutes

GROUP SIZE

15 to 30

LOCATION

Indoors for discussion and mini-lecture with use of indoor or outdoor spider's web activity

EQUIPMENT

- Spider's web adventure activity, common to many ropes courses, or an indoor spider's web
- Retired climbing rope, 150 to 180 feet (45-55 meters) long
- Table 28.2 worksheet (on CD-ROM)

RISK MANAGEMENT CONSIDERATIONS

Some lifting and spotting are required for the Spider's Web activity.

STUDENT PREPARATION

In preparation for this lesson, students should read either one of the following:

- The Background included with this lesson (on CD-ROM)
- Chapter 7, "Facilitating the Adventure Process," by Gass and Stevens (2007)

INSTRUCTOR PREPARATION

- The instructor must be experienced with the first six generations, or levels, of facilitation. The instructor should model to students proper ethical behavior with regard to not exceeding one's level of training.
- Plan for use of an indoor or outdoor spider's web.

LESSON CONTENT AND TEACHING STRATEGIES

Ask students to recall that adventure education is about using adventure pursuits to help people learn and grow, to focus on interpersonal and intrapersonal relationships. Read the following quote:

> People simply don't learn, grow, or change without reflection on their experiences; evaluating the good and bad; analyzing mistakes, failures, or successes; considering the impact of actions or decisions; anticipating consequences or committing to new behaviors; and understanding how they can use new learning, growth, and change. You can facilitate these gains by escorting and accelerating people through the change process. (Priest and Gass 2005, p. 184)

Mention that it is the responsibility of the adventure educator to escort people through the process of learning and growth, to help clients transfer learning from the adventure experience to other aspects of their lives at home, school, or work.

Tell the students that today they will explore how to escort people through this change process using the first six of eight levels of facilitation—the levels most often used by beginning and intermediate adventure facilitators with educational and developmental programs. Levels 7 and 8 have been more recently developed and are most often used with therapeutic populations and with mature clients learning self-facilitation. These advanced levels require facilitators to have more advanced client assessment and clinical skills.

Activity 1: Spider's Web

To illustrate how the eight levels of facilitation are used in adventure activities, conduct the activity (the Spider's Web) or a variation using a climbing rope (the Spider's Web Reweave) at each level. Either version of the Spider's Web is used to illustrate the first six of the current eight generations of facilitation. To use time more efficiently and avoid six repetitions of the same activity, the instructor can describe how the first two levels of facilitation are used with the spider's web rather than actually conducting the activity at these two basic levels, then begin with third-level facilitation. Alternatively, the instructor can conduct the activity once, at level 1 or level 3. The instructor then asks students to imagine themselves back at the conclusion of that activity but demonstrates the next level of facilitation, and so on through the remaining levels.

Level 1: Letting the Experience Speak for Itself At the spider's web, give students the following instructions: "Your task is to pass this entire length of uncoiled climbing rope through each opening in the web, without you or the rope touching any part of the web in the process. You must use every opening, and at least 3 feet (1 meter) of each end of the rope must end up coming out of the first and the last holes in the web. If any touches of the web occur (by people or rope), you must take the rope out of the web and start over."

At the completion of the activity, say nothing, or perhaps refer to how much fun the group seemed to have or encourage the group to move on to new levels of the activity.

Hand out the observation worksheet shown in table 28.2 (also on CD-ROM). Ask students to record their observations for facilitation level 1 about what the facilitator said or did; whether they think the facilitation style used was facilitator centered, client centered, or both; and their reactions to the facilitation.

Level 2: Speaking on Behalf of the Experience Conduct the Spider's Web Reweave activity with the instructions already described. Or simply ask students to reflect back on or imagine themselves back at the conclusion of the activity they just experienced.

TABLE 28.2 Observation Worksheet: Six of Eight Facilitation Levels

Facilitation level	What did the facilitator say or do?	The facilitation level used was . . . (check one)	My reactions to the facilitation
1. Letting the experience speak for itself		Facilitator centered Client centered Facilitator and client centered *Why?*	
2. Speaking for the experience		Facilitator centered Client centered Facilitator and client centered *Why?*	
3. Debriefing the experience		Facilitator centered Client centered Facilitator and client centered *Why?*	
4. Directly front-loading the experience		Facilitator centered Client centered Facilitator and client centered *Why?*	
5. Isomorphically front-loading the experience		Facilitator centered Client centered Facilitator and client centered *Why?*	
6. Indirectly front-loading the experience		Facilitator centered Client centered Facilitator and client centered *Why?*	

After the activity or the students' reflection on the first experience with the activity, provide feedback and observations on what the group did well, their communication, what you think they need to work on, and how they can apply what they learned. Be sure to *tell* the group what you think the group learned rather than asking the group to respond to leading questions.

Ask students to record their observations for facilitation level 2 about what the facilitator said or did, as well as their reactions to the facilitation, on the observation worksheet shown in table 28.2 and on the accompanying CD-ROM.

Level 3: Debriefing the Experience Conduct the Spider's Web Reweave activity with the same instructions. Or, again ask students to reflect back on or imagine themselves back at the conclusion of the activity they just experienced.

After the activity or the students' reflection on their experience with the activity, conduct a debrief using open-ended questions such as "What happened?"; "What did you notice about leadership during the activity?"; and "What did you learn that you can use elsewhere in your life?"

Ask students to record their observations for facilitation level 3 about what the facilitator said or did, as well as their reactions to the facilitation, on the observation worksheet shown in table 28.2 and on the accompanying CD-ROM.

Level 4: Directly Front-Loading the Experience This time, begin by introducing the Spider's Web activity or the variation, the Spider's Web Reweave activity, with the instructions described for level 1, but add a series of questions to focus learning prior to the activity. It can be useful to ask one or two students to take notes, perhaps on large newsprint, on the groups' responses to the front-loading questions; these notes can be used for reference later in the debriefing. The following are examples of front-loading questions:

- What would you like to use this activity to work on?
- What did you learn from your previous involvement in this activity that you can apply to this attempt?
- Why might experiencing this activity be important and how does it relate to everyday life? (Gass and Stevens 2007, p. 104)
- What behaviors might bring about success, and how can the group optimize these behaviors? (Gass and Stevens 2007, p. 105)

After the activity, remind students that because discussion about what the group could learn occurred before the activity, the debrief after the activity focuses on applying the information from the earlier front-loading discussion. Refer to the newsprint notes on preactivity comments. For example, a postactivity question might be, "You said you wanted to try these behaviors for optimizing success; how did these work for you?"

Ask students to record their observations for facilitation level 4 about what the facilitator said or did, as well as their reactions the facilitation, on the observation worksheet shown in table 28.2 and on the accompanying CD-ROM.

Level 5: Isomorphically Framing the Experience (Reminder: This lesson focuses on an introduction to the first six levels of facilitation, not on creating expertise at each level. Levels 5 and above require that the instructor have more advanced training, including experience with client assessment or therapeutic practices. To properly learn facilitation level 5, students should be enrolled in a comprehensive course or training that covers metaphors in adventure activities.)

In this rendition, use the traditional spider's web instead of the spider's web reweave mentioned earlier. Here the instructor or facilitator demonstrates metaphors or parallel structures between the web and other aspects of students' lives. If, for example, you have a group of college students with whom you have been meeting for several weeks or months, you can use a facilitator-created metaphor based on your assessment of student needs. Mention to students that the language for framing the metaphor is important for properly creating the parallel structures, and therefore you are using written notes as a tool that students learning about this level of facilitation should also consider using. The following is an example of language that frames this activity as a facilitator-created metaphor:

> In front of you [point to openings in the web] are the opportunities and challenges you can expect to encounter during the first year of college, and there are a variety of ways to approach these. We are often successful because friends, family, college faculty and staff, and others help and support us in finding opportunities and overcoming challenges, which you can do here by passing successfully through an opening in the web. Success here means going through an opening without touching any part of the web. Sometimes people will just naturally see that you need help and they'll jump right in and help you. Other times they may be busy or involved in their own challenges. And sometimes you may need to ask for help, tell them specifically what you need. The help you need might be help in making decisions about how to handle a challenge. Or it might be actual physical support. Or it might be moral support and verbal encouragement. And then, of course, there are those challenges that you just decide to tackle on your own, without anyone's help at all. You can do all of that here, experimenting with different ways to embrace the opportunities and take on some of the challenges of college. Let's see what you do. (Thanks to Plymouth State University students Chris Mulcahy, Ryan McMahon, and Dwayne Mann, who helped develop this metaphorical structure.)

You can also use the traditional Spider's Web or the Spider's Web Reweave to demonstrate metaphors cocreated by you and the students. Instead of presenting the facilitator-created framework, ask students, before beginning the activity, questions such as the following:

- How can this activity represent something in your life?
- What does the web represent? What do the holes represent?
- [If doing Spider's Web Reweave] What does the rope represent? What does passing the rope through the opening represent?
- What should the consequences be for touching the web, and what does a touch represent?
- What will a successful resolution be in this activity and in what the activity represents for you?

Now have students begin the activity. It may be useful to occasionally reinforce the parallels between the web and college, or the cocreated structures, during the activity.

After the activity, remind students that because discussion about what the activity represents occurred before and during the activity, the debrief focuses on applying the metaphor, or isomorphic framework; students "will discuss the close similarities between the frame and their experience and see the obvious connections for themselves. For example, clients think, 'If a strategy works here, I can see how it will work in my life as well'" (Gass and Stevens 2007, p. 105).

Ask students to record their observations for facilitation level 5 about what the facilitator said or did, as well as their reactions to the facilitation, on the observation worksheet shown in table 28.2 and on the accompanying CD-ROM.

Level 6: Indirectly Front-Loading the Experience Using the classic spider's web activity, the contributor of this lesson employed a variation of the framework provided by Gass (1995, pp. 6-7) with a mixed-gender group of college athletes. Present the following introduction to students:

> Your task here is to get yourselves through the web without touching. Each hole can be used only once. Most groups like you tend to approach this in a particular way. In the beginning everybody offers lots of suggestions at the same time, but many of the suggestions aren't heard or are ignored. After a while, a couple of dominant males take charge. They get a few men to the other side of the spider's web and then throw some women through like sacks of potatoes, often making embarrassing remarks. Then the same group of dominant males decides how to do the hardest part of the task, which is getting the last person through. In the discussion afterward, everyone agrees that the leadership was sexist and not inclusive. However, there are other ways to do the spider's web. Let's see what this group does.

Have students begin the activity, and debrief it afterward, focusing on gender roles, communication, and leadership. If the group has indeed performed the activity using the male-dominated approach mentioned in the briefing, point out that they succeeded in highlighting some issues they may now want to work on. If the group performed in a more equitable and nonsexist manner, point out their success in using new behaviors. For students to understand this "double bind," point out the two options they had—dysfunctional behaviors or more functional behaviors—and mention that either provides a win–win situation that is integral to indirect front-loading.

Ask students to record their observations for facilitation level 6 about what the facilitator said or did, as well as their reactions the facilitation, on the observation worksheet shown in table 28.2 and on the accompanying CD-ROM.

CLOSURE

Summarize for students that they have just experienced the first six of eight generations of facilitation—the levels most often used by beginning and intermediate adventure facilitators with educational and developmental programs. Levels 7 and 8 have been more recently developed and are most often used with therapeutic populations and with mature clients learning self-facilitation. These advanced levels require facilitators to have more advanced client assessment and clinical skills.

Divide the class into six subgroups, one for each level of facilitation presented. Ask students to look at the facilitation worksheet on which they have been recording their observations of the facilitation levels, and to focus particularly on the comments they made for the level their small group is now looking at. Ask each group, in order of level, to comment on what the facilitator said or did; whether they observed the facilitation to be facilitator centered, client centered, or a combination of facilitator and client centered; and what their reactions were to the facilitation used.

After the first three groups comment about facilitation levels 1 through 3, ask students if they see any common thread among these first three levels of facilitation. They should note, or you can point out, that at these levels the activity was conducted and facilitation was used afterward to bring about change. Provide examples. One example is a question asked at level 3, debriefing the activity: "What did you learn that you can use elsewhere in your life?"

After the second three groups comment about facilitation levels 4 through 6, ask students if they see any common thread among these second three levels of facilitation. They should note, or you can point out, that at these levels facilitation occurred before, during, and after the activity to bring about change. Provide examples. One example is a question asked just before the spider's web was experienced at level 5, isomorphic framing: "How can this activity represent something in your life?"

As student groups are commenting, ask what they noticed about the degree to which each level was facilitator centered versus client centered. A basic distinction concerns the extent to which the discussion of learning from the activity came from the facilitator compared the extent to which it came from the client or student group, with the facilitator doing more listening than talking. Point out that in adventure education, more lasting learning usually occurs when facilitation of activities is more student centered.

Mention that "the adventure facilitator should choose a facilitation style based on the situation, clients' readiness and abilities, and facilitators' skills and experience level" (Gass and Stevens 2007, p. 107).

ASSESSMENT OF LEARNING

- **Objective 1:** Observe how accurately students are able to conduct and debrief the activity according to the practices and framing presented at six different generations or levels of facilitation.
- **Objective 2:** In the discussion or mini-lecture review, observe how student groups are able to describe their observations of facilitator language, style, and actions for six generations of facilitation.
- **Objective 3:** Observe whether students are able to accurately describe the common threads among facilitation levels 1 through 3 and among levels 4 through 6.

LESSON 29

Visual Reflections

Using Photographs to Facilitate Adventure Experiences

Jacquie Medina

Taking and using photographs during an adventure activity can provide instructors and participants with an effective means of developing questions and discussions to process the adventure experience. Photos provide a concrete reference point in the experience and promote individual sharing of thoughts and stories. Reflection-on-action is a common method of processing and occurs after the experience through discussion and journal writing. Reflection-in-action occurs while the activity is still happening; an example is "thinking on your feet." Photographs can be used to develop reflection-in-action skills by capturing the moment and allowing individuals to process the activity while it is still occurring, and also to apply new ideas and strategies as they continue the experience. This lesson is designed to foster reflection-on-action and reflection-in-action skills using photographs as a processing tool.

Background

Reflective learning has been recognized as an integral component of the processes and concepts of learning from experience (Boud, Keogh, and Walker 1985; Dewey 1938/1952; Kolb 1984). Boud and colleagues (1985) emphasized three elements as essential to the reflective process: (a) returning to the experience to recollect events and replay the experience; (b) attending to feelings, both positive and obstructive; and (c) reevaluating the experience. Boud and colleagues' proposed elements of the reflective process are consistent with Schon's (1983) theory of reflection-on-action.

Reflection-on-action is the process of thinking about an experience after it has happened. When people are presented with an uncertain situation resulting in confusion, they draw on past experiences to relate to the current situation in order to create new ways of thinking and doing. Using methods of reflection-on-action is a common practice in the debriefing and processing of adventure activities;

journal writing, debriefing circles, and processing activities including drawing are some examples.

Schon's (1983) theory of *reflection-in-action* involves thinking about an experience while it is happening. Phrases such as "thinking on your feet" and "learning by doing" represent the concept of reflection-in-action (p. 54). While specific activities to promote reflection-in-action are less common, the skills of reflection-in-action are essential to leading and facilitating adventure education.

Methods of using visual imagery provide resources for implementing both reflection-on-action and reflection-in-action strategies. *Visual sociology* is a methodological approach that involves using visual images as data. Sources of visual imagery include photographs, slides, film, video, and drawings. Visual images can serve as a means of communication between people themselves and the experience or event being studied.

Photo elicitation is the process in which either the facilitator or the participant produces images that are interpreted by the participant (Collier and Collier 1986; Harper 1994).

The use of photographs in adventure activities can foster facilitation. Harper (1994) states that "interview/discussion is stimulated and guided by images" (p. 410). Photos can also help to develop the participant's point of view and to define the meaning of the photograph for the participant (Harper 1988). In addition, a photograph encourages individuals to tell their own stories spontaneously and sharpens their memory (Collier and Collier 1986).

Participants are able to reflect on their experiences as documented in the photographs immediately following or during the activity. Because the pictures can stimulate individuals to share their stories, the experience becomes their own instead of an interpretation of the facilitator's observations. The facilitator can then reflect-in-action on the stories, images, and points of view being shared and pull from an individual's comments the processing questions and lines of discussion most applicable to the individual's experience.

RESOURCES

Boud, D., R. Keogh, and D. Walker. 1985. *Reflection: Turning experience into learning.* New York: Nichols.

Bunting, C. 2006. *Interdisciplinary teaching through outdoor education.* Champaign, IL: Human Kinetics.

Collier Jr., J., and M. Collier. 1986. *Visual anthropology: Photography as a research method.* Albuquerque, NM: University of New Mexico Press.

Dewey, J. 1938/1952. *Experience and education.* New York: Macmillan.

Harper, D. 1988. Visual sociology: Expanding sociological vision. *American Sociologist,* 19(1):54-70.

Harper, D. 1994. On the authority of the image: Visual methods at the crossroads. In *Handbook of qualitative research,* ed. N.K. Denzin and Y.S. Lincoln, 403-412. Thousand Oaks, CA: Sage.

Kolb, D.A. 1984. *Experiential learning: Experience as the source of learning and development.* Englewood Cliffs, NJ: Prentice Hall.

Loeffler, T.A. 2005. Focusing in: Using photo elicitation to explore the meanings of outdoor experiences. *Research in Outdoor Education,* 7:108-110.

Rohnke, K., and S. Butler. 1995. *Quicksilver.* Dubuque, IA: Kendall/Hunt.

Schon, D.A. 1983. *The reflective practitioner.* New York: Basic Books.

Schon, D.A. 1987. *Educating the reflective practitioner.* San Francisco: Jossey-Bass.

Lesson Plan

PURPOSE

To allow students to develop an understanding of the use of photo elicitation as a method to facilitate the skills of reflection-in-action and reflection-on-action.

OBJECTIVES

As a result of this lesson students will be able to . . .

1. *Cognitive:* apply techniques of photo elicitation to facilitate group experiences.
2. *Cognitive:* explain the theories of reflection-in-action and reflection-on-action.
3. *Cognitive:* demonstrate the ability to apply the theories of reflection-in-action and reflection-on-action in an adventure activity.

DURATION

90 to 120 minutes

GROUP SIZE

8 to 20 students

LOCATION

Indoors or outdoors. Location should be large enough to accommodate participation in the selected adventure activities as well as providing room for "photojournalists" to photograph the activity without getting in the way of the activity process. Indoor and outdoor locations should have adequate light for picture clarity.

EQUIPMENT

- Two instant cameras and instant film (30-40 exposures). Instant cameras produce 3- by 3-inch (8- by 8-centimeter) photographs immediately after shooting.
- Digital camera, laptop, adapter; uploading hardware (if applicable).
- Computer printer or LCD projector or both (if applicable).
- One metal ring approximately 6 inches (15 centimeters) in diameter with 8 to 10 strings of varying lengths attached (5-10 feet [1.5-3 meters] in length).
- One ball that can balance on the metal ring when the metal ring is elevated. To increase the challenge, use lightweight balls or large-size balls. Blow-up balls and Gertie balls work well.
- Two towers on which a ball can be balanced and over which a metal ring can fit; cups, cones, and buckets work well.
- One bicycle inner tube cut in half (with valve removed) and tied into a circle that can be stretched to fit over a bucket and carry the weight of the bucket's contents. Six to 10 lengths of rope or webbing of varying lengths (10-15 feet, or 3-4.5 meters) should be attached to the inner tube.

- Two buckets; large cans also work.
- One length of 30- to 40-foot (9- to 12-meter) rope to create a large circle boundary within which the buckets or cans are located.
- Water to fill and refill the bucket.
- Newsprint.
- Markers and color pens.
- Tape.

RISK MANAGEMENT CONSIDERATIONS

Students may need to complete photo release forms for the school or program. Although photographs are used within the lesson design as described here, selected photos and projects resulting from the lesson may be shared as a wall hanging or used within a slide show. Consider risk management issues related to the activity you select.

STUDENT PREPARATION

Prior readings on reflective learning may be helpful; however, this lesson is also an effective way to introduce students to concepts of reflection.

INSTRUCTOR PREPARATION

Computer, printer, and LCD unit should be set up with appropriate attachments necessary to display or print pictures if a digital camera is to be used in the activity. In addition, all activity props should be available and prior setup completed.

LESSON CONTENT AND TEACHING STRATEGIES

To get the students thinking about photographs, ask the following questions:

- What photographs have you taken throughout your life?
- Why did you choose to take photographs of these moments and people?
- How many of you have collected your pictures and placed them in an electronic photo album? Placed them in a picture frame? Attached them to the refrigerator or a bulletin board?
- What does the photo album represent or communicate for you?
- Why do we hang or post our pictures for us and others to see?

Now that the students have made application of photographs to their own lives, share with them that according to research, photographs can be used to help people capture their experiences, share their stories, and realize potential learning (Collier and Collier 1986; Harper 1988, 1994). Explain that photographs can be useful tools to facilitate group experiences and that this lesson's activities will help them better understand the process of photo elicitation. The lesson will also help them explore photo elicitation as a tool to facilitate adventure activities and implement Schon's (1983) theories of reflection-in-action and reflection-on-action.

Activity 1: PowerPoint on Visual Sociology and Imagery

You can develop your own slide show of photographs to which students can best relate. For example, select photographs of regional locations or images and of events or experiences in which students may have been participants. Or, provide students with a variety of handheld pictures to select and review during this discussion. This presentation of images complements a discussion of the concepts of visual sociology, visual imagery, and photo elicitation.

Have the students view the photographs. Ask the students to partner up with one of their classmates and share with each other what information they gleaned from the photograph(s). Then ask two to three partner groups to share with the rest of the class what meaning the pictures held for them. Briefly discuss with the students how their previous experiences and knowledge contributed to their interpretation of a picture.

Activity 2: Mini-Lecture

Share with the students the following definitions of visual sociology and visual imagery using the students' in-class examples to support or connect to the material.

- **Visual sociology** is a methodological approach using visual images as a source of data. It includes the use of drawings and photographs to educate others and to provide insight into and information on the exploration of different cultures; it also includes the use of photographs to capture the meaning of events, occurrences, incidents, people, and circumstances.
- **Visual imagery** refers to the use of visual images as links and forms of communication within, between, and among individuals, groups, and the environment. Examples include photographs, slides, film, video, and drawings (Collier and Collier 1986).

Following this presentation, explain that the class will now integrate visual imagery into an adventure activity.

Activity 3: Ball Transport

This activity should take about 45 minutes. Divide the class into two groups. One-third of the class will participate in the role of photojournalists, and the remaining two-thirds will be participants in the activity. Inform students of the roles and responsibilities in each group.

The photojournalists will observe and photograph the activity process and the members of the participant group in their efforts to accomplish the task. Photojournalists can move around the group to get the pictures they seek, but they should make a special effort not to interfere with the activity group's efforts to accomplish the task and not to speak or communicate to the activity group at any time. Photojournalists should take notes and should take photographs that they interpret as communicating some aspect of the group process or activity. Encourage the photojournalists to share the role of photographer.

Provide photojournalists with cameras, film (if instant cameras are used), paper, and pens. Predetermine the amount of film you will give the students for this exercise (15-20 exposures), being sure to set aside enough film for use in the second activity. Designate an area where the photographers can lay out the exposed film to develop. Instant film requires 2 to 4 minutes for development.

After instructing the photojournalists in their role, explain the activity to the remaining members of the class. For this lesson, Ball Transport (see handout on CD-ROM) has been chosen as the activity. This is a variation of similar adventure activities sometimes referred to as Life Ring or Toxic Waste (Bunting 2006; Rhonke and Butler 1995). Ball Transport has been selected because it requires students to communicate and work together and has a high rate of completion within the given time frame. However, completion of the task is not necessary in order for the lesson to be effective.

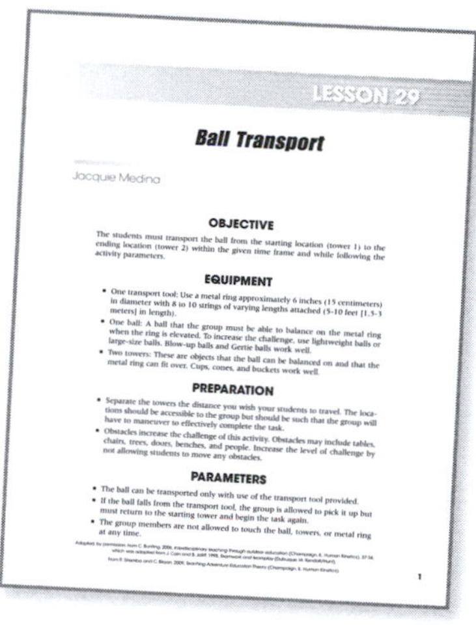

LESSON 29

Ball Transport

Jacquie Medina

OBJECTIVE

The students must transport the ball from the starting location (tower 1) to the ending location (tower 2) within the given time frame and while following the activity parameters.

EQUIPMENT

- One transport tool: Use a metal ring approximately 6 inches (15 centimeters) in diameter with 8 to 10 strings of varying lengths attached (5-10 feet [1.5-3 meters] in length).
- One ball: A ball that the group must be able to balance on the metal ring when the ring is elevated. To increase the challenge, use lightweight balls or large-size balls. Blow-up balls and Gertie balls work well.
- Two towers: These are objects that the ball can be balanced on and that the metal ring can fit over. Cups, cones, and buckets work well.

PREPARATION

- Separate the towers the distance you wish your students to travel. The locations should be accessible to the group but should be such that the group will have to maneuver to effectively complete the task.
- Obstacles increase the challenge of this activity. Obstacles may include tables, chairs, trees, doors, benches, and people. Increase the level of challenge by not allowing students to move any obstacles.

PARAMETERS

- The ball can be transported only with use of the transport tool provided.
- If the ball falls from the transport tool, the group is allowed to pick it up but must return to the starting tower and begin the task again.
- The group members are not allowed to touch the ball, towers, or metal ring at any time.

1

During the activity, monitor the activity and the photojournalists. If instant cameras are used, the exposed film should be located in an area that is accessible to the students for viewing and selecting. Pictures can be taped or tacked to a wall or bulletin board. If students are using a digital camera, have the necessary technology set up and available to upload pictures as quickly and efficiently as possible after the completion of the activity.

When the activity has been completed or when the time is up, let the students know that you will now be assigning a processing activity to each of three different groups to be completed in a designated amount of time. Following the completion of the processing activity, each group will share their product with the rest of the class.

Activity 4: Processing Activities Using Photo Elicitation

Following are three processing activities that can be used to facilitate student understanding of reflection-on-action. Explain each processing activity and provide each group with a written copy of their activity guidelines (see handout on CD-ROM). Begin with the photojournalists, as their activity requires them to select photographs first. After 10 minutes, or when all groups are finished, the students will present their completed activities to their classmates. Students should be seated so that they can optimally see and hear each group present. Students will need to leave their seats to view the pictures in the story line and storyboard activities. The order of presentation may vary.

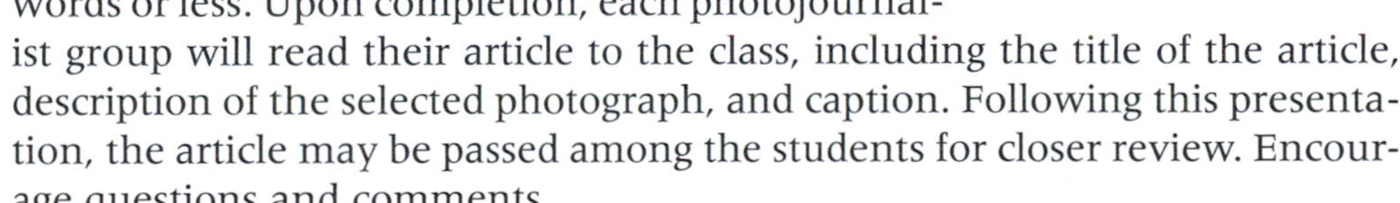

LESSON 29

Processing Activities Using Photo Elicitation

Jacquie Medina

1. Newspaper article. Groups write a front-page article summarizing the group's experience completing the task. Articles must include a succinct headline, one photograph with caption, and a summary paragraph of 200 words or less. Upon completion, each group will share their article with the class.
2. Caption. Participants choose a photograph and create a caption that expresses their experience or the group's experience as captured in the photograph.
3. A story line. Students use pictures to tell a story that communicates their experience as participants in the activity. Using only themselves and the photographs, they create a "chorus line" in which they hold up the photographs for others to see while they communicate their experience through some combination of song, verbal phrases, sounds, and nonverbal communication. They should be creative!
4. Storyboard. Using newsprint, markers, crayons, stickers, or some combination of these, students create a storyboard of pictures and drawings that represents their experience as individuals and as a group in accomplishing the task. The storyboard will be posted and will be viewed by classmates. Students should consider how they can best communicate their experience without using spoken words.
5. Expression. A picture is worth a thousand words—participants select photographs that express their emotions, feelings, thoughts, and ideas.
6. Significant moments. Participants select photographs that capture significant or memorable moments. Possibilities are moments of celebration, frustration, and "light bulb" moments.
7. Problem solving. Participants select photographs that communicate the problem-solving process that the group experienced and that create opportunities to discuss moments of challenge, success, frustration, repetition, and so on.
8. Technology mania! Technological resources allow participants to develop slide shows, iMovies, and CDs documenting their experiences in pictures.
9. Who's the photographer? Group members may play a variety of roles in the activity, including participant, paparazzo, and journalist. Who should take the pictures? Groups should explore this concept. Depending on the activity or experience, participants may take the pictures while participating or observing. Outside

1

1. **Newspaper article (photojournalists).** Divide the photojournalists into groups of two to three students. Each group will write an article summarizing the group's experience in completing the task. Articles must include a succinct headline, one photograph with a caption, and a summary paragraph of 200 words or less. Upon completion, each photojournalist group will read their article to the class, including the title of the article, description of the selected photograph, and caption. Following this presentation, the article may be passed among the students for closer review. Encourage questions and comments.

   Allow the photojournalists to select their pictures first and begin writing their articles while you explain to the remaining participants their processing activities. Divide the remaining participants into two groups and assign one of the processing activities to each group.

2. **A story line.** Give the group their instructions: Your task is to use pictures to tell a story that communicates your experience as participants in the activity. Examples may include the challenges of completing the task, group dynamics issues, communication challenges and strengths, and so on. Review the

photographs taken by the photojournalists and choose no more than half of the remaining photographs (the other group will be using the other half of the pictures). Using only yourselves and the photographs, create a "chorus line" in which you hold up the photographs for others to see while you communicate your experience through song, verbal phrases, sounds, nonverbal communication, or some combination of these. Be creative. Following your presentation of the story line, encourage your classmates to come forward and look at the pictures that you are holding up. Encourage questions and comments.

3. **Storyboard.** Give the group the following instructions: Your task is to use pictures to tell a story that communicates your experience as participants in the activity. Examples may include the challenges of completing the task, group dynamics issues, communication challenges and strengths, and so on. Review the photographs taken by the photojournalists, and choose no more than half of the remaining photographs (the other group will be using the other half of the pictures). Using newsprint, markers, crayons, stickers, or some combination of these, create a storyboard of pictures and drawings that represents your experience as individuals and as a group in accomplishing the task. Consider how you can best communicate your experience without words. Upon completion, display your storyboard for your classmates to view. At this time, refrain from talking or adding oral explanation. Once everyone has had a chance to view the storyboard, encourage questions and comments.

Allow students approximately 10 minutes to complete their processing activities, and then have each group share their activities with the class. Encourage students to ask each other questions about their experiences and use the pictures as a facilitation tool. Consider the following questions:

- What are some of the themes that emerged from the groups' processing activities?
- What themes are similar or different? Why do you think these similarities and differences exist?
- How did the pictures capture and represent your experience?
- Is there any particular picture that captures and best represents your experience? If so, which one? If not, why not?
- Which, if any, pictures surprised you? Why or why not?
- For the activity participants: How did having someone else take the photographs affect the selection of pictures that were available to you? Explain what pictures, if any, were missing from the selection that would have helped you communicate your experience.

Activity 5: Mini-Lecture

Introduce the concept of photo elicitation to the students: the use of images that are produced by either the facilitator or the participant and interpreted by the participant.

The discussion of an experience can be stimulated and guided by images produced during the experience. Photographs provide concrete and explicit reference points and invite people to express thoughts, experiences, and stories spontaneously. Rather than trying to remember what happened, people review the picture; this sharpens their memory, and thus their reconstruction of the experience is more realistic.

Photos can also help to develop the point of view of the participant and define the meaning the participant finds in the photograph. This process fosters the individual's interpretation of the picture and culture rather than the facilitator's interpretation of the participant's experience. Photographs taken by individuals, as opposed to the instructor, during the experience highlight what the individual found interesting or important about the experience. These photographs can help the instructor identify appropriate and effective processing questions and topics that are most applicable to the individual and group.

Refer to the Ball Transport activity as an example: The photojournalists took the photographs for the activity participants, and the photographs were then used within the processing activities to stimulate and guide discussion, allow individuals to tell their own stories, and draw out individual interpretations of the pictures. This demonstrated how photo elicitation can be implemented as an effective technique for facilitating group experiences by fostering reflection-on-action. Schon's theory of reflection-on-action is commonly applied in adventure activities in which processing activities occur following the experience; however, the benefits of photo elicitation also support its use in promoting reflection-in-action.

Reflection-on-action is the process of reflecting on past experiences in relation to a current situation to create new ways of thinking and doing. It is a common reflective practice used in adventure education. Methods of reflection-on-action include journal writing, debriefing circles, and drawings. The photo elicitation activities just completed could also be considered reflection-on-action activities.

Reflection-in-action is the process of thinking about an experience as it is happening. It can be viewed as "thinking on your feet" and "learning by doing." It encompasses problem situations in which learners think about what they are doing while doing it in order to solve the problem.

If processing activities following an adventure experience are a means of reflecting-on-action, then strategies for processing the experience during the activity may be a means of developing the skills of reflection-in-action. Photographs can capture the process that the participant is experiencing by providing immediate and concrete information regarding the problem the participant faces. Reflection-in-action strategies can be implemented to help participants see what they are currently doing or experiencing and make decisions to either modify or maintain the process to accomplish the task.

Tell the class that now they will participate in an activity that will let them put theory into practice.

Activity 6: Toxic Waste

Allot 30 to 40 minutes for this activity. Students will participate in the adventure activity called Toxic Waste, chosen for its similarity to the Ball Transport activity but with more challenging parameters (see handout on CD-ROM). The entire group will participate in this activity, with students taking turns being the photographers. Begin by having two to four students participate as photographers. Explain to the photographers that pictures should be taken that capture the group process and their attempts at activity completion.

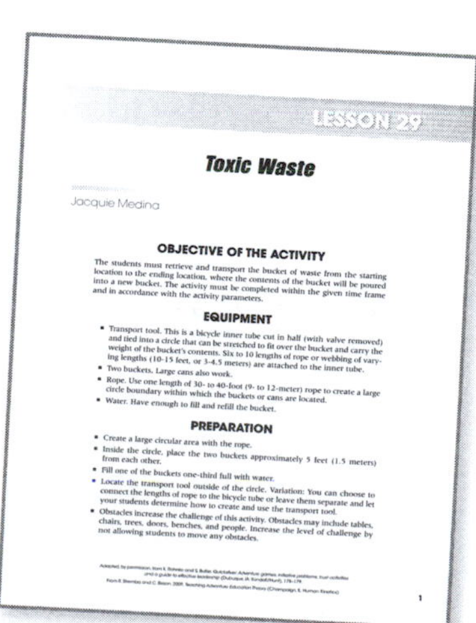
LESSON 29

Toxic Waste

Jacquie Medina

OBJECTIVE OF THE ACTIVITY

The students must retrieve and transport the bucket of waste from the starting location to the ending location, where the contents of the bucket will be poured into a new bucket. The activity must be completed within the given time frame and in accordance with the activity parameters.

EQUIPMENT

- Transport tool. This is a bicycle inner tube cut in half (with valve removed) and tied into a circle that can be stretched to fit over the bucket and carry the weight of the bucket's contents. Six to 10 lengths of rope or webbing of varying lengths (10-15 feet, or 3-4.5 meters) are attached to the inner tube.
- Two buckets. Large cans also work.
- Rope. Use one length of 30- to 40-foot (9- to 12-meter) rope to create a large circle boundary within which the buckets or cans are located.
- Water. Have enough to fill and refill the bucket.

PREPARATION

- Create a large circular area with the rope.
- Inside the circle, place the two buckets approximately 5 feet (1.5 meters) from each other.
- Fill one of the buckets one-third full with water.
- Locate the transport tool outside of the circle. Variation: You can choose to connect the lengths of rope to the bicycle tube or leave them separate and let your students determine how to create and use the transport tool.
- Obstacles increase the challenge of this activity. Obstacles may include tables, chairs, trees, doors, benches, and people. Increase the level of challenge by not allowing students to move any obstacles.

1

Your job as instructor is to facilitate the adventure activity. Create parameters that will challenge the group, making the task difficult to accomplish. Stop the activity at a point at which the group is challenged, introduce the pictures as a means to reflect-in-action, and then have the group attempt the task again implementing the new ideas and strategies. This may occur more than once. When you decide to have the group stop, have them leave everything as it is at that moment. Ask one or two students to objectively summarize what the group is currently doing to accomplish the task. They should identify what is working and what is not working. Allow the students to view the photographs that have been taken. Ask the students what consistencies or inconsistencies exist between the photographs and what they believe to be true about their group's process.

The following are examples of photographs that students may take:

- Pictures of the group standing around discussing versus acting
- Pictures of group members not participating
- Pictures of the transport tool—its physical design, how it is being used in the activity
- Pictures of the group's physical arrangement

All these photographs may represent challenges the group is facing or systems that are or are not working or contributing to the success of the task.

Encourage students to interpret the photographs and glean from them the information that will help them to accomplish their task. Allow only a short amount of time for viewing the pictures and implementing change. Time management is critical to maintaining the spirit of the reflection-in-action concept of "thinking on your feet."

When the activity has been completed or the time is up, process the experience with the group involved in the transport, focusing debriefing questions on the use of photographs to facilitate reflection-in-action. Pose the following questions:

- What examples of reflection-in-action occurred for you while participating in this activity?
- How did the photographs contribute to your ability to "think on your feet" in this activity?
- How often were you experiencing moments of reflection-in-action during this activity?

Lead a discussion of the differences in answers among the activity participants. Consider ways of using photographs to facilitate reflection-in-action and meeting the needs of various learning styles. Guide the students from this discussion to closing and summary statements.

CLOSURE

Returning to the original slide show of photographs, have the students reflect on the pictures and make application to their own lives and experiences. Share again the idea that visual imagery such as photographs can serve as a bridge of communication. Photos can help individuals share their stories with others and connect with an experience, sharpening their memory and encouraging individual interpretation of the experience. Photo elicitation can be used in a variety of ways to foster reflection-on-action. Encourage students to be creative and develop additional methods of using photographs to facilitate an adventure experience.

Ask the students to ponder the challenges of developing the skills of reflection-in-action by posing the following questions:

- What are the challenges we face in trying to develop the skills of reflection-in-action or "thinking on your feet"?
- What role can photographs play in developing reflection-in-action?
- What other methods can be used to foster the skills of reflection-in-action?

ASSESSMENT OF LEARNING

Formative and summative assessment will occur throughout the lesson and during the final summary. Assessments will involve completion of the following:

- Students articulate the differences between reflection-on-action and reflection-in-action, citing examples to support their answers.
- Students demonstrate techniques of photo elicitation to apply the theory of reflection-on-action to facilitating group experiences (newspaper headlines and article, story line, storyboard).
- Students demonstrate the ability to apply the theories of reflection-in-action and reflection-on-action through participation in an adventure activity.
- Students articulate new methods of applying the theories of reflection-on-action and reflection-in-action to adventure activities.

LESSON 30

Growth at the Edge

Expanding Our Comfort Zones

Bob Stremba

Adventure activities, when used to promote change and growth, help individuals expand their comfort zones beyond the adventure itself. What used to be outside one's comfort zone may now be a little more attainable, and what is inside and outside the comfort zone will be different for each individual. So, adventure educators need to be aware of what is happening with their students—their body language, behaviors, and emotions—in order to be able to responsibly invite them into their growth zone but not take them into their panic zone, where fear precludes effective transfer of learning.

Background

John A. Shedd noted, "A ship in harbor is safe, but that is not what ships are built for." The image is often connected to Outward Bound, which has its roots in the use of sailing on the sea as a medium for young people to take risks and discover confidence. Many of the outdoor adventure programs that have evolved from Outward Bound extend the metaphor, using adventure experiences with high perceived risk, but lower actual risk, to promote personal growth in their students.

Adventure educators establish environments in which students may experience a wide range of emotions. When engaging in rock climbing, for example, the student new to this activity is in a state of dynamic tension composed of two conditions (Luckner and Nadler 1997). When he or she is on the ground attached to the belayer, a sense of safety and security exists. This feeling is replaced by a sense of disequilibrium when the student leaves the ground, because there is now a mismatch between old ways of thinking and new information. Luckner and Nadler (1997) describe the process through which the student has moved from his or her familiar comfort zone "into an area that feels uncomfortable and unfamiliar, the groan zone. By overcoming these anxious feelings and thoughts of self-doubt while simultaneously sampling success, individuals move from the groan zone to the growth zone" (p. 20). Jane Panicucci (in Prouty et al. 2007) refers to the groan zone as the "stretch zone." In moving into the groan or stretch zone, individuals have opportunities to expand their comfort zones; what previously elicited anxiety and the temptation to turn back now feels familiar because a sense of mastery and accomplishment has developed. What previously felt risky and produced anxiety now becomes familiar. Adventure educators help students by introducing them to new experiential activities that they may initially be reluctant to engage in. So, the individual's comfort zone at first is rather small with regard to the experience; but after the person has had some degree of success, the comfort zone expands.

So, what happens as individuals leave their comfort zone, move through the groan or stretch zone, and finally emerge in the growth zone? First, they experience a range of feelings—anxiety, fear, or vulnerability initially, followed perhaps by excitement, then feelings of success and competence. Second, a series of defense mechanisms often emerges to protect individuals from at least their own negative feelings. And third, these defense mechanisms are manifested in behaviors that become apparent as the individual moves through the process from the comfort zone to the growth zone. Thus a feeling of fear and vulnerability might be masked by a defense mechanism of denial, which is evidenced when students say "I'm not scared" even though their legs are shaking uncontrollably.

Beyond the growth zone, however, lies the panic zone, the area where the risk exceeds the individual's competence to successfully handle it. Describing the adventure experience paradigm, Priest and Gass (2005) note, "As risk exceeds competence, the potential for misadventure arises; when risk becomes very high and competence is very low, devastation and disaster may occur" (p. 50). In the context of facilitating adventure activities to promote growth, then, little learning can occur in the panic zone because the individual is likely focused on immediate survival issues.

The larger purpose of adventure education is to help people transfer their learning from the adventure experience to other situations in their lives. Adventure educators help students explore connections between their feelings and behaviors on the rock, in the example cited previously, and making changes in their feelings and behaviors in other situations at home, work, or school. "Transfer and generalization occur when the learning in one situation carries over to another. . . . Without such positive transfer, programs that use an experience-based approach have limited long-term value" (Luckner and Nadler 1997, p. 20).

To help students use a rock climbing experience, for example, to attempt previously avoided experiences in other aspects of their lives, the adventure educator can help them become aware of the thoughts and feelings occurring during the climb, along with strategies to change those thoughts and feelings that might be dysfunctional to ones that promote success, or move through the groan or stretch zone into the growth zone. Similarly, we can help people become aware of the thoughts and feelings that do serve them well. The boundaries between the comfort zone and the groan and growth zones are referred to as the "edge." Luckner and Nadler (1997) note, "As people get closer to this unknown, new territory, their sense of disequilibrium increases and a sense of uncertainty exists" (p. 29). The writers go on to describe edge components, along with examples of how the facilitator can help individuals break through their edges:

- As feelings of anxiety, fear, or confusion intensify, physiological symptoms change. Palms sweat, the heart races, and breathing quickens. Facilitators can first help people become aware of their feelings ("What are you feeling right now?"). They can then suggest that the person slow down, take a deep breath, and try to relax.

- Internal conversations (or self-talk) become louder and more frequent. Self-limiting beliefs such as "I can't do this" or "I'll fail" come to mind. Facilitators can invite the individual to change thoughts and self-talk to messages such as "Keep going" or "Just take one step at a time."
- Previous patterns of behavior used in other uncomfortable situations emerge. These behaviors can include avoidance and turning back. Here the facilitator can invite the person to take a new risk, just move forward slowly, or do something that is slightly different than what the person would normally do.
- Mental pictures of previous attempts and failures at new endeavors may develop. The facilitator can suggest that the person create new pictures, asking "What would success look like here?" or suggesting "See yourself achieving the result you want."

Adventure activities, when used to promote change and growth, help individuals expand their comfort zones beyond the adventure itself. What used to be outside one's comfort zone may now be a little more attainable, and what's inside and outside the comfort zone will be different for each individual. So, adventure educators need to be aware of what's happening with their students—their body language, behaviors, and emotions—in order to be able to responsibly invite them into their growth zone but not take them into their panic zone, where fear precludes effective transfer of learning.

RESOURCES

Luckner, J.L., and R.S. Nadler. 1997. *Processing the experience: Strategies to enhance and generalize learning.* 2nd ed. Dubuque, IA: Kendall/Hunt.

Priest, S., and M.A. Gass. 2005. *Effective leadership in adventure programming.* 2nd ed. Champaign, IL: Human Kinetics.

Prouty, D., J. Panicucci, and R. Collinson, eds. 2007. *Adventure education: Theory and applications.* Champaign, IL: Human Kinetics.

Sikes, S. 2003. *Raptor and other team building activities.* Tulsa, OK: Learning Unlimited.

Lesson Plan

PURPOSE

For students to experience the model of "edgework" and comfort zones so that they can teach their own clients or students to expand their comfort zones using outdoor pursuits such as climbing or white-water paddling, or indoor pursuits that involve academic, social, or emotional risk.

OBJECTIVES

As a result of this lesson students will be able to . . .

1. *Cognitive and affective:* describe in writing an experience that expanded their comfort zone, identify their feelings during that experience, and correctly describe at least three components of edgework illustrated by that experience.

2. *Psychomotor:* participate in a kinesthetic model of growth and change and describe physiological, emotional, verbal, and behavioral responses while literally walking through the model.
3. *Cognitive:* describe to other students and the instructor how to use an adventure pursuit to help others expand their comfort zones.

DURATION

40 to 50 minutes

GROUP SIZE

15 to 30

LOCATION

Indoors

EQUIPMENT

- For a large class, use three pieces of webbing (of approximately 15, 30, and 60 feet, or 4.5, 9, and 18 meters); these will form three concentric circles. If the group is small enough, use three shorter pieces of rope or webbing for each student so that three concentric circles can be formed for each.
- Signs to place within the circles (on CD-ROM): "Comfort Zone" (in smallest inner circle), "Groan-Stretch Zone" (in next outer circle), "Growth Zone" (in next outer circle), "Panic Zone" (in space beyond the third circle).
- 50 to 75 basic wooden mousetraps.
- Blindfolds—at least two, or enough for all students if the group is relatively small (fewer than 10).

RISK MANAGEMENT CONSIDERATIONS

There is a perceived risk of walking without shoes through an area strewn with mousetraps that are set to snap shut. In reality, we have never heard of any injuries to toes or feet from this exercise. The activity does, however, raise most students' anxiety level, which is a necessary learning component of the lesson.

STUDENT PREPARATION

- Students can read the Background included with this lesson (on CD-ROM) or pages 17 through 47 in Luckner and Nadler 1997.
- On the basis of this reading, students should write a one- to two-page paper describing a situation that brought them to their "edge" as explained in the reading. They should describe their S–1 moments, the S+1 moments, and the edge components that were occurring for them in this situation.
- Students should bring to class an object that represents something within their comfort zone and another object that represents something outside their comfort zone. Alternatively, they can briefly write on two different pieces of paper something that is within their comfort zone and something that is outside of it.

INSTRUCTOR PREPARATION

- Tie webbing ends together so you have three webbing circles on the floor. The inner circle should be approximately 4 feet (1.2 meters) in diameter; the next circle out is approximately 12 feet (3.7 meters) in diameter; and the outer circle should be approximately 20 feet (6 meters) in diameter. Note that the following explanation of the lesson refers to the alternative for a large class, the use of one set of webbing circles and two volunteers who go through the exercise with the other students observing.
- Become familiar with how to set mousetraps safely so that you can teach this "skill" to your students.

LESSON CONTENT AND TEACHING STRATEGIES

This lesson begins with a series of activities to get students engaged with their own feelings and behaviors about comfort zones; it concludes with a discussion and PowerPoint presentation to explore the theory behind the experience.

Activity 1: Framing the Experience

Describe the definition and nature of comfort zones, represented by the area within the inner circle of webbing (see figure 30.1). Place the "Comfort Zone" sign within the inner circle. A comfort zone is predictable and familiar; it's the known area; it's safe and secure. It feels like home here. Provide examples of things that might be inside one's comfort zone (e.g., friends, family, favorite pillow, favorite outdoor activity) and other things that might be outside one's comfort zone (e.g., a difficult academic course, a new adventure activity).

Brainstorm with students things that can be inside and outside of one's comfort zone.

Have students take out the two objects they have brought to class, one representing something within their comfort zone and the other representing something outside of their comfort zone. As an alternative, have students briefly describe something that is familiar and comfortable (inside their comfort zone) and something that is outside of their comfort zone on two separate pieces of paper. Ask students to consider academic, intellectual, interpersonal, and emotional issues that are inside and outside their comfort zones in order to broaden the thinking about "adventure" beyond just physical risks.

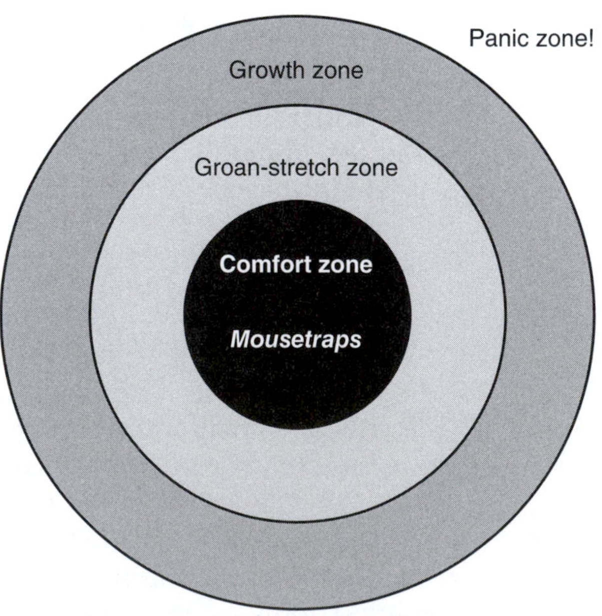

FIGURE 30.1 Arrangement of comfort zone, groan/stretch zone, and growth zone.

Describe the "Groan-Stretch Zone," represented by the circle just beyond the comfort zone. Place the "Groan-Stretch Zone" sign in this circle. The groan zone is unfamiliar, unpredictable, uncomfortable, and unknown. "We might feel insecure out here for a while."

Tell students: "Place within the comfort zone, the inner rope circle, your object or the piece of paper on which you've written about something that is comfortable and familiar. Place within the groan-stretch zone, the next rope circle, your object or the piece of paper on which you've written about something unfamiliar or uncomfortable." Offer students the opportunity to describe what their objects represent or explain what they have written.

Describe the "Growth Zone," represented by the next circle. Place the "Growth Zone" sign in this circle. The growth zone is new territory, the unexplored aspects of our lives, where our future successes will be—the area of new growth. As we spend more time in this territory, it becomes part of our tamed territory. Feelings of mastery, accomplishment, and familiarity develop.

Describe the "Panic Zone," the large area beyond the growth zone. Place the "Panic Zone" sign somewhere out beyond the last webbing circle. "We want to stop short of the panic zone, because no growth occurs here." Ask students for examples of times they have been in the panic zone or have noticed others in this zone.

Explain that the size of each zone and how close it is to the individual vary with the client population and their previous experience. Provide an example or two from your own life or your experience with students who have expanded their comfort zones through outdoor (or indoor) adventure pursuits.

Activity 2: Setting the Stage

Demonstrate how to safely set a mousetrap. Place the mousetrap on the floor or a flat surface; lift the squarish spring-loaded bar over to the other side of the trap, and place the straight bar across the spring-loaded bar so that the straight bar delicately rests under the notch of the copper plate. Be careful not to put the straight bar through the holes on the copper plate. The use of mousetraps for teaching a variety of concepts in adventure education comes from the creative work of Sam Sikes (2003).

This initial mousetrap-setting experience may in itself take some students to the edge of their comfort zones, or beyond, so ask students to notice any symptoms of anxiety—increased heart rate, sweaty palms, self-talk, nervous laughter, and so on.

Have students pick up the mousetraps by their sides with their thumb and forefinger and place the mousetraps so that they are spread out evenly within the groan-stretch zone. Then students should move to a space outside the webbing zones, leaving all the objects and pieces of paper where they were previously placed in the comfort and groan-stretch zones.

Ask for two student volunteers, and have them step inside the comfort zone, being careful not to spring any of the mousetraps on the way. Other students should be fishbowl observers, positioned outside the outer circle. (If each student has his or her own set of circles, have them all step inside their comfort zone at the same time.)

Activity 3: Edgework Experience

Tell students as they stand within the comfort zone: "In a minute, but not yet, I'm going to ask you to leave your comfort zone, then walk through your groan-stretch zone and into your growth zone. You will need to take baby steps and shuffle your feet forward through the groan-stretch zone, the way people often do when traveling through unfamiliar territory. Any questions?" After a slight pause, add, "Oh, yeah, before starting, would you please place this blindfold on?" After students have blindfolds on, add, "Oh, yeah, and would you please take your shoes off and hand them to me [or one of the fishbowl observers]?" This will usually provoke some comments and anxiety, so ask students to again become aware of such signs as increased heart rate, sweaty palms, self-talk, and nervous laughter.

Instructions to those about to leave their comfort zone [and to fishbowl observers]: "Notice what's going during the walk through the mousetraps, through the groan-stretch zone. Notice any signs of anxiety (nervous laughter, hesitation, etc.) and also any signs or behaviors indicating confidence or calmness."

Tell the students still standing inside their comfort zones, "Now, when you're ready, begin to leave your comfort zone and slowly walk through the groan-

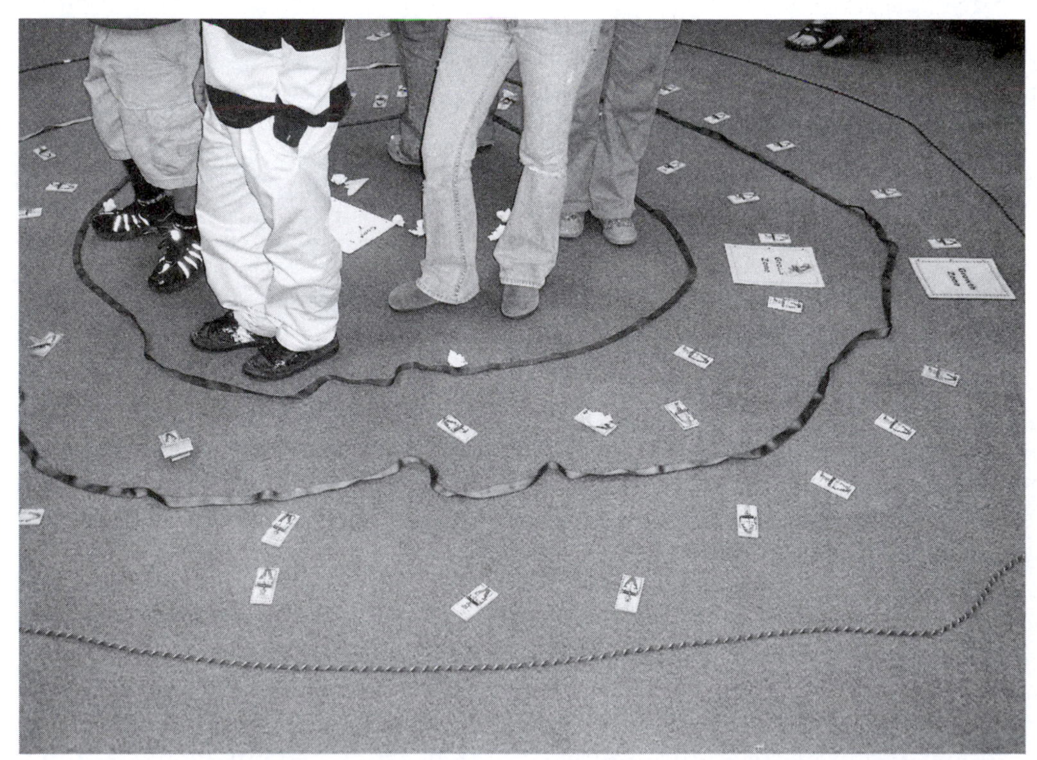

The comfort zone, groan zone, and growth zone represented by webbing and mousetraps.

Bob Stremba

stretch zone. Remember to take baby steps and slowly shuffle your feet forward, and notice what you're feeling and what you may be saying to yourself as you proceed."

When students reach the growth zone, invite them to remove their blindfolds.

After moving through the groan zone, students can remove their blindfolds.
Bob Stremba

Activity 4: Mini-Lecture and PowerPoint on Connecting Experience to Theory

Have students who just walked through the mousetraps, plus the fishbowl observers, review the experience. Much of this review uses probing questions mixed with information provided by the instructor via the PowerPoint presentation (on CD-ROM).

Show slides 1 through 3. "A few minutes ago, you placed an object or a piece of paper outside your comfort zone (show slide 4), in the groan-stretch zone, where there are now mousetraps that also represent things outside the comfort zone. And when you first left your comfort zone and stepped into the groan-stretch zone, you were leaving the familiar and comfortable and moving into the unfamiliar and uncomfortable (show slide 5). That webbing separating the comfort zone from the growth zone is the edge."

"What was your tendency as you got closer to the edge? [To go back to the middle?] This could explain why people sometimes return to old behavior, to what's familiar, and how difficult it is to make changes. What happened at the edge that helped pull you back to the comfort zone or propelled you into the groan-stretch or growth zone?" (Show slides 6-7.)

"Two things can happen at the edge. We can be pulled back into our comfort zone. This is called success minus one (S–1). Or, we can move forward. What helped (or would help) you go beyond your edge into your groan-stretch zone and your growth zone?" Invite student responses. "This moment is called success plus one (S+1). S+1 is the breakthrough to new territory. How can we keep the success factors, so we can again venture into new territory beyond our comfort zone, S+1?" (Show slides 8-10.)

What happens within us at the edge?

Nadler and Luckner (1997) provide a narrative for taking individuals through the edgework process (p. 309). The instructor begins a visual demonstration by returning to the middle of the comfort zone circle. Then he or she walks toward the edge, toward the groan-stretch zone with the mousetraps, and asks the following questions, eliciting quick responses or supplying the answers.

- **Body:** "Will my physiology, my breathing, heartbeats, and sweating, be more frequent or less frequent, more intense or less intense?" [More frequent and intense]
- **Feelings:** "As I walk toward the edge, will my feelings be more or less intense?" [More intense] "What kinds of feelings will I have?" [Anxiety, fear, confusion, etc.]
- **Self-talk and mental pictures:** "Will my self-talk be louder or softer as I approach the edge?" [Louder] "What are some examples of what I may be telling myself at the edge?" [I won't be able to do it, I'll fail and make a fool of myself, I can't, everyone will be looking at me] "What mental pictures might I be seeing?" [Past failures]
- **Behavior:** "Will my old patterns of behavior be more likely or less likely to act up as I approach the edge?" [More likely] "What are some examples of outdated or old patterns?" [Avoidance, anger outbursts, not asking for help, not sharing feelings, isolating]

"What do you think we can do (or help our clients do) at the edge to have a breakthrough from comfort zone to groan-stretch zone to growth zone?"

Changing one or two edge components will help. We can focus in the following ways:

- **Breathing:** Slow down, take a deep breath, relax.
- **Feelings:** Realize that this too will pass; I can tolerate this; just stay with it; it will get less intense.
- **Thoughts (self-talk):** "I can do it;" "Just take one step at a time;" "Keep going."
- **Mental pictures:** Picture what success would look like, how others would see me.
- **Support:** Ask for help, encouragement.
- **Behavior:** Identify patterns of behavior—take a new risk, just keep moving forward slowly, do something that is slightly different from what I would normally do.

Activity 5: Reinforcement Experience (Optional)

If you have access to a ropes course, take students to an element such as the Pamper Pole. Or, in a classroom, use a sturdy table to conduct a trust fall. Conduct a safety briefing before the activity.

Introduce the activity: "Here is an opportunity for you get to your edge and to become aware of what's going on there—and to understand how to offer your clients the opportunity to expand their comfort zones."

Have a rope circle around the ladder going up the Pamper Pole, similar to the rope circle used earlier. Another rope circle under the trapeze can represent the growth zone. Ask each climber before he or she leaves the ground, "Where do you think your edge is here? Stepping onto the ladder? The staples? The platform? Off the platform?"

As they are going up the pole, ask about body (heart racing, breathing), feelings, self-talk, and mental pictures. "What would help? Change some of your edge components. Support from the group? What kind of support would you like?"

After the activity, ask, "What led to your breakthrough, or what happened when you returned to your comfort zone?"

Activity 6: Small Group Discussion

Form pairs or small groups (three or four students). "Think of an adventure pursuit that is already within your own comfort zone. With your group, discuss how you could use this activity to take one of your students or clients, who is new to this pursuit, from his or her comfort zone, through the groan-stretch zone, and into a growth zone. How might you know that the person is moving beyond his or her 'edge' into another change zone? What would you say and do to make this activity a positive, growthful experience for this person?" (Show slides 11-12.)

Ask for examples, without redundant comments, regarding edgework.

CLOSURE

"You have just experienced going from your comfort zone, through the groan-stretch zone, and into a growth zone. What used to be outside your comfort zone may now be a little more attainable. But remember, this is not a blanket invitation to engage in risky behaviors that can be harmful. And what's inside and outside the comfort zone will be different for each individual. So, as an adventure educator you need to be aware of what's happening with your students—their body language, behaviors, and emotions—so you can responsibly invite them into their growth zone but not take them into their panic zone; when we're scared we typically are not able to learn effectively." (Show slide 13.)

ASSESSMENT OF LEARNING

- Check prelesson student understanding through the "edgework" papers they wrote. (See the second assignment in the "Student Preparation" section.) Check postlesson understanding through students' correct responses in the discussion part of the lesson.
- In the small group discussion at the end of the lesson, in which students are asked to apply the model to an adventure experience, check that students are accurately describing how they can tell that someone is at his or her edge; also check that students describe what they as adventure educators can say or do to help clients expand their comfort zone.

PART X

The Human–Nature Connection

The four lessons in part X address the political, emotional, psychological, and ethical connections between our participants and the great outdoors. Because many adventure experiences take place outdoors, it's important that adventure educators understand the psychological and emotional connections between humans and the natural world so that they can help participants develop healthy and rewarding relationships with nature. Furthermore, they should be aware of the political and legal processes that protect and give access to public land.

In lesson 31, "My Land Is Your Land Too: American Public Land and Multiple-Use Policies," Christian Bisson introduces the politics behind the popular land management concepts of multiple-use and sustainable yield found in North America. The lesson introduces the various types of public lands found in the United States and explains who manages them and why they may be accessed by many users. Young adventure educators need to understand why we must share these resources with other users so that misunderstandings, resentment, or even conflicts between users can be avoided. This lesson will help students understand the role played by two of the largest public land agencies in the United States, as well as the dilemma they often experience when trying to meet the needs of all interested groups. The lesson also addresses how students can become involved in the management of these public lands by taking part in the democratic process.

In lesson 32, "Loving Nature Through Adventure: Examining Human–Nature Interaction," Peter Martin reminds us that to develop stewardship for the earth, one must first develop a personal relationship with the planet. The lesson presents a metaphor that promotes acting *for* nature, not just in it, and encourages students to explore how meaningful, caring relationships with nature could be formed and the implications of such relationships for outdoor adventure education.

In lesson 33, "A Walk in the Woods: Teaching Ecopsychology Experientially," Bob Henderson and Deborah Schrader present an engaging lesson that brings the learners in direct contact with the concept of ecopsychology. This lesson employs a simple walk in the woods and sensory activities to reveal a complex set of reflections on the nature of schooling, the nature of cultural sustainability, and the nature of nature. For many students this lesson will serve as a wake-up call about their personal lifestyle and behavior.

Finally, in lesson 34, "Loving the Land for Life: The Vital Role of Recreation Ecology," Kelly Rossiter reminds us that as outdoor adventure pursuits increase in popularity, so too does the strain that visitors place on our natural areas. Though many outdoor adventure enthusiasts and professionals are familiar with Leave No Trace, many are unfamiliar with the area of study undergirding it—recreation ecology. This lesson introduces students to the importance of recreation ecology and enhances their understanding of both the land management practices implemented in natural areas and the important role that they will play as outdoor educators in promoting proper care for our natural areas.

LESSON 31

My Land Is Your Land Too

American Public Land and Multiple-Use Policies

Christian A. Bisson

American and some Canadian adventure educators are bound to deal with public land agencies in America. Most states in the United States provide excellent areas for outdoor recreation and education. Knowing how these various lands are managed and why we need to share these resources with other users is essential so that misunderstandings, resentment, or even conflicts between users can be avoided. This lesson will help your students understand the role played by two of the largest public land agencies in the United States, as well as the dilemma they often experience when trying to meet the needs of all interested groups. The lesson also addresses how students can become involved in the management of these public lands by taking part in the democratic process.

Background

The concept of wildland in America has drastically changed since the establishment of the first 13 colonies and the western expansion by the early European immigrants. At that time, wildlands were often seen as dangerous, inhospitable, and full of untapped resources or wasted spaces. Today, thanks to the work of thinkers like Thoreau, Muir, Leopold, Marshall, Olson, and Carlson and the influence of the first national land ethic, wildlands are now seen as public and cultural values. Public lands are now perceived in the public mind as a heritage for all our children and all the generations to come.

Although the management of this public good is still debated at many levels of administration or as a consequence of different philosophies about nature, many people today agree that public lands provide us with biodiversity, air shed and watershed, recreational opportunities, and goods like timber and minerals.

In the USA, about 30% of all surface land is owned and managed by the federal government. Four large agencies are responsible for managing 93% of the roughly 672 million acres of U.S. federal public lands. These agencies are the U.S. Forest

Service (USFS), the Bureau of Land Management (BLM), the National Park Service (NPS), and the U.S. Fish and Wildlife Service (USFWS) (Martin et al. 2006).

U.S. FOREST SERVICE

The USFS was established in 1905 and is part of the Department of Agriculture. In 2007, it managed 193 million acres or about 28% of all federal land. It supervises 175 units, which are mostly forest and grassland. Its mission is to sustain the health, diversity, and productivity of the nation's forests and grasslands to meet the needs of present and future generations (Lamb and Goodrich 2006).

The phrase "caring for the land and serving people," the Forest Service's motto, captures its mission. As set forth in law, the mission is to achieve quality land management under the sustainable multiple-use management concept to meet the diverse needs of people. In the end, the agency aims at providing service for multiple users while ensuring a sustainable yield.

The concept of multiple users and sustained yield is deeply rooted in the history of the agency. The first chief of the USFS, Gifford Pinchot (chief from 1905 to 1910), who had been trained in a European style of scientific forestry that married conservation and a utilitarian philosophy when it came to public forests, developed and promoted the concept of providing the greatest amount of good for the greatest number of people over the long term (Gookin and Wells 2002).

To this day, the agency provides us with conservation via the establishment of many designated wilderness areas, as well as having a utilitarian commitment to provide management for forest goods and recreation opportunities. Of course, such a diverse set of purposes often places the men and women working for the USFS at the center of requests from diverse advocacy groups.

BUREAU OF LAND MANAGEMENT

The BLM was established in 1946 and is attached to the Department of the Interior. In 2007, it managed the largest portion of public land, 258 million acres or about 38% of all federal land. These lands mostly include deserts, forest, and grassland areas, all located west of the Mississippi River and in Alaska. Quite similar to the USFS mission, the BLM mission reads as follows: To sustain the health, diversity, and productivity of the public lands for the use and enjoyment of present and future generations. The agency also embraces a mixed conservation and utilitarian philosophy and operates under the principles of multiple use and sustained yield of the nation's resources. These resources include recreation, rangelands, timber, minerals, watershed, fish and wildlife, wilderness, air and scenic, scientific and cultural values (Lamb and Goodrich 2006).

For instance, under its multiple-use management mandate, the BLM administers more than 18,000 grazing permits and leases and nearly 13 million authorized livestock animal unit months on 160 million acres of public rangeland. The bureau is also responsible for the leasing of millions of acres of surface and underground land, generating an estimated $4.5 billion in receipts from royalties, bonuses, and rentals that are collected by the Minerals Management Service. The millions of acres supervised by the BLM are also very popular with recreationist and conservation groups.

Again, all these demands from different groups place pressure on a public agency that is legally bound to provide management for multiple users with multiple needs.

NATIONAL PARK SERVICE

The NPS was established in 1916 and is supervised by the Department of the Interior. In 2007, it managed about 84.6 million acres or about 12% of all federal land. The NPS is responsible for 390 distinct units. These units include national parks, monuments, battlefields, military parks, historical parks, historic sites, lakeshores, seashores, recreation areas, scenic rivers and trails, and even the White House (Lamb and Goodrich 2006).

In contrast with the missions of the USFS and BLM, the NPS mission focuses primarily on conservation and on offering recreational and educational experiences to the public. The official mission statement reads as follows: The National Park Service "preserves unimpaired the natural and cultural resources and values of the national park system for the enjoyment, education, and inspiration of this and future generations."

This agency does not have to balance demands between conservation and the sustained yield of natural goods like lumber or minerals. Nevertheless, it often faces a tug-of-war between recreationists advocating the use of outdoor pursuit activities and recreationists requesting the use of motorized vehicles (automobiles, recreational vehicles, planes, helicopters, boats, and snowmobiles). Recreation and education also often conflict with preservation principles when national parks such as Yellowstone, Yosemite, and the Grand Canyon are "loved to death" by the public.

U.S. FISH AND WILDLIFE SERVICE

The USFWS was established in 1956 and is also supervised by the Department of the Interior. In 2007, it managed about 94.3 million acres or about 14% of all federal land. The USFWS includes 632 units, mostly composed of wetlands and seashore areas (Lamb and Goodrich 2006).

In contrast to the other agencies, the USFWS focuses primarily on conservation and restoration of plants and wildlife. Its mission is "to administer a national network of lands and waters for the conservation, management, and where appropriate, restoration of the fish, wildlife, and plant resources and their habitats within the United States for the benefit of present and future generations of Americans."

Although other uses such as hunting, fishing, recreation, grazing, and oil and gas development are sometime permitted, these activities are allowed only if they are compatible with the primary purpose of the agency, conservation.

The USFWS, more than any other agency, benefits from a very focused mandate that protects it from the challenges that a multiple-use and sustainable-yield philosophy can create.

THE MULTIPLE-USE CONUNDRUM

The concept of "multiple use" of public federal lands originated in the desire to apply democratic values to all sectors of the federal government. Unfortunately, when one tries to apply the ideology of "the greatest good for the greatest number" one is also posing the question of what the "greatest good" is. As we have already seen, two agencies in particular, the USFS and the BLM, are constantly struggling with the concept of multiple use.

To understand their struggle we need to look at two pieces of American legislation that define and direct these agencies' actions. These acts are the known as the Multiple-Use Sustained Yield Act (MUSYA) and the Federal Land Policy and Management Act (FLPMA).

MULTIPLE-USE SUSTAINED YIELD ACT

The Multiple-Use Sustained Yield Act was established in 1960 as an official management policy for the USFS. The act states, "It is the policy of the Congress that the national forests are established and shall be administered for outdoor recreation, range, timber, watershed, and wildlife and fish purposes" (Lamb and Goodrich 2006, p. 95). The act further defines the concepts of multiple use and sustained yield as follows.

Multiple use: "The management of all the various renewable surface resources of the national forests so that they are utilized in the combination that will best meet the needs of the American people."

Sustained yield of several products and services: "The achievement and maintenance in perpetuity of a high level annual or regular periodic output of the various renewable resources of the national forests without impairment of the productivity of the land."

FEDERAL LAND POLICY AND MANAGEMENT ACT

The FLPMA was established in 1976 to help define the purpose and goals of the management of public lands by the BLM. According to the act, "The Congress declares that it is the policy of the United States that . . . goals and objectives be established by law as guidelines for public land use planning, and that management be on the basis of multiple use and sustained yield unless otherwise specified by law. . . ." The 1976 act also defines the terms "multiple use" and "sustained yield."

Multiple use: "The term 'multiple use' means the management of the public lands and their various resource values so that they are utilized in the combination that will best meet the present and future needs of the American people; making the most judicious use of the land for some or all of these resources or related services over areas large enough to provide sufficient latitude for periodic adjustments in use to conform to changing needs and conditions; the use of some land for less than all of the resources; a combination of balanced and diverse resource uses that takes into account the long-term needs of future generations for renewable and nonrenewable resources, including, but not limited to, recreation, range, timber, minerals, watershed, wildlife and fish, and natural scenic, scientific and historical values; and harmonious and coordinated management of the various resources without permanent impairment of the productivity of the land and the quality of the environment with consideration being given to the relative values of the resources and not necessarily to the combination of uses that will give the greatest economic return or the greatest unit output."

Sustained yield: "The term 'sustained yield' means the achievement and maintenance in perpetuity of a high-level annual or regular periodic output of the various renewable resources of the public lands consistent with multiple use."

For further information on MUSYA and FLPMA, see copies of these acts on the CD-ROM. In light of these two distinct but very similar pieces of Congressional legislation, we can appreciate the challenge that the men and women working for these agencies face. Some critics of the multiple-use policy feel that such a policy leads not to multiple use of federal lands but instead to "multiple abuses."

The conflicts among stakeholders are various and complex. Disputes are based on ideologies, economic needs, traditions, and local or national political ambitions. Partnerships between various parties are created and broken up when necessary. In some cases, conservationists and the hunting or fishing groups team up against the mining industry, while in other cases the conservationists battle the recreationists. The people involved in the management of public land in America, especially in the western states, differ in background, needs, and goals like night and day. The following is a limited list of stakeholders commonly found participating in the public debate over the multiple use of public federal lands.

- Logging industry
- Mining industry
- Oil industry
- Tourism industry
- Research and science industry
- Livestock industry
- Recreation industry
- Outdoor guiding industry
- Educational services
- Conservation groups

Lamb and Goodrich (2006) propose that because "the Forest Service and the BLM . . . are charged with considering all possible uses of public lands in defining management goals . . . fulfilling the multiple-use mission becomes quite daunting" (pp. 173-174). The authors sadly conclude that although the USFS and the BLM "attempt to handle these challenges through an open planning process that invites all members of the public to voice their needs and concerns . . . In trying to please everyone, the agencies often end up in the unenviable position to please no one" (p. 176).

RESOURCES

Dunsky, S., and D. Steinke. 2005. *The greatest good: A Forest Service centennial film.* Produced by the U.S. Forest Service.

Gookin, J., and D. Wells, eds. 2002. *Environmental education notebook.* Lander, WY: NOLS.

Lamb, J., and G. Goodrich. 2006. *NOLS wilderness ethics: Valuing and managing wild places.* Mechanicsburg, PA: Stackpole Books.

Martin, B., C. Cashel, M. Wagstaff, and M. Breunig. 2006. *Outdoor leadership: Theory and practice.* Champaign, IL: Human Kinetics.

Lesson Plan

PURPOSE

The purpose of this lesson is to allow students to experience the challenge of managing a public land agency such as the U.S. Forest Service or the Bureau of Land Management when the function of these agencies is to ensure multiple use and sustained yield from the land.

OBJECTIVES

As a result of this lesson students will be able to . . .

1. *Affective and psychomotor:* participate in an experience that provides a better appreciation for the challenge that the USFS and the BLM encounter when applying their multiple-use and sustained-yield land management philosophy.
2. *Cognitive:* explain how the multiple-use and sustained-yield land management philosophy came into existence in America.
3. *Cognitive:* explain the process the public land agencies have to go through every 10 to 15 years when developing their respective land management plans.
4. *Cognitive:* explain how, as a consequence of the passage in 1969 of the National Environmental Policy Act (NEPA), each citizen can become involved in the planning and management of public land in America.
5. *Cognitive:* explain why outdoor education and recreation programs must be involved in the planning, management, and conservation of public lands.
6. *Affective:* demonstrate the ability to work within a small group to promote an idea or present an argument supporting a specific political agenda.

DURATION

Two periods of 50 to 60 minutes each

GROUP SIZE

Appropriate for 16 to 30 students

LOCATION

Indoors and outdoors

EQUIPMENT

- 50-foot (15-meter) rope
- Five labels on wooden sticks
- 5 feet (1.5 meters) of miniature railroad made of popsicle sticks
- 12 miniature trees made of popsicle sticks
- Five to 10 overhead transparencies
- Prop labels (on CD-ROM)
- Documentary (optional): *The Greatest Good: A Forest Service Centennial Film,* produced by the U.S. Forest Service (the DVD can be ordered at www.foresthistory.org/Publications/new.html)

RISK MANAGEMENT CONSIDERATIONS

Not applicable

STUDENT PREPARATION

Require students to read the Background (on CD-ROM), or ask them to read either one of the following texts:

- Chapter 13, "Parks and Protected Area Management," in B. Martin, C. Cashel, M. Wagstaff, and M. Breunig, 2006, *Outdoor Leadership: Theory and Practice* (Champaign, IL: Human Kinetics).
- "Wilderness Management in the United States," 2006, in J. Lamb and G. Goodrich, *NOLS Wilderness Ethics: Valuing and Managing Wild Places* (Mechanicsburg, PA: Stackpole Books).

INSTRUCTOR PREPARATION

Outside the classroom and before class, prepare the miniature national forest. See the map of Mount Wow on the CD-ROM. Gather all the necessary materials and the handout. Print the labels and the activity handout (on CD-ROM).

LESSON CONTENT AND TEACHING STRATEGIES

Explain to your students that in this lesson you would like to help them better understand and appreciate the complexity behind the management of public lands in America. Explain that this lesson will help them clarify the recent reading they have done regarding public land agencies in the United States.

Now ask this initial question to build a rationale for the lesson and the content knowledge it includes: "Why should outdoor professionals know about how public lands in America are managed?"

Your class should come up with answers easily since public lands are often used for adventure programming. However, if the class has difficulty finding a rationale for learning about public land agencies and their management practices, ask a few more questions in guided-discovery style to bring out the appropriate answers.

- Where have you been camping recently?
- If you have worked for a camp or outdoor program, where have you run your outdoor pursuit programs?
- Why are you allowed to bring groups onto public lands?
- What other human activities did you see happening on these public lands?
- Why do you think these activities (e.g., logging, off-road vehicle touring, hunting, fishing) are allowed on public lands?

Once their curiosity has been stimulated, explain that to help them answer these questions you would like to lead them in a small simulation having to do with the management of a very special area in the Beau National Forest called Mount Wow National Forest. It just happens that a miniature reproduction of Mount Wow National Forest is right outside the building. But tell the students that before they go out to look at this amazing area, roles have to be established for everyone.

Activity 1: The Beau National Forest Land and Resource Management Plan

Explain that to complete this simulation, you need three volunteers to represent the Beau National Forest district ranger and his or her staff. Explain also that ideally you want three people who can remain neutral throughout the simulation—people who will want to hear and respect the ideas of all stakeholders.

Now enlist the rest of the class into all the interest groups in the following list. Make sure that you ask for volunteers who have a personal interest in the function of the interest group; for instance, ski lovers should volunteer to play the role of the ski industry, students who enjoy motorized outdoor recreation should volunteer to represent the recreation industry, and so on. Try to have students distributed evenly among the interest groups.

- Logging industry: Green Cut Logging Company
- Railroad company: National Heritage Train Company
- Ski industry: Ski-Pro Industry
- Conservation group: Friends of the Earth
- State university: Research Center for the Environment
- Recreation industry: ATV Master Club
- Adventure tourism industry: Rodeo Rafting Company

Now that everyone has a role, distribute labels to use as name tags identifying the various interest groups, move your class outside, and ask them to bring materials for writing (i.e., pens and papers).

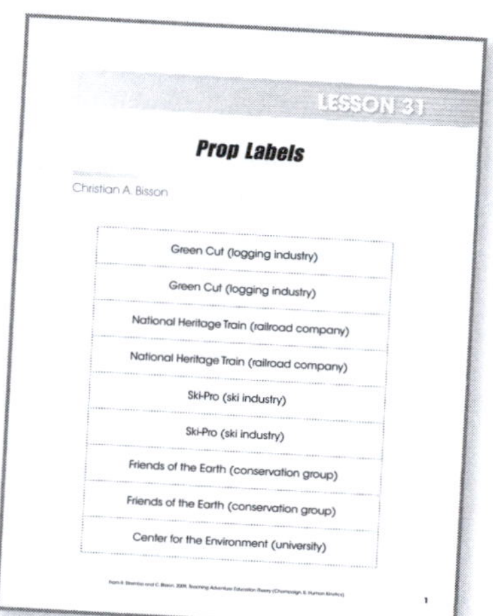
LESSON 31

Prop Labels

Christian A. Bisson

Green Cut (logging industry)

Green Cut (logging industry)

National Heritage Train (railroad company)

National Heritage Train (railroad company)

Ski-Pro (ski industry)

Ski-Pro (ski industry)

Friends of the Earth (conservation group)

Friends of the Earth (conservation group)

Center for the Environment (university)

1

Once outside, gather the students around the miniature of Beau National Forest and use the miniature to explain the following:

This year, the Beau National Forest District from the USFS must review its land and resource management plan. One particular area of the district is attracting a lot of attention from various stakeholders; this area is called Mount Wow National Forest. It is a 500,000-acre area that has been isolated from the public for centuries; but since the completion of the new interstate highway on the western side of the National Forest (NF), accessing the Mount Wow region has been much easier than before.

Mount Wow National Forest is composed of mountains, large valleys, wild rivers, old growth, beautiful scenery, and a second-growth mixed forest. It also features, in the south, an old railroad established by an early logging company that failed due to the increased cost of production in this isolated region. The following are other relevant facts:

- Mount Wow is a 6,320-foot (1,925-meter) mountain located in the northwest corner of the NF. Mount Wow itself is suitable for the development of a ski resort, and many other remote mountains are also suitable for backcountry skiing or heli-skiing.
- The old-growth area is a pristine area of about 80,000 acres located in the northeast and is mainly composed of large conifer trees and very rare fern species.
- A large valley stretches from the north to the south of the NF and contains a wild river called River Wow. River Wow is suitable for paddling and rafting.
- The southern part of the NF reveals a more level landscape with a healthy second-growth mixed forest.

Explain that the Beau National Forest District is now collecting public opinion on the management of Mount Wow National Forest. Tell the students: Your task as invested stakeholders is to come up with proposed actions for the Beau National

Forest District. Obviously your proposed actions should reflect your group's main interest. You will present your proposed actions to the Beau National Forest District staff at a formal public meeting to be held in 15 minutes.

LESSON 31

The Beau National Forest Dilemma

Christian A. Bisson

Size

500,000 acres

Type

Mountains, large valleys, old growth, beautiful scenery, large areas of pristine value

Purpose

Land for multiple uses

Location

A new highway, just developed on the eastern side, is connected to two large metropolitan areas.

Issue

Beau National Forest needs a new management plan. Input is being sought from various groups.

Logging Industry: Green Cut

Wants to have access to 130,000 acres on the western side of Beau National Forest.

Is willing to share the road with recreationists like ATV and hikers.

Railroad Company: National Heritage Train

Wants to rebuild and extend an old railroad that would cross the entirety of Beau National Forest from north to south.

Wants to give all citizens access to the beauty of the land.

Ski Industry: SkiPro

Wants to develop a ski and snowboard center on Mount Wow, the largest mountain in Beau National Forest. Mount Wow is located on the eastern side of the forest.

Also wants to offer heli-ski service on the most remote peaks.

1

At this point, ask if anyone has questions about the role play; then distribute to each interest group the Beau National Forest Dilemma handout (on the CD-ROM).

When every team has completed their survey of the Mount Wow region, return to the classroom and introduce the following tasks:

Task 1: Design a Proposed Action First, draw a map of Mount Wow National Forest and indicate all the pertinent features. Second, start designing your proposed action, that is, how you would like the Beau National Forest District to manage Mount Wow National Forest. Use the handout guidelines to help you come up with your proposed action.

Task 2: Present the Proposed Action Plan your presentation by electing a spokesperson. Draw your proposed action for the management of Mount Wow National Forest on the map transparency provided. Make sure you highlight the benefits of your proposed action.

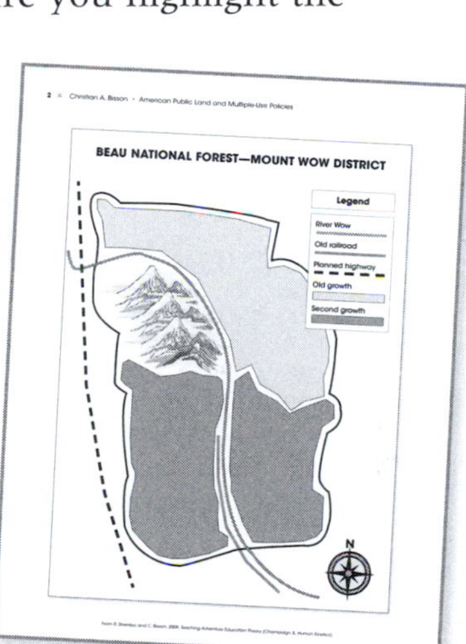

Task 3: Lobby for Your Proposed Action At any time during the simulation, you can lobby the district ranger and his or her staff regarding your proposed action.

Once everyone is ready, rearrange the room as a public meeting place. Place the USFS employees behind a table in the front of the classroom. Use an overhead projector to display the map of Mount Wow National Forest (on CD-ROM).

Now explain that this will not be a debate, but a public hearing, and that all U.S. citizens have a right to propose an action via a special-use permit application for the management of public lands such as those overseen by the USFS or the BLM. Furthermore, explain that in the spirit of the Multiple-Use and Sustained-Yield Act (MUSY) of 1960 for the USFS (on CD-ROM) and the Federal Land Policy Management Act (FLPMA) of 1976 for the BLM (on CD-ROM), public lands shall be administered for outdoor recreation; commercial activities; research; land, watershed, and wildlife conservation; and wilderness preservation.

Invite each special interest group to present their proposed action by using the overhead projector and giving a description of and rationale for their proposal.

Explain that at this stage, only employees of the NF can ask questions regarding the proposed actions.

Once every group has presented their proposed action, allow the students playing the roles of the NF employees to step out of class and come up with a new land and resources management plan for Mount Wow National Forest. Ask them to present their plan by using the transparency map of Mount Wow National Forest.

Note that if you teach the class in a 50- to 60-minute format, this task might have to be completed after class and the presentation by the NF employees made in the next class. If this is the case, remind everyone that appropriate lobbying is allowed until the next class.

When the new NF land and resources management plan is ready, invite the staff of Beau National Forest to present their forest plan by using their map transparency. Ask them to explain their decision and what steps they have taken to come up with their decision (i.e., fictive Environmental Assessment [EA] or fictive Environmental Impact Statement [EIS]).

After the presentation by the NF staff, explain that in accordance with the National Environmental Policy Act (NEPA), the Beau National Forest District must request public opinion on its suggested plan and that it is now appropriate for anyone to support, question, or challenge the NF land and resources management plan. So open the floor to enable everyone to comment on the plan for Mount Wow National Forest. This should engender a lively discussion that might require you to do some moderating.

Once you feel that everyone has had a chance to express his or her opinion, officially close the simulation and congratulate all for their participation; give a special acknowledgment to the students who played the roles of the NF employees.

Activity 2: Discussion on the Public Land Multiple-Use Conundrum

If possible, rearrange the class in a large circle for the class discussion. Use the following questions to help your students express their views on the multiple-use and sustained-yield philosophy of the USFS and the BLM:

- What does multiple use and sustained yield mean to the USFS and BLM?
- What does multiple use and sustained yield mean to you?
- What do you think is the rationale behind multiple use and sustained yield?
- Why is multiple use and sustained yield a conundrum?
- If we had to place groups on a spectrum ranging from anthropocentrism to biocentrism, where do you think your special interest group would place itself? (Note that you can represent this spectrum on the blackboard and allow a representative for each special interest group to place him- or herself on the spectrum.)
- Why are some of the groups at opposite ends of the spectrum?
- If one of the special interest groups was a consortium of outdoor education schools, where do you think we would place it on this spectrum and why?

Activity 3: Documentary

This activity is optional for this lesson, but if you can afford the time and if your library has a copy of the documentary *The Greatest Good*, produced in 2006 for the USFS centennial, the activity is worthwhile since it will help your students better understand how the concept of multiple-use and sustained-yield was developed in the United States.

The documentary presents a wonderful exploration of the history of the USFS. Although it is worthwhile to view the entire documentary, it would not be necessary to show the entire film for the purpose of this class. Since the film comes on a DVD, it would be easy for you to select and present the most appropriate vignettes for this lesson. The following is a list of recommended sections of the documentary that you could present to the class. If you show all the recommended sections from Disc 1, you will have to plan for a viewing time of about 23 minutes.

- Disc 1: Part III—Boom! (1941-1970)
  - Section 7—The "Can Do" Agency (3:38 minutes)
  - Section 8—America's Playground (2:17 minutes)
  - Section 9—Multiple Use (1:00 minute)
  - Section 10—Timber Is King (4:33 minutes)
  - Section 11—The Wilderness Act (1:55 minutes)
  - Section 12—Protest and Transformation (1:34 minutes)
- Disc 1: Part IV—The Greatest Good? (1971-2005)
  - Section 1—Monongahela and Bitterroot (3:30 minutes)
  - Section 2—Environmental Laws (1:38 minutes)
  - Section 3—New Voices and Values (3:28 minutes)

If you have more time or if you want to offer the following as an additional assignment, invite your students to view these sections from the second disc:

- Views of the Forest Service
  - Section 1—The Greatest Good Idea (9:50 minutes)
  - Section 2—Laws and Politics (7:41 minutes)

After the showing, open the floor for any questions or observations that the documentary might have stimulated. Make sure to explain that although this film is about the USFS, the story would be almost the same for the BLM and its evolution toward a multiple-use and sustained-yield mandate.

At the end of the questions or comments session, explain that you would like now to review what students have been learning about public lands and their multiple-use policies via a PowerPoint presentation.

Activity 4: PowerPoint Presentation

As you go through the slides, review the concepts and facts discovered during the simulation and the discussion.

Reviewing U.S. Public Land Agencies Slides 2 to 10 begin the presentation with a review of the most widely known U.S. public land agencies. Explain that the next few slides will help your students summarize what they have learned or read about the following agencies:

- National Park Service
- U.S. Fish and Wildlife Service
- U.S. Forest Service
- Bureau of Land Management

While you are reviewing the agencies, place strong emphasis on the purpose and mission of each agency. By the end of the review, your students should know that only the USFS and the BLM have adopted a multiple-use and sustained-yield approach to public land management; this will set the stage for the last part of the PowerPoint presentation.

U.S. Public Land Management Distribution With slide 11, review and illustrate how much land each of the four major public land agencies manages in the

United States (see figure 31.1). As you will notice, the diagram emphasizes that more than half of the public lands are managed by the USFS and the BLM and that both agencies have a multiple-use and sustained-yield mandate.

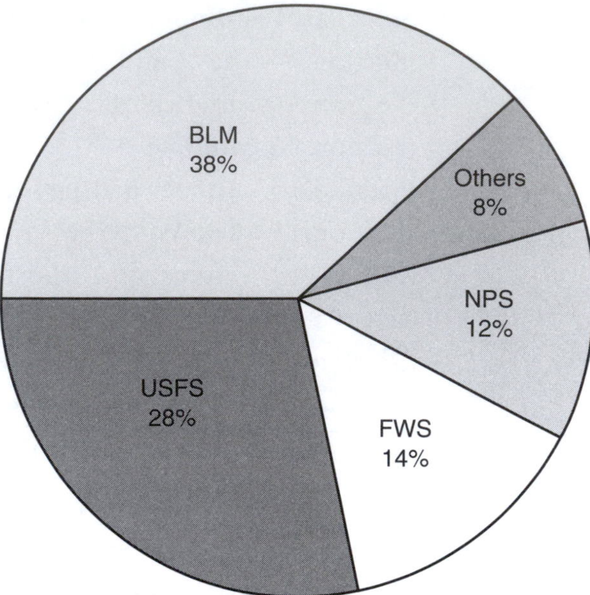

FIGURE 31.1 U.S. federal land management distribution.

Multiple-Use and Sustained-Yield Act (MUSY) Slides 12 through 14 will help your students understand how the MUSY act of 1960 defines multiple use and sustained yield for the USFS. See a copy of the act on the CD-ROM.

Federal Land Policy and Management Act (FLPMA) Slides 15 through 17 will help your students understand how the FLPMA of 1976 defines multiple use and sustained yield for the BLM. See a copy of the act on the CD-ROM.

Public Land Stakeholders and How to Get Involved In closure to the PowerPoint presentation, remind students that their future profession in outdoor or adventure education or recreation is only one stakeholder among many other industries (slide 18). Thus as U.S. citizens and most importantly as young outdoor professionals, they should be aware of and involved in the democratic process of land management in America (slides 19 and 20).

CLOSURE

Ask you students what they will do next. Are they going to get involved? When are they going to get involved? Why are they going to get involved? But most important, how are they going to get involved?

ASSESSMENT OF LEARNING

To assess your students' learning, you can ask them to free write in class about their first impression of the concept of multiple use. Prompt their reflection by asking these types of questions:

- Is a multiple-use and sustained-yield philosophy possible in America?
- Can all interests coexist?
- What role does outdoor education or recreation play in the management of public lands like those overseen by the USFS and the BLM?
- As an outdoor professional, is your public land management opinion biocentric or anthropocentric?

LESSON 32

Loving Nature Through Adventure

Examining Human–Nature Interaction

Peter Martin

As we push into the 21st century, there are increasing signs that humanity is at odds with the well-being of the planet. As a species we have increased our impact on the planet to the extent that it now appears we have fundamentally upset the thermodynamics of the earth and that climate change and its consequences are an increasing reality. In such a world, education that takes students out of doors into more natural settings could well have a mandated role to educate for environmental stewardship. But how in a largely urban society do we educate for a reconnection to nature in a way that promotes acting *for* nature, not just in it? This lesson was developed to encourage students to explore how meaningful, caring relationships with nature could be formed and the implications this has for outdoor experiential education.

Background

While many theoretical contributions underpin this lesson, the three areas of most relevance are concepts of care, metaphorical images of nature, and the conceptualization of language.

Nel Noddings (1984, 1992, 2002) is the originator of several theoretical and philosophical discussions around notions of care. Her writings on care describe how caring exists on a continuum from natural to ethical caring. The best example of natural care, according to Noddings, is the care that a parent exhibits with a newborn infant. In natural caring, an obligation to act on behalf of the other is driven by a powerful subconscious imperative, in which the only decision is how best to enact that caring. As a sense of closeness or proximity to the other decreases, the imperative to act in caring diminishes. The caring then moves toward *ethical* caring, with the individual having to make a conscious decision to act or not act.

Noddings contends that the three primary determinants of caring behavior are proximity, reciprocity, and particular modes of thinking. The role of proximity and closeness is discussed in the lesson outline. The second element, reciprocity, is the degree to which the cared for can reciprocate or respond to the carer's action. According to Noddings, if there is no capacity for response, or if response is weak, then the caring is incomplete and dwindles over time. The ability to learn how to recognize reciprocity, the ability to be open to caring relationships, and knowing how to care effectively underlie the special mode of thinking that Noddings raises as her third element of caring. The particular mode of thinking demanded by caring is the capacity to change between two modes of consciousness, a receptive-intuitive mode and a mode of rational objectivity—or a blending of emotive and rational thought (e.g., Belenky et al. 1986; Knudtson and Suzuki 1992; Sanger 1997; Simpson 1996). This idea has some obvious links to the metaphorical image of nature as a friend, an issue I have written about (Martin 1999a, 1999b). People in outdoor settings who care for nature should recognize how nature responds to or reciprocates that care. Seeing a sunset or the outdoor experience itself as a reward *from* nature may be part of the particular mode of thinking that educators ought to foster to address this issue, and it is clear how a combination of affective and cognitive domains would be involved.

The second theoretical area relevant to the lesson is that associated with metaphorical images of nature. Metaphorical images of nature are pervasive throughout outdoor writing. "Mother Nature," for example, is a common metaphor that implies particular attendant behaviors. Writing in popular outdoor magazines also includes underlying metaphorical imagery, such as cliffs as obstacles or opponents, and magazines can be an interesting source of examples to analyze.

Three useful continuums of human-to-nature relationships use metaphorical imagery and provide interesting ways to conceptualize human-to-nature relationships. The first is the anthropocentric biocentric or ecocentric continuum. Dyer and Gunnel (1993) have developed this continuum by describing a range of differing relationships with nature sketched on a "spectrum of human views of nature" (p. 66). The basis for their spectrum is the assertion that anthropocentrism and biocentrism exist as a continuum of human–nature relationships, not as poles of a dichotomy. Dyer and Gunnel use the light spectrum to represent particular human attitudes to nature. At one end of the continuum, the "infrared fringe" is aligned to totally exploitive behavior; at the other, the "ultraviolet fringe" labels attitudes in which "the rights and interests of other living things are paramount" (p. 66). In describing their spectrum, Dyer and Gunnel outline human attitudes indicative of differing positions on issues such as living parts of nature, energy use, genetic engineering, global population growth, and native peoples. A series of labels describe the differing positions on the spectrum—"Cornucopians, Reformers, Transformers, and Alternativists" (p. 66). The spectral continuum, as well as its language, seems a bit cumbersome and overly complex for ease of use in a classroom. However, the intent of this work is clear: Human relationships and attitudes toward nature vary across a range of possibilities. A specific point stressed by Dyer and Gunnel is that "human-ness" is inescapable; that is, that humans can only know and be human, living as we do in a particular cultural milieu. Any relationship we have with nature, therefore, will be from a perspective of human-ness, hence these authors' choice of a continuum rather than a dichotomy.

A second set of ideas relevant to understanding human–nature relationships is based on the biophilia hypothesis. In 1984 Edward Wilson proposed a theory of biophilia. He hypothesized that humans have a genetically based need for affiliation with life in all its forms, an "innately emotional affiliation of human beings

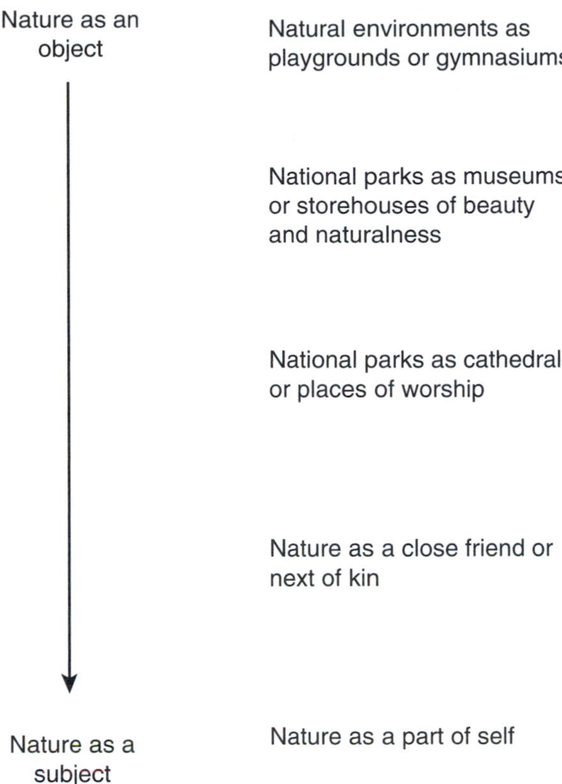

FIGURE 32.1 Metaphorical images of nature.

Adapted, by permission, from P. Martin, 1996, "New perspectives of self, nature and others," *Australian Journal of Outdoor Education* 1(3): 3-9.

to other living organisms" (Kellert and Wilson 1993, p. 31). According to Wilson, this results in a base-level relationship with nature that often occurs subconsciously and affects all human function, including well-being and health, culture, and aesthetic appreciation (Wilson 1984; Kellert and Wilson 1993). Wilson's hypothesis is based on evolutionary logic given that humans have lived as hunter-gatherers for 99 percent of human history. Stephen Kellert (1993, 1996, 1997) proposed a set of nine ways in which humans value nature that support the biophilia hypothesis (Kellert and Wilson 1993). The following two examples illustrate Kellert's concepts. A "negativistic" value reflects the sense that "fear, aversion and alienation" in relation to nature function to ensure "security, protection and safety" of humans (Kellert 1993, p. 59). A "naturalistic" value reflects "satisfaction from direct experience/contact with nature" and functions to ensure "curiosity, outdoor skills, mental/physical development" (Kellert 1993, p. 59). These examples demonstrate both sides of biophilia. Humans can love and hate nature as a consequence of our evolutionary relationship with the natural.

Finally, Martin (1996) after Gough (1990) developed a set of metaphorical images that reflect both objective and subjective images of nature; it is from this material that the lesson was developed. Taken from Martin (1996), figure 32.1 presents some of the metaphorical images that people may have for nature, arranged along a continuum from nature as an object to nature as a subject.

Finally, the lesson challenges students to consider the role of language in shaping beliefs and behaviors in relation to nature. One of the pressing educational dilemmas of our age is how to teach for a sustainable environmental future—in particular, how to educate for the future when the omnipresent growth in consumption and unfettered exploitation of the environment that have characterized past generations are being fundamentally critiqued. Unfortunately, Western culture does not have a good basis in language for conceptualizing and discussing the importance of human-to-nature relationships apart from conceptualizing nature as a resource. This lesson is directed toward that issue and is supported by research that demonstrates how language development and conceptualization of ideas are parallel phenomena. Without the words that enable articulation and dialogue we are stymied so that we cannot deepen our understanding of the underlying concepts; language and depth of understanding must develop together.

Figure 32.2 is taken from Martin (2002). It summarizes diagrammatically a range of differing ideas about human relationships with the natural environment. Each idea has a scholarly literature and discussion potential that could be researched by staff or students interested in exploring further the basic concepts raised in this lesson.

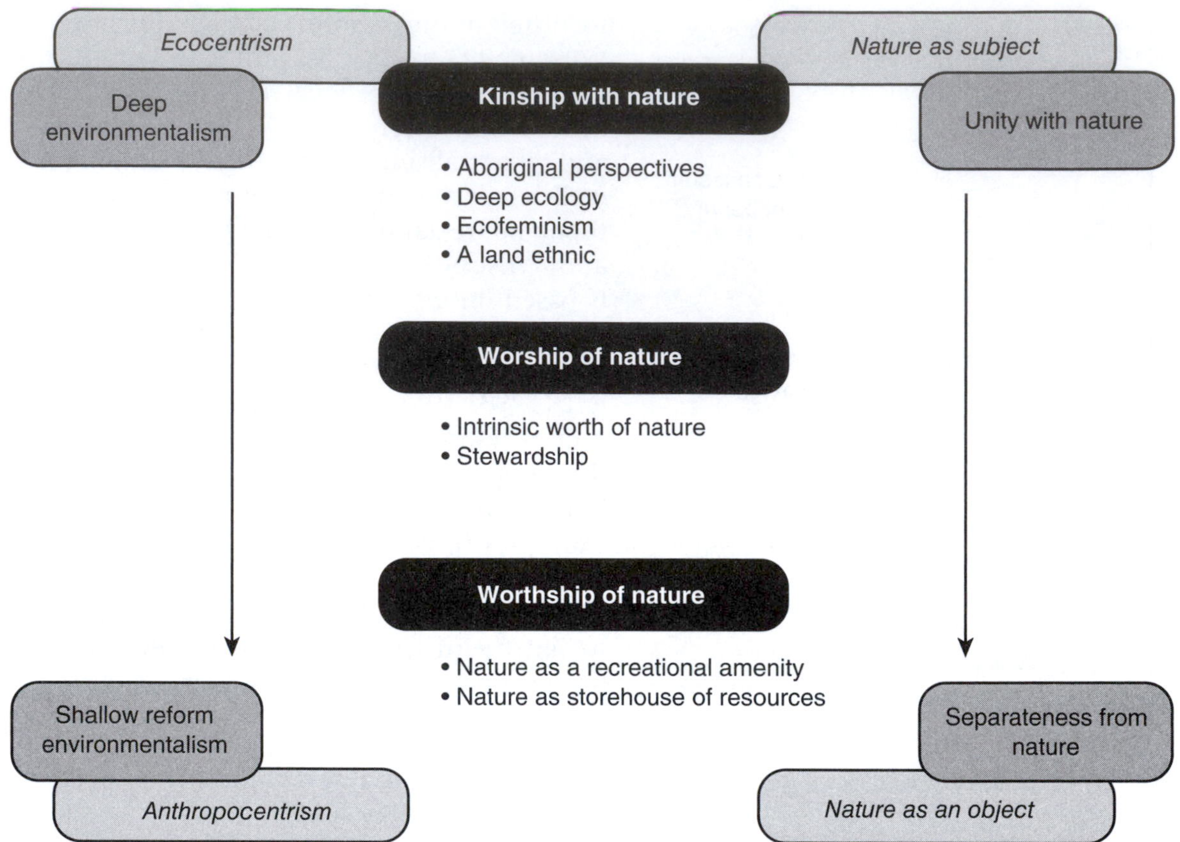

FIGURE 32.2 A summary of conceptions of the human-to-nature relationship.

Adapted from P. Martin, 2002, "A naturalistic inquiry into the role of outdoor education in shaping human to nature relationships" (PhD thesis, La Trobe University).

This type of lesson and the underlying theory are relatively new to adventure programming and outdoor education. No doubt the imperatives of global warming and our deepening ecological crisis will spur us on to find increasingly more effective ways of teaching *for* the natural world in our professional work.

RESOURCES

Belenky, M., B. Clinchy, N. Goldberger, and J. Tarule. 1986. *Women's ways of knowing.* New York: Basic Books.

Chawla, L. 1998. Significant life experiences revisited: A review of research on sources of environmental sensitivity. *Journal of Environmental Education,* 29(3):11-21.

Dyer, K., and P. Gunnell. 1993. Humans and nature: A spectrum not a dichotomy. *Australian Journal of Environmental Education,* 9:53-69.

Gough, N. 1990. Imagining our relationships with nature. Connections: A conference for the environment, the outdoors and camping. Unpublished manuscript, Bendigo, Australia.

Kellert, S. 1993. The biological basis for human values of nature. In *The biophilia hypothesis,* eds. S. Kellert and E. Wilson. Washington, DC: Island Press.

Kellert, S. 1996. *The value of life: Biological diversity and human society.* Washington, DC: Island Press/ Shearwater Books.

Kellert, S. 1997. *Kinship to mastery.* Washington, DC: Island Press.

Kellert, S., and Wilson, E., eds. 1993. *The biophilia hypothesis.* Washington, DC: Island Press.

Knudtson, P., and D. Suzuki. 1992. *Wisdom of the elders.* Sydney: Allen and Unwin.

Martin, P. 1996. New perspectives of self, others and nature. *Australian Journal of Outdoor Education,* 3(1):3-6.

Martin, P. 1999a. Critical outdoor education and nature as friend. In *Adventure education,* eds. J. Miles and S. Priest. 2nd ed. State College, PA: Venture.

Martin, P. 1999b. Daring to care? Humans, nature and outdoor education. *Australian Journal of Outdoor Education,* 4(1):2-4.

Martin, P. 2002. A naturalistic inquiry into the role of outdoor education in shaping human to nature relationships. Unpublished PhD thesis, La Trobe University.

Martin, P. 2005. Human to nature relationship through outdoor education. In *Outdoor and experiential learning: Views from the top,* eds. T. Gray, T. Dickson, and B. Hayllar. Otago, NZ: Otago University Press.

Noddings, N. 1984. *Caring: A feminine approach to ethics and moral education.* Berkeley, CA: University of California Press.

Noddings, N. 1992. *The challenge to care in schools: An alternative approach to education.* New York: Teachers College Press.

Noddings, N. 2002. *Educating moral people: A caring alternative to character education.* New York: Teachers College Press.

Sanger, M. 1997. Sense of place and education. *Journal of Environmental Education,* 29(1):4-8.

Simpson, S. 1996. A Leopold for the nineties: The ecological age and outdoor recreation. *Journal of Experiential Education,* 19(1):14-21.

Wilson, E., ed. 1984. *Biophilia: The human bond with other species.* Cambridge, MA: Harvard University Press.

Lesson Plan

PURPOSE

The purpose of this lesson is to introduce the concept of and language for human relationships with the natural world, for students to begin the process of considering how such relationships are formed and fostered, and for them to reflect on the implications of this for adventure programming.

OBJECTIVES

As a result of this lesson students will be able to . . .

1. *Affective:* feel that relationships with nature are possible and, like interpersonal relationships, are based in the affective domain.
2. *Cognitive:* explain the concept of a relationship with nature using language introduced in the lesson.
3. *Cognitive:* examine the implications of relationships with nature for the planning and conduct of outdoor experiences.
4. *Spiritual:* begin to acknowledge the possibility of affinity between humans and nature.

DURATION

Two 50-minute classes, split after activity 2, either consecutive or separated. A short version could be completed in 50 minutes.

GROUP SIZE

Appropriate for up to 40 students split into smaller groups of four to six

LOCATION

Indoors or outdoors (spaces are needed that will allow groups to work together)

EQUIPMENT

- Large white sheets of paper, two per group minimum
- Felt-tip pens for everyone
- Whiteboard

RISK MANAGEMENT CONSIDERATIONS

Be aware that exploration of deeper personal relationships can be confronting, embarrassing, or upsetting for some people.

STUDENT PREPARATION

The lesson best flows as part of a sequence examining human–environment interactions.

INSTRUCTOR PREPARATION

No preparation required.

LESSON CONTENT AND TEACHING STRATEGIES

This lesson could be introduced in many ways, mostly depending on the context of the program in which it may be useful. For me the course is titled "Ways of Knowing Nature"; students develop a more critical perspective on how knowledge of the natural environment is developed and valued within Western culture. Some of the course touches on history and philosophy of science, but most of the instruction is aimed at developing in students a naturalist's knowledge of the environment founded in lived personal experience and direct inquiry around observations in nature. I usually have preceded this lesson with material from environmental life history research (see Chawla 1980 for an introduction) and with extracts that draw on the life of inspirational environmentalists. (High-profile environmentalists such as Al Gore or David Suzuki can be inspirational. However, for the lesson's intent I find that students identify most with local people who have impact in their hometown and can often be identified in local media coverage.)

Activity 1: Would You Stop?

Set the scene for the lesson by asking students to think about what motivates them to act to help others. You can use the following simplified scenario as a starter.

> You're driving home. You pass a motorist on the side of the road struggling to change what appears to be a flat tire on the rear of the car. It's raining, hard! You see the person slipping in the roadside mud in efforts to position the spare tire. Do you stop?

You can quickly gain responses from a few students about whether they would stop to help or not, and this can be done in a classroom. Alternatively, if space allows, it is more insightful to have students literally take a position on the question. To achieve this, ask students to line up across the room or other space on an imaginary Likert-type scale. A student who would definitely stop would take a space to the far right. A student who would definitely *not* stop would go to the far left. Levels of inclination occur in each direction, or a student who is undecided on the issue can stay in the center. The physical movement allows students some time to interact among themselves on the issue and quickly enables the whole class to see how others respond. This introduction can then become a lesson in its own right as students compare and explore the underlying beliefs and motivations for their respective actions, both within and between the clusters of students across the space. Additional questions can help tease out the underlying issues of importance. For example, students could shift to take up a new position based on the following possibilities:

- As you drive by, you suddenly recognize that the person changing the tire is your neighbor.
- What if the person was your boyfriend, your girlfriend, or your mother?
- What if the person was someone you knew but who you thought was very selfish in his or her own behavior?

The intent of this first exercise is to encourage students to think about how their actions to care for another, to lend assistance in this case, are influenced by a range of factors. Use a whiteboard to list the aspects that students suggest are influential on their decision to stop. This part of the lesson is really exciting as students articulate and explore the impact of differing considerations. Often there are differences between responses from men and women as issues of personal security and capacity to help emerge. The prompting questions help elicit responses about how the strength of the relationship affects the obligation to another.

The most salient factor influencing people's propensity to act in a caring way turns out to be their sense of relatedness, best referred to as their *proximity to the other.* We care most for those with whom we have developed a close relationship (mother and child; best friends). As proximity decreases, so does our obligation to care and act. ("Someone ought do something.") It is important that this exercise distill the importance of proximity. In addition, how safe and competent a person feels is also relevant to help make parallels between emotional relationships and relationships with the natural world.

There is much to discuss here, with plenty of implications for leaders, teachers, and providers of first aid, among others. The activity can also challenge some fundamental beliefs about egalitarianism. While such issues are important, in this lesson you want to move to ultimately consider issues of human relationships to the natural world. This initial exercise is a useful way to raise far more questions than answers and to stimulate thinking about our sense of ethical obligations to others. The next exercise is directed toward considering how close relationships develop.

Activity 2: Developing Friendships

Working in small groups (four to six), students build the stages and contexts in which their own friendships with people have been fostered. Each group has a large sheet of paper and felt-tip pens.

At the top of the sheet they write "A really close relationship." Students then discuss, agree on, and note the sorts of *processes* and *events* that often take place to enable close relationships to materialize. It is often best to initiate the exercise by asking "How do friendships start?" This enables groups to recognize that introductions or initial meetings can take varying forms, which can influence the likelihood of a friendship's growing. The context of a positive initial meeting is noted on the bottom of the sheet, setting the stage for students to suggest the *sequences* appropriate for building toward the goal at the top.

This is a far harder task than some may immediately recognize. It requires students to use their own experiences and to find the language appropriate for description. Encourage the groups to be as specific as possible. For example, someone may suggest, "Spend quality time with the other person." What does this mean? "Okay, time sharing positive experiences. Time with no other pressing distractions." So, does sharing less positive or busy time not help build a relationship? As a teacher you can rotate through the groups, prompting students to explore their ideas in greater depth.

There are clearly no correct answers in this exercise. Similarly, some groups may decide that a sequence implied by placement of the goal at the top of the sheet is constraining and may wish to fashion another model, maybe a spiral. There are two important conclusions to be drawn here.

First, communicating relationship building is complex. We don't have many words or expressions to help us describe the sorts of feelings and growing bonds that are the fabric of relationships. Second, while it is possible to distill some general ideas about how relationships develop, relationships are essentially unique: personal, subjective, and idiographic.

The common outcomes of the exercise are not difficult to envisage, but students may need encouragement to achieve the depth of conceptualization required. Commonly they would list aspects such as a sense of initial attraction, positive friendly first experience, feeling comfortable with the person, shared interests, shared time both good and not so good, lots of time together, meeting the person's family or other friends, learning more about the other's background and likes and dislikes, developing a sense of trust that the person will be supportive, and having an intuitive sort of communication with the other. These are some of the outcomes teachers can prompt students to consider as they move among groups.

Two options are available depending on the time allotment and the number of groups involved. Groups can report to the collective while the teacher develops an amalgamated model on the whiteboard. Or, the groups can immediately move on to the next exercise after a brief introduction. If there are fewer than eight groups it is best to report centrally. It is helpful to draw ideas from the collective, as different groups will have articulated responses in different ways. A good combined model is useful with the next exercise, and as a teacher you can help highlight key aspects.

Activity 3: Nature as a Friend?

The metaphorical image of nature as a friend is the basis for the exercise. The beginning assumption is that people develop relationships with nature in ways similar to how they develop relationships with people. Although contestable, some research evidence suggests that this is the case—consider, for example, the relationships people develop with their pets. The task for the group is to construct another relationship development diagram. This time the top of the sheet is labeled "A close relationship with nature?" Students use the knowledge they have just detailed about interpersonal relationships (either their model or the amalgamated model) to draw parallels to developing a relationship with nature. This is complex but also insightful. The groups should consider each of the elements and brainstorm how the element may transfer to a relationship with nature. Several key realizations ought to be encouraged:

- Relationships can't happen with all of nature, in the same way that people don't develop friendships with all of humanity. Nature needs to be subjectified as individual places or entities. This is why the label at the top of the sheet concluded with a question mark. A relationship with a specific place seems most instructive. During the exercise it is therefore helpful if students can work through this notion and change the statement at the top of their sheet to reflect their new understanding. For example, they might change the label to "A close relationship with Mount Arapiles," now omitting the question mark.

- Introductions to a place become important. Do they stress the dangers and risks of the place or the positive learning and experiences to be gained?
- Encounters with natural environments through recreation are normally confined to certain times of the day and year. The recognition that diverse encounters build relationships carries significant implications for any programming with environmental goals.
- The importance of revisiting places is a core realization. Only through extended repeat encounters with the same place can relationships begin to parallel the depth of interpersonal relationships.
- Comfort and a positive supportive relationship with a place come from having the basic outdoor skills and competence to be at ease in the place. This is akin to the sorts of fundamental interpersonal skills we all learn and develop as children. When we were children, the adults in our lives taught us how to behave in social settings—how to greet and meet people and engage in conversation, for example. Sometimes such teaching was direct, but mostly it was modeled. How to be comfortable outdoors and build a relationship with place also demands skills that can be either directly taught or modeled by the instructor.

There are many other parallels that can carry significant and thought-provoking implications for outdoor adventure programming. There is no right or wrong answer to the issues in this lesson, but the process will inevitably result in students' reevaluating the way in which outdoor and adventure education shapes encounters with natural environments.

CLOSURE

In closure, the learning needs to be brought back to the whole group by way of a summative list of implications. The content of this list will begin to look like an expanded version of the list in the previous section. The intent is to pool the insight that the individual groups developed. The discussion is usually best led by the teacher, using a whiteboard to draw together the contributions from the groups.

A further point can be made about the importance of language and about how a metaphorical image of nature as a friend can help us to understand and reflect on our relationship with nature. This idea can be explored through other metaphorical images used to reflect differing relationships and subsequent behavior. For example, one might use the contrasting metaphors of Mount Arapiles as a *football field* and as a *cathedral*. These two images immediately evoke particular ideas of how people relate to and behave in such settings.

One may also note examples of indigenous language that enable greater understanding of nature (such as the multiple Inuit words for snow). Similarly, outdoor recreation enables us to use words to describe environments in particular ways and often with a depth inaccessible to the uninitiated. For example, the rock climber's vocabulary for the features and lines on a cliff allows a vision of detail far beyond that available to the nonclimber. Such language also allows climbers to understand and relate to rocky places more than those lacking such insight. It is interesting to note that outdoor pursuits enable people to know and to develop a relationship with places in particular ways, both positive and negative, in terms of their environmental sustainability. Not all relationships are supportive and mutually empowering. Those who engage in outdoor recreation have a choice about what sort of relationship they can develop with the places they choose to visit. Guided by *nature as a friend,* adventure programming is ultimately challenged to develop in students the receptivity to a mutually supportive relationship with a place; this relationship demands that they listen to what the place has to say about their presence.

ASSESSMENT OF LEARNING

The exercises have led students through a process of considering how a metaphorical image of nature as a friend, and the language that it enables, could change the way in which people encounter and behave in a specific place. A summative assessment task as homework before the next class can entail asking students to think of another metaphorical image of nature. They should then develop for that image a corresponding set of implied beliefs and behaviors. This is higher-order thinking, but quite appropriate for university students in specialist outdoor programs. Objective images that students sometimes come up with include the outdoors as a play space like a football field, a cathedral or place of worship, a book or source of information, a museum, a supermarket, a storehouse, a refuse dump. Students can also develop subjective images beyond that of nature as a friend, such as that of nature as a mother, an enemy, a confidant, or a master or slave. In each case students need to show that they understand the implications of their image for how people may behave in the outdoors.

LESSON 33

A Walk in the Woods

Teaching Ecopsychology Experientially

Bob Henderson and Deborah Schrader

Take 40 lecture-weary, schedule-fatigued undergraduate students on a walk in the woods with a handful of sensory-building activities, a campfire circle, some sincere story sharing about mystical nonhuman relations, and you don't need to "PowerPoint" ecopsychology. You will be doing it! That was our opinion in creating a 2-hour workshop intended to introduce ecopsychology, deep ecology, ecosophy, and any other "ology" or "osophy" that aspires to suggest the idea that nature is integral to the human psyche. "Walk in the Woods" is what we call it. We know the students respond. It is a consciously simple idea and activity. Yet it reveals a complex set of reflections on the nature of schooling, the nature of cultural sustainability, and the nature of nature. Certainly, for some students the 2-hour class is likely just a walk in the woods with another set of concepts to memorize, another set of words to later recall on a test. But for many (as suggested by varied and informal student feedback), a complex array of reflections revealed through experience might serve as a wake-up call to the consideration of personal practice tied to grounded academic theory.

Background

Theodore Roszak is credited with coining the term *ecopsychology*, popularized through his books *Voice of the Earth* (1992) and *Ecopsychology* (1995), the latter an anthology coedited with Mary Gomes and Allen Kanner. Ecopsychology combines the science of psychology, that of the mind and behavior, with the science of ecology, the study of living organisms in relation to their environment. Ecopsychologists work on the idea that the needs of humans and the needs of the earth fall along the same continuum, resulting in a synergistic relationship between planetary and personal well-being. This relationship is one that has been with humans through all of time, although it is one that has been undermined by Western societies.

The authors would like to thank colleague Liz Newberry for her part in cocreating this workshop.

Through an illusion of separation, we have forgotten that we are simply one part of the huge ecosystem. We have set ourselves apart, collectively naming those "other" species nature.

Chellis Glendinning's notion of *primal matrix* recognizes a relationship between consciousness and our everyday lives, our everyday lifestyle decisions. Glendinning describes the primal matrix as "the state of being of a wholly healthy functional psyche in full-bodied participation with a healthy wholly functioning earth." The primal matrix exists naturally between a healthy person and a healthy earth. This connection really has only to be recalled. This leads to an immutable link between two important social issues of our time—the personal psychological journey that each of us faces and the overwhelming state of ecological crisis that our planet faces. Our "civilized" ways have separated us from the universal ways of "primitive" societies. Ecopsychology stresses that there is no way to understand current environmental issues without asking why they are happening, why each of us continues to make lifestyle choices that endanger the health of the planet that sustains us. It views the trauma of the planet (global warming) as inextricably linked to the trauma of the person (hopelessness, alienation). True and full growth through ecopsychology (ecological healing and social or personal change) returns us to this symbiotic existence and allows us to recall the connection between humans and nature already alive in our genetic makeup.

RESOURCES

Butala, S. 1994. *The perfection of the morning: An apprenticeship with nature.* Toronto: HarperCollins.

Cohen, M. 1987. *How nature works: Regenerating kinship with planet earth.* Portland, OR: World Peace University.

Cohen, M. 1995. *Reconnecting with nature.* Washington, DC: Friday Harbour–Project Nature Connect.

Devall, B., and G. Sessions. 1985. *Deep ecology: Living as if nature mattered.* Salt Lake City: Peregrine Smith Books.

Fisher, A. 2002. *Radical ecopsychology: Psychology in the service of life.* Albany, NY: SUNY Press.

Glendinning, C. 1994. *My Name is Chellis and I'm in recovery from western civilization.* Boston: Shambhala.

Merrill, C. 1991. *The forgotten language: Contemporary poets and nature.* Salt Lake City: Gibbs-Smith.

Roszak, T. 1992. *Voice of the earth.* New York: Simon & Schuster.

Roszak, T., M. Gomes, and A. Kanner, eds. 1995. *Ecopsychology.* San Francisco: Sierra Club.

Lesson Plan

PURPOSE

The purpose of the ecopsychology "Walk in the Woods" class specifically is not to talk about ecopsychology but to "do it." It is a "simple in means, rich in ends" set of activities that should strike a powerful chord with students ready for the simple message "We are of the earth, need the earth, and now the earth needs us." Ultimately, the purpose of the class is to invite students to collectively engage in the reconciliation needed to cultivate ecological consciousness. "I think that we have so allowed the scientific approach to the world to take over our perceptions that we are afraid to mention our experiences for fear of being laughed at or vilified" (Butala 1994, p. 64).

OBJECTIVES

As a result of this lesson students will be able to . . .

1. *Affective and psychomotor:* participate in an experience that provides a better appreciation for nature.
2. *Cognitive:* explain that the planet and humankind have a reciprocal relationship and that anthropocentrism is not sustainable over the long term.
3. *Cognitive:* explain the philosophical tenets behind ecopsychology.
4. *Cognitive:* explain the philosophical tenets behind deep ecology.
5. *Spiritual:* display signs of appreciation for the natural world and its restorative qualities.
6. *Spiritual:* display signs of a renewed sense of wonder toward the natural world.

DURATION

120 minutes

GROUP SIZE

Up to 40 students

LOCATION

A small forest near the campus is perfect.

EQUIPMENT

- Some out-of-place items for the camouflage game—for example, empty pop bottle, crumpled paper, paper clip (about 15 items)
- Some popsicle sticks and string to create the Miniature Park activity
- Firewood and some water for a small campfire experience
- A guitar if you or one of your students is musically inclined
- "Five Minute Field Trip Manual" by Gareth Thompson. This manual can be printed at no cost from www.geoec.org/lessons/5min-fieldtrips.pdf.

RISK MANAGEMENT CONSIDERATIONS

Set boundaries for the student solo time and do a head count to ensure that all students return.

STUDENT PREPARATION

Students must know that for this class, they will be walking and exploring in the woods. Dressing appropriately is important for a successful time for all.

INSTRUCTOR PREPARATION

Gather all the equipment needed for the lesson. Prepare the wooded area for the lesson: (1) Plant the "out-of-place" items along a trail; (2) prepare the material needed to make a campfire. If a fire ring does not already exist, use a fire pan. In either case, make sure you can legally build a fire in this forest.

LESSON CONTENT AND TEACHING STRATEGIES

When everyone is in class, verify whether all students are ready to go outside for the lesson, and check for appropriate clothing and footwear. Once they are all ready, invite them to follow you in a special journey—a journey that will introduce them to a renewed vision of their own campus. Invite them to a "Walk in the Woods."

Activity 1: Spirit Visit

The hike is introduced with a "spirit visit" from any number of ecopsychology-minded writers. You can use authors such as Theodore Roszak, Michael Cohen, and Chellis Glendinning or any other of your liking.

- Theodore Roszak is a cultural historian. He lives in the San Francisco area and has written widely on cultural themes and our need for change to live harmoniously with the earth and each other.
- Michael Cohen was a central figure in creating the Audubon Expedition Institute and the undergraduate and graduate program that travels by bus in regions of North America. He is an outspoken author who promotes the full use of our senses and ecopsychology.
- Chellis Glendinning is a practicing clinical psychologist in the American Southwest who uses nature therapy in addiction counseling.

Other characters who could be presented in a spirit visit for ecopsychology include the cultural anthropologist-philosopher Paul Shepard, the Canadian naturalist John Livingston, and the American author Terry Tempest Williams.

You should know four to six facts and a central philosophical idea for each of these ecopsychology-minded folks.

In character, tell the students about "your" work or writing and hike with them to the edge of the forest. The dramatized character then departs. Now in your normal teaching persona, lead students into the woods and start a short walk.

Activity 2: Sensory Awareness Activities

First, engage your students in a set of 5-minute activities to draw out the senses. You might use ideas from the Institute for Earth Education; you can also use the "Five Minute Field Trip Manual" by Gareth Thompson of the Canadian Parks and Wilderness Society. As students walk along a wooded trail, play a camouflage game. Items that do not really belong are preplanted along the trail. Students walk the trail in silence and try to count all the preplanted items. This activity is simple, easy, and fun. You can also have students map the sounds they hear or smell natural objects found in a forest. These are classic sensory outdoor education activities. With these activities, your students should begin to focus their attention toward their natural surrounding and gain a greater awareness of their senses. Once their awareness level is heightened, move on to the next activity, the miniature park.

Activity 3: The Miniature Park

The Miniature Park activity involves creating groups of three to five students. Each group is invited to create a themed micropark in nature with popsicle sticks and string. Their park or theme trail will showcase specific natural features found in a small patch of ground. Students may build around a small puddle and incorporate a water theme into their micropark. They could also "see" features in the microlandscape that create an adventure park. Students often highlight a single feature—perhaps a rock becomes a mountain range—and build the park around that feature. The smallest fern becomes a giant white pine. They share their created park with other groups. This activity again elicits both an opening of the senses and simple, playful engagement in nature.

Activity 4: Mini-Lecture on Ecopsychology

Next introduce your students to the concept of ecopsychology. Discuss the subject for about 10 minutes. Explain that Theodore Roszak is credited with coining the term ecopsychology. Ask students to guess what this "new" (ancient really) field of study is concerned with. Guide them to discover the answer: Ecopsychology combines the science of psychology, that of the mind and behavior, with the science of ecology, the study of living organisms in relation to their environment.

Now briefly explain that ecopsychologists work on the idea that the needs of humans and the needs of the earth fall along the same continuum, resulting in a synergistic relationship between planetary and personal well-being. This relationship is one that has been with humans throughout time, although it is one that has been undermined by Western societies. Conclude your explanation with this thought: Modern life is has created an "illusion of separation"; we have forgotten that we are simply one part of the huge ecosystem. We have set ourselves apart, collectively naming those "other" species nature.

Activity 5: Mini-Solos

The mini-solo is a simple activity in which students are scattered into the woodlot for 10 minutes, a long time for many. Give them very little direction other than to say that this is intended as a quiet, alone time, one that could be a part of a person's understanding of a needed practice in daily life. Don't forget to establish a special call to bring them back, such as an owl or wolf call. If you can imitate a loon call, that is even better.

Activity 6: Fire and Sharing

While students are on their solo, prepare and light the campfire at a designated and approved site or in your fire pan. This is really the main event. A suitable song could be played with a guitar, or a poem about nature could be shared; but this time is mostly for telling stories concerning exceptional moments you have experienced or follies you have committed within nature.

The following is a useful quote you could share after the solo: "That the self advances and confirms the myriad things is called delusion. That the myriad things advance and confirm the self is enlightenment" (Zen Master Dogen).

A story we have told concerns an eye-to-eye meeting with a wolf on a Labrador River just before a rapid dumped our boat. Was there some warning or intention in the wolf's poignant gaze? Another, urban-based story, similarly concerned with exceptional moments of connection, is about a cyclist who encounters young foxes and shares the experience visually with another person driving by. The goal of telling a story is to have the students loosen up so that they can share their own stories.

Activity 7: Mini-Lecture on the Primal Matrix

When a few have had the opportunity to share, introduce some theoretical concepts relating to what they are presently experiencing. Share with them what Chellis Glendinning calls the "primal matrix." Explain that the primal matrix is "the state of being of a wholly healthy functional psyche in full-bodied participation with a healthy wholly-functioning earth." Add that Glendinning describes one's journey to psychological health, to this primal matrix, as movement through three dimensions of consciousness. The first dimension involves a "sense of belonging and security in the world, trust, faith." This expands one's sense of self through one's relationships. The second dimension nurtures a "sense of personal integrity, centeredness, capability," a conscious process of personal development. The third dimension allows the "capacity to draw vision and meaning from nonordinary states of consciousness." This dimension is also known as the transpersonal, where all is understood as one. Additionally, Glendinning recognizes that experiences within each of these dimensions have the transformative potential toward a fourth dimension, that of a free-flowing, synergistic awareness of interconnectedness. Present these ideas in a very informal manner, as in a casual conversation. Link them back to the shared stories as appropriate.

To close the campfire, ask students if they think this experience was unusual, special, odd for a college class. Of course, all will agree. At this point, you should mention that this is how humanity has functioned in an educational sense for centuries. Telling stories in circles around campfires or the hearth is truly a traditional experience, embedded in our psyche. On the other hand, having students sit in rows, listen, and take notes is a very modern way of conducting the learning process. Reveal that from an anthropological point of view, what we call the "traditional lecture" experience—found in so many universities and colleges—is a recent phenomenon that feels strangely unnatural when compared to our campfire story-sharing circle.

CLOSURE

Class ends at the campfire with students heading off to other classes; or, if they have free time, they may continue the walk. We have observed that unsolicited comments stream in after this experience. Regularly, students comment that they feel refreshed. A student once commented that she had her first good sleep in months the night after the Walk in the Woods. Students often tell us that this lesson has been the highlight of the course and even, on occasion, the highlight of their undergraduate education to date! It seems that a simple walk in the woods might not be so simple. The concepts of ecopsychology become real as a felt experience. An abstract idea comes alive through the walk, a few sensory activities, time alone, and shared stories with friends around the campfire. Two days later in our 1-hour class slot, we lecture on and discuss more of the theory and practice of ecopsychology. But the students already know on a personal level what it is through firsthand embodied learning and understand it as a simple practice that could be part of everyday life. Though it is a modest and short experience, students are attentive to the idea conveyed in this "odd, not so odd" activity that contrasts so sharply with their conventional (but not really traditional) schooling. The experience is at once informal and informative.

ASSESSMENT OF LEARNING

Assess the learning from this activity by observing your students' reactions and participation during the lesson and through the remaining classes that revisit this activity via discussion.

LESSON 34

Loving the Land for Life

The Vital Role of Recreation Ecology

Kelly Rossiter

As outdoor adventure pursuits increase in popularity, so too does the strain that visitors place on our natural areas. Though many outdoor adventure enthusiasts and professionals are familiar with Leave No Trace, many are unfamiliar with the area of study undergirding it—recreation ecology. This lesson introduces students to the importance of recreation ecology and the basic theory involved in this area of study. Equipped with this information, students will have a better understanding of both the land management practices implemented in natural areas and the important role that they will play as outdoor educators in promoting proper care for our natural areas.

Background

The natural character and environmental integrity of public lands in the United States are under increasing strain. This strain is the result of several compounding factors. Most directly, the U.S. population continues to grow, with that growth concentrated on coasts of the continent, where most of the country's wilderness lands are located (Ewert and Hollenhorst 1997). Additionally, outdoor and adventure recreation activities continue to grow in popularity. As our country becomes increasingly urbanized, there appears to be a corresponding increase in our population's drive to experience wilderness (Nash 1967). Today, one in five Americans report camping at least once a year; this constitutes over 60 million user-nights in wilderness lands. With camping predicted to increase by 77% by 2040 and day hiking to explode by almost 200%, a finite amount of wilderness land will experience the strain of an ever-increasing user base (Ewert and Hollenhorst 1997).

These impacts are broadly categorized as either *resource* or *experiential impacts* (Manning and Valliere 1996). Resource impacts are those that alter the physical qualities of the land. Because of their very tangible quality, resource impacts are perhaps the type that most readily comes to mind when we consider "minimum-impact" land use. Perhaps as a result, this is the area in which the majority of impact-related research has been done. The literature offers examples of the wide range of forms these impacts can take. Settina and Marion (2005), in a study of the effects of Leave No Trace educational treatments to state forest visitors, monitored the results in terms of reductions in littering, tree damage, and human waste disposal. Manning and Marion (2005) sought to identify the effects of similar treatments in reducing off-trail travel at Cadillac Mountain, a very popular tour bus destination in Acadia National Park. More drastic—but perhaps less obvious—impacts, such as artifact theft (Widner and Roggenbuck 1999), are also the topic of study in the area of resource impacts.

Though resource impacts may be the most obvious detriment to natural areas, it is important to also consider experiential impacts. Experiential impacts are those that affect the subjective experience of people using the lands. Experiential impacts include such things as crowding in campsites (MacFarlane and Boxall 1998; Manning and Valliere 1996), technological gadgetry, bright colors, and large or loud parties (Waterman and Waterman 1993). Among the many forms of experiential impact, crowding and associated disturbances receive the most research attention. Studies such as that of Hall (2001) have looked at the impact of crowding on visitors' sense of solitude, showing a positive correlation between increased crowding and diminished experiences of wilderness and solitude; 52% of those reporting that they did not have a wilderness experience cited human encounters as the source of that feeling. Schuster and Hammitt (2001) found that such encounters can be the source of "hassles." In that study, 44% of participants cited "noise from other people" as a source of hassle; 36% cited "too many people at campsites"; and 26% cited "too many people on the trail" (p. 27). Table 34.1 presents some examples of resource and experiential impacts (during the lesson, you may want to provide students with one or two examples of each and then see how many more they can brainstorm).

TABLE 34.1 Examples of Resource and Experiential Impacts

Resource impacts	Experiential impacts
Campfires	Crowding
Impacted sites	Excessive control
Too many trails	Noise
Habituated animals	Visual impacts (bright colors, etc.)
Littering	Technology (phones, GPS, etc.)
Vandalism	
Tree damage	
Human waste	
Artifact theft	

Often the two areas overlap (for example, having too many trails causes erosion and leaves a visual impact).

While resource impacts are more permanent than experiential ones, these two types of impacts play an equally important role in the sense of solitude and wilderness that draws people to such lands in the first place. Additionally, there is often an overlap between the two types of impact; for example, impacts to campsites affect both the health of the surrounding ecosystem and the visitors' perception of an area as pristine or not (Farrell, Hall, and White 2001). Thus it is important to take into account both resource and experiential impacts when one is considering how to effectively ensure that visitors minimally affect the areas they go to.

Detrimental visitor actions can be classified into five categories (Marion and Reid 2005):

1. Careless (e.g., accidentally backing into a garbage can because you did not use the rearview mirror)

2. Unskilled (e.g., leaving an ugly fire scar because you did not know how to construct a fire mound)
3. Uninformed (e.g., stepping on cryptobiotic soil because you did not realize how fragile it was)
4. Unavoidable (e.g., cutting down trees in order to build a litter for a rescue)
5. Illegal (e.g., stealing ancient artifacts)

Though education cannot address all five categories, it does play a vital role in ameliorating many of these detrimental actions and their impacts. Visitor education is especially important, considering that mere backcountry experience alone does not impart minimum-impact lessons; a study cited by Marion and Reid (2005) showed that more experienced backpackers were not significantly more knowledgeable about minimum-impact camping skills than less experienced visitors (Thorn 1995). However, education has its limits. The authors write that "Visitor education can only be expected to effectively address unskilled and uninformed actions, and to a lesser extent, careless actions, as these are more highly related to visitor knowledge and skill level" (p. 5).

Factors other than knowledge and skill come into play, affecting visitors' behaviors. Settina and Marion (2005) use the four-stage model of factors first proposed by Harding, Borrie, and Cole (2000) to explain why visitors continue to exhibit depreciative behavior despite education. Beyond knowledge, social and psychological influences play a big role. The following are four factors that can intervene:

1. Lack of skill or willingness to accurately interpret the situation and needed behavior
2. Lack of ability to properly recall the appropriate behavior
3. Influence of ethics on the way a person makes decisions
4. Social pressures that influence behavior choices

Public lands managers seek to mitigate user impacts via three primary avenues:

1. Regulations
2. Site management
3. Education

Each of these avenues has strengths and limitations, as detailed in table 34.2. Regulation (e.g., rules, fines, enforcement) is often the most effective way for dealing with people operating at lower levels of moral reasoning (Marion and Reid 2005); however, it is costly and can adversely affect the visitor experience (Daniels and Marion 2005). Site management techniques, which might include such things as site hardening and installation of restroom facilities, suffer the same limitations.

Visitor education offers an alternative to these measures. In contrast to regulatory measures, "The objective of educational programs is not to 'control' visitor behavior; rather, land managers seek to provide a cognitive basis to encourage appropriate visitor behavior in recreation settings" (Marion and Reid 2005, p. 3). To this end, visitor education offers a mechanism for limiting resource impacts while not creating adverse experiential impacts.

Limiting these resource impacts becomes increasingly important in view of the budget cuts being proposed for federal land management agencies. Already,

TABLE 34.2 Pros and Cons of the Three Different Management Strategies

Pros	Cons
SITE MANAGEMENT	
Often effective at addressing the specific resource/experiential impact	May create other experiential impacts
Works well with uninformed visitors or those with low moral reasoning	Costly
REGULATIONS	
Often effective at addressing the specific resource/experiential impact	May create other experiential impacts
Works well with visitors with low moral reasoning	Often works only when enforcement is present
	Can create defiance
	Costly
EDUCATION	
Empowers visitors to be a part of the solution	May not work with all types of visitors, due to differences in values and/or moral reasoning
Less costly than other methods	Not a one-time "fix-all"

the National Park Service is operating with an estimated $4 to $6 billion deferred maintenance backlog, coming at a time when Congress is wrestling with the prospect of further budget cuts to federal land management agencies (Knickerbocker 2004). In light of such financial challenges and the corresponding need to trim costs associated with the upkeep of management infrastructure (e.g., building and then maintaining new facilities, hiring additional personnel to enforce regulations), and in the face of steadily increasing visitor numbers, effective and efficient education strategies are vital.

METHODS OF DELIVERY OF EDUCATION

Former House of Representatives staff member James Bradley described education as a "pre-emptive strike to teach American peoples how to enjoy the wilderness without destroying it" (Marion and Reid 2001, p. 1).

Recreation ecology education can occur through a wide range of media and methods. The first layer of education methods consists of those that are implemented well in advance of the experience, such as information mailed with permits, public information campaigns, or training received in advance of experiences (e.g., a Leave No Trace trainer course taken so as to disseminate the information to participants). Other delivery methods are targeted toward educating visitors immediately before or during their backcountry experience. Such methods include mailed and on-site brochures, posters, visitor center videos, trailhead signs, and ranger contacts (Yeung and Attarian 2005; Marion and Reid 2005; Settina and Marion 2005). A final method for delivering minimum-impact messages is implemented during the experience, by way of signs on the trail, ranger contacts, and contacts with other independent users or guided- adventure providers.

OUR ROLE IN ASSISTING WITH DELIVERY

Adventure professionals have the potential to be both a major part of the problem in recreation ecology and a major part of the solution. Many people have their first encounters with the natural world under the tutelage of adventure professionals. If adventure professionals do not make a concerted and coordinated effort to teach minimum-impact practices, they become a part of the problem; moreover, they must be prepared to "walk the talk" by educating themselves about the minimum-impact practices particular to the ecologies they are in and the activities they are leading. Finally, they must be prepared to tactfully confront clients and other visitors when they observe minimum-impact lapses. This is obviously a difficult task, and a full analysis of strategies for performing it is beyond the scope of this lesson. Those looking for some brief but helpful materials on providing effective feedback are directed to Priest and Gass (2005, pp. 235-236) or Drury and colleagues (2005, pp. 200-202).

Discussion of adventure professionals as part of the problem and part of the solution often leads people to point out the irony of our work: We love the solace and solitude of wild spaces, yet we make a career out of bringing more people into those places. It is true that if we bring people into the outdoors without engendering a certain respect for it and teaching appropriate behaviors toward it, we have done a disservice; but it is also true that by connecting people to the places we love we have the potential for creating a citizenry that is more prepared to protect these places from farther-reaching and more devastating political impacts (lack of funding, commercialization, loss of land to "development," etc.). Staying aware of both short-term and long-term impacts seems to be the solution, introducing citizenry to their lands and providing them the education necessary to preserve these lands. In the end, it is not a question of "Go or no-go," but one of "How we go." Recreation ecology serves as a useful tool in mapping out that journey.

RESOURCES

Cole, D.N., T.P. Hammond, and S.F. McCool. 1997. Information quantity and communication effectiveness: Low-impact messages on wilderness trailside bulletin boards. *Leisure Sciences,* 8:59-72.

Curtis, R. 1998. *The backpacker's field manual: A comprehensive guide to mastering backcountry skills.* New York: Three Rivers Press.

Daniels, M.L., and J.L. Marion. 2005. Communicating Leave No Trace ethics and practices: Efficacy of two-day trainer courses. *Journal of Park and Recreation Administration,* 23(4):1-19.

Drury, J.K., B.F. Bonney, D. Berman, and M.C. Wagstaff. 2005. *The backcountry classroom: Lessons, tools, and activities for teaching outdoor leaders.* Guilford, CT: Globe Pequot Press.

Ewert, A.W., and S.J. Hollenhorst. 1997. Adventure recreation and its implications for wilderness. *International Journal of Wilderness,* 3(2):21-28.

Farrell, T., T.E. Hall, and D.D. White. 2001. Wilderness campers' perception and evaluation of campsite impacts. *Journal of Leisure Research,* 33(3):229-250.

Hall, T.E. 2001. Hikers' perspectives on solitude and wilderness. *International Journal of Wilderness,* 7(2):20-24.

Harding, J.A., W.T. Borrie, and D.N. Cole. 2000. Factors that limit compliance with low-impact recommendations. In *Proceedings: Wilderness science in a time of change conference, Volume 4: Wilderness visitors, experiences, and visitor management,* eds. D.N. Cole, S.F. McCool, W.T. Borrie, and J. O'Loughlin (compilers), 198-202. Proc. RMRS-P-15-VOL-4. Ogden, UT: U.S. Department of Agriculture, Forest Service, Rocky Mountain Research Station.

Knickerbocker, B. 2004. National parks fast falling into disrepair. *Christian Science Monitor.* www.csmonitor.com/2004/0525/p01s02-usgn.html (accessed December 3, 2005).

LNTCOE. 2005. *What is the Leave No Trace Center for Outdoor Ethics?* http://www.lnt.org/aboutUs/index.php (accessed November 18, 2005).

MacFarlane, B.L., and P.C. Boxall. 1998. Past experience and behavioral choice among wilderness users. *Journal of Leisure Research,* 30(2):195-213.

Manning, R.E., and J.L. Marion. 2005. Cadillac Mountain visitor observation methods. Manuscript in preparation.

Manning, R.E., and W.A. Valliere. 1996. Environmental values, environmental ethics, and wilderness management. *International Journal of Wilderness,* 2(2):27-32.

Marion, J.L., and S.E. Reid. 2001. Development of the United States Leave No Trace program: A historical perspective. In *Enjoyment and understanding of the natural heritage,* ed. M.B. Usher, 81-92. Edinburgh: The Stationary Office.

Marion, J.L., and S.E. Reid. 2001. Development of the U.S. Leave No Trace program: An historical perspective. http://www.bape.gouv.qc.ca/sections/mandats/groulx-levasseur/documents/DD3.pdf (accessed July, 2008).

Marion, J.L., and S.E. Reid. 2005. Minimizing recreation impacts: The efficacy of visitor education programs. Manuscript submitted for publication.

Monz, C.A. 1996. Monitoring recreation resource impacts in two coastal areas of western North America: A preliminary assessment. www.nols.edu/resources/research/Monz_etal.1996a.shtml (accessed November 18, 2005).

Monz, C.A., D.N. Cole, L.A. Johnson, and D.R. Spildie. 1994. Vegetation response to trampling in five native plant communities in the Wind River Range, Wyoming, USA. www.nols.edu/resources/research/Monz_etal.1994a.shtml (accessed November 18, 2005).

Nash, R. 1967. *Wilderness and the American mind.* Binghamton, NY: Vail-Ballou Press.

Priest, S., and M. Gass. 2005. *Effective leadership in adventure programming.* Champaign, IL: Human Kinetics.

Schuster, R., and W.E. Hammitt. 2001. Visitor experiences of stress and reported hassles in the Shining Rock Wilderness Area. *International Journal of Wilderness,* 7(2):26-29.

Settina, N., and J.L. Marion. 2005. Effectiveness of Leave No Trace education treatments at reducing camping impacts in Green Ridge State Forest. Unpublished (in-progress) master's thesis, Frostburg University, Frostburg, Maryland.

Swain, R. 1996. Leave No Trace (LNT)—outdoor skills and ethics program. *International Journal of Wilderness,* 2(3):24-26.

Thorn, T.F. 1995. Teaching low-impact camping practices to wilderness backpackers: An evaluation of trailhead information signing and personal contact. Unpublished master's thesis, University of Utah, Logan.

Waterman, L., and G. Waterman. 1993. *Backwoods ethics: Environmental issues for hikers and campers.* 2nd ed. Woodstock: Countryman Press.

Widner, C.J., and J.W. Roggenbuck. 1999. Reducing theft of petrified wood at Petrified Forest National Park. *Journal of Interpretation Research,* 5(1):1-18.

Yeung, L.F., and A. Attarian. 2005. *Leave No Trace Center for Outdoor Ethics laboratory research findings.* Boulder, CO: Leave No Trace Center for Outdoor Ethics.

Lesson Plan

PURPOSE

Through this lesson's mixture of information, activities, and discussion, students will learn the foundational theories of recreation ecology, consider the role of education in promoting minimum-impact backcountry practices, and explore their role and responsibilities as outdoor educators in that process.

OBJECTIVES

As a result of this lesson students will be able to . . .

1. *Affective and psychomotor:* participate in a range of activities that provide conceptual and emotional linkages to the topics of recreation ecology being presented.
2. *Cognitive:* explain how the various pressures being placed on public lands have brought about the field of recreation ecology.
3. *Cognitive:* explain the two primary types of resource impacts and the five basic classifications of detrimental visitor actions.
4. *Cognitive:* explain the three basic methods for controlling visitor impacts and explain the pros and cons to each approach.
5. *Cognitive:* explain the various methods through which land users can be educated and explain how adventure educators play an important role in the education process.
6. *Affective and cognitive:* express their views about the role that adventure educators play in the care of our public lands and in the education of our clients and other visitors to those places.

DURATION

60 to 90 minutes

GROUP SIZE

Appropriate for 6 to 25 students

LOCATION

Indoors, outdoors, or both (you will need a flat open space large enough to accommodate the group size you are working with)

EQUIPMENT

- Three to four pieces of approximately 2- by 3-foot (0.6- to 0.9-meter) poster board (for making the signs described in the section "Instructor Preparation")
- One permanent marker
- One tent pole per 12 or fewer participants
- Two washers or rings
- One 18-ounce (532-milliliter) beverage bottle (filled with water)
- One 12-ounce (355-milliliter) beverage bottle (filled with water)
- One 10-ounce (296-milliliter) beverage bottle (empty)
- Sponge (to manage water spillage in activity 1 demonstration)
- Small pan (for use with sponge to manage water spillage in activity 1 demonstration)
- Duct tape
- Eight or more balloons (filled with water if outdoor classroom, filled with air if indoor classroom)

- One plastic lunch-type container (about sandwich sized)
- Three large leaves (tree leaves are best, but lettuce or spinach will work)
- One roll of duct tape

RISK MANAGEMENT CONSIDERATIONS

None

STUDENT PREPARATION

No prelesson preparation required

INSTRUCTOR PREPARATION

- So as to demonstrate the various approaches to visitor management, write different kinds of messages on each poster, such as "Please put any gum you are chewing on this poster" (site management); "Do not sit in this chair—$50 fine" (regulation); "So as to improve traffic flow, please don't stand near the entry" (education). Hang the posters in appropriate places prior to the lesson.
- Fill the 12-ounce beverage bottle and the 18-ounce beverage bottle with water. With tape and a marker, label the 12-ounce bottle "Visitors," the 10-ounce bottle "2008," and the 18-ounce bottle "2040."
- Fill balloons with air or water (site dependent) and label them with messages such as "Please stay 3 feet away from this balloon" (site management); "Don't pop—$150 fine" (regulation); and "Popping makes a loud noise that disturbs others—please don't pop the balloon" (education). Strew these about on the floor or ground.
- Take one of the three leaves and put it into the plastic container; take another and put a duct tape tag on the stem that says "Touch stem *only*—or $75 fine"; take the last one and put a duct tape tag on the stem that says "Touching by the stem helps preserve the leaf." These will be used to demonstrate the pros and cons of site management, regulation, and education approaches.

LESSON CONTENT AND TEACHING STRATEGIES

Begin the class with activity 1, without a preface as to the subject matter for the day.

Activity 1: Unconscientious Campers?

This activity follows the basic structure of the initiative commonly known as "helium pole." Divide the class into even groups if possible, with no group larger than 12. Ask participants in each group to form two facing lines, split evenly within the group. (For example, a group of eight people would have four people facing the other four; if the group has an odd number of people, such as nine, having four facing five is all right.) Have them "zipper" their hands together, as for a trust catch, with their index fingers pointing away from them.

Explain that they are on a camping trip, and they need to set up their tent. But, since they are camping in a very fragile environment, they must set up camp very conscientiously. Pick a scenario suitable to your region (for example, in the Northeast, they may be faced with setting up camp in an area with a lot of delicate moss). Together they must work to "get the tent set up" by placing the pole gently on the ground.

However, there are a few guidelines: (1) Everyone must support the group effort by always keeping his or her fingers connected to the pole; (2) because the camping equipment is fragile, no one should attempt to grip the pole by wrapping a finger around it—in other words, the pole should touch only the top side of the index finger; (3) the pole must be set down evenly. Place the washers or rings about 2 inches (5 centimeters) from each end of the pole. If the rings fall off, the "tent setup" was not being supported evenly by all.

Place the pole on the zippered fingers at waist level, and then watch what happens. Inevitably, at first the pole will inexplicably rise up. Use some humor and remind people that they need to set it down. Ask them why they aren't doing what you asked. Ask if they understand what they need to do or other similar questions. After a few responses from the group, invite them to try again. However, unlike the "helium pole" version, this activity is not intended as a team-building initiative, so you can stop it after a few attempts.

To close the activity, ask students the following series of questions:

- Did you intend to push the pole up?
- If not, then why was it going up?
- Did you not understand what you were supposed to do?
- Were you being lazy or careless?

Eventually, explain that just as in this activity, when many people come together to use our public lands—even well-intentioned and conscientious people—the results can often be quite the opposite of what they would hope for or have in mind. This provides a segue into the topic of recreation ecology, which has to do with how to minimize the impacts caused when many people come together to enjoy the outdoors in our finite public land spaces.

Activity 2: Loving Our Parks to Death?

Use the PowerPoint (on CD-ROM) to help your students visualize your presentation. Begin your presentation by sharing the following quote from Marion and Reid (2001): America is in danger of "loving its parks to death." Due to the combination of increased visitation and decreased funding, there are increasingly larger impacts on those areas. Much as in the tent pole activity, even well-intentioned people can be a source of impact. This becomes increasingly problematic when one considers current forecasts calling for camping to increase by 77% before 2040 and day hiking to grow by almost 200%—all in a finite amount of space. Use the following demonstration to illustrate the concepts of carrying capacity and limited natural resources.

Right now, our public lands are barely sufficient—perhaps not even sufficient—to absorb the impacts of the number of people who want to visit them. Demonstrate the current status by attempting to pour the all the water in the 12-ounce bottle into the 10-ounce bottle; there isn't much spillover or damage. Pour the water in the 10-ounce bottle back into the 12-ounce bottle so that the 10-ounce bottle is again empty. Then demonstrate the anticipated number of users in 2040 by trying to pour all the water in 18-ounce bottle into the 10-ounce bottle. Clearly something will need to change if we are to make this work.

Activity 3: Types and Causes of Impact

Explain to your students the two different types of impacts: (1) negative impact on the natural resource and (2) negative impact on the experience of other users. Ask students to share some examples of times when they have experienced either form of negative impact. As you are doing that, begin to pass around the three leaves you have prepared, each representing one land management strategy (i.e., site management, regulation, and education). Request that students continue to pass the leaves around the room while you talk (you will use these leaves in a later demonstration).

Introduce and explain the five classifications of detrimental visitor actions: (1) careless, (2) unskilled, (3) uninformed, (4) unavoidable, and (5) illegal.

Demonstrate a few of these kinds of detrimental actions in the following ways. (1) Pretend you are a tired hiker and carelessly or clumsily trip on a balloon, popping it (careless). (2) Step on one and say, "Oh, I didn't realize that would pop it" (uninformed). (3) Grab the balloon marked "Don't pop—$150 fine" off the floor and—with a mean laugh—pop it in a way that will seem spiteful. Then ask students to link each of these behaviors to a real-life scenario they have experienced or can imagine.

You can use the balloon props in a similar fashion in introducing the four social and psychological influences that can intervene in visitor behaviors: (1) lack of skill or willingness to accurately interpret the situation and needed behavior, (2) lack of ability to properly recall the appropriate behavior, (3) influence of ethics on the way a person makes decisions, and (4) social pressures that influence behavior choices. Use the following demonstration to illustrate the four influences.

1. Grab a balloon and while handling it harshly enough to pop it, ask "Is this one of those balloon things that I'm supposed to handle gently?" (lack of skill in interpreting the situation)
2. Grab another and say, "I know I'm supposed to handle these things gently, but I forget how"; then "accidently" pop it. (lack of ability to recall the appropriate behavior)
3. Pick one up and declare, "I know these things are really fragile and other people enjoy seeing them, but I don't really care about that"; then pop it. (influence of ethics)
4. Pop a balloon while explaining that you're doing it to impress your friends. (social pressures)

Ask students to link each of these behaviors to a real-life scenario they have experienced or can imagine.

Activity 4: Methods for Mitigating Impacts

Explain to your students that there are three primary strategies for mitigating visitor impacts: (1) site management, (2) regulation, and (3) education. As you introduce each method, ask them to look around the room and identify the posters and balloons representing each strategy. Continue forward with the discussion by asking students to identify times in their own experience when they have seen each of the three strategies in action. Ask students what they see as the pros and cons of each strategy. The following demonstration can be useful in helping them to see the pros and cons of each strategy more directly.

Ask students to hold up the three leaves that were passed around earlier in the lesson. Ask them questions such as the following:

1. "Is the 'site management leaf'(in plastic container) still in good shape?" "How connected to it could you feel?" "Did the management method detract from your experience? Why or why not?"
2. "Did anyone mishandle the 'regulations leaf' (with the fine written on it) when I wasn't looking? Why or why not?" "Did the signage detract from your experience? Why or why not?"
3. "Did the leaf with the information tag on the stem make you feel invited to be a part of the solution? Why or why not?" "Did you feel inspired to support the management strategy? Why or why not?"

After all the strategies have been introduced, you can ask some follow-up compare-and-contrast questions, such as "Which approach made you most feel like your intelligence was being respected?" and "Did any of the approaches make you feel like acting out?" Then ask students to start putting the previously presented information together by posing the question, "In what situations or with which type of user do you think that site management, regulation, or education would be the most effective approach?" Ask them to factor in such variables as the five classifications for detrimental visitor actions and the four intervening social and psychological influences.

See if the students can make links between their experiences and feelings during this demonstration and experiences they have had in the outdoors. During this discussion, try to bring out the various pros and cons of each approach. Though each strategy has its downsides, stress that given the current financial constraints on federal lands, education is the most attractive option for many land managers and users.

Activity 5: Education

Explain to your students that as adventure educators, we are on the front line for educating the public about minimum-impact backcountry use. Tell them that education or outreach intervention can be timed to occur (1) well in advance of the experience, (2) immediately before the experience, and (3) during the experience. Ask them to share their experiences with each of these types of education; then ask them to volunteer ideas about how they could use timing when constructing backcountry experiences for clients, for example having pretrip meetings, directing would-be participants to the Leave No Trace Web site, having daily morning meetings during the trip, or intervening when they have observed a client or visitor demonstrating high-impact behaviors. Regarding that last example, this would also be a great opportunity to ask students to share ideas on how to best provide their own students or clients with feedback on their behaviors.

CLOSURE

At this point in the presentation, students should be clear on the different kinds of negative impacts that can occur, some reasons why they might occur, and some ways of managing negative impacts. Revisiting the start of the presentation and considering that there are already perhaps too many people visiting our finite public lands, start a dialogue around the question of whether adventure educators are a part of the problem or a part of the solution. Challenge students also to consider ways in which visitors can have positive impacts. Playing "devil's advocate" helps to start ideas and discussion flowing. You can also use the scenarios in the Group Challenge handout (on CD-ROM) to prompt students as to what their immediate personal responses would be (e.g., "How would you immediately respond to the Lumpy Ridge trundlers to mitigate any impacts?"). Would they attempt to educate or to enforce, and with respect to either choice, how? The ensuing discussion provides students with a context for understanding their responsibilities and vital role as adventure educators in advancing recreation ecology via educating themselves, their clients, and other visitors. The discussion will also allow you to assess how well students have grasped the terms and ideas presented in the lesson.

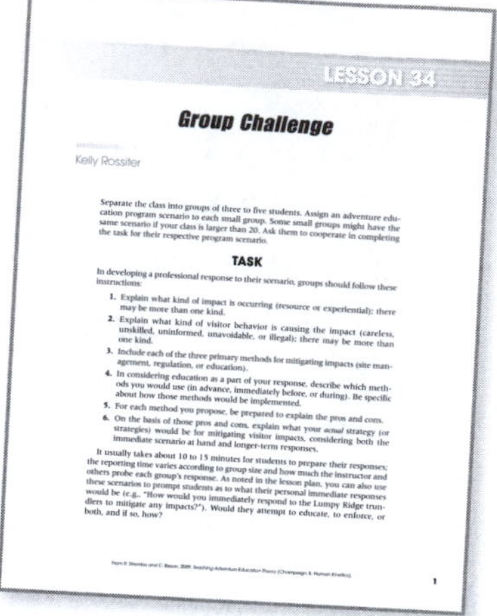

LESSON 34

Group Challenge

Kelly Rossiter

Separate the class into groups of three to five students. Assign an adventure education program scenario to each small group. Some small groups might have the same scenario if your class is larger than 20. Ask them to cooperate in completing the task for their respective program scenario.

TASK

In developing a professional response to their scenario, groups should follow these instructions:

1. Explain what kind of impact is occurring (resource or experiential); there may be more than one kind.
2. Explain what kind of visitor behavior is causing the impact (careless, unskilled, uninformed, unavoidable, or illegal); there may be more than one kind.
3. Include each of the three primary methods for mitigating impacts (site management, regulation, or education).
4. In considering education as a part of your response, describe which methods you would use (in advance, immediately before, or during). Be specific about how those methods would be implemented.
5. For each method you propose, be prepared to explain the pros and cons.
6. On the basis of those pros and cons, explain what your *actual* strategy (or strategies) would be for mitigating visitor impacts, considering both the immediate scenario at hand and longer-term responses.

It usually takes about 10 to 15 minutes for students to prepare their responses; the reporting time varies according to group size and how much the instructor and others probe each group's response. As noted in the lesson plan, you can also use these scenarios to prompt students as to what their personal immediate responses would be (e.g., "How would you immediately respond to the Lumpy Ridge trundlers to mitigate any impacts?"). Would they attempt to educate, to enforce, or both, and if so, how?

1

ASSESSMENT OF LEARNING

Divide students so that they will work in groups of three or four. Hand out the Group Challenge (on CD-ROM). This usually takes about 10 minutes.

About the Editors

Bob Stremba, EdD, is associate professor and director of adventure education in the department of exercise science at Fort Lewis College in Durango, Colorado, where he teaches a wide range of adventure courses both in the field and in the classroom. As a seasonal instructor and course director for Outward Bound Wilderness, Stremba enjoys the opportunity to put the theories of adventure education into action.

Stremba has developed adventure education programs at three universities in the United States and has taught conceptual, theoretical, and technical adventure skills to undergraduates for nearly 10 years, using experiential and hands-on activities to illustrate concepts and theories in his classroom teaching. He has presented his work on experiential education for adventure theory at several conferences for the Association for Experiential Education (AEE) and the Wilderness Education Association.

A member of AEE, Stremba also serves on the board of directors and as a member of four AEE international and regional conference committees, and he is a former member of the AEE's Accreditation Council. He is also a member of the Wilderness Education Association.

Stremba resides in Durango and enjoys backpacking, mountain biking, and snow skiing.

Christian A. Bisson, EdD, is an associate professor of adventure education at Plymouth State University in Plymouth, New Hampshire.

Bisson earned his doctorate in physical education with a specialization in pedagogy. He is a former editor of the *CORE Newsletter* for the Association for Experiential Education (AEE) Schools and Colleges professional group and served on the Educational Resources Information Center (ERIC) Clearinghouse on Rural and Small Schools. Bisson was also an *Outdoor Education* editorial board member from 2001 to 2004. In 2000, Bisson received an Outstanding Teaching Award from Northland College. He also received the Outstanding Experiential Teacher of the Year Award from the Association for Experiential Education in 1997.

He and his wife, Julie, reside in Plymouth. In his free time, Bisson enjoys parenting and, when possible, woodworking, hiking, and paddling.

About the Contributors

Mary Breunig, PhD, began her adventure education career as a wilderness trip guide, leading backpacking, dogsledding, rock climbing, and sea kayaking trips for Outward Bound Australia, Wilderness Inquiry, and Friends Seminary. Mary is an assistant professor in the department of recreation and leisure at Brock University in St. Catharines, Ontario. She teaches courses on outdoor leadership, experiential education, and outdoor and environmental education. Her research interests include experiential education and Freirean praxis, sense of community and group cohesion on wilderness trips, and alternative pedagogies in the K-12 classroom. Mary is the coeditor of the *Journal of Experiential Education*. She earned a PhD in education from Lakehead University, an MS in experiential education from Minnesota State University at Mankato, and a BA from the University of Wisconsin at Madison.

Kate Cassidy is the director of Community Adventure Training Initiatives (CATI) and Youth University at Brock University in St. Catharines, Ontario, Canada. She is also a doctoral student in education at Brock University. Kate's research interests include group development, experiential and holistic learning methodologies, the psychological sense of community, and youth engagement. Kate has more than 15 years of leadership experience in adventure programming and experiential education, working with participants ranging from at-risk youth to corporate clients. She has held a variety of positions within the field and has many years of experience training adventure facilitators and educators. Kate has published in several experiential education journals and books and has presented her work internationally.

Brad Daniel, PhD, is a professor of environmental studies, biology, and outdoor education at Montreat College in North Carolina. He holds an MA in biology from Appalachian State University, an MS in outdoor teacher education from Northern Illinois University, and a PhD in environmental studies from Antioch New England Graduate School, where he also serves as adjunct faculty. Brad was a founder of the bachelor of science program in outdoor education at Montreat College, where he has been lead instructor on many extended wilderness expeditions (longer than 20 days) and numerous shorter trips since 1986. His professional interests include significant life experiences in outdoor settings, environmental philosophy, and field-based environmental education. At Montreat, he has been honored twice with the Distinguished Professor Award and four times as Teacher of the Year.

Alan Ewert, PhD, is a distinguished and titled professor at Indiana University. He is the holder of the Patricia and Joel Meier endowed chair in outdoor leadership and serves as the graduate studies coordinator in the department of recreation, park, and tourism studies. Dr. Ewert's research publications include articles in the *Journal of Leisure Research, Leisure Sciences, Environment and Behavior, Journal of Park and Recreation Administration*, the *Journal of Experiential Education*, and *Society and Natural Resources*. He has published four books: *Outdoor Adventure Pursuits: Foundations, Models, and Theories* (1989); *Culture, Conflict, and Communication in the Wildland-Urban Interface* (1993); *Natural Resource Management: The Human Dimension* (1996); and *Integrated Resource and Environmental Management* (2004). He has authored more than 190 articles and research presentations as well as 14 book chapters. He has instructed in a variety of programs, including Outward Bound, NOLS, and Wilderness Inquiry and has been a survival instructor for the U.S. Air Force.

Aya Hayashi, PhD, is a lecturer of outdoor education in the department of sport for life at Biwako Seikei Sport College, Shiga, Japan. She received a BS in pedagogy from Hiroshima University, an MS in outdoor education from the University of Tsukuba, and a PhD in leisure behavior from Indiana University. Her interests include adventure education, outdoor leadership, diversity, outdoor orientation programs, and curriculum development. She is passionate about rock climbing, mountaineering, wilderness expedition, and international experience. She has also been an instructor in the Wilderness Education Association and Outward Bound Wilderness.

Bob Henderson, PhD, teaches outdoor education and environmental studies at McMaster University in Hamilton, Ontario. He has been editor of *Pathways: The Ontario Journal of Outdoor Education* since 1989 and is author of *Every Trail Has a Story: Heritage Travel in Canada* (2005). Bob will always smile at the delightful faces of students learning experientially.

Peter Martin, PhD, is the former head of the School of Outdoor Education and Environment at La Trobe University in Bendigo, Australia, where he coordinates research. His principal research interests include the development of ecological literacy and sustainable relationships between humans and nature through outdoor adventure experiences. A passionate climber, he teaches climbing with a focus on becoming acquainted with rocky environments.

Jacquie Medina, EdD, is an assistant professor in the outdoor education program at California State University at Chico. Her experience in the field spans over 20 years and includes work administering outdoor adventure programs and challenge courses, leading extended field experiences, and teaching theory and field-based courses in outdoor leadership, group facilitation, and outdoor education and recreation. Medina is a member of the Association for Experiential Education and an instructor for the Wilderness Education Association. She regularly presents at national conferences and pursues research interests in outdoor leadership development, facilitation techniques, and life history narratives. Medina is passionate about teaching, learning, the natural environment, and creating experiential methods for sharing knowledge. She is inspired by her students' curiosity about outdoor education and her son's and dog's fascination with and exploration of everyday life.

Denise Mitten, PhD, teaches at Ferris State University in Big Rapids, Michigan, where she developed a master's program in experiential education. Her research includes efficacy of and attitudes toward complementary and alternative medicine, decision making and ethics, teaching and learning styles in a social context in higher education, and the impact of nature on humans. Denise has worked for the past 30 years in adventure, outdoor, and environmental education with many populations, including youth, homeless people, nuns in recovery, female felons, and men in prison. An experienced adventure guide, Denise has led trips involving scuba diving, mountaineering, rafting, kayaking, rock climbing, and skiing. For 19 years, she worked with Woodswomen, an educational and adventure travel organization for women, in developing and guiding trips in nine countries. In 1992, she received the Excellence in Teaching Award from Metropolitan State University in St. Paul, Minnesota. As a writer and consultant, Denise addresses nature and wellness, ethics, group dynamics, and gender issues.

Marty O'Keefe, EdD, teaches in the outdoor leadership department at Warren Wilson College in Ashville, North Carolina. Her background, interests, and expertise include diversity and social justice issues within the field of outdoor adventure programming, challenge course training, leadership development, and feminist pedagogy.

Maurice Phipps, PhD, is a professor at Western Carolina University. He teaches program planning and outdoor leadership and instruction courses. He has been involved with the Wilderness Education Association for over 20 years and has worked in British mountain centers and directed a commercial outdoor pursuits company in the UK. After graduating from the University of Minnesota, he worked in temporary positions at Iowa State and Cal Poly at San Luis Obispo, then full time at Western State College of Colorado and currently at Western Carolina University, where he has been since 1992. His research interests are in outdoor leadership and instruction.

Ed Raiola, PhD, is the Carol Grotnes Belk chair of the outdoor leadership studies department at Warren Wilson College in Asheville, North Carolina. He teaches courses in outdoor leadership, organizational leadership, and international and cross-cultural experiential education. His research and writing have focused on outdoor leadership education and experiential education.

Leslie Rapparlie obtained her BA degrees in environmental studies and creative writing from Gettysburg College in Pennsylvania. She continued her education at Minnesota State University at Mankato, where she completed an MS in experiential education. After graduation, she directed and coordinated Lynchburg College's Outdoor Program in Virginia. Now a resident of New Jersey, Leslie works in the nonprofit sector and spends her free time writing, teaching, and walking on the trails.

Alison Rheingold is a doctoral student in the education department at the University of New Hampshire. At Project Adventure, she spent her time leading adventure-based professional development for teachers and coordinating school-based adventure implementations. Alison has also used experiential teaching methods as a special education teacher, environmental educator, and wilderness instructor for Outward Bound. She is one of the authors of *Adventure Curriculum for Physical Education* and wrote a chapter titled "Low-Element Challenge Courses" for the Human Kinetics textbook *Adventure Education: Theory and Applications.*

Kelly Rossiter's enjoyment of the outdoors is matched only by his enjoyment of sharing the outdoors with others. Realizing that he and others needed to both enjoy and preserve the backcountry experience, Kel became a master educator. Today he integrates aspects of Leave No Trace into many of the courses he teaches in Lyndon State College's recreation resource department. He is also a doctoral student in the University of Vermont's educational leadership and policy studies program and has focused his studies on recreation ecology, campus sustainability, and environmental leadership. Between—and often during—his teaching and studying about the environment, Kel loves to be out in it, mountain biking, hiking, rock and ice climbing, or just sitting quietly among his joys.

Deborah Schrader teaches outdoor and experiential education at McMaster University in Hamilton, Ontario. She is also a potter, a maker of clay vessels, and an advocate of experiential education.

Karen Warren, PhD, has been an outdoor adventure educator and trip leader since 1974. She has taught in the outdoors program and recreational athletics department at Hampshire College in Amherst, Massachusetts, for almost 25 years. Her teaching, research, and writing interests include outdoor leadership, experiential education, wilderness studies, and social justice issues in the outdoors. She is the editor of *Women's Voices in Experiential Education,* a coeditor of *The Theory of Experiential Education,* and a frequent contributor to the *Journal of Experiential Education*. Karen has been involved for many years with the Association for Experiential Education (AEE). She has received the AEE's 1998 Michael Stratton Practitioner of the Year Award and the 2006 Experiential Teacher of the Year Award as well as the Blair and Carol Brown Outstanding Staff Member Award at Hampshire College.

Martyn Whittingham, PhD, is an assistant professor at Wright State University in Dayton, Ohio, where he teaches in the clinical psychology program. He has a PhD in counseling psychology and a master's degree in therapeutic recreation. He is also a former Outward Bound instructor.

Jackson Wilson is a doctoral student in adventure education at Indiana University. Jackson currently instructs and trains staff for Outward Bound Wilderness, Wilderness Education Association, and Indiana University Outdoor Adventures in the United States and internationally. Jackson's primary research focuses on management practices in adventure education, including the recruitment and retention of adventure education staff.

How to Use the CD-ROM

SYSTEM REQUIREMENTS

You can use this CD-ROM on either a Windows-based PC or a Macintosh computer.

Windows

- IBM PC compatible with Pentium processor
- Windows 98/2000/XP/Vista
- Adobe Reader 8.0
- Microsoft Office PowerPoint 2003 or higher
- 4x CD-ROM drive

Macintosh

- Power Mac recommended
- System 10.4 or higher
- Adobe Reader
- Microsoft Office PowerPoint 2004 for MAC or higher
- 4x CD-ROM drive

USER INSTRUCTIONS

Windows

1. Insert *the Teaching Adventure Education Theory: Best Practices* CD-ROM. (Note: The CD-ROM must be present in the drive at all times.)
2. Select the "My Computer" icon from the desktop.
3. Select the CD-ROM drive.
4. Open the file you wish to view. See the "00Start.pdf" file for a list of the contents.

Macintosh

1. Insert the *Teaching Adventure Education Theory: Best Practices* CD-ROM. (Note: The CD-ROM must be present in the drive at all times.)
2. Double-click the CD icon located on the desktop.
3. Open the file you wish to view. See the "00Start" file for a list of the contents.

For customer support, contact Technical Support:

Phone: 217-351-5076 Monday through Friday (excluding holidays) between 7:00 a.m. and 7:00 p.m. (CST).

Fax: 217-351-2674

E-mail: support@hkusa.com